OXFORD QUICK REFERENCE

A Dictionary of

Social Work and Social Care

John Harris is Emeritus Professor at the University of Warwick. He was a social worker, training officer, and manager prior to moving into social work education.

Vicky White is an independent consultant. She was previously Associate Professor at the University of Warwick and, Principal Social Worker in Children's Services, Coventry City Council.

( ) SEE WEB LINKS

For recommended web links for this title, visit
www.oxfordreference.com/page/socwork
when you see this sign.

The most authoritative and up-to-date reference
books for both students and the general reader.

Accounting
Animal Behaviour
Archaeology
Architecture and Landscape
  Architecture
Art and Artists
Art Terms
Arthurian Literature and
  Legend
Astronomy
Battles
Bible
Biology
Biomedicine
British History
British Place-Names
Business and Management
Card Games
Chemical Engineering
Chemistry
Christian Art and Architecture
Christian Church
Classical Literature
Computing
Construction, Surveying, and
  Civil Engineering
Cosmology
Countries of the World
Critical Theory
Dance
Dentistry
Ecology
Economics
Education
English Etymology
English Grammar
English Idioms
English Literature
English Surnames
Environment and Conservation
Everyday Grammar
Film Studies
Finance and Banking
Foreign Words and Phrases
Forensic Science
Geography
Geology and Earth Sciences
Hinduism
Human Geography
Humorous Quotations

Irish History
Islam
Journalism
Kings and Queens of Britain
Law
Law Enforcement
Linguistics
Literary Terms
London Place-Names
Marketing
Mathematics
Mechanical Engineering
Media and Communication
Medical
Modern Poetry
Modern Slang
Music
Musical Terms
Nursing
Opera Characters
Philosophy
Physics
Plant Sciences
Plays
Pocket Fowler's Modern
  English Usage
Political Quotations
Politics
Popes
Proverbs
Psychology
Quotations
Quotations by Subject
Reference and Allusion
Rhyming
Rhyming Slang
Saints
Science
Scottish History
Shakespeare
Slang
Social Work and Social Care
Sociology
Statistics
Synonyms and Antonyms
Weather
Weights, Measures,
  and Units
Word Origins
Zoology

Many of these titles are also available online at
www.oxfordreference.com

A Dictionary of

Social Work and Social Care

SECOND EDITION

JOHN HARRIS AND VICKY WHITE

OXFORD
UNIVERSITY PRESS

Great Clarendon Street, Oxford, OX2 6DP,
United Kingdom

Oxford University Press is a department of the University of Oxford.
It furthers the University's objective of excellence in research, scholarship,
and education by publishing worldwide. Oxford is a registered trade mark of
Oxford University Press in the UK and in certain other countries

First Edition published in 2013
Second edition 2018

Impression: 1

Published in the United States of America by Oxford University Press
198 Madison Avenue, New York, NY 10016, United States of America

British Library Cataloguing in Publication Data
Data available

Library of Congress Control Number: 2017944693

ISBN 978-0-19-879668-8

Printed in Great Britain by
Clays Ltd, St Ives plc

Preface

The Dictionary is intended primarily for students on social work and social care courses and for qualified social workers. It will also be of use to students of sociology and social policy who are examining issues arising from social care and social work. Other professional groups, for example in health and education, will find it helpful to have a ready source of access to material covering topics that they share with social work and social care, given the increasingly multidisciplinary contexts of practice.

Social work and social care are demanding and their designated tasks and responsibilities are underpinned by the theories, concepts, methods, models, approaches, policies, organizations, and legislation covered in the Dictionary. However, the knowledge base on which they draw in relation to issues and interventions also ranges across other disciplines and, as a consequence, the dictionary extends into relevant aspects of sociology, social policy, and psychology.

An asterisk (*) placed before a word in a definition indicates that there is an entry in the Dictionary for that word and additional relevant material will be found in the entry indicated by the asterisk. Further reading and online resources are given at the end of some entries.

Social work can sometimes seem awash with acronyms. In the appendices there is a glossary of acronyms to which readers can refer when an acronym is encountered in study or practice. From an acronym in the glossary, readers are directed to the relevant entry in the Dictionary.

Social work is rooted in, and often routed through, law and so legislation is encountered throughout the Dictionary. Apart from a handful of exceptions, entries do not bear the titles of specific pieces of legislation, regulations, or codes of practice. Instead, relevant statutory instruments are found under entries dealing with the topics or issues to which they pertain. For example, there is no entry devoted to the Mental Capacity Act (2005) but detailed consideration is given to that Act under the entry on 'capacity'. However, we recognize that readers may encounter an aspect of the statutory framework of social work before they are aware of the areas of policy and practice to which it relates. Accordingly, in the appendices there is an Index of Legislation, Regulations, and Codes of Practice that identifies in which entries particular statutes, regulations, or codes can be found. This is a tool for readers who encounter an aspect of law and who want to identify all of the material relevant to it, wherever it occurs in the Dictionary.

The four countries of the UK have followed different paths since devolution. We would have liked to have included material from all four countries throughout but this would have taken the Dictionary far beyond its allocated length. Hence, substantial standalone entries have been provided on Northern Ireland, Scotland, and Wales.

The Dictionary introduces the reader to contemporary challenges, dilemmas, tensions, and possibilities in social work and social care and will serve as a springboard for extending and deepening knowledge about the issues it raises.

List of Contributors

(Contributors to the second edition.)

Katrin Bain, Independent Consultant.

Derek Birrell, Professor of Social Policy, University of Ulster.

Mark Drakeford, Cabinet Secretary for Finance and Local Government, Welsh Government.

Patrick Finnegan, Operations Manager for Mental Health, Warwickshire County Council.

John Harris, Emeritus Professor, University of Warwick.

Christine Harrison, Associate Professor, Member of the Centre for the Study of Safety and Wellbeing, University of Warwick.

Seth Harris-White, Team Manager, Children's Services, Coventry City Council.

Deirdre Heenan, Professor, Director of Health and Wellbeing Research Centre, University of Ulster.

Makhan Shergill, Senior Lecturer in Social Work, Coventry University.

Mark Smith, Senior Lecturer in Social Work, University of Edinburgh.

Vic Tuck, Freelance Child Protection Trainer.

Karen Ward, Senior Lecturer, Social Work, Coventry University.

Vicky White, Independent Consultant.

****

Special thanks to John Howarth, solicitor, for guidance on legal issues.

Contents

ABC *See* ACCEPTABLE BEHAVIOUR CONTRACT.

ABC model *See* FUNCTIONAL ANALYSIS.

able-bodiedism *Prejudice and/or *discrimination towards disabled people on the basis that their bodies are inferior to those of people without physical impairments and that, as a consequence, they should be accorded lower social status. Although overt abuse directed towards disabled people on the basis of physical impairments has become increasingly socially unacceptable, wider assumptions based on able-bodiedism have proved resistant to change: for example, the tendency to design the physical environment without sufficient regard to disabled people or consultation with them and depictions of disabled people that are designed to elicit pity for them. *See also* ACCESS (DISABILITY); ANTI-DISCRIMINATORY PRACTICE; ANTI-OPPRESSIVE PRACTICE; DIFFERENTLY-ABLED; DISABILITY; DISABLISM; SOCIAL MODEL OF DISABILITY.

able-bodyism *See* ABLE-BODIEDISM.

abortion Planned termination of a foetus. A private member's bill led to the legalization of abortion through the Abortion Act (1967), which covers abortions in England, *Scotland, and *Wales. Abortions can be performed legally if continuing with a pregnancy involves a greater risk to the physical or mental health of the woman or her existing children than having a termination. Abortion is also allowed if there is a substantial risk that were a child born, s/he would suffer 'such physical or mental abnormalities as to be seriously handicapped'. An abortion must be agreed by two doctors (or one in an emergency), and carried out by a doctor in a government-approved hospital or clinic. The Human Embryology and Human Fertilization Act (1990) lowered the time limit for abortions from 28 to 24 weeks. Abortions after 24 weeks are allowed for an unlimited period if there is grave risk to the life of the woman, evidence of severe foetal abnormality, or risk of grave physical or mental injury to the woman or to her existing children.

A woman's inalienable rights over her own body, including the right to control her reproductive processes, have been central to 'pro-choice' feminist campaigning in favour of abortion. Feminist arguments have also emphasized that access to abortion depends on health care making abortion readily available. However, there is no single feminist position on abortion. For example, some feminists argue that abortion is an instrument of male domination, giving control over women to (in the main male) doctors. In addition, feminists from a wide range of positions would stress the need to consider the place of abortion in much wider debates and struggles about family, motherhood, and sexuality. While an emphasis on bodily empowerment is a consistent theme within feminism, there is growing recognition that what this means for women depends on where they are placed in terms of the intersections between age, *class, *disability, *'race', and sexuality. 'Pro-life' and religious organizations, which often have overlapping memberships, argue for foetal rights or, as it is usually expressed, 'the rights of the unborn child'. Some disabled people's groups campaign against abortion on the grounds of foetal 'abnormality'. They consider that this devalues disabled people and their right to exist. They argue that sufficient resources should be available for disabled children and adults so that no woman should need to feel that abortion is the only option available if her foetus has an impairment. *See also* DISABLISM; FEMINISM.

absent without consent Previously called absent without authority or unauthorized absence. *Looked-after children are absent without consent when they absent themselves from their care placement without the agreement of those caring for them.

absent without explanation People who are informally admitted to psychiatric units are not detained under the Mental Health Act (1983) and therefore cannot be *absent without leave. Informal patients who leave inpatient or day services unexpectedly, without explanation or prior notice, are defined as absent without explanation or missing. Being absent without explanation is distinct from 'discharge from hospital against medical advice', as in the latter case the person is providing notice of her/his intention to leave. *See also* INFORMAL ADMISSION.

absent without leave (AWOL) People who are detained in a psychiatric unit under the Mental Health Act (1983) can be granted leave of absence under Section 17 by their *responsible clinician. Patients are absent without leave if such authorized leave has not been granted, or they fail to return from leave when expected, fail to return when recalled from *supervised community treatment, or fail to keep to residential conditions imposed on their leave. Section 18 of the Mental Health Act (1983) allows a detained person who is absent without leave to be taken into custody and returned to a psychiatric unit by any *approved mental health professional, any officer of the staff of the unit (usually nursing staff), any police officer, or any other person authorized in writing by the hospital manager. *See also* ABSENT WITHOUT EXPLANATION.

absolute poverty *See* POVERTY.

abuse Encompasses a wide range of ill-treatment of children and adults. Instances of abuse that emerge into the public domain receive an enormous amount of media attention and this may lead to legislative and/or policy changes. *See also* CHILD ABUSE AND NEGLECT; CHILD ABUSE INQUIRIES; CHILD PROTECTION; SAFEGUARDING ADULTS; SAFEGUARDING CHILDREN.

AC *See* APPROVED CLINICIAN.

acceptable behaviour contract (acceptable behaviour agreement) An acceptable behaviour contract or agreement is a written agreement aimed at engaging someone in acknowledging her/his *anti-social behaviour and its effect on others, with the aim of stopping the behaviour. It is made between a child or young person who has been involved in anti-social behaviour and her/his *local authority, *Youth Inclusion Support Panel, landlord, or the police. Although they are often referred to as contracts, the agreements have no basis in law. *See also* ANTI-SOCIAL BEHAVIOUR ORDER.

access (children) Prior to the Children Act (1989) the legal term for the arrangements whereby a child living with one parent following separation or divorce was
able to see, visit, or stay with the other parent. After the Act came into force, 'access'
was replaced by the term *'contact', though the term 'access' is still encountered in
day-to-day conversation. Access to/contact with children is now dealt with under
*Child Arrangements Orders. *See also* CUSTODY (CHILDREN); FAMILY COURTS;
PARENTAL RESPONSIBILITY; RESIDENCE.

access (disability) Ensuring that disabled people can gain entry to buildings and use
transport, services, leisure, and other facilities. This is seen as a central issue with
regard to the inclusion of disabled people in mainstream activities, rather than their
being segregated into activities designed solely for use by them. The Chronically Sick
and Disabled Persons Act (1970) was the first legislative measure that had requirements in relation to improving access, but only to public buildings. The Disability
Discrimination Act (1995) went further in extending requirements for access to private
businesses, shops, etc. It has been superseded by the Equality Act (2010), which makes
provision for access to goods, services, and facilities. *See also* ABLE-BODIEDISM;
DIFFERENTLY-ABLED; DISABILITY; DISABLISM; SOCIAL MODEL OF DISABILITY.

access to birth records (adoption) *See* BIRTH RECORDS COUNSELLING.

access to records Subject to a small number of exemptions under Part IV of the
*Data Protection Act (1998), anyone who has personal information held by a social
services authority has a right of access to the information, including factual information and expressions of opinion. If access is denied, the person concerned can
appeal to the courts or the *Information Commissioner. There is no right to know
what is recorded about someone else. If disclosing the information requested is not
possible without disclosing information about another person, normally the request
does not need to be met, unless the other person gives consent to the disclosure.
However, there may be occasions where it is 'reasonable in all the circumstances' to
comply without that other person's consent. This includes the disclosure of identifiable details about a 'source' who has contributed information to a social work
record. The right of access extends to children and young people under 18 who
understand what it means to exercise that right. If a child or young person under 18
does not have sufficient understanding to make her/his own request, a person with
*parental responsibility can make the request on the child's behalf. Where granting
access to a parent is likely not to be in the child's interest or is likely to result in
serious harm to anyone, including the child, access can be refused. In that case, a
parent, acting on the child's behalf, may make an application to the courts or to the
Information Commissioner. *See also* CALDICOTT GUARDIAN.

accommodated child *See* CHILD ACCOMMODATED BY A LOCAL AUTHORITY.

accommodation (ethnicity) *See* ASSIMILATION.

accountability Social workers are usually seen as having several lines of accountability. They are expected to act within the law and may have to account for their
actions in court. They are also accountable through managers to the agencies that
employ them, to individual *service users, who have the right to complain as a way
of reinforcing that accountability, and to the *Health and Care Professions Council's
*Standards of Conduct, Performance, and Ethics, as part of a wider accountability to
professional values. There are widely differing views about how these accountabil-
ities should be balanced and which of them should take precedence.

Achieving Best Evidence The principles, processes, and format to be followed by police officers and social workers conducting investigative interviews with child witnesses and vulnerable adults. In the case of children, these interviews may be conducted as part of a *Section 47 (Children Act [1989]) investigation where the child is suspected of having experienced *significant harm. The aim is to enable the child to provide a full account of what may have happened to her/him, recorded on a DVD, and subject to the rules of evidence applied by the criminal courts. For example, the child should be encouraged to provide a free narrative account, followed by non-leading questioning. The account provided by the child will constitute their evidence should the alleged perpetrator of harm be prosecuted. Although this is intended to prevent the child having to give evidence in court, s/he should be capable of being cross-examined and, should this occur, it will usually happen via a video link to the court room.

Further reading: Ministry of Justice (2011) *Achieving Best Evidence: Guidance on Interviewing Victims and Witnesses and Guidance on Using Special Measures.* Available at: http://www.cps. gov.uk/publications/docs/best_evidence_in_criminal_proceedings.pdf.

Action on Elder Abuse An organization that seeks to prevent the abuse of vulnerable older adults and campaigns for effective responses when abuse has occurred. It provides advice and guidance to *older people and others through help-lines, runs staff training courses, raises awareness of the issues, stimulates debate, and undertakes special projects. *See also* SAFEGUARDING ADULTS.

((⊕)) SEE WEB LINKS
• Official site of Action on Elder Abuse.

Action on Hearing Loss A charity (formerly the Royal National Institute for Deaf People) that provides information, advice, and support for people with hearing *loss and tinnitus, day-to-day care for people who are deaf and have additional needs, and practical advice to help people protect their hearing. It also campaigns to change public policy on hearing loss issues and supports research into the search for cures for hearing loss and tinnitus. *See also* DUAL SENSORY IMPAIRMENT; HEARING IMPAIRMENT.

((⊕)) SEE WEB LINKS
• Official site of Action on Hearing Loss.

action research Using evidence gained by using research techniques in order to seek to bring about social change, with the researcher often being involved in the action as much as the research. The issue or problem is researched, findings are presented, and analysed, and courses of action are suggested. The model of action research often put forward is a chain of research-action-research-action (and so on) in an unfolding and continuing process of *feedback between action and research. *See also* APPLIED SOCIAL RESEARCH.

active citizenship A version of *citizenship, usually found on the right of the political spectrum, that achieves greater prominence at certain points in time, for example, as it did in the late 1980s towards the end of *Thatcherism, emerging again in the Conservative Party's manifesto in 2010 in the guise of the *Big Society that was subsequently taken up by the Conservative–Liberal Democrat coalition government following the election. Active citizens are depicted as successful, self-reliant, and enterprising. The concept of the worthy active citizen emphasizes personal, rather than public or state responsibilities, stressing the need for social bonds of obligation, and personal and private, rather than state, responsibilities for providing care. Neighbourliness, kindness, and voluntary action are seen as key, with active citizens taking responsibility for others as well as themselves.

activism Taking collective action in attempting to bring about change as an alternative to seeking change through elected representatives. For an example in social work *see* SOCIAL WORK ACTION NETWORK.

activities of daily living (ADL) An approach that has entered social work via medicine and nursing as a consequence of the development of inter-professional intervention, particularly with *older people, that focuses on the detail of people's daily lives in areas such as self-care and care of their homes. In medicine, nursing, and, increasingly, social work with adults, ADL scales are used to measure the extent of functional ability. There are also ADL scales specifically designed for use with residents in homes for older people. *Occupational therapists often evaluate activities of daily living as part of their contribution to inter-professional hospital or community-based *assessments.

addiction A persistent recurring compulsion to use a substance (such as alcohol, drugs, nicotine) or engage in a specific behaviour (such as gambling, spending, eating, sexual activity) with harmful consequences to the person's health, mental state, or social life, though addiction to physical substances is now more commonly referred to as 'dependence'. If no harm is being suffered by or damage done to the individual or another party, then the activity may be considered compulsive and not addictive. A physiological perspective regards addiction as involving physical dependence, being characterized by withdrawal symptoms when it ceases. A psychological perspective characterizes addiction by the presence of psychological dependence. Addictions often have both physical and psychological components. *See also* ALCOHOLISM; COMMUNITY DRUG TEAM; DRUG AND ALCOHOL PROBLEMS; DUAL DIAGNOSIS.

Further reading: Forrester, D. and Harwin, J. (2011) *Parents who Misuse Drugs and Alcohol: Effective Interventions in Social Work and Child Protection*, Wiley-Blackwell.

ADHD *See* ATTENTION DEFICIT HYPERACTIVITY DISORDER.

ADL *See* ACTIVITIES OF DAILY LIVING.

admission (mental health) *See* COMPULSORY ADMISSION; INFORMAL ADMISSION.

admission for assessment (mental health) *See* COMPULSORY ADMISSION.

admission for treatment (mental health) *See* COMPULSORY ADMISSION.

adolescence The period of life between puberty and early adulthood. (Health, education, and social work services catering for adolescents usually refer to them as young people.) Adolescence can be a challenging developmental stage for parents and young people because of the rapid and profound physical and emotional changes that characterize it. The process of physical changes in adolescence (puberty) starts from around 11 years for girls and 13 for boys. The age at which puberty starts has been falling in most developed countries, probably because of better nutrition. Hormonal changes that underlie the physical developments contribute to periods of moodiness and restlessness associated with adolescence. For girls these changes include the onset of menstrual periods, growth of underarm,

a

body, and pubic hair. For boys their voices 'break' (become deeper), there is growth of underarm, body, pubic, and facial hair, as well as erections and nocturnal emissions ('wet dreams'). For both genders there is likely to be rapid physical growth, but there is considerable individual variation in this.

Psychological changes see adolescents forming close relationships outside the family with friends of their own age. Relationships within the family also change. Parents become less important in their children's eyes as their lives outside the family develop. In this respect, the growth of *independence and a distinctive identity, linked substantially with a sense of solidarity with peers, is a major feature of this phase of human development. This can lead to conflicts between parents and their adolescent children, particularly as young people may increasingly challenge their parents by their behaviour and attitudes, and try out new experiences. However, this is often accompanied by lack of confidence and vulnerability, leading to withdrawn and incommunicative behaviour at home.

While most adolescents emerge from the emotional upheaval that can be associated with this stage of their life, those experiencing difficulties may exhibit deeper problems, such as *eating disorders, excessive sleepiness, *anxiety, possibly linked to *phobias, and panic attacks. Emotional problems may not be easy for parents to recognize and may lead to *depression, and in more serious *cases the involvement of specialist services such as *Child and Adolescent Mental Health Services. Experiencing *bullying and *cyber-bullying may be a major source of emotional difficulties in adolescence. This period of life is a time of powerful and rapid sexual development. More than half of young people in the UK are likely to have their first experience of sex before the age of 16. Teenagers are able to obtain confidential advice on contraception from their general practitioner. Following the emergence of the *Fraser guidelines, arising from the establishment of *Gillick competency in respect of young people seeking contraceptive advice, it is not necessary for doctors to inform parents that such advice is being given providing certain criteria are met. *See also* CHILD DEVELOPMENT.

adoption The process of changing the legal status of a child so that s/he becomes a full member of a new family in which s/he has one or two new parents. An adoption order is the legal provision that transfers *parental responsibility and all the rights and duties associated with this from the child's *birth parent(s) to the adoptive parent(s). Only a court can make an adoption order following consideration of an application from prospective adoptive parents at an adoption hearing. Once the court has made the order, the child takes the surname of her/his adoptive parents and may also change her/his first name in some circumstances, particularly if it is distinctive. Following the making of the adoption order the child and adoptive parents have the same rights as if the child had been born to them, including rights of inheritance.

The Adoption and Children Act (2002), the Adoption Regulations (2005), and the Adoption Agencies Regulations (2005) define the legal framework for adoption and adoption services in England and *Wales, the intention being to improve the performance of adoption services and promote the greater use of adoption. The 2002 Act aligns adoption law with the Children Act (1989) in order to ensure that the child's welfare is the paramount consideration in all decisions relating to adoption (*see* PARAMOUNTCY PRINCIPLE). The *welfare checklist (*see* WELFARE CHECKLIST 2) is applied by the court and adoption agency in determining the best interests of the child in any decision but is tailored to address the particular circumstances of adoption.

Individuals who wish to become adoptive parents apply to an adoption agency and undergo a comprehensive assessment. An adoption agency is defined in the Adoption and Children Act (2002) as either a local authority or a registered adoption society. The latter is a body whose functions consist of or include making arrangements for the adoption of children. The assessment will comprise statutory checks, including those made with the police, and a home study completed with applicants by qualified social workers employed by the agency. This explores with applicants their domestic circumstances, personal history and background, and motivation for wishing to adopt a child. It examines what they can offer a child awaiting adoption and normally takes six months to complete.

An adoption panel constituted by the adoption agency considers each assessment and makes a recommendation to the agency as to whether or not the applicants should be approved. The panel comprises senior social workers, other professionals, including a medical advisor and a legal representative, and independent people. It meets on a regular basis to consider applications. Panels also consider the appropriateness of placing individual children for adoption, if their circumstances indicate this is in their best interests. Once approved, a social worker from the adoption agency is linked with the prospective adoptive applicants and seeks to identify a suitable child to be placed with them. In the case of a local authority adoption agency, children awaiting placement in an adoptive home from within the area will be considered. If a suitable placement cannot be identified, enquiries may be made with neighbouring authorities. If this proves unsuccessful, details of the prospective adoptive applicants will be circulated through the National Adoption Register in search of a suitable match. The register has been operated by the British Association for Adoption and Fostering Services (now *CoramBAAF) on behalf of the government since 2004.

Once a match is made the details are considered by the adoption panel to ensure its suitability. Careful plans are then made to set up the placement and if successful the child moves into the home of the prospective adoptive applicants. The placement is supervised in accordance with the Adoption Regulations (2005). When the child has been successfully settled into the family, social workers and prospective adopters agree when the latter should submit to the court their adoption application in respect of the child. The child will need to have lived with the applicants for at least three months. To assist in making its judgment on the application, the court will call for a confidential report from the social worker concerned, known as a Schedule II Report. It will also appoint a court officer who will meet with the applicants, child, and birth family before presenting a report to the court. When all reports have been submitted, a date for an adoption hearing is fixed, to be attended by the applicants and child, social worker, and, if necessary, a legal representative. The adoption takes legal effect with the granting of an Adoption Order.

Under the 2002 Act, local authorities must continue to provide an adoption service within their areas that is designed to meet the needs of children who may be adopted, their parents and guardians, persons wishing to adopt a child, and adopted persons, their parents, natural parents, and former guardians. Facilities must include not only making and participating in arrangements for the adoption of children, but also for the provision of adoption support services. These include ongoing support for placements and *birth records counselling for adopted adults wishing to find out more about their birth family, and possibly meeting with adult birth relatives. The Registrar General maintains an Adoption Contact Register, which allows an adopted adult and their birth relatives to register their details if

a

they would welcome contact or wish to stipulate no contact. *See also* AGENCY DECISION-MAKER; INTER-COUNTRY ADOPTION; OPEN ADOPTION.

Adoption Contact Register *See* ADOPTION; BIRTH RECORDS COUNSELLING.

Adoption Order *See* ADOPTION.

Adoption Panel *See* ADOPTION.

AdoptionUK Provides support and gives a voice to adoptive families. Experienced adoptive parents offer their knowledge and experience to adopters and prospective adopters. The charity provides peer support through online information, message boards, a helpline, and individual support. It seeks to influence decision-makers through its research and the knowledge and experience of its members. It offers training and publications that inform adopters, carers, and professionals about the neurological and psychological effects of early childhood trauma and attachment difficulties.

(((()))) SEE WEB LINKS
• Official site of AdoptionUK.

adoption welfare checklist *See* ADOPTION; WELFARE CHECKLIST 2.

adoptive parents *See* ADOPTION.

adult abuse *See* SAFEGUARDING ADULTS.

adult family placement Placing people in families that are not their own, with the family being paid for providing the accommodation and day-to-day support. Originally referred to as 'adult fostering' but this was thought to *infantilize the people concerned. Most commonly a service associated with people with *learning disabilities, but can also include placements for *older people and people with mental health problems. Social workers usually run such schemes, so in addition to the person placed having a social worker, there will be a social worker who has oversight of the placement itself. Sometimes such placements are also used to provide short *respite breaks for someone's usual *carers.

adult fostering *See* ADULT FAMILY PLACEMENT.

adult protection *See* SAFEGUARDING ADULTS.

advance decisions (advance directives) *See* CAPACITY.

advice centre (advice service) The provision, most commonly in the *voluntary sector, of advice and assistance to people with problems. Advice services have been set up in relation to specific issues, such as *welfare rights, *asylum, rape, and homelessness. Some organizations, such as *Citizen Advice Bureaux, offer assistance across a broad range of issues such as debt, welfare rights, housing, employment, and consumer issues. Other organizations, such as *Age UK, offer an advice service as part of a wider range of services. Some *local authorities have introduced advice centres called *'one-stop shops', either in a central location or in particular neighbourhoods, which provide advice in relation to the full range of the services they provide. *See also* ADVICE WORKER.

advice worker Someone who works in an *advice centre/service. In many advice centres/services in the *voluntary sector there is a mix of paid and unpaid staff who may all be referred to as advice workers. *See also* ADVICE CENTRE.

advocacy Helping and supporting people to speak up for what they want or speaking on their behalf when they find it difficult or impossible to do that for themselves. This can involve access to information and services; being involved in decisions; expressing and representing views; securing services; defending interests; exercising rights; making choices; ensuring procedures are followed.

An advocate should be free from conflicts of interest and should represent the other person's interests as if they were the advocate's own. Social workers are expected to be able to advocate on behalf of *service users and may use advocacy skills in order to make sure that service users' views and opinions are heard and understood, thus enabling them to participate in assessments and decision-making, for example. However, social workers are often in situations that make it impossible for them to concentrate on independent representation of service users for a number of reasons, such as: working with family members who have conflicting interests; making an assessment of what is in the interests of the service user that conflicts with the service user's views; not being able to meet the wishes of the service user within the priorities established for the allocation of limited resources. In such circumstances, service users may have access to independent advocacy services. Social workers need to have knowledge of these services in order to be able to advise service users where they can find an independent advocate. There are several types of advocacy:

Self-advocacy involves service users speaking up for themselves and representing their own interests.

Peer advocacy uses advocates who have experienced or are experiencing similar issues to the person on whose behalf they are advocating.

Group advocacy brings together people who have similar issues or concerns so that they can speak up collectively.

Citizen advocacy is a one-to-one (usually) long-term *partnership between a trained unpaid citizen advocate and a service user.

Professional advocacy involves a trained paid worker.

Legal advocacy introduces a lawyer to act on a service user's behalf.

Section 12 of the Health and Social Care Act (2001) places a duty on the Secretary of State to arrange for the provision of independent advocacy services in connection with adult service users making complaints. Such services should be 'independent of any person who is the subject of a relevant complaint or who is involved or who is investigating such a complaint'. Section 26 of the Children Act (1989, as amended 2004) requires local authorities to make arrangements for the provision of advocacy services for children and young people making or intending to make representations, including complaints.

In 2002, Action for Advocacy launched the Advocacy Charter, a document that defines and promotes ten principles of advocacy: clarity of purpose; putting people first; empowerment; equal opportunity; accountability; accessibility; *confidentiality; independence; supporting advocates; complaints. Action for Advocacy closed in 2013 but the Charter is still a useful reference point for advocacy practice. *See also* ADVOCACY (ADULTS).

Further reading: Action for Advocacy (2002) The Advocacy Charter. Available at: http://www. aqvx59.dsl.pipex.com/Advocacy%20Charter2004.pdf.

Donnison, D. (2009) *Speaking to Power: Advocacy for Health and Social Care*, Policy Press.

a

advocacy (adults) There is a duty to provide independent *advocacy for adults, placed on local authorities by the Care Act (2014). Under Sections 67 and 68 of the Care Act (2014) an independent advocate can be arranged to facilitate the involvement of a person in their *assessment, in the preparation of their *care and support plan, in the *review of their care and support plan, in *safeguarding enquiries, and in *Safeguarding Adults Reviews. There are two conditions to be met in order for the local authority to provide an independent advocate:

- that if an independent advocate were not provided the person would have substantial difficulty in being fully involved;
- that there is no appropriate individual available to support and represent the person's wishes who is not paid or professionally engaged in providing care or treatment to the person or their carer.

The judgement about whether a person would have substantial difficulty in engaging with a *local authority's processes is informed by four considerations, in any one (or more) of which a substantial difficulty might be found:

- understanding relevant information;
- retaining information;
- using or weighing up information;
- communicating views, wishes, and feelings.

When a local authority considers that a person has substantial difficulty in being involved, before it appoints an independent advocate it must consider whether there is anyone appropriate who can support the person's involvement. This could be a *carer (who is not employed or paid), a family member, or a friend. If the person does not wish to be supported by an individual identified by the local authority and if the person has *capacity, their wishes should be respected. If the person has been judged to lack the capacity to make a decision, then the local authority must be satisfied that it is in her/his *best interests to be supported and represented by the individual it has identified. When a person does not wish to be supported by a relative, for example, because they want to move towards *independence from their family, a relative cannot be considered as appropriate. If there is no one appropriate, then the local authority must arrange for an independent advocate. Someone who is to undertake the role of independent advocate cannot be someone who is already providing the person with care or treatment in a professional capacity or on a paid basis (regardless of who employs or pays for them). If assessments are being carried out on two people in the same household, they can have the same advocate if both agree and there is no conflict of interest between them or either of them and the advocate.

The role of the independent advocate is to support and represent the person and to facilitate their involvement with the local authority and other organizations. If a decision is made not to offer an independent advocate at the assessment and/or care and support planning stages, an advocate can still be appointed subsequently. For example, an independent advocate can be offered at the point a care and support plan is being reviewed if a person's ability to be involved in the process without an advocate has changed, or the circumstances have changed (for example, the person's involvement was previously facilitated by a relative who is no longer able to perform that role), or it now appears that an advocate should have been involved at an earlier stage but was not.

Advocates must have:

- a suitable level of appropriate experience;
- appropriate training;

- competency in the task;
- integrity and good character;
- the ability to work independently of the local authority or body carrying out assessments, planning, or reviews on the local authority's behalf;
- arrangements for regular supervision.

The role of the independent advocate includes assisting the person to:

- understand the assessment, care and support planning, review and safeguarding processes. This requires advocates to understand local authority policies, and other agencies' roles, and processes, the available assessment tools, the planning options, and the options available at the review of a care or support plan and *good practice in safeguarding enquiries and Safeguarding Adults Reviews. It may involve advocates spending considerable time with the individual, considering their communication needs, their wishes and feelings, and their life story, and using all this to assist the person to be involved and, where possible, to make decisions;
- communicate their views, wishes, and feelings to the staff who are carrying out an assessment or developing a care or support plan or reviewing an existing plan, or to communicate their views, wishes, and feelings to the staff who are carrying out safeguarding enquiries or Safeguarding Adults Reviews;
- understand how their needs can be met by the local authority or otherwise—understanding, for example, how a care and support or support plan can be personalized, how it can be tailored to meet specific needs, how it can be creative, inclusive, and how it can be used to promote a person's rights to liberty and to family life (*see* HUMAN RIGHTS);
- make decisions about their care and support arrangements—assisting them to weigh up various care and support options and to choose the ones that best meet their needs and wishes;
- understand their rights under the Care Act (2014), to an assessment that considers their wishes and feelings and that considers the views of other people; to have their *eligible needs met, and to have a care or support plan that reflects their needs and their preferences; and in relation to safeguarding, to have their concerns about *abuse taken seriously and responded to appropriately. Also assisting the person to understand their wider rights, including their rights to liberty and family life (*see* HUMAN RIGHTS);
- challenge a local authority decision or process, and where a person cannot challenge the decision even with assistance, then to challenge it on their behalf.

In safeguarding situations there are additional important issues for advocates to address. These include assisting a person to:

- decide what outcomes/changes they want;
- understand the behaviour of others who are abusive and/or neglectful;
- understand actions of their own that may expose them to avoidable abuse or neglect;
- understand what actions they can take to safeguard themselves;
- understand what advice and help they can expect from others, including the criminal justice system;
- understand what parts of the process are completely or partially within their control;
- explain what help they want in order to avoid a recurrence of, and to recover from, the experience.

Many people who qualify for advocacy under the Care Act (2014) also qualify for advocacy under the Mental Capacity Act (2005) from an Independent Mental Capacity

Advocate (*see* CAPACITY). The same advocate can provide support as an advocate under the Care Act (2014) and under the Mental Capacity Act (2005). Under the Mental Health Act (1983) certain people, known as 'qualifying patients', are entitled to help and support from an *Independent Mental Health Advocate (IMHA). Those people with mental health problems who do not have a right to an IMHA and whose care and support needs are being assessed, planned, or reviewed are considered for an advocate under the Care Act (2014), if they have substantial difficulty in being involved and if there is no appropriate person to support their involvement. Whichever legislation the advocate is acting under, they should meet the appropriate requirements for an advocate under that legislation.

Further reading: Department of Health (2016) *Care and Support: Statutory Guidance*, Chapter 7. Available at: https://www.gov.uk/government/publications/care-act-statutory-guidance/care-and-support-statutory-guidance#person-centred-care-and-support-planning.

Advocacy Quality Performance Mark Published in 2014 by the National Development Team for Inclusion. The QPM is a tool for use by providers of independent *advocacy to show their commitment and ability to provide high-quality advocacy services.

advocate *See* ADVOCACY; ADVOCACY (ADULTS).

AEA *See* ACTION ON ELDER ABUSE.

affect (mental health) The outwardly observable representation of feeling or emotion displayed to others through facial expressions, tone of voice, laughter, tears, etc. The normal range of affect, termed the broad affect, is culturally defined and relative. The term is associated with mood and mood disorders in psychiatry, in which it is used to describe the person's emotional state from an observer's (usually a doctor's) perspective. *See also* AFFECTIVE DISORDER; BIPOLAR DISORDER.

affective disorder (affective mood disorder) An overarching category that refers to a group of mental health problems involving thoughts, behaviours, and emotions in which a person's mood is involved. A person's *affect is her/his expression of emotion so affective disorder indicates an abnormal and persistent change in an individual's emotional state, usually elevated (manic), or depressed, or both alternately. The most common affective disorders are major depressive disorder (also known as clinical *depression, uni-polar depression, or major depression), *bipolar disorder (formerly known as manic depression), and *anxiety disorder. Symptoms of affective disorder range from mild and inconvenient to severe and life-threatening, and can lead to suicide in serious *cases. *Psychotic symptoms (*hallucinations and/or *delusions) can accompany severe cases.

affirmative action Actions taken to address discrimination, and the monitoring of their impact, which focus on achieving equality of outcome not *equality of opportunity. *See also* POSITIVE ACTION/DISCRIMINATION.

after-care Follow-up services after a period in a range of settings (for example, children leaving care, *older people leaving hospital, people discharged from in-patient mental health services) in order to provide ongoing support after the provision of the previous service has ended. *See also* AFTER-CARE (MENTAL HEALTH).

after-care (children) *See* LEAVING CARE.

after-care (mental health) The care provided to certain categories of psychiatric
patient when discharged from *compulsory admission to hospital. Section 117 of
the Mental Health Act (1983) places a specific duty on health and social services
authorities to provide after-care to a patient who has been detained for treatment,
under Sections 3, 37, 45A, 47, or 48, when s/he leaves hospital. After-care also
applies to people granted leave from hospital under Section 17, during their period of
leave; discharged from their treatment section but who remain in hospital voluntarily
before leaving; and individuals placed on *supervised community treatment. After-
care services are defined by the Care Act (2014) as services that meet a need arising
from or related to the person's mental disorder and reduce the risk of a deterioration
of the person's mental condition (and, accordingly, reduce the risk of the person
requiring admission to a hospital again for treatment for the disorder). The range of
services that can be provided under S117 is broad, and can include residential care
services. There is no power to charge individuals for Section 117 services. However,
an individual with Section 117 entitlements may pay a top-up fee for their preferred
accommodation, if this is more than the local authority would usually pay.

The purpose of after-care is to meet someone's immediate social and health care
needs, to support them in regaining or enhancing their skills, and to assist them in
learning new skills in order to cope with life outside hospital. The care should be
provided until both health and social services authorities are satisfied that the
individual concerned no longer needs the services. Even if the individual becomes
well, services may need to continue to prevent deterioration in her/his mental
health. An individual cannot be discharged from Section 117 after-care in their
absence nor without a formal discharge meeting at which they must be present. An
individual does not have to accept Section 117 services offered to them, but
declining services does not end entitlement should the person change her/his
mind at a later date. Proper implementation of the *Care Programme Approach
should ensure that the legal requirements of Section 117 are met. Comprehensive
practice guidance on after-care duties can be found in the *Code of Practice to the
Mental Health Act (1983)*. *See also* AFTER-CARE.

Further reading: Department of Health (2015) *Code of Practice to the Mental Health Act (1983)*,
Chapter 33. Available at: https://www.gov.uk/government/uploads/system/uploads/
attachment_data/file/435512/MHA_Code_of_Practice.PDF.

age-appropriate 1. Encouraging people with *learning disabilities to behave in
accordance with their chronological age, rather than their developmental stage, and
discouraging behaviour not associated with their chronological age (for example, an
adult not carrying a doll or a teddy bear) in order to increase their status in the wider
society.

2. Also used in relation to *child development with reference to whether particular behaviour is appropriate to a particular stage of development. For example,
walking at twelve months would be regarded as age-appropriate, heavily sexualized
behaviour on the part of an eight-year-old would be regard as age-inappropriate.

age assessment Undertaken when someone who is an unaccompanied asylum-
seeker or who has been trafficked states that s/he is under 18 years old but her/his
appearance suggests strongly that s/he is over 18. Department for Education statutory guidance (2014) states that when someone's age is uncertain and there are
reasons to believe that s/he is under 18, s/he should be presumed to be a child in
order to receive immediate access to assistance, support, and protection in accordance with Article 10(3) of the Council of Europe Convention on Action against

Trafficking in Human Beings (2005). Age assessments should only be carried out where there is significant reason to doubt that someone is under 18. Such assessments should not be a routine part of a *local authority's assessment of unaccompanied or trafficked children. Where age assessments are conducted, they must follow the guidance given in the case *R. v Merton LBC* (2005). (Following this guidance is referred to as being 'Merton-compliant'.) Some young people may genuinely not know their age and this should not be misread as lack of cooperation. The advice of a paediatrician with experience in considering age may be needed to assist with an age assessment. However, the High Court has ruled that, unless a paediatrician's report can add something specific to an assessment of age undertaken by an experienced social worker, it is unnecessary. Someone having an age assessment should be offered an *independent visitor and if s/he declines, her/his reasons should be recorded. An independent visitor who is appointed should have appropriate training and demonstrate an understanding of the needs faced by unaccompanied or trafficked children. *See also* UNACCOMPANIED ASYLUM-SEEKING CHILDREN.

Further reading: Association of Directors of Children's Services (2015) *Age Assessment Guidance: Guidance to Assist Social Workers and their Managers in Undertaking Age Assessments in England*. Practice guidance that is not binding on local authorities but is the ADCS's recommended approach. Available at: http://adcs.org.uk/assets/documentation/Age_Assessment_Guidance_2015_Final.pdf.

Council of Europe Convention on Action Against Trafficking in Human Beings (2005). Available at: https://rm.coe.int/CoERMPublicCommonSearchServices/DisplayDCTMContent?documentId=090000168008371d.

Department for Education (2014) *Care of Unaccompanied and Trafficked Children: Statutory Guidance for Local Authorities on the Care of Unaccompanied Asylum Seeking and Trafficked Children*. Available at: https://www.gov.uk/government/uploads/system/uploads/attachment_data/file/330787/Care_of_unaccompanied_and_trafficked_children.pdf.

age discrimination *See* AGEISM.

age-inappropriate *See* AGE-APPROPRIATE.

ageing *See* THEORIES OF AGEING.

ageism A process of systematic stereotyping of and discrimination against people because they are older that legitimates inequalities based on age. Ageism stems from the social construction of ageing through the combination of a range of factors and is manifested in policy, personal values, and the experiences of *older people. First coined by the American gerontologist Robert Butler (1927–2010) in 1969 in an article in *The Gerontologist* ('Ageism: another form of bigotry', 9, 4, 243–6). He defined ageism as 'a process of systematic stereotyping and discrimination against people because they are old, just as racism and sexism accomplish this for skin colour and gender. Older people are characterized as senile, rigid in thought and manner, and old-fashioned in morality and skills.' He saw ageism as arising from a combination of stereotyping and myths about old age because of lack of knowledge of and insufficient contact with a wide variety of older people and partly 'a deep and profound dread of growing old'. He argued that ageism can be a convenient means by which society can relinquish a sense of responsibility towards older people, while at a personal level it can shield young and middle-aged people from thinking about ageing and death. He noted the irrationality of ageism since most people will become old and yet through the lens of ageism older people are seen as 'somehow different from our present and future selves and therefore not subject to the same

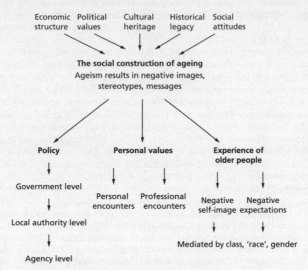

Ageism
Adapted from Hughes, B. *Older People and Community Care* (1995) p. 45

desires, concerns or fears'. Ageism is rooted in thought patterns and implicit assumptions. It operates at intrapersonal, interpersonal, and institutional levels, for example in medicine, social services, and politics.

It is easy to assume that ageism is a universal phenomenon, but in some cultures older age may lead to a more valued status or it may not be seen as a source of status at all. However, in Western societies older age is often constructed as a social problem, resulting in *loss of status and devalued identity. This has consequences in terms of older people's self-perception, how they are perceived by others, their exclusion from some social activities and relationships, and the approaches taken to policy and practice in health and social services. A number of factors contribute to ageism:

Economic Older people are seen as unproductive.

Cultural Youth is highly valued; in contrast, older age is associated with decline and decrepitude.

Interpersonal Older people may be put at a distance and treated as '*other' in order to protect against fears about ageing.

See also OBJECTIFICATION; OLDER PEOPLE; REMINISCENCE GROUP; THEORIES OF AGEING.

Further reading: Macnicol, J. (2006) *Age Discrimination: An Historical and Contemporary Analysis*, Cambridge University Press.

agency decision-maker The designated person within a fostering service or an adoption agency who makes decisions about the acceptance of foster or adoptive parents on the basis of recommendations made by a Fostering Panel (in relation to a fostering service) and an Adoption Panel (in relation to an adoption agency). The agency decision-maker will take into account the Panel's recommendation before making a decision but is not bound to follow it. *See also* ADOPTION; FOSTERING.

agency social work The supply of contracted qualified social workers by private recruitment agencies predominantly to the *statutory sector, a growing phenomenon from the 1990s onwards. The hourly rates of agency social workers are higher than social workers on permanent contracts but agency staff do not have employment benefits such as paid holidays and pensions provision. There have been contrasting reports of agency social workers not being valued and being treated as outsiders by staff on permanent contracts and of their contribution being welcomed by hard-pressed teams. Contrasting views have also been put forward about the nature of agency social work, some seeing engagement in a range of different work placements with new challenges as a positive portfolio career choice, with others seeing the tasks given to agency social workers as repetitive, perhaps involving less *service user contact time, as well as such workers having fewer opportunities for training and professional development. Some see it as an escape from the oppressive nature of state employment and/or as choosing an employment option that is better fitted to someone's life circumstances at a certain point, rather than constituting a strategic career choice. Research indicates that there may be particular pressures on agency social workers to deliver services at speed in unfamiliar surroundings, leading to a working environment in which they find it essential to conform quickly to organizational and group norms and engage in superficial relationships with colleagues and service users. One reading of agency social work is to see it as a further extension of *neo-liberal *managerialism, with the ability to hire and fire at short notice and narrow instrumental perspectives on social work that are well-suited to a workplace increasingly dominated by a culture of *performance management. *See also* GIG ECONOMY.

Further reading: Unwin, P. (2009) 'Modernisation and the Role of Agency Social Work' in Harris, J. and White V. (eds) *Modernising Social Work*, Policy Press.

agency theory Conceptualization of services and their management in terms of principal–agent relationships. Control resides with the 'principal' (service purchaser) who has the power to make decisions and see them carried through. The 'agent' (service provider) has to implement the principal's decisions. This centralizes strategic control over services while decentralizing responsibility for service delivery. The introduction of *New Right ideas into social work, from the late 1980s onwards, led to increasing separation of the roles of principal and agent in the provision of services. This was often referred to as the 'purchaser–provider split' and was implemented through the introduction (and continuing use) of service specifications and contracts. *See also* CONTRACT STATE.

agents of social control A critical view of occupations that contribute to securing people's conformity with the established structure of society, diverting them from questioning whether their difficulties may be caused by the way in which society is structured and functions. The police, courts, and prisons are examples of 'hard' agents of social control, whereas social workers are seen as softer versions and are sometimes referred to as 'soft police' in order to indicate that while their controlling role may not be as obvious, it is nonetheless significant.

age of criminal responsibility No child under 10 years of age in England, *Wales, and *Northern Ireland can be found guilty of a crime. (In *Scotland, the age of criminal responsibility is 12.) The law assumes young children do not sufficiently understand the difference between 'right' and 'wrong' to be responsible for what they have done. However, they can be given a Local Child Curfew, under which the police can ban children from being in a public place between 9.00 p.m. and 6.00 a.m., unless accompanied by an adult. This can last for up to ninety days. If a child breaks the curfew, s/he can be given a Child Safety Order if s/he has engaged in behaviour that would have been criminal had s/he been above the age of criminal responsibility. This Order places the child under the supervision of a *youth offending team. The Order normally lasts for up to three months, but in some cases it can last for up to twelve months. If a child does not stick to the rules of a Child Safety Order, the court can consider if s/he should be taken into care or if her/his parents should be held responsible for the child's behaviour. The latter can result in parents being asked to attend a *parenting programme or enter into a *parenting contract or being made the subject of a *Parenting Order.

Children between 10 and 17 can be arrested and taken to court if they commit a crime. They are treated differently from adults in being dealt with by youth courts, given different sentences, and sent to special secure centres for young people, not prisons.

Young people aged 18 are treated as adults by the law. However, if they are sent to prison, they will be sent to a specialist facility for those 18 to 25 years old, not a full adult prison.

Age UK An organization, which resulted from the merger of Age Concern and Help the Aged in 2010, that provides information, advice, and commercial products to *older people, conducts campaigning activity on issues of concern to them, funds research on later life, and provides training for those working with older people.

(⊕) SEE WEB LINKS
• Official site of Age UK.

aggravating factor *See* HATE CRIME.

aggression Hostile behaviour and/or attitude towards an individual or group that results in verbal and/or physical attacks. *See also* ANGER MANAGEMENT.

AIDS *See* HIV/AIDS.

aids and adaptations Equipment provided to people in their own homes (aids) or physical alterations to the accommodation itself (adaptations), which make it easier and safer to live there, usually following an assessment by an *occupational therapist. This could be something simple like a grab rail to help with getting in and out of the bath or more extensive changes such as installing a stairlift or a shower room.

The previous duty placed on local authorities under Section 2 of the Chronically Sick and Disabled Persons Act (1970) to assist disabled people with aids and adaptations has been replaced by the requirements of the Care Act (2014), which apply to services for adults in England. The guidance on the Act includes the provision of minor adaptations and equipment as part of preventive services that are aimed at maximizing *independence. When provided by a local authority as a preventive service, a minor adaptation costing £1,000 or less and equipment aids must be free of charge. If aids and adaptations are not provided as preventive services, they come under the Act's arrangements for assessment and care planning (*see* CARE AND SUPPORT PLANNING [ADULTS]; NEEDS ASSESSMENT [ADULTS]).

The Housing Grants, Construction and Regeneration Act (1996) is unaffected by the Care Act (2014). This contains provision for Disabled Facilities Grants, which are for major adaptations up to a maximum of £30,000, subject to a means test. In addition, the Regulatory Reform (Housing Assistance) (England and Wales) Order (2002) gives local authorities wide discretion to assist with housing locally, including home adaptations, for example being able to provide extra funding on top of the £30,000 maximum awarded for a Disabled Facilities Grant or for an adaptation not falling within the DFG scheme. Therefore, if someone's needs in relation to an adaptation cannot be met in full or at all under the 1996 Act, the 2002 Order could be used. If this were the case, adult social care services would not need to consider stepping in under the Care Act (2014). However, as the 2002 Order is discretionary, in times of *austerity it is likely to provide diminishing assistance.

Section 2 of the Chronically Sick and Disabled Persons Act (1970) continues to apply to children, despite no longer applying to adults. In legal cases, Section 2 has been regarded as in effect an extension of Part 3 of the Children Act (1989). The wording of Section 17 of the 1989 Act (the general duty to safeguard and promote the welfare of children in need) can cover the provision of major adaptations. Under the Children and Families Act (2014) when a child has special educational needs, over and above those the school is able to meet from its own resources, s/he will have an *Education, Health and Care (EHC) plan. Anything provided for the child, under Section 2 of the Chronically Sick and Disabled Persons Act (1970), must be in the EHC plan (Section 37, Children and Families Act (2014)). *See also* ASSISTIVE TECHNOLOGY; TELECARE.

Alcoholics Anonymous Describes itself as a 'fellowship of men and women who share their experience, strength and hope with each other that they may solve their common problem and help others to recover from alcoholism'. It is concerned solely with the personal recovery and continued sobriety of individual alcoholics who turn to it for help. It has remained focused on this core purpose by not engaging in alcoholism research, medical or psychiatric treatment, education, or advocacy in any form, although some of its members participate in such activities as individuals. It does not seek or accept financial support from outside sources and members' anonymity is preserved. *See also* ALCOHOLISM.

(⊕) SEE WEB LINKS
• Official site of Alcoholics Anonymous.

alcoholism An *addiction involving craving for, dependence on, and compulsive consumption of alcohol. A term still in widespread use though in medical and other professional circles the terms alcohol abuse and alcohol dependence are more likely to be used. The key characteristic is that someone's use of alcohol has repeatedly caused problems in her/his health, work and personal life, and/or for family and friends. The key issue is not the amount of alcohol that is consumed but the loss of control over its consumption and the attendant consequences. Long-term abuse produces physiological changes in the brain, such as increased tolerance for alcohol and physical dependence, which maintain the compulsive inability to stop drinking. *See also* ADDICTION; ALCOHOLICS ANONYMOUS; DRUG AND ALCOHOL PROBLEMS; DUAL DIAGNOSIS.

alienation Seen as estrangement from nature by Hegel and reworked by Marx to refer to the separation of people from their human nature because of having to sell their labour power under capitalism. Marx argued that this results in their being alienated from: the products of their labour, because they have no control over what they produce; the work itself, because labour is a commodity that is bought; their humanity, because work lacks creativity; others, because market relations eclipse social relations. Feminists have used the term to refer to women's experience of oppression not only in work but also in other settings, such as the home. Now used in a general way to cover estrangement of many kinds (from others, from oneself, from a specific situation) and the negative feelings associated with it, for example, when reference is made to a child being alienated from her/his parent(s). *See also* ANOMIE; FEMINISM.

allocation The distribution of work, such as assessments, to social workers. Traditionally this occurred in a *collective forum, such as a team meeting, but is now more likely to take place on an individual basis with managers, administrators, or computer software allocating work directly to individual social workers.

altruism Putting other people's interests before one's own. Often presented as the opposite of self-centredness and as the motivation for volunteering or charitable activity.

Alzheimer's Disease A progressive deterioration of the brain as a result of the *loss of brain cells. *See also* ALZHEIMER'S RESEARCH UK; ALZHEIMER'S SOCIETY; DEMENTIA.

Alzheimer's Research UK Charity that funds research into *dementia. *See also* ALZHEIMER'S DISEASE; ALZHEIMER'S SOCIETY.

(⊕) SEE WEB LINKS
• Official site of Alzheimer's Research UK.

Alzheimer's Society A charity providing support for people with *dementia, their *carers, families, and professionals. It provides local services, engages in campaigning and lobbying to influence government policy, raises awareness generally about dementia, and funds research. *See also* ALZHEIMER'S DISEASE; ALZHEIMER'S RESEARCH UK.

(⊕) SEE WEB LINKS
• Official site of the Alzheimer's Society.

ambivalence The state of experiencing co-existing but competing or conflicting emotions, for example, when an adolescent wishes to break free of her/his parents but wants the security provided by their support.

AMHP *See* APPROVED MENTAL HEALTH PROFESSIONAL.

analysis The examination of an issue, problem, topic, or situation that goes beyond describing it and includes (one or more of) theories, thoughts, opinions, and judgements.

anger management (anger management programmes) Approaches to dealing with unpredictable and powerful emotions that lead to a state of being out of control and that have a destructive impact on relationships at work and/or in personal life. The focus is on reducing the feelings and physiological arousal associated with anger so that excessive and disruptive reactions are brought under control by finding out what triggers the anger and then developing strategies to deal with those triggers, such as:

Relaxation Techniques such as deep breathing and use of relaxing imagery. Once the techniques have been mastered they can be recalled when needed.

Cognitive restructuring Changing thoughts so that feelings change. For example, changing exaggerated 'it's the end of the world' thinking and replacing it with a more measured approach.

Problem-solving When anger is aroused by a problem, focusing on how to face and handle the problem.

Communication Avoiding immediate responses, listening to other people, thinking things through, and taking time before answering.

Anger management programmes are used with violent offenders in attempting to make them more aware of the effects of their anger on themselves and others, to teach them the strategies already mentioned, and to practise those strategies in a controlled environment such as role play in a group setting. *See also* COMMUNITY SENTENCES.

Anglocentrism *See* ETHNOCENTRICITY/ETHNOCENTRISM.

anomie Confusion and/or breakdown as a result of the absence of societal norms or conflict about them. (Now used more generally to refer to negative experiences associated with breakdown.) Most associated with the work of Émile Durkheim (1858–1917), particularly in *The Division of Labour in Society* (1893) and *Suicide* (1897), in which he argued that in a stable society people internalize norms about their aspirations that fit the circumstances of their lives. These societally produced norms and aspirations can be disrupted by economic, political, and social change. For example, Durkheim argued that suicide rates not only go up at times of economic depression, as we might expect, but also at times of economic boom, when cultural norms break down and people feel psychologically adrift, experiencing the condition he called anomie. Robert Merton (1910–2003), in *Social Theory and Social Structure* (1957), used anomie to refer to the experience of a disjunction between society's *goals and the means of realizing them. For example, the economic structure, for the most part, enables only privileged groups to succeed. This creates feelings of deprivation amongst those denied access to such success and pushes them towards deviance from societal norms. Although both Durkheim's and Merton's work has been re-evaluated, they offer support to the view that the individual problems to which social workers respond are located in wider social, political, and economic processes. *See also* AGENTS OF SOCIAL CONTROL; ALIENATION.

anorexia nervosa An eating disorder characterized by a severe and persistent disturbance in eating attitudes and behaviour as a consequence of experiencing an intense fear of gaining weight and a disturbance in the perception of body shape or weight. The intake of calories is severely restricted and excessive exercise may be undertaken, leading to malnutrition, serious physical health complications, and an abnormally low body weight, all of which can be life-threatening. The condition can cause acute psychological distress and significantly interfere with daily living. There is debate about the causes but most experts believe that an interaction of social, cultural, interpersonal, and biological factors contribute to its development.

anti-ageist practice Social work characterized by perspectives, attitudes, and actions that seek to counter *ageism. *See also* ANTI-DISCRIMINATORY PRACTICE; ANTI-OPPRESSIVE PRACTICE.

anti-disablist practice Social work characterized by perspectives, attitudes, and actions that seek to counter *able-bodiedism. *See also* ANTI-DISCRIMINATORY PRACTICE; ANTI-OPPRESSIVE PRACTICE; DIFFERENTLY-ABLED; DISABILITY; DISABLISM; SOCIAL MODEL OF DISABILITY.

anti-discriminatory practice (ADP) A social work stance that seeks to address individual *service users' experiences of instances of unfair treatment on the basis of age, *class, *disability, *ethnicity, *gender, *'race', and sexuality. Often used interchangeably with *anti-oppressive practice, but while anti-oppressive practice encompasses concern with individual experiences of discrimination, it has a much wider analysis of the sources of those experiences in the social divisions that create oppression and the measures needed to address them. *See also* CONSCIENTIZATION.

anti-discriminatory social work *See* ANTI-DISCRIMINATORY PRACTICE.

anti-oppressive practice (AOP) An overarching framework that encompasses a range of struggles for social justice in response to the social divisions in society and the oppressions that stem from them. Its roots lie in 1970s *radical social work, with its analysis of the structural basis for what are experienced as personal problems and its opposition to complete reliance on the tradition of individual *casework, rooted in seeing people's problems as *pathological. Critiques of radical social work from a number of perspectives alleged that it was too focused on *class at the expense of consideration of the impact of other social divisions. For example, feminist social workers identified an insufficient emphasis on gender and Black social workers criticized the lack of attention to *'race'. Over time, despite some continuing tensions and debates, a range of critical perspectives have placed themselves within the framework of anti-oppressive practice, united by commitments to *empowerment, inclusion, and greater equality. Power and its operation through oppression are central to the analyses of these perspectives.

In addition to challenging, or as it is sometimes put 'speaking to', power, there is a concern with focusing on the knowledge, experiences, and accounts of those who have been marginalized and seeking to work collaboratively with them. There are differences of opinion about the potential of social work in combating oppression. While some see its potential as great, others point to the marginal position in society occupied by social work itself and/or to its functions as an *agent of social control. There are also differences about the social work methods that are seen as fitting within this framework. Some advocate that only collective forms of social work, such as *community work and *group work, are appropriate, not least because by bringing people together their consciousness of their oppressed position may be raised and they are then enabled to address together the injustices they experience. Others see a place for continuing to work with people on a one-to-one basis, providing that individuals' problems are approached in terms of their being shaped by the social and economic circumstances within which they are located. *See also* ANTI-DISCRIMINATORY PRACTICE; CONSCIENTIZATION.

anti-oppressive social work *See* ANTI-OPPRESSIVE PRACTICE.

anti-poverty strategies Seeking to improve material circumstances by ensuring *service users have all of the social security and other benefits to which they are entitled, providing information on work and training opportunities, and conducting campaigns. There was a tendency for anti-poverty strategies to be adopted across the whole of *local authority provision, rather than being seen as the sole concern of social work in its work with service users. These local strategies sought to coordinate and integrate the contributions of all the departments of a local authority with the aims of meeting disadvantaged citizens' needs, improving their economic position, and promoting their social inclusion. Such initiatives have been increasingly difficult to sustain in the context of *austerity. *See also* CHILD POVERTY; POVERTY.

anti-psychiatry The ideas of a number of critics of conventional psychiatry that emerged in the 1960s. While there would be disagreement about which critics to include, in the UK the leading figures in both theory and practice were Ronald Laing, David Cooper, and Aaron Esterson. Wider critical contributions were provided by French theorists Michel Foucault and Jacques Lacan, and by Thomas Szasz in the US, particularly through his influential *The Myth of Mental Illness* (1961). Anti-psychiatry is not so much a coherent perspective as an umbrella term under which a range of different ideas about psychiatry have been debated. However, a common idea in anti-psychiatry is that the physical concept of illness and conventional medicine cannot be applied to social and psychological problems, bringing into question fundamental assumptions and practices of psychiatry, such as the authority of the psychiatrist and mainstream psychiatric treatments. The anti-psychiatry movement in the UK reached its height in the 1970s and is now usually presented as a historical phenomenon. However, the Critical Psychiatry Network was established in 1999 by a group of psychiatrists in the UK to develop contemporary critique of the bio-medical approach. The Network's criticism of psychiatry has resurrected the debates originally set in motion by the advocates of anti-psychiatry.

(⊕) SEE WEB LINKS
• Official site of the Critical Psychiatry Network.

anti-psychotics A group of medicines developed in the 1950s and used to treat severe mental disorders, primarily *psychoses, including *schizophrenia and *bipolar disorder. Also known as neuroleptic drugs and major tranquillizers, the introduction and eventual widespread use of anti-psychotic medication played a significant role in the shift in the treatment of conditions such as schizophrenia from being hospital-based to community-based.

anti-racist practice (ARP) Combating negative attitudes and treatment on the basis of *'race' and/or *ethnicity. The starting point is that the UK is a society in which *racism continues to exist and that social work has to recognize and address its impact. This involves addressing: social (and other) workers' perspectives; organizational policies and practices, for example, with regard to recruitment and employment issues; and aspects of service provision, such as monitoring trends and responding to them, as in the case of court disposals of white and minority ethnic young offenders. *See also* ANTI-DISCRIMINATORY PRACTICE; ANTI-OPPRESSIVE PRACTICE; BLACK PERSPECTIVES.

anti-social behaviour An act that causes a nuisance or disturbance to those living in and around a specific area and is grounds for an *Anti-social Behaviour Order. Such acts can take many different forms, such as graffiti, vandalism, destruction of property, intimidating language, threatening body language, noise, and consuming alcohol or drugs in a public area.

Anti-social Behaviour Order (ASBO) Introduced under Section 1 of the Crime and Disorder Act (1999), ASBOs were intended to reduce the likelihood of *anti-social behaviour and/or offending. Anyone over 10 can be given an ASBO, which lasts for at least two years but can be reviewed if behaviour improves. An Order can be issued if someone is charged and taken before a magistrate, who can instigate proceedings to have an ASBO put in place, An ASBO is a legal and binding contract between someone who has committed acts of anti-social behaviour and the police. The terms of an ASBO can incorporate an exclusion area, barring an individual from being in or around a particular area, or a curfew, banning an individual from being out after a designated time, or both. It can also include stipulations about particular behaviours such as not associating with particular people or not drinking in the street. The Anti-social Behaviour Act (2003) widened the powers to use fixed penalty notices for noise, nuisance, graffiti, etc.; introduced a power to disperse groups in designated areas; and strengthened the power to enforce *parental responsibility for children who behave in an anti-social way.

Breaching an ASBO is a criminal offence that can result in an individual being returned to court, where a harsher punishment may be imposed. The possible sentences depend on someone's age. Young offenders aged 10 to 14 can be fined up to £250 rising to £1,000 if aged 15 to 17. The fine may have to be paid by parents if someone is under 16. There is also the possibility of a *community sentence or a *Detention and Training Order for up to twenty-four months if someone is over 12. Adult offenders can be fined up to £5,000 or sentenced to five years in prison, or both. *See also* ACCEPTABLE BEHAVIOUR CONTRACT; YOUTH INCLUSION SUPPORT PANEL.

anti-social personality disorder (ASPD) *See* PERSONALITY DISORDER.

anxiety Feelings of uneasiness, apprehension, or fear aroused by a perceived sense of threat or danger. Anxiety is considered to be a biological life-preserving response involving a combination of biochemical changes in the body. Factors affecting anxiety also include the individual's personal history, experience, and memory. The physical and psychological symptoms of anxiety can be unpleasant and can include headache, nausea, trembling, fainting, chest tightness, and tingling in hands or feet. The distinction between anxiety as a commonplace and normal feeling or experience, and *anxiety disorder is important. A person may feel anxious without having an anxiety disorder. In addition, anxiety frequently occurs as an aspect of other mental health problems.

anxiety disorder A mental health problem characterized by *anxiety as a central feature. Typical signs include a state of unease, fear, or apprehension with or without a recognizable cause. Physical symptoms include sweating, palpitations, difficulty breathing, trembling, and feelings of unreality. Anxiety is a normal response to stress or danger and is a commonplace experience. For a diagnosis of anxiety disorder, the anxiety must be severe and persistent enough to interfere with daily functioning and customary activities. The *Diagnostic and Statistical Manual of Mental Disorders* (*DSM-5*) recognizes the following types of anxiety disorder: separation anxiety disorder, selective mutism, specific phobia, social phobia, panic disorder, agoraphobia, and generalized anxiety disorder. (*Obsessive-compulsive disorders and trauma/stressor-related disorders are treated as separate conditions.) *See also* AFFECTIVE DISORDER; ANXIETY.

applied social research The use of systematic investigation to increase knowledge that will improve the social conditions and wellbeing of people in society. The research may be about, for example, groups of people, cultures, health and social problems, social trends, social policies, and programmes. Applied social research can include, but is not limited to, identifying the prevalence of a social concern or problem, raising awareness of the social issue or problem, examining the impact of social and personal conditions on affected individuals, examining the effectiveness of policies, programmes, and interventions in addressing social or personal problems, and identifying strategies for the prevention of social problems and social disadvantage. The range of research methods used in applied social research is the same as those used in other forms of research. However, social work values and ethics may at times prevent the use of some methods. For example, it may be considered unethical to employ a control where this involves excluding a group from receiving support. Applied social research has been used by social workers to advocate for social change; in these cases it has an explicit value base about the promotion of equality and social justice. In general, most social work research is applied social research as the purpose is ultimately to improve the existing social and personal conditions of individuals and groups. *See also* ACTION-RESEARCH.

appropriate adult Someone who attends police interviews conducted with people in custody who are identified as being vulnerable. This vulnerable status refers to people with mental health problems or *learning disabilities who exhibit communication difficulties. It also encompasses children and young people under the age of 17 years. The responsibility for identifying a person as vulnerable rests with the police custody officer, who, once this status has been assigned, seeks out a responsible adult, known as the appropriate adult, to join the police interview. This person can be a family member, a friend, a volunteer, a social worker, or another professional from health or social services. Full details of the responsibilities of this person to provide support and advice to the vulnerable person are set out in the Police and Criminal Evidence (PACE) Code of Practice, published in conjunction with the Police and Criminal Evidence Act (1984). The role is one that essentially seeks to ensure that the rights of the individual in custody are maintained.

(⊕) SEE WEB LINKS
• Official site of the National Appropriate Adult Network.

approval panel *See* RESOURCE PANEL.

approved clinician A role introduced by the Mental Health Act (2007). A mental health professional who has been approved, for the purposes of the Act, to undertake Mental Health Act (1983) *assessments and who understands the range of treatment options available. Approved clinicians may be doctors, psychologists, nurses, *occupational therapists, and social workers. *See also* APPROVED MENTAL HEALTH PROFESSIONAL.

approved doctor *See* SECTION 12 APPROVED DOCTOR.

approved mental health professional (AMHP) A role created by the Mental Health Act (2007) to replace the role of the approved social worker, which was introduced by the Mental Health Act (1983). Approved mental health professionals may be social workers, nurses, *occupational therapists, or psychologists and are approved by a local social services authority to undertake functions under the Mental Health Act (1983) in relation to making applications for admission to hospital under sections of the Act. To qualify as an AMHP a recognized course in a higher education institution must be undertaken. In practice the AMHP role is mainly carried out by social workers. *See also* APPROVED CLINICIAN; COMPULSORY ADMISSION; INFORMAL ADMISSION.

approved social worker *See* APPROVED MENTAL HEALTH PROFESSIONAL.

Area Child Protection Committee *See* LOCAL SAFEGUARDING CHILDREN BOARD.

area teams The decentralized work units of social workers, located in the areas they served, were accorded a central place in *Social Services Departments in accordance with the recommendations of the *Seebohm Report (1968). These were generic teams, covering the full range of service-user groupings (people with *learning disabilities, children and young people, people with physical disabilities, *older people, people with mental health problems). There was considerable delegation to this level of the organization rather than the work of area teams being directed by more senior managers. As a result, there was a high degree of autonomy for the teams and the social workers within them, which was consistent with the proposals of the Seebohm Committee concerning the importance of flexible decentralized services. Area teams gradually disappeared and were replaced by teams of specialist social workers or multidisciplinary teams. *See also* COLLABORATIVE WORKING; DECENTRALIZATION.

Arnstein's Ladder An influential typology that can be helpful in clarifying the degree of citizen and/or *service user *participation involved in particular services or contexts. Arnstein identified eight levels of *citizen participation, classified according to whether she regarded them as examples of non-participation, tokenism, or citizen power.

On the lowest rungs of the ladder, she considers therapy and manipulation to be concerned with education and cure rather than participation. Therapy and manipulation are followed by three forms of tokenism, through which citizens can be informed and advised, but cannot make decisions. At the top of the ladder are

Ladder of citizen participation
Arnstein, S. (1969) 'A ladder of citizen participation', *Journal of the American Institute of Planners*, 35, 4, 217

three forms of citizen power: *partnership, delegated power, and citizen control; these involve the redistribution of power.

Asperger's Syndrome A condition associated with difficulties with communication and social skills that can lead to isolation and emotional problems. Although seen as falling within the *autism spectrum, people with the syndrome are usually less affected than those with autism. Children with the syndrome are often of average or above average intelligence and may be adept at factual learning and mathematics. *See also* NATIONAL AUTISTIC SOCIETY.

assertive community treatment (assertive outreach) Providing intensive multidisciplinary support services to adults with severe and enduring mental health problems in order to enable them to live independently in the *community and reduce hospital admissions. The model was first developed in the US in the 1970s and became a significant influence on UK policy and practice from the late 1990s. It targets severely mentally ill adults who do not engage effectively with mental health services and whose symptoms result in significant difficulties that interfere with many aspects of their lives.

assertiveness training Programmes for people who experience difficulty in putting forward their interests and needs, which use exercises to teach strategies that enable them to state their position firmly but not aggressively.

Assessed and Supported Year in Employment (ASYE) A programme of support and assessment for all newly qualified social workers in the statutory, voluntary, and private sectors that was introduced in 2012. Since then, newly qualified social workers have been assessed against ASYE capabilities as part of the overarching *Professional Capabilities Framework (PCF). The AYSE capabilities were augmented in 2015 by the inclusion of the *Knowledge and Skills Statements for Social Workers. The ASYE is intended to provide newly qualified social workers with regular and focused support during their first year of employment so that they continue to develop their skills, knowledge, and values and strengthen their professional confidence. *See also* CONTINUING PROFESSIONAL DEVELOPMENT; HEALTH AND CARE PROFESSIONS COUNCIL.

(())) SEE WEB LINKS
- Guidance and resources for the ASYE in adult services.
- Guidance and resources for the ASYE in child and family services.

assessment Collecting, analysing, and recording information about people, their circumstances, and the context of their lives in order to reach an understanding of their situation and to inform decisions about whether further intervention is necessary and, if so, to propose what form(s) it should take. It can be an event that occurs at a recognizable point in time or an ongoing process, a combination of the two, or can move between event and process as circumstances change.

The form a particular assessment takes will be shaped by the purpose it performs. It may be concerned with the assessment of *need, a decision about *eligibility for a particular service, *gate-keeping resources, evaluating *risk, prioritizing *referrals according to urgency, or a combination of any or all of these purposes. The purposes of assessment in specific circumstances will be shaped by legislation, national policy, and local policies and procedures, all of which identify the role assessment is expected to play in relation to the provision of particular interventions and service provision. This is often seen as introducing a tension in terms of the extent to which the social worker is concerned with the needs and interests of the *service user, up to and including advocacy on their behalf, versus the social worker's role as a representative of the employing organization and the functions it performs on behalf of the state.

Assessment is increasingly undertaken on an inter-professional and inter-organizational basis as multidisciplinary responses have become a growing feature of policy and practice, with the recognition that assessment is a key element in the work of many professionals and a function of a range of organizations. Multidisciplinary assessments have the potential for developing shared perspectives and concerns between social workers and other professionals, but also reveal professional differences that have to be considered and negotiated. Recognition that a number of professional views may need to be represented has led to an emphasis on the service user not having to repeat information to different professionals.

Service user involvement in assessment has been an increasingly significant issue in policy and practice. For example, in adult services, service users and *carers are regarded as integral participants in forms of assessment that seek to recognize their strengths, knowledge, abilities, and successes in contrast to models of assessment dominated by professionals. Service users and carers are now portrayed in policy documents as involved in collaborative exchanges with social workers in which they contribute their knowledge and expertise about themselves and their situations, and social workers negotiate solutions and access resources. However, while recognizing the central importance of service user and carer views it is important to acknowledge that the statutory duties of social workers remain, with consequent obligations to make professional judgements, particular in circumstances of *abuse.

Service user involvement has been pushed further in a vocal movement for user-led assessment in accessing services for adults. This has been seen in service users and carers being involved in designing the assessment process itself and, more significantly, in dispensing with the professional role as a result of forms of *self-assessment, reinforced by *direct payments and *personal budgets. Self-assessment moves beyond the service user or carer being involved in assessment to a position in which they take responsibility for the process. Web-based forms of self-assessment have appeared on some *local authority sites, which provide immediate decisions on eligibility for services. A range of developments includes self-directed assessment, peer-supported self-assessment, and professionally supported self-assessment. There are limits to self-assessment in circumstances of abuse or where the implementation of some statutory duties is concerned. *See also* COLLABORATIVE WORKING; EXCHANGE MODEL OF ASSESSMENT; HOLISTIC APPROACH; NEEDS ASSESSMENT; RESIDENTIAL ASSESSMENT.

assessment (adults) *See* EXCHANGE MODEL OF ASSESSMENT; NEEDS ASSESSMENT (ADULTS).

assessment (children) Under the Children Act (1989), *local authorities are required to provide services for children for the purposes of *safeguarding and promoting their *welfare. Social workers undertake *assessments of the *needs of individual children to determine which services to provide and what action to take. A number of different assessments are conducted under the Act:

a

- A *child in need* is defined under the Act as a child who is unlikely to achieve or maintain a reasonable level of health or development (*see* CHILD DEVELOPMENT), or whose health and development is likely to be significantly or further impaired, without the provision of services; or a child who is disabled. Children in need are assessed under *Section 17 of the Children Act (1989)*.

- When undertaking an assessment of a *disabled child*, a local authority must also consider whether it is necessary to provide support under *Section 2 of the Chronically Sick and Disabled Persons Act (1970)*. If a local authority is satisfied that services and assistance can be provided under Section 2 of the CSDPA, and they are necessary in order to meet a disabled child's needs, the authority must arrange to provide that support.

- Where there are concerns about a *child being maltreated* or concerns arise while services are being provided to a child and family, a local authority must initiate enquiries to find out what is happening to the child and whether the child needs to be protected. Local authorities have a *duty to make enquiries under *Section 47 of the Children Act (1989)* if they have reasonable cause to suspect that a child is suffering, or is likely to suffer, *significant harm, in order to decide whether they should take any action to safeguard and promote the child's welfare. There may be a need for immediate protection whilst the assessment is carried out (*see* EMERGENCY PROTECTION ORDER).

- Some *children require accommodation* because there is no one who has *parental responsibility for them, because they are lost or abandoned, or because the person who has been caring for them is prevented from providing them with suitable accommodation or care. Under *Section 20 of the Children Act (1989)*, a local authority has a duty to accommodate such children.

- If a local authority considers that a *young carer* may have support needs, they must carry out an assessment under *Section 17ZA of the Children Act (1989)*. The authority must also carry out such an assessment if a young carer, or the parent of a young carer, requests one. Such an assessment must consider whether it is appropriate or excessive for the young carer to provide care for the person in question, in the light of the young carer's needs and wishes (*see* TRANSITION TO ADULT CARE AND SUPPORT). The Young Carers' (Needs Assessment) Regulations (2015) require local authorities to consider the needs of the whole family when carrying out a young carer's assessment. Young carers' assessments can be combined with assessments of adults (*see* NEEDS ASSESSMENT; TRANSITION TO ADULT CARE AND SUPPORT) in the household, with the agreement of the young carer and adults concerned.

- If a local authority considers that a *parent carer of a disabled child* may have support needs, it must carry out an assessment under *Section 17ZD of the Children Act (1989)*. The local authority must also carry out an assessment if a parent carer requests one. Such an assessment must consider whether it is appropriate for the parent carer to provide, or continue to provide, care for the disabled child, in the light of the parent carer's needs and wishes.

Assessment is a dynamic and continuous process which should build upon the history of an individual child, responding to the impact of any previous services and analysing what further action might be needed. Social workers should build on this history with assistance from other professionals. Accordingly every assessment should draw together relevant information gathered not only from the child and her/his family but also from relevant professionals including teachers, early years workers, health professionals, the police, and adult services. The aim is to use all the information gathered to identify difficulties and *risk factors as well as developing a picture of strengths and *protective factors.

The purpose of an assessment is to:

- gather information about a child and family, to analyse their needs and/or the nature and level of any risk and harm being suffered by the child;
- to decide whether the child is a child in need (Section 17) and/or is suffering, or likely to suffer, significant harm (Section 47); and
- to provide support to address needs in order to improve the child's *outcomes and/or to make her/him safe.

Where a child becomes *looked-after, the assessment becomes the baseline for work with the family. Any needs that have been identified are addressed before decisions are made about the child's return home. A further assessment by a social worker (under the Care Planning, Placement and Case Review [England] Regulations [2010]) is required before the child returns home.

The *Working Together* (2015) statutory guidance sets out the principles and parameters of high-quality assessments. They:

- are child-centred. Where there is a conflict of interest, decisions should be made in the child's *best interests;
- are rooted in child development and informed by evidence;
- are focused on action and outcomes for children;
- are *holistic in approach, addressing the child's needs within her/his family and wider community;
- ensure equality of opportunity;
- involve children and families;
- build on strengths as well as identifying difficulties;
- are integrated in approach;
- are a continuing process, not an event;
- lead to action, including the provision of services;
- review services provided on an ongoing basis; and
- are transparent and open to challenge.

As well as setting out the principle and parameters of high-quality assessments, *Working Together* advocates adopting a systematic approach using a conceptual

Assessment Framework

model as the best way to produce comprehensive assessments for children. It states that a good assessment is one that investigates the three domains set out in the *ecological approach utilized by the Assessment Framework: parental capacity to care for the child; the child's development needs; and wider family and environmental factors. (The way in which the domains are presented is often referred to as the 'assessment triangle'.)

These domains are divided into a series of dimensions that encourage specific information to be gathered. Under the ***child's developmental needs***, information can be sought on the child's health, education, emotional and behavioural development, family and social relationships, self-care skills, and identity. Under the ***parenting capacity*** domain, consideration can be given to the child's basic care, safety, emotional warmth, stimulation, guidance, and boundaries. The domain of ***family and environmental factors*** focuses on community resources, the family's social integration, employment and income, housing, family history and functioning, and wider family. The interaction of the domains requires careful consideration during an assessment. The aim is to reach a judgement about the nature and level of needs and/or *risks that a child may be facing within her/his family. The analysis of the domains is intended to provide the basis for judgements and decisions as to how best to safeguard and promote the welfare of a child and, where possible, to support parents in contributing towards achieving this aim. The end product of the assessment is an analysis of a child's needs, a description of the intervention needed, and a plan specifying who will do what within what time frame, including the arrangements for reviewing the progress of the plan.

An assessment should be child-centred. Where there is a conflict between the needs of the child and those of her/his parents or *care-givers, decisions should be made in the child's best interests. Local authorities have to give due regard to a child's age and understanding when determining what (if any) services to provide under Section 17 of the Children Act (1989), and before making decisions about action to be taken to protect children under Section 47 of the Children Act (1989). Wherever possible, an assessment should be informed by the views of the child (according to her/his age and understanding) as well as the family. Children should, wherever possible, be seen alone and social workers have a duty to ascertain the child's wishes and feelings regarding the provision of services to be delivered. Culture, religion, ethnic origin, and other characteristics should be respected.

Working Together stresses that the timeliness of an assessment is a critical element for its quality and the *outcomes for the child. The speed with which an assessment is carried out should be determined by the needs of the individual child and the nature and level of any harm, or risk of harm, faced by the child. However, there are laid-down time limits.Within one working day of a *referral being received, a local authority social worker should make a decision about the type of response that is required and acknowledge receipt of the referral to the referrer. For children who are in need of immediate protection, action must be taken by the social worker, or the police or the *NSPCC if removal of a child is required, as soon as possible after the referral has been made (Sections 44 and 46 of the Children Act [1989]). The maximum time frame for an assessment to conclude, so that it is possible to reach a decision on the next steps, is forty-five working days from the point of referral. If an assessment exceeds forty-five working days, the social worker should record the reasons for exceeding the time limit.

Local authorities determine their own assessment processes, which are published in local protocols. A local protocol should set out clear arrangements for how *cases will be managed once a child is referred to the local authority and be consistent with the requirements of *Working Together*, as this is statutory guidance. The protocol is agreed with the relevant *Local Safeguarding Children Board.

Chapter 1 of *Working Together* sets out detailed processes and flow charts to guide the management of individual *cases.

Further reading: HM Government (2015) *Working Together to Safeguard Children: A Guide to Inter-agency Working to Safeguard and Promote the Welfare of Children*, Chapter 1. Available at: https://www.gov.uk/government/uploads/system/uploads/attachment_data/file/419595/Working_Together_to_Safeguard_Children.pdf.

Assessment Framework *See* ASSESSMENT (CHILDREN).

assessment models (adults) *See* EXCHANGE MODEL OF ASSESSMENT.

assessment of capacity *See* CAPACITY.

assessment triangle *See* ASSESSMENT (CHILDREN).

ASSET A structured assessment tool used by *Youth Justice Services in England and *Wales with all *young offenders who come into contact with the criminal justice system. Described by the *Youth Justice Board as a Young Offender Assessment Profile, it aims to look at the young person's offences and identify the *risk and *protective factors that may have contributed to the offending behaviour. These may, among others, be associated with mental health problems, educational attainment issues, or difficulties at home. The information gathered as a result of the application of this tool is used to inform court reports prepared by youth justice professionals and frame recommendations for intervening in the life of the young person. These interventions are likely to seek to address the factors identified in the assessment as having contributed to the offending behaviour. The tool is also used to measure the progress made by the young person and the risk of further offending over time.

Further reading: Youth Justice Board (2014) *Forms for the Assessment of Young Offenders with Guidance for Youth Offending Teams*. Available at: https://www.gov.uk/government/publications/asset-documents.

assimilation (ethnicity) The process by which a ethnic minority group is absorbed into the majority population, thereby losing its distinctiveness. In postwar mainstream politics this was seen as a desirable *goal with regard to immigrants from Commonwealth countries. Such attitudes were also prevalent in social work, for example, in the assumption that ethnic minority groups should adapt to mainstream services rather than vice versa, as when it was thought in the best interests of Black children to be placed with white adoptive parents. In recent years, this assumption has been questioned with an emphasis on accommodation replacing assimilation. Accommodation celebrates difference, stresses ethnic groups finding ways of co-existing, and seeks to develop services that are attuned to their distinctive characteristics. *See also* ANTI-RACIST PRACTICE; MULTICULTURALISM; SAME RACE PLACEMENT.

assistance *See* CARE.

assisted suicide *See* EUTHANASIA.

assistive technology An umbrella term for which the most widely used definition is that adopted by the Royal Commission on Long-term Care: 'any device or system that allows an individual to perform a task that they would otherwise be unable to do, or increases the ease and safety with which the task can be performed' (Royal Commission on Long-term Care 1999). This includes a wide range of devices from simple low-tech items to sophisticated high-tech integrated systems. *See* AIDS AND ADAPTATIONS; TELECARE.

asylums Institutions built to segregate people with mental health problems from society. Developed across Europe and America from the mid-1750s onwards, asylums were gradually replaced by psychiatric hospitals during the early part of the twentieth century.

asylum-seeker A person who has made a formal application for asylum and is waiting for a decision. If a claim is accepted by the Home Office, there are three possible statuses that can be granted: *refugee status for five years; *humanitarian protection for three years; *discretionary leave to remain for three years. All three of these statuses give the same welfare rights as those of UK citizens but do not confer UK citizenship. *See also* NATIONAL ASYLUM SUPPORT SERVICE; UNACCOMPANIED ASYLUM-SEEKING CHILDREN.

at risk Commonly used term when social workers or other professionals are concerned that someone may come to harm and usually indicating that action needs to be considered. A wide range of *service users, for example, people with mental health problems, *older people, and children may be at risk as a result of their own actions or the actions of others in many different ways. As a result, the term can be used so broadly that care needs to be taken to define precisely what it means in specific contexts. Someone may be at risk but what needs to be clarified is at risk of what and how likely is it that the threat posed by the risk will materialize? *See also* DANGEROUSNESS; RISK.

attachment (attachment theory) Concerned with ties between a child and an attachment figure who meets the child's need for safety, security, and protection, particularly in stressful situations. A perspective first formulated by psychologist John Bowlby (1907–1990) that is primarily concerned with early emotional bonds between children and their adult caregivers. The central tenet of attachment theory is that caregivers who are available and responsive to their child's needs establish a sense of security in the child as s/he develops. The child knows that the caregiver is dependable and this creates a secure base from which the child can move out to explore the wider world. The key characteristics of secure attachment are seen as:

Safe haven When the child feels afraid, s/he can obtain comfort from the caregiver.

Secure base The caregiver provides a dependable base from which the child can explore outwards.

Proximity maintenance The child seeks to stay within reach of the caregiver.

Separation distress When separated from the caregiver, the child becomes upset but not overwhelmed.

Other psychologists have elaborated types of insecure attachment: ambivalent-insecure attachment; avoidant–insecure attachment; disorganized–insecure attachment. Children who are ***ambivalently attached*** tend to be very suspicious of strangers. They become extremely distressed when separated from a caregiver but do not seem comforted by their return, in some cases rejecting them by refusing comfort or directing aggression towards them. Children with ***avoidant attachment*** tend to avoid their caregiver, especially after a period of absence. They show no preference when having a choice between a caregiver and a complete stranger. The actions and responses of children with *disorganized attachment* to caregivers are often a mix of behaviour, including avoidance and/or resistance. They can seem confused or apprehensive in the presence of a caregiver.

Attachment theory has sometimes been interpreted in social work as suggesting that attachment is an early once-and-for-all event whose absence justifies permanent removal of a child from a caregiver. There is now widespread recognition that attachment is a more complex and ongoing process so that if there is a break in the formation of attachment, even early in a child's life, it should not be necessarily assumed to mean that attachment will not develop.

Further reading: Howe, D. (2011) *Attachment across the Lifecourse: A Brief Introduction*, Palgrave Macmillan.

attendance at school *See* COMPULSORY SCHOOL AGE.

attention deficit hyperactivity disorder (ADHD) A collection of childhood-onset behavioural difficulties resulting in significantly reduced ability to maintain attention without being distracted, and being impulsive and restless. There is debate about the causes of ADHD and whether there are neuro-biological differences between children with and without ADHD. For example, it has been suggested that problems with neurotransmitters (the chemicals that transmit nerve signals in the brain) are involved, resulting in an inability to filter stimulation from the outside world. However, such suggestions remain controversial. Diet may be implicated, as research has shown that certain combinations of artificial food colours and preservatives are linked to increases in hyperactivity. It is important not to confuse ADHD with boisterous behaviour. Although the manifestations may be similar (having difficulty waiting in turn, following instructions, playing quietly, concentrating, and so on) for the child with ADHD the severity of the problems will make everyday functioning at school or at home very difficult and will be extremely disruptive for those around them. Behaviour management and educational support are the most likely responses, along with medication. There are four licensed drugs in the UK for the treatment of ADHD.

Audit Commission A *non-departmental public body that pursued the three 'c's (*economy, efficiency, and effectiveness) in the delivery of local public services (local government, health, housing, community safety, and fire and rescue services). It was central to the development of a *business orientation in public services, including social work. It began work in April 1983, having been established by the Local Government Finance Act (1982), as part of the Thatcher government's programme for introducing private sector disciplines and styles of management into the public sector. Under the Local Government Act (1999) *local authorities were required 'to secure continuous improvement in the way in which their functions [were] exercised, having regard to a combination of economy, efficiency, and effectiveness'. The Audit Commission was given the power to carry out inspections of local authorities' performance of their functions, including their compliance with this duty. This maintained pressure on local authorities, including with regard to their social services functions, to continuously strive for *'value for money'. The Audit Commission was abolished following the Comprehensive Spending Review undertaken by the Conservative–Liberal Democrat Coalition Government in 2010 but has had a deep and enduring influence. *See also* BUSINESS ORIENTATION; MANAGERIALISM.

austerity Used as shorthand for the principle that underpins policies and pro-grammes that have been put in place following the crisis in the financial system in 2007–8. The crisis was originally located in the banking and financial sectors of the USA and UK but rapidly became global in scope. While the initial focus was on how to rescue the banks from disaster and restore financial stability, the economics and politics of austerity quickly shifted to a concern with government debt, which included the phenomenal amounts involved in saving the banks. In the process, the cause of and blame for the crisis shifted from the private sector (the high-risk strategies employed by the banks) to the public sector (the 'wasteful' and 'expensive' *welfare state). As a consequence, austerity has amplified existing *neo-liberal themes in which public spending, public debt, and public benefits and services are viewed as problematic and as obstructing growth and enterprise. In this view, fiscal constraint is seen as having the potential to expand economic growth through greater private consumption and investment. If this does not happen, rather than being questioned, austerity is restated and asserted more strongly. The UK has cut public benefits and services more deeply than most European countries, justified by the argument that this is both economically necessary and morally desirable, as the actions of citizens are called upon to replace the activities of the state (*see* BIG SOCIETY.) A key component of austerity has been welfare state reform, reducing or removing altogether public services and benefits (for example, *youth services and/or *education social work have been disbanded by some local authorities), with such developments often presented as opportunities for *modernization. This has resulted in workers in the *public sector and recipients of its benefits and services bearing the brunt of austerity. For example, workers have experienced wage cuts or freezes and as women predominate in public sector employment, these measures have affected them disproportionately. Women have also been disproportionately affected by cuts in public services because the gendered roles in caring for children, older, and disabled people mean that women rely on public services and related aspects of the social security system more than men. Given that services and benefits are already targeted on vulnerable and financially impoverished citizens, cutting them increases suffering still further. What this suggests is that while at first sight austerity may seem to belong to the realm of economics and to have little to do with social work, its impact has been far-reaching in shaping the politics, policies, and practice of social work following the financial crash.

authorized person *See* DIRECT PAYMENT.

autism spectrum A range of life-long developmental disabilities characterized by difficulties with communication, interaction, and imagination. The term has replaced 'autism' in order to recognize that although these three main areas of difficulty are common, they affect different people in different combinations and in different ways:

> **Communication** For example, problems with facial expressions, voice tones, and jokes. Some people may not speak or may have quite limited speech, in which case they usually understand what other people say but may prefer to use sign language or visual symbols themselves. Others have good language skills but may repeat what the other person has just said.
> **Interaction** Difficulty recognizing or understanding other people's emotions and feelings and expressing their own. This can make it difficult to fit in socially and social rules may not be picked up. Can appear insensitive because of

having no sense of how others are feeling. May appear to behave 'strangely' because of problems in expressing feelings, emotions, or needs.

Imagination Finding it hard to imagine situations outside the immediate daily routine. This means there may be difficulty in anticipating what might happen next, in understanding the idea of *risk, or in dealing with unfamiliar situations. In other areas of imagination, there can be particular strengths, for example, in art or music.

While some people have no specific support targeted at their difficulties, others need intensive assistance. There is a range of interventions including behavioural, dietary, medical, relationship-based, and skills-based approaches. *See also* ASPERGER'S SYNDROME; NATIONAL AUTISTIC SOCIETY.

aversion therapy An approach to eradicating behaviour by associating it with an unpleasant event. It has tended to fall into disrepute because of the notoriety it achieved through controversial applications, such as showing gay men pictures of naked men to the accompaniment of electric shocks. However, some applications continue to be used. For example, the drug Antabuse (also known as Disulfarim) is used to treat *alcoholism. If alcohol is consumed, Antabuse causes an extreme physical reaction. The longer the drug is taken, the more severe the reaction becomes. *See also* BEHAVIOUR MODIFICATION; BEHAVIOURISM.

AWOL *See* ABSENT WITHOUT LEAVE.

BAAF *See* CORAMBAAF.

backward chaining *See* CHAINING.

bail A court releasing an alleged offender, instead of sending her/him to prison, while s/he waits for the date of her/his trial. Bail may have conditions attached, such as specifying where the alleged offender must live, or only be granted if a surety is lodged—a sum of money that is forfeited if the alleged offender does not turn up for the trial. The expectation is that bail will be granted unless it is believed that the alleged offender may not appear for her/his trial, is likely to offend again, or may intimidate witnesses.

Barclay Report (1982) The outcome of a two-year national enquiry into the roles and tasks of social workers commissioned by the Secretary of State for Social Services in the first Thatcher government and produced by a working party convened by the National Institute for Social Work in 1980, chaired by Peter Barclay (1926–2014). The Report particularly emphasized the need for social work to promote community networks and engage in social care planning in cooperation with *voluntary organizations and *informal carers. It advocated augmenting the existing individual *casework with roles of *brokerage and negotiation, using knowledge of community resources to develop *community social work. This form of social work was seen as requiring workers to see individual *service users as citizens, in the context of their local communities and networks. It envisaged a redistribution of power through greater delegation to front-line social workers and evinced a belief in the capacity of ordinary people to make decisions for themselves. The report advocated that social workers should develop detailed knowledge of local areas and use that knowledge to encourage local community *participation in social services, focusing on strengths and resources. The abilities identified as necessary for community social workers were to work in *partnership, understand local communities, and develop networks. After initial enthusiasm in some local authorities for community social work, often referred to as *patch-based social work, experiments with its implementation dwindled, partly in the face of the continuing existence of social work's statutory roles and duties, a reality that Robert Pinker, in a minority report, had suggested would fly in the face of attempts to develop the more ambitious and expansive approach represented by community social work.

Barnardos A *voluntary organization founded by Dr Thomas Barnardo (1845–1905) when he set up the Ragged School in 1867 in the East End of London as a response to children's poverty. For many years its primary focus was on children's homes (Barnardo's Homes), sometimes provided in large establishments or 'villages'. From the 1880s children began to be sent to Canada and Australia where there were work opportunities, in search of a better life. Their experiences varied from becoming fully part of the family they joined to being exploited and/or abused. Over its more recent history, Barnardos has evolved into an organization running community-based projects across the UK, directed at a range of issues affecting children and young people, such as crime, mental health problems, *abuse, and poverty. Barnardos also provides *counselling and *advocacy for vulnerable children and young people.

(((⊕))) SEE WEB LINKS
• Official site of Barnardos.

'battered baby' The original term, used initially by doctors and then widely, to describe the physical abuse of children. It was only in the late 1950s that doctors began to accept that parents might inflict harm on their children. Before that time, doctors were puzzled by children being brought to hospital with a succession of different injuries. The term is no longer in professional use but may be encountered colloquially or in the media. *See also* CHILD ABUSE AND NEGLECT.

'battered wife' *See* DOMESTIC VIOLENCE.

'battered woman' *See* DOMESTIC VIOLENCE.

behavioural family therapy (BFT) (mental health) A particular form of *family therapy that is widely used as a short-term intervention. It focuses on positive communication, problem-solving skills, and stress management within the family. The needs of all family members are addressed and each family member is encouraged to identify and work towards clear personal *goals. Families are asked to undertake work on recognizing early signs of relapse in the person with mental health problems and to develop a clear staying-well plan. BFT can be practised by a range of professionals who have undertaken training and is recommended by the *National Institute for Health and Care Excellence for use in families where a member has a severe mental health condition such as *schizophrenia. *See also* DIALECTICAL BEHAVIOUR THERAPY.

behavioural psychology *See* BEHAVIOURISM.

behaviourism A psychological theory based on the proposition that all behaviour is learned through conditioning processes as the individual interacts with her/his environment. It sees no need to engage in analysis of internal mental states because it considers that behaviour can be studied and analysed systematically based on scientific observation. Conditioning processes are divided into two main types:

Operant conditioning (instrumental conditioning) Learning that results from rewards and punishments for behaviour. There is a learned association between the behaviour itself and the consequence that follows it through *reinforcers* and *punishment.* Reinforcers increase behaviour, punishment decreases behaviour. *Positive reinforcers* are favourable responses to behaviour, whereas *negative reinforcers* involve removing unfavourable responses. Punishment institutes adverse responses to the behaviour it follows. *Positive punishment* involves an unfavourable response. *Negative punishment* occurs when a favourable response is removed. These techniques can be found in a wide range of applications with children, young people, and adults.

Classical conditioning A naturally occurring (unconditioned) stimulus produces an unconditioned response. A previously neutral stimulus is then associated with the naturally occurring stimulus. Eventually the previously neutral stimulus comes to evoke the response previously produced by the naturally occurring stimulus and becomes a conditioned stimulus, capable of eventually producing the original unconditioned response as a conditioned response. Pavlov's experiments with dogs are often used to illustrate this process. The unconditioned stimulus was the sight and smell of food. The unconditioned response was that the dog would salivate. Pavlov rang a bell—a neutral stimulus—when the food was produced for the dog. Over time, the ringing bell became a conditioned stimulus producing the learned (conditioned) response of salivating, even when food was not present. These techniques can be used in the treatment of *phobias or *anxiety disorders. For example, by juxtaposing an anxiety-provoking or phobia-inducing situation with pleasant surroundings and/or sensations, new associations can be learned. *See also* BEHAVIOUR MODIFICATION; FUNCTIONAL ANALYSIS; TOKEN ECONOMY.

Further reading: Skinner, B. F. (2006) *About Behaviourism*, Random House.

behaviour modification Applying the operant and classical conditioning processes of *behaviourism in order to change behaviour. The emphasis is on measuring observable behaviour that is the focus of the intervention, such as the amount of alcohol that has been consumed, the number of angry outbursts that have taken place, and so on. Unwanted behaviour is extinguished and/or wanted behaviour is promoted by the use of reinforcers and punishment. A number of other techniques have been developed, particularly for the treatment of *anxiety disorders or *phobias. For example, *modelling* involves watching another person producing the behaviour that is the object of the intervention as a way of learning how to respond differently. *Desensitization* exposes the person seeking assistance to gradually increasing 'doses' of the object, event, or situation (or visualizations of it) that is feared, usually combined with relaxation techniques, so that the stress associated with it is replaced by a more relaxed response. *Flooding* subjects someone to the full force of that which they fear, often producing an initial sense of being overwhelmed, in the knowledge that this feeling will subside, particularly if the process also involves relaxation techniques. *See also* FUNCTIONAL ANALYSIS; TOKEN ECONOMY.

Further reading: Schinke, S. (ed.) (2008) *Behavioral Methods in Social Welfare: Helping Children, Adults, and Families in Community Settings*, Aldine Transaction.

behaviour therapy *See* BEHAVIOUR MODIFICATION.

benchmarking A standard against which performance is measured or judged. Originally a mark used in surveying, carpentry, and other areas of work as a reference point. In *private sector business it came to refer to the measurement of rival companies' products or services according to specified standards in order to compare it with and improve one's own product or service. A similar approach has been increasingly prevalent in the *public sector. For example, comparing the average cost of a place in a residential establishment in a particular *local authority with the average cost in all local authorities or the average in a sample of similar local authorities. *See also* PERFORMANCE MANAGEMENT.

benefit cap A limit on the total amount of *benefits that most people aged 16 to 64 can get.

benefits Financial payments made through the social security system.

bereavement The *loss of someone through death, resulting in a sense of absence and longing for the dead person, followed by a period of adjustment that can be prolonged. Grief can be expressed in a range of feelings:

Stunned Disbelief that the death has occurred.

Numbness Feelings of unreality.

Yearning Wanting to see the dead person again.

Anger Directed at medical staff, or friends and relatives, or the person who has died.

Guilt Ruminating about things one would have liked to have said to or done with the dead person.

Relief If someone has died after a painful or distressing illness or because of release from an oppressive relationship.

Mood swings For example, agitation alternating with sadness or *depression.

There are various models that present accounts of these feelings in terms of stages through which bereavement passes. However, there is increasing recognition that the feelings often do not occur in distinct and discrete stages but rather overlap and can manifest themselves differently in different people. Eventually there is a sense of letting-go the person who has died and the start of a new phase of life.

There are people who depart from these feelings and processes, for example, people who do not seem to grieve and get back to normal quickly. For some people, this reflects their usual way of dealing with losses, but for others, who have not grieved in the way that they needed, perhaps because responsibilities prevented them from doing so, physical and emotional symptoms may emerge later. Some people may find it hard to grieve because their loss is not seen as a 'proper' bereavement, for example, those who have had a miscarriage or stillbirth. Some people may begin to grieve, but get 'stuck', in which case the early sense of disbelief continues, sometimes for years. Others may be unable to think of anything else, perhaps turning their home into a 'shrine' to the dead person.

Although the feelings occasioned by bereavement may be similar, they will be expressed differently as people from different cultures deal with death in their own distinctive ways. In some communities, death is seen as part of the cycle of life rather than as 'the end'. Mourning rituals and funeral ceremonies may be public and demonstrative, or private and restrained. The period of mourning may be fixed or open-ended.

Children and young people feel the loss of people to whom they are close in much the same way as adults. However, given their different experience of time they may mourn more quickly. Some children and young people may feel responsible for the death that has taken place. The grief of children and young people and their need to mourn has been increasingly recognized. *See also* DEATH AND DYING.

Further reading: Murray Parkes, C. and Prigerson, H. G. (2010) *Bereavement: Studies of Grief in Adult Life*, Penguin.

best interests An implicit principle underpinning the practice of social work that emphasizes acting in ways that benefit the *service user. In some areas of practice it is stated explicitly, for example when conducting a best interests assessment under the Mental Capacity Act (2005). The *paramountcy principle in the Children Act (1989) is sometimes referred to as the 'best interests principle'. *See also* CAPACITY; DEPRIVATION OF LIBERTY SAFEGUARDS.

best interests assessment *See* DEPRIVATION OF LIBERTY SAFEGUARDS.

best interests assessor *See* DEPRIVATION OF LIBERTY SAFEGUARDS.

best practice 1. [Organizational level.] Techniques for or approaches to achieving the best *outcome in a given situation. The concept originated in management literature in relation to organizational *performance management and *quality improvement and has had an increasing influence on social work services. Best practice is associated with measuring, *benchmarking, and identifying processes that lead to desired outcomes. Actions instituted in response to the data resulting from these processes are seen as the route to best practice in organizational learning and improved organizational performance.

2. [Practice level.] A method or technique that is generally accepted as better than alternative options because it produces superior results or because it has become the preferred approach to an aspect of practice, for example in complying with *statutory duties. *See also* EVIDENCE-BASED PRACTICE.

Best Value '...a statutory duty to deliver services taking into account quality and cost by the most effective, economic, and efficient means possible' (Local Government Act [1999] Annex A). First flagged up in a *New Labour White Paper on *local government in 1998, in which it was described as standing for continuous improvements in both quality and cost at the local level, it became a statutory duty on 1 April 2000. From that point all *local authority services had to be reviewed within a five-year period and Best Value Performance Plans had to be produced, with user satisfaction indicators for all services. Social work, located in the then *Social Services Departments, was included in the Best Value regime, with requirements to deliver services to clear standards, paying attention to quality and cost, and to demonstrate a commitment to continuous improvement in the efficiency and effectiveness of its performance, in pursuit of national standards and targets. Four principles underpinned the introduction of Best Value:

Challenge why and how a service is provided.

Compare with others' performance, including the use of performance indicators in *benchmarking exercises.

Consult local taxpayers, *service users, and the business community in setting performance targets.

Competition as the means to efficient and effective services.

These four principles emphasized the ethos of Best Value as placing 'everything up for grabs'. There was no assumption that a particular service should continue to be provided, there was no notion that services that were to be provided had to continue to be provided in the same way as previously, and there was a driving dynamic of saving money. Although the Best Value regime ended, it has had an enduring influence on how services are viewed and managed. *See also* PERFORMANCE MANAGEMENT.

Better Care Fund *See* JOINT FINANCE.

Better Government for Older People (BGOP) A programme set up by the *New Labour government in 1998 to oversee 28 research projects on the engagement of *older people (defined as those aged 50 and above) in a variety of services. The programme ended after the research projects were completed. 'Network' was then added and the BGOP Network took into membership 350 local member organizations to share *good practice. The members—*local authorities, health agencies, and *voluntary organizations—received a range of services to help them to work together with the aims of encouraging older people to achieve greater *participation as citizens and to bridge the gap between the policy intentions of local and central government and their implementation. The BGOP initiative emphasized the importance of older people having a direct *voice in national and local policy and service provision for older people.

Beveridge Report (1942) On 1 December 1942 the wartime coalition government published the report *Social Insurance and Allied Services* (Beveridge Report), the outcome of a committee set up at the request of the trade unions and chaired by Sir William Beveridge, a Liberal economist and expert on unemployment. The Report identified 'five giants' that obstructed the path to the post war reconstruction of British society—'want, disease, ignorance, squalor, and idleness'—and became the blueprint for the post-war *welfare state that would tackle these. Although it ran to more than 300 pages, its publication was a huge success, selling 635,000 copies. Opinion polls reported that the majority of the public welcomed the Report and wished to see it implemented as quickly as possible. The first post-war election, in June 1945, resulted in a landslide victory for the Labour Party, which had established itself as the party of Beveridge when the Report was produced. The principle of 'individual liberty' was now being challenged by a stronger emphasis on collective welfare rights 'from the cradle to the grave', provided through a comprehensive system of social insurance, *means-tested social assistance, family allowances, and the establishment of a free, universal, and comprehensive national health service. All working people were to pay a weekly insurance contribution to the state. In return, benefits would be paid to the unemployed, the sick, the retired, and the widowed, aimed at ensuring there was an acceptable minimum standard of living below which nobody would fall. The post-war Labour government (1945–51) led by Clement Attlee, deputy prime minister during the war and previously a social worker in the East End of London, passed the legislation that put the Beveridge Report into effect: the Family Allowances Act (1945), the National Insurance Act (1946), the National Health Service Act (1946), and the National Assistance Act (1948). *See also* CITIZENSHIP; WELFARE STATE.

BGOP *See* BETTER GOVERNMENT FOR OLDER PEOPLE.

Big Society Presented as a key concept in the Conservative party's manifesto in 2010 and a central theme in its election campaign of that year, then taken up following the election by the Conservative–Liberal Democrat coalition government in the context of *austerity. It emphasized giving citizens and communities power and information so that they could come together and solve problems themselves. Families, networks, and neighbourhoods were presented as needing to be stronger in order to take more responsibility and as the route to achieving fairness and opportunity for all. Examples given of what this meant included local groups running post offices, libraries, and transport services. The coalition government acknowledged that one of the motivations for attempting to create a culture of volunteerism was to save money by getting people to do things for nothing that otherwise would require paid workers. A variant emerged with the election of Theresa May as Prime Minister in 2016: the Shared Society, based on the 'bonds of family, community, citizenship and strong institutions'. *See also* ACTIVE CITIZENSHIP; ALTRUISM; COMMUNITARIANISM; CO-PRODUCTION.

binary opposite *See* DECONSTRUCTION.

biographical approaches Understanding and responding to *service users through accounts of their past and present life experiences. This is contrasted with collecting information from service users according to narrow managerially-defined criteria, which ignore broader social and emotional dimensions of experience, and risk overlooking or misinterpreting issues that are crucial to the service user. It is an approach rooted in people's sense of themselves evolving as time passes, with the personal biography being regarded as an essential aspect of the sense of self.

Such an approach is seen as having a number of benefits: it leads to a better understanding of and respect for the individual's unique situation and characteristics, and an appreciation of issues of diversity; it contributes to a relationship of trust and generates feelings of value and self-worth; and it can have a direct bearing on making better decisions about appropriate service provision. However, there are often difficulties in applying a biographical approach in practice because it can be time-consuming and it may be necessary to respond to acute needs before or alongside adopting a biographical approach. *See also* NARRATIVE APPROACHES; THEORIES OF AGEING.

biological determinism Seeing men's and women's relationships with each other and wider social, economic, political, and cultural processes as rooted in their physiological differences, resulting in differing instinctive needs and drives. This powerful perspective can consciously or unconsciously influence a social worker's practice, for example, in assuming when undertaking an *assessment of a family with heterosexual parents that it is natural for a man to be the breadwinner and a woman to be the homemaker. Most feminists strongly contest biological determinism, arguing that women and men are socialized into their roles and relationships with each other and into seeing them as natural and inevitable, through patriarchal ideology that exploits women and privileges men. However, some feminists believe that biology does determine some or all aspects of women's nature (biological essentialism), such as women being more peaceful, cooperative, and nurturing than men. *See also* FEMINISM; PATRIARCHY.

biological essentialism *See* BIOLOGICAL DETERMINISM.

bio psycho social approach A development that moves away from the traditional *medical model, with its focus on physical causes and treatments, and is seen as providing a more holistic perspective on health and illness because of its stress on the inter-relationships between physical, psychological, and social functioning. Social workers based in health settings may be involved in making use of this perspective and it has become prominent in the mental health field, particularly where *community psychiatric nurses and social workers are working closely together in multidisciplinary teams. *See also* CARE AND TREATMENT PLAN.

bipolar affective disorder *See* BIPOLAR DISORDER.

bipolar disorder A type of *affective (or mood) disorder characterized by abnormally intense emotional states occurring in distinct phases or episodes. Moving back and forth between high (mania) and low (*depression) moods, with a period of stability in between, is experienced in some, but not all, cases. Mania and depression are seen as being at opposite ends of a continuum, hence the term 'bipolar'. Rapid cycling is the term used when the disorder is not interrupted by periods of mood stability. Some people experience a simultaneous combination of symptoms of high and low mood, without the development of distinct episodes of mania or depression, and this is defined as a mixed episode. Sometimes mania is the predominant experience, hence the term unipolar.

Symptoms of bipolar disorder are severe and interfere with many aspects of daily living. In a manic episode, feelings of intense joy and euphoria may be experienced, while others may experience severe anxiety and intense irritability. There may be an increase in energy and sexual drive, a decreased need for sleep, rapid speech, racing thoughts, impaired judgement leading to damaging behaviours such as substance and alcohol abuse, excessive spending sprees and other extravagances, and intrusive behaviours towards others such as *aggression and irritability. At its most extreme, *psychosis may be experienced where thought is affected as well as mood, and the individual is unable to distinguish reality. Individuals may feel out of control and experience *hallucinations and grandiose and delusional ideas, for instance, that they have been chosen for a special mission. In the depressive episode, symptoms include persistent feelings of hopelessness, sadness, anxiety, guilt, anger, and isolation. Sleep and appetite may be affected, and fatigue, lack of motivation, apathy, chronic generalized pain, and self-loathing may also be experienced. In severe *cases, morbid *suicidal thoughts may be present. As with mania, thought may become affected, leading to psychosis, and unpleasant hallucinations and *delusions can be experienced. Bipolar disorder is difficult to diagnose in its early stages and symptoms may appear as separate problems that can last for years before a diagnosis is made. Once diagnosed, the condition can be managed with medication known as mood stabilizers. Difficulties can occur when those experiencing mania consider themselves to be well and not in need of treatment. Bipolar disorder is usually considered to be caused by a mixture of genetic and environmental factors.

birth family A family consisting of a child's biological, as opposed to adoptive, parents and their offspring plus other relatives. *See also* ADOPTION.

birth parent(s) An individual's biological as opposed to adoptive parent(s). *See also* ADOPTION.

birth protection plan (birth safety plan) Devised by a children's services social worker in conjunction with other professionals and the family prior to the birth of an unborn child who is the subject of a *Child Protection Plan. The plan may set out who can visit the baby at the hospital, levels of supervision, and the plan for the baby when s/he is ready for discharge.

birth records counselling The Adoption and Children Act (2002) gives an adopted person the legal right, on reaching the age of 18, to apply to the General Register Office for a copy of their original birth certificate. It provides for adopted adults to obtain their birth record information to enable them to obtain a copy of their original birth certificate. Access to information and birth record *counselling enables adopted adults to understand the circumstances of their *adoption and enhance their sense of *identity. There are different procedures to be followed, depending on the date of a person's adoption:

- People adopted before 12 November 1975 who do not know their birth name make an application to the General Register Office (GRO). They are given information on where they can receive a counselling interview. They must attend a counselling interview before the GRO releases the information. Only people adopted prior to 12 November 1975, and who do not know their original name, are required by law to have counselling before being given access to their birth records.

- People adopted before 12 November 1975 who know their birth name may apply for a copy of their original birth certificate from the GRO, as they have the information necessary to make the application. When they do so, the GRO informs them of the counselling services available.
- People adopted on or after 12 November 1975 and before 30 December 2005 are not required to attend a counselling interview but this service is available to them. They can apply to the GRO for a copy of their original birth certificate whether or not they know their birth name.
- People adopted after 30 December 2005 have a right, on reaching the age of 18, to receive a copy of everything that the adoption agency was required to give to their adoptive parents at the time they were placed for adoption. This will be the information contained in the *Child's Permanence Report, which includes identifying information about the child, the *birth parents, birth siblings, and possibly other members of the *birth family. It also includes information about the child's early life and family history, their social, emotional, and behavioural development, and other matters. The application for this information must be made to the appropriate adoption agency because the adoption agency is considered best-placed to disclose sensitive information, to consult interested parties, and to arrange for the provision of counselling and support, if required. The appropriate adoption agency will usually be the agency that placed the child for adoption or, if different, the agency that holds the relevant adoption case records. It may also be the *local authority to which notice of intention to adopt was given.

Birth record counselling can only be undertaken by a qualified social worker with knowledge and experience of adoption work and all the issues involved.

Further reading: Department for Children, Schools and Families (2008) *Adoption: Access to Information and Intermediary Services. Practice Guidance.* Available at: https://www.gov.uk/government/uploads/system/uploads/attachment_data/file/459609/Adoption_-_Access_to_Information_and_Intermediary_Services.pdf.

Black Used to group together people of colour in a broadly encompassing way. Initially adopted as a progressive replacement for pejorative terms, such as 'negro' or 'coloured', subsequently its use has itself been subject to controversy. It has been objected to on the basis of its treating as homogeneous people whose origins are in, for example, Africa, the Caribbean, India, and Pakistan. The counter-argument is that retaining a Black/white dichotomy reflects the crude construction and experience of *racism based on skin colour. The use of the term 'Black' (i.e. with a capital 'B') is a convention employed to indicate that its user acknowledges the limitations of the Black/white dichotomy in terms of its inability to recognize diverse *ethnicities but that s/he is using the term consciously in order to stress the reality and unacceptability of *discrimination based on skin colour. This is one example of the need for social workers to be aware of the terms they use to group people together and to be sensitive about how such terms may be interpreted and understood by others. *See also* BLACK AND MINORITY ETHNIC GROUPS; BLACK PERSPECTIVES.

Black and minority ethnic groups Categories that describe people who have a common experience of discrimination because of their *'race' and/or *ethnicity' and who are not from the majority white group in the UK. The term ethnicity refers to sharing a cultural heritage with a common language, values, religion, customs, and attitudes, whereas 'race' is based on differences in outward appearance, such as skin colour. *See also* BLACK; BLACK PERSPECTIVES.

Black feminism *See* FEMINISM.

Black perspectives A range of stances informed by Black people's diverse experiences of 'race' and *racism that challenge the assumption that Black people have the same experiences and needs as white people and/or the making of assumptions from white perspectives about the experiences, needs, and cultures of Black people. These perspectives promote the views and analyses of Black people themselves in asserting the significance of their *identities in their histories, languages, cultures, religions, and traditions. *See also* ANTI-DISCRIMINATORY PRACTICE; ANTI-OPPRESSIVE PRACTICE; ANTI-RACIST PRACTICE; BLACK; BLACK AND MINORITY ETHNIC GROUPS.

blame culture A set of *collective attitudes and behaviours characterized by an unwillingness to take risks or accept responsibility for mistakes because of a fear of criticism or reprimand.

block contract A binding agreement made by an organization *commissioning the purchase of a large volume of services from a particular provider for many *service users. This became the dominant arrangement in adult services following the *community care reforms and resulted in a tendency towards standardized services. Although the model underpinning the reforms was the spot-contract (individual social workers purchasing single services for individual users), the attractions of block contracts to commissioners were clear: lower unit costs, reduced transaction costs, and ease of monitoring quality, as compared with overseeing a succession of specific spot-contracts. The priority was achieving economy and efficiency by seeking high volume from a limited range of standardized services. In addition, providers were resistant to offering the small units of service required by spot-contracts, and preferred the guaranteed level of funding available to them under block contracts. As a result, *assessments and *care plans were increasingly shaped by social workers' awareness of the services that were available. One of the arguments in favour of *Direct Payments and *Personal Budgets, particularly in the context of the implementation of the Care Act (2014), has been that individualizing provision through their use will curtail the use of block contracts and lead to more individually attuned services.

blocked beds Pejorative expression for hospital places taken by patients, predominantly *older people, who have been medically assessed as fit for discharge but who cannot leave hospital because the necessary social and other services are not in place.

body language The signals people give off through physical expressions and gestures that may confirm or disconfirm what they are communicating verbally. *See also* NON-VERBAL COMMUNICATION.

borderline personality disorder (BPD) *See* PERSONALITY DISORDER.

bounded rationality A limited way of thinking that does not appear to be so because its constraints are concealed to those operating within it. For example, *managerialism may dominate a social work organization and shape the *identities and social relations of managers, social workers, and *service users according to the limitations of its rationale, but those located within this bounded rationality may assume that this is simply 'how things are'.

Bournewood gap (Bournewood safeguards) The position of someone in a hospital or a care home who does not actively object to being there but lacks the *capacity to consent to the decision. This situation became known as the 'Bournewood Gap' following the case of a man with autism who was detained in Bournewood Hospital without having consented to the detention or being made subject to compulsory admission under the Mental Health Act (1983), which brings with it legal safeguards but is generally used only when someone objects to detention. This gap allowed situations in which it may have been possible for professionals and others to cajole people into entering a care home or into going into hospital for *assessment or treatment related to their mental health but in which the person could not be regarded as having freely given informed consent and hence was effectively deprived of her/his liberty. The European Court of Human Rights ruled that being in a hospital or care home without having consented does not necessarily amount to a deprivation of liberty under Article 5 of the Human Rights Act (1998) and that whether or not deprivation of liberty has occurred has to be decided by examining the circumstances in each individual case. The illegality that the case identified was not the deprivation of liberty per se, but the fact that it did not follow a legally recognized and fair process subject to review by the courts. To address the Bournewood Gap, 'Bournewood safeguards' were introduced and designated the *Deprivation of Liberty Safeguards in order to safeguard the position of those who lack capacity to make decisions about their care and who are being deprived of their liberty outside of the remit of the Mental Health Act (1983).

Braille A writing and reading system for visually impaired people, named after its nineteenth-century inventor Louis Braille, that consists of patterns of raised dots which are read by touch through the fingertips.

breach proceedings Legal process under which someone who has been made the subject of a *community sentence and has failed to meet (i.e. 'breached') some or all of its requirements, can be taken back to court to be resentenced, fined, or receive a warning.

brief intervention (brief therapy, brief treatment) Working with a *service user over a short timescale, usually for between three and six sessions. In the context of traditional long-term *casework, brief intervention was regarded as having little value, but with the advent of research into the efficacy of short-term approaches such as *crisis intervention and *task-centred casework, its credibility grew. Such research emphasized the value service users placed on more focused short-term problem-solving approaches. *See also* SOLUTION-FOCUSED THERAPY.

British Association for Adoption and Fostering *See* CORAMBAAF.

British Association for Adoption and Fostering Form F (Fostering) *See* FORM F.

British Association for Counselling and Psychotherapy Largest of the professional associations for counsellors and psychotherapists, established in 2000 after a change of name from the previous British Association of Counselling, indicating a broader remit following the inclusion of psychotherapy. It produced Ethical Standards for Counselling in 2016.

((⊕)) SEE WEB LINKS
• Official site of the British Association for Counselling and Psychotherapy.

British Association of Social Workers A professional organization for social workers, founded in 1970, which unified a wide range of specialist professional bodies. *See also* CODE OF ETHICS.

((⊕)) SEE WEB LINKS
• Official site of the British Association of Social Workers.

British Sign Language A visual method of communication, used by 50,000 to 70,000 people who have hearing impairments, that employs gestures, facial expressions, and body language, and has its own structure and syntax. After a long campaign, the UK government recognized it as a minority language in 2003, according it the same status as Welsh and Gaelic. *See also* MAKATON.

brokerage Arranging the support set out in a *care and support plan or support plan under the Care Act (2014). It can include helping people to identify the changes they want to make to their lives, finding support services and community opportunities, negotiating with service providers, and initiating the implementation of the plan. Brokerage can be undertaken by the person concerned her/himself or, in consultation with the person, by people employed or volunteering as brokers in *local authority services or independent organizations.

bullying Behaviour by an individual or group that intentionally hurts others on a physical or emotional basis, usually over an extended period of time. It can range from teasing and rumours to physical injury. Recognition of bullying has been extended to encompass the misuse of technologies, known as *cyber-bullying. The impact of bullying is harmful to those experiencing it and can lead to damaging emotional effects. Although bullying is usually thought of in relation to children and young people, it can also be experienced by adults. For example, many workplaces now have anti-bullying policies and procedures.

burden of care 1. The strain experienced as a result of looking after someone. While recognizing the physical and emotional demands that providing care can make on a carer, 'burden of care' is regarded by many as a questionable term because of its tendency to stigmatize the 'cared-for' person.
   2. Also used pejoratively to describe the 'burden' placed on society by *older people. *See also* DEMOGRAPHIC TIME-BOMB; INTER-GENERATIONAL CONTRACT.

bureaucracy A pyramid-shaped form of organization with laid-down roles, procedures, and tasks for its personnel. Max Weber (1864–1920) identified it as a form of legitimized and institutionalized power based on rational–legal principles with characteristics that included the following: a defined division of labour; a high degree of specialization; a hierarchical structure of authority with clear lines of control; a body of rules governing the operation of the organization; effective record-keeping; promotion on the basis of merit or seniority. Although it has become a largely pejorative term, Weber saw bureaucracy as having advantages in its commitment to efficiency, predictability, and fairness, but was also pessimistic about where the rationalization it represented would lead, anticipating that it might become an 'iron cage'. Characteristic elements of bureaucracy can be seen in statutory social work organizations that are granted *powers and *duties by law, which they execute through laid-down social work roles, procedures, and tasks within hierarchical structures. The omnipresent danger is that *service users will be constrained simply to fit in and comply with the demands of this form of organization, given the difficulty it has in being attuned to the needs of individuals. At the extreme, service users can be objectified and seen as *'cases' or 'files', as a consequence of social workers being subjected to the instrumental rationality bureaucracy produces. *See also* BOUNDED RATIONALITY; BUREAUCRATIZATION; BUREAU-PROFESSIONAL REGIME; MCDONALDIZATION.

bureaucratization Introducing the characteristic features of *bureaucracy to an organization or processes previously structured more loosely, with implications of unwarranted inflexibility.

bureau-professionalism *See* BUREAU-PROFESSIONAL REGIME.

bureau-professional regime An organizational form associated with public services in the post-war *welfare state that brought together two key aspects of state welfare: the rational administration of bureaucratic systems; and professional expertise in control over the content of services, thus allowing professionals like social workers considerable discretion within which to operate. In the case of social work, this type of regime was particularly connected with the implementation of the *Seebohm Report and the setting up of *Social Services Departments, which fused the interests of social work attempting to organize as a *profession and the *bureaucracy associated with the *local authorities in which the departments were located. *See also* BOUNDED RATIONALITY; BUREAUCRACY; BUREAUCRATIZATION.

burn-out An enduring state of physical and emotional exhaustion involving lack of interest, disillusionment, helplessness, feeling overwhelmed, and being fearful of making mistakes. It is associated with excessive and prolonged stress, resulting from working under difficult and demanding conditions, such as a chaotic and/or high-pressure environment. Social workers are susceptible to it because of the emotionally taxing nature of their work, but this can be exacerbated in situations where there are inappropriate allocation of *cases, unmanageable workloads, lack of supervision, and unsympathetic line management. Signs include chronic fatigue, short-temper, suspicion, and excessive susceptibility to colds and headaches. Many writers identify the state developing progressively, as the culmination of a number of phases such as:

• A compulsion to prove oneself.
• Working harder and harder.
• Neglecting one's own needs.
• Displacement of conflicts (not realizing the cause of the distress).
• Revision of priorities (friends and interests are neglected).
• Denial of emerging problems.
• Withdrawal (reducing social contacts to a minimum, becoming walled off).
• Inner emptiness.
• *Depression.

The signs and symptoms are subtle at first, but get worse as time goes on.

Remedies are seen as lying in a combination of organizational change and interventions with individuals, but the overwhelming emphasis in the literature is on the latter, for example in the three 'r's approach:

Recognize Watch for the warning signs of burnout.

Reverse Undo the damage by managing stress and seeking support.

Resilience Build resilience to stress by taking care of physical and emotional health.

As far as social work is concerned, there is considerable concern about burn-out among social workers, but the concept may be just as or more applicable to *service users, such as a lone parent caring for children in poor material conditions or the *carer of someone with dementia. *See also* ROUTINIZATION.

business excellence An approach to social work that stresses the need for it to excel in business terms, that is, in terms of organizational concerns, often set out in the form of *performance indicators. There is pressure on managers to be less concerned with supporting the quality of social workers' practice than with seeing social work as a series of service transactions that are geared to the achievement of corporate objectives. *See also* AGENCY THEORY; BUSINESS ORIENTATION; EUROPEAN FOUNDATION OF QUALITY MANAGEMENT MODEL; MANAGERIALISM; NEW PUBLIC MANAGEMENT; PERFORMANCE MANAGEMENT.

Business Excellence Model *See* EUROPEAN FOUNDATION OF QUALITY MANAGEMENT MODEL.

business orientation An approach to the provision of *social work and *social services in the *public and *voluntary sectors that treats them as far as possible as though they were profit-making activities operating in the market and uses managerial knowledge and techniques taken from the private sector. *See also* AGENCY THEORY; BUSINESS EXCELLENCE; MANAGERIALISM; NEW PUBLIC MANAGEMENT; PERFORMANCE MANAGEMENT.

C4EO *See* CENTRE FOR EXCELLENCE AND OUTCOMES IN CHILDREN'S AND YOUNG PEOPLE'S SERVICES.

CAF *See* COMMON ASSESSMENT FRAMEWORK.

CAFCASS *See* CHILDREN AND FAMILY COURT ADVISORY SUPPORT SERVICE.

Caldicott Guardian A senior person appointed by every National Health Service organization and *local authority who is responsible for safeguarding the *confidentiality of patient and *service user information, enabling appropriate information-sharing, and advising on lawful and ethical processing of information. The role was recommended by a committee charged with examining confidentiality issues, chaired by Fiona Caldicott, which reported in 1997. The committee made sixteen recommendations and formulated six principles relating to data handling and use, on which the Guardian role is based:

- Justify the purpose(s) for using confidential information.
- Only use confidential information when absolutely necessary.
- Use the minimum that is required.
- Access should be on a strict need-to-know basis.
- Everybody must understand her/his responsibilities.
- Understand and comply with the law.

Since the Caldicott Report was produced there has been a plethora of legislation, either directly concerned with the handling of confidential information or with implications for it. As a consequence, the role and responsibilities of Caldicott Guardians, for what is now usually referred to as information governance, have grown significantly. The UK Caldicott Guardian Council (UKCGC) is the national body for Caldicott Guardians. *See also* ACCESS TO RECORDS; CONFIDENTIALITY; DATA PROTECTION; INFORMATION COMMISSIONER'S OFFICE; INFORMATION-GIVING; INFORMATION-SHARING.

Further reading: NHS England (2014) *Guidance for Caldicott Guardians*. Available at: http://www.england.nhs.uk/wp-content/uploads/2014/08/guid-acm-auth-proc.pdf.

call centre A centralized office location that receives all telephone calls made by consumers to a business or service, for example, in relation to sales, product support, or information enquiries. Usually organized through large open workspaces with individual work stations that include a computer and a telephone headset, and most often using scripted interaction with customers. Visual display boards are common, giving information about the number of calls waiting, the average waiting time, and the average call duration. The facility for supervisors to listen in to calls without call-centre workers' knowledge and the sophisticated nature of the technology mean that close monitoring of staff's performance is easy and widespread, and this, together with the stressful nature of the work, has led to

widespread depictions of them as dehumanizing. They originated in major businesses such as utility and mail order companies but have been increasingly adopted
in the *public sector, including for use by people making contact with social work
services. The *New Labour governments (1997–2010) promoted call centres as part
of an emphasis on the use of *information and communication technology in its
*modernization agenda, with *local authorities being urged to use call centre
technology to deliver social services from the late 1990s onwards. Call centres are
now firmly established in social services, as elsewhere in the public sector. In official
policy, the use of call centres has been presented as a key aspect of attempts to
change the relationship between *service users and social workers by treating the
former as 'customers'. The centres have been portrayed as one of the principal
routes towards increasing the accessibility and efficiency of public services.
A central claim is that they are a key aspect of 'joined-up' working and this is
seen as a vastly superior alternative to the old system of central and local government organization, characterized as 'silo culture', with individual departments
working in isolation. Call centre staff are often organized in a tiered system. The
first tier consists of workers who handle simple requests for information and
redirect callers. If a caller requires more assistance, the call is forwarded to the
second tier. In the case of social work, the first tier is often staffed by people who
have been redeployed from clerical and administrative posts elsewhere in social
services or the local authority more widely, together with people with experience
of call centre work in banking, insurance, and retail. The second tier consists of
social workers to whom the more complex calls will be referred. *See also* CONTACT
CENTRE 2.

Further reading: Coleman, N. and Harris, J. (2008) 'Calling Social Work', *British Journal of Social
Work*, 38, 3, 580–99.

CAMHS *See* CHILD AND ADOLESCENT MENTAL HEALTH SERVICES.

capacity The ability to make decisions. Whether or not an individual is deemed
to have this ability will be the key factor influencing a social worker's response to a
particular situation. For people whose mental capacity is impaired, the Mental
Capacity Act (2005) provides a legal framework for decision-making. The legal
protection of people who lack capacity was further strengthened in that the
neglect or ill-treatment of someone who lacks capacity is a criminal offence,
punishable by up to five years' imprisonment. Prior to the Act, provisions existed
for other people to manage the property and financial affairs of someone who
lacked mental capacity, but there was no legislation for decision-making in respect
of other matters. The Act covers decision-making in relation to welfare, health,
and financial affairs. It is relevant to decisions about day-to-day matters, such as
the support services or dental care someone needs, as well as decisions relating to
major life changes, such as a move to residential care. Section 1 of the Act sets out
five key principles:

- All people over 16 are presumed to have capacity to make their own decisions
  unless it is proved that they lack capacity.
- Individuals should be given all possible help to make their own decisions before
  they are treated as though they are not able to make their own decisions.
- Making what others perceive as unwise decisions does not indicate a lack of
  capacity to make those decisions.
- Any action taken or decision made on behalf of someone who lacks capacity
  under the Act must be made in their *best interests.

- Any action or decision taken on behalf of someone who lacks capacity should be the option that is the least restrictive on their basic rights and freedoms.

The five principles of the Act should inform all actions when working with a person who may lack or have reduced capacity and should be evidenced in taking decisions or actions on behalf of a person who may lack or have reduced capacity.

Section 2(1) of the Act defines what is meant by lack of capacity:

For the purposes of this Act, a person lacks capacity in relation to a matter if at the material time he [sic] is unable to make a decision for himself in relation to the matter because of an impairment of, or a disturbance in the functioning of, the mind or brain.

There is, therefore, no blanket judgement about someone's level of mental capacity; this is decided in relation to specific decisions. For example, someone may have the capacity to make minor decisions, such as what they want to eat, but lack the capacity for making major decisions, such as those involved in making a will. It also reflects the fact that a person who lacks capacity to make a decision for themselves at a certain time may be able to make that decision at a later date. This may be because they have an illness or condition that means their capacity changes. Alternatively, it may be because at the time the decision needs to be made, they are unconscious or barely conscious, whether due to an accident or being under anaesthetic or their ability to make a decision may be affected by the influence of alcohol or drugs. It reflects the fact that while some people may always lack capacity to make some types of decisions—for example, due to a condition or severe *learning disability that has affected them from birth—others may learn new skills that enable them to gain capacity and make decisions for themselves. As these considerations indicate, the Act applies to those whose lack of capacity is both temporary and permanent. Therefore, whenever the term 'a person who lacks capacity' is used, it means a person who lacks capacity to make a particular decision or take a particular action for themselves at the time the decision or action needs to be taken.

To help determine if a person lacks capacity, the Act sets out a two-stage test:

Stage 1 Does the person have an impairment of, or a disturbance in the functioning of, their mind or brain?

Examples include:

- conditions associated with some forms of *mental illness;
- dementia;
- significant learning disabilities;
- the long-term effects of brain damage;
- physical or medical conditions that cause confusion, drowsiness, or loss of consciousness;
- delirium;
- concussion following a head injury;
- symptoms of alcohol or drug use.

If a person does not have such an impairment or disturbance of the mind or brain, they do not lack capacity under the Act.

Stage 2 Does the impairment or disturbance mean that the person is unable to make a specific decision when they need to?

The impairment or disturbance of the mind or brain must be the direct cause of their inability to make a decision. In addition the person must first be given all practical and appropriate support to help them make the decision for themselves.

A person is considered to be unable to make a decision if they cannot:

- understand relevant information about the decision to be made;
- retain that information in their mind;
- use or weigh that information as part of the decision-making process;
- communicate their decision (by talking, using sign language, or any other means).

The person who wishes to take a particular action or decision on behalf of the person thought to lack mental capacity must make the judgement about capacity. For legal matters, this is likely to be a solicitor; for medical matters, it is likely to be a doctor; for many matters of everyday living, it is likely to be a *carer, family member, or social worker. A decision may also, at times, be made jointly by a number of people. For example, when a *care and support plan for a person who lacks capacity is being developed, different health care and/or social care staff might be involved in making decisions or recommendations about the *care package, based on what the team has ascertained to be the person's best interests.

Those making decisions on behalf of someone who lacks capacity must work through a checklist in determining what is in the person's best interests. This includes not making assumptions on the basis of age, appearance, condition, or behaviour; considering all of the relevant circumstances; considering whether and when the person is likely to regain capacity (and, therefore, be able to resume decision-making); encouraging the person to participate as fully as possible in decision-making; not making a decision about life-sustaining treatment motivated by a desire to bring about the person's death; taking account of the person's past and present wishes and feelings, beliefs, and values in decision-making; and taking account of the views of carers or other interested parties, as appropriate. Anyone, including both informal and professional carers, who acts in the reasonable belief that someone lacks capacity and that they are acting in the person's best interests cannot be held legally liable, unless they can be shown to be negligent.

Under the Act, people can plan ahead and appoint an attorney to act on their behalf, if at some point in the future they were to lose capacity. This is called a Lasting Power of Attorney. (A Lasting Power of Attorney is similar to the Enduring Power of Attorney, which existed previously, but it applies to health and welfare matters as well as financial affairs.) People can also make advance decisions regarding future medical treatment. However, an advance decision can only specify treatment that someone wishes to refuse, not treatment that they would like to have. If the decision concerns refusal of life-sustaining treatment, it must be in writing, signed, and formally witnessed, and include a statement that the decision stands 'even if life is at risk'. Both a Lasting Power of Attorney and an advance decision can only be made if the person has mental capacity at that time. For someone in the early stages of dementia, therefore, it will be important that the potential benefits of a Lasting Power of Attorney and/or advance decision are considered while the person still has the capacity to consent to these decisions.

The Mental Capacity Act (2005) also established a new *Court of Protection that has overall responsibility for the Act, with its own procedures and nominated judges. The Court can make decisions and orders regarding complex issues on behalf of those who lack capacity, and it can appoint court deputies to take decisions regarding property and financial affairs and health and welfare matters but not the refusal of life-sustaining treatment. Deputies are only appointed if the Court cannot make a one-off decision to resolve the issues. An Office of the Public Guardian supports the Court of Protection, acting as the registering body for Lasting

Powers of Attorney and deputies, overseeing the work of deputies, and providing information to assist the Court of Protection in its decision-making.

For people who lack capacity but do not have family, friends, or others to advocate for them, an Independent Mental Capacity Advocate can be appointed. However, an IMCA can be appointed even if family and friends are available, if that is thought to be in the person's interests. The areas of decision-making in which an IMCA may be used are *safeguarding situations, changes in accommodation, care and support planning, care and support *reviews, serious medical treatment, and circumstances involving the *Deprivation of Liberty Safeguards (DoLS). The Independent Mental Capacity Advocate acts on what can be established about the person's wishes, beliefs, feelings and values, brings to the attention of the decision-maker all relevant factors to the *case, and ensures the person's rights are upheld in any decisions that are made. This may involve challenging the person appointed to make decisions on their behalf. IMCA services are provided by organizations that are independent of the NHS and local authorities.

A detailed Code of Practice was issued alongside the Mental Capacity Act (2005) and it is periodically reviewed and updated. Social workers have a duty to have regard to the provisions of the Code and their failure to do this could be used in legal proceedings.

Further reading: Department of Constitutional Affairs (2007) *Mental Capacity Act (2005): Code of Practice.* Available at: http://www.justice.gov.uk/downloads/guidance/protecting-the-vulnerable/mca/mca-code-practice-0509.pdf.

capacity assessment *See* CAPACITY.

capitalist society A system based on the majority of the population selling their labour by working for wages and producing commodities for sale in the *market, rather than for their own immediate use. Their labour is sold to the owners of the means by which commodities are produced in order to make profit for them. Marxists view this system as the basis of inevitable and enduring class conflict between the owners of the means of production and wage-labourers, whose labour is treated as simply another commodity. Some Marxist analysts of capitalist society have regarded social work as an *agent of social control that contributes to the maintenance of capitalist society in the interests of the few and disguises the exploitation of the many. *See also* CLASS; COMMODIFICATION; MARXIST SOCIAL WORK.

capital threshold *See* CHARGING FOR SERVICES.

cardio vascular accident (stroke) The sudden death of cells in a localized area of the brain due to inadequate blood flow. It occurs when blood supply is interrupted to part of the brain because of clots that block an artery, either in the brain itself or in the neck, or when a blood vessel bursts around or in the brain. Without blood to supply oxygen and nutrients, and to remove waste products, brain cells quickly begin to die. Symptoms may include blurring or decreased vision in one or both eyes; severe headache; weakness, numbness, or paralysis of the face, arm, or leg, usually on one side of the body; dizziness, loss of balance, and/or coordination. Depending on the region of the brain affected, it may cause paralysis, speech impairment, loss of memory, and reasoning ability, coma, or death. It is a medical emergency requiring immediate treatment, which improves the chances of survival and increases the degree of recovery that may be expected. Treatment to break up a blood clot must begin within three hours to be effective. There are more than

100,000 strokes each year in the UK. People are twice as likely to survive a stroke today than they were twenty years ago, but stroke remains the fourth single largest cause of death in the UK. *See also* STROKE ASSOCIATION.

care Used in a general sense to mean the presence of an emotional bond but in social work usually refers to the act or process of looking after people by undertaking tasks that they are unable to do for themselves. It is increasingly rejected as a term and a concept by the Disabled People's Movement because of its connotations of dependency and passivity. It is seen as oppressive, representing *service users as dependent and subordinate, with overtones of monitoring, supervision, and control. 'Assistance' has been proposed as an alternative that signifies a form of support that is under the control of the person receiving it. Others argue that rather than rejecting the notion of 'care' as oppressive, we need to retain it and revalue it in positive terms. It has been suggested that rather than viewing the receipt of care as a negative quality of those who have failed to match up to an ideal of *independence, it should instead be recognized as a universal characteristic of *interdependence in relationships. Social workers can play an important role in challenging the ideal of the independent individual and the assumption that dependency is necessarily something to be eliminated or managed. *See also* CARER; CARE RECIPIENTS.

care and repair agencies *See* HOME IMPROVEMENT AGENCIES.

care and support plan (care and support planning) (adults and carers) Following a *needs assessment or a *carer's assessment and a determination of *eligibility under the Care Act (2014), a written care and support plan (for an adult with care and support needs) or a support plan (for a *carer) must be provided where a *local authority has agreed to meet a person's needs. (In what follows, 'plan' encompasses 'care and support plan' and 'support plan', unless otherwise stated.) The process of developing the plan is meant to be person-centred and person-led in order to meet the *needs and achieve the *outcomes of the person in ways that work best for them as an individual or as part of a household. The planning process and its outcomes are built around people's wishes, feelings, needs, values, and aspirations. Everyone whose needs are being met by a local authority, regardless of the setting in which the needs are met, should have a care and support plan.

'Meeting needs' through care and support planning is an important concept under the Care Act (2014) and is intended to be broader than a duty simply to provide or arrange a particular service. Because a person's needs are specific to them, there are many ways in which their needs can be met. The purpose of the care and support planning process is to agree how a person's needs should best be met. There are a number of options for how needs can be met, depending on the person's circumstances, including:

• the local authority directly providing some type of support, for example by providing a *reablement or short-term *respite service;
• making a *direct payment, which allows the person to purchase their own care and support;
• an *individual service fund with the budget held by a service provider and the person having control of it;
• a combination of the above, for example the local authority arranging a home-care service whilst providing a direct payment for the person to meet other needs.

Individuals choosing options for meeting needs that are suitable but cost more than the local authority has budgeted can contribute additional resources or personal funding towards arranging this support. (This is often referred to as 'topping-up'.)

A local authority does not have to meet any needs that are being met by a *carer. However, the local authority must identify, during the assessment process, the needs of the person that are being met by a carer at that time, and whether those needs meet the eligibility criteria. Any eligible needs met by a carer are not required to be met by the local authority, for so long as the carer continues to do so, but the care and support plan should record the needs being met by a carer, and contingency plans to respond to any breakdown in the caring relationship should be considered.

When a local authority is not required to meet needs, it may still use its legal *powers to meet them, for example meeting needs that do not meet the eligibility criteria, or meeting eligible needs in circumstances where the duty does not apply, for example when the person is *ordinarily resident in another area. Where a local authority exercises such a discretionary power to meet other needs, they must be included in a care and support plan.

If a local authority decides not to use its powers to meet other needs, it must give the person a written explanation for taking this decision and should give a copy to her/his *advocate if the person requests. If the person cannot request this, then a copy should be given to the person's advocate or appropriate individual if this in the *best interests of the person. This explanation must also include information and advice on how the person can reduce or delay their needs in future. This has to be personal and specific advice based on the person's *needs assessment and not a generalized reference to *prevention services or signposting to a general website. The explanation should be accessible to the person.

The plan must:

- identify the needs to be met;
- detail how the needs will be met;
- link back to the outcomes that the person wishes to achieve in day-to-day life as identified in the *assessment process;
- reflect the person's wishes, needs, and aspirations;
- state what is important to and for the person, where this is reasonable.

Information must be made available in ways that are meaningful to the person, and s/he must have support and time to consider options. A named contact or lead professional should be considered as part of the care and support planning process, so that the person knows how to contact the local authority. The planning choices offered could include:

- support for the person to develop their plan jointly with the local authority alone or with their family, friends, or whoever they may wish to involve;
- written information and peer support;
- one-to-one support from a paid professional, such as a social worker, who may be the same person who undertook the assessment.

Where the person has substantial difficulty in being actively involved with the planning process, and they have no family and friends who are able to support them, the local authority must provide an independent *advocate (*see* ADVOCACY [ADULTS]). Likewise, where a person with specific expertise or training in a particular condition (for example, deaf-blindness) has carried out the assessment, someone with similar knowledge (and preferably the same person to ensure continuity) should be involved in production of the plan.

There are certain elements that must always be incorporated in the plan:

- the needs identified by the assessment;
- whether, and to what extent, the needs meet the eligibility criteria;
- the *indicative amount;
- the needs that the authority is going to meet, and how it intends to do so;
- for a person needing care—for which of the desired outcomes care and support could be relevant;
- for a carer—the outcomes the carer wishes to achieve, and her/his wishes with regard to work, education, recreation, and providing care, where support could be relevant;
- the *personal budget;
- *information and advice on what can be done to reduce the needs in question, and to prevent or delay the development of needs in the future;
- where needs are being met via a direct payment, which needs are to be met via the direct payment and the amount and frequency of the payments.

Consideration of the needs to be met should take a holistic approach that covers aspects such as the person's wishes and aspirations in their daily and community life, rather than a narrow view purely designed to meet personal care needs. If the person has fluctuating needs, the plan should accommodate them, as well as indicating what contingencies are in place in the event of a sudden change or emergency. This should be an integral part of the planning process, and not something decided when someone reaches a crisis point. Specific consideration should be given to how planning is conducted in end-of-life care. Consideration of needs should also include the extent to which the needs or a person's other circumstances may reveal a *safeguarding issue, and lead to a requirement to carry out a safeguarding enquiry. Where such an enquiry leads to further specific interventions being put in place to address a safeguarding issue, these may be included in the plan.

A local authority must involve the person the plan is intended for, the carer (if there is one), and/or any other person the person requests to be involved. Where the person has *capacity, the local authority must involve any person who appears to be interested in the welfare of the person and any person who would be able to contribute useful information. Where the person lacks capacity, the local authority should make a *best interests decision about who else should be involved. An independent advocate must be provided where the criteria apply (*see* ADVOCACY [ADULTS]; CAPACITY). Support of speech therapists or other specialists such as interpreters may also be needed. Some people will need little help to be involved; others will need much more. Social workers or other relevant professionals should get a sense of the person's confidence and what support they feel they need in order to be meaningfully involved.

Plans should not be developed in isolation from other plans (such as plans for carers or family members) and should have regard to all of the person's needs and outcomes, rather than just their care and support needs. Where other plans are present or are being completed, these can be combined if appropriate. This should be considered early on in the planning process (at the same time as considering the person's needs and how they can be met) to ensure that the package of care and support is developed in a way that fits with what support is already being received and/or developed. The plan should only be combined if all parties to whom it is relevant agree and understand the implications of sharing data and information. Consent should be obtained from all parties involved, and the combination of plans should aim to maximize outcomes for all involved. Plans can be combined in cases where the person is receiving both local authority and NHS support, for example a person with mental health problems who meets the criteria for care and support under the multi-agency *Care Programme Approach.

Upon completion of the plan, the local authority must give a copy of the final version to the person in a format that is accessible to her/him, to any other person that the person requests should receive a copy, and to the person's independent advocate if s/he has one and the person agrees. Consideration should also be given to sharing key points of the final plan with other professionals and supporters, with the person's consent (for example, as part of the person's health record), or sharing the plan in the best interests of a person who lacks capacity.

A 'light touch' review should be considered six to eight weeks after the plan and personal budget have been signed off, with the plan then being reviewed no later than every twelve months. *See also* REVIEW OF CARE AND SUPPORT PLANS.

Further reading: Department of Health (2016) *Care and Support: Statutory Guidance*, Chapter 10. Available at: https://www.gov.uk/government/publications/care-act-statutory-guidance/care-and-support-statutory-guidance#person-centred-care-and-support-planning.

care and treatment plan (mental health) A plan directed towards meeting a person's psychiatric, psychological, and social needs, including the impact of medication. It includes the management of any significant *risk factors and a crisis and contingency plan. *Refocusing the Care Programme Approach* (2008), which updated policy and set out practice guidance for mental health services, suggested a number of other elements for inclusion in a person's care and treatment plan, such as needs arising from *co-morbidity; personal circumstances; housing; financial circumstances; employment, education, and training; equality and diversity issues; social inclusion and social contact; and *independence. Furthermore, it stated that 'the care and treatment plan should focus on the person's aspirations, outcomes and strengths, not just on needs and difficulties'. *See also* BIO-PSYCHO-SOCIAL APPROACH.

Further reading: Department of Health (2008) *Refocusing the Care Programme Approach*. Available at: http://webarchive.nationalarchives.gov.uk/20130107105354/http://www.dh.gov.uk/prod_consum_dh/groups/dh_digitalassets/@dh/@en/documents/digitalasset/dh_083649.pdf.

care coordination *See* CARE COORDINATOR.

care coordinator (mental health) The role of bringing together services when there is a high degree of complexity in the range and number of services involved. This role, formerly *'key worker' until a government review of the *Care Programme Approach in 1999, is closely associated with mental health services. The role is recognized as central to the CPA but has no formal definition, leading to local variations in its application. Nonetheless, the role is generally recognized as serving two important functions. The first involves establishing and sustaining professional relationships with the *service user and significant others. The second involves coordinating, monitoring, and recording the *assessment, planning, delivery, and review of services, including considerations of *risk. The role is typically undertaken by the professional who is best placed to oversee the management of *care and organization of resources. This can be a professional of any discipline and does not have to be the person most heavily involved in providing services.

cared-for *See* CARE RECIPIENTS.

career *See* MORAL CAREER.

care-giver (care-taker) Anyone who is the main *carer of a child, whether a parent or not. However, sometimes (confusingly) used to indicate that a person caring for a child is not the child's birth parent.

care-giving *See* CARE; CARER; CARE RECIPIENTS.

care-leavers *See* LEAVING CARE.

care management An integrated and circular process for identifying and addressing the needs of individuals within available resources, which recognizes, at least rhetorically, that those needs are unique to the individuals concerned. First introduced by the *community care reforms in the early 1990s, it comprised seven distinct stages: the publishing of information, determination of the level of *assessment, assessment, *care planning, implementation of the care plan, *monitoring, and *review.

The stage of determining the level of assessment, along with that of publishing information, occurred outside the circular process formed by the other five stages. At the stage of determining the level of assessment, some *referrals were screened out of the process altogether, if the referred *need was seen as not requiring social work assessment. How need was defined and interpreted at this stage of the process was therefore of crucial significance in terms of the eventual service response.

Originally called case management, care management was based on a model of service provision developed in North America. Prior to the community care

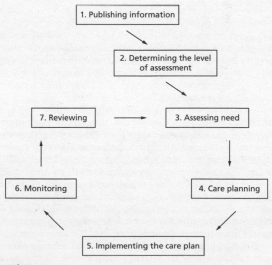

Care management process

reforms, research on how the model could be developed and applied in the UK was carried out by the Personal Social Service Research Unit. The PSSRU evaluated a number of pilot projects including a project in Kent concerned with evaluating the purchase of intensive home-based care by social workers as an alternative to the admission of *older people to residential care, and a project in Darlington concerned with evaluating schemes to facilitate the discharge of older people from hospital. There were a further 28 projects focused on the discharge of people from long-stay hospital care and their resettlement in the community. Common to all of the projects was the use of care management as a process for matching needs with resources. A quasi-experimental design was used in the studies, making comparisons between individuals receiving the care management approach with matched control groups. Evaluation encompassed both cost-effectiveness and care process issues. The overall framework of the projects was the 'production of welfare' model, adopted and adapted from economic theories of production. Within this production model, care management was a process explicitly concerned with managing the tension between need on the one hand, and limited resources on the other. The PSSRU's positive findings from the pilot projects were taken as evidence that similar gains could be achieved if care management were to be adopted nationally.

After the implementation of the NHS and Community Care Act (1990), rather than being a targeted response to particular types of need and situations, as in the pilot projects, care management was applied to all adult *service users accessing services. In 1997, the Annual Report of the Chief Social Services Inspector noted that *local authorities were failing to differentiate between different levels of intervention, with all users in need of services receiving care management in many authorities. The report recommended three distinct types of care management: administrative, where the need was for advice or information; coordinating, where a single service or straightforward response was required; and intensive, where planning and coordination of services needed to be combined with supportive or therapeutic objectives. The latter was seen as a response that would apply to a small number of service users with complex or changing needs. In addition to the lack of targeting of care management, there were other differences between the features of the pilot projects and mainstream care management practice. The pilot projects tended to involve highly motivated staff given preferential workloads and extra resources, features not typical of the general care management system introduced after the implementation of the NHS and Community Care Act (1990). In addition, the pilot project reports struck notes of caution about whether devolving control of resources to the level of front-line workers could be achieved in mainstream *local authority structures without the introduction of controls that would lead to routinization and inflexibility. Therefore, while the PSSRU projects demonstrated the effectiveness of care management, this was under particular conditions, which were largely absent from care management as later developed in community care practice after the Conservatives' reforms.

The NHS and Community Care Act (1990) was accompanied by detailed guidance for managers and practitioners. This guidance emphasized that care management was a process for tailoring services to individual need by focusing holistically on the uniqueness of the person concerned and by keeping assessment of needs distinct from preoccupation with what services might be available. Instead of determining whether people met the criteria for a particular service, beginning with a set of criteria for services and deciding whether and, if so, how the person fits within them, care management was supposed to begin from the needs of the individual; it was supposed to be needs-led rather than service-led. However, the use of *eligibility criteria and *block contracts tended to militate against this aspiration. Over time, the criticisms of inflexibility and routinization that began to be levelled at care management increasingly echoed those that were used to castigate the system prior to the implementation of the NHS and Community Care Act (1990). Eventually this led to disillusionment with the care management system and its replacement by *care and support planning with the implementation of the Care Act (2014). The latter has a similar emphasis to that found in the original formulations of care management on being needs-led and tailoring responses to people's individual needs. *See also* BROKERAGE; CARE AND SUPPORT PLAN; CARE MANAGER; CARE MARKET; CARE PACKAGE; FAIR ACCESS TO CARE SERVICES; PERSONALIZATION.

care manager A social worker, or more rarely another professional, who was responsible for providing *care management. Although the *community care reforms stressed customer choice for *service users, a theme that has since remained central to services for adults, at least rhetorically, it was envisaged that judgements about their needs would still be made by social workers but in their new role as care managers. The care manager was charged with realizing customer *choice by providing an individualized service to meet the needs of a particular person, rather than requiring the person to fit whatever was already available. Increased customer choice was, therefore, not to be exercised directly by service users but was to emerge from the actions of care managers as champions of the service users' interests. The care manager role required a shift in orientation from social workers with the Griffiths Report (1988) (*see* COMMUNITY CARE REFORMS) stressing that social workers were to have a more managerial function, for example, needing to develop the skills to buy services. This took social work in adult services away from traditional *casework and towards a view of the social worker as a broker of services. Social workers as care managers had to develop capacities and dispositions made necessary by new activities such as managing budgets, which exposed them directly to the costs of the services that they arranged. An orientation of care managers to micro-management was encouraged and has remained, with an emphasis on scrupulous *gate-keeping and strict rationing of scarce resources; decisions, based on managerial criteria, have to be matched with financial data. Care management introduced complex procedures for regulating social workers in their distribution of services, based primarily on budgetary considerations. Skills traditionally associated with social work, such as forming relationships with service users, no longer seemed to be highly valued. The highly valued skills became managing budgets and understanding management information systems. Through the introduction of the care manager role social workers were pressured to develop a managerial orientation to their day-to-day work that has had an enduring impact. *See also* BROKERAGE; CARE AND SUPPORT PLAN; CARE MANAGEMENT.

care market The arrangements through which services are provided for purchase by social workers, or others in their employing organizations, from a number of different sources in the *private and *voluntary sectors. It replaced a system in which *local authorities were the direct providers of most services from in-house. Originally a feature of services for adults as a result of the *community care reforms but now prominent across all services, for example, as in the development of private foster care services that compete with placements provided by *local authority foster parents. As a result of the introduction of care markets, the role of local authorities in directly providing services has decreased significantly while that of the private and voluntary sectors has increased. For example, in *domiciliary services for adults the number of home care hours provided by private sector agencies has increased dramatically, as has the number of places provided in private sector care homes. Despite, or as a consequence of, this rapid growth there have been recurrent crises in care markets that have not been in the interests of *service users. In addition, increasing monopolization of care markets by large providers has diminished *choice for *service users and reduced responsiveness to *diversity and minority needs.

These problems with the operation of the care market led to the Care Act (2014) imposing a general duty on local authorities to promote sustainability, diversity, and quality in their local areas, ensuring the efficient and effective operation of the market for adult *care and support. This can be considered as a duty to facilitate the market, in the sense of using a wide range of approaches to encourage and shape it, so that it meets the needs of people in a local authority's area who need care and support, whether arranged or funded by the state, by the individual themselves, or in other ways. Local authorities must ensure that a range of providers are available, shaped by demands of individuals, families, and *carers, and that services are of high quality and meet the needs and preferences of those wanting to access services. In the Care Act (2014) guidance, the role of the local authority is seen as critical to achieving 'a vibrant responsive market of service providers', both through its *commissioning of services and its involvement in market shaping.

Market shaping involves a local authority in collaborating with its partners in order to facilitate the market in its area for *care and support services. This includes:

- services arranged and paid for by the state through the local authority itself;
- those services paid for by the state through direct payments;
- those services arranged and paid for by individuals from whatever sources (*self-funders);
- services paid for by a combination of these sources.

Market-shaping activity is intended to stimulate a diverse range of high-quality services, both in terms of the types, volumes, and quality of services and the types of provider organization. This means the local authority has to engage with stakeholders to develop understanding of supply and demand and to understand likely trends that reflect people's needs and aspirations. It is meant to be based on evidence and to signal to the market the types of services needed now and in the future, encouraging innovation, investment, and continuous improvement. In the Care Act (2014) guidance, local authorities' commissioning of services is seen as the prime way to affect market shaping. Commissioning is a cyclical activity to assess the needs of a local population for care and support services. It involves demand, market and supply analysis, market structuring and interventions, resource allocations and procurement, and contract management. Commissioning has increasingly been shaped more by the outcomes commissioners identify, rather than volumes of activity expected from service providers. In the guidance, market shaping and commissioning are seen as promoting a market for care and support that broadens, supplements, and supports a wider system in which much of the need for care and support is met by people's own efforts, by their families, friends, or other carers, and by community networks.

Local authorities have to produce a 'market position statement'. This should contain the local authority's direction of travel and policy intent; key information and statistics on needs, demand, and trends (including for specialized services, *personalization, integration, housing, community services, *information services and advocacy, and carers' services); information from consumer research and other sources about people's needs and wants; information to put the authority's needs in a national context; an indication of current and future authority resourcing and financial forecasts; a summary of supply and demand; the authority's ambitions for quality improvements and new types of services and innovations; and details or cross references to the local authority's own commissioning intentions, strategies, and practices. *See also* CARE MANAGEMENT; CARE PACKAGE; COMMODIFICATION; COMPETITION; MIXED ECONOMY OF CARE; QUASI-MARKETS.

Further reading: Department of Health (2016) *Care and Support: Statutory Guidance*, Chapter 4. Available at: https://www.gov.uk/government/publications/care-act-statutory-guidance/care-and-support-statutory-guidance#person-centred-care-and-support-planning.

Care Order Granted under Section 31 of the Children Act (1989) when a designated local authority is given *parental responsibility (Section 33) for a child by a court. A Care Order (or *Supervision Order) may only be granted by a court if it is satisfied that the child concerned is suffering or is likely to suffer *significant harm and this significant harm or likelihood of significant harm is attributable to the care given to the child or likely to be given to her or him if the Order were not made. This care is defined as not being what it would be reasonable to expect a parent to provide to a child. A Care Order (or Supervision Order) may also be made in circumstances where a child is beyond parental control. The child made subject to a Care Order must be under 17 years of age or under 16 years if married. Care Orders may be discharged by the court under Section 39 of the Children Act (1989) on the successful application of any person with parental responsibility, the child or relevant *local authority. Courts may substitute a Supervision Order for a Care Order, rather than discharging it, when an application is made. *See also* INTERIM CARE ORDER; THRESHOLD CRITERIA (CHILDREN).

care package The services provided to an adult *service user following a *needs assessment under the Care Act (2014). This term was originally introduced as part of the new market-oriented language that was associated with the implementation of the *community care reforms following the NHS and Community Care Act (1990), as a result of which social workers were required to put together services for people from what was available in the local *care market. *See also* CARE MANAGEMENT; CARE MANAGER; COMMODIFICATION; COMPETITION; MIXED ECONOMY OF CARE; QUASI-MARKETS.

care plan (children) The Arrangements for Placement of Children (General) Regulations (1991) place a duty on *local authorities to draw up individual care plans for *looked-after children. They state that a care plan should: set realistic specific objectives; set out the manner in which the objectives are to be achieved; set a timetable; identify a person to undertake necessary tasks; and identify the source of any funding required. This was intended to avoid the setting out of vague/general *goals, without describing precisely how they were to be achieved. The Review of Children's Cases (Amendment) (England) Regulations (2004) set out the procedure for regular review of care plans to ensure they continue to meet a child's needs: the first review must take place within four weeks of the child becoming looked after; the second review must be no more than three months after the first review; subsequent reviews must take place at intervals of no more than six months. At these reviews, contributions should be made by social workers, the parents, and other professionals working with the family (for example, from health and education and foster carers), as appropriate. *See also* SECTION 31A PLAN.

Further reading: Arrangements for Placement of Children (General) Regulations (1991). Available at: http://www.legislation.gov.uk/uksi/1991/890/regulation/5/made#regulation-5-1-a. Review of Children's Cases (Amendment) (England) Regulations (2004). Available at: http://www.legislation.gov.uk/uksi/2004/1419/pdfs/uksi_20041419_en.pdf.

care planning *See* CARE AND SUPPORT PLAN; CARE PLAN.

Care Proceedings Initiated under Section 31 of the Children Act (1989), only a local authority or the NSPCC can apply for a *Care Order or *Supervision Order on the grounds that a child known to them is suffering or is likely to suffer *significant harm. The Children and Families Act (2014) set a target of twenty-six weeks within which care proceedings should be concluded. *See also* INTERIM CARE ORDER; SECTION 31A PLAN.

Care Programme Approach A framework introduced in 1990 to formalize and strengthen systems of community support to people with mental health problems, underpinned by collaboration between health and social services. The four corner-stones of the CPA are the *assessment of health and social care *needs; a formal *care plan; care coordination undertaken by a designated *care coordinator; and regular reviews. Since its introduction, the CPA has been subject to government review and modification. Following criticisms of poor collaborative arrangements between health and social services and a lack of overall coordination as intended, the government integrated what had been two separate processes of the CPA and *care management in 1999. This gave the CPA the care management function for people of working age in contact with specialist mental health services, regardless of setting, so that support extends to hospitals, residential care settings, and prisons. Two levels of CPA were also introduced. The standard level applied to those receiving services from one provider who were able to manage their own care and maintain contact with services. The enhanced level was developed to target people with complex and multiple needs who receive support from more than one service provider and who are considered to be a higher *risk and more likely to disengage from services. Formal risk assessments were introduced for those on the enhanced CPA.

In 2008 the CPA was subjected to a refocusing exercise and the term CPA is no longer used to describe the care provided to those receiving the standard level of support. Responsibility for facilitating the care of those with straightforward needs who have contact with only one service provider is instead undertaken by an appropriate professional from within the providing agency, and formal care planning and review are no longer required. Although no longer eligible for the CPA unless their needs change, these individuals are entitled to: an identified lead professional; a full assessment of their needs; a formal statement of care agreed by them; ongoing review as required; the identification of their carers (if any); information about their rights; and a brief central record carrying essential information. The CPA is now frequently termed the '(new) CPA' in practice and in policy documents to clarify the application of the new arrangements. The (new) CPA continues to support those eligible for the former enhanced CPA in the same way as before. Hence the (new) CPA targets those who need multi-agency support, intensive intervention, and support with *dual diagnosis, and those who are difficult to engage or considered to be at higher risk. The underpinning principle of the CPA as a framework remains unchanged. As such, it is still an approach to providing care to those considered to be at greatest risk but its *eligibility criteria are not intended as a measure of eligibility to services. Eligibility for service provision continues to be defined in accordance with statutory responsibilities and the assessment of individual need.

The refocusing exercise introduced a statement of values and principles to the CPA. These include putting the individual at the centre of their care and support planning; recognizing the individual as a person first and patient/*service user second; recognizing the individual's wider roles, relationships, and networks; the promotion of self-determination and the individual's control over their support and care; the need to recognize and support carers' needs; the importance of developing therapeutic relationships and *partnership working with individuals; the importance of building long-term relationships based on trust. The (new) CPA also promotes the broader integration of the CPA with assessment and care planning systems present in adult care, older adult care, services for children and young people, *learning disability services, substance misuse services, and the criminal justice system.

Further reading: Department of Health (2008) *Refocusing the Care Programme Approach*. Available at: http://webarchive.nationalarchives.gov.uk/20130107105354/http:/www.dh.gov. uk/prod_consum_dh/groups/dh_digitalassets/@dh/@en/documents/digitalasset/ dh_083649.pdf.

Care Quality Commission (CQC) The body that regulates all health and social care services in England: hospitals, dentists, ambulances, *care homes, and care given in people's own homes. Different services are inspected and regulated in different ways but some aspects of the CQC's work apply across all services:

- Registering people that apply to provide services;
- Examining data, evidence, and information;
- Using *feedback from *service users;
- Carrying out inspections;
- Taking action when services need to improve and making sure those responsible for poor care are held accountable for it;
- Publishing information on judgements reached about services, including giving ratings.

There are four ratings:

Outstanding The service is performing exceptionally well.

Good The service is performing well and meeting the CQC's expectations.

Requires improvement The service is not performing as well as it should and the CQC has told the service how it must improve.

Inadequate The service is performing badly and the CQC has taken action against the person or organization that runs it.

When undertaking inspections of services and deciding on a rating, the CQC focuses on five questions:

Are they safe? Are their users protected from abuse and avoidable harm?

Are they effective? Does the care, treatment, and support provided achieve good outcomes, help to maintain quality of life, and use best available evidence?

Are they caring? Do staff involve users and treat them with compassion, kindness, dignity, and respect?

Are they responsive to people's needs? Are services organized so that they meet users' needs?

Are they well-led? Does the leadership, management, and governance of the organization make sure it is providing high-quality care that is based around individual needs, encourages learning and innovation, and promotes an open and fair culture.

Each of the five key questions is broken down into a further set of more detailed questions that the CQC calls 'key lines of enquiry'. It uses different key lines of enquiry for different services.

(⊕) SEE WEB LINKS

• Official site of the Care Quality Commission.

carer An unpaid member of a household or informal support network who assists or looks after someone else. It has been estimated that around 6.8 million carers (12 per cent of the UK population in 2015) save the taxpayer £132 billion a year, almost double what the saving was in 2001 and close to the total annual cost of health spending in the UK (£134.1 billion in the year 2014–15). Carers are providing more care for two main reasons: because care *needs are greater, due to an increasingly ageing population, and because there is less home care support. Between 2001 and 2015, the number of people aged 85 and over increased by over 431,000 (38 per cent) and the number of people with a limiting long-term illness increased by 1.6 million (16 per cent). Between 2010–11 and 2013–14, less home care support was provided by local authorities to people with care needs in England (where the reduction was greatest) and in *Scotland. Numbers of home care clients and hours of home care increased in *Wales and *Northern Ireland, but still did not keep pace with rising care needs. Between 2001 and 2015, those carers providing substantial amounts of care (twenty to forty-nine hours per week) rose by almost 43 per cent to 940,000 and those caring intensively (for fifty or more hours per week) rose by almost 33 per cent to 1,655,100 (Carers UK 2015).

Despite the central contribution made by such informal support to many people's lives, it is only in recent years that this contribution has been recognized. The voices of carers, through national organizations such as *Carers UK and local carers' groups, have been increasingly influential in bringing to public attention the often undervalued work of carers and the substantial saving in public spending that they represent.

Early work on the needs of carers emphasized gender inequalities in caring, premised upon stereotypical assumptions about the roles of women and men, and the impact of *community care policy on the level of caring undertaken by women. Subsequent critiques highlighted the significance of other social divisions, such as disability and *ethnicity, for caring and how this is experienced. Another social division impacting on caring is age; many *older people are carers. These older carers may experience multiple and overlapping inequalities. Health problems are more likely to be experienced by those providing high amounts of care and older carers tend to be most concentrated in areas of social and economic disadvantage.

Following the *community care reforms, the contribution of carers was slotted into the assembly of 'packages of care' by social workers and government guidance stipulated that social workers should take account of the support from carers that was available or could be arranged, being careful only to supplement carers' likely future ability to care. As a consequence, the positioning of caring shifted from its being an implicit to an explicit resource. The assumptions that caring—as an expected standard of behaviour predicated on individual willingness and a sense of responsibility—would be the first port of call, and that it required active management by social workers, became prominent in practice. The government declared that this was 'both right and a sound investment'. Subsequently three pieces of legislation—Carers (Recognition and Services) Act (1995); Carers and Disabled Children Act (2000); Carers (Equal Opportunities) Act (2005)—were passed that addressed the needs of carers and these were consolidated in the Care Act (2014), with the avowed aim of placing carers on the same footing as those they care for.

Under the Care Act (2014), a *local authority does not have to meet any needs that are being met by a carer. However, the local authority must identify, during the assessment process, the needs of the person that are being met by a carer at that time, and whether those needs meet the *eligibility criteria. Any eligible needs met by a carer are not required to be met by the local authority, for so long as the carer continues to do so, but the *service user's *care and support plan should record the needs being met by a carer and contingency plans to respond to any breakdown in the caring relationship should be considered. In addition, local authorities have been encouraged to engage in targeted interventions to identify carers, including those who are taking on new caring responsibilities. The focus has been on helping carers to continue to care, enabling them to have a life of their own alongside caring, facilitating breaks from caring, assisting them to develop mechanisms to cope with the stress associated with caring, and developing awareness of their own physical and mental health needs. Services, facilities, and resources have been identified that contribute to preventing, delaying, or reducing the needs of carers, helping them to:

- care effectively and safely—both for themselves and the person they are supporting—for example by providing interventions or advice on moving and handling items safely or avoiding falls in the home, or training for carers to feel confident performing basic health care tasks;
- look after their own physical and mental health and wellbeing, including developing coping mechanisms;
- make use of IT and assistive technology;
- make choices about their own lives, for example managing care and paid employment;
- find support and services available in their area;
- access the advice, information, and support they need, including information and advice on social security benefits and other financial information; entitlement to a *carer's assessment; breaks from caring; *advocacy; and caring and employment.

Social workers and others can make a difference by simply listening to carers and valuing what they do. They can offer emotional support and validation of the carer's role and contribution, recognizing the expertise of the carer and harnessing this in the planning and monitoring of support arrangements. They also need to act as a resource bank, linking carers to sources of information, advice, and support that are pertinent to their specific needs. In particular, carers need to be made aware of and encouraged to have a *carer's assessment under the Care Act (2014) in order to utilize services that will support their own health and wellbeing. This includes educational, leisure, and employment opportunities. However, in the context of cuts in expenditure in an era of *austerity there is likely to be a gap between the rhetoric and the reality of what should be available for carers.

Studies of kinship obligations have found that involvement in caring does not follow a straightforward trajectory. Carers are negotiated into the caring role through family processes arising from specific social and biographical contexts, rather than being derived from an abstract set of moral values. Requiring a family member to provide intimate care can undermine the relationship that already exists, and public services are often seen by service users as preferable to care by relatives, counter to official policy. Every caring situation is unique and full consideration needs to be given to the individual needs and preferences of those involved in caring, the needs and preferences of the person cared for, and the nature and dynamics of the caring relationship. In such situations, there are often dilemmas for social workers in acting on behalf of two (or more) individuals, a service user and a carer(s), who may have competing needs and interests. The Care Act (2014) guidance stresses the responsibility of social workers to involve *service users and carers, and take account of their views. However, balancing service users' needs and concerns with those of carers is often not straightforward. It is important that service users' needs are not conflated with those of their carers, and vice versa, and that the individual support requirements and perspectives of both parties are considered, while avoiding extreme polarization of service users' and carers' *identities and needs in seeking to address and balance the needs and interests of both parties. A number of issues arise.

First, the term 'carer' implies that the relationship is one-way, rather than one that involves, or has the potential for, reciprocity and interdependence between carer and service user. Secondly, service users, particularly older people, as we have seen, may themselves be significant resources in giving care and support to others. Thirdly, focusing too heavily on supporting carers fosters an uncritical acceptance of the conditions that have created the need for care in the first place; attention should also be directed at addressing the factors that contribute to people's need for care. Fourthly, often neither service users nor those in their informal networks who are involved in providing support define this as '*care'; care is often an intrinsic part of the interpersonal relationship but not its defining characteristic. These issues reinforce the importance of evaluating what is seen as 'good' care from the perspectives of both (or all) parties to the care arrangements. They emphasize that in seeking to address the needs and concerns of both service users and carers, it is not simply a case of establishing each party's practical needs, but reaching an understanding of how each party perceives and experiences the relationship and the impact it has on her/his sense of self. *See also* CARE; CARE RECIPIENTS; YOUNG CARERS.

Further reading: Barnes, M. (2006) *Caring and Social Justice*, Palgrave Macmillan.
Carers UK (2015) *Valuing Carers 2015: The Rising Value of Carers' Support*. Available at: http://www.carersuk.org/for-professionals/policy/policy-library/valuing-carers-2015.

care recipients Campaigns for *carers' rights have tended to neglect the position and experience of those receiving *care, as well as the *interdependence of the giver and the recipient of care. For example, the allegation has been made that caregiving has become a central feminist issue but care-receiving has not. While some feminist writers have asserted that 'collective' (i.e. institutional) forms of care for older and disabled people are the only way to prevent the exploitation of women as carers, the *Disabled People's Movement has challenged this construction of disabled people as passive bodies in need of placement and 'tending' elsewhere.

carer's assessment An *assessment of a *carer's need for support as a result of her/his looking after someone else, which is undertaken under the Care Act (2014). When someone provides or intends to provide *care for another adult, *local authorities must consider whether to carry out a carer's assessment if it appears that the carer may have any level of need for support. Where an adult provides care under contract or as part of voluntary work, they are not normally regarded as a carer. There may be circumstances where the adult providing care, either under contract or through voluntary work, is also providing care for the adult outside that. In such a circumstance, a *local authority may consider whether to carry out a carer's assessment for the part of the care the person is not providing on a contractual or voluntary basis.

The assessment is the key interaction between a local authority and a carer. As well as being a gateway to the support a carer needs, it can be an intervention in its own right, which can help a carer to understand her/his situation and the *needs s/he has and reduce or delay the onset of greater needs. The aim of the assessment is to identify what needs the carer may have and what *outcomes s/he wants to achieve to maintain or improve her/his *wellbeing. It provides a full picture of the carer's needs so that a local authority can provide a response that meets the level of the needs. This might range from offering guidance and information to arranging for services to meet the needs. The assessment may be the only contact a local authority has with the carer at that point in time, so it is critical that the most is made of the opportunity it presents.

A carer's assessment establishes not only the carer's needs for support but also the sustainability of the caring role, which includes the practical and emotional support the carer provides to the person cared for. Therefore, a carer's assessment includes consideration of the carer's potential future needs for support. Consideration is given to whether the carer is currently willing and/or able, and whether the carer will continue to be willing and/or able, to care for the person needing care. The aim is to produce a realistic evaluation of the carer's present and future needs for support and whether the caring relationship is sustainable. The assessment must also consider the carer's activities beyond her/his caring role and the impact of caring upon those activities. This includes considering the impact of caring on a carer's desire and ability to work, to partake in education, training, or recreational activities, and to have time to themselves. The impact of caring on the carer's life is considered in both the short and long term. Furthermore the assessment must consider a carer's support needs over a sufficient period of time to get a complete picture of any fluctuating needs. This could be because at specific times a carer needs more support than at others. For example, if they share responsibility for looking after their children with a former spouse, they may need more support in their caring role when they are the primary *care-giver to their children. The carer's support needs could also fluctuate based on the needs of the person receiving care. For example, if that person's needs fluctuate, the carer might provide additional care at certain times.

To help a carer prepare for an assessment a local authority should provide in advance, and in accessible format, the list of questions to be covered in the assessment so that the carer can prepare for the assessment and think through what her/his needs are and the outcomes s/he wants to achieve. A local authority must offer a carer the choice of a supported self-assessment if s/he is able and willing to undertake it. This means that the carer completes the assessment using the same schedule that the local authority uses. Before offering a supported self-assessment, local authorities must ensure that carer has *capacity in accordance with the Mental Capacity Act (2005) to assess their own needs. Local authorities may combine a carer's assessment with a *needs assessment of an adult needing *care and support, where both the individual concerned and the carer agree to this, to avoid carrying out two separate assessments. If either of the individuals concerned does not agree to a combined assessment, the assessments must be carried out separately. A carer must be given a record of her/his assessment. A copy must also be shared with anybody else that the carer requests the local authority to share a copy with. *See also* CARE RECIPIENTS; CARERS UK; YOUNG CARERS.

Further reading: Department of Health (2016) *Care and Support: Statutory Guidance*, Chapter 6. Available at: https://www.gov.uk/government/publications/care-act-statutory-guidance/care-and-support-statutory-guidance#person-centred-care-and-support-planning.

Carers UK An organization that acts as a pressure group in seeking to gain greater recognition for the contribution made by *carers and campaigns for the practical, financial and emotional support they need. Carers UK advocates five measures that would improve the situation of carers:

- Address urgently the underfunding of social *care.
- Improve financial support for carers.
- Promote a carer-friendly National Health Service.
- Introduce a right to paid care leave.
- Recognize that flexible and affordable care services are a condition for carers to stay in work.

See also CARE RECIPIENTS; CARER'S ASSESSMENT; YOUNG CARERS.

(((⊕))) SEE WEB LINKS
- Official site of Carers UK.

care versus control The tension between two main facets of social work. *'Care' is used in this phrase as a shorthand expression for all of the ways in which social workers seek to work alongside and with people, as much as possible on their own terms. However, social workers are also *agents of social control. This can be seen in their *statutory powers to intervene in people's lives in order to protect them from themselves or from others, or as part of a wider analysis of the role social workers play in turning the difficulties caused by wider social issues, such as poverty, into their representation as individual problems. *See also* INDIVIDUAL PATHOLOGY.

care village *See* RETIREMENT COMMUNITY.

caring *See* CARE; CARER; CARE RECIPIENTS; CARER'S ASSESSMENT; CARERS UK; YOUNG CARERS.

case There is a tendency to regard and/or refer to *service users as 'cases', whatever the official current parlance is for them, because of the way in which social work organizations document them in hard copy or electronic case files. *See also* CASE CONFERENCE; CASE HISTORY; CASEWORK; CHARITY ORGANISATION SOCIETY.

case conference A meeting of a number of professionals and, usually, *service users and *carers (in adults' services), or parents or other *care-givers (in children's services), who come together to pool information about the circumstances of an individual or a family and decide upon a course of action, including how services will be coordinated. Case conferences may be convened in a wide range of situations but have a particularly significant role in relation to *safeguarding children or vulnerable adults (*see* SAFEGUARDING ADULTS). Periodically, case conferences may be held to *review the work that has been undertaken since an initial case conference or since an earlier review. These may be termed 'case reviews', rather than case conferences. New or amended plans may result from reappraisal in a case review.

case file *See* CASE; CASE HISTORY; CASEWORK.

case finding An aspect of *care management which existed in US models that were imported to the UK in the 1990s concerned with locating adults who had not been referred for *assessment but who might benefit from it. The aim was to identify people needing assistance early in order to put preventive interventions in place. There was a tension between case finding and the emphasis in services for adults on prioritizing the provision of services by targeting those with high-level *needs. As a consequence, although case finding was part of the official framework of care management, it was usually seen as an optional extra and was little practised. *See also* CARE MANAGER; COMMUNITY CARE REFORMS; SCREENING.

case history An account of the difficulties being experienced by a family or an individual that sets problems in a historical context. Many years ago case histories were in common use, being seen as an essential social work tool for exploring and explaining problems by focusing on significant events and formative developments. In recent years, recording has tended to be much briefer, often constrained by software programmes that have a tick-box format or allow little scope for elaboration. Running counter to this trend is the recognition of the importance of full background knowledge about children in the care system, particularly those being placed permanently somewhere other than with their *birth parent(s), for example, through *adoption. In other areas of practice, for example with *older people or people with *learning disabilities, a full understanding of someone's history can be the basis for responding to her/him on an individual basis. *See also* ASSESSMENT; BIOGRAPHICAL APPROACH; CASE; CASEWORK; CHARITY ORGANISATION SOCIETY; CHILD'S PERMANENCE REPORT; CHRONOLOGY.

case law Legal cases that establish precedents requiring social workers, with advice from lawyers, to apply the law guided by how the law has been used to interpret previous cases.

caseload management Systematic measurement and monitoring of the amount and nature of a social worker's (or other worker's) *workload, often involving the allocation of points for particular types of work so that an overall numerical score can be applied. *See also* WORKLOAD MANAGEMENT.

case management A term used in the US and initially used in the UK at the beginning of the *community care reforms, but dropped and replaced by *'care management' as a result of *service users' organizations insisting that they were not *'cases' to be managed but people for whom services needed to be managed or who could manage their own services.

case management hearing Part of the court procedures for dealing with *public law children's cases under the *Public Law Outline. At the case management hearing, the court gives detailed directions about how the case will be progressed, with the aim of completing cases within twenty-six weeks. *See also* CARE ORDER; CARE PROCEEDINGS; SUPERVISION ORDER.

case review *See* CASE CONFERENCE.

casework An influential approach to social work initiated by the *Charity Organisation Society in the nineteenth century, first in London and then spread nationally and internationally by the Society. The emphasis was on responding to people with problems on the basis of an *assessment of an individual's *needs. The approach was originally steeped in the assumptions of the COS concerning individual culpability and moral responsibility but in the twentieth century, particularly from the end of the Second World War to the 1970s, casework was concerned with addressing *individual pathology within a *psycho-dynamic framework that sought to assist a person to gain insight into the sources of and solutions to their problems. Such casework was critiqued from the right on the grounds of its moral relativism and from the left because it located people's problems within themselves rather than in the external factors created by social divisions in society, such as *poverty, *class, *'race', and *gender. It fell into disfavour, although work with individuals remains the dominant form of social work, particularly in *statutory settings, and key elements of the approach's focus on the individual as the source of and solution to problems are still found.

cash for care *See* DIRECT PAYMENT.

cash limits Ceilings placed on the budgets available to *local authorities for the provision of local services as a result of restrictions on the amounts available from central government funds. These ceilings have frequently contained assumptions about efficiency gains in percentage terms. For example, a budget might be reduced by 5 per cent on the assumption that this loss of funding can be made up by finding ways of running services more efficiently. Such measures have exerted strong pressure to reduce the costs of services, emphasizing the need for constant cost-consciousness, which has become a key theme in social work.

caution A warning given verbally to an offender by a police officer as an alternative to court proceedings, which can only be used if the offence has been admitted. For young offenders (under 18), the caution has been replaced by a *reprimand and a *final warning (Crime and Disorder Act 1998).

CBT *See* COGNITIVE BEHAVIOURAL THERAPY.

CDT *See* COMMUNITY DRUG TEAM.

centile chart A graph against which a child's development can be assessed. It comprises a series of lines showing average measurements of height, weight, and head circumference (see illustration). The lines of growth on the graph are called centiles (or percentiles), and the number of a centile predicts the percentage of children who are below and above that measurement at a given age. For example, the tenth centile means that 10 per cent of the age- and sex-matched population will be smaller and 90 per cent bigger. The charts are a useful tool for health professionals who may have concerns about the growth of a particular child and how s/he is faring compared with what might be reasonably expected of a child of similar age, keeping in mind the wide scope for variation in *child development. Alongside other assessments the charts can provide an important indicator of whether developmental milestones are being achieved. Problems in meeting these milestones may be due to many factors including illness, disability, an underlying organic condition, poor *attachment, or *child abuse and neglect.

Centre for Excellence and Outcomes in Children's and Young People's Services (C4EO) Provides a range of products and services to support the children's services sector in areas including *fostering, *adoption, *looked-after children, *early intervention, *safeguarding, *disability, and *early years.

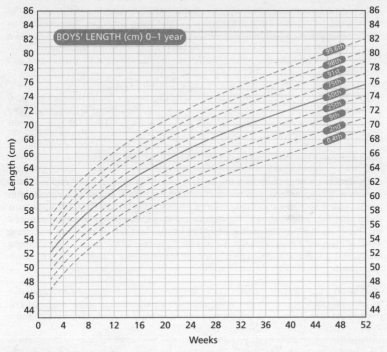

Centile chart

(🌐) SEE WEB LINKS

• Official site of the Centre for Excellence and Outcomes in Children's and Young People's Services.

chaining Breaking down an activity into a series of small cumulative steps and learning each step, one at a time, until it is thoroughly mastered, before moving on to the next, until the entire activity (or chain) can be carried out. An approach often used with people with *learning disabilities as a way of their learning daily life skills. A variant is 'backward chaining', a technique in which the steps are mastered in reverse order, so that, for example, if someone were learning to tie shoelaces through backward chaining, the initial stage would be to complete the final step of tightening the completed knot to secure the shoe.

challenging behaviours A range of responses (such as head-butting, kicking, spitting, biting, screaming) that can put the person concerned and/or others at *risk and/or prevent a person participating in activities associated with day-to-day life. Behaviours can be destructive and violent, and can lead to self-harm. Less extreme behaviour can still be distressing and disruptive to those affected by it. In many cases these behaviours are a result of difficulty with understanding and communicating, and are not under the control of the person involved. Originally used predominantly in relation to children or adults with *learning disabilities, the use of the term has gradually been extended to people with severe mental health problems, *older people with *dementia, and, more recently, children and young people. The person involved needs to be supported in attempting to communicate without resorting to challenging behaviour. *Behaviour modification may be used to address the behaviour and medication may be prescribed.

Channel Panel Under the Counter-Terrorism and Security Act (2015), *local authorities are required to have Channel Panels. The Panels assess the extent to which identified individuals are vulnerable to being drawn into terrorism and arrange for support to be provided to those individuals. Panels must include the local authority and the chief officer of the local police. Whilst the Channel Panel provisions are counter-terrorism measures, the way in which the Channel Panel operates can overlap with the implementation of wider safeguarding duties, especially where there are vulnerabilities requiring social work intervention or where the individual is already known to social workers. If the individual to be discussed is a child known to social workers, or if there is a concern that a child might be at *risk of *significant harm, as defined by the Children Act (1989), then the relevant social worker has to be present at the Panel and be involved in the decisions about the child. Channel Panels assess vulnerability using a vulnerability assessment framework built around three criteria: engagement with a group, cause or ideology; intent to cause harm; and capability to cause harm.

Further reading: HM Government (2015) *Channel Panel Guidance. Protecting Vulnerable People from Being Drawn into Terrorism. Statutory Guidance for Channel Panel Members and Partners of Local Panels.* Available at: http:www.gov.uk/government/publications/channel-guidance.

charging for services (adults) Residential and non-residential services arranged by *local authorities for adults are charged for, while services provided by the National Health Service are free at the point of delivery (*see* NHS CONTINUING HEALTH CARE; NHS-FUNDED NURSING CARE). The Care Act (2014) guidance states that *local authorities should take into account the following principles when making decisions on charging:

- Ensure that people are not charged more than it is reasonably practicable for them to pay.
- Be comprehensive to reduce variation in the way people are assessed and charged.
- Be clear and transparent so people know what they will be charged.
- Promote wellbeing and social inclusion and support the vision of *personalization, *independence, *choice, and control.
- Support *carers to look after their own health and wellbeing and to care effectively and safely.
- Be person-focused, reflecting the variety of *care and caring journeys and the variety of options available to meet needs.
- Apply the charging rules equally so that those with similar *needs or services are treated the same and minimize anomalies between different care settings.
- Encourage and enable those who wish to stay in or take up employment, education, or training, or plan for the future costs of meeting their needs to do so.
- Be sustainable for local authorities in the long term.

Regulations determine the maximum amount a local authority can charge a person. Partners cannot be assessed according to their joint resources; each person must be treated individually. A financial limit, known as the 'upper capital limit', exists for the purposes of the financial assessment. Below this level, a person can seek *means-tested support from the local authority. This means that the local authority will undertake a financial assessment of the person's assets and will make a charge based on what the person can afford to pay. There is also a 'lower capital limit' and if someone falls below that limit, s/he will not need to contribute to the cost of her/his *care and support from her/his capital. A person with more in capital than the upper capital limit can ask her/his local authority to arrange care and support. However, the person is not entitled to receive any financial assistance from her/his local authority and will pay the full cost of her/his care and support until her/his capital falls below the upper capital limit. A local authority cannot charge more than the cost that it incurs in meeting someone's assessed needs. It cannot recover any administration fee in relation to arranging care and support. The only exception is in the case of a person with *eligible needs and assets above the upper capital limit who has asked the local authority to arrange care and support on her/his behalf. In such cases, the local authority may apply an administration fee to cover its costs. However this must not be higher than the cost the local authority has incurred in arranging that care and support.

A local authority must carry out a financial assessment of what a person can afford to pay and, once complete, it must give a written record of that assessment to the person. It explains how the financial assessment has been carried out, what the charge will be, and how often it will be made, and if there is any fluctuation in charges, the reason for the fluctuation. In some circumstances, a local authority may undertake a 'light-touch' financial assessment, i.e. it may choose to treat a person as if a financial assessment had been carried out. In order to do so, the local authority must be satisfied on the basis of evidence provided by the person that they can afford, and will continue to be able to afford, any charges due. The main circumstances in which a local authority may consider carrying out a light-touch financial assessment are:

• Where a person has significant financial resources, and does not wish to undergo a full financial assessment for personal reasons, but wishes nonetheless to access local authority support in arranging their care. In these situations the local authority may accept other evidence in lieu of carrying out the financial assessment and consider the person to have financial resources above the upper limit;
• Where the local authority charges a small or nominal amount for a particular service which a person is clearly able to meet and carrying out a financial assessment would be disproportionate;
• Where an individual is in receipt of benefits which demonstrate that they would not be able to contribute towards their care and support costs.

A local authority may be satisfied that a person is able to afford any charges due because a person has property or savings clearly worth more than the upper capital limit or sufficient income left following the charge due in the case of small or nominal charges. The person has to be told that s/he has the right to request a full financial assessment.

The local authority cannot charge for certain types of care and support that must be arranged free:

• *Intermediate care including *reablement (for up to six weeks);
• Community equipment (*aids and minor adaptations). Aids must be provided free of charge whether provided to meet or prevent/delay needs. A minor adaptation is one costing £1,000 or less;

- Care and support provided to people with Creutzfeldt-Jacob Disease;
- *After-care services/support provided under Section 117 of the Mental Health Act 1983;
- Any service or part of service that the NHS is under a duty to provide. This includes *Continuing Health Care;
- Any services a local authority is under a duty to provide through other legislation.

Whereas charging policies for meeting care and support needs in someone's home are a matter of local authority discretion, within the parameters of the regulations, there is a national charging policy for people in residential care according to which they contribute most of their income towards the cost of their care and support. However, a local authority must leave the person with a specified amount of her/his own income so that the person has money to spend on personal items such as clothes and other items that are not part of their care. This is known as the personal expenses allowance. It is adjusted annually by the government to ensure it maintains its value.

When the care planning process has determined that a person's needs are best met in a care home, a local authority must offer at least one option that is affordable within someone's *personal budget. However, a person can choose alternative options, including a more expensive setting, if a third party and/or the resident is willing and able to pay the additional cost (referred to as a 'top-up'). Such an additional payment must always be optional.

Where a local authority meets a carer's support needs, it has the *power to charge the carer. However, a local authority must not charge a carer for care and support provided directly to the person they care for under any circumstances. When deciding whether to charge, and in determining what an appropriate charge is, a local authority has to consider how it wishes to express the way it values carers within its local community and recognize the significant contribution carers make. Local authorities have to consider carefully the likely impact of any charges on carers, including their willingness and ability to continue caring. A nominal charge may be appropriate, for example to ensure sufficient numbers participate in an activity specifically arranged for a group of carers. A local authority has to ensure that any charges do not negatively impact a carer's ability to look after their own health and wellbeing and to care effectively and safely.

Further reading: Department of Health (2016) *Care and Support: Statutory Guidance*, Chapter 8. Available at: https://www.gov.uk/government/publications/care-act-statutory-guidance/care-and-support-statutory-guidance#person-centred-care-and-support-planning.

charitable organization *See* CHARITY.

charity A non-profit organization that provides services or money to people in need. Some charities are run on a shoestring in a particular local area. Others are well-funded and have a national or international remit. Charities are run by trustees, who form the governing body or 'board' of a charity, and they carry ultimate responsibility. Most trustees are volunteers and receive no payment other than expenses. Charities cannot be involved in party political activity, but they can lobby or campaign in the political realm in order to further their objectives or to provide information to people involved in politics that is relevant to their objectives. Most of the *voluntary organizations employing social workers are charities. Social workers in *statutory settings may have to make applications to charities on *services users' behalf or assist service users to do so in their own right, when there are gaps in state provision. *See also* CHARITY COMMISSION.

Charity Commission An organization responsible for registering and regulating charities. It offers charities advice and guidance, and keeps the Register of Charities, which provides information about each of the registered charities. Most charities with an annual income of over £5,000 have to register with the Charity Commission and all charities have to abide by charity law, under the regulation of the Commission. *See also* CHARITY.

(⊕) SEE WEB LINKS
• Official site of the Charity Commission.

Charity Organisation Society The COS, founded in 1869, sought to reform what it depicted as the directionless chaos of existing charitable activities. By coordinating and concentrating charities' resources so that they were distributed systematically, it was thought that those best able to make use of assistance would become self-supporting. In addition to coordinating charitable effort, the COS dovetailed its work with the Poor Law; the COS was keen to ensure that the Poor Law operated effectively, by not helping people regarded as undeserving and passing them on to the Poor Law authorities. The Society was only concerned with assisting the *'deserving poor', people who were seen as victims of circumstance and who had the moral character to use charitable assistance to restore themselves to *independence. The assessment of moral character (thrift, sobriety, industriousness, decency) became central to the COS's work and was undertaken through *casework, which involved regular visiting and a relationship that combined support and surveillance. This required careful enquiry into the backgrounds of applicants for assistance to see whether they were worthy of help, as well as building up detailed knowledge of a person's character (morals, habits, lifestyle) and circumstances, documenting any help already being given and assessing the nature and amount of help still needed in order to achieve character transformation. Although casework was advocated before the COS, the COS systematized and codified its techniques in order to pass them on as a foundation for social work and to support its claims for treating social work as a profession. Thus, the COS's casework was the key to the shift from charity as an unskilled duty of the rich, to social work as an expert and professional activity, undertaken by those educated in its theory and methods. Though the language has changed, the enduring *'cases' mentality that continues to characterize social work dates back to the COS's work in the nineteenth century. *See also* CASE.

Cheshire West Used as a shorthand term to refer to the Supreme Court Judgment of March 2014, *P v Cheshire West and Chester Council and another and P and Q v Surrey County Council*. The judgment clarified what constituted a deprivation of liberty. *See* DEPRIVATION OF LIBERTY SAFEGUARDS.

child 1. Denotes developmental stage and/or age and/or legal status. The *United Nations Convention on the Rights of the Child* defines it thus: 'A child means every human being below the age of 18 years unless, under the law applicable to the child, majority is attained earlier'. The definition of child varies in different jurisdictions and under legislation enacted for different purposes. In the Children Acts (1989 and 2004), a child is anyone who has not yet reached her/his 18th birthday. The fact that a child has reached 16 years of age, may be living independently, is in further education, is a member of the armed forces, is in hospital, or in custody does not change her/his status or entitlement to services or protection under the Children Act (1989). The entitlement to services is extended to those children for whom *local authorities have had responsibility up to the age of 16 in the requirement to provide some services for them up to the age of 21. *See also* CHILDHOOD; LEAVING CARE.

2. It may also be used to define the legal and/or biological relationship to a parent, as in 'child of'.

child abuse and neglect Forms of maltreatment that constitute a violation of human and/or civil rights through the infliction of harm or the failure to prevent harm either deliberately or through negligence. They may occur in a family, or in an institutional or community setting, and be carried out by another child or children, or an adult or adults known to the child, or, more rarely, by a stranger, for example, via the Internet. Official definitions of physical abuse, emotional abuse, sexual abuse, and neglect are used by social workers and other professionals to make judgements as to whether a child is experiencing *significant harm, and to determine whether protective action, including the implementation of a *child protection plan, is required.

Physical abuse This is defined as situations involving hitting, shaking, throwing, poisoning, burning, or scalding, drowning, suffocating, or otherwise causing physical harm to a child. Physical harm may also be caused when a parent or *care-giver fabricates the symptoms of or deliberately induces illness in a child.

Emotional abuse This is the persistent emotional maltreatment of a child such as to cause severe and persistent adverse effects on the child's emotional development. It may involve conveying to children that they are worthless or unloved, inadequate, or valued only insofar as they meet the needs of another person. It may include not giving the child opportunities to express their views, deliberately silencing them, or making fun of what they say, or how they communicate. It may feature age or developmentally inappropriate expectations being imposed on children. These may include interactions that are beyond the child's developmental capacity, as well as overprotection, and limitation of exploration and learning, or preventing the child participating in normal social interaction. It may involve seeing or hearing the ill-treatment of another. It may involve serious *bullying (including *cyber-bullying), causing children frequently to feel frightened or in danger, or the exploitation or corruption of children. Some level of emotional abuse is involved in all types of maltreatment of a child, though it may occur alone.

Sexual abuse This involves forcing or enticing a child or young person to take part in sexual activities, not necessarily involving a high level of *violence, whether or not the child is aware of what is happening. The activities may involve physical contact, including assault by penetration (for example, rape or oral sex) or non-penetrative acts such as masturbation, kissing, rubbing, and touching. They may also include non-contact activities, such as involving children in looking at or in the production of sexual images, watching sexual activities, encouraging children to behave in sexually inappropriate ways, or grooming a child in preparation for abuse (including via the Internet). Sexual abuse is not solely perpetrated by adult males. More rarely, women can also commit acts of sexual abuse, as can other children.

Neglect This is the persistent failure to meet a child's basic physical and/or psychological needs, which is likely to result in the serious impairment of the child's health or development. Neglect may occur during pregnancy as a result of maternal substance misuse. Once a child is born, neglect may involve a parent or care-giver failing to:

• Provide adequate food, clothing, and shelter (including exclusion from home or abandonment).

- Protect a child from physical and emotional harm or danger.
- Ensure adequate supervision (including the use of inadequate care-givers).
- Ensure access to appropriate medical care or treatment.
- Respond to a child's basic emotional needs.

See also CHILD ABUSE INQUIRIES; CHILD PROTECTION; CHILDREN AND DOMESTIC VIOLENCE; CHILD SEXUAL EXPLOITATION; CHILD TRAFFICKING; SECTION 47 ENQUIRY.

Further reading: Howe, D. (2005) *Child Abuse and Neglect: Attachment, Development and Intervention*, Palgrave Macmillan.

child abuse inquiries Panels of inquiry that have usually been constituted as a full public inquiry ordered by central government and conducted in accordance with legal processes and principles to establish the circumstances surrounding well-publicized deaths of children at the hands of their parents. These have tended to be held in response to public, political, and media reaction to the horrific nature of a child's death, and have sought to identify failings that may have contributed to the tragedy, and any lessons for professional and organizational practice that need to be learned and acted upon. Examples of these have been Denis McNeill (1945), Maria Colwell (1974), Jasmine Beckford (1985), Tyra Henry (1985), Kimberley Carlisle (1987), Victoria Climbié (2003), Peter Connolly (2007), and Daniel Pelka (2013). The common feature of the reports published at the end of these inquiries has been the perceived failure of professionals to intervene sufficiently early or robustly enough to safeguard the child and prevent their death, with many opportunities to decisively safeguard the child deemed to have been lost. Social workers have been the main targets of criticism. By contrast, the public inquiry into the events in Cleveland in 1987, where significant numbers of children were medically diagnosed as having been sexually abused and were subsequently removed from home, concluded that professional interventions may on occasions be premature, even over-zealous. This inquiry was followed by others that drew similar conclusions in relation to the investigation by professionals of alleged organized sexual abuse (Rochdale [1990], Orkney Isles [1991]).

Inquiries have had a major impact on the development of policy and practice in *child protection. The death of Maria Colwell led to the first government-published inter-agency guidance for professionals and agencies working with children, *Working Together to Safeguard Children*, and to the establishment of Area Review Committees as the forerunners of *Local Safeguarding Children Boards, to promote inter-agency cooperation in local areas. The inquiries during the 1980s had a major influence on the emergence and content of the Children Act (1989), which, among many provisions, set out the *duty to investigate, or *Section 47 enquiries, and identified, under Section 17, a new category of child that should be provided with help and support, namely a *child in need. Although not directly referred to in the Act, professionals were also encouraged to work in *partnership with parents where there were concerns about their children, as a way of trying to achieve a balance between safeguarding children and supporting families.

The costs and repetitive nature of the findings associated with high-profile child abuse inquiries has resulted in reluctance by government to establish them in recent years. The death of Peter Connolly in 2007 led to a report published in 2009 by the author of the Victoria Climbié Inquiry Report, Herbert Laming. However, rather than this being the outcome of a public inquiry into the circumstances surrounding Peter Connolly's death, findings were presented as a progress report on child protection in England since the Victoria Climbié Inquiry. In June 2010 the

Conservative–Liberal Democrat coalition government established a review of child protection under the leadership of Eileen Munro to explore barriers to effective professional practice and how these might be removed. One of the core premises of this review was that the well-intentioned improvements, prompted to a large extent by earlier child abuse inquiries, had not resulted in the desired changes and a fresh approach was needed. *See also* CHILD ABUSE AND NEGLECT; MUNRO REVIEW; SAFEGUARDING CHILDREN; SERIOUS CASE REVIEW; SIGNIFICANT HARM.

Further reading: Butler, I. and Drakeford, M. (2005, 2nd edn.) *Scandal, Social Policy and Social Welfare*, Policy Press.

child accommodated by a local authority (voluntary admission to care)
Under Section 20 of the Children Act (1989), a child may be accommodated by a *local authority if s/he has no parent or is lost or abandoned or where her/his parents are not able to provide her/him with suitable accommodation and they agree to the child being accommodated. A child who is accommodated under Section 20 becomes a *looked-after child. Section 20 agreements are not valid unless the parent giving consent has capacity to do so and their consent is properly informed and fairly obtained. The parent of an accommodated child may at any time remove them from accommodation provided by a local authority. The accommodation will usually take the form of *foster care or, less commonly, a *children's home. When a child is accommodated, the parents retain full and exclusive *parental responsibility rather than this being shared with the local authority as with a *Care Order. The local authority has a duty to inform the parents where the child is residing and to maintain *contact between the parents and the child. In situations where a child is the subject of a *Section 47 enquiry and the level of *risk to the child indicates that it may not be appropriate for them to remain at home while an *assessment is completed, a local authority will usually seek to reach agreement with the parents for the child to be accommodated. If agreement is not possible or the level of risk is especially grave, then social workers may make an application to the courts for an *Emergency Protection Order.

Child and Adolescent Mental Health Services (CAMHS) Used in one sense to refer to all services that contribute to mental health care for children and young people, including health, education, and social services, even if their primary function may not be mental health care. Also refers more narrowly, but more commonly, to specialist child and adolescent mental health services whose primary function is the promotion of children's and young people's mental health, including direct work with them and their families. Accordingly, child and adolescent mental health services are divided into four tiers of service provision. The first tier comprises non-specialist practitioners whose professional roles bring them into contact with children and young people, and who may notice early signs of mental distress. This tier includes GPs, teachers, school nurses, health visitors, and social workers. The second tier comprises educational psychologists, clinical child psychologists, child psychiatrists, community children's nurses, and social workers. This tier provides outreach services, consultation, and training services. The third tier is a specialist service whose primary function is targeted intervention for children and young people who have developed severe and complex mental health problems. Typically organized as a specialist multidisciplinary team, the third tier comprises social workers, child and adolescent psychiatrists, clinical psychologists, *occupational therapists, and art and music therapists. The fourth tier provides access to child psychiatric services, including in patient and residential services for children and young people who are severely mentally ill or at risk of serious *self-harm or *suicide. The Mental Health Taskforce's Report (2016) identified child and adolescent mental health services as a priority area, and pledged that at least 70,000 additional children and young people would have access to high-quality mental health care by 2020–1, if they needed it.

Child and Family Reporter An officer of the *Children and Family Court Advisory Support Service who seeks to assist families in agreeing arrangements for their children following separation and divorce where issues of *contact and *residence are contested. The Reporter will usually meet with the adults concerned to see if issues can be agreed without going to court, a process known as *mediation. If no agreement can be reached, the Reporter will write a report for the court which explains what enquiries have been made and what s/he thinks is in the *best interests of the children. Usually in these cases, Child and Family Reporters from CAFCASS are the sole representatives of the child's best interests and source of independent advice to the court. This mediation service is not available for *public law cases (for example, where applications for a *Care Order are being considered by the *family courts) or in cases of *adoption. *See also* CHILDREN'S GUARDIAN.

Child Arrangements Order A *private law order introduced in April 2014 by the Children and Families Act (2014), which amended Section 8 of the Children Act 1989 (under which a Child Arrangements Order is made) in order that the CAO could replace Contact Orders and Residence Orders. A CAO sets out who the child is to live with and/or who the child will spend time with, and can be granted to more than one person whether they live together or not. If a CAO states that the child will live with a person, that person will have *parental responsibility for that child until the Order ceases. Where a person is named in an Order as a person with whom the child is to spend time or otherwise have *contact, but is not named in the Order as a person with whom the child is to live, the court may provide in the Order for that person to have parental responsibility for the child while the Order remains in force. Contact with a child can either be in direct face-to-face meetings or indirect, for example by letter or exchange of cards. Some Orders will make very specific arrangements for the child; other Orders will be more open with detailed arrangements to be made between the parties by agreement. CAOs are not only made in respect of parents; there can also be Orders for arrangements between siblings and other family members. Sometimes an Order will give directions that contact is to be supervised by another person or that contact is to take place in a specific location. Where a child is the subject of a *Care Order, there is a general duty on the local authority to promote contact between the child and the parents.

Child Assessment Order A rarely used provision in Section 43 of the Children Act (1989), which makes it possible for a *local authority or authorized person to apply to a court for a child to be presented for an assessment of their health or development or of the way s/he has been treated in order to enable the applicant to determine whether or not the child is suffering or likely to suffer *significant harm. A court has to be satisfied that it is unlikely such an assessment will be made in the absence of the Order. The Order will specify the date when the assessment is to begin and how long it will last, for a period not exceeding seven days. The parent or *care-giver is required to produce the child for the assessment and comply with its requirements. The granting of this Order does not remove the child's right to contribute to an assessment, as long as s/he is of sufficient age and understanding.

child care 1. The care provided for children by a parent or other *care-giver.

2. Services provided by the *public, *private, or *voluntary sectors or *childminders to look after children, usually during the daytime, for example day nurseries. Child care services in the UK have been poorly developed compared to some other countries, most notably the services in Scandinavia. There was resistance to their development in the UK after the Second World War, with the emphasis being on children staying at home with their mothers. This position was influenced by John Bowlby's work on *maternal deprivation (*Child Care and the Growth of Love* [1953]). Feminists attacked this position because it reinforced the idea that women should be the sole carers for children and should be located primarily in the sphere of home and family, seeing this as contributing to women's inferior status. Other feminists have argued that women should be able to choose to undertake child care on the basis of being paid a proper wage for doing so.

child care services A predecessor term for children's services that disappeared in the late 1990s/early 2000s.

child-centred approach Ways of working with children that promote their right to choose, make connections, and communicate. They encourage children to think, experience, explore, ask questions, search out answers, and be creative. It is an approach that is widely seen as promoting healthy *child development and learning, and accordingly is one that is favoured in settings in which young children are cared for and educated, for example, nurseries. It is also seen as having wider significance in the development of policies and programmes for children. *See also* CHILD DEVELOPMENT.

Child Death Overview Panel *See* CHILD DEATH REVIEW.

Child Death Review A requirement that, from 2008, *Local Safeguarding Children Boards make arrangements for the review of all child deaths in their area, with a view to exploring how similar deaths may be prevented. The Children Act (2004) established LSCBs and empowered the Secretary of State to make regulations setting out their functions. The regulations that were issued require LSCBs to undertake CDRs and *Serious Case Reviews. Guidance that sets out the particular duties and processes to be undertaken to carry out CDRs is contained in *Working Together to Safeguard Children and their Families* (2015), issued under the Children Act (1989). An inter-agency Child Death Overview Panel considers all the information gathered on the circumstances surrounding a child's death, determines the causes as far as possible, and considers future action that may need to be taken by agencies and professionals. Reviews are conducted on all children who have died, not just those whose death is a consequence of *child abuse and neglect. The latter are considered under the processes established for Serious Case Reviews. *See also* RAPID RESPONSE.

Further reading: HM Government (2015) *Working Together to Safeguard Children: A Guide to Inter-agency Working to Safeguard and Promote the Welfare of Children*, Chapter 5. Available at https://www.gov.uk/government/uploads/system/uploads/attachment_data/file/419595/ Working_Together_to_Safeguard_Children.pdf.

child development The biological and psychological changes that take place in human beings from birth until the end of *adolescence, a period characterized by progression from dependency to increasing levels of autonomy. While the quality of nurturance provided to the child throughout this time is seen as crucial to their healthy development, the impact of genetic factors and events during the pre-natal period are generally also regarded as important factors in child development. There are many strands in the study of child development: for example, Piaget's theory of cognitive development, in which children are seen as learning through the process of play; Erikson's stages of psycho social development, which focus on the tasks that need to be completed by human beings at different stages of life; and the behaviourist school pioneered by Watson and Skinner. A further strand is Vygotsky's cultural-historical psychology, which accepts that while children learn through experience, adults may greatly assist this by supporting children to learn new tasks. The work of Bronfenbrenner has also been influential in recognizing the significance of interlocking environmental systems for human growth, with writers such as Garbarino building on this work to elaborate the importance of social ecology—the wider physical and social environment in which children are reared—for healthy child development.

The study of development is usually linked to *attachment theory, which regards the development of healthy relationships between human beings, most significantly between the infant and at least one primary *care-giver, as the most crucial element in the quality of a child's development. A knowledge of and focus on child development is regarded as an essential aspect of the work of professionals who seek to protect children and promote their welfare. This is underlined by the concept of *significant harm, introduced by the Children Act (1989), which requires that when professionals make judgements about whether a child is experiencing harm, they need to weigh the impact of harm on her/his health and development. This judgement needs to encapsulate what would reasonably be expected of a child of similar age and development. To inform this judgement, professionals apply knowledge of developmental milestones in childhood, which refer to the changes in physical and mental capacities that characterize the end of one stage of child development and the beginning of another. While it is widely accepted that child development is subject to considerable variation, influenced by the quality of the child's direct care, the wider environment, the presence of *disability, and many other factors, developmental milestones have come to be associated with typical chronological ages. However, the attainment of some milestones may be more variable than others, for example, expressive speech.

The importance attached to child development is underlined in government guidance for those involved in safeguarding children. It stipulates that *child protection training should equip professionals with this knowledge. *See also* ADOLESCENCE; CENTILE CHART; CHILD-CENTRED APPROACH.

Further reading: Crowley, K. (2014) *Child Development: A Practical Introduction*, Sage.

childhood Although regarded in contemporary life as a 'natural' stage in human development, writers (most notably Ari, P. *Centuries of Childhood*, 1962) have shown that childhood is an institution that began to develop from the eighteenth century onwards, initially in bourgeois families as a form of socialization of infants into the family. *See also* CHILD.

child in need Defined in Section 17 of the Children Act (1989) as a child unlikely to reach or maintain a satisfactory level of health or development, or whose health or development will be significantly impaired without the provision of services. This definition includes children who are disabled. The critical factors to be taken into account in deciding whether a child is in need are what will happen to a child's health or development without services being provided; and what are the likely effects services will have on the child's standard of health and development? *Local authorities have a duty to safeguard and promote the welfare of children in need (*see* TARGET DUTY). A child in need plan (sometimes referred to as a child's plan) is drawn up for a child who is not *looked after but who is identified as a child in need requiring services to meet her/his needs. It is completed following an *assessment in which services have been identified as necessary. A child in need of protection, who is at risk of *significant harm, will always be regarded as a child in need, but not all children in need are children in need of protection.

child maintenance Financial support provided by a parent without the day-to-day care of their child (the non-resident parent), and paid to the parent with the day-to-day care (the parent with care) to help cover the child's living costs. In some cases the person receiving child maintenance may be a grandparent or a guardian. Parents who no longer live together may agree these financial arrangements privately. In circumstances where this is not possible, maintenance is likely to be arranged through the *Child Maintenance Service.

Child Maintenance Service (CMS) Since 2012, the successor agency to the *Child Support Agency. When arrangements for child maintenance are made through the CMS, it takes steps to take payments from the non-resident parent (the parent without day-to-day care of the child) and pass them to the parent with care (the parent who provides the child with day-to-day care). The CMS can:

- try to find the other parent, if the parent seeking maintenance does not know where they live;
- sort out disagreements about parentage;
- work out how much child maintenance should be paid;
- arrange for the 'paying' parent (who does not have the main day-to-day care of the child) to pay maintenance;
- pass payments on to the 'receiving' parent (who has the main day-to-day care of the child);
- look at the payments again when changes in parents' circumstances are reported;
- review the payment amount every year;
- take action if payments are not made.

(⊕) SEE WEB LINKS
- Official site of the Child Maintenance Service.

childminders Individuals who work in their own homes providing care for other people's children. A registered childminder looks after one or more children for more than two hours a day for payment. Before a person can become a childminder they must be registered with *Ofsted, the government regulatory body for schools and children's social care services, which maintains two registers: the Early Years Register for children from birth to 31 August following their fifth birthday, and the Childcare Register, for childminders caring for children from 1 September following their fifth birthday and up to and including age 7. In registering for the first register, childminders need to demonstrate their ability to meet the requirements of the Early Years Foundation Stage. Most childminders are registered on both registers as this allows them to care for children of all ages. Ofsted manages and approves applications from prospective childminders. Childminders in England and *Wales may receive help and support from the Professional Association for Childcare and Early Years. *See also* CHILD CARE 2.

(⊕) SEE WEB LINKS
- Official site of the Professional Association for Childcare and Early Years.

child neglect *See* CHILD ABUSE AND NEGLECT.

child placement plan *See* PLACEMENT PLAN.

child poverty One in four children in the UK are in *poverty, according to the Child Poverty Action Group, one of the highest rates in the industrialized world. Child poverty has profound impacts on the health and *well-being of children, denying their rights, such as the right to be healthy. The Child Poverty Act (2010) set out the *New Labour government's commitment to eradicate child poverty by 2020, seeking to ensure sustained action by successive governments, local authorities, and other agencies. The Act sought to establish a Child Poverty Commission tasked with providing expert advice to government. In 2012 the Coalition government (2010–16) amended the Child Poverty Act (2010) to establish a Social Mobility and Child Poverty Commission. The Conservative government's Welfare Reform and Work Act (2016) abolished the Child Poverty Act (2010), including the targets to reduce poverty and the measure of poverty based on family income, and the Social Mobility and Child Poverty Commission became the Social Mobility Commission. After a prolonged campaign, the Conservative government agreed to commit in law to regularly publishing data on the number of children in poverty. *See also* ANTI-POVERTY STRATEGIES.

(⊕) SEE WEB LINKS
• Official site of the Child Poverty Action Group.

child protection The aim, activities, and processes involved in *safeguarding individual children who are specifically identified as either suffering, or likely to suffer, *significant harm as a result of *abuse or neglect. It is part of a wider concern with safeguarding and promoting the welfare of all children through *agencies and individuals proactively seeking to obviate the need for action to protect children from harm. *See also* CHILD ABUSE AND NEGLECT; CHILD PROTECTION CONFERENCE; CHILD PROTECTION PLAN; CHILD PROTECTION REGISTER; SAFEGUARDING CHILDREN.

child protection conference An inter-agency meeting convened after an investigation by social workers and police officers into allegations of child abuse. When concerns are substantiated and the child is judged to be suffering *significant harm or likely to be suffering significant harm, professionals from different agencies involved with or having knowledge of the child and family meet to discuss the child. Parents or *care-givers normally attend the conference. The conference decides if the child needs to be the subject of an inter-agency *child protection plan, tailored to safeguard her/him and promote her/his welfare. The first conference held about a child is called an 'initial child protection conference' and follow-up meetings where the progress of the plan is reviewed, are called 'child protection review conferences'. *See also* CHILD PROTECTION; CHILD PROTECTION PLAN; CHILD PROTECTION REGISTER; CHILDREN AND DOMESTIC VIOLENCE; SAFEGUARDING CHILDREN.

Further reading: HM Government (2015) *Working Together to Safeguard Children: A Guide to Inter-agency Working to Safeguard and Promote the Welfare of Children.* Chapter 1, gives an overview of the responsibilities of and timescales for child protection conferences (pp. 43–4) and child protection review conferences (pp. 47–8). Available at: *https://www.gov. uk/government/uploads/system/uploads/attachment_data/file/419595/ Working_Together_to_Safeguard_Children.pdf.*

child protection inquiry *See* SECTION 47 INQUIRY.

child protection plan A document that sets out the steps to be taken by professionals and parents to safeguard a child and the services that will be provided to the family. A plan is put in place when children are assessed by members of a multi-agency *child protection conference as requiring further action to safeguard and promote their welfare. The aim is to reach a point where a child protection plan is no longer necessary to safeguard the child. *See also* CHILD PROTECTION; CHILD PROTECTION REGISTER; SAFEGUARDING CHILDREN.

Further reading: HM Government (2015) *Working Together to Safeguard Children: A Guide to Inter-agency Working to Safeguard and Promote the Welfare of Children.* Chapter 1, sets out the purpose and function of a child protection plan and the roles of those involved in it (pp. 45–6). Available at: *https://www.gov.uk/government/uploads/system/ uploads/attachment_data/file/419595/Working_Together_to _Safeguard_Children.pdf.*

child protection register Until 2006, a list held by every *local authority of all the children in its area who were subject to *child protection plans. From 2006, the register was replaced by a 'record' of all such children in each local authority. Criticized by many in the child protection field at the time as undermining a clear focus on protecting children, this move was seen as necessary by the then government to ensure professional attention centred on the plan rather than the child's status as a 'registered' child. However, the term 'child protection register' remains in widespread use by the public, politicians, and the media. *See also* CHILD PROTECTION; CHILD PROTECTION PLAN; SAFEGUARDING CHILDREN.

children and domestic violence Living with the impact of *domestic violence can have serious consequences for children's health, wellbeing, and development. That domestic violence often commences or escalates during pregnancy makes it a dual attack on mother and foetus and a form of *child abuse, as well as of gendered *violence. Women are also at greater risk after childbirth, including attacks on women holding babies, often involving men undermining parenting and the mother–child relationship. Despite their living with the impact and consequences of domestic violence, the ways in which women protect and nurture their children are often underestimated.

Given the extent of male violence towards women partners and ex-partners, it is not surprising that, despite women's efforts, this violence constitutes a major source of adversity and harm for children and young people in terms of both direct and indirect effects on their health and wellbeing. There are many ways in which children can be negatively affected by violence: they can see and hear violence; they can get caught up in violence; they can suffer because they live in a violent atmosphere where their mother is constantly afraid. They may be exposed to perpetual criticism of their mother and hear her being labelled as mad, and they may suffer as a result of the economic deprivation and social isolation that is very often an aspect of domestic violence. Even children who are indirect witnesses are likely to be aware of domestic violence and they will be affected if it has eroded their mother's ability to care for them.

Children's distress may be evident in a range of emotional, psychological, and behavioural responses to the complicated and traumatic impact of exposure to violence. Children react individually and age, *gender, *disability, and stage of development will all affect the consequences for them. There may be externalized responses, such as *aggression, destructiveness, and defiance, and internalized responses, such as *anxiety, *depression, fear, and low self-esteem. There may also be other signs of distress, such as stomach aches, headaches, and difficulties in social interaction. Children witnessing severe violence may experience *post-traumatic stress disorder. Not only may children affected in this way display the more intense forms of the above internalized and externalized behaviours, but also they may have to deal with intrusive recall of events, 'flashbacks', avoidant or numbed responses, hyper-vigilance, inability to concentrate, watchfulness, or disturbed sleep.

The inter-connections between violence towards women and child abuse have been increasingly recognized. Domestic violence towards a mother increases the likelihood of violence towards her child, and the severity and length of time over which violence has occurred increase the *risks for children. The impact on children and women facing additional forms of adversity, like *racism, may be compounded, and they confront barriers to recognition of their experiences.

For many women and children, violence intensifies after separation and it has been found that a large proportion of women using domestic violence outreach centres have experienced further abuse, including a sizeable minority that have suffered persistent post-separation violence. A number of studies demonstrate that child *contact arrangements, including court-ordered contact, are used to track women to perpetuate domestic violence, even when there are high levels of super-vision. Murders of women and children where there is a history of domestic violence frequently take place at the point of separation, including during child contact, as do child abductions. The *Domestic Abuse, Stalking and Harassment and Honour-based Violence Risk Identification, Assessment and Management Model (endorsed by the Association of Chief Police Officers), which provides a framework for the analysis of risk to improve law enforcement and to contribute to safety planning for victims, identifies separation with disputes about contact or *residence as high-risk factors for serious escalating domestic violence.

For children (and women) the costs of domestic violence are high and those enduring post-separation violence may be among the most distressed in the popu-lation, with the highest levels of behavioural and emotional disturbance and *depression. For these children, contact with violent men may be of little benefit and may impede their recovery. Conversely, where children have no contact with violent fathers, the harm they have sustained can be ameliorated. A child's recovery has been found to be related to that of her/his mother; continuing threats or contact proceedings used to protract conflict often mean that mothers are unable to recover and this has an indirect effect on children.

While children may face many potentially traumatic events in their lives, domes-tic violence is particularly pernicious. It is rarely only one form of *abuse and tends to escalate over time. It occurs where children are meant to be safe and undermines those aspects of children's lives that might otherwise confer protection and *resili-ence. Its pervasiveness can affect every aspect of a child's life. At the same time, it is also important to acknowledge the strengths of women and children (both separ-ately and together), and to recognize the importance of their own coping and survival strategies. Focusing on *resilience and *protective factors is the foundation of children's recovery and does not assume that damage is inevitable or permanent. The responses of statutory *child protection agencies have not always been found to be helpful. Research involving women and children, as well as with the voluntary agencies that have provided the highest levels of support and assistance to them, have helped to identify what is considered important to the recovery process. Safety—feeling safe and being safe—is a prerequisite for all other interventions, and the minimizing of disruption is also critical. Children themselves have confirmed that a significant factor in building resilience is a strong and emotional bond with a significant non-abusing person, usually with the mother. In addition, women and children need a range of opportunities to restore self-confidence and self-esteem. These include individual work and group work, with the involvement of survivors being highly valued. Most of all, children and young people want to be informed and actively involved.

Knowledge about domestic violence, and the needs of women and children for safety and support, has demonstrated the importance of comprehensive and coordinated responses across health, social care, and law enforcement agencies. It has also highlighted the central role played by voluntary agencies representing women survivors and women survivors themselves. *See also* CHILD ABUSE AND NEGLECT; DOMESTIC VIOLENCE FORUM; WOMEN'S AID.

Further reading: Stanley, N. (2011) *Children Experiencing Domestic Violence: A Research Review*, Research in Practice.

Children and Family Court Advisory Support Service (CAFCASS) An independent organization established by the Criminal Justice and Court Services Act (2000) that is responsible for representing the interests of children and young people involved in family court proceedings. From the 1930s onwards, the Probation Service provided a social work service to the divorce courts that involved providing reports on the welfare of children and working with families experiencing divorce. The Probation Officers who specialized in this area of work were called Family Court Welfare Officers. In 2001, the launch of CAFCASS brought together into the work of this one organization the work previously undertaken by the FCWOs in the context of divorce and that of the guardians ad litem (working for Social Services Departments), acting as independent social workers and representing the interests of the child in other court proceedings (for example, *adoption and *care proceedings), thus bringing together all of the *child welfare services associated with court proceedings, whether arising from divorce proceedings or under the Children Act (1989). CAFCASS is staffed by qualified social workers who assess children and families involved in court proceedings and recommend to courts what is in the *best interests of individual children.

CAFCASS's functions are to: safeguard and promote the welfare of children; give advice to family courts; arrange for children to be legally represented, where necessary; provide information, advice, and support to children and their families. The main types of cases in which the courts ask CAFCASS to become involved are when: there is the possibility of children being adopted; social workers have become involved and children may be removed from their parents' care for their protection; parents or care-givers are separating or divorcing and they have not reached agreement about arrangements for their children. Thus the service may be involved in two types of case: *public law cases and *private law cases. Public law cases are those which involve applications, usually by the *local authority, for an *Emergency Protection Order; *Care Order; *Supervision Order, or *Secure Accommodation Order, for the purposes of safeguarding and promoting the welfare of the children involved. In all these cases the child is regarded as a party to the proceedings and is represented by a *Children's Guardian appointed by CAFCASS. Private law cases are those involving *residence, *contact, and *parental responsibility. They are cases that involve private individuals usually under Section 8 of the Children Act (1989). In private law cases a child is not automatically deemed a party to the proceedings and will not automatically be represented by a guardian. However, a court may request a welfare report either from the local authority or from a *Child and Family Reporter appointed by CAFCASS.

Children and Young People's Plan The Children Act (2004) requires that each *local authority leads the production of a single, strategic, overarching plan for all services for children and young people in its area. The aim is to promote the development of more integrated and effective services. It identifies where *outcomes need to be improved and the means by which these improvements will be achieved.

children leaving care *See* LEAVING CARE.

Children's Centres Established from 1998 onwards by the New Labour government (1997–2010) in different localities under the *Sure Start programme and funded through *local authorities, the centres were seen as a means of bringing together all of the different support agencies in one place to offer a range of services to meet the needs of young children and parents. Eventually almost 4,000 were established in England. Each was developed in line with the particular needs of its local community, but had to provide a core set of services:

• Child and family health services;
• *Child care and early learning;
• Advice on parenting, local child care options, and access to specialist services for families such as speech therapy, healthy eating advice, or help with managing finances;
• Help to find work or training opportunities.

Following the financial crash in 2007–8 and the *austerity policies that followed, funding for Sure Start was slashed. In the first two years of the Coalition government (2010–16) more than 400 Children's Centres were closed, with many more to follow. Many of those that remain have been denuded of services because of government cuts and are shadows of their former selves.

Children's Commissioner A role created by government to promote the views of children and young people from birth to 18 years and up to 21 years for *looked-after children or those with *learning disabilities. There are four commissioners, one each for England, *Northern Ireland, *Scotland, and *Wales, which established the first commissioner. Each produces an annual report documenting their work, including the findings of studies commissioned to explore aspects of the lives of children and young people, and highlighting what are seen as pressing issues for promoting their wellbeing.

( ) SEE WEB LINKS
• Official site of the Children's Commissioner for England.
• Official site of the Children's Commissioner for Northern Ireland.
• Official site of the Children's Commissioner for Scotland.
• Official site of the Children's Commissioner for Wales.

Children's Guardian Previously known as a 'guardian ad litem', appointed by a court to represent independently the rights and interests of a child during cases where *local authority children's services have instigated *public law proceedings in the *family courts, such as making an application for a *Care Order, or in a contested *adoption. A Children's Guardian appoints a solicitor for the child who specializes in family law, advises the court about what needs to be done before the court makes a decision, and writes a report for the court saying what s/he thinks would be best for the child. This report must include the wishes and feelings of the child, where the child is of an age to provide them. Compiling the report requires the Guardian to spend time getting to know the child and members of the family. Guardians are qualified in social work, and trained and experienced in working with children and families. They work for the *Children and Family Court Advisory Support Service or may be self-employed and contracted by CAFCASS. Guardians have their own professional association, the National Association for Children's Guardians, Family Court Advisors, and Independent Social Workers. *See also* CHILD AND FAMILY REPORTER.

((⊕)) **SEE WEB LINKS**

• Official site of the National Association of Children's Guardians, Family Court Advisors, and Independent Social Workers.

children's home Owned by *local authorities or *private or *voluntary organizations, and offering help and support to children who may have suffered *abuse and neglect or other traumas and emotional problems, or who may have no family to care for them. Children's homes broadly fall into two categories: respite care and residential care. Respite care is intended to support parents of children who may have *disabilities or behavioural difficulties. In these circumstances the children may be looked after for a short time to allow their parents or *care-givers to have a break from caring for them. Residential care provides longer-term care for children or young people with serious emotional or behavioural difficulties, which their parents or care-givers feel unable to manage. This is likely to have followed a period when steps taken to assist the family have proved unsuccessful. However, some admissions to residential care may arise from a crisis or emergency within the family. Children's homes are regulated according to the Department for Education's *Children's Homes Regulations* (2015) and inspected on behalf of the government by Ofsted.

Further reading: Department for Education (2015) *Guide to the Children's Home Regulations Including the Quality Standards.* Available at: http://www.gov.uk/government/uploads/system/uploads/attachment_data/file/463220/Guide_to_Children_s_Home_Standards_inc_quality_standards_Version__1.17_FINAL.pdf.

Children's Pledge The White Paper *Care Matters: Time to Deliver for Children in Care* (2008) required every *local authority to set out a pledge to children and young people in care in the form of a statement that covers the care, support, parenting, and range of services that they can expect to receive, how they will be enabled to influence decisions about their care, and how the pledge and its implementation will be monitored.

children's rights The human rights of children, with particular emphasis on the special protection and care they require as a result of their dependency on adults, and the means employed to promote these rights. The best-known articulation of children's rights appears in the *United Nations Convention on the Rights of the Child* (UNCRC) which applies to all children and young people aged 17 and under. The Convention has 54 articles, most of which give children social, economic, cultural, civil, or political rights, while others set out how governments should publicize and implement the Convention. The UK ratified the Convention on 16 December 1991. *Children's Commissioners are in place in the four countries of the UK with a remit to promote and protect children's rights. Their role has been mirrored by the appointment of *Children's Rights Officers in some local authorities to advocate on behalf of children and young people.

Children's Rights Alliance *See* UNITED NATIONS CONVENTION ON THE RIGHTS OF THE CHILD.

Children's Rights Officer Appointed in some *local authorities to give a voice to children and young people in their areas and to promote and protect their rights. Components of the role are to support and advocate for young people, to explain to them what their rights are, to make sure that those caring for children and young people listen to what they have to say, and to put children in touch with others who can give them advice. There is likely to be a particular focus on the needs and rights of *looked-after children in the area. *See also* CHILDREN'S RIGHTS; *UNITED NATIONS CONVENTION ON THE RIGHTS OF THE CHILD.

child safety An approach that institutes measures to keep children safe from accidents. The most common types of accidents affecting children in the home are exposure to poisonous substances, used, for example, as cleaning agents; trips and falls; burns and scalds arising from spilt hot drinks, cooking, and kitchen equipment; injuries arising from poor fire safety. Outside the home, poor road safety, road traffic collisions, or incidents relating to pond or pool safety are sources of potentially serious injury to children. While the child safety movement is mainly focused on the prevention of accidental injury, injuries associated with these factors may in some circumstances be linked to child neglect if they arise from poor parental supervision. *See also* CHILD ABUSE AND NEGLECT.

Child Safety Order *See* AGE OF CRIMINAL RESPONSIBILITY.

Child Sex Offenders Disclosure Scheme *See* CHILD SEX OFFENDERS POLICE DISCLOSURE SCHEME.

Child Sex Offenders Police Disclosure Scheme Under the scheme, a parent, carer, guardian, or other interested party can check whether someone who has access to their children has a record of committing child sexual offences. If they are found to have convictions for sexual offences against children, and pose a *risk of causing serious harm to the child or children concerned, then this information may be disclosed. The Scheme is sometimes referred to as 'Sarah's Law', named after 8-year-old Sarah Payne, who was abducted and murdered by Roy Whiting, a man who had already been placed on the *Sex Offenders Register for previous offences. Sarah's mother, Sara Payne, campaigned for a number of years for the government to allow the public controlled access to the Sex Offenders Register, so parents could know if a child sex offender was living in their area.

child sexual exploitation (CSE) A form of child sexual abuse (*see* CHILD ABUSE AND NEGLECT) that occurs when an individual or group takes advantage of an imbalance of power in exploitative situations, contexts, and relationships in order to coerce, manipulate, or deceive a child or young person under the age of 18 into sexual activity in exchange for something the victim needs or wants, and/or for the financial advantage or increased status of the perpetrator or facilitator. Victims may be given food, accommodation, drugs, alcohol, cigarettes, affection, gifts, or money as a result of engaging, or agreeing to engage, in sexual activities. The victim can be sexually exploited even if the sexual activity appears consensual. CSE does not always involve physical contact; it can also occur through the use of technology, for example when a child is persuaded to post sexual images on the Internet or send them via mobile phones without immediate payment or gain. Those exploiting the children and young people have power over them by virtue of their age, *gender, intellect, physical strength, or economic or other resources. *Violence, coercion, and intimidation are common. Perpetrators seek out children with limited choices and opportunities because of their social, economic, and emotional circumstances. The publicity given in the media to high-profile cases, such as Operation Span and Operation Retriever (Rochdale) and Operation Bullfinch (Oxfordshire), has brought CSE into the public domain. It is not a new phenomenon, but was hidden or denied before the emergence of the high-profile cases. One of the shocking aspects of those cases was the lack of recognition and concern that had existed previously on the part of social work organizations and the police. This has now been remedied and CSE is a high-profile area of work in children's services. *See also* CHILD ABUSE AND NEGLECT; CHILD PROTECTION; CHILD TRAFFICKING; ORGANIZED CHILD ABUSE; SAFEGUARDING CHILDREN; SECTION 47 ENQUIRY.

Further reading: Department for Education (2017) *Child Sexual Exploitation: Definition and a Guide for Practitioners, Local Leaders and Decision-makers Working to Protect Children from Child Sexual Exploitation*. Available at: https://www.gov.uk/government/uploads/system/uploads/attachment_data/file/591903/CSE_Guidance_Core_Document_13.02.2017.pdf.

child's permanence report Written and presented by a child's social worker to an Adoption Panel when the Panel's recommendation is being sought that a child should be placed for *adoption. *See also* BIRTH RECORDS COUNSELLING.

child support *See* CHILD MAINTENANCE SERVICE.

Child Support Agency Established by the government in 1993 to ensure that parents who lived apart from their children contributed financially to their upkeep by paying *child maintenance, implementing the Child Support Act (1991) and subsequent legislation. It was replaced in 2012 by the *Child Maintenance Service, to which all new applications have been made since then. The CSA continues to work on pre-2012 *cases but is gradually transferring them over to the CMS, a process which should be completed by 2017–18.

child's welfare A child's wellbeing and *best interests. The concept of a child's welfare has been central to the legislation under which social work with children is conducted since the implementation of the Children Act (1989) and has been the main principle underpinning social work practice. In court proceedings, a child's welfare must be the court's paramount consideration (*see* PARAMOUNTCY PRINCIPLE) and social workers reporting to a court must reflect that consideration in what they present with respect to a child. Although welfare is not defined in legislation, courts have to have regard to a *welfare checklist in their decision-making. Increasing resource constraints in the context of *austerity can result in social workers feeling they cannot do what is necessary to promote a child's welfare. *See also* CHILD ABUSE AND NEGLECT; CHILD DEVELOPMENT; CHILD PROTECTION; GOOD-ENOUGH PARENTING; PARENTING SKILLS; SAFEGUARDING CHILDREN.

child trafficking The recruitment, transport, transfer, harbouring, or receipt of a child for the purpose of exploitation. This can involve moving a child within a country, town, or city, or across national borders, whether by force or not. It includes sexual exploitation, forced labour, such as domestic servitude, and forced criminality, such as begging, pickpocketing, or cannabis cultivation. Any form of trafficking OG children is *abuse. Children are coerced, deceived, or forced into the control of others who seek to profit from their exploitation and suffering. There is a wide range of UK legislation (one review identified twenty-five statutes) and guidance relevant to trafficked and exploited children. The Modern Slavery Act (2015) consolidated and clarified offences specifically related to trafficking and slavery, increased the penalties associated with them (up to life imprisonment), and introduced a number of measures focused on supporting and protecting victims, including special measures for witnesses in criminal proceedings, independent child trafficking advocates, non-prosecution of victims compelled to commit crimes, and a presumption that a victim is under 18 until appropriate *age assessments have been carried out. *See also* CHILD ABUSE AND NEGLECT; CHILD PROTECTION; CHILD SEXUAL EXPLOITATION; ORGANIZED CHILD ABUSE; SAFEGUARDING CHILDREN; SECTION 47 ENQUIRY.

Further reading: Department for Education and Home Office (2011) *Safeguarding Children Who May Have Been Trafficked: Practice Guidance.* Available at: https://www.gov.uk/ government/uploads/system/uploads/attachment_data/file/177033/DFE-00084-2011.pdf.

child welfare A wide-ranging term that has had greater currency in the US than in the UK. It is used to refer to the continuum of services impacting on children's wellbeing: universal services available to all children and families such as schools, primary health care, and services providing advice and guidance for parents; those services designed to promote *early intervention and *prevention, when emerging vulnerability in the child requires more targeted assistance; and those services of a more specialist nature designed for families experiencing difficulties of greater severity and complexity. The last include social work with children and families where interventions seek to protect a child who may be at risk of *significant harm or who is defined as a *child in need under Section 17 of the Children Act (1989), and children with psychological and behavioural problems who may require services such as *Child and Adolescent Mental Health Services. The Children Act (1989) defines a *child's welfare as the paramount consideration in making decisions about children (*see* PARAMOUNTCY PRINCIPLE). This legal mandate is not only the focus of *intervention in relation to specific children (*see* CHILD'S WELFARE) but also should underpin the design and delivery of services at policy and organizational levels in the child welfare system as a whole. *See also* CHILD PROTECTION; CHILDREN'S CENTRES; EARLY YEARS FOUNDATION STAGE; EARLY YEARS SERVICES; EXTENDED SERVICES; FAMILY INFORMATION SERVICES; HOME START; SAFEGUARDING CHILDREN; SURE START.

choice Selection between different options. An oft-repeated buzzword associated with *neo-liberalism and a key concept in relation to the *public sector for all governments, from the first Thatcher government onwards. The assumption is that people's experience of choice in the *private sector is overwhelmingly positive and that they increasingly expect a similar experience from public services, to which they bring a rational and calculating orientation. Public sector choice can be divided into economic choice, where money follows the *service user's choice, as in the case of *direct payments, and non-economic choice, where choice is not followed by financial payments but involves selection between alternatives, for example, with options such as the timing of a hospital appointment or choices about treatment. In the Care Act Guidance (2016), choice is seen as central to having a positive experience of *care and support. The neo-liberal embrace of choice in public sector services such as social work ignores the constraints on choice, including its unequal distribution—for example only those with sufficient financial resources can choose to *top up care home fees and get a higher standard of accommodation; the reality for many people of choice about services in the context of *austerity being little more than a choice to 'take it or leave it'; choice being an anxious and uncertain experience in the fraught circumstances often faced by *service users, rather than a positive expression of self-identity. In addition, there are limitations on choice for many of social work's service users, most obviously in *child protection situations. Most parents do not choose to become involved with social workers about child protection issues, as the majority of referrals received by children's services come from other agencies, such as nurseries and schools. Once they are known to social workers, their non-compliance with the services offered might be interpreted as neglecting the children or putting them at risk, which then allows for compulsory intervention into family life, about which there is no choice. *See also* CITIZEN'S CHARTER; CONSUMERISM.

chronology A document in which a social worker sets out significant events and changes in the life of a child or young person. It is an analytical tool that helps social workers to understand the impact, both immediate and cumulative, of events and changes on the child or young person. A significant event is an incident that impacts on a child's safety and/or welfare, circumstances, or home environment, and professional judgement is required about what is seen as significant for each child. A chronology is a sequential narrative through which current events are understood in the context of historical information. It should be *succinct*: if every issue and contact is recorded without the exercise of discrimination on the part of the social worker, the value of the chronology will be diminished; *simply formatted*, ensuring that information is efficiently sorted and set out; *informative*, so that it assists with decision-making. While it is possible to suggest a number of issues that might be considered, they are not necessarily relevant for every case, nor are they necessarily the only considerations, and professional judgement is needed regarding what to include:

- Birth of significant persons;
- Death of significant persons;
- Education, training, and employment;
- Changes of school and *school attendance issues;
- Referrals to children's services;
- *Strategy discussions;
- *Section 47 enquiries;
- *Child Protection Conferences;
- Admissions to the care of a *local authority;
- Child missing from home or care of a local authority;
- Discharges from the care of a local authority;
- House moves;
- People moving in and out of the household;
- Significant incidents of anti-social behaviour;
- Significant assessments by any professional agency;
- Significant referrals to partner agencies;
- Criminal proceedings;
- Incidents of domestic violence;
- Mental health issues;
- Other significant health issues.

The disadvantage with checklists of this nature is that they all too easily consist of events and changes in a child's life that only address negative aspects and *risk factors. It is important, where possible, to counterbalance this by drawing out other aspects that highlight strengths, *resilience, and *protective factors.

Citizens Advice *See* CITIZENS ADVICE SERVICE.

Citizens Advice Bureau(x) *See* CITIZENS ADVICE SERVICE.

Citizens Advice Service The membership organization, Citizens Advice, has 400-plus local Citizens Advice Bureaux. Each bureau, and the membership organization, is a registered *charity in its own right. Together they make up the Citizens Advice Service. The Bureaux help people resolve their legal, money, housing, consumer, and other problems by providing free, independent, confidential information, and advice about their rights and responsibilities using face-to-face, telephone, email, and online services. They also seek to improve policies and procedures by campaigning when they become aware that these are impacting adversely on people's lives.

(⊕) SEE WEB LINKS
• Official site of Citizens Advice Service.

citizen participation Processes through which individuals contribute to decision-making about issues that affect them and/or their *communities as a way of making government more responsive to their wishes. Usually associated with the local government level but there are examples of central government initiatives of this kind, such as *Better Government for Older People. Ideally, such involvement can provide people with opportunities to influence policy development and implementation, and the allocation of resources, as envisaged in relation to social work services in the *Seebohm Report, with its proposal for local advisory fora of citizens who would contribute to the work of *area teams of social workers. Ideally, citizen participation is seen as making public *bureaucracies more responsive to the *needs of those they serve, and more open to alternative views and approaches. In practice, citizen participation has usually fallen far short of this ideal, at least in the public sector (Seebohm's advisory fora never materialized, for example), though there are recent examples of advisory groups of *service users working with children's and adults' services. In some parts of the *voluntary sector there is a well-established practice of including service user representatives on decision-making bodies as a matter of course. *See also* ARNSTEIN'S LADDER.

Citizen's Charter A series of laid-down expectations of the standards services should meet, sometimes with compensation if the standards fell below a specified level. The Conservative government's *Citizen's Charter* (1991) was the originator of this development. It was ostensibly concerned with the transplantation of best *private sector customer-centred practice into the *public sector, and set out the means by which services were to be made more responsive to their users. It had four main themes:
• *Quality* A sustained programme for improving the quality of public services.
• *Choice* Whenever possible between competing providers; choice is the best spur to quality improvement.
• *Standards* The customer must be told what service standards are and be able to act when services are unacceptable.
• *Value* The customer is also a taxpayer; public services must give value for money within a tax bill the nation can afford.
The means set out to advance the customer's interests covered a range of initiatives including: privatization of services; increased competition; the publication of

national and local performance standards; publication of information on the standards achieved; more effective complaints procedures; and tougher and more independent inspectorates. The original *Citizen's Charter* was followed by more specific charters. By 1996 there were forty-two central government charters for public services, accompanied by over 100,000 local charters. The *Community Care Charter* (1994) fleshed out the original *Citizen's Charter* themes in relation to social work. The emphasis was on customer vigilance, operating from the basis of rational self-interested calculation, as it was seen as desirable for the service-customer relationship to be treated as if it were taking place on a commercial basis in the private sector. The *Citizen's Charter* initiative was a turning point in terms of embedding official promotion of *consumerism in public services, not least because of the political consensus that emerged in support of it. For example, the Labour Party also produced a *Citizen's Charter* (1991) and introduced consumerist ideas during its time in power as *New Labour from 1997 to 2010. As a consequence of the *Citizen's Charter*, consumerism became, at least rhetorically, a core component in the culture of social work and an enduring theme came to the fore of the *service user functioning as a customer in a *mixed economy of social services. *See also* QUALITY ASSURANCE.

citizenship The status of members of a nation state that accords civil, political, and social rights. The most influential contribution to theorizing citizenship was that of T. H. Marshall (*Citizenship and Social Class* 1950). His three-pronged framework identified the development of *civil rights*, associated with individual freedom and protected by the law courts, in the eighteenth century; *political rights*, the exercise of political power by voting or by being elected, in the nineteenth century; and *social rights*, to a certain standard of living and a range of state-provided services through the *welfare state, in the twentieth century. This evolutionary approach to citizenship was regarded as having reached a pinnacle, with the concluding contribution made by the establishment of social rights signalling a broad consensus on citizenship and the approach of the end of ideology. Marshall included in this broad consensus agreement by governments that the *personal social services had to be provided on the welfare principle as public, non-profit, non-commercial services available to all at a uniform standard, irrespective of means. His view was that there would 'always be casualties to be cared for' and it was a social right to receive such care. Critics have argued that Marshall's account of citizenship is Anglocentric and that he assumed that increasing rights through citizenship were on an upward trajectory, whereas the election of *New Right-influenced governments seeking to replace citizenship with *consumerism questioned this. The account has also been criticized for not taking account of differential experiences of citizenship according to age, *class, *disability, *ethnicity, *gender, *'race', and sexuality, and the negative experiences of citizenship that result from immigration laws. In relation to social work, Marshall's account of citizenship rests on a notion of the state providing services to passive citizens. An alternative conception of citizenship regards it as an active practice of seeking to secure and consolidate rights. For example, struggles for recognition and negotiation of claims to social rights have increasingly had a cultural dimension that rests on three claims: the right to presence and visibility (*vs.* marginalization); the right to dignifying representation (*vs.* stigmatization); the right to identity and maintenance of lifestyle (*vs.* assimilation). Social workers, whether they are aware of it or not, are enmeshed in reproducing day-to-day experiences of citizenship, as they engage in mediating between the state and *service users.

civil proceedings Court cases that are not concerned with criminal acts. They cover a wide spectrum of law, but for social workers are usually encountered in cases concerned with children's welfare. *See also* CIVIL STANDARD OF PROOF.

civil rights Entitlements that are struggled for on the basis that they should be possessed by everybody in a society. The idea took on a particular force with the development of civil rights movements in the 1960s, such as that in the US in relation to *Black people and in Northern Ireland in relation to Catholics. *See also* CITIZENSHIP; CIVIL SOCIETY.

civil society The intermediate sphere between the public world of the state and the private world of households and individuals. It encompasses a range of educational, political, economic, cultural, and social institutions, such as *voluntary organizations, religious groupings, and trade unions. A flourishing civil society is usually depicted as a positive element in society, as it is seen as indicative of individuals coming together outside their households in a way that counterbalances the power of the state. In contrast, the most influential formulation of civil society in the twentieth century, that of Antonio Gramsci (1891–1937), argued that civil society makes a fundamental contribution to the maintenance of *hegemony and thus is supportive of the state. However, he also saw civil society as a space in which counter-hegemonic ideas can be developed and different practices can be tried out—the women's movement provides a good example of this, as do many grass-roots service user movements and initiatives. *See also* IDEOLOGICAL STATE APPARATUSES.

civil standard of proof In non-criminal cases the standard of proof is the balance of probability as opposed to the standard of 'beyond reasonable doubt' that is used in criminal cases. The civil standard is used in non-criminal proceedings involving children and young people, such as *care proceedings. *See also* CIVIL PROCEEDINGS.

Clare's law *See* DOMESTIC VIOLENCE DISCLOSURE SCHEME.

class In everyday usage refers in a general and often imprecise way to a group of people of similar economic and social standing. In contrast, Marxist analysis views classes as specific antagonistic formations created and maintained by the organization of the process of production. In this formulation, there are two classes: the owners of the means of production, the capitalist class; and those who live by selling their labour, the proletariat or working class. Neo-Marxists, such as Poulantzas (1936–79), have sought to explain the phenomenon of the professional middle class by broadening out considerations of class position to other factors beyond the relationship to the means of production. Bourdieu (1930–2002) emphasized the importance of social capital—the access to resources and networks that privileges some and excludes others. He investigated how social and cultural status and attainments are associated with class position, and contribute to enduring socio-economic advantage or disadvantage. For example, he highlighted the meaning and function of taste in maintaining distinctions between individuals and classes. Some analysts argue that social work functions in ways that obscure class inequality and contribute to maintaining *hegemony. In social work's *anti-oppressive *discourses, class has largely disappeared. The impact on *service users' lives of the demonstrable pattern of enduring material differences associated with class position is marginalized because it cannot easily be fitted into notions of *difference, *diversity, and unstable, shifting *identities that underpin the dominant approach in social work to the existence of social divisions. *See also* AGENTS OF SOCIAL CONTROL; CAPITALIST SOCIETY; CLASS POSITION.

classical conditioning *See* BEHAVIOURISM.

class position A person's location in the distribution of wealth, property, and income that has a predominant effect on life chances and opportunities. Emphasized in *radical social work in relation to users of social work and the role that economic disadvantage plays in constructing what are usually seen as their individual problems. *See also* AGENTS OF SOCIAL CONTROL; CAPITALIST SOCIETY; CLASS; INDIVIDUAL PATHOLOGY.

client The term preferred by social workers for many years to refer to a person who uses social work services. The intention behind the use of the term was to convey a sense of respect and, for social workers practising in health or mental health settings, to differentiate their approach from the narrowness of the medical model signified by its reference to people as patients. However, there were difficulties with the use of the term in practice as it implied a relationship with social work services that had been entered into freely, when the reality was that many clients had experienced compulsion or control through their contact with social work, for example, parents having their children removed, or people with mental health problems being compulsorily admitted to psychiatric hospital. It gradually fell into disuse, by some social workers because it was not seen as reflecting the reality of the relationship between the social worker and the user of social work services, and by others because it implied that users of social work were passive. However, it is still used by some social workers in preference to *service user as they consider it to be more respectful and because it emphasizes that social work should be a personally attuned service. The term has been retained in *counselling.

Clinical Commissioning Group (CCG) Clinical Commissioning Groups were created by the Health and Social Care Act (2012) and replaced Primary Care Trusts from April 2013. They are National Health Service bodies responsible for planning and *commissioning health care services for their local areas. CGCs assess local *needs, decide priorities and strategies, and buy services on behalf of their local population from providers such as hospitals, clinics, and community health organizations. They are measured by how much they improve outcomes. There are 209 CCGs in England.

CCGs are:

- Made up from local *GP practices;
- Led by an elected governing body made up of GPs, other clinicians, and lay members;
- Responsible for approximately two-thirds of the total NHS budget in England;
- Responsible for health care commissioning, for example mental health services, urgent and emergency care, hospital services, and community care;
- Independent, and accountable to the Secretary of State for Health through NHS England;
- Responsible for the health of populations ranging from under 100,000 to 900,000; the average population covered by a CCG is about 250,000 people.

CCGs work with *local authorities through *Health and Wellbeing Boards, developing joint needs assessments and strategies for improving public health.

clinical depression *See* DEPRESSION.

clinical judgement A decision made by a doctor based on medical knowledge and expertise that determines the kind of treatment and care a patient receives. Such a decision can have a considerable impact on *service users' lives. The decisions are rarely open to challenge, even in legal proceedings, unless a clinical judgement itself is under scrutiny in a medical negligence case, when other expert medical evidence will be heard in order to decide whether the basis of the original decision was correct.

clinical social work (clinical social work practice) Encountered to a far greater extent in other parts of the world, particularly in North America, and often associated with private practice, clinical social work refers to direct practice with individuals, couples, families, and groups with a focus on intra-personal and interpersonal problems. It has much in common, therefore, with the UK practice of *casework, though its proponents usually have greater aspirations, some would say pretensions, to professional status. The use of the word 'clinical', with its medical overtones, contributes to such aspirations. Although clinical social work can be seen as encompassing a range of roles, including *care management, the emphasis is predominantly on the clinical social worker acting as a therapist or counsellor.

Further reading: Corcoran, J. and Walsh, J. (2006) *Clinical Assessment and Diagnosis in Social Work Practice*, Oxford University Press.

clitoridectomy *See* FEMALE GENITAL MUTILATION.

closed questions *See* QUESTIONS.

CMHN *See* COMMUNITY PSYCHIATRIC NURSE.

code of ethics A set of principles of conduct produced by a profession (or other form of organization) in a formal document that is meant to guide decision-making and behaviour. The purpose of the code is to provide the professionals concerned with guidelines for making ethical choices in their work. National organizations of social work around the world produce their own codes. The *British Association of Social Workers' Code of Ethics is built on three values and the principles that underpin them:

Human rights
- Upholding and promoting human dignity and wellbeing;
- Respecting the right to self-determination;
- Promoting the right to *participation;
- Treating each person as a whole;
- Identifying and developing strengths.

Social justice
- Challenging discrimination;
- Recognizing *diversity;
- Distributing resources;
- Challenging unjust policies and practices;
- Working in solidarity.

Professional integrity

- Upholding the values and reputation of the profession;
- Being trustworthy;
- Maintaining professional boundaries;
- Making considered professional judgements;
- Being professionally accountable.

See also CODE OF PRACTICE; HEALTH AND CARE PROFESSIONS COUNCIL; INTERNATIONAL FEDERATION OF SOCIAL WORKERS; KNOWLEDGE AND SKILLS STATEMENTS; PROFESSIONAL CAPABILITIES FRAMEWORK.

Further reading: British Association of Social Workers (2014) *The Code of Ethics for Social Work: Statement of Principles*. Available at: http://www.basw.co.uk/codeofethics.

Code of Practice 1. Guidance on how to implement legislation in practice, such as the Code of Practice issued in relation to the Mental Capacity Act (2005) (*see* CAPACITY). *See* TABLE OF LEGISLATION, REGULATIONS AND CODES OF PRACTICE.

2. Statement of what is expected in terms of professional conduct, for example as in the *Health and Care Professions Council's Standards of Conduct, Performance and Ethics* and *Standards of Proficiency*, both of which apply to social workers in England. For social workers in *Northern Ireland, *Scotland, and *Wales, the Codes of Practice, originally produced by the (now defunct) General Social Care Council in 2002 under Section 62 of the Care Standards Act (2000), still apply: one for staff (*Code of Practice for Social Care Workers*) and one for their employers (*Code of Practice for Employers of Social Care Workers*).

Codes of practice set out the standards of practice and conduct workers and their employers should meet. They are intended to regulate the workforce, and contribute to increasing levels of professionalism and public protection. The Codes are meant to give: social care workers guidance for their practice and clarity about standards of conduct that are required; employers expectations of their role in the regulation of the workforce and the support of high-quality services; members of the public knowledge of how social care workers should behave, and how employers should support social care workers to do their jobs well. Registered social care workers who breach the codes can be referred for a conduct hearing with the possibility of being deregistered. *See also* CODE OF ETHICS; HEALTH AND CARE PROFESSIONS COUNCIL; INTERNATIONAL FEDERATION OF SOCIAL WORKERS; KNOWLEDGE AND SKILLS STATEMENTS; PROFESSIONAL CAPABILITIES FRAMEWORK.

cognition (cognitive) Processes of mental life involving thinking and knowing, as opposed to *affect or feeling. *See also* COGNITIVE BEHAVIOURAL THERAPY; COGNITIVE FUNCTIONING ASSESSMENT; COGNITIVE THEORY.

cognitive behavioural therapy (CBT) The application of *cognitive theory with individuals or in groups that seeks to change the ways in which people think as the basis for changing their feelings and behaviour, their responses to themselves, and their responses to others. Thought patterns are seen as central to blocking change, for example, in overcoming *depression or dealing with inappropriate anger, and as needing to be the primary focus of intervention. CBT teaches people to identify embedded and repetitious thinking patterns that hold them back, to challenge them, and to replace them with different ways of thinking. The positive experience of the resultant changes in feelings and/or behaviour reinforces the process as the new ways of thinking and the associated feelings and changes in behaviour become rewarding, not least because of positive responses from others. As well as being used in mental health settings, CBT has been employed extensively with offenders, particularly young offenders, for example, in *anger management programmes. *See also* BEHAVIOURISM; BEHAVIOUR MODIFICATION; COGNITIVE THEORY; DIALECTICAL BEHAVIOUR THERAPY.

Further reading: Sheldon, B. (2011) *Cognitive-Behavioural Therapy: Research and Practice in Health and Social Care*, Routledge.

cognitive dissonance The concept proposed by Leon Festinger (1919–89) in *When Prophecy Fails* (1956) that human beings have a psychological *need for consistency and that where there is a clash between knowledge and behaviour, they will seek to meet this need, rather than rely on logical thought, by either changing behaviour or reshaping what they know. For example, a parent who believes that abusing children is unacceptable but who abuses her/his child may see the child as an exception to the general unacceptability of child abuse because s/he thinks some children, including her/his own child, are evil. *See also* COGNITION; COGNITIVE THEORY.

cognitive functioning assessment Completed by a psychologist to determine whether a person has a learning need or difficulty and to provide advice about effective methods of working with that person. A cognitive functioning assessment is usually sought when there are concerns about a *service user's level of under-standing and a *local authority wants to ensure that social workers are able to work with the person in an effective way.

cognitive theory Originated in social psychology and developed in a number of specific directions, each of which focuses on the links between mental processes, such as attitudes, perceptions, or ways of thinking, and behaviour. In contrast to *behaviourism, it sees human beings as active in constructing their identities and the meaning of events as they make sense of their world. *See also* COGNITIVE DISSONANCE; COGNITIVE BEHAVIOURAL THERAPY.

cohabitation Living together without being married - can be used with overtones of moral disapproval. The phenomenon is now so widespread that the term has almost fallen out of use, except for in the social security system in relation to *means-testing. Here a couple is considered to be two people aged over 16 who are married or in a civil partnership and living in the same household or, if not married or in a civil partnership, 'living together as if husband and wife or as if in a civil partnership'. The latter is usually referred to as the 'cohabitation rule'. To be defined as cohabitating under the rule, the two people should mean their relation-ship to be a long-term mutual commitment. In deciding whether a relationship does amount to cohabitation, the Department of Work and Pensions and the Tax Credit system consider a number of factors:

• Is the relationship stable?
• How is money managed?
• Do others think the two people are a 'couple'?
• Do the two people 'share a household'?
• Is there a sexual relationship?
• Do the two people have children together?

collaborative working (collaborative workers) Used to describe forms of social work that engage with a wide variety of other professionals and organizations. An approach to practice that emphasizes the need to work jointly with others, valuing the contributions that they make, in order to produce coordinated, coherent, and holistic responses to *service users' *needs, achieving more together than the practitioners would have done separately. In order to move in this direction, social workers, and others, have been enjoined to work in new ways, to change what are depicted as unhelpful working practices and cultures, and to reconstruct professional and practice relationships.

Three factors have been regarded as significant in the shift towards a much greater emphasis on collaborative working in policy and practice: the need for multi-agency responses to address multi-dimensional needs in an increasingly complex society; changes in the structures, roles, and functions of statutory agencies that have made them potentially more fluid, flexible, and better able to work in cooperation with other agencies; political drivers within policy requiring agencies to work in *'joined-up' ways to deliver 'seamless services'.

Despite collaborative working being promoted heavily in policy and practice, there is little consensus about what it actually means. Common elements are a desire to achieve benefits that could not be attained by a single agency working on its own; a recognition that some services are interdependent, and that action in one part of the system will have a 'knock-on effect' somewhere else; some sort of shared purpose or shared vision of the way forward.

However, there are a number of potential barriers to collaboration being achieved in practice. These are *structural*, for example, fragmented responsibilities for services both between different *agencies and within them; *procedural*, for example, differences in planning and budget cycles; *financial*, for example, differences in funding mechanisms and the way service costs are paid by users of services and retrenchment in resources leading to cuts and restrictions in service provision; *defensiveness*, in response to perceived threats to professional status, autonomy, and legitimacy; *professional*, for example, differences in ideologies, values, and professional interests; *power differences* between occupational groups and the competition for territory between them. Different organizational *audit and *performance management systems may also lead to conflicting priorities, as each organization is working to achieve different targets and meet different performance measures, the achievement and meeting of which are likely to be affected and possibly compromised by the policies and practices of other organizations. These factors all threaten to undermine collaborative working, fostering blame and antagonism rather than goodwill between *agencies. In addition, there have been concerns that although there may be benefits in working more closely with other professionals, this may pose a threat to social workers' professional identity and the *values they espouse. A prime example is the conflicting beliefs and values underpinning the medical and *social models of *disability. Another is different professional perspectives on what constitutes acceptable *risk and risk-taking.

It is important to evaluate collaboration in terms of *outcomes, rather than assuming that it is in itself 'a good thing'. Collaboration can be ineffective or even have deleterious consequences: a focus on collaborative working can be used to conceal inadequate funding for services; it can easily come to be seen as an end in itself rather than as a means to the delivery of services that are responsive to *service users' *needs; it can silence the voices of small *voluntary sector agencies or *community groups. *See also* TEAM AROUND THE CHILD.

collaborative working with service users A stance towards *service users in which social workers see them as contributing as experts on their own lives. *See also*

CO-PRODUCTION; EXPERTS BY EXPERIENCE; PARTICIPATION; PARTNERSHIP WITH SERVICE USERS; SERVICE USER INVOLVEMENT.

collective A group working together collaboratively for the mutual support and/or advancement of the interests of its members, as when feminists have rejected authoritarian male-dominated organizational forms in favour of more egalitarian forms of organization. *Service user organizations may adopt collective forms in seeking to overcome the isolation of their individual members and understand their difficulties in terms of their (collective) *social construction rather than in relation to *individual pathology. *See also* COLLECTIVISM; COLLECTIVE ACTION; COLLECTIVE WELFARE; COLLECTIVE WORK.

collective action Joint attempts to address and/or seek remedies for a specific perceived wrong, such as the successful campaign by Prostitutes for Reform of the Law on Soliciting (a *collective of sex workers) against sex workers being jailed for soliciting. The collective action's aim of abolishing imprisonment for soliciting was realized with the passing of the Criminal Justice Act (1982). Collective action can also involve working more generally towards a broader *goal, such as the *Disabled People's Movement's opposition to widespread *discrimination and *oppression on the basis of *disability. *See also* COLLECTIVE; COLLECTIVISM; COLLECTIVE WELFARE; COLLECTIVE WORK.

collective welfare Advocacy of communal bonds between citizens as the basis for welfare provision. This concept underpinned the establishment of the post-war *welfare state, which saw *welfare in terms of the mutual obligations of strangers to each other as an expression of collective responsibility, social solidarity, and *altruism, rather than calculated self-interest. This approach was based on an assumed set of collectivist values that were seen as embodied in and represented by the welfare state. It has been increasingly challenged and is largely viewed as discredited by the mainstream political parties. *See also* CITIZENSHIP; COLLECTIVE; COLLECTIVE ACTION; COLLECTIVE WORK; COLLECTIVISM; CONSUMERISM.

collective work Seeking to undertake day-to-day work in the manner suggested by *collective forms of organization. In the past, some teams of social workers sought to operate in this way, allocating work and taking decisions about the running of the team collectively. The consolidation of *managerialism in social work has militated against such attempts to work in a more egalitarian fashion. *See also* CITIZENSHIP; COLLECTIVE; COLLECTIVE ACTION; COLLECTIVE WELFARE; COLLECTIVISM; EGALITARIANISM.

collectivism Political, social, or economic theories and/or practices that advocate communal or state ownership of the means of production and distribution, and the provision of social and other services as a public good. *See also* CITIZENSHIP; COLLECTIVE; COLLECTIVE ACTION; COLLECTIVE WELFARE; COLLECTIVE WORK.

combined predictive algorithm *See* VIRTUAL HOSPITAL WARD.

coming out The open acknowledgement of a lesbian, gay, or bisexual identity. First used in the 1960s to indicate the first time that someone's gay, lesbian, or bisexual identity was revealed to another person(s), but increasingly seen as a process rather than a one-off event.

Commission for Local Administration *See* LOCAL GOVERNMENT OMBUDSMAN.

commissioning The process of assessing the needs for which services are required, procuring the services, and managing the subsequent relationships with service providers. *See also* CARE MARKET.

commodification A component in Marxist analysis of capitalist economies that sees one of their distinguishing features as workers producing commodities for sale at a profit in the market for a capitalist, rather than producing goods and services to meet their own needs. Also regarded as the tendency to treat as economic commodities what previously would have been seen as emotional and relationship-based. For example, in the past social work was seen as a personal service rooted in the relationship between the social worker and the *service user, which included concern with the *service user's emotional needs. However, it is increasingly seen as a series of transactions in the *care market that involves the social worker putting together a combination of commodities, as when a social worker acting as a *care manager arranges what is referred to as a *care package. *See also* CAPITALIST SOCIETY.

Common Assessment Framework for Children and Young People (CAF)
This was previously a framework, accompanied by national practice guidelines, that was used for early identification of children with additional *needs, sharing of information between organizations, and coordination of service provision. Needs were assessed according to the framework and decisions made about how best to respond to them. An *assessment under the CAF was coordinated by a lead professional. Any agency that identified a child as having additional needs could initiate a common assessment and the lead professional could be a teacher, health visitor, or other professional involved with the child and family. The intention was that the CAF would identify what help the child and family required to prevent needs escalating to a point where intervention would be needed via a statutory assessment under the Children Act (1989).

The *Munro Review recommended that the government should not prescribe national models for assessments. Accordingly, the national status of the CAF was withdrawn, though it is still in use by some local authorities when assessing a child's additional needs at an early stage. *See also* ASSESSMENT (CHILDREN); CHILD IN NEED; CHILD PROTECTION; INITIAL ASSESSMENT; SAFEGUARDING CHILDREN.

Further reading: Guidance on the CAF. Available at: http://webarchive.nationalarchives.gov.uk/20090608182316/http:/dcsf.gov.uk/everychildmatters/strategy/deliveringservices1/caf/cafframework.

communication skills Interpersonal, written, and verbal abilities, and the capacity to adapt them to different contexts, that are central to social work both in direct work with *service users and when working with other social workers and professionals. Communication plays a crucial role in *assessment, planning, intervening, and reporting on actions taken. In addition, initial access to services depends upon communication of information about them in a variety of languages and formats (including Braille, taped versions, on the Internet, etc.). *See also* COLLABORATIVE WORKING.

Further reading: Koprowska, J. (2014, 4th edn.) *Communication and Interpersonal Skills in Social Work*, Learning Matters.

communitarianism The belief that contemporary social problems such as crime and social isolation stem from the interrelationship between the decline of supportive communities and the weakening of families within them. The ideas underpinning this belief came to prominence in the 1990s, mainly in the US, as a reaction against *neo-liberalism, but have had a much wider influence. For example, Amitai

Etzioni (1929–), one of the main US proponents of communitarianism, advised *New Labour after it came to power in 1997. Communitarians favour policies that support the family, often embodying a traditional conception of the *nuclear family, and that allow the *community to decide for itself what is good for it and how its aspirations can be achieved, without what they see as interference from the state. This leaves some questions unanswered. For example, what if the community adopts as a *goal that it only wants to have heterosexual people living within it? Communitarian ideas can be found in the values underpinning some social work practice, but may not be articulated as such. *See also* BIG SOCIETY; COMMUNITY; COMMUNITY ACTION.

community Usually seen as typified by social relationships based on commonality, either derived from living in a particular geographical location, such as a defined urban neighbourhood or a village, or sharing a particular interest(s) or *goal(s), for example, on the basis of *ethnicity, *gender, religion, or membership of a professional association. It often has powerful symbolism and rhetoric attached, often functioning as an *ideal-type, and conveying notions of engagement, cohesion, solidarity, and continuity, its existence seen as reflecting well on the society in which it is located. Less often articulated are the ways in which close communities can result in pressure to adopt conventional and conservative values. *See also* COMMUNITARIANISM; COMMUNITY ACTION.

community action The coming together of people in a local area in order to achieve a common *goal such as preventing a road being built or a hospital from being closed, seeking the allocation of resources for housing improvements, or obtaining increased funding for services in the locality. Actions taken can include petitions, lobbying councillors and MPs, media campaigns, demonstrations, or direct action, such as occupying *local authority offices or lying in the path of earthmoving equipment when a road is about to be built. *See also* COMMUNITARIANISM; COMMUNITY; COMMUNITY WORK.

community care Originally contrasted with 'out of sight, out of mind' *institutional care in long-stay, large-scale institutions and used to refer to services and support provided to people living in the *community, either in smaller scale provision, such as hostels or *group homes, or in their own homes. Although the term has strong rhetorical resonance, it has been open to a wide range of interpretation. It came to prominence as a major policy direction in the 1960s, in relation to moving people out of large psychiatric hospitals, and soon became the central approach in all services for adults, with the aim of avoiding institutional care whenever possible. The services typically associated with community care have been *mobile meals, *day care, and *home helps. Feminists have highlighted the extent to which community care has relied far more heavily on households than on service provision, and within those households it has predominantly involved women. From 1979 to 1997, under Conservative governments, this was reinforced by the insistence that care *in* the community should be replaced by care *by* the community; in other words that, wherever possible, services should be replaced by support provided by relatives, friends, and neighbours, the assumption being that providing care in the community was not to be seen as the state's responsibility. In recent years, community care has been redefined in terms of *personalization, stressing arrangements for support being made on an individual basis, for example, using *direct payments or *personal budgets, rather than the use of standardized services. This approach underpins the Care Act (2014), which is the legislation under which community care services are provided. *See also* CARE MANAGEMENT; CARER; CARER'S ASSESSMENT; COMMUNITY CARE REFORMS; NEEDS ASSESSMENT.

Further reading: Means, R., Richards, S., and Smith, R. (2008, 4th edn.) *Community Care: Policy and Practice*, Palgrave Macmillan.

community care assessment *See* CARER'S ASSESSMENT; NEEDS ASSESSMENT.

community care reforms The restructuring of services for adults that took place in the early 1990s under the Conservative government and that had a profound and lasting impact. Driven by economic pressures, coupled with increased demands being made on services, and consequent resource constraints, the rationale for the reforms was that a policy was needed that would target services to those in greatest need. Matters came to a head with the publication of *Making a Reality of Community Care* (Audit Commission 1986), which identified the massively increased spending on residential care for adult *service users, under arrangements introduced by the Conservative government in 1980, when the policy was ostensibly one of community care. These arrangements meant that the social security system paid for people with assets under £3,000 to be in residential care. In many circumstances, the easiest service provision to arrange for someone who needed day-to-day support was a place in a private care home at central government's expense. As well as opening up this avenue for use directly by relatives, there was what the Audit Commission described as a 'perverse incentive' for *local authorities to place people receiving financial support from social security in residential and nursing homes, where their care would be funded by central government, rather than to support them living in the community, when the costs would fall on local authorities themselves. In response to the Audit Commission's report, the Conservative government commissioned a review undertaken by Sir Roy Griffiths, which was delivered in his report *Community Care: An Agenda for Action* (1988). He recommended that the then *Social Services Departments should have the lead role in assessing need, and planning and coordinating services, including those provided by the *private and *voluntary sectors. It was proposed that the perverse incentive to use residential care should be removed by transferring funding from the social security system to Social Services Departments and by imposing an *assessment 'gateway' for those needing to access this funding. This was intended to establish greater control over the finances committed to residential care and to use the resources transferred to open up greater possibilities for developing community-based alternatives. Following on from the Griffiths Report, the White Paper, *Caring for People: Community Care in the Next Decade and Beyond* (Department of Health 1989) incorporated the recommendations contained in the Report that Social Services Departments should assess individual need, design tailor-made *care packages, and ensure appropriate service provision by acting as *enablers and *purchasers rather than providers. The White Paper also reflected the political objective of restricting the role of local authorities by requiring them to stimulate what became known as the *'mixed economy of care', that is, providing services by a mixture of *statutory, private, and voluntary sector agencies, alongside support for *carers. The stated objectives of *Caring for People* were to:

- Promote development of domiciliary, day, and respite care to enable people to live in their own homes.
- Provide support for carers.
- Make proper assessment of need and good case management 'the cornerstone of high quality care'.

- Promote a flourishing independent sector.
- Clarify the responsibilities of agencies, especially between the NHS and local authorities.
- Secure better value for money.

There has always been a mixture of provision between the state, the *market, the voluntary sector, and carers, and in this respect the mixed economy of care was not new. However, the community care reforms reflected a significant shift in the role of the state from an institutional to a residual one. Key to achieving this shift in community care provision was the separation of assessment of *need from the provision of services. Although there was no requirement for local authorities to organize according to what was referred to as the *'purchaser–provider split', the respective functions of *assessment and direct service provision had to be clearly distinguished, and most authorities did opt for the split in the purchasing and providing functions. The stated rationale for this distinction was to free the process of assessing the appropriate provision to meet need from service considerations, and to enable private and voluntary sector providers to compete on equal terms with services provided in-house by the local authorities' Social Services Departments. The 'mixed economy of care' was presented as a way of improving standards through introducing competition. Stimulation of the mixed economy was ensured by the stipulation that 85 per cent of monies transferred to local authorities from central government in the form of a 'special transitional grant' had to be spent on services provided by the *independent sector. A further rationale for the reforms was the empowerment of service users and carers through their new status as 'consumers' of services. The *care market was represented as enabling them to exercise increased *choice and control over the services they received, with the right of redress through new complaints procedures. Section 47 of the NHS and Community Care Act (1990), which followed the *Caring for People* White Paper, set out the 'gateway' to community care services, namely the duty of local authorities to assess an individual's need for services. The system ushered in by the reforms was itself increasingly criticized as having a narrow and instrumental approach to assessment and service provision and the NHS and Community Care Act (1990) was replaced by the Care Act (2014). This introduced *needs and *Carer's Assessments and the use of *care and support plans. *See also* AGENCY THEORY; CARE MANAGEMENT; COMMUNITY CARE.

community care services *See* CARE AND SUPPORT PLAN; CARER'S ASSESSMENT; NEEDS ASSESSMENT.

community care worker Job title often used for unqualified staff in social work teams providing services for adults, or by agencies for workers in *domiciliary services. *See also* COMMUNITY CARE.

community development Practice aimed at assisting people to improve the quality of their lives in their neighbourhoods, by identifying, building, and utilizing social networks and community assets to give them more autonomy, capacity, and control. *See also* COMMUNITY; COMMUNITY WORK.

Community Development Programme (Community Development Projects) *See* COMMUNITY WORK.

Community Drug Team (CDT) A unit within the National Health Service that delivers services for drug users in a local area on a *multidisciplinary basis. The services provided can include needle exchange schemes, supervised use of *methadone, work in prisons, following up referrals after arrest, *counselling, arrangements for admission to *detoxification units, and outreach work, for example, in night clubs and at festivals. *See also* ADDICTION.

community equipment *See* AIDS AND ADAPTATIONS.

community health services The *NHS continuing health care services provided to people in their own homes, or in residential or nursing homes under the NHS Act (1977).

community interest company (CIC) Introduced in 2005 under the Companies Act (2004) and designed for companies using their profits and assets for the public good, so that there would be a legal vehicle for non-charitable social enterprises. They vary in size from small *community organizations to multi million-pound companies. They operate in a range of areas, including education, health, and social work. Some local authorities have transferred their adults' and/or children's social work and social care services to CICs. Profits have to be used for the good of the community; they cannot usually be distributed to members or shareholders. The main difference between *charities and CICs is that charities must in most circumstances have voluntary boards, whereas the directors of a CIC can be paid salaries.

Community Mental Health Nurse (CMHN) *See* COMMUNITY PSYCHIATRIC NURSE.

community organization As originally developed by the *Charity Organisation Society, this involved the upper and middle classes employing what was seen as a scientific organized response to the *poverty and social disintegration that characterized nineteenth-century capitalist industrial society. In its present form it still tends to be a top-down rather than a bottom-up approach. It may involve a local organization or proposed organization identifying a social need and putting together a service to address that need. Existing resources will be identified that might be able to help in addressing the problem. When information has been collected on the need and the existing resources, a set of recommendations and/ or an action plan will be put together, bringing together the existing resources and representatives of organizations that might contribute and form a working group to develop strategies to lead to action and community change in relation to the task or problem. An open meeting may then be held and some sort of either informal association or formal organization be formed. *See also* COMMUNITY; COMMUNITY DEVELOPMENT; COMMUNITY WORK.

community patient *See* COMMUNITY TREATMENT ORDER.

Community Payback *See* COMMUNITY SENTENCES; UNPAID WORK.

community psychiatric nurse (CPN) A qualified nurse with specialized training and education for work in mental health settings. CPNs usually work in a Community Mental Health Service or GP practice and may act as an ongoing contact point for someone under the care of a psychiatrist. The CPN plays a significant role in the supervision and treatment of individuals with a diagnosis of *mental illness who are living in the community. CPNs administer but generally do not prescribe medication. There have, however, been developments in nurse prescribing by those who have undertaken and achieved the necessary qualification. Many CPNs are trained to provide *cognitive behavioural therapy.

community sentences A court can decide on a community sentence if someone is convicted of a crime but not sent to prison. A community sentence is more likely if it is a first offence; if the person has a mental health condition that affects her/his behaviour; or if the court thinks the person is more likely to stop committing crime than if s/he went to prison.

The sentence of Community Payback is unpaid work, typically removing graffiti, clearing wasteland, or decorating public places and buildings. It usually involves the person in work in her/his local area, managed by a Community Payback supervisor. A high-visibility orange vest has to be worn while the work is carried out. The length of sentence ranges from forty to 300 hours, depending on how serious the crime was. If the person is unemployed, s/he has to work three or four days per week. If the person has a job, Community Payback work is arranged outside the person's working hours.

A court can also stipulate treatment or programmes that address problems that may have led to the person having committed the crime, with the aim of preventing the committing of further crimes. These can be focused on addiction, mental health problems, or obtaining skills and qualifications, and can include:

• counselling sessions;
• drug testing;
• programmes, such as *anger management courses, aimed at changes in behaviour;
• mental health treatment;
• improving reading and writing;
• getting help with a job application;
• learning interview skills;
• meeting people who were affected by the offence, as part of a *restorative justice programme. (This involves the person meeting the victim[s], listening to their side of the story, and apologizing to them, either in writing or face-to-face.)

If a treatment or programme is not completed or a drugs test is failed, the person can be sent back to court and the sentence can be increased.

Community sentences for young people under 18 are different from those given to adults. There are three main community sentences for young people:

  __Referral Order__ The person agrees to a programme of work to address her/his behaviour with a panel of people from the local community and youth justice workers.

  __Reparation Order__ The person makes up for the harm caused by the crime, for example by repairing any damage done to a victim's property.

  __Youth Rehabilitation Order__ The court decides on what the person has to do or must not do for up to three years.

Alternatively, young people under 18 can be given a discharge when the court decides that the experience of being arrested and going to court has been enough of a punishment.

Detailed conditions can be attached to any community sentence either by the court when sentencing takes place or by the person, called an offender manager, dealing with the sentence once it is under way. This can include:

• a curfew—staying in at a particular place at certain times;
• being stopped from going to certain places or areas;

- being stopped from taking part in certain activities;
- being told where to live;
- wearing an electronic tag to check that the person does not go to particular places or go out at certain times;
- appointments with an offender manager.

If the conditions of a community sentence are broken, a warning can be issued or the person can be sent back to court and the sentence can be increased.

community services *See* CARE AND SUPPORT PLAN; CARER'S ASSESSMENT; NEEDS ASSESSMENT.

community social work *See* BARCLAY REPORT.

Community Treatment Order (CTO) Introduced by the Mental Health Act (2007), it requires certain categories of people with mental health problems to receive compulsory care and treatment within the community under powers set out by the Mental Health Act (1983). The aims of a CTO are to ensure that patients are not left untreated in the community and to prevent the *revolving door syndrome. The provisions were a diluted version of *New Labour's original intentions, which attracted considerable controversy and criticism from those concerned about civil liberty and *human rights principles. The framework replaces Supervised Aftercare (also known as Supervised Discharge), which had been introduced by the Mental Health (Patients in the Community) Act (1995), following a series of highly publicized cases. A CTO can be applied to patients of any age who are liable to be detained under Sections 3, 37, 45A, 47, and 48 and who meet the grounds set out in Section 17A(5) of the Mental Health Act (1983), as amended by the Mental Health Act (2007). Patients who are subject to a CTO are referred to in the legislation as community patients. Legally, the effect of a CTO is to suspend two requirements set out by the original treatment section (*see* COMPULSORY TREATMENT). The first is the liability to be detained in hospital. The second is the requirement to take medication and related powers of *compulsory treatment as set out under Part IV of the Act. Patients on a CTO are instead subject to Part IVA under which there are no powers to give treatment without consent. The CTO is made by the patient's *Responsible Clinician (RC) and requires the agreement of an *Approved Mental Health Professional (AMHP). The CTO sets out mandatory conditions requiring patients to make themselves available for examination. Further discretionary conditions can be specified by the RC if the agreement of the AMHP is obtained. Failure to comply with a mandatory condition provides grounds to recall a patient to hospital for treatment. There is no such power with discretionary conditions and in this case the RC would need to believe that the patient required treatment in hospital and that there would be a risk of harm to the health or safety of the patient or to others if they were not recalled to hospital for treatment. A CTO lasts for six months in the first instance, but can be extended for a further six months, and then yearly if the criteria are still met. The RC may revoke the CTO with the agreement of the AMHP. This has the effect of making the patient subject to their original treatment section and the detention period will be started anew. The patient remains in hospital as long as the detention period lasts. Revocation triggers an automatic *First-tier Tribunal. The RC can also discharge the CTO completely if the grounds are no longer met. The patient can apply for a First-tier Tribunal hearing that has the power to discharge the CTO, but it does not have the power to vary the conditions. *Hospital managers' hearings also have the power to discharge the CTO (under Section 23) and patients may request a hearing. The *nearest relative (NR) can discharge certain categories of patient from a CTO but NR discharge can be blocked by the RC in certain circumstances. Discharge from a CTO has the effect of discharging the initial liability for detention. *See also* COMMUNITY PSYCHIATRIC NURSE; COMPULSORY ADMISSION; SUPERVISED COMMUNITY TREATMENT.

community work A form of practice focused on the people living in a particular geographical area, usually experiencing poverty and disadvantage. It is based on involving people in seeking solutions to the problems they are experiencing in their locality. In the early 1970s the government, through the Home Office, sponsored a number of community development projects in disadvantaged areas of England. These were initially based on a model of people in these communities being assisted to help themselves, although support was provided through the employment of community workers and additional services were put in place such as social security benefits advice and housing improvements. As time went on the projects became increasingly critical of the extent to which problems in such areas could be solved at the local level and developed analyses that placed the *poverty and disadvantage the areas experienced in the context of wider political, economic, and social forces. The government was not receptive to these analyses and the Home Office closed down the projects in the mid-1970s. In the same period, many *Social Services Departments also employed community workers, in accordance with the promotion of community work in the *Seebohm Report, but they, too, were a short-lived phenomenon. *See also* COMMUNITY ACTION; COMMUNITY DEVELOPMENT.

Further reading: Twelvetrees, A. (2008, 4th edn.) *Community Work*, Palgrave.

co-morbidity When two disorders or illnesses occur in the same person, usually simultaneously but sometimes sequentially, they are described as co-morbid. Co-morbidity implies interactions between the illnesses that affect the course and prognosis of both.

competence An individual's ability to perform work activities to the standards required by the employer. The stress on competence began in the 1980s and early 1990s, when the Conservative governments were keen to place competence at the centre of training, learning, and *assessment for employment across a wide range of occupations. It has remained an enduring emphasis in social work, currently embodied in the *Professional Capability Framework and the *Knowledge and Skills Statements for social workers in children's and adults' services.

competing interests The stakes that different people have in situations that may be opposed or in tension. For example, when working with *older people, social workers are exhorted to adopt a person-centred approach, but as well as focusing on the older person, they have to take account of the interests and potentially conflicting needs of *carers, other members of informal networks, other professionals and agencies, and their employing organizations. These competing interests mean that social workers' different responsibilities and concerns can come into conflict. Promoting the autonomy of one individual may infringe the needs and interests of another. Conflict may arise when the rights and freedom of one individual are in opposition to those of others. For example, an older person may choose to live with very low standards of cleanliness within their home, but this may have environmental health consequences for those living next to them. In their practice, social workers frequently have to negotiate competing interests, and the conflicts and dilemmas they raise. *See also* CARE; CARER; CARE RECIPIENTS.

competition The introduction of *care markets, initially via the *community care reforms, installed competition between service providers as part of the strong Conservative commitment to a common policy of *market-oriented reform across a range of services. As far as social work was concerned, the Conservative government instigated competition by stipulating that 85 per cent of the funds transferred from central government's Social Security system to *local authorities for *community care services had to be spent on the *independent sector so that there would be competition to provide services between the *private, *voluntary, and *public sectors. In addition, local authorities were required to make clear what steps they were taking to make increased use of service providers outside the public sector or, where such providers were not available, how they proposed to stimulate such activity, including by floating off some of their own services. Competition was seen and continues to be seen as essential to the development of cost-effective services. Even if 'proper' competition within a market is not possible, then competition for a market itself, through tenders for contracted-out services, still tends to produce 'efficiency gains' by driving down costs such as wages. The markets within which competition operates are steered by local authorities, which, through their *commissioning activities, can usually manage the terms of competition. Such markets can shape the decisions and actions of organizations and *service users just as much as public services. For example, they can guide service providers to do or insist that they do more at less cost. In conditions in which a particular service provider has become dominant and it is more difficult for a local authority to steer a market, the private sector can produce inefficient and expensive services. *See also* AGENCY THEORY; CARE MARKET; COMMUNITY CARE REFORMS; CONTRACT STATE.

complaints *See* COMPLAINTS PROCEDURE.

complaints procedure A formal process for hearing allegations about a service being unsatisfactory or a *service user being mistreated, which is the responsibility of a senior manager. It is intended as a last resort, at least within the social work organization, if complaints have not been resolved informally at an earlier stage. (Further avenues outside the social work organization include the Commission for Local Administration [*Local Government Ombudsman] or *judicial review.) Complaints procedures are meant to be written in plain English and to have clear time limits. When a decision has been reached about the complaint, it is communicated in writing. If it is upheld, the decision can be accompanied by an explanation, an apology, compensation, or information about changes in practice and procedure. Annual reports are compiled about the number and nature of complaints and how they have been dealt with. The Children Act (1989) makes provision for complaints in relation to children's services, and the Care Act (2014) does likewise with regard to services for adults.

complex child abuse *See* ORGANIZED CHILD ABUSE.

compulsive–obsessive disorder *See* OBSESSIVE–COMPULSIVE DISORDER.

compulsory admission (mental health) An individual can be compulsorily admitted to hospital under the Mental Health Act (1983). Part II of the Act applies to civil admissions (also known as sectioning). Part III of the Act sets out the circumstances in which criminal courts can order individuals to be detained. The two main civil sections in Part II are Sections 2 and 3, and both must be agreed by three professionals (usually an *Approved Mental Health Professional, a *Section 12 approved doctor, and a registered medical practitioner). The individual's *nearest relative (as defined by the Act) can also make the application for detention, but the Approved Mental Health Professional is the preferred applicant. In practice applications by the nearest relative are rare. Section 2 (admission for assessment followed by treatment) allows for an individual to be detained for up to 28 days if they have a mental disorder and need to be assessed for their own health or safety, or for the protection of other people. Section 2 cannot be renewed at the end of 28 days, but an assessment for Section 3 may be considered. Section 3 (admission for treatment) allows for an individual to be detained for up to six months if they have a mental disorder and it is necessary for their own health or safety, or for the protection of other people, and treatment cannot be provided unless they are detained in hospital. After six months, Section 3 can be renewed for six months initially and for twelve months at a time subsequently. Individuals can be detained under other sections set out in Parts II and III of the Act if they meet the legal grounds for compulsory admission, but Sections 2 and 3 are the most widely used. *See also* COMMUNITY TREATMENT ORDER; COMPULSORY TREATMENT; INFORMAL ADMISSION.

compulsory detention (mental health) *See* COMPULSORY ADMISSION.

compulsory school age The ages between which a child must attend school or be in some other approved form of education such as home schooling. Compulsory school age is defined by Section 8 of the Education Act (1996), as amended by Section 52 of the Education Act (1997), and the Education (School Leaving Date) Order (Statutory Instrument 1997 no.1970). It begins when a child is aged five and s/he must start school in the term following her/his fifth birthday. It ends on the last Friday in June in the school year in which a child reaches the age of 16. Parents of children of compulsory school age are required to ensure that they receive a suitable education, usually by regular attendance at school. Failure to comply with this duty can lead to parents being prosecuted. Schools are required to take attendance registers twice a day. Where a child of compulsory school age is absent, schools have to indicate in the register whether the absence is authorized by the school or unauthorized. Local authorities are legally responsible for making sure that children attend school. *See also* SCHOOL ATTENDANCE; SCHOOL ATTENDANCE ORDER.

compulsory treatment (mental health) Circumstances in which medical treatment for mental disorders may be given where a patient who is compulsorily detained either refuses to give, or is incapable of giving, consent as set out by the provisions in Part IV of the Mental Health Act (1983). (Not all detained patients are included but most are; Part IV of the Act applies to patients detained under Sections 2, 3, 36, 37, 38, 44, 45A, 47, and 48.) Any treatment can be given without the patient's consent, unless the Mental Health Act or Department of Health regulations specify otherwise.

However, under Section 57, psychosurgery and other serious treatments that give rise to special concern (such as hormone implantation) can only be given if:

- the patient consents *and*
- a panel of three independent people appointed by the Care Quality Commission (in England; in *Wales by the Welsh Ministers) confirms that her/his consent is valid *and*
- the doctor on the panel certifies it is appropriate for the treatment to be given. Before doing so, he or she must consult two people who have been concerned with the patient's treatment. One of these must be a nurse and the other neither a nurse nor a doctor.

As any treatments covered by Section 57 give rise to particular concern, the arrangements for giving consent, as above, apply to all voluntary and detained patients. Under Section 58A, *electro-convulsive therapy can be given with the patient's consent, or if the patient lacks *capacity, with the approval of a *Second Opinion Appointed Doctor. Any treatment can be given without consent in specific emergencies, subject to restrictions when a treatment is irreversible or hazardous (Section 62). If a person continues to withhold consent to the medication they are being given for a period of three months, a Second Opinion Appointed Doctor must, at this point, be arranged to decide whether this treatment should continue.

Patients who are not covered by the provisions for compulsory treatment set out in Part IV of the Mental Health Act (1983) cannot be treated without their consent except where the Mental Capacity Act (2005) (*see* CAPACITY) applies, or where common law would allow it, for example, in an emergency. The fact that a person is mentally disordered does not mean that they necessarily lack capacity to give or withhold valid consent to particular forms of treatment. Consent needs to be based on an adequate and broad knowledge of the proposed treatment and the person should understand what is likely to happen if the treatment is not given. Consent should not be given under duress and it can be withdrawn at any point.

computerization Originally the introduction of standardized procedures for information processing in connection with electronic recording on *case files, information technology has played an increasing part in shaping and monitoring social workers' practice. For example, in services for adults, information technology systems take every social worker in a particular *local authority step-by-step through the same process for every *service user, usually marrying financial and other information so that it is impossible for a service user to receive a service unless the social worker complies with every requirement of the software. This has resulted in practice being welded inseparably to the computer and software technology through which it has been codified and turned into a set of requirements. Debates about social work methods and theoretical perspectives have increasingly been replaced by computer systems controlled by managers, with staff following through the actions required by the information technology system, in the space previously largely controlled by the *discretion of social workers. Thus the developmental work in preparation for the introduction or updating of a computer system involves careful description and categorization of work practices, breaking them down into discrete and measurable elements, as a preliminary step to computer programming. This reduces the social workers' scope for interpretation or judgement because there are stipulations in the software, inserted at the design stage, about what can or cannot be done. *See also* COMMODIFICATION; DESKILLING.

conciliation 1. A process in which an independent impartial person (the conciliator) facilitates a meeting between people in dispute to seek a resolution. The parties in dispute are responsible for deciding how to resolve the dispute, assisted by the conciliator. Conciliation agreements can be made into legally binding settlements if both parties agree.
2. The initial stage of *complaints procedures is sometimes called 'conciliation'. When the term is used in this context, the conciliator is not independent but represents the organization against which the complaint has been made. *See also* CONFLICT MANAGEMENT; FAMILY MEDIATION; MEDIATION.

conditional positive regard *See* UNCONDITIONAL POSITIVE REGARD.

conditioning The connection(s) between stimuli (observable inputs) and responses (observable outputs) in the production and shaping of specific behaviours. *See also* BEHAVIOUR MODIFICATION; BEHAVIOURISM.

confidentiality There are a number of legal imperatives concerning the protection of confidentiality. In general terms, Article 8 of the Human Rights Act (1998) states that 'everyone has the right to respect for his [*sic*] private and family life'. The Data Protection Act (1998) imposes specific requirements concerning the processing, sharing, and security of sensitive personal data. Local authorities are required to appoint a *Caldicott Guardian to safeguard confidentiality. Their role is to act as the 'conscience' of an organization, actively supporting, facilitating, and enabling information-sharing and advising on lawful and ethical processing of information. However, these mandates have to be set against policy and practice requirements to collaborate closely with other agencies and professionals. As a consequence, *service users' right to have information about them treated in confidence is not absolute. Whilst there is a general expectation that social workers will respect confidentiality, they must also work openly and cooperatively with colleagues, for example ensuring that they inform them about the implications and outcomes of *risk assessments. Four models of information-sharing have been identified that strike differing balances between protecting confidentiality on the one hand, and openly sharing information with other professionals and agencies on the other:

   Ideal Information is shared appropriately but only when necessary.
   Over-open Information is shared when this is not always necessary or
      appropriate. This model is likely to breach confidentiality but unlikely to lead to
      important information being withheld.
   Over-cautious Information is withheld when it is necessary or appropriate to
      share it. This creates a high risk of failure to communicate necessary
      information but a low risk of breaching confidentiality.
   Chaotic The sharing and withholding of information is indiscriminate, leading to
      high risks of both not communicating important information and breaching
      confidentiality.

Although there is limited evidence concerning the influence of professional culture on information-sharing, it has been suggested that health professionals, influenced by the medical model, may be more inclined to adopt an 'over-cautious' model, prioritizing the protection of confidentiality over the need to communicate with other professionals, while the police may adopt an 'over-open' approach when communicating with health and social care agencies. As well as professional values and culture, the level of trust between professionals is also likely to bear directly on willingness to share information. *See also* COLLABORATIVE WORKING; DATA PROTECTION.

conflict Struggle between opposing attitudes, beliefs, identities, interests, or values. Social workers will encounter conflict when their interventions go against the wishes of *service users, as is often the case, for example, when children are removed from their parents. *See also* CONFLICT MANAGEMENT.

conflicting interests *See* COMPETING INTERESTS.

conflict management Usually collaborative processes through which a facilitator assists individuals or groups to resolve their differences through voluntary agreements. Some caution needs to be exercised in relation to their 'voluntary' nature as power imbalances between the parties may be masked but still shape the final outcome. Social workers often encounter situations in which they are attempting to facilitate conflict management and resolution. For example, when working with a family in which a young person and her/his parents are in *conflict. In such circumstances, social workers will often attempt to help people to communicate with each other and seek to create an environment within which that can happen. The approaches adopted can range from *task-centred to *therapeutic. *See also* CONCILIATION.

conflict resolution *See* CONFLICT MANAGEMENT.

conflict theories Perspectives that are centred on a view of society as fundamentally shaped by conflicting interests, for example the concept of class conflict in the case of Marxism, between those with wealth, property, status, and power, and those without. *See also* CAPITALIST SOCIETY; CLASS.

connected person A relative, friend, or other person with a pre-existing relationship with a child. A child may be placed with a connected person as an alternative to being placed with a birth parent. This can take place via *Special Guardianship or the connected person being approved by the *local authority as a foster carer. Placements of *looked-after children with connected persons who have not been approved as foster carers can be made under *Regulation 24 of the Care Planning, Placement and Review Regulations (2010).

conscientization A form of *consciousness-raising set out by Paulo Freire (1921–97) in *Pedagogy of the Oppressed* (1970), and developed through his involvement in literacy programmes in South America, which began with key words from people's own experiences. It involved assisting oppressed people to recognize their position and to build on their strengths as a basis for seeking to improve their lives. His methods, using critical dialogue and consciousness-raising, were not only seen as applicable in South America but also exerted an influence on social and community workers in deprived neighbourhoods across poor and rich countries, particularly during the 1970s. *See also* CONSCIOUSNESS-RAISING.

consciousness-raising Activities and discussion, usually in small groups, in which people increase their awareness and knowledge of their oppression by exchanging their individual experiences and feelings as the starting point and moving towards *collective articulation and critique of prevailing *ideologies. A key component in second-wave feminism, captured in its insistence that 'the personal is political'. *See also* CONSCIENTIZATION.

consensus Agreement about attitudes, ideas, norms, and values in a group or a whole society. In some accounts, the history of social work is depicted as resulting from a slowly developing societal consensus about the role of the state in providing support to disadvantaged people and people in need of protection that institutionalized humanitarian values and norms. *See also* CONFLICT THEORIES; HEGEMONY.

consent to treatment (mental health) *See* COMPULSORY TREATMENT.

Conservative Government's community care reforms *See* COMMUNITY CARE REFORMS.

constructionism *See* SOCIAL CONSTRUCTIONISM.

constructive social work An approach that draws on *social constructionism and *narrative approaches to analyse, understand, and develop social work practice. In addition to 'constructive' making reference to social constructionism, its proponents also see the approach as constructive in its building on and being positive about what they see as distinctive about social work, a distinctiveness they see as in danger of being lost. In their emphasis on work with individuals in their immediate relationships, they stress evidence from studies of what *service users find valuable in social work. This is not the particular theories or techniques used by the social worker but the quality and value of the experience of using active conversation to make sense of what is going on and feeling that this enables them to take control. Service users value social workers perceived as warm, trustworthy, non-judgemental, and empathetic who encourage them to tell their stories in their own terms, listening to them respectfully, as a necessary ingredient for change to occur. Proponents of the approach are concerned that social work has become so preoccupied with assessing, managing, planning, monitoring, and accounting that it is in danger of losing the core of what it has to offer in terms of encouraging narrative and interacting with service users. Meaning and understanding are seen as negotiated between the social worker and service user in this interaction, making the use of language crucial to the helping process. Thus the approach argues for the centrality language, listening, and talking in social work, but in a way that is theoretically informed.

Further reading: Parton, N. and O'Byrne, P. (2000) *Constructive Social Work: Towards a New Practice*, Macmillan.

consultation Seeking the views of *service users and/or the general public on a specific issue(s). This typically happens when a development is about to take place, such as planning to introduce a new service, or cutting back or closing an existing one. It usually takes the form of a public meeting and/or completion of questionnaires to gauge opinion. The options are usually limited and the people consulted are not being given the power to make decisions. They are simply expressing opinions that the decision-makers may or may not take into account subsequently. The increased use of consultation has led some service user groups to complain of 'consultation fatigue' and there has also been cynicism about decision-makers who have been perceived as simply seeking to co-opt opinion in support of decisions that in reality have already been taken. *See also* ARNSTEIN'S LADDER; CITIZEN PARTICIPATION.

consumerism Previously only associated with the purchase of goods and services from the *private sector, in recent years there has been official encouragement of *service users to act as customers, taking on greater involvement in choosing and arranging the services they receive. This has been advocated by Conservative, *New Labour, and Conservative–Liberal Democrat Coalition governments as the central theme in the reform of *public sector services. These services, such as social work, are depicted as locked into their post-war *welfare state origins and are portrayed as inflexible and uniform. This portrayal of public sector provision is contrasted with what is presented as the responsiveness, fluidity, and flexibility of contemporary consumer culture. Businesses operating within that culture are seen as having much to teach the public sector about how to transform its services. At the centre of the transformation is the customer, seen as having high expectations that have been forged in the society's wider consumer culture, straining at the leash to make *choices that result in the receipt of individually-attuned services. Citizens, as customers, are seen as only having their individual interest in getting the best deal they can, rather than services being seen as rooted in *collective *citizenship. The rhetoric about consumerism has grown steadily louder, particularly in services for adults with the introduction of *direct payments and *personal budgets. The adoption of consumerist *discourse in services like social work raises a number of issues.

First, consumerism is not a ready-made experience that all possess, simply waiting to be unleashed by stating in policy documents that henceforth it will be the basis for engagement with public services. Consumption is a skilled accomplishment. People learn to behave as consumers and their learning is located within a *class position that intersects with a range of other social divisions (age, *disability, *gender, *'race', and sexuality) in their biographies. The extent to which consumerism is embraced also varies according to the roles of others, authority relations, and users' experiences of earlier situations, as well as the amendment and application of any skills already acquired to a particular service context. (For example, the consumer has to consume the fire service, the library, and social work in different ways.) The impact of all of these variables on the extent to which consumerism can be accomplished by a particular *service user will shape the range and content of the services that are secured.

Secondly, in any market, active choice from options is seen as the key to the authority of the consumer but people in receipt of public services may well have no choice of provider or no provider at all. In the case of social work, most service users are not in a position where they can shop around and take their 'custom' elsewhere and they may well be told that they will not receive a service at all until they get worse.

Thirdly, if consumerism were embraced significantly it would lead to an ever-increasing demand for public services, particularly as choice can only operate in the context of surplus capacity, and for that to be achieved, services would have to be expanded. This is clearly not the intention as there is concern to keep a firm grip on public expenditure. In the private sector market place the intention is to encourage as much consumption (and profit generation) as possible. In public services, however, the relationship between demand and resources is usually fraught and subject to active management; only people whose needs are defined as satisfying certain policy criteria receive a service. In the context of social work, the state is concerned predominantly with restricting demand, through mechanisms like *eligibility criteria, *needs assessments, *charging policies, and prioritizing service allocation through *resource panels, and so on. Social workers are usually preoccupied with managing scarce resources, the excessive demand for those resources, and what it is 'reasonable' for someone to expect by way of a response to their *needs, in the light of what is available. As consumerist rhetoric has been turned up in volume, services have been increasingly targeted, *means-tested, and *risk-assessed, with attention focused more sharply on the most disadvantaged through *rationing and the ranking of competing risks and needs.

Fourthly, consumerism hides the reality of how many people come into contact with social work. Most of them are not choosing to use social work in the first place. Often, they are approaching services in a stressful state, contact with social work might be misunderstood and/or unwelcome, it might well have been initiated by someone else, and some people involved with social work are a more or less captive clientele as a result of their life experiences, or through aspects of their social context that have a coercive element. Once in contact with social work, many of their lives are subjected to surveillance and regulation. The consumerist rhetoric of service users as enterprising, active, choice-making consumers isolates its idealized depiction of their experiences from such material and emotional circumstances and is at odds with references to their being in control of their own lives through a series of rational transactions. *See also* CARE MARKET; CARE PACKAGES; CHOICE; CITIZEN'S CHARTER; CUSTOMER SATISFACTION; MANAGERIALISM; MODERNIZATION; MYSTERY SHOPPER; PERSONALIZATION.

Further reading: Harris, J. (2003) *The Social Work Business*, Routledge.

contact 1. A legal term that describes the arrangements whereby a child living with one parent is able to see, visit, or stay with the other. Before the Children Act (1989), which introduced the term, contact was known as 'access'. Contact arrangements are likely to be made in situations where parents are separated or divorced. Most such arrangements are mutually agreed by the parents of the child. However, in circumstances where there is a dispute between the child's parents or guardians about contact and mediation proves unsuccessful in resolving this dispute, courts may make a *Child Arrangements Order under Section 8 of the Children Act (1989), specifying the nature of future contact arrangements. The *Children and Family Court Advisory Support Service may be required by the courts to become involved in these situations to seek a solution and report to the court.

2. The term also applies where the child is *looked after by a *local authority as the result of being accommodated (*see* CHILD ACCOMMODATED BY A LOCAL AUTHORITY) or the subject of a *Care Order, and arrangements are subsequently made for the parent or guardian to have contact with the child. Local authorities are required to allow a child reasonable contact with guardians, anyone with parental responsibility, or anyone named in a *Child Arrangements Order that is in force as someone with whom the child should live (Section 34, Children Act [1989]). Where there have been concerns about the child experiencing *significant harm, this contact may be supervised by the local authority rather than the parent or *care-giver being permitted to see the child alone. In addition, contact describes other arrangements that enable a child to maintain links with a parent(s) or a care-giver(s) with whom s/he does not live, through letters, telephone calls, electronic communications, and photographs.

3. Telephone calls or meetings with *service users that are recorded on their files are often referred to as contacts. *See also* CHILDREN AND DOMESTIC VIOLENCE; CONTACT CENTRE; CUSTODY; RESIDENCE.

contact centre 1. A facility provided by *local authorities, the *private sector, or *voluntary organizations in which a child can meet parents, siblings, or other relatives. Anyone can approach a contact centre and request use of the facilities it provides. However, centres are more commonly used for this purpose for *looked-after children and children who are the subject of a *Child Arrangements Order. In addition, contact centres are sometimes used by local authorities for *contact between children and birth family members when the child is subject to an *Interim Care Order or *Care Order. If there is *risk to the child, contact takes place under supervision. If the child is still living with a parent who mainly cares for the child, s/he takes the child to the centre and leaves her/him there with the staff. The other parent arrives and has contact with the child at the centre. S/he will not usually be able to take the child out of the centre, unless this has been agreed. When the contact visit is over, the main carer will leave with the child.

2. The term has also been employed in the *public sector since the mid-1990s as an alternative to *'call centre'. This seems to be intended as a way of dissociating public sector call centres from the unfavourable experiences people have of private sector call centres. Strictly speaking, a contact centre (or 'customer interaction centre') is a unit from which all customer contacts for a particular organization are managed, handling not only telephone calls but also letters, faxes, and emails at one location. *See also* CHILDREN AND DOMESTIC VIOLENCE; CONTACT; CUSTODY.

Contact Order 1. An Order made prior to April 2014 by a *family court in circumstances where separated or divorced parents were in dispute about *contact arrangements for their child. The Order could be phrased in general terms, for example stipulating 'reasonable contact', or could specify the arrangements by which the parent not living with the child (or some other person) would see her or him and the circumstances in which the child would visit and stay with this parent (or other person) or have contact by telephone, letter, or electronic means. Most contact arrangements are agreed on a voluntary basis and a Contact Order was made only in situations where all attempts to achieve a voluntary agreement had failed. Contact Orders were made under Section 8 of the Children Act (1989), as was also the case with *Residence Orders that stipulated where and with whom the child would live. From April 2014, Contact and Residence Orders were replaced by *Child Arrangements Orders, introduced by the Children and Families Act (2014). From 22 April 2014, existing Contact Orders and Residence Orders were deemed to be Child Arrangements Orders. They remain valid and any arrangements in them are not affected by the change.

2. An Order can be made under Section 34 of the Children Act (1989) requiring a *local authority to allow a child to have contact with a named person. On an application made by the authority or the child, the court may make an Order with respect to the contact which is to be allowed between the child and any named person. Or, on an application made by the authority or the child, the court may make an Order authorizing the authority to refuse to allow contact between the child and any person who is named in the Order. In response to an application from parents, guardians, anyone with parental responsibility, anyone named in a Child Arrangements Order that is in force as someone with whom the child should live, or any other person who has obtained the leave of the court to make an application, the court may make an Order with respect to the contact which is to be allowed between the child and that person. When making a Care Order with respect to a child, or in any family proceedings in connection with a child who is in the care of a local authority, the court may make an Order about contact, even though no application has been made for an Order, if it considers that the Order should be made. *See also* CONTACT; CONTACT CENTRE.

contact session (contact visit) *See* CHILD ARRANGEMENTS ORDER; CONTACT; CONTACT CENTRE; CONTACT ORDER.

contingency plan (contingency planning) *See* PARALLEL PLAN.

continuing care *See* NHS CONTINUING HEALTH CARE.

continuing health care (CHC) *See* NHS CONTINUING HEALTH CARE.

continuing professional development (CPD) 1. Generally used to refer to continued learning beyond the point of initial qualification as a social worker (or other professional).

2. Specifically refers to the *Professional Capabilities Framework, which focuses on social workers developing their capabilities, deepening their knowledge, and extending their skills to deal with increasingly complex and specialist work. It is intended to promote employers' and social workers' responsibilities for CPD and give greater priority to social workers' on going learning and development. *See also* ASSESSED AND SUPPORTED YEAR IN EMPLOYMENT.

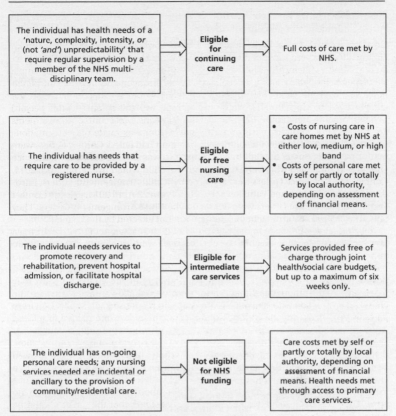

The individual has health needs of a 'nature, complexity, intensity, *or* (not *and*') unpredictability' that require regular supervision by a member of the NHS multi-disciplinary team.	**Eligible for continuing care**	Full costs of care met by NHS.
The individual has needs that require care to be provided by a registered nurse.	**Eligible for free nursing care**	• Costs of nursing care in care homes met by NHS at either low, medium, or high band • Costs of personal care met by self or partly or totally by local authority, depending on assessment of financial means.
The individual needs services to promote recovery and rehabilitation, prevent hospital admission, or facilitate hospital discharge.	**Eligible for intermediate care services**	Services provided free of charge through joint health/social care budgets, but up to a maximum of six weeks only.
The individual has on-going personal care needs; any nursing services needed are incidental or ancillary to the provision of community/residential care.	**Not eligible for NHS funding**	Care costs met by self or partly or totally by local authority, depending on assessment of financial means. Health needs met through access to primary care services.

Funding arrangements for different types of care
Tanner, D. and Harris, J. (2008), *Working with Older People*, Routledge, p. 158

continuity theory *See* THEORIES OF AGEING.

contract state The form of the state advocated by *agency theory in which social and political life can be understood as a series of contracts in which the agent agrees to perform tasks on behalf of the principal, and in return the principal agrees to reward the agent. The parties to an exchange and their interests are made distinct from each other and exchanges become more specific and concrete. Shared values and interests are replaced by contractual sanctions and incentives. Evaluation criteria become more specific and measurable, with evaluation on the basis of being a party to a contract. *See also* PERFORMANCE MANAGEMENT.

Control Order *See* ELECTRONIC TAGGING.

conversion disorder *See* HYSTERIA.

coordination of services and/or strategy An increasingly advocated solution to more efficient and effective delivery of a wide range of services. Two areas of particular relevance to social work are closer working relationships between health and social services, for example, the provision in the Health and Social Care Act (2001) for the setting-up of joint Health and Social Care Trusts and calls for greater cooperation in the Care Act (2014) (*see* JOINT FINANCE); and between education and social work, which led to the integration of the two services at local authority level as a result of the Children Act (2004). *See also* COLLABORATIVE WORKING.

co-production *Partnerships between the state, citizens, and public services in order to tackle social problems and achieve outcomes that citizens want. This increasingly prominent approach in policy is seen as encouraging citizens to contribute more of their own resources and giving them greater control over decisions and resources associated with services, for example, through passing over responsibility for budgets to *service users through *personal budgets and *direct payments. Co-production is seen as a trade-off: citizens contribute more resources to achieving an outcome, share more responsibility, and manage more *risk in return for greater control over resources and decisions. *See also* ACTIVE CITIZENSHIP; BIG SOCIETY.

CoramBAAF An independent membership organization for professionals, foster carers, and adopters, and anyone else working with or looking after children in or from care, or adults who have been affected by adoption. It is a successor organization to the British Association for Adoption and Fostering (BAAF). It has adoption agency and fostering service corporate members from the *public, *private, and *voluntary sectors. Other organizations, for example legal practices and children's organizations, have associate membership. Individual members include social workers, trainers, adopters, foster carers, therapists, lawyers, *looked-after children nurses, and researchers. It has four aims:

- to promote and encourage the highest standards of practice in adoption, *fostering, and social work with children and families through support to social workers, health professionals, and legal practitioners;
- to promote public and professional understanding of *adoption and fostering, and the resulting lifelong implications for children separated from their birth families, including their needs for safety, security, and a positive *identity;
- to act as an independent voice in the field of child care, to inform and influence policy-makers and legislators, and all those responsible for the welfare of children and young people;
- to be an umbrella body that provides overall coordination and a concerted voice for all member agencies and all those working with children.

(⊕) SEE WEB LINKS
- Official site of CoramBAAF

core assessment This involved a detailed analysis of a child's circumstances where it appeared s/he might be 'in need' within the meaning of the Children Act (1989), undertaken using the national *Framework for Assessment of Children in Need and their Families* (*see also* ASSESSMENT). A core assessment had to be completed within thirty-five working days of the decision to initiate it. A local authority children's social worker led the assessment and involved relevant professionals in gathering information.

The *Munro Review recommended that the government should not prescribe national models for assessments and should replace core and *initial assessments with a single assessment. Accordingly, the national status of the *Framework for Assessment of Children in Need and their Families* was withdrawn, as were core assessments. However, *Working Together* (2015) statutory guidance states that all assessments under the Children Act (1989) should be completed with reference to the three domains in the Assessment Framework (*see* ASSESSMENT). *See also* CHILD IN NEED; CHILD PROTECTION; SAFEGUARDING CHILDREN.

core group A group of professionals identified by a *child protection conference as responsible for implementing the *child protection plan agreed at the conference. The core group meets on a regular basis to review the progress of the plan and reports on this to subsequent child protection conferences. Parents and carers will be members of a core group whenever possible.

core group meeting *See* CORE GROUP.

corporate parent When a *local authority assumes the role of parent to a child, it becomes her/his 'corporate parent', and is required to demonstrate the characteristics associated with being a good parent. Whatever the child's *placement, corporate parenting must assist her/him to achieve her/his potential. Inspections by *Ofsted of a local authority's *safeguarding and *looked-after children arrangements assess the effectiveness of its corporate parenting approach and that of its key partners, notably health and education services.

cost-benefit analysis An approach that originated in the *private sector and is used in the *public sector to set out factors to be taken into account in deciding whether to initiate, extend, reduce, or cease providing public services. It involves allocating financial values to all social and economic costs and benefits of the proposed course of action in order to see whether the benefits outweigh the costs and justify a decision being made to go ahead. The main problem is how to place a financial value on costs and benefits that are social. Critics argue that it gives a gloss of rational objectivity to decisions that are not just economic but also social and political.

cost-effectiveness Seeking maximum value for any money expended, for example when weighing up the needs of a *service user against the efficient use of resources. Demands for increased cost-effectiveness impact on social work as a result of shortage of resources, with *local authorities only being able to target those in most need in both children's and adults' services, particularly in the context of *austerity. *See also* ECONOMY, EFFICIENCY, AND EFFECTIVENESS.

costs of personal care *See* CHARGING FOR SERVICES; NHS CONTINUING HEALTH CARE; NHS-FUNDED NURSING CARE.

Council of Voluntary Service The organization within a particular area that coordinates the activity of *voluntary organizations. Many CVSs have a volunteer bureau that acts as a clearing house, putting people wishing to volunteer in touch with voluntary organizations affiliated to the CVS. Some collect data about needs and services in their areas, for example, through the compilation of community profiles.

councillors Politicians elected to local government to represent people from their wards and to elaborate policies, allocate resources, and institute procedures so that their *local authority complies with statutory *duties placed upon it by central government legislation. Some of them take responsibility for particular aspects of their local authority's services, acting together as a cabinet. Others scrutinize the work of cabinet members and seek to hold them to account.

counselling A process involving a counsellor and a *client in a professional relationship that seeks to assist the client to address a problem, issue, or personality trait that is impacting on the client and/or her/his relationships with other people, or that seeks to support someone who has experienced a traumatic event such as being a victim of crime or being bereaved. In whatever circumstances counselling is provided, the aim is for the client to gain greater control over her/his life. The client-centred or *person-centred approach of Carl Rogers (1902–87) was enormously influential in establishing counselling as different from therapy. He saw the counsellor's responsibility as providing empathy, genuineness, and *unconditional positive regard as the basis for a relationship in which the client would be able to work though her/his issues and find her/his own solutions. In contrast, therapy was premised on the treatment of the client's pathological condition. Therapy is generally seen as a more complex process than counselling, with a therapist needing to have more knowledge and be more intensively trained than a counsellor. While counselling is seen as a practice apart from social work, which functions with a mandate that cannot be exclusively client-centred in the way counselling can, social work nevertheless incorporates counselling elements and roles within its broader reach. Approaches to both counselling and counselling elements within social work are located within a wide range of theoretical perspectives (for example, *psychodynamic, *gestalt, transactional analysis, *cognitive behavioural therapy), with some practitioners adhering to a particular theory and some adopting an *eclectic approach. *See also* BRITISH ASSOCIATION FOR COUNSELLING AND PSYCHOTHERAPY.

Further reading: Miller, L. (2006) *Counselling Skills for Social Work*, Sage.

Court Deputy *See* CAPACITY; COURT OF PROTECTION.

Court of Protection A specialist court created by the Mental Capacity Act (2005) for all issues relating to people who lack *capacity to make specific decisions. The court makes decisions and appoints deputies to make decisions in the *best interests of people without capacity. The decisions can concern their property, financial affairs, health, or welfare. The court can:

- Decide whether a person 'has capacity' (i.e. is able) to make a particular decision for her/himself;
- Make declarations, decisions, or orders on financial or welfare matters affecting people who lack capacity to make these decisions;
- Appoint a deputy to make ongoing decisions for people lacking capacity to make those decisions;
- Decide whether a *Lasting Power of Attorney is valid;
- Remove deputies or attorneys who fail to carry out their duties;
- Hear cases concerning objections to registering a Lasting Power of Attorney.

An order from the court is usually required for any matters related to property and financial decisions for people who lack capacity to make specific decisions themselves. Someone *caring for someone else who lacks capacity can carry out tasks and make decisions about health or personal care without asking the court, providing that what they do or decide is in the person's best interests.

CPN *See* COMMUNITY PSYCHIATRIC NURSE.

credit union A financial cooperative that offers savings investments and low-interest loans to its members. The members own and manage the credit union themselves. The aims of a credit union are to encourage its members to save regularly; provide loans to members at low rates of interest; and give members assistance managing their finances, if required. The members of a credit union have to have a 'common bond', for example, through living in the same locality. They save money with the credit union, and once they have reached a personal target for saving, and the credit union's overall fund has reached its target, they can borrow. The amounts borrowed are usually small, with low rates of interest. Credit unions have a particularly important role to play for people living in or on the margins of *poverty because banks and other organizations will usually not make loans to them. Having access to a credit union can help people stay out of the reach of money lenders (or 'loan sharks') who charge exorbitant rates of interest.

crime Breaking laws to which punishments are attached following the intervention of the state through the police and the courts. Intent (or at least the conscious abandoning of intent, i.e. recklessness) is usually seen as a key component. The absence of intent, for example, because of a child's age or because of an adult's *insanity, will be seen as justifying not treating an action as a crime that would normally be seen in that way. This *normative and conventional definition disguises the social construction of crime, as it passes through a number of stages. A crime may or may not be reported by a member of the public, may or may not be seen as it happens by a member of the police, or may or may not be detected following its execution. It may or may not be officially recorded, and if it is recorded, it may or may not be followed up. If it is followed up, it may or may not be taken to court. At each stage, decisions are being made that determine whether an action or event is seen as a crime and whether it is recorded in the crime statistics. When self-report studies of the experience of crime are undertaken, unreported and hence unrecorded crime is revealed in relation to *domestic violence, rape, and attacks on members of *ethnic minority groups. In addition, middle class (or 'white collar') crime, such as stealing from work or submitting fraudulent expenses claims, may be regarded as scarcely criminal. *See also* AGE OF CRIMINAL RESPONSIBILITY; CRIMINAL STANDARD OF PROOF.

Criminal Records Bureau (CRB) *See* DISCLOSURE AND BARRING SERVICE.

criminal responsibility *See* AGE OF CRIMINAL RESPONSIBILITY.

criminal standard of proof The standard for a conviction in a criminal case is that the jury is satisfied that the facts of the case have been proven by the prosecution 'beyond reasonable doubt'. *See also* CIVIL STANDARD OF PROOF.

crisis *See* CRISIS INTERVENTION.

Crisis Care Concordat (mental health) The Crisis Care Concordat (2014) is a national agreement that sets out how organizations will work together so that people get the help they need when they are having mental health crises. Most local areas have multi-agency action plans detailing how they are implementing the Concordat.

(⊕) SEE WEB LINKS

• Official site of the Crisis Care Concordat.

crisis intervention A crisis is usually seen in terms of someone's reaction to a stressful situation, or event, and/or experience that causes upset and a sense of vulnerability, of things being shaken up and out of the usual pattern. Crisis intervention is an approach that, while acknowledging the possibility that things might deteriorate further and focusing on providing immediate relief, sees a crisis as an opportunity for turning things round, as many people are more amenable to assistance during such periods. For example, mental health provision usually offers a crisis response service aimed at stabilizing a *service user in crisis and either returning her/him to her/his previous level of functioning, or assisting her/him to develop different coping strategies. There is a wide range of services that respond to crises such as the *Samaritans, rape crisis centres, and help-lines taking calls about *domestic violence. In addition, the opportunities that crises present across social work are widely recognized. In crisis intervention, the social worker may work in a directive way, seeking to achieve specific *goals and may coordinate resources that will enable the service user to get through the crisis. Typically, crisis intervention models see social work responses as moving through a succession of stages, such as establishing rapport, assessing the crisis and its impact on the service user, providing immediate support, considering alternatives, formulating an action plan, and follow-up. Critics have suggested that crisis intervention is a superficial 'sticking plaster' response that has tended not to engage with the roles played by structural factors and social divisions in producing crises. *See also* CRISIS INTERVENTION TEAM.

Further reading: Thompson, N. (2011) *Crisis Intervention*, Russell House.

crisis intervention team A multidisciplinary unit that provides intensive, usually 24-hour support services to adults with severe and enduring mental health problems, who are experiencing a relapse in their condition, and/or where there is an increased risk of hospital admission without intensive support. The model was introduced to the UK in the late 1990s following a review of mental health service provision. The objective is to treat people in the least restrictive environment possible and to prevent their admission to hospital, with support continuing until the crisis is resolved. A key feature of the approach is that it bolts on to existing service provision. Overall case responsibility is retained during the crisis by the pre-existing designated *key worker or *care coordinator. This means that other teams such as *assertive outreach, case management, or adult mental health teams will remain involved. *See also* CRISIS INTERVENTION.

crisis resolution *See* CRISIS INTERVENTION; CRISIS INTERVENTION TEAM.

critical realism *See* POSTMODERNISM.

Cruse Bereavement Care A charity that promotes the wellbeing of bereaved people by helping them to understand their grief and cope with their *loss. It also provides information, support, and training services for organizations and professionals. The name of Cruse is derived from a passage in the Old Testament about a widow's cruse (jar of oil) that never ran out. This represents the charity's aspiration that support should be given for as long as it is needed. Although the name of the charity is derived from this Bible story, Cruse is a non-religious organization.

(SEE WEB LINKS)

• Official site of Cruse Bereavement Care.

CSE *See* CHILD SEXUAL EXPLOITATION.

CTO *See* COMMUNITY TREATMENT ORDER.

cultural capital Assets other than economic capital that differentiate social *classes and are acquired through the family and education. A concept introduced by Pierre Bourdieu (1930–2002) to refer to the attributes, ideas, and tastes associated with middle-class culture and the ways in which these reinforce distinctions between classes. Thus, he asserts that there is a middle-class *'habitus', a disposition to think, feel, and act in particular ways that are inaccessible to working-class people and that enables the middle class to compete successfully and make themselves distinctive. The cultural capital that is accumulated is the source of the habitus of the next generation, thus reproducing the privileged position of the middle class.

cultural pluralism A term used to describe a situation in which a variety of subcultures, characterized by different *ethnicities, religions, and language, exist in a whole society or a particular location within it, such as a city.

culture In everyday speech, this tends to refer to the arts but in sociology (and social work) is seen as everything in society that is social rather than biological, such as language, history, knowledge, and the norms and values into which people are socialized.

culture of dependency *See* DEPENDENCY.

Curfew Order *See* YOUTH REHABILITATION ORDER.

custodial sentence A period of imprisonment imposed as a punishment after conviction for committing a *crime. Criminal offences that can result in custodial sentences are termed 'imprisonable offences', which means that a custodial sentence can be imposed but does not have to be. For young people aged between 12 and 17 the main custodial sentence is the *Detention and Training Order and this will be served in either a *young offender institution, *secure training centre, or a *local authority secure children's home. *See also* CUSTODY (IMPRISONMENT).

custody (children) The legal and practical arrangements agreed by separated or divorced parents for the care of their children, including the right and responsibility of the parent with custody to care for the children and make decisions for them. The legal terminology changed as a result of the Children Act (1989) in which a child is said to 'reside' with a parent, rather than the parent 'having custody' of the child. However, in everyday speech, the term 'custody' is still commonly encountered. A further but less-used application of 'custody' relates to shared custody of children according to which a child alternates living with each parent. This is an idea that has been more popular in continental Europe and the US than in the UK. *See also* CHILD ARRANGEMENTS ORDER; CONTACT; RESIDENCE.

custody (imprisonment) May be used in relation to children, young people, or adults who are the subject of a *custodial sentence, as in 'He is in custody.'

customer choice *See* CHOICE; CONSUMERISM.

customer interaction centre *See* CONTACT CENTRE 2.

customer satisfaction Originally associated with the degree to which a consumer was content with the purchase of goods and services from the private sector in the *market, but introduced into the public sector under the influence of *consumerism. Use of standardized customer satisfaction measures assume that organizations know what being treated well as a consumer means, narrowly defined, and do not question their underlying power relations with *service users. *See also* CONSUMERISM; MYSTERY SHOPPER.

CVA *See* CARDIO-VASCULAR ACCIDENT.

CVS *See* COUNCIL OF VOLUNTARY SERVICE.

cyber-bullying A form of *bullying that involves the use of mobile phones or the Internet. It may include sending offensive text messages and emails, circulating degrading images, or impersonating someone on social networking sites such as Facebook.

cycle of deprivation A concept popularized in the 1970s by Sir Keith Joseph, a prominent Conservative politician, that explains *poverty in terms of its being passed from generation to generation by values, attitudes, and behaviours, mainly in families but reinforced by the communities in which they live. The cycle is regarded by its proponents as explaining a range of aspects of living in poverty such as low educational performance, poor housing, and unemployment. Services that have been based on this concept have focused on intervention with young children and their parents in attempts to break the cycle, as in the *Sure Start programme. Critics of such approaches suggest that they ignore the impact of social *class and other social divisions on the origins and perpetuation of poverty. The presence of significant social, economic, and political inequalities is regarded as secondary to the negative attributes of the poor. *See also* UNDERCLASS.

dangerousness The threat of inflicting injury on others. The concept originated in the nineteenth century in relation to the urban poor who were seen as the 'dangerous class'. In contemporary use it is most often associated with mentally disordered offenders. Under Part III of the Mental Health Act (1983), courts have powers to remand or detain mentally disordered offenders in hospital, including secure psychiatric hospitals such as Rampton or Broadmoor. Although the term 'dangerousness' is not used in the Act, these legal provisions and their connection in some cases with secure psychiatric units have led to a more general and unwarranted association between mental disorder and *violence in popular perception. Dangerousness has come to be used more widely to incorporate psychological as well as physical injury and has been broadened to encompass the threat posed by perpetrators of *domestic violence and *sex offenders. In addition, in social work with families decisions about children's safety are often made on the basis of the perceived dangerousness of their parents, given that such decisions revolve around the question of *significant harm to the child.

dashboard A commonly used management tool in the *private sector, where they are used to gauge performance and progress towards selected business *goals (see illustration). As part of drawing on approaches and techniques used in the private sector, the use of dashboards has been imported into social work. They enable managers to monitor the work of individual social workers and teams of social workers (see fig.). *See also* BUSINESS EXCELLENCE; BUSINESS ORIENTATION; MANAGERIALISM; NEW PUBLIC MANAGEMENT; PERFORMANCE MANAGEMENT.

data controller *See* DATA PROTECTION.

data protection The security and safeguarding of personal information is governed by the Data Protection Act (1998), which applies to the way personal data is gathered, stored, used, and shared in social work, as elsewhere. The Act defines personal data as that which relates to a living individual who:

- Can be identified from that data; or
- Can be identified from that data and any other information in the possession of or likely to come into the possession of the data controller; and
- Includes any expression of opinion about the individual and any intentions of the data controller or any other person in respect of the individual.

Data is defined as information which is:

- Processed automatically or recorded with the intention to process automatically; or
- Recorded as or with the intention that it be part of a manual filing system; or
- Contained in a health, educational, or social services record.

All handling of data that is covered by the Act must comply with eight principles. The data must be:

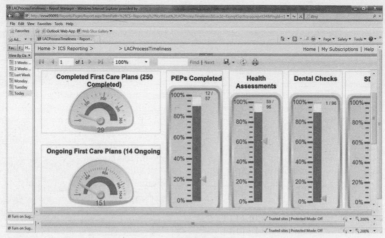

Dashboard

- Processed fairly and lawfully;
- Obtained only for one or more specified and lawful purposes and not be further processed in any manner incompatible with that purpose or those purposes;
- Adequate, relevant, and not excessive in relation to the purpose or purposes for which they are processed;
- Accurate and, where necessary, kept up-to-date;
- Not kept for longer than is necessary for the purpose or purposes for which they were collected;
- Processed in accordance with the rights of data subjects under the Act;
- Protected against unauthorized or unlawful processing, accidental loss, destruction, or damage;
- Not transferred to a country or territory outside the European Economic Area unless that country or territory ensures an adequate level of protection for the rights and freedoms of data subjects in relation to the processing of personal data.

The Act gives individuals rights to access personal information about themselves, held in computerized or manual form, whenever the information record(s) was created. This is known as 'subject access'. The rights are to:

- Be informed about whether personal data is processed (which includes being held or stored);
- Have a description of the data held, the purposes for which it is processed, and to whom the data may be disclosed;
- Have a copy of the information constituting the data;
- Receive information as to the source of the data.

Adults without *capacity can exercise these rights through their representatives. In such circumstances the request must be genuinely made on behalf of the data subject, not the representative. An immature child exercises her/his rights through an adult with parental responsibility. When a social worker believes that a child is mature enough to exercise her/his rights, the parent should be asked to provide proof that s/he is acting with the child's consent. If a social worker believes a child is mature enough to understand the nature of the data request and the nature of the information that may be disclosed, then careful consideration must be given to any instructions received from the child, for example, if the child has given information to a social worker and specifically asked for this to be withheld from a parent. The child's wellbeing should also be taken into account if information disclosed to the parent might have a detrimental effect, or might undermine the ability of a social worker to work with the child. This is particularly important if the file contains details of a child's concerns or allegations about *abuse by parents.

There are exceptions to the *duty of data controllers to supply information. For example, a request can be refused if disclosing the personal data would reveal information that relates to and identifies another person (for example, that a relative had provided certain information), unless that person has consented to the disclosure or it is reasonable to comply with the request without that consent. Or if the request for access to personal data is made by another person on behalf of the data subject, such as a parent for a child, access can be refused if the data subject had either provided the information in the expectation it would not be disclosed to the applicant, or had indicated it should not be disclosed, or if the data was obtained as a result of any examination or investigation to which the data subject consented on the basis that information would not be disclosed. There are specific exceptions that apply to social work: a *local authority may refuse access to information if access 'would be likely to result in serious harm to the person requesting the data or some other person' or where the data subject is incapable of managing her/his own affairs and expressly indicated that the data should not be disclosed (Data Protection [Subject Access Modification] [Social Work] Order [2000]).

A subject access request has to receive a response within forty days. This is a statutory requirement and there are no exemptions or exceptions. Calculation of the forty days begins when:

- It has been confirmed that the person making the subject access request, or their representative, is being dealt with;
- The relevant fee (if any) has been received;
- Any information needed to assist in finding the information requested has been obtained.

Social work records often contain information from a wide range of sources, for example, from schools, doctors, or the police. The practitioners who supply this type of information are usually referred to as 'relevant professionals'. Medical or health information is the only type of information in social work records from relevant professionals where the decision to disclose will not always rest entirely with the data controller. The Data Protection (Subject Access Modification) (Health) Order (2000) sets out additional requirements in respect of subject access requests for medical information. It defines medical or health information as 'consisting of information relating to the physical or mental health or condition of the data subject'. This includes any medical or health information that is contained within social work records. It exempts from disclosure any medical or health information that has been included in reports made to courts dealing with children and young people. It also exempts from disclosure any medical or health information where disclosure 'would be likely to cause serious harm to the physical or mental health or condition of the data subject or any other person'. The Order prohibits a data controller who is not a health professional from withholding information under this exemption unless they have first consulted with the 'appropriate health professional' to determine whether this exemption applies. The exemption will only apply in the most serious *cases. In open or recent social work records, it is likely to be possible to identify the relevant health professional and get their opinion on the possibility of harm as a result of disclosure. When records are old and/or closed the relevant practitioner may not be available. In these cases it may be possible to get an opinion from the person's *general practitioner or from another practitioner in a particular medical speciality. Where it is not possible to consult a medical practitioner without disclosing some information about the person, the information should, as far as is practicable, be anonymized. It is not necessary to get someone's consent to consult in this way, as the consultation is necessary to fulfil the legal obligation to respond to the subject access request.

Records are likely to contain information about other individuals, for example, the person's parents, siblings, or other family members. These individuals are often referred to as 'third parties'. If a response cannot be made to a subject access request without disclosing information about a third party, who could then be identified from that information, there is no obligation to disclose it, unless the third party consents or unless it is reasonable in all the circumstances to disclose it without consent. In deciding whether to disclose information about a third party, a social worker should consider what the person making the subject access request is already likely to know. It may be helpful to meet with them or their representative to check whether they are in contact with any siblings, other relatives, or family friends who are mentioned in their records. In the light of what is discovered, it may not be necessary to remove all the information about family members that is contained in the records. Contact details may also be obtained at such a meeting that may enable consent to disclose to be obtained from third parties. In the case of old closed records, third parties may have died. If an individual is dead their personal information is no longer covered by the Act. Third parties may have changed their names or contact details but reasonable efforts to get consent should be made. Some third parties may not consent to the disclosure of their personal information. However, this does not mean that this information cannot be disclosed. The Act makes clear that information about a third party must be disclosed if 'it is reasonable in all the circumstances' to do this without their consent. The impact that disclosure will have on the third party has to be weighed against the impact that non-disclosure will have on the person making the subject access request. Before a final decision is made about what information about third parties should be disclosed, all of the matters that have been considered, and all of the efforts that have made to get consent should be reviewed. Decisions on whether to disclose or not and the reasons behind them should be recorded.

Some social work records will contain information that may be so complex that it needs to be explained and/or be so serious that disclosure may well be a difficult or traumatic experience for the person concerned. *Good practice in these cases is to offer the person the opportunity to consider the information during a supportive interview with a social worker. *See also* ACCESS TO RECORDS; CALDICOTT GUARDIAN; CONFIDENTIALITY; INFORMATION COMMISSIONER'S OFFICE; INFORMATION-GIVING; INFORMATION-SHARING.

data subject *See* DATA PROTECTION.

day care *See* DAY SERVICES.

day centres *See* DAY SERVICES.

day services Encompass a range of *public, *private, and *voluntary provision, covering a wide spectrum of *service user groups (*older people, people with mental health problems, people with *learning disabilities, disabled people, people who are terminally ill, pre-school children). Day care, a term that is gradually passing out of use, is associated with bringing people together into the same location where they might benefit from contact with others and/or participate in activities, sometimes for the purpose of *rehabilitation, for example, after a stroke, and is also associated with giving *carers the opportunity to have a break. Day care is either provided at day centres, for example, those for people with learning disabilities that were previously designated Adult Training Centres and often had work-based activities, or is attached to other services, for example, when it is provided within residential establishments for older people living in their own homes. More recently, there has been a concern in policy and practice to move away from the segregation of *service users in specific locations and towards their integration into *universal services, sometimes with the assistance of former day services staff, and towards the purchase of individualized options using *direct payments or *personal budgets.

With regard to children, the implementation of the Children Act (1989) promoted the expansion of day services in the form of *family centres for them and their parents. In the late 1990s the *Sure Start initiative rapidly expanded day services for the under-fives and their parents, with these services subsequently being incorporated as family centres into mainstream provision. Some family centres only work with children and parents who are referred to them because of specific problems that have been identified, often where there are concerns about *abuse of the children. Such centres may be involved in a range of activities such as supervising *contact between parents and children, contributing to social workers' *child protection assessments, conducting their own *assessments, and running *parenting classes. Many family centres were closed with the onset of *austerity. *See also* DROP-IN CENTRE.

deafblind (deaf-blind) *See* DUAL SENSORY IMPAIRMENT.

Deafblind UK A charity offering a wide range of services to support people with a *dual sensory impairment (combined sight and hearing) and to train professionals and others.

 SEE WEB LINKS
• Official site of Deafblind UK.

deafness *See* HEARING IMPAIRMENT.

death and dying There has been an increasing tendency to bracket together death and dying in order to recognize that the lead-up to someone's death involves processes that need to be understood and addressed. Influential in this regard are the five stages of emotional responses in dealing with dying that were set out in a book by Elisabeth Kübler-Ross (1926–2004), *On Death and Dying*, first published in 1969:

Denial The person who is dying cannot accept this, for example, thinking that there must be some kind of mistake.
Anger Often expressed in terms of 'why me?'

> ***Bargaining*** The person begins to accept that death is inevitable but hopes that s/he can survive for long enough to attend an event that is important to her/him, or to be able to see particular people.
>
> ***Depression*** As the reality of death sinks in, depression may be experienced.
>
> ***Acceptance*** Preparing for death and putting affairs in order.

Not everyone who is dying experiences all five of the responses, nor are they necessarily experienced chronologically. However, recognizing and reacting to the emotional responses of the dying person is crucial, if s/he is not to be prevented from articulating her/his needs and obtaining the support s/he requires. The failure to acknowledge what is happening to and for the dying person can result in a conspiracy of silence in which the person languishes in emotional isolation. *Palliative care was pioneered by the *hospice movement and is a *holistic approach that takes full account of the dying person's emotions and focuses on making dying as pain-free as possible. (Social workers may be part of palliative care teams.) In a multi-ethnic society it is important to recognize that there is a range of culturally-shaped ways of dealing with death and dying, but equally important for social workers not to make assumptions about what these are for the person dying and those close to them. In all aspects of this area of work, great sensitivity is needed in recognizing what is being communicated by the dying person and those close to her/him, and responding openly without embarrassment or awkwardness. *See also* BEREAVEMENT.

Further reading: Kübler-Ross, E. (2008) *On Death and Dying: What the Dying Have to Teach Doctors, Nurses, Clergy, and their Own Families*, Routledge.

debt advice Advice for people in financial difficulty provided through organizations such as *Citizen Advice Bureaux. Advice may include matters pertaining to benefits or tax, or about how to negotiate repayment arrangements with companies to which money is owed. Advisors may move beyond advice-giving into representing the person in debt in relation to creditors or court proceedings.

decarceration Policies that involve releasing people from prisons and using community-based punishments or rehabilitative measures as alternatives to incarceration. *See also* DEINSTITUTIONALIZATION.

decentralization The process of moving social workers and other staff from central locations, such as town or county halls, to local offices. This approach was first advocated by the *Seebohm Report (1968), which accorded a central place to the establishment of *area teams in the new *Social Services Departments it proposed. After area teams were set up there was considerable delegation to this level, rather than direction of their work by senior centrally-based management or by middle managers. As a result, the area teams had a high degree of autonomy, which was consistent with the proposals of the Seebohm Committee concerning the importance of decentralization and delegation. The *Barclay Report (1982) called for decentralization to be taken further and for social work to be located in neighbourhoods, perhaps consisting of just a few streets. Although some *local authorities experimented with decentralized neighbourhood social work, these experiments were short-lived. Following massive Labour Party gains in the early 1980s, during the first Thatcher government, 'urban Left' local authorities developed more integrated decentralized services, for example, bringing together housing and social services in the same local base. In more recent years, some local authorities have developed *'one-stop shops', which offer a first point of contact for all local authority services, and *family centres have offered decentralized access to child health and family support services. With increasing financial stringency and efficiency drives there has been a reduction in the amount of decentralized social work provision and a swing back towards larger teams covering bigger geographical areas, or even one team covering the whole of a local authority, for example, a city council may have one team for *older people across the whole of the city.

decision-making Making decisions or making contributions to decision-making is an integral component of social work. When things go wrong, for example, when decisions concerning the safety and wellbeing of children are examined in detail by *child abuse inquiries, social workers are expected to have made decisions based on what is currently regarded as *good practice and to demonstrate that they were the best decisions that could have been made in the circumstances, though what constitutes good practice may itself be contested. There is also an expectation that decisions will be made in line with any regulations, requirements, and guidelines that have a particular purchase on an area of practice. There is an increasing emphasis on seeking to enable *service users to make as many decisions as possible for themselves, but this is still framed within regulations, requirements, and guidance. *See also* DEFENSIVE PRACTICE.

deconstruction This involves ideas associated initially with the work of the French philosopher Jacques Derrida (1930–2004) in his uncovering of contradictions within texts that had been written in a wide range of disciplines. The conventional focus on the author of a text and the text's obvious meaning(s) are rejected in favour of searching for hidden meanings and assumptions. The 'text' has come to be used to refer to much more than written materials; for example, some would argue that social relations can be treated as a text and be deconstructed. Proponents of deconstruction argue that a primary way in which meaning is constructed is by contrasting what are presented as binary opposites, such as man/woman or white/Black, and that seeing one of these terms as positive (man or white) depends on the negation of the other term (woman or Black). Deconstruction takes apart the processes that have resulted in the setting up of these binary opposites and their presentation as natural and inevitable. As a result, deconstruction undermines the notion that individuals have fixed and stable *identities and that concepts have essential and enduring meanings, for example, as in the binary social worker/service user.

defence mechanisms Psychological responses, postulated by Sigmund Freud (1856–1939) and developed by his daughter Anna (1895–1982) that are seen as performing the function of protecting an individual from anxiety, usually without the awareness of the person utilizing them. Although almost universally depicted as unhealthy, they can be useful in allowing people to function normally when under stress, at least for short periods:

Repression Unwittingly holding down information beneath an individual's conscious awareness, which, nevertheless continues to affect emotional responses; for example, a social worker who has repressed memories of *child abuse that affect her/his current working relationships with *service users. When information is consciously placed out of awareness this is known as suppression.

Sublimation Acting out unacceptable impulses by converting them into a more acceptable form; for example, an individual who experiences anger might take up boxercise as a means of venting her/his frustration.

Reaction formation Reducing anxiety by producing the opposite feeling, impulse, or behaviour; for example, a social worker treating a service user in a very friendly manner, thus disguising her/his dislike of the person.

Intellectualization Responding to anxiety-provoking events in an unemotional way, thus avoiding the stressful aspects and focusing only on the intellectual component. For example, an individual who has been diagnosed with a terminal illness might focus on gaining knowledge about the disease and distance her/himself from what s/he is feeling.

Denial Complete lack of recognition that something has occurred or is occurring; for example, the person who has alcoholism but is unable to see it, or the person who has experienced a trauma but denies that the event that caused it ever occurred.

Projection Attributing qualities or feelings in oneself to other people; for example, a social worker who is insecure seeing a service user as being insecure.

Rationalization Avoiding the reasons for behaving in a certain way or that have resulted in certain occurrences; for example, a social worker who does not have the skills to undertake a particular piece of work might rationalize the lack of progress in terms of the service user's lack of commitment to change.

Displacement Redirecting feelings to people or objects that are less threatening than the people and/or situations that have provoked those feelings; for example, aggression felt by a social worker towards a team manager who has overridden her/his decision may be displaced on to a partner or pet when s/he gets home.

Regression Reverting to patterns of responses used earlier in development; for example, an individual might sulk when unable to get what s/he wants immediately.

Since these defence mechanisms were first outlined by Sigmund and Anna Freud, others have identified further responses to defend the self against anxiety, including:

   *Altruism Satisfying personal needs by helping others.
   Compensation Overachieving in one area to compensate for failure in another.
   Acting out Engaging in actions rather than reflecting on feelings.
   Passive-aggression Expressing anger in a muted or indirect form.
   Avoidance Not dealing with unpleasant situations or difficult relationships.

Much of the language associated with defence mechanisms has passed into popular use, for example, 'S/he's in denial.' The mechanisms are also employed within social work as a way of understanding individual or family dynamics, often without direct awareness of their origins. *See also* PSYCHO-DYNAMIC CASEWORK.

defensive practice Working in a way that avoids *risk as far as possible, following procedures rigidly, and taking primary account of how the practice will appear to someone outside the situation, particularly should things go wrong, so that the social worker would be able to defend her/himself against potential allegations of poor practice. *See also* DECISION-MAKING.

deferred sentence When a court sets a waiting period of up to six months before making a final decision about what sentence to impose for an offence, as long as the offender agrees to this, and the court believes that this is in the interests of justice. If the offender commits another offence during the deferment, s/he will be brought back to court, and the court will deal with sentences for both offences at once. The offender must agree to comply with any requirements concerning her/his conduct that the court imposes for the period of deferment, such as *reparation activities. The *Probation Service oversees the offender's compliance with the requirements and a probation officer prepares a court report in readiness for consideration of sentencing at the end of the deferment period. Failure to comply with a court requirement will result in the offender being brought back to court for sentencing before the deferment period has ended. *See also* COMMUNITY SENTENCES.

deinstitutionalization Moving *older people, people with *learning disabilities, disabled people, and people with mental health problems out of large institutions, usually long-stay hospitals, often built in the Victorian era, into a variety of smaller more community-based settings, such as group homes, foster placements, or independent accommodation. This was justified on humanitarian grounds, after critiques of the negative features of institutions, such as standardization and uniformity, which led to passivity and dependence on the part of inmates, analysed by Russell Barton as *Institutional Neurosis* (1959). Deinstitutionalization received added impetus following a series of scandals about poor standards of provision in institutions in the 1950s and 1960s. It was also advocated on the basis that more community-based provision would be less expensive. Other factors were of particular relevance to specific *service user groups. For example, disabled people campaigned for different lifestyles to those offered in large institutions, advances in medication were significant to the development of deinstitutionalization in the mental health field, and the concept of *normalization played a role in relation to the relocation of people with learning disabilities. For a range of reasons, then, closing institutions attracted the support of social workers and politicians. The results were patchy. Some service users were able to lead a far more satisfying life with the support they needed. Others found themselves poorly prepared for the drastic changes involved in the change in location and some ended up in a 'care-gap', perhaps living rough on the streets, as it proved more expensive than anticipated to provide community resources. *See also* DECARCERATION.

delayed discharge (from hospital) 'Blockages' in the hospital system when patients have been medically assessed as fit for discharge but discharge is delayed and the bed is 'blocked' because the necessary social services are not in place. *Older people are primarily affected and targeted as 'bed-blockers'. This is ageist in deeming older people's needs for careful *discharge planning and proper *rehabilitation as being less significant than those of younger people. In effect it places the blame on older people for the failure to provide appropriate and timely services for them.

Hospitals receive payments for individual patients, regardless of the amount of time they occupy a bed, so this increases the incentive for hospitals to increase their rates of admission, which, in turn, necessitates speedier discharges. Accelerated discharges have direct consequences on the demand for community care services. Concerns with targets and budgets have led to a focus on the speed of discharge. Factors unrelated to whether the patient is ready to be discharged, such as pressure on beds, influence decision-making, which is primarily in the hands of doctors, with the role of social workers being seen as to respond quickly to pressure for discharge, leaving them with limited time to see the person concerned. However, the level and quality of post-discharge support services is crucial to achieving positive outcomes. With increased pressures on social workers to bring about the swift discharge of (mainly older) people from hospital, the consequences may be that they are discharged directly to *care homes without the benefit of a period of rehabilitation that might have enabled them to recover sufficiently to return home. Alternatively, they may be discharged home before they are ready, creating physical, psycho-logical, and emotional risks, the prospect of early readmission and imposition of additional pressure on *carers. The central focus for practitioners can easily become managerial-driven processes and requirements pertinent to their particular organ-ization, such as reaching targets, rather than achieving user-centred outcomes related to their wellbeing. NHS financing, priorities, and provision have a direct impact on social work and 'cost-shunting' can increase inter-agency conflict about boundaries and responsibilities. Different organizational *audit and *performance management systems may also lead to conflicting priorities, as each organization is working to achieve different targets and meet different performance measures, the achievement and meeting of which are likely to be affected, and possibly comprom-ised, by the policies and practices of other organizations. The *voluntary sector may be pushed into the position of compensating for deficits in the statutory system, which in turn may generate pressure on its own resources and undermine its *goals. These factors all threaten to undermine *partnership working, fostering blame and antagonism, rather than collaborative goodwill between *agencies. For hospital discharge services to be effective in terms of both conserving costly resources and promoting *independence, an integrated whole-system approach is needed. Unless these services are supported by adequate and appropriate provision at other stages in the service pathway, including *preventive and longer-term rehabilitative sup-port, there is a danger that problems will simply be forced from one part of the system to another by targeted and time-limited intervention.

The concern with accelerating the discharge from acute medical care of (mainly older) people who were assessed as medically fit for discharge resulted in the Community Care (Delayed Discharges) Act (2003), implemented in 2004. The Act introduced a reimbursement policy whereby *local authorities were obliged to reimburse the National Health Service for the costs incurred through 'blocked beds'. This was superseded by a new system introduced by the Care Act (2014) (*see* HOSPITAL DISCHARGE). *See also* DEMOGRAPHIC TIME BOMB.

deliberate self-harm *See* SELF-HARM.

delinquency Sometimes used interchangeably with crime but usually refers to behaviour in which children and young people engage (hence references are often to *juvenile* delinquency) that is troublesome but not seen as serious crime. Delin-quency has also been largely regarded as a passing phase, perhaps involving resistance to dominant values, en route to adulthood. The term is falling into disuse as a consequence of increased attention being paid to what were previously seen as minor infractions through their designation as *anti-social behaviour with specific measures targeted at them such as *anti-social behaviour orders.

delusion A belief considered to be false because it is not based in reality and may be contradicted by other evidence. The belief, often bizarre or irrational, is strongly held and cannot be altered by proof presented that disputes the belief. Delusions are commonly associated with psychotic conditions such as *schizophrenia and may be features of *affective disorders such as *bipolar disorder and severe *depression. They may also be evident in people with brain injuries or brain tumours and in people with *dementia as a result of deterioration of brain tissue. Non-bizarre delusions can be a feature of *delusional disorder.

delusional disorder A mental health disorder characterized by a noticeable system of delusional beliefs that are persistent, of at least one month's duration, and recurrent. They may be bizarre or non-bizarre in content. Types of delusional disorder include grandiose, jealous, persecutory, and mixed. Delusional disorder is diagnosed when the *delusions cannot be better accounted for by another disorder such as schizophrenia. Unlike other psychotic disorders the person with delusional disorder may not appear obviously odd, strange, or markedly impaired in their daily social or family functioning. Therefore individuals may not come to the attention of services unless their delusions result in illegal behaviour, severe distress, or other problems.

dementia A group of symptoms caused by a range of organic disorders that affect the brain. There are around 750,000 people with dementia in the UK with numbers set to rise to one million by 2021. Symptoms include a progressive decline in cognitive functions, including memory, attention, concentration, planning, thinking, problem-solving, language, and the ability to make judgements. Dementia is associated with the ageing process and the clinical definition of senile (i.e. old age) dementia is commonly accepted to be 65 years and older. Dementia can involve the destruction of tissue in any area of the brain, but this is especially prevalent in the frontal lobes, which support *personality and memory. As a consequence, the symptoms of dementia significantly affect personal *identity, which can be distressing to family and friends. Symptoms are progressive and start with a gradual decline in the memory of recent events and the ability to retain new information. This can lead to wandering, disorientation, and confusion. As more brain tissue dies, more complex cognitive functions, such as the capacity for abstract thought, language, and memory, are also affected. Because the frontal lobes also support social behaviour and awareness of social rules, those affected may lose their usual and long-standing social and emotional responses to social situations. Physical and verbal behaviour may become disinhibited and inappropriate, and might include urinary and bowel incontinence. In advanced stages, recognition of friends and family may be entirely lost and personal identity further diminished. Usually this signifies the onset of the final stages of physical withdrawal and a decrease in physical function, which can eventually lead to death from associated illnesses such as bronchopneumonia. The disease is life-shortening, but the life expectancy of a person with dementia is difficult to predict. The progress of the disease can last up to ten years.

Different types of dementia have been identified. *Alzheimer's disease is the most common and involves brain shrinkage and the deposit of a substance that kills brain cells. Age and ageing is the greatest risk factor associated with Alzheimer's. Physical causes can include serious head injury and boxers carry a greater risk of developing Alzheimer's. Some evidence seems to indicate a genetic link but this appears to be very small, while other studies suggested a causative link with aluminium, since discounted. On the whole, firm evidence about causes remains weak. Lewy Body dementia is less common and is related to the ageing of the brain. In Lewy Body dementia, abnormal structures known as Lewy bodies develop gradually inside the brain over several months. Multi-infarct dementia, also known as vascular dementia, is caused by a lack of blood supply (infarction) to the brain, and is often caused by cerebrovascular disease. High blood pressure (hypertension) can also cause small bleeds into the brain; the progress of this type of dementia can be delayed if hypertension is treated. Multi-infarct (vascular) dementia can either develop suddenly and progress rapidly or can take many months to develop. Early onset dementia is far less prevalent and refers to any dementia that begins before the age of 65 years. Individuals can develop dementia, including Alzheimer's, in their 30s, 40s, and 50s. Because it is uncommon, it is difficult to diagnose and can be confused with *depression or a brain tumour. Pick's disease is an uncommon type of dementia that affects adults under the age of 65 years. It is one of a range of uncommon dementias called fronto-temporal dementias and the cause is unknown, although studies indicate there may be a genetic link. Early onset dementia can also be caused by chronic alcoholism and its progress can be reduced by ceasing alcohol intake. Korsakoff's dementia can also result from prolonged excessive alcohol use, which diminishes thiamine levels in the body. Korsakoff's dementia is partially reversible in certain cases.

Drug treatment can help delay the progress of dementia by delaying cognitive damage, but there is no cure. Drug treatments are not always effective and in some cases only a temporary improvement is possible. Individuals with dementia may also develop symptoms of depression, *anxiety, and *psychosis, and are frequently prescribed medication to reduce these symptoms. However, side-effects such as confusion or sedation have attracted criticisms of their use in practice. People who care for individuals with dementia benefit from psychological support and advice, and a support network is important to those with the disorder in addition to drug treatment.

Skills and values for communicating effectively with people with dementia are important for social workers and others working with them. Tom Kitwood has been an influential figure in highlighting the essential 'personhood' of someone with dementia, implying recognition, respect, and trust. He refers to negative interaction with people with dementia as based on 'malignant social psychology', including forms of communication such as treachery (using forms of deception in order to distract or manipulate), disempowerment (not allowing a person to use the abilities that s/he has), and stigmatization (treating someone as a diseased object or outcast). In contrast, Kitwood identifies positive ways of communicating with people with dementia that recognize and affirm personhood. These types of interactions contribute to what he calls 'positive person work'. The positive communications he identifies include recognition (acknowledging someone as a person, by name, affirming her/his uniqueness), facilitation (enabling a person to do what otherwise they would be unable to do), and negotiation (consulting people about their preferences and needs in a way that gives them some degree of power and control). Kitwood's argument is that communication has a central role in sustaining personhood. *See also* ALZHEIMER'S DISEASE; ALZHEIMER'S RESEARCH UK; ALZHEIMER'S SOCIETY.

Further reading: Baldwin, C. and Capstick, A. (2007) *Tom Kitwood: A Critical Reader in Dementia Theory and Practice*, McGraw-Hill.

Dementia Friends People who have undertaken a brief information and awareness-raising session about dementia and who commit to taking practical action, in however small a way, to improve the lives of people with dementia. The scheme is run by the *Alzheimer's Society and originated from the national dementia strategy *Living Well with Dementia* (2009).

democratic-welfare-capitalism A societal arrangement, described by T. H. Marshall (1893–1981), whose term it is, as the 'hyphenated society', in which capitalism is accepted as the economic system and parliamentary democracy as the political system, with the promotion of welfare being a function of the state as it constrains the imbalances produced by capitalism in order to promote social stability. This requires balancing the socially divisive effects of market-based inequalities with the integrative experience of social solidarity. Marshall laid a strong stress on the hyphen between 'welfare' and 'capitalism'. There was a private market and there were public services, with the latter seen as a means of attempting to stabilize capitalism and regulate, at least to some extent, its impact on people's lives. Social work was established by and firmly embedded in the post-war social democratic *welfare state, as a component in the 'hyphenated society' of democratic-welfare-capitalism, and until the mid-1970s it was insulated from the market and to a large extent from political intervention. *See also* NEO-LIBERALISM.

d

demographic time bomb A pejorative way of referring to the increasing proportion of *older people in the population that represents them as dependent people for whom 'wasteful' social and economic provision has to be made by the rest of society because they represent a *'burden of care'. This concern about the consequences of population ageing is rooted in political anxiety about the costs of welfare provision. At times, something approaching a *'moral panic' has been engendered by lurid accounts of the dire consequences of older people continuing to be a 'drain' on the public purse and costing the young dear in terms of paying for older people's support. Running parallel with this concern about the costs of population ageing has been the promotion of the virtues of self-responsibility and self-reliance, with 'dependency' on others being seen as having very negative cultural connotations. This perspective on population ageing ignores the ways in which older people (as *carers for other older people and children) are resources for, rather than consumers of, welfare, and deflects attention from their rights as citizens. *See also* DEPENDENCE; DEPENDENCY RATIO; INTER-GENERATIONAL CONTRACT.

demonization Extreme negative responses to a particular group of people, for example, as encountered in the tabloid press, in which social workers may be demonized by being portrayed as universally inept, meddling, and misguided. It serves to distract attention from problems or issues that need to be addressed.

dependence (dependency) Simultaneously being connected and subordinated to someone or something; often contrasted with *independence, which is seen as a state of autonomy and self-reliance. In recent years the issue of whether welfare measures, including social work, induce a state of dependency in people has been a central political concern, particularly with regard to people in receipt of social security benefits, the latter issue often being criticized as a key element in a growing 'culture of dependency'. However, dependency is used in more specific contexts. It can refer to women's economic dependence on men. For example, the *Beveridge Report assumed the existence of the *nuclear family in which the husband supported the wife financially. Feminists highlighted and challenged the way in which such assumptions limited the autonomy and options of women, as in the case of women who had experienced *violence. In social work, there may be reference to 'emotional dependency' in situations in which someone is in a relationship that is thought to be damaging, but it seems impossible for them to break the connection with the other person. Dependency is also a key theme in relation to drug and alcohol use, and services that attempt to counter people's *addiction to them. There has been growing concern about the 'dependency' of *older people (*see* BURDEN OF CARE; DEMOGRAPHIC TIME BOMB). Thus, the *goal of recent policy for older people to rely on services from the market instead of the state is referred to as being independent, not being dependent on the market. The construction of a binary opposite (*see* DECONSTRUCTION) between dependency and independence undermines the possibility of thinking about relationships in terms of *interdependence, a concept that is potentially more helpful in social work. *See also* DEPENDENCY RATIO.

dependency ratio A way of referring to the age composition of the population in terms of the number of young and old 'dependents', divided by the population of working age, not those actually working. The precise way in which the ratio is calculated varies, for example: the number under 16 plus the number 65 and over divided by the number 16–64, or the number under 20 plus the number 60 and over divided by the number 21–59. The increasing proportion of *older people in the population has focused the spotlight on them, rather than children and young people, so that calculations of the dependency ratio are now also produced that compare the number of working age with the number of non-working age, which can be misleading because of the increasing fluidity between the two categories. *See also* BURDEN OF CARE; DEMOGRAPHIC TIME BOMB; INTER-GENERATIONAL CONTRACT.

depot *See* DEPOT MEDICATION.

depot anti-psychotics *See* DEPOT MEDICATION.

depot injection *See* DEPOT MEDICATION.

depot medication A way of administering medication as an injection that results in long-acting, slow, and consistent release of the prescribed drug. It is most commonly associated with the medical treatment of people with mental health problems. Injections are usually intra-muscular and administered into the buttocks by a doctor or nurse. Medications most commonly administered by injection are older ('first-generation') anti-psychotics such as Modecate, Haldol, and Depixol. These can have unpleasant side effects such as lasting pain at the site of the injection, feelings of restlessness, dizziness upon standing, weight gain, blurred vision, memory impairment, sexual dysfunction, sedation, and stiffness in the limbs, neck, or mouth. Long-term effects can be irreversible in some people and include involuntary twitches around the mouth, known as tardive dyskinesia. It is also possible to receive newer anti-psychotic medication in depot form, such as Risperdal, Consta, and Abilify. These tend to be less associated with side effects. Depot injections are normally prescribed to people who may be unable to take oral medication on a daily basis or where daily oral dosage is impractical. The *service user's compliance with medication is often a clinical consideration in the decision to administer drugs by injection. A significant disadvantage is that any adverse effects of injected drugs are not immediately reversible. Pre-treatments with small test doses are, therefore, usually administered to assess tolerability. Depot medication is administered in accordance with strict clinical prescribing guidelines and as part of a range of interventions available to the service user as part of their *care plan. There should be written evidence of the person's consent to receive the treatment, or if detained under the Mental Health Act (1983), evidence that the person's consent to treatment exists. Although depot medication is predominantly associated with psychiatry, it is used in other fields, for example, prostate cancer patients being treated with hormone therapy are given depot injections and depot contraception can be prescribed as an alternative to oral contraception.

depression A group of common mental disorders characterized by mood change, hence sometimes referred to as mood or *affective disorder. Symptoms of depression include low mood such as prolonged sadness and a *loss of interest and enjoyment in ordinary experiences. These symptoms can impair emotional and physical wellbeing, and may also include feelings of guilt or low self-worth, disturbed sleep or appetite, irritability, low energy, pessimism, withdrawal, chronic physical pain, poor motivation, and poor concentration. Different types of depression are associated with specific psychiatric disorders such as *bipolar disorder (manic depression), post-natal depression, and clinical or major depression. However, symptoms of depression can be experienced by an individual at any age in the absence of a diagnosis of serious psychiatric disorder. There are three clinical categories which indicate levels of severity and which tend to guide intervention: mild, moderate, or severe. Mild depression may last for a few days or weeks, and if necessary can be treated by the individual's *general practitioner with anti-depressant medication. Moderate depression may require additional psycho social support that enables an individual to continue their employment, and social and domestic lives. If the severity increases or the duration of the episode is prolonged, clinical intervention may be necessary as the risk of *suicide is greater with severe (major) depression. Public understanding of and attitudes towards depression have tended to be dismissive, and individuals with depression can be perceived to have a weakness in succumbing to moods that should be shaken off, and yet without treatment the condition can be disabling and persist for years.

deprivation Taking something away from someone or their not having something that would be expected to be present, for example, as in Bowlby's concept of *maternal deprivation. Also used in relation to whole communities—'deprived community'—to reflect a lack of economic resources.

Deprivation of Liberty Safeguards (DoLS) The Deprivation of Liberty Safeguards (DoLS) were introduced into the Mental Capacity Act (2005) by the Mental Health Act (2007) and came into force in April 2009. The DoLS are intended to protect the human rights of people who lack the *capacity to consent to care or treatment in a hospital or care home, when they receive care that amounts to a *deprivation of liberty (as defined by Article 5, Right to Liberty, *Human Rights Act [1998]). When introduced, the DoLS applied to incapacitated adults (over 18) with a *mental disorder or disturbance of the mind, which can include profound *learning disability, who were deprived of their liberty in a hospital, residential care, or nursing home, but who were not subject to the provisions of the Mental Health Act (1983). The Safeguards, developed in response to the *Bournewood Gap, protect someone who lacks capacity to consent to detention by providing a formal *assessment process in connection with authorizing deprivation of liberty. When a hospital or care home wishes to keep someone in circumstances that amount to deprivation of liberty, authorization must be obtained. Anyone subject to an assessment is entitled to an Independent Mental Capacity Advocate (*see* CAPACITY) and to a Relevant Person Representative to represent their wishes and feelings. Everyone who is subject to a deprivation of liberty authorization will be appointed a Representative, who must maintain contact with them in person, and represent and support them in all related matters, including requesting a review or applying to the Court of Protection to present a challenge to a DoLS authorization. If there is no family member, friend, or informal carer suitable to be the Representative, a paid Representative will be appointed. Through the Advocate or Representative, the person can apply to the Court of Protection to challenge a decision authorizing deprivation of liberty or any part of the process.

In March 2014, a ruling of the *Supreme Court (in the cases of *P v Cheshire West and Chester Council and another* and *P and Q v Surrey County Council*) had a significant impact on decisions about arrangements made for the care and/or treatment of people who might lack the capacity to consent to their living arrangements. The ruling concerned the criteria for judging whether the living arrangements of a person without capacity amount to deprivation of her/his liberty. The Court widened these criteria by setting out a revised test. It stated that when people lack capacity to consent to *care or treatment arrangements and they are the responsibility of the state, the issue of whether they are deprived of their liberty should be determined by asking two questions:

Is the person subject to continuous supervision and control?

All three elements must be present: the oversight must be continuous (though it does not have to be 'in line of sight'), it must amount to supervision, and it must have a clear element of control.

AND

Is the person free to leave?

The person may not be asking to go or showing by their actions that they want to go but the issue is about how staff would react if the person did try to leave or if relatives/friends asked to remove them.

The Supreme Court held that a deprivation of liberty can also occur in domestic/home-type settings where the state is responsible for making such arrangements. This can include a placement in a supported living arrangement in the community or situations where a person is intensively supported in their own home. These deprivations of liberty must be authorized by the Court of Protection.

The Supreme Court also ruled that the following factors, which were previously seen as relevant to decisions about deprivation of liberty, should no longer be taken into consideration:

- The person's compliance or lack of objection;
- The suitability or relative normality of the placement (after comparing the person's circumstances with another person of similar age and condition);
- The reason or purpose leading to a particular placement.

The Supreme Court ruling extended the scope of the DoLS to many more health and social care *service users than previously. The cases heard by the Supreme Court related to people with *learning disabilities. However, the majority of people who are subject to the DoLS are *older people and the ruling had significant implications for them. The impact of the judgment's extension of the definition of deprivation of liberty has been a substantial increase in the number of DoLS applications. *Local authorities have struggled to cope with the increased volume of work, and to adhere to the statutory timescales.

A further judgment, by the *Court of Protection in January 2016 (*Birmingham City Council v D*), widened the Supreme Court's test to include 16- and 17-year-olds who lack *capacity. It also widened the accountability of the state in relation to the test so that it applies to all those people who may be deprived of their liberty in the community, whose deprivation of liberty the state has a duty to authorize. This does not just apply to persons who are in receipt of an *assessment and/or a *care package but to anyone 'who lacks capacity to decide on their place of care and residence, is under continuous supervision and control and is not free to leave'. Accordingly this judgment widened the test to include private living arrangements.

If an assessment is made that the living arrangements of a person who lacks capacity amount to a deprivation of liberty, this must be authorized through the Deprivation of Liberty Safeguards process (for hospitals and care homes) or the Court of Protection (for domestic settings). Once agreed, the deprivation of liberty must be subject to regular independent checks.

What is referred to as the 'managing authority' is the body managing the care of the adult concerned; for example, the managing authority may be a care home. Where a managing authority thinks it needs to deprive someone of their liberty under the test, it has to request the authorization from what is referred to as the 'supervisory body'. It can do this up to twenty-eight days in advance of when it plans to deprive the adult of their liberty. The supervisory body supervises the assessment process and signs off the final order. The local authority where the person is *ordinarily resident is the supervisory body for care homes. This will usually be the local authority for the area in which the care home is situated, unless the person is funded by a different local authority. The local *Clinical Commissioning Group is the supervisory body for hospitals.

When a managing authority (care home) requests a 'standard authorization', it is sent to the supervisory body, which has twenty-one days in which to decide whether the person can be deprived of their liberty. Before a local authority, as the supervising authority, can grant an authorization, it will arrange the following assessments:

- mental health assessment: to confirm whether the person has an impairment/disturbance in the mind or brain;
- eligibility assessment: to confirm the person's existing or potential status under the Mental Health Act (1983), and whether it would conflict with a DoLS authorization;
- mental capacity assessment: carried out by either the Mental Health Assessor or *Best Interests Assessor to determine the person's capacity to consent to the care proposed;
- best interests assessment: to confirm whether deprivation of liberty is occurring, whether it could be avoided, and whether it is in the person's best interests. The Best Interests Assessor also recommends how long the authorization should last and who should act as a person's representative throughout the period of authorization;
- no refusals assessment: to confirm whether there is any valid advance decision which would conflict with the authorization, or whether a person has a valid and registered *Lasting Power of Attorney (*see* CAPACITY) with authority over welfare decisions.

If any of the above conditions are not met, deprivation of liberty cannot be authorized. This may mean the care home has to change its *care plan. If all the conditions are fulfilled, the supervisory body must authorize the deprivation of liberty, for up to one year. The supervisory body must inform the adult and the managing authority in writing. The restrictions should cease as soon as the adult no longer requires them; they do not have to be in place for the full period of the authorization. The supervisory body can set certain conditions on the authorization, which must be fulfilled by the managing authority. At the end of the authorization period, if it is believed the adult still needs to be deprived of their liberty, the managing authority must request another authorization.

If it is believed an adult needs to be deprived of her/his liberty before the supervisory body can respond to a standard authorization request, the managing authority can use an urgent authorization. The managing authority can deprive a person of her/his liberty for up to seven days using an urgent authorization. It can only be further extended (up to another seven days) if the supervisory body agrees to such a request from the managing authority. When requesting an urgent authorization, the managing authority must also request a standard authorization.

The managing authority must reasonably believe a standard authorization would be granted when requesting an urgent authorization.

Before granting an urgent authorization, the managing authority should try to speak to the family, friends, and carers of the person. Information they provide may assist in preventing the adult being deprived of their liberty. Efforts to contact family and friends and any discussions had with them should be documented in the person's case records.

Applications to authorize a deprivation of liberty in the community are made to the Court of Protection. In most cases this involves a paper-based application that does not require a court hearing.

A care home or hospital must monitor and review the care needs of an adult with a DoLS authorization on a regular basis and report any changes in needs or circumstances that would affect the authorization or any of the conditions attached to it. A care home or hospital must request a DoLS review if:

- the person no longer meets any of the qualifying requirements;
- the reasons the person meets the qualifying requirements have changed;
- it would be appropriate to add, amend, or delete a condition placed on the authorization due to a change in the person's situation;
- the person or their representative has requested a DoLS review, which they are entitled to do at any time.

Further reading: Lord Chancellor (2008) *Deprivation of Liberty Safeguards: Code of Practice to Supplement the Main Mental Capacity Act (2005) Code of Practice.* Available at: http://webarchive.nationalarchives.gov.uk/20130107105354/http://www.dh.gov.uk/prod_consum_dh/groups/dh_digitalassets/@dh/@en/documents/digitalasset/dh_087309.pdf.

deprofessionalization A reduction in professional discretion and control over practice. What does reduced discretion and lack of control over work mean in a professional context? Following Braverman's work on *deskilling, writers have identified two components of control in a professional setting: lack of control over the process of work; and lack of control over the use to which work is put. The first component is about the means, and the second component is about the ends of professional work. Employed professionals have traditionally had a considerable degree of autonomy about how they go about their work so long as the *goals of their work are aligned with their employing organization's interests. For example, in the post-war *welfare state, social workers' concerns for the *wellbeing of *service users could be accommodated in forms of practice that served the purposes of the state, for example, through carrying out legislative mandates, and the welfare state gave considerable discretion to professionals in how they undertook their work in return for their working towards state goals. From the advent of the *New Right onwards, a process of deprofessionalization ensued in that not only did control over the goals of social work tighten but also so did the control over the means by which social work was undertaken, through the introduction of information technology systems and technocratic systems of *care management that rationalized practice, resulting in the *deskilling of social work, and the curtailment of discretion. In addition, successive reforms of social work education have focused on training and assessing students against first *competencies, and then *key roles, means of classification by which social work is broken down into sets of functional tasks.

deputy *See* CAPACITY; COURT OF PROTECTION.

desensitization *See* BEHAVIOUR MODIFICATION.

deserving poor The impact of the Poor Law Amendment Act (1834) was to divide poor people into the deserving poor (for example, *older people, widows, disabled people), who were seen as responsive to charitable assistance, and the undeserving poor (for example, single mothers, the unemployed), who were to be consigned to the workhouse. Ideas concerning who is seen as deserving of assistance and who is seen as needing to be disciplined have persisted, though precisely who is placed in which category can vary. *See also* CHARITY ORGANISATION SOCIETY; POOR LAW.

deskilling Designing work processes so that they are fragmented into smaller, less skilled tasks that are more susceptible to managerial coordination and control. The most celebrated critique of trends in the deskilling of work is that of Harry Braverman in *Labor and Monopoly Capital* (1998, first published 1974). He sought to counter the apparent neutrality of management techniques and argued that they are moulded in a direct way by the demands of capitalism through the deliberate control and deskilling of labour, with the employers' need to maximize profits dictating the necessity of gaining control over work processes. As part of this strategy, the scope for workers' control of and discretion in undertaking work had to be severely limited. As a result, only managers have a grasp of the overall business, with the workers engaged in fulfilling their fragmented roles, a process that Braverman described as the separation of conception and execution, of thinking and doing. As execution becomes increasingly separated from conception, the bulk of employees are involved in simple mundane tasks. Some writers have drawn on Braverman's thesis and argued that social workers have been subjected to deskilling, with some of the *radical social work literature of the 1970s and early 1980s referring to the 'industrialization' of social work, with the introduction of *Social Services Departments or *'Seebohm factories', as they were sometimes called. The Conservative governments' advocacy of the three 'e's—*economy, efficiency, and effectiveness—in the public sector during the 1980s and 1990s resulted in more overt control over the process of social work, eroding the previous distinction between the *private and *public sector with regard to the way in which work was organized and managed. This trend intensified under *New Labour governments with the use of *information technology for the surveillance and *rationalization of social workers' practice, and the drive for productivity in social work pursued by the emphasis on *performance indicators, *audit, *inspections, and star-rating systems. Some argue that deskilling is most advanced in the introduction of *call centres into social work and that in this setting the separation of conception and execution of work is sharply defined, with managerial surveillance and control being at its most explicit. Critics of Braverman's account of deskilling, and of its derivatives in fields like social work, have argued that it pays insufficient attention to subjectivity and individual agency, portraying workers as essentially passive in the face of managerial subordination. *See also* DEPROFESSIONALIZATION; FRAGMENTATION OF ROLES AND TASKS.

Further reading: Harris, J. (2003) *The Social Work Business*, Routledge.

detention Depriving an individual of her/his liberty. **1.** The police can arrest people they suspect of criminal offences and keep them in detention for set periods (Police and Criminal Evidence Act 1984). If a custodial sentence is passed on conviction for a criminal offence, this can be referred to as a period of detention.

2. Outside of criminal processes, someone with mental health problems can be subject to a period of detention in psychiatric provision (Mental Health Act 1983).

3. Detention can also refer to a child or young person being kept at school after the end of the school day, usually in secondary schools, for misbehaviour or being late. Parents have to be given 24 hours' notice. *See also* COMPULSORY ADMISSION; DEPRIVATION OF LIBERTY SAFEGUARDS; DETENTION AND TRAINING ORDER.

Detention and Training Order (DTO) The main *custodial sentence for young people aged between 12 and 17. The DTO (made under the Powers of Criminal Courts [Sentencing] Act [2000]) is a two-part sentence served partly in custody, and partly under supervision in the community by a *Youth Offending Team, with a strong emphasis on training and *rehabilitation. It has a minimum term of four months and a maximum of two years. Early release of one or two months is possible depending on the length of the sentence, and someone who is released early is monitored using an electronic tag. A court can only make a DTO if the offence is punishable with imprisonment in the case of a person aged 21 or over, or the court decides only a custodial sentence reflects the seriousness of the offence, or where the person is aged 12–15 at the time of conviction and is a persistent offender. Young people under the age of 18 who are found guilty of the most serious crimes, such as murder and serious assaults, can be detained for longer periods. *See also* DETENTION; ELECTRONIC TAGGING; LOCAL AUTHORITY SECURE CHILDREN'S HOME; REHABILITATION ORDER; SECURE TRAINING CENTRE; YOUNG OFFENDERS' INSTITUTION.

determinism The theories, and accounts and explanations of behaviour based upon them, which contend that people have little or no conscious choice over what they do because they are shaped by forces or processes that are beyond their control. A concept that is pertinent to social work because the extent to which social workers embrace determinist perspectives will influence how they assess, define, and respond to problems.

detox *See* DETOXIFICATION.

detoxification The process of removing toxins from the body as a consequence of ceasing to use alcohol or some other drug, until the body functions without relying on the substance to which the person was physically addicted. Usually medication is prescribed to assist with the symptoms experienced as withdrawal from the substance occurs, as these effects can be severe. Alongside the detoxification of the body, psychological *dependency on the substance is usually also addressed in individual and/or group sessions. Detoxification can be undertaken while the person continues to live at home, under the medical supervision of a general practitioner, or in an outpatient unit, or may involve admission to a residential detoxification unit. *See also* ADDICTION.

developmental milestones *See* CHILD DEVELOPMENT.

developmental psychology The study of psychological changes that originally focused predominantly on children, and still has a heavy emphasis on childhood and adolescence, but which also encompasses the psychological development of adults and the psychology of ageing. *See also* CHILD DEVELOPMENT; THEORIES OF AGEING.

deviance (deviancy) Can refer to crime, but also used much more widely in relation to breaking social rules and/or flouting conventional expectations, for example, people with mental health problems may be portrayed as deviant. The concept can be powerful in normalizing certain views and actions, and stigmatizing others. For example, heterosexuals can be presented as 'normal' with gay men and lesbian women presented as 'deviant'. In the 1960s the sociological study of deviance questioned its being seen as an inherent attribute and focused instead on societal reaction to it, for example, through the use of *labelling theory. This led to concern with how judgements are made about when deviance has occurred and how rules are applied when it is judged to have occurred. 'Deviancy amplification' described the ways in which the responses of state agents, such as the police, psychiatrists, the courts, and social workers may serve to reinforce a deviant *identity, sustaining that identity rather than deterring the 'deviant' from further acts. For example, taking young offenders to court and imposing a punishment may alienate the young person and make her/him feel more like a criminal and encourage her/him to identify more with others who feel likewise. If the young person reoffends, the official agents feel confirmed in their original view of her/him and the court process is repeated, amplifying the deviance still further (and so on). A policy that attempts to prevent this type of deviancy amplification occurring is *'diversion', which seeks to keep young people who have committed offences out of the courts whenever possible. *See also* SYSTEMS MANAGEMENT.

deviancy amplification *See* DEVIANCE.

devolution The process of passing areas of government from the Westminster Houses of Parliament to the assemblies of *Northern Ireland and *Wales, and to *Scotland's Parliament. This has led to differences in social work policies and practices, a trend that is likely to continue.

devolved budgets Placing the allocation of money for the purchase of services lower in the organizational hierarchy. A core component of the *community care reforms was the idea of placing budgets for *community services in the hands of *care managers so that services that were more responsive to need could be purchased close to the *service user. This was briefly realized in some areas, but almost everywhere budgets still remain in the hands of team managers, or more rarely, are located at the management level above team managers. Wherever the responsibility for agreeing the allocation of money is located, social workers/care managers will be constrained to be 'budget-conscious' especially under the influence of *austerity, assembling *'care packages' on the basis of the unit costs of services within *cash limits. *See also* RESOURCE PANELS.

diagnosis The identification of a specific disorder, syndrome, or disease following a process of clinical *assessment and information-gathering. Usually a diagnosis is made by a doctor, and in the case of mental disorder, a psychiatrist, using medical reference texts or information technology resources to guide professional judgement. However, the concept has also been adopted by some social workers, mainly in North America and particularly in *clinical social work, in relation to the initial processes of engagement and assessment with a *service user and the judgements made through those processes, which serve as the basis for the work undertaken subsequently. The use of the term in social work is contested, with many arguing that it has been borrowed inappropriately from medicine and misused by social work, resulting in a social work version of the *medical model that identifies pathological characteristics of disorders in service users' lives and treats service users as quasi-patients. *See also* DIAGNOSTIC AND STATISTICAL MANUAL OF MENTAL DISORDERS; INDIVIDUAL PATHOLOGY; INTERNATIONAL CLASSIFICATION OF DISEASES.

Further reading: Corcoran, J. and Walsh, J. (2006) *Clinical Assessment and Diagnosis in Social Work Practice*, Oxford University Press.

Diagnostic and Statistical Manual of Mental Disorders (DSM or DSM-5)
One of two reference texts containing standardized criteria for the classification of mental disorder and used in the UK by psychiatrists to assist the process of *diagnosis. (The other reference text used is the *International Classification of Diseases*: *ICD* or *ICD-10*.) First published by the American Psychiatric Association in 1952, the fifth edition of the *DSM* was published in 2013. Mental disorders are classified in groups or syndromes based on clusters of symptoms. If a pattern of symptoms experienced by a person fits the criteria set out by a classification, such as *bipolar disorder or *schizophrenia, a diagnosis will be made. Classifications are also used by psychiatrists to guide decisions about treatment and to predict outcomes. Each revision of the manual has included more classifications of mental disorder, though some controversial classifications, such as homosexuality, have been removed. Social workers do not use the *DSM*. However, for social workers in mental health settings, awareness of the use of the *DSM* and familiarization with its features can assist in understanding the process of psychiatric diagnosis.

dialectical behaviour therapy (dialectical behavioural therapy) (DBT)
Based on *cognitive behavioural therapy techniques, which it combines with elements of *mindfulness. It is increasingly used in mental health services with people who have borderline *personality disorder (BPD). The aim is to help people to modify patterns of behaviour that are unhelpful, such as self-harm and substance misuse. The therapy focuses on the intense emotional arousal that many people with BPD experience. It encourages people to understand more about the triggers that lead to these responses and to develop a greater degree of emotional regulation. DBT helps people to develop coping skills that they can apply in practice when they experience emotional surges. *See also* BEHAVIOURAL FAMILY THERAPY; FAMILY THERAPY.

diaspora
The dispersal of a people who originated in a particular geographical location to different parts of the world. Originally used in relation to Jewish people, a number of other ethnic groups are now considered as diasporas, maintaining a sense of solidarity and keeping their cultures alive, despite being dispersed widely. However, questions of *identity within a diaspora community may be complex and diverse, as social workers often discover, particularly when working with young people.

difference
The generation of any social category (women, *older people, etc.) can lead to the assumption that all of those within a particular category are the same. For example, early second-wave *feminism emphasized the sameness of those within the category of 'woman' and their difference from men, whereas later feminism moved towards exploring different and distinctive women's voices, and emphasized the differences of and intersections between age, *class, *disability, *ethnicity, *'race', and sexuality. Thus, in some cases, those within a category will have a strong sense of sharing key aspects of *identity with people outside the category as much as or more than with those within it and, as a consequence, will experience themselves as different from others who are placed within the same category. For example, a Black or disabled identity may be more salient for a person's sense of self than being placed within the category of older people. As well as assuming sameness, social categories also tend to separate certain groups from others. This *'othering' process can be used as a basis for *exclusion and

subordination, with certain categories of people having a negative social evaluation applied to them because they are seen as different (*see* DECONSTRUCTION; SOCIAL CONSTRUCTIONISM). To counteract this tendency, some postmodernist ideas have stressed the plurality of difference, rather than its operation in the binary opposition of the 'other'.

The concept of difference has occupied a central position in social work in recent years, with social workers' being enjoined to inform their understandings of people's experiences and situations in the light of their *diversity rooted in difference, making no assumptions about the precise way in which difference operates in particular situations, or about how difference is experienced by the individuals concerned. Accordingly, recognizing and valuing difference has become the central component of *anti-oppressive practice. However, concentrating solely on individual differences can obscure shared interests, weakening the potential for people to acquire strength through uniting against common sources of injustice and oppression. In this respect, the social construction of alternative identity categories, such as, in the case of older people, the Gray Panthers, or Hell's Geriatrics, challenges dominant discourses in potentially empowering ways. Some writers have suggested that instead of seeing 'unity' and 'diversity' as opposites, we could talk about 'unity in diversity' or 'diversity in unity', with people from diverse backgrounds seen as unified on the basis of their shared experience of marginalization and devalued identities. While this approach has much to offer, it rests upon the significance of culturally constructed and negotiable identities. Material differences rooted in *class result in significant differences and inequality that this approach finds difficult to address. As a consequence, class is rarely given the same attention in social work, if it is given any attention at all. If class is addressed, it is seen as being capable of accommodation as simply another difference, another aspect of individual identity. In some approaches to difference, there is little recognition that the existence of difference—any difference, not just class—takes place within power relations. More critical approaches assert that differences between people belong to and are located in the social divisions created by the economic, ideological, and political world and that difference results from the power relationships that are embedded in these divisions. *See also* DISTINCTION; DIVERSITY.

differently abled An alternative to 'disabled' or *'disability', as in 'a differently abled person' instead of 'a disabled person', that seeks to move away from the notion of deficit that can be imputed to 'disabled', and towards a more positive connotation of *difference between people. *See also* ABLE-BODIEDISM; DISABILITY; DISABLISM.

digital government *See* ELECTRONIC GOVERNMENT.

dignity (being treated with) Usually seen in social work as a *service user's right to be treated with respect on the basis that s/he has inherent human rights. *See also* CODES OF PRACTICE; DIGNITY IN CARE; HUMAN RIGHTS.

Dignity in Care A campaign initiated in 2006 by the Department of Health in response to evidence of the persistence of negative cultural attitudes towards *older people, reflected in poor standards of practice, in particular, lack of respect and dignity in the way older people are treated in hospitals. The campaign declared the intention 'to put dignity at the heart of care'. After holding listening events about what dignity in care meant to people, the 'Dignity Challenge' stated that high-quality services that respect people's dignity should:

- Have zero tolerance of all forms of abuse;
- Support people with the same respect you would want for yourself or a member of your family;
- Treat each person as an individual by offering a personalized service;
- Enable people to maintain the maximum possible level of *independence, *choice, and control;
- Listen and support people to express their needs and wants;
- Respect people's right to privacy;
- Ensure people feel able to complain without fear of retribution;
- Engage with family members and *carers as care partners;
- Assist people to maintain confidence and positive self-esteem;
- Act to alleviate people's loneliness and isolation.

The Dignity in Care Campaign has continued as a freestanding *network, based on these ten principles, and has over 60,000 individual and organizational supporters. The network seeks to change the culture of services and emphasizes improving the quality and experience of them, in hospitals, community services, and care homes.

(⊕) SEE WEB LINKS
- Official site of the Dignity in Care Network.

direct action Protests that confront and challenge attitudes, *ideologies, or decisions with varying levels of conflict but usually falling short of the advocacy of *violence. For example, people with disabilities who have thrown themselves from their wheelchairs into the road in protest at the physical barriers to having equal access that they face.

Directions Hearing A court hearing that is held before a full hearing that enables a court to give directions to the parties about how the case should proceed. The precise purpose of such a hearing is determined by the nature of the case, but generally a Directions Hearing will be concerned with issues relating to the provision of evidence and the timetabling of the proceedings. However, in a *family court directions can be issued on any matter relevant to the welfare of the child, including *contact, *residence, and any other specific issues that the court considers need to be explored to assist it in arriving at decisions about the child, including whether a court order needs to be made. A Directions Hearing may be held in respect of a child subject to *public law proceedings (for example, an application by a *local authority for a *care order or *supervision order), or *private law proceedings (for example, where divorcing parents are contesting issues of *contact and *residence).

direct payment Following campaigns by *disability activists, who saw direct payments as a means of gaining greater control over their lives and escaping institutionalized services, the Community Care (Direct Payments) Act (1996) introduced monetary payments made by *local authorities to individuals to meet some or all of their *eligible *care and support *needs (at that time under Section 47 of the NHS and Community Care Act, [1989]) in order to enable them to purchase their own services, rather than having services arranged by the local authority. Initially, people over the age of 65 were excluded from receiving direct payments and local authorities only had a *power, rather than a *duty, to make payments to them. Additional regulations extended direct payments to *older people in 2000. Then, the Health and Social Care Act (2001, Sections 57 and 58) superseded the Community

Care (Direct Payments) Act (1996). It placed a duty on local authorities to make direct payments to *service users who fulfilled the criteria and consented to receiving a direct payment 'equivalent to the reasonable cost of securing the provision of the services concerned' (Health and Social Care Act 2001, Section 57). The Adult Social Care Green Paper, *Independence, Well-Being, and Choice* (Department of Health 2005), advocated increasing the use of direct payments. The Green Paper's proposals were taken forward in the White Paper, *Our Health, Our Care, Our Say* (Department of Health 2006), which announced the intention of increasing the take-up of direct payments, requiring local authorities to be proactive in their promotion of direct payments as a first option with everyone, at each assessment and each review. The Carers and Disabled Children Act (2000) extended direct payments to *carers and to 16- and 17-year-old disabled young people for services to meet their assessed needs. Since then, in government policy, most notably the Care Act (2014) under which direct payments are now provided, they have increasingly been the preferred means of providing personalized care and support. They are seen as providing *independence, *choice, and control by enabling people to meet their eligible needs through *commissioning their own care and support. (What follows is written to address how direct payments operate for people in need of care and support but is equally applicable to carers' support needs.)

The availability of direct payments should be included in the *information and advice service that a local authority provides. The information about direct payments should set out:

- what direct payments are;
- how to request one, including the use of a nominated person (someone who agrees to manage a direct payment on behalf of a person with *capacity) or an authorized person (someone who agrees to manage a direct payment for a person who lacks capacity) to manage the payment;
- explanation of the direct payment agreement and how the local authority monitors the use of the direct payment;
- the responsibilities involved in managing a direct payment and being an employer;
- making arrangements with social care providers;
- signposting to local organizations such as *voluntary and *user-led organizations and the local authority's own support which offer assistance to direct payment holders;
- information about local providers;
- case studies and evidence on how direct payments can be used locally to meet needs innovatively.

This information is geared to making people fully aware about what direct payments are so that they can decide whether they are interested in them. In addition to provision of this general information, during the *care and support planning process an explanation is given to people about how needs can be met by direct payments. As a result, most requests to receive direct payments occur during the care and support planning stage but requests for direct payments can be considered at any time. For example, a person may request a direct payment before a scheduled *review and, if so, it can be considered at the same time as the care and support plan is reviewed, with the review brought forward, if necessary, so that the consideration of the direct payment request is not delayed.

The steps followed after receiving a request for a direct payment depend on whether the person has been assessed as having *capacity to make a decision about direct payments or not, which will have taken place as part of the *assessment of *needs. Where the person has capacity to make a request for direct payments to cover some or all of her/his care needs, four conditions have to be met fully. A failure to meet any one of them will result in the person's request for a direct payment being declined. The conditions are:

- The adult has capacity to make the request, and where there is a nominated person, that person agrees to receive the payments.
- The local authority is not prohibited (by regulations under Section 33 of the Care Act) from meeting the adult's needs by making direct payments to the adult or nominated person.
- The local authority is satisfied that the adult or nominated person is capable of managing direct payments, either by himself or herself or with whatever help the authority thinks the adult or nominated person will be able to access.
- The local authority is satisfied that making direct payments to the adult or nominated person is an appropriate way to meet the needs in question.

The person requesting the direct payment can ask for it to be received by a nominated person, in which case that person is involved as appropriate in the care planning process, such as in the development of the care plan, as long as the person with care needs agrees. Where the person does not request the nominated person's involvement, the local authority should consider whether to encourage the person to make that request. During this process, the nominated person is given information and advice on managing the direct payment, so that s/he understands her/his legal obligations as the direct payment recipient to act in the *best interests of the person requiring care and support.

In cases where the person in need of care and support has been assessed as lacking capacity to request a direct payment, an authorized person can request the direct payment on the person's behalf. In these cases, the local authority must satisfy itself that five conditions are met in full. Failure to meet any of the conditions will result in the request being declined. The conditions are:

- Where the person requesting the direct payment is not authorized under the Mental Capacity Act (2005) but there is at least one person who is so authorized, the person who is authorized supports the person's request.
- The local authority is not prohibited by regulations under Section 33 of the Care Act from meeting the person's needs by making direct payments to the authorized person, and if regulations under that section give the local authority discretion to decide not to meet the adult's needs by making direct payments to the authorized person, it does not exercise that discretion.
- The local authority is satisfied that the authorized person will act in the person's best interests in arranging for the provision of the care and support for which the direct payments would be used.
- The local authority is satisfied that the authorized person is capable of managing the direct payment by himself or herself or with whatever help or support the authority thinks the authorized person will be able to access.
- The local authority is satisfied that making direct payments to the authorized person is an appropriate way to meet the person's needs in question.

With regard to the fourth condition about the help or support someone needs to manage a direct payment, a local authority must take all reasonable steps to provide this support to whoever requires it. There are usually contracts with voluntary and/or user-led organizations that provide support and advice to people interested in receiving direct payments or to direct payment holders.

After considering the suitability of the person requesting the direct payment against the five conditions, the local authority decides whether to provide a direct payment. When the decision is to make a payment, it is recorded in the care and support plan. When the request is declined, the person in need of care and support, and any other person involved in the request, receive the reasons for rejection of the request in a format that is accessible to them. This sets out which of the five conditions have not been met, the reasons why they have not been met, and what the person may need to do in the future to obtain a positive decision. (The Care and Support [Direct Payments] Regulations [2014] state that direct payments cannot be made to people subject to a court order for a drug or alcohol treatment programme or similar schemes.)

The amount of the direct payment is derived from the *personal budget as set out in the care and support plan and has to be sufficient to meet the needs the local authority has to, or has chosen to, meet. The direct payment amount reflects whether the person is required to make any financial contribution or is requesting a direct payment for only a part of their care and support requirements. The local authority cannot require financial contributions to a direct payment for *after-care services under Section 117 of the Mental Health Act (1983).

Where a direct payment is used to employ a *personal assistant or other staff, the local authority ensures that clear plans are in place for how needs will be met in the event of the personal assistant being absent, for example due to sickness, maternity leave, or on holiday. These should be detailed in the care and support plan. Direct payment holders who are employers are required to comply with the duty to enrol eligible workers into a qualifying workplace pension scheme and to meet the minimum contributions required (more information is available at http://www.thepensionsregulator.gov.uk). They also have to have plans in place for redundancy payments due to circumstances such as moving home, a change in care and support needs, or because of the death of the direct payment holder or care recipient. If the person meets needs by directly employing someone, s/he is responsible for all employment costs including redundancy payments. This is made clear to people as part of the information and advice process before a decision is made by them to request direct payments. The direct payment is set at a level that is sufficient to meet these costs, if it is appropriate for the person to meet their needs by employing someone.

Normally, if someone dies, any employment liabilities are met by the person's estate but with direct payments there is freedom to develop other arrangements, for example using any unspent direct payment to contribute to any redundancy costs, having insurance in place that covers redundancy, or the local authority agreeing to cover redundancy payments through the direct payment amount. Decisions are recorded in care plans. Whatever arrangements are made, the local authority and direct payment holder need to be clear about their responsibilities in order to avoid any disputes at a sensitive time for family and *carers.

All direct payment recipients are given information about having the correct insurance cover in place and are supported in sorting it out so that they understand the benefits that insurance cover can provide and the direct payment should include an amount to cover the cost of employers' liability insurance and any other insurance that is required in order that the person can meet their needs in the way specified in the care plan.

The Care and Support (Direct Payments) Regulations (2014) exclude the direct payment from being used to pay for care from a close family member living in the same household, except where the local authority decides this is necessary.

However, it provides a distinction between 'care' and 'administration/management' of the direct payment. This allows people to pay a close family member living in the same household to provide management and/or administrative support to the direct payment holder in cases where this is necessary. This reflects the fact that in some cases, especially where there are multiple complex needs, the direct payment amount may be substantial. The management and administration of a large payment, along with organizing care and support, can be a complex and time-consuming task. Family members performing this task can be paid a proportion of the direct payment, similar to that paid by direct payment holders to third-party support organizations, as long as the local authority allows this. The local authority has to be satisfied that it is necessary to make the payment to the family member to provide this service and that the direct payment will only be used for administration and management of the payment. The circumstances and payment amount is decided and agreed with the person requiring care and support, the family member, local authority, and an *advocate (if any). These decisions are recorded in the care plan and include the amount of the payments, their frequency, and the activities that are covered. This arrangement is also taken into account during allocation of the personal budget so that the amount remains sufficient to meet the person's needs. An agreement is put in place between all parties about what steps to take in case of a dispute regarding the management of the payment by a household family member. This is especially relevant where the person managing the payment is also the nominated direct payment recipient.

Direct payments can be made to enable people to purchase short stays in care homes, provided that any stay does not exceed a period of four consecutive weeks in any twelve-month period. This can be used to provide a respite break for a carer, for example. When the interim period between two stays in care homes is less than four weeks, the two stays are added together to make a cumulative total, which should also not exceed four weeks if it is to be paid for with direct payments. As long as each stay is less than four weeks and there is an interim period of at least four weeks between two or more stays which added together exceed four weeks, then the service recipient may use their direct payments to pay for residential breaks throughout the year. People can receive additional weeks in a care home once they have reached the four-week maximum. In this situation, they cannot purchase additional weeks using their direct payments, but if the local authority and the person agree that a longer stay is needed, the authority can arrange and fund it. There is no restriction on the length of time for which the local authority may arrange such accommodation.

People who are living in care homes may receive direct payments in relation to non-residential care services. For example, they may have temporary access to direct payments to try out independent living arrangements before making a commitment to moving out of a care home. Direct payments can also be used by people living in care homes to take part in day time activities. Direct payments cannot be used at present for long-term stays in a care home, though the government plans to introduce this in 2020.

When direct payment holders are in hospital, payments do not have to be suspended. Where the direct payment recipient is also the person requiring care and support, consideration is given to how the direct payment may be used in hospital to meet non-health needs or to ensure employment arrangements are maintained. This avoids suspending or even terminating the payment, which may result in the person having to break an employment contract with a trusted personal assistant, causing distress and a lack of continuity of care when they are discharged from hospital. In these circumstances, the local authority explores the options with the person, their carer, and the NHS to ensure that both the health and care and support needs of the person are fully met in the best way possible. For example, the person may prefer the personal assistant to visit hospital to help with their personal care, alongside health staff, especially where there has been a long relationship between the direct payment holder and the personal assistant. In some cases, the nominated or authorized person managing the direct payment may be in hospital, in which case an urgent review is conducted to ensure that the person continues to receive care and support to meet their needs. This may be through a temporary nominated or authorized person or through short-term care and support arranged by the local authority.

As a general rule, direct payments should not be used to pay for local authority-provided services from the person's 'home' local authority. Where a person wishes to receive care and support from their local authority, it is easier to provide the service direct to the person. This also avoids possible conflicts of interest where the local authority would be providing the direct payment and their services for people to purchase. There may be *cases where the local authority exercises discretion to provide care and support by receiving a direct payment amount, for example where a person who is using direct payments wants to make a one-off purchase from the local authority such as a place in day care. Someone can use their direct payment to purchase care and support from a different local authority. For example, a person may live close to local authority boundaries and another local authority may be able to provide a particular service that their 'home' authority does not provide.

Where it is in the person's interest to combine the direct payment with another form of state support (such as personal health budgets), and the person agrees that plans should be combined, consideration is given to whether the person is receiving direct payments from partner organizations, such as the NHS. If so, attempts are made to harmonize the direct payments so that the person does not have multiple payments each with their own monitoring regime. For example, the local authority can work with the NHS partner to agree on a 'lead organization' that oversees the overall budget and monitors the direct payments to ensure they are being used to meet both health and care needs, while still allowing both bodies to satisfy themselves of their statutory responsibilities.

The Care and Support (Direct Payments) Regulations (2014) state that the local authority must review the making of direct payments initially within six months. This is intended to be a 'light-touch review' to ensure that the person is comfortable with using the direct payment, and experiencing no initial issues. It can be incorporated in the initial review of the care and support plan, six to eight weeks after it has been signed off. It includes aspects such as managing and using the direct payment and a discussion of any long-term support arrangements that may be necessary, such as payroll, insurance cover, and third-party support. This review is not a full review of the person's care and support plan. However, if this review raises concerns or requires actions that affect the detail recorded in the care plan, then a full review of the plan is carried out. Following the initial review, no later than six months, the direct payment is reviewed no later than every twelve months. After the six-month review, the annual review of the direct payment will usually be aligned with the general review of the care plan. The reviews must not require information to be provided more often and in more detail than is reasonably required for the purpose of enabling the authority to know that making a direct payment is still an appropriate way of meeting the needs and that the conditions upon which it is made are being met. Monitoring requirements for people who have been managing direct payments without issues for a long period may be lowered. Where a direct payment is allocated to a nominated or authorized person, or where a family member is being paid for management/administrative support, a review includes all of the parties as well as the person in need of care and support in order to ensure the views of everyone involved in the direct payment are heard and any issues can be resolved. The outcomes of the review are recorded and a copy given to all parties. Where there are issues that require resolution, agreement is sought with all parties involved, as far as is reasonably practicable. Where appropriate, people are advised of their rights to access the local authority *complaints procedure.

Direct payments are only terminated as a last resort or where there is clear and serious contradiction of the Direct Payment Regulations or where the conditions (see above) are no longer met, except in cases of fluctuating capacity (see below). All reasonable steps are taken to address any situations without the termination of the payment. Effective, but proportionate, monitoring processes are routinely used to identify potential issues before a termination is necessary. When a direct payment is terminated, the care and support plan is revised to ensure that the plan is appropriate to meet the needs in question.

A person to whom direct payments are made, whether to purchase support for themselves or on behalf of someone else, may decide at any time that they no longer wish to continue receiving a direct payment. In these cases, any outstanding contractual liabilities are considered and the care plan is reviewed to consider alternative arrangements to meet the person's needs. A direct payment is also discontinued if the person no longer appears to be capable of managing it or of managing it with whatever support is necessary. Furthermore, a direct payment is also discontinued when a person no longer needs the support for which the direct payment was made. This might happen in situations where the direct payment was for short-term packages when leaving a care home or hospital. Direct payments for mental health after-care services under Section 117 of the Mental Health Act (1983) also cease when the *Clinical Commissioning Group and the local authority are satisfied that the person concerned is no longer in need of such services.

Direct payments may be discontinued temporarily, for example when an individual does not require assistance for a short period because their condition improves and they do not require the care and support that the direct payments cover. A discussion takes place with the person, their carer, and any other person involved about how best to manage this. The person is allowed to resume responsibility for their own care after the interruption, if that remains their wish, unless there has been a change of circumstances which means that the conditions (see above) are no longer met. If there is a change of circumstances that affects the care and support plan, it is revised to ensure that it is still meeting needs.

A direct payment can also be discontinued if the person fails to comply with a condition to which the direct payment is subject or if for some reason the local authority no longer believes it is appropriate to make the direct payments. For example, the local authority might discontinue the direct payment if it is apparent that it has not been used to achieve the *outcomes of the care plan.

Where someone with capacity is receiving a direct payment but then loses capacity to consent to a direct payment, the direct payment is discontinued and consideration is given to making payments to an authorized person instead. In the interim, alternative arrangements are made to ensure continuity of support for the person concerned. If the *loss of capacity to consent appears to be temporary, payments may continue to be made if there is someone else who is willing to manage payments on the person's behalf. This situation should be treated as temporary and should be closely monitored to ensure that when the person has regained capacity, s/he is able to exercise control over the direct payments as before. The local authority should make clear that the arrangement is designed to be temporary, so that the person managing the direct payment does not enter into any long-term contractual arrangements. If the person's loss of capacity to consent becomes prolonged, consideration is given to making more formal arrangements for an authorized person to take over receipt of the direct payment on behalf of the person.

In the case of someone lacking capacity to consent to a direct payment, the payment is discontinued if the authorized person is no longer acting in the best interests of the person for whom the direct payment is made. A direct payment can also be discontinued if it appears that the conditions imposed on the authorized person are not being met. Consideration may be given to someone else acting as an authorized person for the person lacking capacity or the local authority may have to arrange services for them in place of the direct payment. Direct payments to an authorized person are discontinued when someone who had lacked capacity to consent to direct payments has regained that capacity on a long-term or permanent basis and wishes to take over responsibility.

If consideration is being given to discontinuing a direct payment, discussion takes place as soon as possible with the person, their carer, and any person managing the direct payment in order to explore all available options before making the final decision to terminate the direct payment. For example, if ability to manage the payment is an issue, the person can be given an opportunity to demonstrate that s/he can continue to manage the direct payment, albeit with greater support, if appropriate. When problems arise, it is not automatically assumed that the only solution is to discontinue direct payments.

If a decision is made to discontinue direct payments, a review of the plan is conducted and alternative care and support provision is agreed with the person, their carer, and their advocate if they have one, unless the discontinuation follows a review in which the local authority concluded that the services were no longer needed. A period of notice will normally be given before direct payments are discontinued. It is extremely unlikely that direct payments will be discontinued without giving notice, although in serious cases this may be warranted, for example if the nominated or authorized person are not acting in the *best interests of the person.

In circumstances where the person has lost the capacity to manage the direct payment and there is no one else to manage the payment on their behalf or where the person needs additional support to terminate arrangements, the local authority can consider stepping in or providing support to ensure that any contractual arrangements are appropriately terminated so that additional costs are not incurred.

Access to and take-up of direct payments are not just a matter of law and policy but also of practice, and writers have emphasized the potentially key role played by front-line social workers in giving information, advice, and support in relation to them. It has been argued that the success of direct payments depends on social workers being well-informed about them, having the time to talk through the options and implications with service users, and ensuring that those who wish to use them have access to effective support, including peer support. Consultations with people who use direct payments, local and central policy-makers, and researchers have highlighted the low level of awareness and understanding of direct payments by social workers and the lack of information, *advocacy, and support for direct payments users. Other barriers identified include negative attitudes of social workers about the capabilities of service users and their reluctance to relinquish power. Difficulties have also been noted in recruiting, employing, and retaining personal assistants to provide good quality support. It seems that additional barriers are faced by *Black and minority ethnic people who are considerably underrepresented amongst direct payment users, despite the potential of direct payments to deliver a more culturally responsive service.

Critics of direct payments have argued that their effects are to increase the individual responsibility of service users for arranging their own support, thus transferring risk from the state to the service user; neglect poverty and inequality, and their impact on service users' lives; promote the *deprofessionalization of social work; cut the costs of services; undermine collective service provision; introduce more *privatization and market forces into social services; and produce poor conditions for personal assistants who are employed using direct payments. Furthermore, as direct payments do not bypass *assessment and are only received when needs have been assessed according to *eligibility criteria, they do not increase the resources available to promote wellbeing; that would require increased funding and a widening of eligibility criteria. It has been argued that the promotion of direct payments, as 'cash for care' policy, is motivated by concerns to contain costs and that the funding made available through direct payments does not reflect the real costs of the care required, with the consequence that service users may end up paying additional costs themselves. Critics have argued that these effects suggest that direct payments should not be accepted uncritically by social workers and service users and that many of the same problems arise with direct payments as with traditional *care management. In addition, critics have argued that although direct payments appear to meet service users' requirements for increased *choice and control, they are primarily about promoting the role of the *private sector consistent with a model of individual *consumerism. *See also* CARER'S ASSESSMENT; NEEDS ASSESSMENT.

Further reading: Care and Support (Direct Payments) Regulations (2014). Available at: http://www.legislation.gov.uk/uksi/2014/2871/pdfs/uksi_20142871_en.pdf.
Department of Health (2016) *Care and Support: Statutory Guidance*, Chapter 12. Available at: https://www.gov.uk/government/publications/care-act-statutory-guidance/care-and-support-statutory-guidance#person-centred-care-and-support-planning.
Glasby, J. and Littlechild, R. (2016, 3rd edn.) *Direct Payments: Putting Personalization into Practice*, Policy Press.

direct practice Face-to-face social work with *service users, as opposed to activities carried out on behalf of or with regard to service users. There has been growing concern about the shrinking proportion of time social workers spend in direct practice as their administrative burden has grown.

direct work with children Techniques and approaches used by social workers working with children who have experienced major change and trauma, including *child abuse and neglect. The aim is to enable children and young people to talk about and make sense of what has happened to them, an experience that is intended to be of therapeutic value. The work undertaken may involve *looked-after children, for whom opportunities to reflect on how they have come to live in a *placement away from their *birth family are deemed beneficial to their emotional and psychological wellbeing with regard to making this major transition, particularly if they are subject to *permanency planning. Direct work may also be undertaken with children who continue to live at home, including those who are the subject of a *child protection plan, a component of which may involve face-to-face work undertaken by the *lead social worker or a colleague. In a narrower sense, the term may be used to describe attempts by professionals to communicate with children during the course of a social work *intervention or at the request of the *family courts to obtain their wishes and views about what has happened or may happen to them in the future. Direct work can be used to give attention to the wishes and feelings of children as an aspect of *assessment and planning, as their wishes and feelings are given considerable weight by the Children Act (1989), and in the application by the courts of the *paramountcy principle to decide what is best for a child. For examples of specific techniques *see* ECO MAP; GENOGRAM; LIFE STORY WORK; PLAY THERAPY. *See also* CHILD-CENTRED APPROACH.

disability Conventionally understood as the condition of someone who is not able to use a part or parts of her/his body and depicted primarily in terms of its being an individual tragedy. The focus of social work that proceeded from this understanding of disability was on the individual accepting and coming to terms with the *loss of function. This conventional perspective has been extensively challenged, not least by disability activists, with physical limitations being termed 'impairment' and 'disability' referring to the societal barriers faced by people with impairments that result in their being disabled. In the Equality Act (2010) a person has a disability if:

• They have a physical or mental impairment.
• The impairment has a substantial and long-term adverse effect on their ability to perform normal day-to-day activities.

For the purposes of the Act:

• 'Substantial' means more than minor or trivial.
• 'Long-term' means that the effect of the impairment has lasted or is likely to last for at least twelve months. (There are special provisions covering recurring or fluctuating conditions.)
• 'Normal day-to-day activities' include everyday things like eating, washing, walking, and going shopping.

There are additional provisions relating to people with progressive conditions. People with HIV, cancer, or multiple sclerosis are protected by the Act from the point of their diagnosis. People with some visual impairments are automatically deemed to be disabled. *See also* DIFFERENTLY ABLED; DISABILITY DISCRIMINATION; DISABLISM; DISCRIMINATION; NEEDS ASSESSMENT; SOCIAL MODEL OF DISABILITY.

disability discrimination Under the Equality Act (2010) a person discriminates against a disabled person if s/he treats the disabled person unfavourably because of something that is a consequence of the *disability and s/he cannot show that the discrimination is a proportionate means of achieving a legitimate aim. There is no discrimination if someone does not know and could not reasonably be expected to know that another person has a disability. A person has a disability if s/he has a physical or mental impairment, and the impairment has a substantial and long-term adverse effect on her/his ability to carry out normal day-to-day activities. There is a duty to make 'reasonable adjustments' for disabled people:

• Where a 'provision, criteria, or practice' puts a disabled person at substantial disadvantage to take such steps as are reasonable to avoid the disadvantage;
• Where a physical feature puts a disabled person at a substantial disadvantage to take such steps as are reasonably necessary to avoid the disadvantage;
• Where but for the provision of auxiliary aids a disabled person is at a substantial disadvantage to take reasonable steps to provide auxiliary aids.

Failure to comply with the duty to make reasonable adjustments is discrimination against a disabled person. *See also* ABLE-BODIEISM; ANTI-DISCRIMINATORY PRACTICE; DIFFERENTLY ABLED; DISABILITY; DISABLISM; DISCRIMINATION; SOCIAL MODEL OF DISABILITY.

Disability Movement *See* DISABLED PEOPLE'S MOVEMENT.

disabled children Government guidance emphasizes that a key issue for disabled children is *safeguarding and promoting their welfare, for example, understanding the impact of *abuse or neglect on a child's health and development, and how harm is best prevented. Moreover, while children's impairments can create genuine difficulties in their lives, many of the problems they face are not caused by their conditions or impairments, but by negative attitudes, prejudice, and unequal access to those things necessary for a good quality of life. In this respect the issues for disabled children are the same as those encountered by disabled adults. Government practice guidance for social workers and other professionals does not identify specific groups of disabled children but, given the importance of communication in relation to safeguarding and *child protection, children with speech, language, and communication needs are referred to in discrete terms. Children with these needs are seen as including those who use non-verbal means of communication as well as a wider group of children who have difficulties in communicating with others. This issue is of major importance for the effective protection of disabled children because the available UK evidence suggests that they are at increased risk of abuse and that the presence of multiple disabilities, including difficulties associated with communication, appears to increase the risk of both abuse and neglect. There is also evidence that disabled children are underrepresented in safeguarding systems. Early indicators that might suggest abuse or neglect can also be more complicated for disabled children. This requires professionals to have the necessary expertise and commitment in relation to both child protection and disability in order to ensure that disabled children receive the same levels of protection from harm as non-disabled children. However, important as these safeguarding issues are, promoting the welfare of disabled children goes beyond their need for protection from harm. As the Council for Disabled Children asserts: 'We want a society in which disabled children's needs are met, aspirations supported and their rights respected.'

Under the Equality Act (2010), it is against the law for schools and other education providers to discriminate against disabled children. Examples of discrimination include a school refusing to admit a disabled child because of her/his disability or stopping a disabled pupil going outside at break time because it takes them longer to get there. Schools have to make 'reasonable adjustments' for disabled children. These can include changes to physical features, for example installing a ramp, changes to assessment, and providing extra support, for example specialist teachers or equipment. Some children may have special educational needs because their disabilities affect their ability to learn. *See also* CHILD ABUSE AND NEGLECT; CHILD PROTECTION; DIFFERENTLY ABLED; DISABILITY; EDUCATION, HEALTH AND CARE PLAN; INDIVIDUAL EDUCATION PLAN; SAFEGUARDING CHILDREN; SCHOOL ACTION; SCHOOL ACTION PLUS; SIGNIFICANT HARM; SOCIAL MODEL OF DISABILITY; SPECIAL EDUCATIONAL NEEDS.

Further reading: Department for Children, Schools and Families (2009) *Safeguarding Disabled Children*. Available at: https://www.gov.uk/government/uploads/system/uploads/attachment_data/file/190544/00374-2009DOM-EN.pdf.

- Official site of the Council for Disabled Children, providing discussion, development, and dissemination of policy and practice issues relating to service provision and support for disabled children.

Disabled Movement *See* DISABLED PEOPLE'S MOVEMENT.

disabled people, register of *See* REGISTER OF DISABLED PEOPLE.

Disabled People's Movement Describes the totality of organizations consisting of and controlled by disabled people themselves, rather than organizations that purport to speak on their behalf. The UK Disabled People's Council (formerly the British Council of Disabled People, founded in 1981) forms an umbrella group for these organizations. The movement's interests are pursued through political lobbying and other channels by which its views are communicated to central government and *local authorities, as well as its being involved in campaigns and demonstrations. UKDPC in turn belongs to Disabled People's International, an umbrella group of national organizations of disabled people that has representation from over a hundred countries and is recognized by the United Nations as the voice of disabled people internationally.

The organization Disabled People Against Cuts (DPAC) was set up in October 2010 after protests against how the politics and policies of *austerity were affecting disabled people:

DPAC is for everyone who believes that disabled people should have full human rights and equality. It is for everyone that refuses to accept that any country can destroy the lives of people just because they are or become disabled or have chronic health issues. It is for everyone against government *austerity measures which target the poor while leaving the wealthy unscathed. It is for everyone who refuses to stay silent about the injustices delivered by wealthy politicians on ordinary people and their lives.

DPAC has produced a comprehensive Charter of Rights for disabled people.

Social workers can increase their appreciation of the perspectives of disabled people by attending disability equality training run by disabled people, based on the *social model of disability. Although there are clearly organizational constraints on social workers' freedom of action, they can seek to work in *partnership with disabled people, recognizing the expertise that they bring from their experiences, and, where necessary, assisting them to achieve their *goals in a way that gives the disabled person maximum control over her/his life.

- Official site of Disabled People Against Cuts (includes the Charter of Rights).

disablism Discrimination against disabled people. The definition proposed by *SCOPE in its 'Time to Get Equal' campaign was 'discriminatory, oppressive, or abusive behaviour arising from the belief that disabled people are inferior to others'. Social work can compound disablism or it can challenge the discrimination that disabled people experience. *See also* ABLE-BODIEDISM; ANTI-DISCRIMINATORY PRACTICE; ANTI-OPPRESSIVE PRACTICE; DIFFERENTLY ABLED; DISABILITY; DISABILITY DISCRIMINATION; DISCRIMINATION; SOCIAL MODEL OF DISABILITY.

disadvantaged To be in a position that is unfavourable when compared with others and/or in relation to future prospects. For example, children in *poverty are disadvantaged in comparison with children who are not in terms of their prospects in and beyond childhood. Also used to refer to geographical localities, for example, disadvantaged neighbourhood or disadvantaged *community.

discharge from hospital *See* DISCHARGE PLANNING; HOME IMPROVEMENT AGENCIES; HOSPITAL DISCHARGE; HOSPITAL SOCIAL WORK.

discharge notification *See* HOSPITAL DISCHARGE.

discharge planning The importance in principle of planning discharges from hospital sensitively and effectively for the person concerned has tended to be overshadowed by the focus on speed of discharge and the emphasis on targets and penalties. Although discharge planning can involve people of any age, *older people constitute the overwhelming majority of those with whom social workers make plans. The consequences for older people of hospitals exerting increased pressure on social workers to ensure their swift discharge may be that they are discharged directly to care homes without the benefit of a period of rehabilitation that might have enabled them to recover sufficiently to return home. Alternatively, they may be discharged home before they are ready, creating physical, psychological, and emotional *risks, the prospect of early readmission and the imposition of additional pressures on *carers. Such consequences of inadequate discharge planning run directly counter to supporting older people's control over their life planning processes. Work by the now-defunct Commission for Social Care Inspection employed a wider remit than speed of discharge in an examination of the experiences of older people who needed social services support on discharge from hospital. It found that where there was access to good community support services, older people recovered well. However, where community services were unavailable or inadequate, older people's recovery was undermined. It appeared that some older people were propelled into making hasty decisions to enter residential care while others were readmitted to hospital as a result of premature discharge or inadequate post-discharge support. A number of points were identified:

- Continuity in terms of a named person with responsibility for monitoring and reviewing care is important to older people. People moving frequently between hospital and home particularly benefited from there being one person with whom they had a longer-term relationship and who had knowledge of their needs and preferences.
- Many hospital readmissions could potentially be avoided with improved risk assessment and forward planning to prevent and respond to crises.
- An orientation towards *rehabilitation can result in long-term improvements in people's lives. Positive outcomes for people were more common in places where rehabilitation was seen as a principle underpinning all services rather than as a specialist service with a limited intake of *service users.
- On going coordination of community health and social services is vital to successful outcomes for older people with multiple needs. Effective multidisciplinary working was more common at acute stages than in longer-term management and support.
- A focus on preventive services was eclipsed by the concern to reduce pressures on hospital resources. Coordination of a wide range of services across all *local authority services is needed to address quality-of-life issues for older people.
- More effort is needed to ensure a consistently high quality of home care.
- Care homes need to play a more flexible role in supporting *independence, alongside other community services, for example, by offering shared care.

- Hospital or care home admissions that arise through breakdowns in the caring network can be prevented by the provision of more practical and flexible support for *carers.
- Improvements are needed in meeting individuals' cultural needs and preferences.
- Strategic *partnerships between health and social services are vital.

Discharge planning illustrates the interdependence of health and social services, and the potentially adverse consequences for people when 'joined up' services are not delivered.

Attention has tended to be concentrated on the nature and extent of joint working between the National Health Service and social services in relation to discharge planning, with less attention being given to working relationships in this context with the *voluntary sector. This sector plays a significant and increasing role in delivering services related to discharge planning that would once have been provided by statutory agencies. *Voluntary organizations may be contracted to provide services such as hospital after-care under the remit of *intermediate care but can also be a significant source of support more generally for older people discharged from hospital: providing help with practical domestic tasks, such as shopping and cleaning; undertaking an *advocacy role to help the older person gain access to particular resources, such as social security benefits advice; and providing assistance that enables the older person to develop or regain skills necessary for their independence, for example, restoring confidence in using public transport or using a telephone following a stroke. However, the voluntary sector can be pushed into the position of compensating for deficits in the statutory system, which in turn can generate pressure on its own resources, and undermines its *goals. *See also* COLLABORATIVE WORKING; DELAYED DISCHARGES; HOME IMPROVEMENT AGENCIES; HOSPITAL DISCHARGE; HOSPITAL SOCIAL WORK.

disciplinary gaze (disciplining power) *See* GAZE; GOVERNMENTALITY.

disclosure A child telling someone that s/he is being or has been abused. This may occur in an unplanned way, for example, a child may disclose to a teacher, or it may happen in a situation in which abuse is suspected and a social worker is working with a child, using drawing or play, in order to provide an opportunity for disclosure to take place. It can be part of a police investigation, with a social worker and police officer jointly interviewing a child, and recording the interview as a possible source of evidence. When abuse is suspected, great care has to be taken not to lead the child into giving the 'right answers'. This is a highly skilled area of social work. However, unanticipated disclosure can happen to anybody, though it is unlikely to take the form of a child telling someone like a teacher or a social worker immediately and directly that s/he has been abused. Disclosure may be difficult for a child for a number of reasons: feelings of shame may be associated with the abuse; there may be a sense of loyalty to the abuser; there may be a fear of not being believed; there may be a fear of the consequences of disclosure to the child or other people, for example, fearing that s/he or a parent may be removed from the family home. In the case of sexual abuse, the child may feel under direct threat because s/he has been told that the abuse is a secret and that bad things will happen to her/him if what has happened is disclosed. All of these factors make it unlikely that a child will disclose abuse directly and is more likely to drop hints ('X is bothering me'), to disguise the circumstances ('What would happen if my friend told someone that she was being touched where she shouldn't be by her dad?'), or to seek to prevent any consequences ('I want to talk to you about something but only if you promise not to tell anybody else'). Judging the response to make can be difficult. If the response is insufficiently supportive, the child can feel abandoned, but if the response is dramatic, it can frighten the child, and make her/him inhibited about talking further. It is important to remain calm and listen carefully to the child, using the child's style and form of language as far as possible, encouraging the child to say what has happened, but not pressing for details the child does not seem ready to provide. The child needs to know that s/he is not to blame for what has happened, and to be clear about what will happen next.

Disclosure and Barring Service (DBS) Began work in 2012, replacing and taking over the functions of the Criminal Records Bureau (CRB) and the Independent Safeguarding Authority (ISA). The DBS seeks to prevent unsuitable people from entering or remaining in paid or voluntary work with children, young people, or vulnerable adults. The Safeguarding Vulnerable Groups Act (2006) sets out the scope and operation of the vetting and barring scheme the DBS operates. Anyone wanting to work with children, young people, or vulnerable adults must declare any criminal convictions. The provisions of the Rehabilitation of Offenders Act (1974) that normally allow convictions to be 'spent' and not disclosed do not apply. Only those thought not to pose a *risk, after criminal and other records have been checked, should be engaged in paid or voluntary work. The DBS is responsible for processing requests for criminal records checks (DBS checks) and deciding whether it is appropriate for a person to be placed on or removed from the DBS children's barred list and adults' barred list for England, *Wales, and *Northern Ireland, that is, the lists of those not allowed to work with children and/or adults. The DBS searches police records and, where relevant, barred list information, and then issues a DBS certificate to the applicant. Access to the DBS checking service is only available to registered employers who are entitled by law to ask someone to reveal their full criminal history, including spent convictions. The minimum age at which someone can be asked to apply for a criminal record check is 16 years old. In addition, referrals can be made to the DBS when an employer or an organization, for example a regulatory body, has concerns that a person has caused harm, or poses a future risk of harm to vulnerable adults and/or children. An employer must make such a referral to the DBS, though this is not obligatory for regulatory bodies.

( ) SEE WEB LINKS
• Official site of the Disclosure and Barring Service.

discourse Linguistic systems through which the social world is experienced and understood. In critical theory usually associated with the work of Michel Foucault (1926–84) and seen as the characteristic ways of describing and explaining the social world through which power is sustained. Foucault undertook historical analyses, which he called 'archaeologies', into subjects such as sexuality, punishment, and madness, and identified the discourse within which the phenomenon under investigation was classified and ordered in a particular era, arguing that people were subject to the discourse and largely unable to exist outside it, though he did, to a lesser extent, acknowledge the possibility of resistance. An example relevant to social work is the former (male-dominated) dominant discourse of *domestic violence, couched in terms of 'women asking for it', and a response of non-intervention, and the resistant feminist discourse of domestic violence as a form of unacceptable male domination, which enabled the construction of new responses to abused women. *See also* DISCOURSE ANALYSIS; DISCURSIVE FORMATION; DOMINANT IDEOLOGY; HABITUS; HEGEMONY; IDEOLOGY.

discourse analysis The study of *discourses through analysis of what is said and written, usually assuming that the influence of the discourse is greater than the participants in it are aware of because of their location within its power structures and assumptions. For example, in some *local authorities, people who use social work are no longer referred to as *service users but as customers, a change of terminology that interprets and represents the position and role of service users within the discourse of *consumerism. *See also* DISCURSIVE FORMATION; DOMINANT IDEOLOGY; HABITUS; HEGEMONY; IDEOLOGY.

discretion (local authority) *Local authorities can exercise judgement and make choices about how they implement their *statutory duties, and this has implications for social workers; for example, in relation to *policies and procedures when an assessment is made of an adult's *care and support needs under the Care Act (2014) (*see* NEEDS ASSESSMENT). Local authorities have to have policies that are flexible enough to make decisions in relation to an individual's circumstances but discretion cannot be exercised too loosely; a local authority cannot do whatever it wants, even if its intention is 'good', but has to act within the legislation that applies to an individual's circumstances. *See also* DUTY; ELIGIBILITY CRITERIA; EXCEPTIONS; FETTERING DISCRETION; JUDICIAL REVIEW; NEEDS ASSESSMENT; POWER; REASONABLENESS; RELEVANT FACTORS; RIGID POLICIES; TARGET DUTY.

discretion (social workers) The latitude to decide what should be done in a particular situation. Following the establishment of *Social Services Departments in the early 1970s, social workers had considerable freedom in defining problems and the priority allocated to them, choice over their preferred methods, and control over how they rationed their time and paced their work. *Supervision of social workers by team leaders was predominantly consultation about professional practice, with the agenda largely initiated by the social worker. Social workers' discretion was embodied in *casework which, despite critical assault, held on to its position as the main form of practice after the establishment of Social Services Departments and underpinned the organization of work in personal caseloads. As a result, the individual social worker retained a degree of personal decision-making substantially greater in terms of the consequences for the *service user affected by her/his decisions, than was true for most occupational groups. This meant that Social Services Departments were a striking departure from the classic model of a *bureaucracy because of the absence of detailed rules and regulations for dealing with each service user. The social worker assessed the service users' needs, arranged any services that were needed, and when necessary, maintained a continuing relationship with the service user as part of her/his caseload. Social workers were directly involved with service users and acted as their advocate to a variety of agencies.

The Conservative governments (1979–97) introduced wide-ranging reforms of social work that had a marked impact on social workers' use of discretion. Constraining expenditure was achieved either in spite of social workers' *assessments or by constraining their assessment decisions. Either way, the role of the social worker in allocating resources was undermined. In tandem, other external forces operated to impose constraints on social worker decisions, often in the form of public inquiries, and the legislation, and/or guidelines that arose from them. High-profile cases of *child abuse, for example, frequently resulted in official inquiry reports (*see* CHILD ABUSE INQUIRY) that detailed the failures of social work and made procedural recommendations without considering fully the implications for social work practice. More routinely, inspections of social work reported on a range of issues, with a major focus on the closer management of social workers. The implication of these developments was increased control and oversight, and decreased discretion for social workers. This was to enable scarce resources to be directed at 'core business' and to increase efficiency. These trends continued under successive governments and now much of this control is expressed in manuals, procedures, directions, and guidelines that limit professional discretion and set up; standardized and repetitive systems; tightly defined criteria for eligibility for services; standardized assessment tools; interventions that are often determined in advance from a limited list; minimization of contact time; and pressure for throughput. However, arguments have continued about whether or not a degree of discretion continues to be exercised in social workers' everyday decision-making. Some have argued that the increase in *performance management and greater proceduralization have heavily constrained and regulated discretion, and resulted in 'people-processing'. Others that a degree of discretion cannot be eliminated from social work because it would seize up without it. Much of the argument has taken Lipsky's work on 'street-level bureaucracy' as its starting point. Lipsky (1940–) sees the work of street-level bureaucrats (front-line workers) as happening in services in which discretion is necessary to meet a variety of human needs; discretion is necessary simply to do the job. However, the vague, ambitious, and often contradictory *goals of street-level bureaucracies create another area of discretion: the space in which to translate nebulous policy into practice. Finally, Lipsky recognized the discretion street-level bureaucrats themselves have to create space to advance their own values, interests, and needs. *See also* BUREAU-PROFESSIONAL REGIME.

Further reading: Lipsky, M. (2010, 30th-anniversary edn., first published 1980) *Street-level Bureaucracy: Dilemmas of the Individual in Public Services*, Russell Sage.

discretionary leave to remain Allows an *asylum-seeker to remain in the UK, despite not qualifying for *refugee status or *humanitarian protection.

discretionary service A service provided by a *local authority under a *power rather than a *duty, and different from the exercise of *discretion by a local authority with regard to fulfilling *statutory duties.

discrimination Practices that involve treating people unfairly on the basis of a characteristic they share with others. Discrimination is located in patterns of *power and privilege associated with social divisions such as age, *class, gender, *'race', and sexuality, though these may be obscured and the focus may remain on the individual consequences for the person experiencing discrimination and/or the individual characteristics of the person discriminating, with an emphasis on the latter's personal prejudice.

Over time, legislation concerning individuals' experiences of discrimination has made different types of discrimination unlawful, for example the Equal Pay Act (1970), the Sex Discrimination Act (1975), the Race Relations Act (1976), and the Disability Discrimination Act (1995). Each Act established an organization to enforce its provisions, for example, the Disability Rights Commission. The Equality Act (2006) abolished those other bodies and created a single *Equality and Human Rights Commission to receive and investigate complaints and to take steps to promote equality and human rights. The Equality Act (2010) brought together and restated the earlier legislation, and strengthened the law in a number of areas. The role of the Equality and Human Rights Commission was unaffected.

The Equality Act (2010) identifies 'protected characteristics': age; *disability; gender reassignment; marriage and civil partnership; pregnancy and maternity; *'race'; religion or belief; sex; sexual orientation. A public authority must have due regard to the 'public sector equality duty', which involves:

- Eliminating conduct prohibited under the Act;
- Advancing equality of opportunity between people who share a 'protected characteristic' and people who do not share it;
- Fostering good relations between people who share a 'protected characteristic' and people who do not.

Conduct prohibited by the Act includes:

Direct discrimination (Section 13) A person discriminates against another person if s/he treats the other person less favourably than s/he would treat others because of the other person's protected characteristic. (Someone can be treated more favourably on the basis of disability as a protected characteristic, allowing positive discrimination in relation to this characteristic.)

Indirect discrimination (Section 19) A person discriminates against another person if s/he applies to the other person a provision, criteria, or practice that is discriminating in relation to a protected characteristic of the other person.

Harassment (Section 26) A person discriminates against another person if s/he engages in unwanted conduct in relation to a protected characteristic and the conduct has the effect of violating the other person's dignity or creating an intimidating, hostile, degrading, humiliating, or offensive environment for the other person.

Victimization (Section 27) A person victimizes another person if s/he subjects the other person to a detriment (i.e. damage, harm, or loss) because: the other person brings proceedings under the Act; gives evidence or information in connection with proceedings under the Act; makes an allegation that a person has contravened the Act; or does anything else in connection with the Act.

The Act applies to provision of services; public functions; premises; employment; employment services; terms of employment; trade organizations; occupational pensions; associations and political parties; schools; further and higher education; qualification bodies; transport. *See also* ANTI-DISCRIMINATORY PRACTICE; DISABILITY DISCRIMINATION.

discursive formation Foucauldian term for the loosely structured amalgam of themes, concepts, issues, and concerns in a particular historical era within which specific *discourses are located. *See also* DISCOURSE ANALYSIS; DOMINANT IDEOLOGY; HABITUS; HEGEMONY; IDEOLOGY.

disempowering (disempowerment) Depriving *service users of power or influence in matters that affect them. *See also* EMPOWERING.

disengagement theory *See* THEORIES OF AGEING.

Disneyization (Disneyfication) Using the processes that characterize Disney theme parks as metaphors for wide-ranging social changes and processes, particularly in consumption, Alan Bryman argued that Disneyization is the process by which four dimensions exemplified in the Disney parks—theming, dedifferentiation, merchandising, and emotional labour—are found increasingly in other sectors of society. *Theming* establishes coherence. The Disney corporation divides its parks into different 'lands' that make connections between rides and attractions through themes depicted in architecture, merchandising, costumes, and music. *Dedifferentiation* interlocks different forms of consumption with each other. The Disney parks exploit their potential for selling food and various goods, for example, by leading visitors to shops when leaving attractions. They incorporate ideas from rides into restaurants and provide Disney hotels. *Merchandising* promotes goods with particular images. In the early days, Walt Disney took control of merchandising from other companies and made it integral to his operation, including the use of copyright images and logos. A whole area of the Disney parks, Main Street, is devoted solely to merchandising, which also occurs throughout the rest of the parks' 'lands'. *Emotional labour* requires staff to demonstrate particular emotions during service transactions such as being cheerful and friendly. Disney employees are taught to use happy phrases and behave as though they are having fun and not engaging in real work. The Disney corporation seeks to control their interaction with visitors, as well as how they view themselves, and how they feel. Bryman locates Disneyization in literature that emphasizes the significance of the consumption of goods and services for individual lifestyles, and the cultivation of personal *identity projects, and regards Disneyization as an analysis of a fundamental shift to the central role of consumption in society. Arguments based on this shift underpin the introduction of *consumerism and *personalization into social work.

Further reading: Bryman A. (2009, 3rd edn.) 'The Disneyization of Society', in Ritzer G. (ed.) *McDonaldization: The Reader*, Pine Forge Press.

displacement *See* DEFENCE MECHANISMS.

dissonance *See* COGNITIVE DISSONANCE.

distinction A key component in Pierre Bourdieu's (1930–2002) theory of culture that he used to elaborate the ways in which social *discrimination and exclusion, rooted in *class position, are generated and sustained in everyday life and across generations, resulting in differing degrees of a sense of belonging (or a sense of not belonging at all). In any particular field he sees those who hold power as conferring recognition of the existence of distinction, thus legitimizing those who possess it, and excluding those who are found lacking in distinction. Although his analysis was developed in relation to markers of taste (in art, music, literature, hobbies, food, and so on) it has potential for application to the field of social work in terms of the generation and maintenance of legitimation and recognition of some, and the exclusion of others. *See also* DIFFERENCE; DIVERSITY; HABITUS; OTHER.

diversion A policy of dealing with offenders in ways that, where possible, keep them out of the criminal justice system. It is based on the assumption that *labelling minor offenders as criminals is counter-productive, as it can serve to confirm them in a deviant identity. In addition, avoiding court proceedings saves the system time and money. *Cautions and *final warnings are the main alternatives to prosecution for an offence. *See also* DEVIANCE; MINIMUM INTERVENTION; SYSTEMS MANAGEMENT.

diversity One of the major changes in social work education and training from the mid-1990s onwards has been a tendency to move away from emphasizing *anti-discriminatory and *anti-oppressive practice towards the need for students to develop knowledge and understanding of diversity, seen as the ways that people are different from one another, concentrating on how those *differences shape a range of ways of living and thinking, and generate different assumptions, values, and beliefs. The *assessment of a student's ability to be a social worker in this regard has been couched increasingly in terms of how s/he approaches diversity using an individualistic approach that sees diversity as stripped of critical aspirations for social change, stressing that everyone's *needs are unique. For example, social work undertaken from this perspective with women stresses sensitivity to the experience of women and the issues they face in their particular social and cultural location, whereas critical *feminist social work practice would suggest identifying and challenging the oppressive nature of male domination in patriarchal cultures, structures, and systems. This individualistic perspective on diversity can encompass the possibility of multiple oppression, given that everyone is seen as unique, but finds it difficult to embrace *intersectionality because of its individualization of experiences of oppression. Rather than locating oppression in social divisions built around, for example, *class, *gender, and *'race', the individualistic perspective explores diversity as reflected in religion, *ethnicity, culture, language, social status, family structures, and lifestyle, encouraging students to respect such differences and not to compound any *disadvantage or *stigma that people's diversity may have attached to it, while acting in accordance with their social work role and the organizational context. Whilst valuing and respecting the diversity of *service users is *good practice and can be a component in engaging in more critical forms of practice, on its own it falls short of engagement with issues of *discrimination and *oppression in ways that are central to more critical radical perspectives. *See also* DISTINCTION.

division of labour Dividing the workforce so that people specialize in particular tasks. The establishment of *Social Services Departments in the early 1970s minimized the division of labour in social work with either generic social workers, who covered a range of different *service user groups, or generic teams, which brought together specialist workers. In recent years the trend has been back to specialist social workers in specialist teams for specific service user groups or multi-professional teams, for example, Community Mental Health Teams, which bring together nursing and social work, or *Youth Offending Teams, which bring together the police, social work, probation, and other agencies.

The division of labour has also been applied to the breaking down of complex tasks into their components in order to increase efficiency by improved productivity. For example, an adult service user, instead of being dealt with by the same social worker throughout, may have contact with a worker initially, possibly through a *call centre, another worker may carry out an *assessment, another worker may bring together the services recommended by the assessment (*brokerage), and a further worker may *review the services provided after a designated period of time. This example raises the question of who benefits from the efficiency sought by the division of labour, as the service user may experience this as inefficient in terms of the consequent fragmentation s/he encounters.

Increasing attention has been drawn to the sexual division of labour in social work in which the majority of social workers are women, and the majority of managers are men. *See also* DEPROFESSIONALIZATION; DESKILLING; GENERICISM.

divorce The legal ending of a marriage. The Divorce Reform Act (1969) introduced irretrievable breakdown as the basis for divorce. This could be established on the grounds of adultery, cruelty, desertion, two years' separation with the consent of both parties, or five years' separation. The Matrimonial Causes Act (1973) introduced a process that allowed uncontested cases not to go before the courts, making the majority of divorces much more straightforward procedurally. The Family Law Act (1996) set out irretrievable breakdown—so-called 'no fault' divorce—as the only grounds for divorce but opposition to removal of the grounds for establishing irretrievable breakdown meant that this aspect of the Act has never been implemented. The Act also introduced funding for *mediation services as a means of encouraging parties to reach agreement and reducing conflict.

In addition to the social work contribution in the legal context of divorce (*see* FAMILY COURT WELFARE SERVICES), social workers encounter problems in family relationships and children's welfare issues arising from divorce (and other parental separation) that are referred to them in the normal course of their work. The impact of divorce (or other parental separation) on children and young people varies widely. They need to be given information about the reasons for divorce, and what the consequences will be for them, and their voices need to be heard fully as part of the process. The implications for children and young people depend on: the nature and extent of their preparation for the break-up; the new living arrangements, including transition to a lone-parent or step-parent household; *contact with the parent who is no longer living with them; the nature of the relationship between the separated parents. Moving out of a marital (or other) relationship, and having to restructure parenting usually results in considerable stresses on the adults involved. It is in the interests of children and young people for the adults not to embroil them in any battles that ensue.

Divorce Court Welfare *See* FAMILY COURT WELFARE SERVICES.

DoLS *See* DEPRIVATION OF LIBERTY SAFEGUARDS.

domestic abuse *See* DOMESTIC VIOLENCE.

Domestic Abuse Forum *See* DOMESTIC VIOLENCE FORUM.

Domestic Abuse, Stalking and Harassment and Honour Based Violence Risk Identification, Assessment and Management Model Used by all police services and a large number of their partner agencies across the UK to identify and assess *risk in the situations with which the Model is concerned. *See also* CHILDREN AND DOMESTIC VIOLENCE; DOMESTIC VIOLENCE; HONOUR-BASED VIOLENCE.

(((⊕))) SEE WEB LINKS

• Official site of the Domestic Abuse, Stalking and Harassment and Honour Based Violence Risk Identification, Assessment and Management Model. The Model's risk checklist.

domesticity An ideology supportive of the *domestic division of labour that sees the household sphere as the proper place for women, and the basis for the construction of their identity as wives and mothers in their devotion to the harmonious functioning of the home. The ideology was invoked with particular vigour during the establishment of the post-war *welfare state as part of prising women out of the paid work roles they had occupied during the Second World War. *See also* BEVERIDGE REPORT; CARERS; KIN-WORK.

domestic labour (domestic division of labour) Unpaid housework and caring for children. The term is used deliberately in *feminist analysis to indicate that this is *work*, still predominantly undertaken by women, and its demands and contribution should not be marginalized. The division of labour in the domestic sphere is concerned with the distribution of tasks necessary to sustain a household and the people living in it. Sometimes this is referred to as the sexual or gendered division of labour because of the disparities in contribution between men and women. A range of theories has developed to account for these disparities. Some suggest that the domestic division of labour primarily benefits capitalism because housework and nurturing revive men's capacity to work. Others point to *patriarchy predating capitalism, through which men controlled the work of women and children within the family, and that men's exploitation of women's domestic labour, then and now, directly benefits men. Others see domestic labour as benefiting both capitalism and patriarchy in a mutually supportive network. Despite women's involvement in paid work, they usually shoulder a 'double burden', remaining responsible for the bulk of domestic labour, even when men are unemployed or when both work full-time. In better-paid households, one 'solution' has been to pay another woman to do the work, which is indicative of the extent to which women's paid work in cleaning and caring often mirrors their unpaid domestic labour. The predominant emphasis on housework and child care for many years tended to obscure the physical and emotional labour involved in caring for adults, but this is now recognized as another significant aspect of women's domestic work. *See also* CARERS; DOMESTICITY; KIN-WORK.

domestic space Although 'home' can be a threatening place (*see* DOMESTIC VIOLENCE), for many it can be a significant source of stability and continuity, and a site of self-determination. For example, a sense of a secure domestic space can be significant for *older people with regard to maintaining their *identity, and as a base within which they can feel confident, and from which they can engage in their neighbourhoods.

domestic violence A term that can be used in a general sense to refer to any *violence in the home, though violence against children is usually termed *child abuse. When used in this general sense, it can involve the exercise of power and control by one partner over another in any intimate relationship: by a man over a woman; by a woman over a man; or by one partner over another in same-sex relationships. It can also include abuse by a relative other than a partner, an adult child, for example, in the context of working to *safeguard adults. The government's definition is consistent with this general sense in which the term is used, and is found repeated on many *local authority websites: 'Any incident of threatening behaviour, violence, or abuse (psychological, physical, sexual, financial, or emotional) between adults who are or have been intimate partners or family members regardless of gender or sexuality'. Most commonly, however, domestic violence indicates a specific concern with male violence against women by partners or ex-partners, not only in the home, as 'domestic' implies, but also in public places and *refuges, if women are tracked down by ex-partners. It can involve physical, sexual, or emotional abuse or intimidation, and is often a combination of these. Domestic violence often begins or intensifies during pregnancy, and women are at greater risk after giving birth. The term was promoted by women's organizations in the 1970s as part of a campaign to make male violence in the domestic setting seen as a public issue, and as an alternative to 'battered wives' and 'battered women', because those earlier terms were considered to divert attention from male violence as the key issue. An alternative term, 'domestic abuse', is still occasionally encountered but has been largely rejected on the grounds that it minimizes the extent and severity of male violence, though it does have the merit of emphasizing the breadth of abuse that goes beyond overt violent acts. Domestic violence is the most common form of violence, with a consensus emerging around estimates of one in four women being affected and an average of two deaths per week. Such violence represents the extremities of gender inequality and the exercise of male power and oppression.

Traditionally, the police, social work, and other services were reluctant to intervene in domestic violence, sometimes portraying the family as a private realm that should be free of outside interference. The bulk of provision has been specialist services established by *voluntary sector women's organizations, most notably *Women's Aid, which, amongst many other things, has a network of refuges. Social work often downplayed the significance of domestic violence by not following up male violence against women unless a child had also been harmed; not taking seriously the impact on children of witnessing domestic violence; concentrating on whether the woman had tried to protect her children rather than addressing the man's violence; and not recognizing links between domestic violence and child abuse. In recent years this has changed significantly, though responses to domestic violence can still be patchy, despite the fact that social workers in a range of settings will have contact with women who are experiencing or have experienced domestic violence. For example, a significant number of women with mental health problems are in this position. Patchy service provision is compounded by resource shortfalls. For example, the Adoption and Children Act (2002) refers to the 'impairment suffered from seeing or hearing the ill-treatment of another'. This suggests that there is a strong case for children in households that have experienced domestic violence being eligible for social work assistance as *'children in need', but resource constraints may mean that they do not receive a service unless they have experienced or are likely to experience *'significant harm'.

Although all social workers are likely to encounter domestic violence to varying degrees, its incidence and impact is most pronounced in children's services, with children, as well as women, experiencing serious consequences from: seeing and/or hearing violence; being caught up in violence, or targeted at the same time; living in an atmosphere of intimidation and fear; experiencing their mother being constantly vilified. Children's reactions to the distress caused by domestic violence can be wide-ranging, from *aggression through to *depression, as well as physical symptoms. They may become numb and withdrawn as a result of constant exposure, or be agitated and unable to concentrate. In addition to the impact of violence against women on children, the links between violence towards women and child abuse have been increasingly recognized. Domestic violence towards a woman increases the likelihood of violence towards her child. Many women and children experience an intensification in violence after separation occurs. Contact arrangements with children can be used to continue violence against women or can result in children being seized. Despite the often-catastrophic impact of abuse on women's and children's lives, it is important to move beyond a view of them as victims, and to acknowledge their strengths as survivors, not assuming that damage will be permanent.

There are two areas of law relating to domestic violence: criminal and civil. Criminal proceedings can be instigated by the police and the Crown Prosecution Service in response to behaviour that is criminal conduct and most forms of domestic violence involve criminality. Traditionally, prosecution of offenders was dependent on the willingness of the woman to make a formal complaint and attend court to give evidence. This hardly ever happened because women were too afraid or disempowered. The Domestic Violence, Crime, and Victims Act (2004) encourages prosecution regardless of the woman's wishes, and the situation is gradually changing with the police and the CPS more willing to pursue cases. During the period between the offender being charged and his case being dealt with in court, conditions can be attached to the granting of *bail to protect the victim(s) (Special Measures [Youth Justice and Criminal Evidence] Act [1999]). Attempts are being made to improve the way in which the courts handle criminal cases involving domestic violence through the introduction of specialist court systems aimed at providing more support to women during the trial. The features of these courts include:

- Magistrates specially trained in dealing with domestic violence;
- Separate entrances, exits, and waiting areas so that women do not come into contact with offenders;
- Cases fast-tracked through the system, limiting the likelihood of further incidents as a result of delays in cases coming to trial;
- Support and advice from *Independent Domestic Violence Advisors.

A multi-agency approach involves the police, prosecutors, court staff, the probation service, and specialist support services attempting to work together to identify, track, and assess risk in domestic violence cases, to support victims, and share information. Following conviction, apart from the normal range of criminal penalties the court can make a Restraining Order through which restrictions can be imposed on the offender's freedom to go to specified areas or to contact named individuals.

Civil remedies are available to women by making an application to a *family court for an *injunction (Family Law Act [1996]; Domestic Violence Crime and Victims Act [2004]), though they may incur expenses that they cannot recover in doing so. This is a court order that instructs a person not to do specified acts, or compels them to do others:

Non-molestation Order Prohibits molesting an adult or child associated with the person subject to the order. It can be a general injunction not to molest, or it can refer to particular acts, or it can include both. As well as being applied for specifically, it can be granted during the course of other proceedings.

Occupation Order Can order a person to: leave a home; stay a certain distance from a home; stay in certain parts of a home; allow someone back in a home; continue paying mortgage, rent, or bills. In deciding who lives in the home, an Occupation Order provides an important alternative to removal of women and children from the home.

Although injunctions are made in civil proceedings, breach of an injunction is a criminal offence that can result in sanctions including imprisonment. The police will respond where an injunction with a power of arrest is breached.

The injunctions are available in relation to 'associated' persons who are or were: married; civil partners; cohabiting; living in the same household; relatives; parents of the same child; having *parental responsibility for the same child; parties to the same court case; in an intimate relationship of significant duration. The orders can be extended to 'relevant' children. Remedies for non-associated people may be available under the Protection From Harassment Act (1997).

Further measures are available through the Domestic Violence Protection Notice (DVPN) and the Domestic Violence Protection Order (DVPO). Initiated by Sections 24 to 33 of the Crime and Security Act (2010), which were implemented in March 2014, the DVPN/DVPO process builds on existing measures and procedures in relation to domestic violence and provides immediate emergency protection for the victim, allowing a period of protected space in which to explore the options available and make informed decisions regarding future safety. A DVPO is a civil order that provides protection to victims by enabling the police and *magistrates' courts to put in place protective measures in the immediate aftermath of a domestic violence incident where there is insufficient evidence to charge a perpetrator and provide protection to a victim by imposing bail conditions. A DVPN is an emergency non-molestation and eviction notice that can be issued by the police to a perpetrator when attending a domestic violence incident. Because a DVPN is a police-issued notice, it is effective immediately from the time of issue, giving the victim the immediate support they require in such a situation. Within forty-eight hours of the DVPN being served on the perpetrator, an application by police to a magistrates' court for a DVPO must be heard. A DVPO can prevent the perpetrator from returning to the residence and from having contact with the victim for up to twenty-eight days. This allows the victim breathing space to consider options with the help of a support agency such as *Women's Aid. Both the DVPN and DVPO contain a condition prohibiting the perpetrator from molesting the victim. *See also* CHILDREN AND DOMESTIC VIOLENCE; DOMESTIC VIOLENCE DISCLOSURE SCHEME; DOMESTIC VIOLENCE FORUM; HONOUR-BASED VIOLENCE.

Domestic Violence Disclosure Scheme Introduced in 2014, and often referred to as 'Clare's law', after Clare Wood who was murdered by her ex-boyfriend, the Scheme allows the police to disclose information on request about a partner's previous history of *domestic violence or other violent acts.

Domestic Violence Forum Each *local authority area has a Domestic Violence or Domestic Abuse Forum where *statutory and *voluntary agencies develop strategies to identify, prevent, and respond to *domestic violence. Such *multi-agency *collaboration can involve social workers in contributing to the development of more systematic and responsive services. Knowledge about domestic violence and the needs of women and children for safety and support has demonstrated the importance of comprehensive and coordinated responses across health, social services, and the police. It has also highlighted the central role played by voluntary agencies representing women survivors and by women survivors themselves. Feeding into DVFs is the requirement placed on local authorities to draw up *community safety plans under the Crime and Disorder Act (1998) that include estimates of the incidence of domestic violence. *See also* CHILDREN AND DOMESTIC VIOLENCE.

domestic work *See* DOMESTIC LABOUR.

domiciliary care *See* DOMICILIARY SERVICES.

domiciliary care agency *See* DOMICILIARY SERVICES.

domiciliary services Any service provided in a person's own home. Although in principle the definition is broad, the term most often refers to services provided for assistance with daily living or *personal care, in the majority of cases to *older people. The traditional *local authority *home help service, which in the main provided assistance with cleaning, cooking, and shopping, disappeared following the *community care reforms, and because of the impact of *eligibility criteria introduced by the reforms, such assistance is now only provided as part of an overall *'care package' arranged to meet more complex needs and usually supplied by a *private or *voluntary agency. Before private and voluntary providers became dominant there were extensive debates about the boundaries between what should be considered health (National Health Service) and social services (local authority) responsibilities, the most infamous of these being whether a bath was a 'social bath' or a 'medical bath'. Such disputes have lessened as responsibility for service provision has shifted away from statutory providers. Studies have shown that satisfaction or otherwise with domiciliary services is determined by the nature of the relationship with the staff providing it and the way in which the service is provided. Factors highlighted have included staff reliability and continuity, characteristics of the staff such as kindness and understanding, and their knowledge of *service users' *needs.

Historically, domiciliary services were slow to develop. There were concerns that extending services to support older people at home would encourage families (for which read women) to relinquish what were regarded as their rightful responsibilities to care for their older relatives. Domiciliary care was also not seen as effective in supporting more vulnerable older people. Accordingly, when the National Assistance Act (1948) was passed, local authorities merely had *powers to arrange for the provision of meals and recreational services by making grants to voluntary organizations. The need for local authorities to assume a more significant role in providing domiciliary services was only gradually accepted, and in 1962 the National Assistance Act (1948) was amended to allow the direct provision of *mobile meals services by local authorities. While domiciliary services gradually increased from the 1940s to the 1970s, they remained discretionary and were patchy geographically. The needs of older people were recognized specifically in the Health Services and Public Health Act (1968), implemented in 1971. This Act was concerned with promoting the welfare of older people. It was aimed at older people who were not 'substantially handicapped' but who nevertheless would benefit from the provision of services due to age-related frailty. It enabled local authorities to adopt a *preventive rather than reactive approach, giving them *powers, for example, to make arrangements for 'practical assistance in the home' and for 'meals and recreation'. However, these remained powers rather than *duties, so local authorities were not obliged to provide a service for older people who did not meet the definition of disability, at that time contained within Section 29 of the National Assistance Act.

Legislation and national standards are now in place with regard to domiciliary services (Health and Social Care Act [2008] [Regulated Activities] Regulations [2014]) and responsibility for the registration and inspection of domiciliary care providers lies with the *Care Quality Commission. There are minimum standards for domiciliary care agencies grouped under the headings of user-focused services; personal care; protection; managers and staff; organization, and running of the business. To be registered, providers must demonstrate that they meet the legal requirements and national minimum standards. All services have to be inspected at least once every three years, involving scrutiny of documents, visits to people's homes, and interviews with staff, *service users, and families. These inspections contribute to a quality rating of the service and determine the frequency of future inspections. *See also* AIDS AND ADAPTATIONS.

Further reading: Health and Social Care Act 2008 (Regulated Activities) Regulations (2014). Available at: http://www.cqc.org.uk/content/regulations-service-providers-and-managers.

domiciliary support *See* DOMICILIARY SERVICES.

dominant ideology A body of ideas, belief systems, values, and culture that portrays and promotes a world view in which its dominance appears natural and inevitable. Marx and Engels' dictum 'The ideas of the ruling class are in every epoch the ruling ideas' (*The German Ideology*) is the most well-known expression of the proposition that social order rests not only on forms of overt control, such as the police, but also is achieved by persuading people through commonly-held ideas and assumptions that the present form and organization of society, and the consequent distribution of power, privilege, and wealth, is a natural and legitimate state of affairs. The dominant ideology is seen as functioning in a way that incorporates dominated and oppressed groups into society in a way that is more cohesive than relying on direct repression. Some would argue that the concept of *citizenship—the formal equality of all members of a nation state—serves an important function in dominant ideology in masking the inequalities that exist. Others argue that social work serves a function within dominant ideology of ensuring that problems experienced by people are understood at the levels of the individual and the family, obscuring their relationship to wider social forces and social divisions. *See also* AGENTS OF SOCIAL CONTROL; DEMOCRATIC-WELFARE-CAPITALISM; DISCOURSE; DISTINCTION; DOMINATION; HEGEMONY; INDIVIDUAL PATHOLOGY.

domination The exercise of power by force or because the power is accepted as legitimate by those who are subjected to it. Max Weber (1864–1920) outlined three types of what he referred to as 'legitimate domination': rational-legal (derived from rules and procedures); traditional (from continuity over time); and charismatic (based on exceptional qualities of a leader). Domination by force occurs at different levels, from the domination of whole societies to the domination of individuals. For example, a small, close-knit community may force the acceptance of certain values and practices, and harm or reject those who deviate from them. At the individual level, domination by force can take many forms; for example, male domination expressed and upheld through *violence against women. *See also* DIFFERENCE; DISCOURSE; DISTINCTION; DIVERSITY; DOMESTIC VIOLENCE; DOMINANT IDEOLOGY; HEGEMONY.

double-bind A concept developed by Gregory Bateson (1904–80) to describe an emotional dilemma created when two (or more) conflicting messages are received, so that whatever response is given will be wrong but there is no way of opting out of the situation. For example, a child is placed in a double-bind if a parent clasps her/him tightly by the hand, trembling as s/he does so, and says that the child has to go to school because the child and the parent will be in trouble if s/he doesn't go to school, and that the parent will be fine while the child is at school, and the child should not worry about the parent. The child cannot resolve or opt out of this situation. If s/he responds to the signals that the parent is not OK at the prospect of being left, s/he will cause trouble for her/himself and the parent by not going to school. If the child goes to school, then s/he is abandoning the parent who needs her/him.

double standard Informal rules, ethics, or principles that are defined by dominant groups and applied to some people and not others, or applied more strictly to some people than others. One example is the double standard that operates for heterosexual women and men with regard to sexual behaviour. Another is gendered differences in pay and conditions for work that is the same or the different expectations of women and men with regard to *domestic labour or caring. The concept has also been used in relation to ageing, with women and men evaluated by different standards, men being less evaluated by how they look as physical signs of ageing are less penalized for men than for women (grey hair, for example).

Down's syndrome A genetic condition ('trisomy'), named after Victorian phys-
ician John Langdon Down, which involves having an extra copy of one chromosome—
three copies of chromosome 21 rather than two. It occurs in around one in a thousand
babies born in the UK. It is the most common inherited cause of *learning disability,
which people with Down's syndrome have to varying degrees. The chance of having a
baby with Down's syndrome increases with the age of the mother, especially over the
age of 35 (20 years: 1 in 1,500; 45 years: 1 in 30). Down's syndrome affects people from
all ethnic groups. Heart problems, some of which can be treated, affect almost half of
people with Down's syndrome. Gut problems are common, which can cause difficulties in eating, as well as meaning that constipation and thyroid gland disorders are
more likely. Sight and hearing difficulties, vulnerability to infections, and *autistic
spectrum disorders can also occur. Many people with the syndrome are able to lead
independent lives, while some need full-time care. Physiotherapy, speech therapy,
and special educational programmes are important, and social workers may be
involved with children and adults with Down's syndrome and their families. It is not
possible to prevent the genetic condition that results in Down's syndrome but during
pregnancy it is possible to identify the likely risk that a baby will be affected.

Down's Syndrome Association An association that began in 1970 as a local
parent support group and is now a national charity. The DSA provides information
and support for people with Down's syndrome, their families and carers, and
professionals who work with them, and champions the rights of people with the
syndrome. Its services include a help-line that provides information about all
aspects of living with the syndrome, including social security benefits, education,
and health, and advises new parents or anyone experiencing difficulties. The DSA is
also concerned with getting information to the media, public, and professionals,
and influencing policy-making. It runs courses throughout the UK for members,
professionals, and carers.

(SEE WEB LINKS)
• Official site of the Down's Syndrome Association.

dramaturgy Originating in the micro-sociological work of Erving Goffman
(1922–82) and using metaphors of social life from drama, theatre, and stage. For
example, Goffman contrasts 'frontstage' and 'backstage' areas to analyse how behaviour changes and impressions are managed when social actors 'go on stage'. This can
be seen in the contrast between social workers' behaviour backstage in the office, and
frontstage when working with *service users. *See also* ENCOUNTERS.

drop-in centre Open accessible place offering informal support for which no
*referral is necessary. Different drop-in centres cater for a wide range of people,
such as new parents, children, young people, *older people, people with mental
health problems, or anyone in a particular neighbourhood. They are often the
initiative of local *community groups or *voluntary organizations, and meet
people's needs at a grass-roots level. *See also* DAY SERVICES.

drug and alcohol problems Although the majority of people who use drugs or
alcohol do not develop long-term problems, there are persistent if fluctuating levels
of concern about drug and alcohol use when it does have a problematic impact on
the individuals concerned, as well as its wider economic and social repercussions,
such as crime, *poverty, ill-health, mental health problems, and damage to households and *communities. Although use of drugs and alcohol is governed by

legislation and potential prosecution of users, *harm reduction has been a principle that has underpinned policy and practice for many years. This principle is pursued through a number of strategies: seeking to restrict the supply of drugs; referring for *assessment on arrest; providing access to treatment such as *detoxification or methadone, including through the criminal justice system; working with families that have parents using drugs and/or alcohol; supplying sterile syringes at needle exchanges to minimize syringe reuse and sharing. Many social workers will encounter issues arising from the use of drugs and alcohol in their work, such as the impact it has on someone's parenting capacity or a young person's propensity to offend. In addition, specialist teams focused on drug and alcohol problems exist within local health service provision and often include social workers specializing in these areas of work. *See also* ADDICTION; ALCOHOLISM; COMMUNITY DRUGS TEAM; DUAL DIAGNOSIS.

Further reading: British Association of Social Workers (2012) *Alcohol and Other Drugs: Essential Information for Social Workers*. Available at: http://cdn.basw.co.uk/upload/basw_31759-10.pdf. Harris, P. (2007) *Empathy for the Devil: How to Help People Overcome Drug and Alcohol Problems*, Russell House.

SEE WEB LINKS
- Official site of Alcohol Concern.
- Official site of DrugWise, an independent centre of expertise on drugs, alcohol, and tobacco.

DSM (DSM-5) *See* DIAGNOSTIC AND STATISTICAL MANUAL OF MENTAL DISORDERS.

dual diagnosis In psychiatry this refers to the coexistence of mental disorder and other disorders. In recent years, dual diagnosis has come to be most commonly associated with the coexistence of mental disorder and substance misuse, and less commonly to the coexistence of mental disorder and *learning disability. Dual diagnosis can present professionals with serious challenges. There is a complex interaction between the two aspects, leading to difficulties in care and treatment: certain substance misuse can precipitate the onset of mental disorder and psychological symptoms and vice versa; symptoms of mental disorder can be worsened by the effects of substance misuse; and withdrawal symptoms from substance misuse can result in psychiatric symptoms. There is an increased risk of *suicide in individuals with a dual diagnosis, and they can fall between mental health and substance misuse services. In recent years attempts have been made to provide a more coherent response through the development of dual diagnosis and *assertive outreach teams.

dual sensory impairment In principle any combination of two sensory impairments but usually refers to being both blind and deaf, and is often used interchangeably with 'deaf-blind'. Some would see the latter term as objectionable but it is the term used in the Care Act (2014) guidance. The impairment does not have to involve total blindness or complete deafness. The Department of Health has stressed someone's 'combined sight and hearing impairment caus[ing] difficulties with communication, access to information, and mobility' (*Social Care for Deafblind Children and Adults*, 2001). Thus the severity of impairment for each separate sense, and the relationship between the two can vary considerably between the partial and complete *loss of one or both senses. However, most often it is people with complex needs who receive specialist services, and many of these people have been dual-sensory impaired from birth or early childhood. While people who

acquire dual sensory impairment during adulthood are also likely to receive services, *older people in that position are often not recognized as having an identifiable *disability, as there is a general assumption that sensory impairment is an
inevitable aspect of growing older, and there is a far higher risk that their sensory
impairment will not be investigated, and they will not receive services. *See also*
DEAFBLIND UK; SENSE.

duty of realism A notional 'duty' to take account of what is achievable in social
work. In examining social workers' dual and conflicting responsibilities to advance
*service users' interests on the one hand, and to be accountable to employing
organizations on the other, some have argued that social workers have a duty to
advocate for their service users, and a duty to contribute to their agency's agenda of
using resources as fairly, efficiently, and effectively as possible. Given that resources
are finite, this involves weighing up the relative benefits of different ways of
deploying resources. However, a duty of realism does not imply simply accepting
the status quo as the argument includes the need to state publicly when resources
are inadequate to the task and be clear about the duties that are not being
discharged and the *risks that are being taken. This suggests that social workers
should challenge the breaching of *statutory duties, the disregarding of central
government policy directives, and the interpretation of the law in ways that have
negative implications for service users, rather than accepting them with resignation
as the inevitable realities of practice. There are a number of prerequisites for social
workers to be able to fulfil the duty of realism in this way: a detailed working
knowledge of legislation and policy; a commitment to retaining social work *values
at the forefront of their work; critical reflection on their practice; and building up
forms of *collective support.

duty (specific) If legislation mandates a specific action then it must be done and a
legal duty is placed on the public authorities concerned, such as *local authorities or
the National Health Service. Such duties are often referred to as *statutory duties. In
legislation a duty is often triggered by the words 'shall' and 'any person'. With
increasing pressure on resources, social workers usually find themselves in the
position of only being able to carry out work where there is a strong specific
statutory duty towards an individual person. In addition to these duties to individuals there are general duties (sometimes referred to as *target duties) that are
directed at local populations rather than individuals. Specific duties are more
precise and give rights that are more enforceable, for example, through *judicial
review. *See also* POWER.

duty to assess *See* CARER'S ASSESSMENT; NEEDS ASSESSMENT.

duty to investigate The duty of a *local authority to make or cause to be made
such enquiries as it considers necessary if it is informed that a child found in its area
is the subject of an *Emergency Protection Order or is in *police protection, or the
authority has reasonable grounds to suspect that the child is suffering or likely to
suffer *significant harm (Children Act 1989 Section 47). Commonly referred to as a
*Section 47 enquiry by professionals and in government guidance, the legislation
describes this provision as the 'local authority's duty to investigate'.

dysfunction (dysfunctional) Used with regard to individuals, families, households, groups, or communities to refer to a pattern of activity or behaviour that has
unpleasant or harmful consequences. In relation to an organization, signifies that it

is not achieving the purposes for which it exists. Used in a general sense to refer to an aspect of society, or even to a whole society, that is not thought to be working well.

dyslexia Literally 'difficulty with words' (from Greek), a general term that covers a range of information-processing disorders. It is identified as a disability in the Equality Act (2010). Ten per cent of the UK population is dyslexic; 4 per cent severely so. Many dyslexic adults or children are unable to fulfil their potential as a large percentage of the population still do not understand what dyslexia is or know the difficulties that it presents. This is compounded by dyslexia being a hidden disability. As a result, people with dyslexia have to overcome numerous barriers. Dyslexia affects people in many different ways. Frequently encountered problems are difficulties in learning to read, spell, and write. (Less frequently encountered is a specific difficulty with numeracy.) Several areas in the brain interact to coordinate the manipulation of words needed for reading, writing, and spelling. Brain-imaging scans show that the brains of those with dyslexia work differently from those without dyslexia when processing information, but the features of any one person's dyslexia will depend on which areas of the brain are affected and how. There may be difficulties with reception of sensory information through sight or hearing, information processing speed, retaining, structuring, or retrieving information. This has nothing to do with intelligence. Dyslexia has an inherited component and other family members are often affected. Dyslexia is diagnosed on the basis of testing by a psychologist. Appropriate teaching methods and support can help, and coping strategies can be developed.

SEE WEB LINKS
• Official site of the British Dyslexia Association.
• Official site of Dyslexia Action.

early intervention (children) Intervening as soon as possible to tackle problems that have already emerged. It can apply to any *service user group but most commonly refers to targeting specific children who have an identified need for additional support, when their problems have begun to develop but before they become serious. Early intervention aims to prevent problems from becoming entrenched by promoting the strengths of children and families, and enhancing their *'protective factors' and, where necessary, by providing them with support from education, health, or social work services. The distinction between early intervention and *prevention, the latter referring to provision aimed at limiting the emergence of problems in the first place, is often blurred, as some programmes for children adopt both strategies at the same time. *See also* CHILDREN'S CENTRES; EARLY INTERVENTION (MENTAL HEALTH); EARLY YEARS SERVICES; EXTENDED SERVICES; FAMILY INFORMATION SERVICES; HOME START; LEAD PROFESSIONAL.

early intervention (mental health) A policy and practice approach aimed at improving the early detection and treatment of *psychosis during the critical early phase. The peak age-band for onset of the first episode of psychosis is 14 to 25 years and specialist early intervention services usually target people between the ages of 14 and 35. Psychosis can be symptomatic of the development of psychiatric disorders such as *schizophrenia and *bipolar disorder. Studies have shown that early detection and treatment can significantly reduce the risk of relapse and greatly improve the long-term *prognosis. For adolescents and young adults, undetected episodes of psychosis can have a devastating effect on the development of *identity, on intellectual and social development, on family life, on educational achievement, and on the ability to form lasting relationships. Evidence indicates that without early detection and treatment, the longer-term likelihood of unemployment, *depression, substance misuse, law-breaking, *self-harm, and *suicide is increased, and these interrelated patterns are difficult to interrupt once established. Delayed treatment also leads to reduced rates of *recovery and the course of the disorder, once established, is more serious and harmful to the individual in the long term. Early intervention services provide a holistic long-term approach, usually for up to three years, working with the young person, their family or significant others, education services, and any other important networks. The sustenance of existing relationships and the support of the young person's *goals and aspirations are considered vital to promote treatment and recovery, and to limit the potentially damaging impact psychosis can have on a young person's life. Specific interventions may include *family therapy and *cognitive behavioural therapy. *See also* EARLY INTERVENTION (CHILDREN).

Early Years Foundation Stage Statutory framework for the structure and standards of learning, development, and care for children from 0 to 5 years, which aims to lay the foundation for future learning and development, planned around the individual needs and interests of the child. The framework sets out six areas of learning and six stages of development against which children are assessed. *See also* CHILDREN'S CENTRES; NURSERIES; SURE START; UNDER-FIVES PROVISION.

Early Years Partnerships *See* EARLY YEARS SERVICES.

Early Years Services *Partnerships between local authorities and organizations in the *voluntary and *private sectors that provide a range of services for the under-fives and their families, including children with special educational needs. Early years services aim to give children a sound foundation for learning, combining nursery education and day care. They are an integral part of the *Early Years Foundation Stage framework. *See also* CHILDMINDERS; CHILDREN'S CENTRES; EXTENDED SERVICES; NURSERIES; SURE START; UNDER-FIVES PROVISION.

eating disorders Conditions characterized by persistent and severe disturbance in attitudes towards eating and the act of eating that significantly interfere with daily functioning, causing damage to an individual's physical, psychological, and emotional wellbeing. While it is not fully understood how these conditions arise, there is agreement that most eating disorders are characterized by a complex combination of physical and psychological factors, with intervention usually addressing both of these aspects so that people are assisted in developing healthier coping strategies. Traumatic events may contribute to the onset of an eating disorder and there is some evidence that genetic factors may have a small impact on whether someone develops the condition. Any person may develop an eating disorder regardless of age, *gender, cultural, or ethnic background, but the most vulnerable group tends to be young women between the ages of 12 and 25 years; women and younger people are more likely to be affected than men and *older people. The most well-known eating disorders are either eating excessively (bulimia nervosa) or insufficiently (*anorexia nervosa). Eating disorders are often accompanied by acute psychological distress and serious physical complications such as gastrointestinal problems and osteoporosis. The disorders can become chronic with poor recovery rates. Death can result from associated physical complications and research indicates that people with eating disorders have the highest mortality rates of all people with mental health problems. Those living with eating disorders often experience significant and long-term disruption to employment, relationships, fertility, family life, and parenting. In the UK it is widely recognized that there is under-detection of eating disorders, in part because those affected often conceal their condition from others, and can be reluctant to seek help. Treatment options depend on the nature and development of the disorder. *General practitioners are often the first port of call and are in a position to make an assessment that may lead, in the case of a child or young person, to referral to *Child and Adolescent Mental Health Services. Specialist assessments draw on contributions from clinical, social, and psychological perspectives in an *interdisciplinary team approach. Nutritional guidance and counselling may be provided and in some cases hospitalization may be necessary if the individual's health is at serious risk. Specialist clinics may provide treatments. In extreme cases, the Mental Health Act (1983) affords powers to administer force-feeding. *See also* CHILD DEVELOPMENT.

Further reading: Alexander, J. and Treasure, J. (eds) (2012) *A Collaborative Approach to Eating Disorders*, Routledge.

(((⊕))) SEE WEB LINKS

• Official site of Beating Eating Disorders (BEAT), which provides helplines, offers support online, and has a network of self-help groups.

eclecticism Drawing on a number of different theories and methods, and using parts of them in combination. The argument in support of eclecticism is that social workers encounter a wide range of people and circumstances, and that no single theory or method is likely to be capable of underpinning their practice. Advocates of eclecticism claim that it allows social workers to draw on the best mix of theories and methods in each situation they encounter.

ecological approach Perspective used in social work practice that seeks to understand and interpret the functioning of individuals and families in terms of their relationships with the wider community, and the cultural and socio-economic context in which the individual and family are located. There may be many factors to consider as part of this complex interaction. Advocates of the approach contend that in adopting this broader view of children, parents, and families, one that moves beyond a consideration of individual and family *pathology alone, social workers and those who frame social policy may be better placed to identify and build upon strengths within individuals, families, neighbourhoods, and *communities, and may meet their needs more effectively. In direct practice with children and families, the main impact of this approach can be seen in the format of the Assessment Framework (*see* ASSESSMENT [CHILDREN]), which social workers and other professionals draw on when compiling holistic assessments of children and families. Information about families is collated using the Framework under three domains, which are divided into a series of dimensions that reflect both the immediate and wider context of the child's environment and their interrelationship. The ecological perspective can be traced back to biological theories that sought to explain how organisms adapt to their environment. The classic exponent of this perspective as applied to the social sciences was Urie Bronfenbrenner (1917–2005), who identified five ecological levels that facilitate understanding of how individual and family processes are influenced by the environmental systems in which they function. This work was developed by James Garbarino in relation to child maltreatment. *See also* CHILD DEVELOPMENT; CHILD POVERTY; CHILD WELFARE; CYCLE OF DEPRIVATION; ECO MAP; PROBLEM FAMILY.

Further reading: Garbarino, J., Eckenrode, J., and Barry, F. (1997) *Understanding Abusive Families: An Ecological Approach to Theory and Practice*, Jossey Bass.
Greene, R. (2008, 3rd edn.) 'Ecological Perspective: An Eclectic Theoretical Framework for Social Work Practice', in Greene, R. (ed.) *Human Behavior Theory and Social Work Practice*. 199–236, Aldine Transaction.

ecological map *See* ECO MAP.

eco map A diagrammatic representation of all the relationships identified in a person's or family's life. This technique is used in social work, individual *counselling, and *family therapy to indicate, for example, all the individuals who are significant to a child, such as parents who care directly for the child and other *carers living in the household; parents living elsewhere; full and half siblings; grandparents and other members of the *extended family; other significant individuals. In this way, the entire set of relationships surrounding the child is graphically depicted for the purposes of *direct work with the child and her/his family, and as a tool to assist planning and *decision-making. Eco maps were developed by Hartman as a means of depicting the ecological system that surrounds a family or individual. *See also* CHILD-CENTRED APPROACH; ECOLOGICAL APPROACH; GENOGRAM; KINSHIP NETWORKS; LIFE MAP; LIFE STORY WORK; PLAY THERAPY.

Note: The stronger the line linking to the applicant, the greater the degree of support.

Mary and Peter Jones
Julie's parents.
White/British.
Live in same town as Julie. Daily contact by phone or visit. Currently offer practical and emotional support. Babysit Julie's children and would include any foster child. Peter enjoys DIY and making things and would share this with any foster child and would be a good role model.

David and Joanne
David is Julie's brother and Joanne his partner.
White/British.
Live in Devon (200 miles from Julie). Contact by telephone monthly and see each other 2/3 times a year. Have two children aged 18 and 16. Offer Julie moral support but unlikely to play any major role in fostering.

JULIE
(Applicant)

Winston and Claudine
Next-door neighbours.
African-Caribbean/British
Daily contact.
Offer practical and emotional support. Would be positive support to Julie if she was caring for an African-Caribbean child. Have two children, Duane (13) and Alisha (11), who play with Julie's children and would help any foster child to settle into the neighbourhood.

Anne
Julie's best friend from school days. Lives on same estate as Julie.
White/British.
Contact 2/3 times a week. Offers Julie lots of moral and emotional support. Was main source of support when Julie's marriage broke up. Anne is a single parent of two children, Anthony (9) and Suzie (7), who are of dual African-Caribbean/White British heritage. The two families do lots of social activities together so would play a large role in the life of any foster child.

Yoga class
Meets weekly in local community centre. Provides Julie with valuable 'me-time' as well as helping to maintain fitness and wellbeing.

Meera and Susan
Two friends from Julie's work. Meera is Indian/British and Susan is White/British.
Live in same town as Julie and meet up for occasional meals and nights out. Would offer Julie 'time-out' from fostering.

Eco map for a person applying to be a foster carer

Further reading: Hartman, A. (1995), 'Diagrammatic Assessment of Family Relationships', *Families in Society*, 76, 111–122.

economic determinism A view of Marx's position that the relations of production produce social relations. He regarded the relations of production as the base on which the political and legal superstructure rests. Thus social work exists in the superstructure but takes particular forms in capitalist societies as a consequence of the economic base, rooted in the relations of production. In this formulation, social workers are often seen as *agents of social control. Since Marx there has been a great deal of debate about the extent of economic determinism, some arguing for strong determinism, others for relations of production to be seen as a looser framework from which the superstructure develops relatively autonomously, and others have stressed individual resistance and/or the collective power of oppositional ideas and consciousness. Each of these positions has been applied to social work. *See also* HEGEMONY; MARXIST SOCIAL WORK; RADICAL SOCIAL WORK.

economy, efficiency, and effectiveness (the three 'e's) First promoted by the Thatcher governments, the three 'e's, as they are commonly called, are now an established part of received wisdom as the principles that should guide the provision of public services, including social work. Official definitions stress the following:

Economy means ensuring that the assets of a *local authority (or other body), and the services it purchases, are procured and maintained at the lowest possible cost consistent with a specified quality and quantity.

Efficiency means providing a specified volume and quality of services with the lowest level of resources capable of meeting that specification.

Effectiveness means providing the right services to enable the local authority (or other body) to implement its policies, meet its objectives, and achieve the desired outcomes.

See also NEO-LIBERALISM; NEW PUBLIC MANAGEMENT.

ECT *See* ELECTROCONVULSIVE THERAPY.

educational inclusion *See* INCLUSION.

educational psychologist A psychologist, usually employed by a *local authority, who works in schools, colleges, nurseries, or special units, helping children and young people experiencing problems in an educational setting, with the aim of enhancing their learning and addressing social or emotional problems, or learning difficulties. This involves working with individuals or groups and advising teachers, parents, social workers, and other professionals. Direct work with the child or young person involves *assessment, observation, *interview, or use of test materials to uncover the nature and source of the problem. Some educational psychologists work as independent private consultants. *See also* EDUCATION, HEALTH AND CARE NEEDS ASSESSMENT; EDUCATION, HEALTH AND CARE PLAN; EDUCATION SOCIAL WORKERS; INDIVIDUAL EDUCATION PLAN; PUPIL REFERRAL UNIT; SCHOOL ACTION; SCHOOL ACTION PLUS; SCHOOL ATTENDANCE; SPECIAL EDUCATIONAL NEEDS; TRUANCY.

education and looked-after children *See* LOOKED-AFTER CHILD (EDUCATION).

Education, Health and Care Needs Assessment An *assessment undertaken by a *local authority under the Children and Families Act (2014) of the education, health, and care needs of a child or young person aged 0–25 with special educational needs or disabilities to determine whether it is necessary to make provision for those needs with an *Education, Health and Care Plan. The following have a specific right to ask a local authority to conduct an Education, Health and Care Needs Assessment:

- A child's parent;
- A young person over the age of 16 but under the age of 25;
- A person acting on behalf of a school or post-16 institution (this should be with the knowledge and agreement of the parent and young person where possible).

In addition, anyone else can bring a child or young person who has (or may have) special educational needs to the attention of the local authority, for example foster carers, health and social care professionals, education staff, *youth offending teams, *probation services, or a family friend. Following a request, or a child having come to its attention, the local authority must (unless it has already undertaken such an assessment during the previous six months) determine whether an Education, Health and Care Needs Assessment is necessary and communicate that decision within six weeks.

Education, Health and Care Plan Introduced by the Children and Families Act (2014) and replacing *Statements of Special Educational Needs from 1 September 2014. (Children and young people who already had Statements of Special Educational Needs at the changeover date move to Education, Health and Care Plans in spring 2018). The Plan details the education, health, and social care support that is to be provided to a child or young person aged 0–25 who has special educational needs or a *disability. It is drawn up by the *local authority after an *Education, Health and Care Needs Assessment of the child or young person has determined that such a plan is necessary and after consultation with relevant partner agencies.

education social workers They work with schools, pupils, parents, and other professionals, dealing with problems and issues that prevent children from attending school or that are related to or emerge in the school context. Promoting school attendance is seen as a component in assisting children considered to be at *risk of *social and educational exclusion. In response to *austerity, some local authorities have drastically reduced or completely cut education social work provision. *See also* EDUCATIONAL PSYCHOLOGIST; EDUCATION, HEALTH AND CARE NEEDS ASSESSMENT; EDUCATION, HEALTH AND CARE PLAN; EDUCATION SUPERVISION ORDER; INDIVIDUAL EDUCATION PLAN; PUPIL REFERRAL UNIT; SCHOOL ACTION; SCHOOL ACTION PLUS; SCHOOL ATTENDANCE; SPECIAL EDUCATIONAL NEEDS; TRUANCY.

Education Supervision Order An order specified under Section 36 of the Children Act (1989) that empowers *local authorities to apply to courts for this Order in respect of children of *compulsory school age who are not being educated. If a court makes an Education Supervision Order, it requires the local authority to appoint a named education supervisor, usually an *education social worker, to work with the child and her/his parents, usually for up to a year. The Order places the child under the supervision of the local authority with the aim of ensuring s/he receives full-time education suited to her/his age, ability, and aptitude, taking into account any special educational needs. There is an expectation that support, advice, and guidance is provided to the parents and the child, and the parents and child must comply with any reasonable directions given by the supervisor. *See also* PARENTING CLASSES; PARENTING ORDER.

effectiveness *See* ECONOMY, EFFICIENCY, AND EFFECTIVENESS.

efficiency *See* ECONOMY, EFFICIENCY, AND EFFECTIVENESS.

egalitarianism The belief that all people are of equal worth, which takes different forms when its implications are discussed. Some hold that egalitarianism means that equality is a desirable *goal towards which to work, but divide on whether that means equality of opportunity (making competition fairer) or of outcome (redistribution of wealth); others that equality means that everybody should enjoy the same human rights.

ego In Freud's model of the personality having three components, the ego is the component that deals with reality, trying to reconcile the demands of the id for pleasure or gratification with the censure of the superego acting as the 'conscience'. *See also* PSYCHODYNAMIC CASEWORK.

egocentric network analysis *See* ECO MAP.

e-gov (e-government) *See* ELECTRONIC GOVERNMENT.

85% rule Under the Conservatives' *community care reforms the stipulation made to ensure the development of a market in services: 85 per cent of the funds transferred to *local authorities from central government's social security system for providing *community care services had to be spent on services provided by the *independent sector. This led local authorities to float off some of their domiciliary and residential services as independent not-for-profit operations.

elder abuse Mistreatment of an older person. *See also* SAFEGUARDING VULNERABLE ADULTS.

electroconvulsive therapy (ECT) A psychiatric treatment that has attracted much controversy. It consists of passing an electrical current through the brain, while the patient is anaesthetized, in order to produce a seizure (fit), with the aim of relieving severe *depression, mania, or catatonia. ECT was first introduced in the 1930s and its use was most common between the 1940s and 1960s. It is now used less often, possibly because of better psychological and drug treatments for depression. It is not clear how ECT works. Many medical experts believe that severe depression is linked to problems with chemicals in the brain. They consider that ECT helps to restore the proper function of these chemicals and so aids recovery. ECT is usually considered only when other treatments have failed. Under Section 58A of the Mental Health Act (1983), ECT can only be given with the person's consent, or—if s/he lacks the *capacity to consent—where a Second Opinion Appointed Doctor certifies that it is appropriate for her/him to receive this treatment. The SOAD is unable to provide a certificate if ECT conflicts with an advance decision (*see* CAPACITY), with a decision of a deputy (*see* COURT OF PROTECTION) under the Mental Capacity Act (2005), or with an order of the *Court of Protection. In restricted emergency situations ECT can be administered without consent under Section 62 of the Act, if treatment is required to save the patient's life, prevent the condition from worsening, or prevent serious harm to others.

electronic government The provision of access to central and local government information and services via computer and telephone, creating digital interaction between government and citizens. As part of its *modernization agenda, the *New Labour government (1997–2010) promoted the use of information and communication technology for this purpose, presenting ICT as the way to 'reinvent' government. This top-down initiative forced *local authorities to rethink and reorganize their services, including social work, not least because New Labour required all services to be 'e-accessible' by 2005. Electronic government powerfully symbolized New Labour's promotion of technological approaches as part of its advocacy of 'modern management' with supposedly sophisticated 'leading-edge' solutions, services, or institutions. 'E-government' was accompanied by the creation of an 'e-minister', 'e-envoys', and 'information champions'. Although electronic government can be situated at a particular moment in the development of New Labour, the technological scope of electronic government has since increased with the growing sophistication of ICT and it endures as a significant force in how social services are accessed and delivered. *See also* CALL CENTRE; COMPUTERISATION.

electronic monitoring (electronic tagging) A form of surveillance that involves the attachment of an electronic device to individuals convicted of criminal offences in order that their whereabouts can be monitored. Used by the courts and penal institutions to manage individuals who have been released back into the community, ensuring their compliance with the requirements of a court order or parole conditions. In England and *Wales, this method may also form part of a *community-based sentence or fall under the conditions of Home Detention Curfew, which requires someone to remain in their home during specified hours. These uses are mainly covered by the Criminal Justice Act (2003). Separate legislation applies in *Scotland. The Prevention of Terrorism Act (2005) extended the use of tagging to individuals made the subject of a Control Order, an order made by the Home Secretary to restrict an individual's liberty for the purpose of 'protecting members of the public from a risk of terrorism'.

eligibility assessment *See* DEPRIVATION OF LIBERTY SAFEGUARDS; ELIGIBILITY CRITERIA.

eligibility criteria (eligibility threshold) Statements that set out the basis on which decisions are made about whether adults are entitled to receive social care services.

Following the implementation of the NHS and Community Care Act (1990), central government indicated that criteria for providing services should be drawn up independently by each *local authority, with reference to the resources each local authority had available. Local authorities had considerable discretion to set their own eligibility criteria but this resulted in widespread geographical variation and a 'postcode lottery' in the provision of services. Some local authorities had different criteria for different *service user groups, and also different criteria to access particular services, such as day care or residential care. A significant legal case (the Gloucestershire judgment) confirmed that local authorities could take account of their resources in deciding whether to meet *need, but clarified that this decision-making had to be carried out with reference to general publicized eligibility criteria, applied consistently to each individual *case. Thus, the purpose of eligibility criteria was and is to manage the deficit between demand for services and the resources available to provide them. They operate as a *rationing device, directing resources to individuals who meet particular conditions and withholding them from others who do not satisfy the criteria laid down. From April 2003, a national framework for eligibility criteria for adult social care services was introduced under *Fair Access to Care Services* guidance, issued by the Department of Health. This imposed one set of criteria for all adult *service users and for access to all types of service, with local authorities deciding at which level of need they would provide services within the framework. FACS was replaced in 2010 by: the Department of Health's *Prioritising Need in the Context of Putting People First: A Whole System Approach to Eligibility for Social Care—Guidance on Eligibility Criteria for Social Care*. However, the approach was essentially the same as that in FACS. This framework was replaced by national eligibility criteria under the Care Act (2014), which set minimum thresholds for adult *care and support needs and *carer support needs and stipulated that needs that reach the thresholds must be met.

After an *assessment (*see* CARER'S ASSESSMENT; NEEDS ASSESSMENT) has been completed, a social worker has to decide, on the basis of the eligibility criteria, whether the person in question should receive services. In this process, a distinction is made between 'presenting needs', that is, someone's comprehensive needs that may have been identified when carrying out the assessment, and 'eligible needs', that is, those needs that meet the eligibility criteria. There is a statutory *duty on local authorities to meet eligible needs that meet the national thresholds, but not presenting needs. In theory under the Care Act (2014) local authorities can also decide to meet needs that are not deemed to be eligible according to the national threshold but this was not happening prior to the onset of *austerity and the likelihood of it ever happening has now receded out of sight. Thus, the use of eligibility criteria cloaks what is moral, ethical, and political decisions in a technical-managerial guise. By gradually redrawing (and reducing) the parameters of what is available, incrementally and away from public view, eligibility criteria make it difficult to identify groups of people who are suffering as a result of the operation of the criteria and to point to patterns in resource shortfalls.

Adults with care and support needs The national eligibility criteria for adults with care and support needs set a minimum threshold that must be met. The threshold is based on identifying how a person's needs affect their ability to achieve relevant *outcomes and how this impacts on their wellbeing. All of the following three conditions have to be met for an adult who has care and support needs to be considered as having eligible needs:

- The adult's needs arise from or are related to a physical or mental impairment or illness.
- As a result of the adult's needs s/he is unable to achieve two or more of the specified outcomes (see below).
- As a consequence of being unable to achieve these outcomes there is, or there is likely to be, a significant impact on the adult's wellbeing.

Condition 1 The adult's needs arise from or are related to a physical or mental impairment or illness
The adult's needs for care and support are due to physical, mental, sensory, learning, or cognitive disabilities or illnesses, substance misuse, or brain injury and they are not caused by other circumstantial factors. A formal diagnosis is not required. The judgement about the presence of a condition is based on the assessment that is undertaken (*see* NEEDS ASSESSMENT).

Condition 2 As a result of the adult's needs, s/he is unable to achieve two or more of the outcomes set out in the regulations
The adult is unable to achieve two or more of the outcomes set out in the eligibility regulations. Being unable to achieve an outcome describes the situation of someone who:

- *Is unable to achieve the outcome without assistance*. This would include where the adult is unable to do so even when assistance is provided. It also includes when an adult needs prompting. For example, some adults may be physically able to wash but need reminding about the importance of doing so;
- *Is able to achieve the outcome without assistance but doing so causes the adult significant pain, distress or anxiety*. For example, an older person with severe arthritis may be able to prepare a meal, but doing so leaves them in severe pain and unable to eat the meal;
- *Is able to achieve the outcome without assistance, but doing so endangers or is likely to endanger the health or safety of the adult, or of others*. For example, if the health or safety of another member of the family is endangered when an adult attempts to complete a task or an activity without support;

- *Is able to achieve the outcome without assistance but takes significantly longer than would normally be expected.* For example, an adult with a physical *disability who is able to dress themselves in the morning, but it takes a long time to do this, it leaves them exhausted, and it prevents them from achieving other outcomes.

The next stage is to assess whether or not someone is unable to achieve two or more of the following outcomes:

(a) *Managing and maintaining nutrition*
The adult has access to food and drink to maintain nutrition and is able to prepare and consume the food and drink.

(b) *Maintaining personal hygiene*
The adult is able to wash themselves and launder their clothes.

(c) *Managing toilet needs*
The adult is able to access and use a toilet and manage their toilet needs.

(d) *Being appropriately clothed*
The adult is able to dress themselves and to be appropriately dressed, for instance in relation to the weather.

(e) *Being able to make use of the home safely*
The adult is able to move around the home safely, which could, for example, including getting up steps, using kitchen facilities, or accessing the bathroom. This also includes the immediate environment around the home such as access to the property, for example steps leading up to the home.

(f) *Maintaining a habitable home environment*
The condition of the adult's home is sufficiently clean and maintained to be safe. A habitable home is safe and has essential amenities, such as water, electricity, and gas.

(g) *Developing and maintaining family or other personal relationships*
The adult is not lonely or isolated. S/he is able to maintain the personal relationships s/he has and/or is able to develop new relationships.

(h) *Accessing and engaging in work, training, education, or volunteering*
The adult has an opportunity to engage in work, training, education, or volunteering, if s/he wishes to do so.

(i) *Making use of necessary facilities or services in the local community, including public transport and recreational facilities or services*
The adult is able to get around in the community safely and use facilities such as public transport, shops, or recreational facilities.

(j) *Carrying out any caring responsibilities the adult has for a child*
The adult is able to carry out caring responsibilities s/he has for a child/children.

Condition 3 As a consequence there is, or there is likely to be, a significant impact on the adult's wellbeing

The adult's needs and their inability to achieve two or more of the outcomes above cause or *risk causing a significant impact on their wellbeing. The impact of being unable to achieve the outcomes does not have to be considered individually; a significant impact on wellbeing can be the result of the cumulative effect of being unable to achieve outcomes. Decisions also involve consideration of whether the adult's inability to achieve the outcomes impacts on at least one of the areas of wellbeing in a significant way or whether the effect of the impact on a number of the areas of wellbeing means that there is a significant impact on the adult's overall wellbeing.

The term 'significant' is not defined by the Eligibility Regulations and therefore has its everyday meaning in relation to the adult's needs and their consequent inability to achieve the relevant outcomes that have important consequences for their daily lives, their *independence, and their wellbeing. In deciding the impact on an adult's wellbeing, the adult's needs have to be understood in the context of what is important to them. Needs may affect different people differently because what is important to an individual's wellbeing varies; circumstances that create a significant impact on the wellbeing of one person may not have the same effect on another.

People with fluctuating needs may have needs that are not apparent at the time of the assessment, but may have arisen in the past and are likely to arise again in the future. Therefore the local authority must consider an individual's needs over an appropriate period of time to ensure that all of their needs have been accounted for when eligibility is being determined. Where fluctuating needs are apparent, they should be included in the *care plan, detailing the steps the local authority will take to meet needs in circumstances where these fluctuate. In such situations, the nature of the adult's needs over the past year should be considered in order to get a complete picture of the adult's level of need.

Carers with support needs Carers can be eligible for support in their own right. The carers' threshold is based on the impact a carer's need for support has on her/his wellbeing. All of the following three conditions need to be met for a carer with support needs to be considered as having eligible needs:

- The needs arise as a consequence of providing necessary care for an adult.
- The effect of the carer's needs is that any of the circumstances specified in the Eligibility Regulations apply to the carer.
- As a consequence of that fact there is, or there is likely to be, a significant impact on the carer's wellbeing.

Condition 1 *The needs arise as a consequence of providing necessary care for an adult*
The carer's need for support arises because they are providing care to an adult. They can be eligible for support whether or not the adult for whom they care has eligible needs. The decision about a carer's eligibility is based on the carer's needs and how these impact on their wellbeing. The care provided has to be 'necessary'. If the carer is providing care and support to meet needs that the adult is capable of meeting themselves, the carer may not be providing necessary support. In such circumstances, *information and advice are provided to the adult and carer about how the adult can use their own strengths or services available in the community to meet their needs.

Condition 2 *The effect of the carer's needs is that any of the circumstances specified in the Eligibility Regulations apply to the carer*
Consideration has to be given to whether the carer's physical or mental health is either deteriorating or is at *risk of doing so, or whether the carer is unable to achieve one of a list of other outcomes that may apply. Being unable to achieve an outcome describes the situation of a carer who:

- *Is unable to achieve the outcome without assistance.* This includes where the carer would be unable to achieve an outcome even if assistance were provided. A carer might, for example, be unable to fulfil her/his parental responsibilities unless they receive support in their caring role.
- *Is able to achieve the outcome without assistance, but doing so causes or is likely to cause significant pain, distress, or anxiety.* A carer might, for example, be able to care for the adult and undertake full-time employment, but doing both causes the carer significant stress.
- *Is able to achieve the outcome without assistance but doing so is likely to endanger the health or safety of the carer or any adults or children for whom the carer*

provides care. A carer might, for example, be able to provide care for her/his family and provide necessary care for the adult, but, where this endangers the adult with care and support needs, for example because the adult receiving care has to be left alone while other responsibilities are met, the carer should not be considered able to meet the outcome of caring for their family.

A carer has eligible support needs, if s/he is unable to achieve any of the following outcomes, set out in the Eligibility Regulations, and as a result there is, or there is likely to be, a significant impact on their wellbeing:

(a) *Carrying out any caring responsibilities the carer has for a child*
Any parenting or other caring responsibilities the carer has for a child in addition to their caring role for the adult. For example, the carer might be a grandparent with caring responsibilities for their grandchildren while the grandchildren's parents are at work.

(b) *Providing care to other persons for whom the carer provides care*
Any additional caring responsibilities the carer may have for other adults. For example, a carer may also have caring responsibilities for a parent in addition to caring for the adult with care and support needs.

(c) *Maintaining a habitable home environment*
Whether the condition of the carer's home is a safe and an appropriate environment to live in and whether it presents a significant risk to the carer's wellbeing. A habitable home should be safe and have essential amenities such as water, electricity, and gas.

(d) *Managing and maintaining nutrition*
Whether the carer has the time to do essential shopping and to prepare meals for her/himself and her/his family.

(e) *Developing and maintaining family or other significant personal relationships*
Whether the carer is in a position where her/his caring role prevents them from maintaining key relationships with family and friends or from developing new relationships where the carer does not already have other personal relationships.

(f) *Engaging in work, training, education, or volunteering*
Whether the carer can continue in her/his job or undertake education, engage in voluntary work, or have the opportunity to get a job if s/he is not already in employment.

(g) *Making use of necessary facilities or services in the local community*
Whether the carer has the opportunity to make use of the local community's services and facilities, for example whether the carer has time to use recreational facilities such as gyms or swimming pools.

(h) *Engaging in recreational activities*
Local authorities should consider whether the carer has leisure time, which might, for example, mean having some free time to read or engage in a hobby.

Condition 3 As a consequence of that fact there is, or there is likely to be, a significant impact on the carer's wellbeing

Where the carer is unable to achieve one or more of the above outcomes, the impact of each does not have to be considered individually; a significant impact on well-being can be the result of the cumulative effect of being unable to achieve those outcomes. Decisions also involve consideration of whether the carer's inability to achieve the outcomes above impacts on at least one of the areas of wellbeing in a significant way or whether the effect of the impact on a number of the areas of well-being means that there is a significant impact on a carer's overall wellbeing.

The term 'significant' is not defined by the Eligibility Regulations and therefore has its everyday meaning in relation to a carer's needs and her/his consequent inability to achieve the relevant outcomes that have important consequences for her/his daily life, independence, and wellbeing. In deciding the impact on a carer's wellbeing, the carer's needs have to be understood in the context of what is important to her/him. Needs may affect different people differently because what is important to an individual's wellbeing will vary so that circumstances which create a significant impact on the wellbeing of one person may not have the same effect on another. Therefore, it should be noted that there is no hierarchy of needs or of the areas of wellbeing.

Carers with fluctuating needs may have needs that are not apparent at the time of the assessment, but may have arisen in the past and are likely to arise again in the future. Therefore the carer's needs must be considered over an appropriate period of time to ensure that all of their needs have been accounted for when their eligibility is being determined. A carer's needs can fluctuate, irrespective of whether the needs of the adult for whom they care fluctuate. For example, if the carer is a parent of schoolchildren, they may not have the same level of need for support during term time as during school holidays. Where fluctuating needs are apparent, these should be included in the support plan, detailing the steps local authorities will take to meet needs in circumstances when they fluctuate. Consideration is also given to how the carer's needs may change as a result of the fluctuation in the needs of the person they are caring for. Authorities must get a complete picture of the carer's level of need over an appropriate period.

After the decision about eligibility The decision about eligibility is based on the adult's needs for care and support and how these impact on their wellbeing. Account is only taken of whether the adult has a carer or what needs may be met by a carer, after the eligibility decision has been made at the point when a *care and support plan is prepared. At that point, if the adult does have a carer, the care they are providing will be taken into account when considering whether needs have to be met. Eligible needs that are being met by a carer do not have to be met but those needs are recognized and recorded as eligible during the assessment process (*see* NEEDS ASSESSMENT). This is to ensure that should there be a breakdown in the caring relationship, the needs are already identified as eligible and steps can be taken to meet them without further assessment.

When a decision has been made about eligibility, a copy of the decision is provided to the person to whom the decision applies, whether that is an adult with care and support needs or a carer with support needs.

Where a person is found to have no eligible needs, information and advice are provided on what can be done to meet or reduce the needs that remain (for example, what support might be available in the *community to help the adult or carer) and to prevent or delay the development of needs in the future. This information and advice is tailored to the needs the person has, with the aim of delaying deterioration and preventing future needs, as well as reflecting the availability of local support.

If an adult has eligible care and support needs, an agreement is reached with them about which of her/his needs s/he would like the local authority to meet. The person may not want to have local authority support in relation to all of her/his needs. They may intend to arrange alternative services themselves to meet some needs. Others may not want the local authority to meet any of their needs, having approached the authority only for the purpose of an assessment. For any needs that someone wants to have met by the local authority, consideration will be given to how the local authority might meet those needs. This consideration does not replace or pre-empt the care and support planning process. It is an early consideration of the potential support options in order to determine whether some of those may be services for which the local authority makes a charge. Where that is the case, the local authority must carry out a financial assessment.

If a person has eligible needs, it has to be established whether they meet the residence requirement. This applies differently to adults with care and support needs and to carers with support needs. In the case of an adult, they must be ordinarily resident in the local authority's area. In the case of a carer, the person for whom they provide care must be ordinarily resident in the authority's area. This is because a carer's needs are met by the local authority where the adult with the need for care and support lives, not the authority where the carer lives, if they live elsewhere. *See also* CARER'S ASSESSMENT; NEEDS ASSESSMENT; THRESHOLD CRITERIA (CHILDREN).

Further reading: Department of Health (2015) *Care and Support (Eligibility Criteria) Regulations*. Available at: http://www.legislation.gov.uk/uksi/2015/313/pdfs/uksi_20150313_en.pdf.
Department of Health (2016) *Care Act (2014) Guidance*, Chapter 6. Available at: http://www.gov.uk/government/publications/care-act-statutory-guidance/care-and-support-statutory-guidance.

eligible needs (adults) *See* CARER'S ASSESSMENT; ELIGIBILITY CRITERIA; NEEDS ASSESSMENT.

elite Used loosely to refer to any group with privileges not shared by others, but strictly speaking a powerful ruling minority group whose composition reflects the balance of power between competing social groups and forces in society. *See also* ESTABLISHMENT.

emancipatory perspectives Stances with regard to social work that emphasize the presence of oppressive power relations in people's lives and the need to free them from the impact of those power relations. Social work is seen as having the potential to unmask power relations and to contribute to freeing *service users from oppressive circumstances and relationships. Stances vary according to the different weight they place on *participation, justice, and equality, either separately or in combination. The principle of participation is seen as fundamental to developing emancipatory practice with service users, though there may be differences concerning whether participation is seen as referring simply to work with individual service users at an interpersonal level, often referred to as *partnership, or whether it is seen as extending to wider issues such as planning and evaluating services (*see* ARNSTEIN'S LADDER). Justice is concerned with ensuring that people realize their rights. Equality is concerned not with 'treating everyone the same', but with providing the means by which people can achieve either equality of opportunity or equality of outcomes (*see* EGALITARIANISM). Although emancipatory social work perspectives originally had far-reaching *goals, and some versions of them in different parts of the world still do, in UK social work they have tended to be diluted as they have been fitted to the parameters of practice in *statutory settings and are usually confined to a concern with the immediate constraints affecting people's lives. *See also* ANTI-DISCRIMINATORY PRACTICE; ANTI-OPPRESSIVE PRACTICE; DISCRIMINATION; EMPOWERMENT; SERVICE USER PARTICIPATION.

emergency duty team (EDT) A team of social workers, employed by a *local authority, which works when social work offices are closed (overnight, at weekends, and during Bank Holidays). Such a team usually covers the whole of the local authority's area, such as a city or a county. Rather than undertaking the full range of social work duties, it responds only to urgent crisis situations, such as *compulsory admission to a psychiatric unit or removal of an abused child from her/his parents.

emergency placement *See* PLACEMENT.

Emergency Protection Order (EPO) An order made under Section 44 of the Children Act (1989) that is intended for situations in which it is necessary to secure the immediate safety of a child. A court will only grant an Order if it has been satisfied by the applicant, usually a *local authority, that a child is likely to suffer *significant harm if not removed to accommodation provided by or on behalf of the applicant, and enquiries are being made with respect to the child under *Section 47 of the Children Act (1989). This Order may only be made for a period not exceeding eight days, after which time a local authority will decide if further legal action is needed to safeguard the child. It may then enter *care proceedings and make an application for an *Interim Care Order. Courts are unlikely to make an EPO unless the threat to the child's safety is clear and imminent. A local authority is more likely to seek the agreement of a parent or care-giver to place the child away from the family should her/his immediate safety needs indicate the necessity for this. *See also* FAMILY COURTS; POLICE PROTECTION; SECTION 47 ENQUIRY; STRATEGY DISCUSSION; STRATEGY MEETING.

emotional abuse *See* CHILD ABUSE AND NEGLECT.

emotional intelligence An important attribute in social work that involves the ability to be aware of and monitor one's own and others' emotions and to use this information to steer one's emotional responses, thinking, and actions in formulating *assessments and plans. The ability to build relationships with children and adults is at the heart of social work and this requires empathy, genuineness, warmth, acceptance, encouragement, and sensitivity. *See also* EMOTIONAL LABOUR; EMOTIONAL RESILIENCE; RESILIENCE.

Further reading: Ingram, R (2015) *Understanding Emotions in Social Work: Theory, Practice and Reflection*, McGraw Hill.

emotional labour 1. Work roles that require not simply face-to-face contact with people, but the sustained performance or withholding of certain emotions. The term was first used by Arlie Hochschild (1940–) in *The Managed Heart* (1983) to refer to the expression of 'commodified emotions', such as those required to be displayed by airline cabin staff. Social workers carry a heavy load of emotional labour with work requirements such as not displaying shock or revulsion, and remaining calm in the face of anger directed towards them. *See also* DISNEYIZATION; EMOTIONAL INTELLIGENCE; EMOTIONAL RESILIENCE.
2. Used by feminists to describe the work that women do as partners and relatives, in part compensating for the alleged inability of men to express their own emotions and respond to the emotions of those around them. *See also* DOMESTIC LABOUR; EMOTIONAL INTELLIGENCE; EMOTIONAL RESILIENCE; RESILIENCE.

Further reading: Hochschild, A. (2012, first published 1983) *The Managed Heart: Commercialization of Human Feeling*, University of California Press.

emotional neglect *See* CHILD ABUSE AND NEGLECT.

emotional resilience An important attribute in social work that involves an individual's capacity to manage external and internal demands and pressures and is characterized by an ability to emerge strengthened and more resourceful, some-times described as the ability to 'bounce back'. Being resilient does not mean that a social worker never experiences stress or distress or feels emotional pain and sadness. Emotional resilience refers to the process of adapting to difficult situations, learning from the experience, and being able to develop an increased ability to cope with adversity in the future. The *Professional Capabilities Framework identifies emotional resilience as a key professional attribute for social workers throughout their careers. The *Health and Care Professions Council, the professional regulator for social workers, also emphasizes the importance of their being able to manage the emotional impact of practice and sustain their health and *wellbeing. There have been a number of research studies on the personal qualities that underpin emotional resilience in practitioners, for example the ability to:

- Reflect on practice by utilizing a range of skills;
- Understand the impact of emotions on the self and others and the implications for practice;
- Respond to service users with empathy and avoid over-involvement;
- Draw on a flexible repertoire of coping strategies;
- Communicate effectively and confidently with service users and colleagues from a range of different backgrounds;
- Utilize organizational support, such as supervision, confidently and effectively;
- Maintain a strong value base and professional capability in the face of challenging circumstances.

See also EMOTIONAL INTELLIGENCE; EMOTIONAL LABOUR; MINDFULNESS; RESILIENCE.

emotional work *See* EMOTIONAL LABOUR.

empathy The ability to imagine oneself in the position of another person and to be able to understand how the other person is feeling. Social workers have traditionally been encouraged to respond empathetically to *service users in order to appreciate fully the situation they are in, though this is not seen as necessarily requiring social workers to approve of the emotions that they seek to understand. *See also* EMOTIONAL INTELLIGENCE; WARMTH.

empirical When used in relation to research, it indicates the detail of the approach taken to acquiring the data or an emphasis on the data that is produced. It implies, therefore, a concern with evidence and how the evidence was generated. It is sometimes contrasted with 'theoretical' in order to emphasize a close relationship with the findings of research and how they were derived. It can be used in a critical way to mean a lack of interest in theory as in 'mindless empiricism' or 'abstracted empiricism'. *See also* EVIDENCE-BASED PRACTICE.

empowering (empowerment) The processes through which people who lack power become more powerful, not in the sense of having power over others but in working towards or achieving their aims. This concept has achieved a prominent position in social work in recent years. Its origins lie in seeking to connect the personal problems in people's lives, seen as their private troubles, to wider social, political, and economic forces (or public issues), as a way of bringing about change in the lives of the less powerful. In much mainstream social work it has been diluted to mean a social worker helping people to become more powerful in their transactions with social services through such means as having more say in plans that are being made to address issues in their lives or taking part in *case conferences. While such an approach to involve *service users is *good practice, to call it empowerment is perhaps a misnomer. Giving people power, itself somewhat a contradiction in terms, in the sense of assisting their *participation in social work processes, is a long way from earlier aspirations for people to develop strategies to understand what needs to change, not just in themselves but in the wider society, if they are to become more powerful. Thus while earlier approaches asserted that people had to address both their personal problems and wider issues, contemporary mainstream empowering practice frequently stops short at the level of addressing personal problems. Notwithstanding the limitations of this approach, it is clearly important for social workers to seek to work with service users in ways that do not compound their experiences of *oppression so that people can have as much say as possible in decisions that affect their lives. In so doing, they need to be keenly aware of how power permeates social worker–service user relationships. *See also* ADVOCACY; ANTI-DISCRIMINATORY PRACTICE; ANTI-OPPRESSIVE PRACTICE; DISCRIMINATION; SERVICE USER PARTICIPATION.

Further reading: Adams, R. (2008, 4th edn.) *Social Work and Empowerment*, Palgrave Macmillan.

enablement (enablement service) *See* REABLEMENT.

enabling authority Conceiving of the roles of a *local authority as being to purchase and oversee the provision of services such as *residential care and *domiciliary services through contracts and regulation of contract compliance, rather than as primarily a direct provider of services itself. *See also* AGENCY THEORY; COMMUNITY CARE REFORMS; CONTRACT STATE.

encopresis Faecal incontinence/soiling. Children usually have control over their bowels by the age of four, though some children take longer. Soiling can happen for a number of reasons. Some children develop at a slower rate but they will eventually develop the ability not to soil. Other children are worried about using the toilet. A specific occurrence may have started this response, such as having been constipated and experienced pain in the past. Others may be unable to go to the toilet because of fear or *anxiety. In the case of some of the children social workers meet, severe cases of soiling can be as a consequence of *abuse and/or neglect and/or trauma. A child with prolonged encopresis should be taken to see her/his doctor so that the possibility of a physical cause can be investigated.

encounters Social work involves a series of face-to-face encounters. The detail of encounters in everyday life was extensively explored in the work of Erving Goffman (1922–82) in terms of the social rules governing verbal and non-verbal behaviour, such as turn-taking in conversation, body stance, and frequency of eye contact. Conscious or unconscious familiarity with and the ability to act within these 'rules' is essential for social workers, if they are to be able to negotiate the encounters in which they are engaged. *See also* DRAMATURGY.

endogenous depression A form of *depression that emerges from within rather than as a reaction to external events.

Enduring Power of Attorney *See* LASTING POWER OF ATTORNEY.

enterprise culture A concept found in *New Labour (1997–2010), Conservative–Liberal Democrat coalition (2010–15), and Conservative (2015–) policies that extols the qualities of self-reliance and individual achievement. Reforms to the *public sector, including social work, were seen as necessary to instil these qualities in workers and *service users, and locate both within a different and more enterprising organizational culture. Such policies were seen as being needed in order to promote economic competitiveness, reduce state intervention and expenditure, and encourage people to take responsibility for their own lives within *market or market-like arrangements. *See also* CARE MARKET; COMMUNITY CARE REFORMS; PERSONALIZATION; QUASI-MARKETS.

enuresis Wetting by children during the night or day, usually considered to require intervention if it occurs after the age of five. Bedwetting at night is far more common than wetting during the day. It can be a sign of *anxiety or result from a delay in maturation. *Intervention is usually aimed at modifying the behaviour through using star charts or an alarm. *See also* BEHAVIOUR MODIFICATION.

epidemiology The study of the prevalence and distribution of disease in populations.

EPO *See* EMERGENCY PROTECTION ORDER.

Equality and Human Rights Commission (EHRC) A commission established by the Equality Act (2006) and operating from 1 October 2007, the EHRC combined the work of three previous commissions: the Equal Opportunities Commission, the Commission for Racial Equality, and the Disability Rights Commission. It has also assumed responsibility under the Equality Act (2010) for promoting equality in relation to age, sexual orientation, religion or belief, and for *human rights. *See also* DISCRIMINATION.

(⊕) SEE WEB LINKS
• Official site of the Equality and Human Rights Commission.

equality of opportunity *See* EGALITARIANISM.

equality of outcome *See* EGALITARIANISM.

equal opportunities policy A statement of commitment on the part of an organization to its countering *discrimination in recruitment and employment practices, and, possibly, also in relation to service provision and the treatment of *service users.

ESO *See* EDUCATION SUPERVISION ORDER.

establishment A loose way of describing the holders of power and influence in society and the sense of their shared interests overall in maintaining things as they are, particularly their secure and privileged position, even if they may not always act as a bloc on individual issues. Radical critics of mainstream social work have accused it of serving the needs of the establishment by containing and stabilizing potentially disruptive social problems. *See also* ELITE; RADICAL SOCIAL WORK.

ethical code(s) *See* CODE OF ETHICS; ETHICAL ISSUES.

ethical issues Matters concerning the principles to be followed in determining a social worker's response(s) in a particular situation. These principles may be shaped by accepted social work concepts such as fair distribution of available resources, social justice, and seeking to pursue what is in a *service user's *best interests. They may also be influenced to a greater or lesser extent by the personal commitments of social workers such as religious or political beliefs or cultural traditions. Such personal ethics may conflict with generally accepted professional ethics. An ethical issue is rarely straightforward and will often be referred to as an ethical dilemma, for example when a social worker is faced with a *conflict of interest between different people in a family. In many situations, the ethical issue (s) will not appear as something separate that the social worker needs to address; rather there will be ethical dimensions to many of the decisions that social workers make every day. A framework for social workers to reflect on ethical issues is provided by working through the following questions:

- What is the ethical issue?
- What are the principles that have a bearing on this ethical issue?
- What are the courses of action that would follow from adopting particular principles?
- What other issues have to be taken into account (for example, legislation)?
- What action would you choose?
- What are the likely outcomes of the action chosen?

Further reading: Beckett, C. and Maynard, A. (2013, 2nd edn.) *Values and Ethics in Social Work: An Introduction*, Sage.

ethnically sensitive practice Social work that takes into account the linguistic and cultural traditions associated with a particular ethnic background. Whilst *advocacy of ethnically sensitive practice was an attempt to overcome previous tendencies in social work to neglect the impact of *ethnicity on people's lives, there have been criticisms of its counter-tendency to stereotype particular ethnicities and to make assumptions about what people's ethnicity means to them, for example, assuming that religion will play a central role in their lives or that their family will be structured in a particular way. This points to the danger of ethnically sensitive practice being something that is 'done to' people, a contradiction in terms. As a consequence, the notion that the cultural traditions of a particular *ethnic group could be learned by social workers and then applied to that group in their practice has been largely discredited. The emphasis now is on a dialogue with people that seeks to establish their view of the significance of their cultural traditions and their interpretation of them in their lives, and determining how these need to be taken into account in their contact with a social worker. This is not to be regarded as an 'add-on' but simply part and parcel of *good practice. Although including positive regard for ethnicity as part of mainstream practice is for the most part not problematic, in certain situations it has limits, for example, when confronted by practices such as *female genital mutilation or *honour-based violence. *See also* ANTI-RACIST PRACTICE; ETHNIC MINORITY GROUP.

ethnic group Individuals who share distinctive origins, history, culture, and linguistic heritage. *See also* ETHNICALLY SENSITIVE PRACTICE; ETHNICITY; ETHNIC MINORITY.

ethnicity Often used in preference to *'race' because of the latter's biological connotations, such as skin colour and physical appearance, and attempts to associate different 'races' with different levels of intelligence and other measures of supposed superiority and inferiority. Ethnicity may involve racial attributes but places more emphasis on historical, cultural, and linguistic characteristics. Although ethnicity may be used in preference to 'race', because of the latter's susceptibility to negative overtones, it, too, can be converted into the basis for *oppression, subordination, and exploitation. *See also* ANTI-RACIST PRACTICE; ETHNICALLY SENSITIVE PRACTICE; ETHNIC GROUP; ETHNIC MINORITY.

ethnic minority group An *ethnic group that is in a minority within a particular society or community. *See also* ETHNICALLY SENSITIVE PRACTICE; ETHNICITY.

ethnocentricity (ethnocentrism) The belief that a dominant *ethnic group is superior to other ethnic groups, and that its perspectives should be adopted at the individual and societal levels. This belief assumes that the characteristics, attitudes, and practices of the dominant ethnic group should be adopted by other ethnic groups and should be the organizing principles for the society as a whole, forming the basis of its culture. Other ethnic groups are expected to expunge their beliefs, attitudes, and practices, and to adopt those of the dominant culture. Ethnocentrism often has connotations of being inadvertent or (wrongly) well-intentioned in comparison with deliberate discrimination as in the case of *racism. Eurocentrism is a form of ethnocentrism that involves privileging the standpoint of (white) Europeans. Anglocentrism privileges the standpoint of (white) British people. As social workers operate in the context of a diverse multi-ethnic society it is important that they should not practise from an ethnocentric perspective but should be responsive to the *values and expectations of different ethnic groups. *See also* ANTI-DISCRIMINATORY PRACTICE; ANTI-OPPRESSIVE PRACTICE; ANTI-RACIST PRACTICE; ETHNICALLY SENSITIVE PRACTICE; RACE.

eugenics Manipulation of a population in order to 'improve' its genetic stock, an idea promoted vigorously in an 'enlightened' form by the Eugenics Society in the early twentieth century. This can be achieved through pre-birth screening and selective abortion, or by preventing certain individuals or groups from reproducing, for example, through sterilization, or by programmes of extermination as in Nazi Germany. Recent advances in genetic testing of foetuses and the possibility of aborting those with genetic 'defects' have been regarded by, for example, some disabled people's groups, as a modern-day form of eugenics that seeks to eliminate those with potential disabilities. *See also* EUTHANASIA.

eurocentrism *See* ETHNOCENTRICITY.

European Foundation of Quality Management Model A framework that is extensively used in the *private and *public sectors to enable an organization to

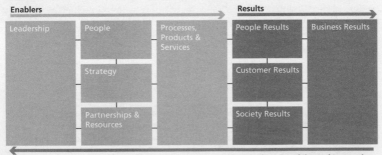

European Foundation of Quality Management Model
Available at http://www.efqm.org/efqm-model/model-criteria

assess and improve the quality of its performance. The framework comprises nine criteria against which organizational performance is assessed. The first five criteria are referred to as 'enablers', inputs that are needed in any organization: leadership; people; strategy; *partnerships and resources; processes, products and services. The other four criteria are referred to as 'results' achieved by the activities of the organization: people results, customer results, society results, and business results. There is a system of scoring how well the organization performs against each of the criteria and how well the criteria interrelate with each other, particularly with regard to enablers and results. The criteria have different weightings within the scoring system to reflect their differing importance. An EFQM assessment starts with the organization producing a submission document against the criteria. This is assessed by a team of EFQM assessors who also visit the site. A final score is awarded to the organization and *feedback arrangements are made. The assessment identifies the organization's strengths and the areas for improvement so that it can plan accordingly. Progress is measured by subsequent submissions and assessments.

euthanasia Originally associated with the *eugenics movement, and notoriously associated with the extermination regime in Nazi Germany, it has come to mean almost exclusively someone choosing to die as painlessly as possible, usually in response to an incurable disease that has resulted or will result in pain and/or incapacity. This is often referred to as 'assisted suicide'. It is illegal in the UK, leading to people going to the Netherlands, Belgium or Switzerland to die because it is legal in those countries providing the legal system's requirements are met. The arguments for and against euthanasia are deeply held on both sides and often hotly contested. They centre round whether a person has the right to decide when s/he wants to die, whether someone should have to tolerate severe pain if s/he does not wish to do so, and whether modern pain relief, for example, in a hospice, can relieve much or all of the pain that has prompted the contemplation of euthanasia. There is concern from those opposed to euthanasia not just about the 'sanctity' of life but also that if it were legalized, people who would not have chosen this option might be pressured by relatives to consider it for reasons affecting them, such as financial gain, rather than because euthanasia would be in the *best interests of the person concerned. *Living wills sometimes identify the circumstances in which a person would wish to die in the future, either through assisted suicide or the withdrawal of life-prolonging treatment. There has been controversy concerning the role played by friends or relatives in helping people to die, either directly or by taking them abroad, usually following decisions about whether or not to prosecute them. The Crown Prosecution Service has produced guidance about such cases: *Policy for Prosecutors in Respect of Cases of Encouraging or Assisting Suicide* (2010).

evaluation The process of seeking to review systematically the effectiveness and consequences of a policy or a practice intervention including making an *assessment of whether and to what extent stated *goals have been achieved. Consideration will usually be given to inputs, *outputs, and *outcomes, with decisions made about what will be considered to be indicators of successful outcomes. One component may be to adopt *benchmarks against which services can be measured, for example, the proportion of children looked after by a *local authority may be compared against the average for a group of similar local authorities. *See also* EVIDENCE-BASED PRACTICE.

Every Child Matters A Green Paper, published in 2003 by the *New Labour government, that represented the official response to the report published by Lord Laming into the death of Victoria Climbié at the hands of her *care-givers, which considered the failure of a variety of organizations to protect her. The Green Paper defined the priorities for government policy in respect of vulnerable children and families in the aftermath of the Laming Report, encapsulated in five outcomes that were seen as key to children and young people's wellbeing, and to giving them the opportunity to achieve their full potential:

- Be healthy.
- Stay safe.
- Enjoy and achieve.
- Make a positive contribution.
- Achieve economic wellbeing.

The Children Act (2004) subsequently set out these outcomes in statute. Within days of the election of the Conservative–Liberal Democrat coalition government in 2010, it moved away from the term *Every Child Matters*, but in pursuance of its responsibility as a *corporate parent, a *local authority must still ensure that *looked-after children have the opportunity to achieve the five outcomes *Every Child Matters* originally set out, given that these are enshrined in the Children Act (2004). *See also* CHILD ABUSE AND NEGLECT; CHILD IN NEED; CHILD PROTECTION; SAFEGUARDING CHILDREN.

evidence (legal) Written material and verbal statements presented in court. There are strict rules concerning what counts as evidence and about the process by which evidence is obtained. Concerns about the latter in child or adult *safeguarding cases has led to the widespread practice of social workers and police officers undertaking *joint interviews with victims. In response to concerns about children giving evidence in court as victims or witnesses, there is provision for evidence to be given on video recordings or through live video links with the child outside the courtroom. Courts hearing cases concerning children must reach decisions based on the evidence presented by the different parties and the recommendations of the *children's guardian. There are different kinds of evidence: *direct evidence* is about something that someone has actually witnessed, for example, 'I saw Mr Smith punch his son'; *hearsay evidence* is when someone repeats what somebody else has said to them, for example, 'Ms Smith told me that Mr Smith had punched their son'; *opinion* evidence is when someone gives an opinion, for example, 'I do not think that it is safe for Mr Smith to look after his son'. In cases concerning children all evidence is admissible but a court will attach more weight to some types of evidence than others. *See also* EXPERT WITNESS.

evidence-based practice (EBP) The pursuit of effective outcomes in social work that are to be achieved by utilizing research evidence from studies that have used rigorous methodologies, such as systematic evaluative measurement of a particular intervention. An approach with its origins in medicine but now promoted in many fields including education, *child welfare, mental health, and criminal justice, as well as social work. Professionals are seen as needing to intervene in *service users' lives on the basis of the best evidence available about what the consequences of their practice are likely to be, being centrally concerned with the question of 'what works'. This involves using research evidence concerning the effectiveness of interventions, which is usually referred to as *outcomes research, evaluating the quality of relevant evidence, as well as its applicability to the intervention, applying the evidence in the intervention, and then evaluating its effectiveness.

There are three main criticisms of evidence-based practice. First, that its positivist stance and its emphasis on *empirical science, both derived originally from the natural sciences and embodying a view of reality as data waiting to be collected, have been seen as flawed by a range of social theories, not least *postmodernism. Secondly, that it is founded on misconceptions about the nature of social work that mean the use of evidence in practice and the operation of decision-making processes do not work in the way it suggests. Social workers, like human beings generally, it is argued, are not rational processing agents, sorting and prioritizing evidence, shaping their work to achieve ends under the guidance of technical rules and empirical facts as they seek to improve their practice. Rather, the world of practice is located in legislation, and intra- and inter-agency policies and dynamics, and is infused with moral and political issues. In such a context, interventions are not value-free and objective. Accordingly, social workers make decisions by deliberating, and in their deliberations evidence is just one component, which they interpret in accordance with its relationship to their practical concerns, their conception of how things are, what is feasible, and what they want to do. Thus *decision-making in social work is not and cannot be based on certainty rooted in objective evidence. The proponents of evidence-based practice argue that it is because social workers function in this way that evidence-based practice is important; its scientific approach requires changing the mind set and getting these characteristics of social work under control by systematically checking the evidence base for practice. The third criticism is that evidence-based practice plays into and enhances increased managerial control of social workers by only legitimizing scientific-technical ideas and interventions, intensifying the pressure to move social work in a more technocratic routinized direction that fits with the *performance management culture, valuing the aspects of social work that are instrumental and externally measurable, and undermining *practice wisdom and professional judgement.

In the debate about evidence-based practice, in addition to the proponents of evidence-based practice and its detractors, there is an alternative conception of the research-minded social worker in which the social worker is seen as combining use of well-researched interventions with practice experience, ethics, and a consideration of the wishes and preferences of *service users. The implication for social workers is that they must be skilled in *assessment in order that the *interventions they select are appropriately matched to the *needs and circumstances of the service user, taking into account any cultural considerations. The difficulty facing practitioners when the available evidence in a particular field may be contentious, of variable quality, contradictory, or incomplete is acknowledged in this perspective. Research-mindedness is, therefore, often presented as a developing concept, rooted in advances in professional knowledge and expertise, which are in turn likely to be influenced by developments and shifts of thinking in social work's culture, values, and ethics.

The *Centre for Excellence and Outcomes in Children's and Young People's Services (C4EO) adopts an evidence-based perspective. Its aim is to gather and share evidence about what makes the most difference to outcomes for vulnerable groups of children, young people, and their families, and in this way support those who work in children's services to 'narrow the gap in society'. C4EO publishes and makes available online a range of research documents to further this objective. *See also* EVALUATION; NATIONAL INSTITUTE FOR HEALTH AND CLINICAL EXCELLENCE; RESEARCH-MINDEDNESS; SOCIAL CARE INSTITUTE OF EXCELLENCE.

Further reading: Roberts, R. and Yeager, K. (2006) *Foundations of Evidence-based Social Work Practice*, Oxford University Press.

(⊕) SEE WEB LINKS

• Official site of the Centre for Excellence and Outcomes in Children's and Young People's Services (C4EO).

exceptions *Local authorities have to be able to show that their policies and priorities allow for exceptions, that is exceptional cases, because they cannot be seen to have constrained their *discretion in cases taken to *judicial review, for example, when the application of *eligibility criteria are challenged. *See also* DISCRETION (LOCAL AUTHORITY); DUTY; ELIGIBILITY CRITERIA; FETTERING DISCRETION; JUDICIAL REVIEW; NEEDS ASSESSMENT; POWER; REASONABLENESS; RELEVANT FACTORS; RIGID POLICIES; TARGET DUTY.

exchange model of assessment A much-cited approach to the *assessment of adults in which the social worker is encouraged to undertake an assessment by working alongside the person and other significant people in her/his life in order to arrive at a mutual understanding of the problem(s) and negotiate who might do what to help. This approach is seen as allowing the service-user-as-citizen to be a full partner in the process of negotiating about the nature of her/his problem(s) and possible solutions. In addition to highlighting that the *service user is the expert about her/his own situation, the social, as opposed to a preoccupation with the individual, focus of assessment is stressed. This is seen as including local and cultural expectations about 'normal' patterns of *care and support, *service users', *carers', and other significant people's perceptions of needs and available resources, and the nature and quality of the *care relationships that exist. The response(s) to the problem(s) is seen as needing to be drawn from a combination of people's personal networks, and voluntary and statutory services.

The exchange model was developed originally by Smale *et al.* (1993) in the aftermath of the *community care reforms, and in that context was specifically concerned with the skills required for effective assessment in the context of *care management. They (and Smale *et al.* 2000) identified two other models of assessment: the procedural model, which is governed by the needs of the organization or system, and the questioning model, in which the worker's role is that of the professional expert. The three models are relevant to the values and principles of *anti-oppressive practice, since each is concerned with different constructions of the power dynamics in an *assessment and the role of the worker vis-à-vis the service user.

The exchange model has been compared and contrasted with the questioning model and the procedural model:

Exchange model
- The worker's role is to act as facilitator, generating an exchange of information between the people involved.
- The work depends on establishing respect and trust.
- Understanding is negotiated between the parties, rather than information being passed in linear fashion from one person to another.
- The worker draws on wider information about the social situation in order to enhance understanding.
- People are seen as the experts on themselves, their situation, their relationships, what they want and *need.
- The social workers' responsibility is to contribute to, not take over from, people exercising their own problem-solving skills.

Questioning model
- The worker's role is diagnostic; the worker takes responsibility for making an accurate assessment and taking appropriate action.
- The worker is assumed to be the expert about people and their needs.

- The worker's role is to ask questions that reflect the worker's view of the nature of the problem/situation and what should be done.
- The assessor's judgement and actions are seen as objective.
- The model is relatively quick and straightforward compared with the exchange model.

Procedural model

- The worker's role is to act as guide through the system, gathering information to see if the person meets the criteria that would make them eligible for services.
- The information regarded as relevant is determined by organizational policies.
- The organization remains central to how problems are defined and the range of solutions available for dealing with them.
- The model tends to focus on dependency, needs and difficulties, rather than strengths and coping strategies.
- The model is simple and quick.
- The model tends to lead to standard packages rather than innovative or individually-tailored responses.

Although the exchange model is frequently cited as the basis for good assessment practice with adults, it was developed in the particular context of the community care reforms. In those reforms, the original objectives of care management included separating out assessment of need from considerations about service provision and reconfiguring service users of social work as consumers or customers who, once their needs had been assessed in *partnership with the social worker, could exercise choice in the *care market about how their needs were to be met. Smale *et al.* (1993) sought to provide guidance about the skills and values required by workers to achieve these objectives. The exchange model is, if anything, even more influential in the guidance to the Care Act (2014). Even if it is not named as such, the principles underpin the approach to practice that it advocates.

What is missing from the model is the economic, political, or organizational context in which assessment of adults is carried out, in particular the central conflict between empowering service users and constrained resources. This context means that in practice, there are a number of factors that inhibit the use of the exchange model as originally envisaged, and as presented in the Care Act (2014) guidance, with the service user taking the lead role in assessment and planning services, and the social worker seeking to arrive at a mutual understanding with the service user:

Organizational There are likely to be a number of organizational barriers to a genuine exchange model being realized in practice. These include constraints on the time that is available to undertake a 'person-led' assessment and the barriers that may be presented by the requirements of the organization in terms of particular information that has to be gathered (for example, financial details), or the forms that have to be completed. The demand for high throughput of work, based on standardized computer-formats, may conflict with conducting thorough assessments.

Policy and legislative The social worker may, with great skill and sensitivity, elicit the person's understanding of the nature of the problem and the assistance required, but policy and resource obstacles may prevent this from being provided. In addition, the way *need and *risk are constructed in individual terms in legislation and policy tends to obstruct recognition of the significance of social factors in assessment and intervention.

Services Services that are responsive to someone's needs may not be available. The social worker's knowledge of these restrictions may intrude into the assessment process since it is difficult in practice to free an assessment from service considerations.

Professional The social work role often involves conflicting duties and obligations. Sometimes there will be a professional and legal obligation to act in ways that conflict with an individual's expressed needs and wishes.

Communication There may be communication barriers operating between the social worker and the person being assessed that impede an 'exchange' of information and understanding. These may include language barriers, or cultural differences, or the impact of sensory impairments, or *learning disabilities.

Network The interests of other people within the care network may have to be counterbalanced with those of the person. Sometimes needs and interests of the different parties will be in conflict, and the social worker will have to negotiate with the individuals concerned, and try to reach a resolution that involves balance and compromise.

Personal Because of their personal biographies, experiences, and attitudes, people may not want or feel able to take a lead role in the assessment process. They may adopt passive roles in the process, grateful for whatever help they are offered.

Social work based on the exchange model of assessment has to work within and around the obstacles and constraints raised by such factors. *See also* CARER'S ASSESSMENT; ELIGIBILITY CRITERIA; EXPERT BY EXPERIENCE; NEEDS ASSESSMENT.

Further reading: Smale, G., Tuson G., Biehal, N., and Marsh, P. (1993) *Empowerment, Assessment, Care Management and the Skilled Worker*, HMSO.
Smale, G., Tuson G., and Statham, D. (2000) *Social Work and Social Problems: Working towards Social Inclusion and Social Change*, Macmillan.

exclusion *See* EXCLUSION FROM SCHOOL; SOCIAL EXCLUSION.

exclusion from school Sanction available to head teachers if a child or young person gets into serious trouble at school. Exclusions can be for a fixed period or permanent, and apply to situations where a child has broken the rules, where allowing them to stay in school would seriously harm their education or welfare, or that of other children or young people. A school should only permanently exclude as a last resort, having tried to resolve problems through other means. There may be exceptional circumstances when the seriousness of an incident may result in permanent exclusion for a single transgression, such as serious actual or threatened *violence, sexual abuse or assault, supplying an illegal drug, or carrying an offensive weapon. The head teacher's decision has to be ratified by the school governors. The governors or a designated committee must meet to consider permanent exclusion. Parents and the child have a right to attend and make representations. Head teachers are required to pay particular attention to the position of vulnerable children, such as *looked-after children and children with special educational needs. If the governors uphold the head teacher's decision, the parent(s) can appeal to an Independent Appeal Panel. The panel must decide, on a balance of probabilities, whether the child was responsible for the behaviour alleged. Evidence is presented by the head teacher and by the parent(s), and the panel must make a decision on the basis of that evidence. The panel can make three decisions: to uphold the decision to exclude; to order reinstatement immediately or at some future date; to decide if reinstatement at a future date would be appropriate and order reinstatement but because of exceptional circumstances the reinstatement will not be put into effect. The latter could happen if the relationship between the school and the child and/or her/his family had completely broken down and it would not be in the child's interest to return but the exclusion will in effect be removed from the child's record. Reinstatement does not necessarily mean complete reintegration. It reinstates the school's duty to educate the child, which may be off the school site or in isolation from other children. *See also* EDUCATIONAL PSYCHOLOGIST; EDUCATION SOCIAL WORKER; EDUCATION SUPERVISION ORDER; PARENTING CLASSES; PARENTING ORDER; PUPIL REFERRAL UNIT; SCHOOL ATTENDANCE; TRUANCY.

exit *See* VOICE.

exogenous depression *See* REACTIVE DEPRESSION.

experiential learning Knowledge and skill that comes from the practice of doing something rather than from books or the classroom. Experiential learning has a long tradition in social work, which from its nineteenth-century origins onwards has emphasized the learning that needs to be gained from undertaking periods of assessed practice in order to become a social worker. *See also* LEARNING LOG; LEARNING STYLES; REFLECTIVE PRACTICE; REFLEXIVITY.

expert by experience Sometimes used in preference to *service user in order to signify that people are to be seen as experts on themselves, their situation, their relationships, and what they want and need in order to address issues in their lives. *See also* EXCHANGE MODEL OF ASSESSMENT.

expert witness Someone who has special expert knowledge of the subject about which s/he testifies in a court. The person must be accepted by the court and testify about facts and/or opinions rather than the law. It is not unusual for *care proceedings to involve the calling of expert witnesses, particularly if medical *evidence relating to a child's injuries or condition is contested. A medical practitioner regarded as having particular expertise with regard to the injury or condition may be called to provide an expert opinion to assist the court in its decision-making. *See also* FAMILY COURTS.

expulsion from school *See* EXCLUSION FROM SCHOOL.

extended family Originally referred to a family that had different generations living together in one household, but now usually used to refer to the wider family structure that exists outside the immediate family of parents and children. Given renewed emphasis in the *ecological approach and *family group conferencing. *See also* ECO MAP; GENOGRAM; NUCLEAR FAMILY.

extended schools *See* EXTENDED SERVICES.

extended services Range of services provided by schools that go beyond the school day and are aimed at meeting the needs of children, families, and the wider community. Extended services can include child care, adult education, parenting support programmes, community-based health and social services, and behaviour management programmes. *See also* EARLY INTERVENTION; PREVENTION.

extroversion *See* INTROVERSION AND EXTROVERSION.

Fabianism A standpoint on the centre left of the political spectrum that prizes pragmatic, rational, evolutionary development of social policy through direct government intervention based on *empirical research. It takes its name from the Fabian Society, which was founded in 1884 by Beatrice and Sidney Webb, George Bernard Shaw, and H. G. Wells as a group promoting non-Marxist socialism. It was one of the founding groups of the Labour Party, to which it remains affiliated, but it is organizationally independent. Its ideas were at their most influential during the establishment of the post-war *welfare state. All Labour prime ministers have been members of the Fabian Society. The Society continues to play a role as a think tank in the development of political ideas, as well as conducting research into policy reform.

fabricated and induced illness A rare form of *child abuse and neglect that covers specific situations, which, as a result of a *care-giver's behaviour, give cause for concern that a child is suffering or may suffer *significant harm. These are situations where there is suspicion that a care-giver is fabricating signs, symptoms, and medical history; falsifying hospital charts and records, letters, and documents; tampering with specimens of bodily fluids; and inducing illness in the child by a variety of means. These situations may lead to the child experiencing unnecessary invasive and potentially traumatic medical investigations, procedures, and treatment that cause them to become ill or more ill. This form of harm used to be commonly referred to as 'Munchausen Syndrome by Proxy', named after Baron von Munchausen, an eighteenth-century German with a reputation for telling far-fetched stories. The syndrome referred to an adult who wanted to be in regular contact with medical institutions and personnel by using another person, usually a child, and fabricating and/or inducing illness in order to achieve this. 'Munchausen Syndrome by Proxy' is now regarded by many as too restrictive on the grounds that it refers to only one aspect of fabricated and induced illness, and others doubt that it is even a recognizable condition. *See also* CHILD PROTECTION; FAILURE TO THRIVE; SAFEGUARDING CHILDREN.

Further reading: Department for Children, Schools and Families (now the Department for
Education) (2008) *Safeguarding Children in whom Illness is Fabricated or Induced:
Supplementary Guidance to Working Together to Safeguard Children* describes the action to
be taken by practitioners when this form of harm is suspected. Available at: https://www.gov.
uk/government/uploads/system/uploads/attachment_data/file/277314/
Safeguarding_Children_in_whom_illness_is_fabricated_or_induced.pdf.

failure to thrive Refers to children whose current weight or rate of weight gain is significantly below that of other children of similar age and gender. Tending to be applied to young children, especially babies, rather than older children, failure to thrive is a way by which health professionals and others may express their concern that a *child's development is faltering. The condition is not a disease. Its cause needs to be established in each *case in order that appropriate medical care can be provided for the child. If the cause is attributable to *child abuse and neglect, for example if a parent is knowingly providing a child with inadequate nutrition when in a position to provide adequate nutrition, then action to safeguard the child and promote her/his welfare may need to be taken. However, there is a range of reasons why children may fail to thrive, many of which are associated with organic factors. A common approach to measuring whether or not a child is failing to thrive is to use a *centile chart. If a child continues to fall below the third centile in one or more of the measures of height, head size, and weight, this acts as an alert to the possibility of failure to thrive. *See also* CHILD ABUSE AND NEGLECT; CHILD PROTECTION; FABRICATED AND INDUCED ILLNESS; SAFEGUARDING CHILDREN.

Fair Access to Care Services (FACS) *See* ELIGIBILITY CRITERIA.

falls There is growing recognition of the role falls can play in reducing the health and wellbeing of *older people and an attempt to shift the view that they are an inevitable concomitant of growing older towards preventive strategies. *See also* HOME IMPROVEMENT AGENCIES.

false memory syndrome Refutes memories of child sexual abuse that have been recovered by adults (predominantly women) in therapy by suggesting that the events recalled did not occur. Many feminist commentators see the syndrome as a backlash against revelations of the extent of male sexual abuse inflicted on girls and young women.

family *See* EXTENDED FAMILY; NUCLEAR FAMILY.

Family Assistance Order Can be made by a *family court in any family proceedings, under Section 16 of the Children Act (1989). The aim of the Order is to provide short-term assistance to families who need help coping with the effects the proceedings are having on them. Such Orders are most likely to be made in contested *private law cases involving children. The Order requires a social worker to 'advise, assist and befriend' the family for a period of up to six months, providing short-term help in relation to conflict between parents or assisting with other problems arising from separation or *divorce. (The work is usually undertaken with the parents rather than the child.) An Order is only made 'in exceptional circumstances' and if a court considers that granting an Order will be in the interests of the child's welfare. It can only be made if the parents agree. These Orders have not been widely used.

family centre Originally referred to a *community resource that provided support to parents, *carers, and children but increasingly replaced by or developed into a *children's centre with a wider remit, though some have argued that there is still a role for smaller, more grass-roots family centres. *See also* SURE START.

family courts Created by the Children Act (1989) and located within the Family Division of the High Court, they deal with family law cases and all non-criminal matters relating to children: *matrimonial matters*, including *Child Arrangements Orders; *child welfare concerns*, including *Care Orders, *Supervision Orders, *Emergency Protection Orders, and *Secure Accommodation Orders; and *adoption*. In contested applications for *Child Arrangements Orders, under Section 8 of the Children Act (1989), a family court can ask for a social work report on issues relating to a child's *needs and welfare. A child can be made a party to the proceedings and a *child and family reporter can be appointed as a social worker for the child. The principles underpinning the Children Act (1989), which are usually encountered in *local authority children's services, apply equally in the family courts in the legal context of *divorce: the child's welfare is the paramount consideration (*see* PARAMOUNTCY PRINCIPLE); parents retain responsibility for their children after separation (*see* PARENTAL RESPONSIBILITY); parents should be as involved as possible in making decisions about their children; courts should only make an Order if they are satisfied that this will have a positive impact on the child (*see* NO ORDER PRINCIPLE); delay in court proceedings should be avoided as far as possible as it is not usually in a child's interests. *See also* CARE PROCEEDINGS; CHILD ASSESSMENT ORDER; CHILDREN AND FAMILY COURT ADVISORY AND SUPPORT SERVICE; FAMILY DRUG AND ALCOHOL COURTS; INTERIM CARE ORDER; PARAMOUNTCY PRINCIPLE; WELFARE CHECKLIST.

Family Drug and Alcohol Courts (FDAC) Specialist courts launched in 2008 for dealing with *care proceedings when parental substance misuse causes harm to children. The court aims to help parents stabilize or stop their use of drugs and/or alcohol and, where possible, keep families together. *See also* FAMILY COURTS.

family group conference (family group conferencing) Originating in Maori communities in New Zealand, a meeting championed by some *voluntary organizations for children in the UK and operating in some *local authorities, in which the decision-makers are the family members, participating on a voluntary basis, rather than professionals, with parents, grandparents, aunts, and uncles encouraged to discuss and decide how to resolve the *child welfare issues with which they are faced. The idea is that families have the opportunity to come together to make the best possible plan for the children concerned. A family group conference may also be offered in situations where *youth justice issues arise, with the same principles and practices applied. The *Children and Family Court Advisory Support Service, the service which supports the work of *family courts, also uses family group conferences in situations where parents separate or *divorce, and issues of *contact and *residence are being contested. In this setting the conference provides family members with an opportunity to discuss how to resolve these problems as an alternative to potentially acrimonious and expensive court proceedings. There are usually three stages in a family group conference:

Information-giving A coordinator explains any legal issues and tells the family what resources they may be able to draw on.

Private time The family meets on its own to discuss the issues and devises a plan to address them.

Presenting plans The family shares its plan with the coordinator and any other professionals who are involved.

See also CHILD AND FAMILY REPORTER; EARLY INTERVENTION; FAMILY SUPPORT MEETING; PARENTING PLAN; PREVENTION; WORKING AGREEMENT.

Further reading: Barnardos, Family Rights Group, NCH (2002) *Family Group Conferences: Principles and Practice Guidance.* Available at http://www.frg.org.uk/images/e-publications/fgc-principles-and-practice-guidance-english.pdf.

family information services The Child Care Act (2006) requires *local authorities to provide high quality, accurate, and timely information and advice to parents on child care and other services that they may need to support their children up to their 20th birthday. Family information services are the main means by which local authorities fulfil this duty in relation to areas such as:

- How to find child care.
- The average cost of child care in the local area and how to claim financial help for it.
- Information on quality standards and how to check if a child care provider is registered.
- Information and signposting to national and local support agencies.
- Advice and information on where to go for help and support if a child has an additional *need.
- Information on leisure activities and groups.
- Leaflets and booklets on a range of subjects for the family and young people.

See also CHILDMINDERS; CHILDREN'S CENTRE; EARLY INTERVENTION; EARLY YEARS SERVICES; EXTENDED SERVICES; HOME START; NURSERIES; PREVENTION; UNDER-FIVES PROVISION.

Further reading: Then the Department for Children, Schools, and Families, now the Department for Education (2008) *Duty to Provide Information, Advice, and Assistance: Guidance for Local Authorities—Child Care Act 2006.* Available at: https://www.cumbria.gov.uk/elibrary/Content/Internet/537/1459/4126295139.pdf.

family placement *See* ADOPTION; FOSTERING.

family placement team A specialist team in children's services that recruits, prepares, and supports families who provide *foster care (short-term, long-term, and respite) and *adoption placements. In some *local authorities the same family placement team(s) provides all of these services; in others one team deals with short-term foster carers and a permanency team looks after long-term fostering and adoption; and in others one team deals with short-term and long-term foster carers and a permanency team deals with adoption. A family placement team publicizes the need for foster and adoptive parents and seeks to recruit them from a diverse range of communities and backgrounds. People who are interested in becoming foster or adoptive parents attend group meetings run by family placement team social workers to find out more about what is involved and if they pursue an application, continue to attend group meetings that prepare them for the role. At the same time, a team social worker undertakes a series of interviews in the family home. The social worker writes a comprehensive report to the fostering or adoption panel, and the panel recommends to a senior manager whether to accept or reject the application. Once approved, foster carers are linked to a social worker in the team, who sorts out payments and training, and provides support if a placement proves difficult. Increasingly, private sector agencies are moving into foster care and they usually pay foster parents considerably more than local authorities.

family support If a child is assessed as 'in need' (Children Act 1989, Section 17), services can be provided to any member of the family provided that the *child in need benefits. These services can be practical, supportive, or therapeutic, and either offered individually or in combination. The Children Act (1989) stipulates the services that should be in place to support families when they have a 'child in need', including day care, out-of-school care, activities, holidays, *respite accommodation, and practical help in the home. Short-term *fostering can also be used for the purpose of family support. The extent to which local authorities have developed family support services varies considerably. Attempting to prioritize family support to children in need is constantly threatened or undermined by the prominence of *child protection work for children suffering or likely to suffer from *significant harm (Children Act 1989, Section 47). When research in the 1990s demonstrated that the vast majority of child protection investigations did not result in children being placed on the *child protection register nor to their receiving services, there were attempts to rebalance services by moving the emphasis significantly in the direction of family support. This achieved patchy results and child protection still occupies a dominant position. *See also* CHILDREN'S CENTRE; FAMILY CENTRE; SURE START.

family support meeting A gathering of professionals and family members in circumstances where it is agreed that a more coordinated approach to meeting the *needs of a child and family is needed. The meeting may also consider whether additional services are required. These meetings are distinguished from a *family group conference where the focus is essentially on family members identifying solutions to the problems faced by the family. *See also* LEAD PROFESSIONAL; WORKING AGREEMENT.

family therapy Work with families, rather than individuals, to promote change and development, and find constructive solutions to problems within relationships so that the family functions more smoothly. There is a variety of approaches but a *systems perspective is often employed that views the family as an interdependent self-governing system, which runs according to 'rules' developed over time and which has a number of sub-systems, each affecting the other sub-systems and the family system as a whole. Family members are encouraged to share their beliefs, perspectives, experiences, and narratives in moving towards unpicking habitual destructive behaviour patterns. The skills of the family therapist lie in engaging family members in the therapeutic process, harnessing the family's strengths, so that rigid behaviour patterns and family scripts can be interrupted and change can be brought about. As family therapy has developed, some versions of it have moved beyond an enclosed view of the family in the direction of supporting change in relationships that go beyond the immediate family members. This may entail involving other people important to family members including those with whom there may be no blood tie. Such an approach is based on the recognition that different groups and cultures have different interpretations about what a 'family' means. Accordingly, the Association for Family Therapy and Systemic Practice regards a family as any group of people who define themselves as such and who care about and care for each other. Critics point to the 'neutral' stance towards family dynamics occupied by many family therapists, arguing that this fails to question the operation of power in families, for example, the ways in which men oppress and subordinate women in families. *See also* BEHAVIOURAL FAMILY THERAPY; DIALECTICAL BEHAVIOUR THERAPY; DIRECT WORK WITH CHILDREN; ECOLOGICAL APPROACH; KINSHIP NETWORKS; MULTI-SYSTEMIC THERAPY; PSYCHOANALYSIS.

Further reading: Goldenberg, H. and Goldenberg, I. (2008) *Family Therapy: An Overview*, Thomson Brooks/Cole; *Journal of Family Therapy* is published four times a year on behalf of the Association for Family Therapy and Systemic Practice.

(⊕) SEE WEB LINKS
• Official site of the Association for Family Therapy and Systemic Practice.

feedback Comments given about how well a task has been carried out. For example, after a social work student's practice has been observed as evidence for her/his assessed practice portfolio, s/he will be given verbal and written feedback on her/his performance.

female Literally an individual who possesses certain biological characteristics. In *feminism, usually used in this way to emphasize women's purely biological differences from men. Many feminists have argued that women are estranged from their female nature; instead of being a positive concept in its own right, female exists in a position of inferiority as the *binary opposite of male. *See also* BOUNDED RATIONALITY; DECONSTRUCTION; FEMININITY; FEMINISM; FEMINIST SOCIAL WORK; FEMINIST THERAPY; GENDER; GENDER DIFFERENTIATION; INTERSECTIONALITY; MASCULINITY; OTHER; SOCIAL CONSTRUCTIONISM.

female circumcision *See* FEMALE GENITAL MUTILATION.

female genital mutilation (FGM) Sometimes and originally used to refer to the removal of the tip of the clitoris but more often now used in a broader sense to describe any actions that involve cutting a woman's genitalia. The most extreme procedure is the removal of the clitoris and the inner and outer lips of the vagina. The resulting wound is pulled together so that only a small hole remains for passing urine and menstrual blood. Previously thought of as a practice confined to some areas of the so-called Third World, the incidence of genital mutilation has been rising in the UK because of migration. Almost 140,000 women and girls in the UK are estimated to have undergone female genital mutilation. Social workers may encounter its use, for example, if it is practised on young women and is referred to them as *abuse. Female genital mutilation is illegal (Female Genital Mutilation Act [2003]), and social workers are under a mandatory duty to report *cases of FGM involving girls under 18 to the police. The Serious Crime Act (2015) introduced other measures in relation to female genital mutilation:

- An offence of failing to protect a girl from the risk of FGM;
- Extra-territorial jurisdiction over offences of FGM committed abroad by UK nationals and those habitually (as well as permanently) resident in the UK;
- Lifelong anonymity for victims of FGM;
- FGM Protection Orders, which can be used to protect girls at risk.

If a vulnerable adult is identified as having had or being at risk of FGM, this is responded to within existing *safeguarding processes to protect vulnerable adults. If an adult discloses that a child has had FGM, it is a report of *child abuse and local safeguarding processes should be followed, including a mandatory report to the police. If there is a suspicion that a child or vulnerable adult may have had FGM, or is at serious or imminent risk of FGM having considered her family history or other relevant factors, local safeguarding responses will be initiated as is the procedure with other instances of *abuse. If a child or vulnerable adult has a family history that mean she may be at risk of FGM, but the risk is not imminent or serious, local processes for sharing information between professionals and agencies are followed. There is no requirement for automatic referral of adult women who have had FGM to the police. Any disclosure may be the first time that a woman has discussed her FGM with anyone and referral to the police should not be an automatic response. Women can be supported by offering referral to *community groups which can provide support or to the NHS for medical follow-up at an FGM clinic. The wishes of the woman must be respected at all times. If a woman discloses that she has an adult daughter over 18 who has already had FGM, even if the daughter does not want to take her case to the police, it is likely to be important to establish when and where this took place. This should lead to enquiries about other girls in the family. FGM is a complex area and some women may have greater influence in decision-making with regards to FGM when they are outside their country of origin and may decide to discontinue FGM practice.

Further reading: Department of Health (2016) *Female Genital Mutilation Risk and Safeguarding: Guide for Professionals.* Available at: https://www.gov.uk/government/uploads/system/uploads/attachment_data/file/525390/FGM_safeguarding_report_A.pdf.

HM Government (2016) *Multi-agency Statutory Guidance on Genital Mutilation.* Available at: http://www.gov.uk/government/uploads/system/uploads/attachment_data/file/512906/Multi_Agency_Statutory_Guidance_on_FGM__-_FINAL.pdf.

Home Office (n.d.) *Mandatory Reporting of Female Genital Mutilation: Procedural Information.* Available at http://www.gov.uk/government/uploads/system/uploads/attachment_data/file/469448/FGM-Mandatory-Reporting-procedural-info-FINAL.pdf.

RCM, RCN, RCOG, Equality Now, UNITE (2013) *Tackling FGM in the UK: Intercollegiate Recommendations for Identifying, Recording, and Reporting.* Available at: http://cdn.basw.co.uk/upload/basw_112818-5.pdf.

femininity A set of socially constructed images of supposedly 'natural' woman-hood to which women are subjected, governing their appearance, behaviour, and feelings: 'One is not born but becomes a woman' (Simone de Beauvoir, *The Second Sex*, 2009, orig. 1969). Femininity has been the focus of much feminist critique, for example, in relation to the heavy emphasis on the role of appearance in creating women's *identity and the pressure to make women conform to men's ideas of sexual attractiveness. This critique has pointed to the damage sustained by women in attempts to achieve femininity. In addition, feminists have stressed that the association between femininity and passivity, dependence, and weakness serves to make masculinity appear more masterly and competent. *See also* DECONSTRUCTION; FEMALE; FEMINISM; FEMINIST SOCIAL WORK; FEMINIST THERAPY; GENDER; GENDER DIFFERENTIATION; INTERSECTIONALITY; MASCULINITY; SOCIAL CONSTRUCTIONISM.

feminism This is often represented in social work writing as a single entity, united by its concern with combating women's oppression, contesting ideas that gender relations stem from fixed natural differences between the sexes and promoting *gender equality. However, the perspectives encompassed within feminism occupy a range of different positions, as soon as they move beyond general assertions about *oppression and inequality. The perspectives can be broadly classified into three loose groups: liberal, socialist, and radical.

Liberal feminism argues for individual fulfilment for women on the basis of their equal *citizenship with men. Liberal feminists argue for women's rights in terms of their welfare needs, equal opportunities in employment, education, and health services. Socialist feminists argue that the interweaving of Marxism and feminism is crucial to the emancipation of women. Socialist feminists link gender inequality and women's oppression to the capitalist system of production and the division of labour within this system. In contrast, radical feminists stress the primacy of gender relations and argue that women's oppression stems from men's domination of women through *patriarchy as the key defining characteristic of society. In a similar way to, but to a greater extent than, other feminist perspectives, radical feminism asserts that the personal is political and that woman-centeredness can be the basis of a more equal society. Although these three perspectives have been the most significant historically, other perspectives have emerged, for example, post-modernist, post-structuralist, Black, and lesbian feminisms. A strong dynamic in the emergence of other perspectives has been criticism of feminism for regarding the category 'woman' as unitary. In opposition to this view, it has been argued that women comprise a diverse group, with significant sub-divisions resulting from women's various positioning in relation to age, *class, *disability, *ethnicity, *'race', and sexuality. These alternative perspectives led to debates about how to negotiate such multiple subjectivities and the potential fragmentation they produce in pursuing social justice for women. Some feminists have argued that instead of seeking social cohesion through a consensus that masks *differences, strategic alliances and coalitions need to be formed in relation to specific actions and campaigns. Coalition-building as a strategy is seen as acknowledging women's occupation of many subject positions, personally, socially, and politically. *See also* DECONSTRUCTION; FEMALE; FEMININITY; FEMINIST SOCIAL WORK; FEMINIST THERAPY; FIRST-WAVE FEMINISM; GENDER; GENDER DIFFERENTIATION; INTERSECTIONALITY; MASCULINITY; SOCIAL CONSTRUCTIONISM.

Further reading: David, M. (2016) *Reclaiming Feminism: Challenging Everyday Misogyny*, Policy Press.

feminist social work Women working with women has been regarded by many writers as at the heart of feminist social work. A shared experience of oppression between women social workers and women *service users has been seen as the impetus for seeking egalitarian *relationships. The feminist social work literature has suggested that women social workers can engage in such egalitarian relationships with women service users with the *goal of the latter's *empowerment. This depiction of feminist social work has been criticized for not being grounded in the realities of practice, particularly within *statutory settings.

Women social workers have been urged to embrace a feminist identity that has been characterized as rooted in *eclecticism. In the literature's elaboration of this eclecticism, it is common for the diverse perspectives that fed into the origins of feminist social work to be mentioned, for example, liberal, radical, socialist, Black, anti-racist, and postmodernist feminisms. However, there tends to be little precision about the specific legacies of these different perspectives and a broad measure of consensus about the nature of feminist social work as rooted in common principles, with which women social workers are called to align themselves as the basis for their practice:

• Upholding the right of women to be free from oppression.
• Having women speak for themselves in their own voices.
• Listening to what women have to say.
• Creating alternative lifestyles.
• Integrating feminist theory with practice.
• Seeking compatibility between the ends and the means of practice.
• Seeking collective solutions that respect the individuality and uniqueness of each woman.
• Valuing women's contributions.
• Using women's individual experiences to make sense of social realities.

Underpinning these principles is the straightforward proposition that everyone is equal, irrespective of gender. Gendered inequality and its elimination are seen as the starting points for feminist social work.

Some writers have viewed such an eclectic approach as being in the interests of the development of feminist social work because it means that as many women as possible can think of themselves as feminists. This has led most feminist social work writers to stress the breadth of possibilities offered by feminism and to emphasize common goals. However, with the greater emphasis on *diversity within feminist analysis more generally, some social work writers have placed greater emphasis on *differences between women—mediated by age, *class, *disability, *'race', and sexuality—that work against the idea of a shared experience of oppression on the basis of gender alone, and highlight women's varied and complex social realities. Attempts by some feminist social work writers to accommodate difference and diversity amongst women have been seen as insufficient by some Black, lesbian, and disabled women who have criticized the dominant eclectic approach for its alleged *racism, *ethnocentrism, *heterosexism, and *able-bodiedism.

In the feminist social work literature, the articulation of diversity and difference has been addressed largely through the refinement of eclecticism. In response to critiques of eclecticism, the main stance has been to view such challenges as capable of being used to revise and extend feminist social work *identity. It has been argued that through this process of refinement, a feminist stance can endorse *egalitarianism across all social divisions and not simply those based on *gender. Thus, the inclusion of different women's experiences and standpoints has not necessarily been seen as undermining the unifying identity for women that has emerged from the feminist social work agenda. Some commentators argue that a dual stress on unity and diversity encourages women social workers to respect difference and uniqueness, while also seeing similarities and wholeness. By this means, there has been a sense of confidence that routes through to an eclectic identity could still be found. In relation to 'race', for example, feminist social work writers have suggested that although Black and white women have different experiences of *oppression, these can be incorporated into feminist practice and ultimately transcended because Black and white women are also grappling with experiences of *sexism that they have in common. In this way, a refined version of eclecticism is seen as still offering the basis for feminist social work. While there is increasing acknowledgement that a single feminist social work standpoint cannot readily encompass the wide range of women's lives, women are still seen as having common experiences and common goals, with the promise of still attaining a unifying feminist identity.

In contrast to these attempts by feminist social work writers to refine eclecticism and rescue a unifying feminist identity, some writers have developed wider *anti-oppressive forms of social work theory and practice that recognize the complexity and diversity of the oppressions that affect women's lives. Rather than seeing feminist social work as capable of expanding its eclecticism to incorporate challenges from a range of oppressions, such writing has argued for the necessity of developing anti-oppressive and *anti-discriminatory practice that is relevant to all spheres of social work. *See also* FEMALE; FEMININITY; FEMINISM; FEMINIST THERAPY; GENDER; GENDER DIFFERENTIATION; INTERSECTIONALITY; MASCULINITY.

Further reading: White, V. (2006) *The State of Feminist Social Work*, Routledge.

feminist therapy Therapeutic practices that developed from feminist perspectives, initially closely associated with the Women's Therapy Centre, which was established in London in 1976 as a reaction against the widespread failure of traditional therapies to incorporate the significance of the experience of *gender *oppression in the production of women's 'problems'. *See also* FEMALE; FEMININITY; FEMINISM; FEMINIST SOCIAL WORK; GENDER; GENDER DIFFERENTIATION; INDIVIDUAL PATHOLOGY; INTERSECTIONALITY; MASCULINITY.

fettering discretion (local authority) When implementing legislation, whether with regard to *duties or *powers, it is unlawful for a *local authority to have inflexible policies, priorities, or *eligibility criteria that restrict discretion in ways that prevent decisions being made that might be appropriate in individual *cases. There must be sufficient flexibility to decide individual cases on their own merits. A policy stating that a specified group of people are not eligible for a service in any circumstances or that a particular service, *aid or adaptation will never be provided, fetters the discretion of a decision-maker such as a social worker or team manager, because the policy makes up their mind in advance, not allowing their exercise of discretion. Such a rigid policy may cause unfairness in individual cases and as a consequence is vulnerable to legal challenge through *judicial review. General policies, priorities, and eligibility criteria have to leave sufficient room for the carrying out of an *assessment that is capable of taking account of an individual's *needs. *See also* DISCRETION (LOCAL AUTHORITY); DUTY; ELIGIBILITY CRITERIA; EXCEPTIONS; JUDICIAL REVIEW; NEEDS ASSESSMENT; POWER; REASONABLENESS; RELEVANT FACTORS; RIGID POLICIES; TARGET DUTY.

fieldwork 1. Social work carried out in the *community, usually in *service users' homes.

2. Face-to-face methods of collecting data for research, such as participant observation or interviewing. Also used more generally to include any activity that takes the researcher into the field under study.

final warning Used along with *reprimands instead of *cautions since the implementation of the Crime and Disorder Act (1998). If someone under the age of 18 admits an offence, the police can decide to issue a final warning as an alternative to court proceedings. The final warning can either be given for a serious first offence or when a young person has already received a reprimand for an earlier offence. After receiving a final warning, a young person is referred to a *youth offending team for a programme aimed at preventing further offending.

financial abuse *See* SAFEGUARDING ADULTS.

financial assessment When undertaking *needs assessments with adults, there is a financial assessment of capital and income, usually conducted by a social worker in association with the *assessment. This boosts *local authorities' interest in maximizing the income of *service users through benefit checks to ensure they are receiving all of the social security *benefits to which they are entitled, as this may increase the charges that the local authority can set for the services provided. Unlike *benefit rates, which are set nationally, charges for services in people's homes are decided by each local authority, resulting in considerable inequity. *See* CHARGING FOR SERVICES; ELIGIBILITY CRITERIA.

finding of fact hearing A court hearing where allegations that a child has experienced *domestic violence or *child abuse and neglect are examined by a judge in order to find whether the alleged events occurred. These hearings may follow the initiation of *care proceedings by a *local authority when it has grounds for believing a child has experienced *significant harm but this is contested by the parents of the child. After hearing the different versions of events provided by each of the parties to the proceedings, if the judge concurs with the local authority, the case then proceeds as usual with the court's findings being taken into account. *Expert witnesses may be called to assist the judge in determining her/his finding.

fine A court sentence that requires an offender to pay money as a punishment. The amount of any fine is meant to take into account the seriousness of the offence and the financial circumstances of the offender.

First-tier Tribunal (Mental Health) In England what was previously known as a Mental Health Review Tribunal is now called a First-tier Tribunal (Mental Health). These Tribunals have powers to discharge patients from detention in hospital under the Mental Health Act (1983), from *Community Treatment Orders, and from *guardianship. They *must* exercise these powers if the statutory criteria, set out in Section 72 of the Mental Health Act, are met. Tribunals may also direct the discharge of a patient from hospital at a future date, and can recommend the granting of *leave of absence, or transfer to another hospital or into guardianship. Hospital managers have a statutory obligation to inform detained patients of their right to apply to a tribunal for a review and to ensure patients are given every opportunity to exercise their rights, including assistance with representation. Managers are also obliged to appoint a member of staff to assist patients with tribunal applications. Patients, and in some cases *nearest relatives, may apply for a review in respect of guardianship and Community Treatment Orders. Reviews may also be requested in respect of changes to a *care and treatment plan, for example when a doctor reclassifies a mental disorder. Timescales apply to applications. The Secretary of State may in some circumstances and at any time refer a patient to a tribunal. Hospital managers have a duty to automatically refer *cases of patients detained under some sections of the Act when they have not exercised their right to apply within the timescale permitted. This provision ensures safeguards against patients being detained for unduly long periods. Hearings are normally held in private. Tribunal rules stipulate that hearings must be conducted by a judge, a registered medical practitioner, and a layperson with experience of health and social care matters. Patients are represented at tribunals by solicitors who have expertise in the mental health field. In some cases, a registered medical practitioner authorized by or on behalf of the patient may undertake an independent medical examination of the patient and may inspect any medical or nursing records. A social circumstances report is usually required and often provided by a social worker. The Tribunals, Courts and Enforcement Act (2007) also created an Upper Tribunal. Decisions of a First-tier Tribunal can be appealed to the Upper Tribunal on points of law. In certain limited cases decisions of the Upper Tribunal can be appealed to the Court of Appeal. *See also* MENTAL ILLNESS.

first-wave feminism Usually refers to the first organized movement for reform to women's unequal social and legal position, strongly focused on the campaign for women's suffrage in the late nineteenth and early twentieth centuries. Although the struggle was built substantially around the demand for the vote, campaigns also focused on property rights, widening access to the professions (especially medicine), family allowances, contraception, *abortion, and *welfare rights. *See also* FEMALE; FEMININITY; FEMINISM; FEMINIST SOCIAL WORK; FEMINIST THERAPY.

fit for purpose Suitable for the use for which it is intended. The term began life in the field of consumer protection, where it is used to refer to manufactured goods being required to do what they are designed to do. With the growth of *managerialism in the public sector and its commitment to *consumerism, 'fit for purpose' became a phrase that could be applied to any aspect of any service, for example, 'our child protection procedures are fit for purpose'.

flooding *See* BEHAVIOUR MODIFICATION.

fluctuating needs (adults) *See* CARER'S ASSESSMENT; ELIGIBILITY CRITERIA; NEEDS ASSESSMENT.

forced marriage A marriage that has taken place or is due to take place under coercion, either as a result of physical *violence, or threats, or other forms of psychological pressure, usually from family. A court can grant a Forced Marriage Protection Order to protect a person from being forced into a marriage, or to protect someone who has already been forced into a marriage and to help remove them from the situation. (Forced Marriage [Civil Protection] Act [2007]). Anyone not obeying an order can be found in contempt of court and sent to prison for up to two years. Each Forced Marriage Protection Order contains terms that are designed to protect the victim in their particular circumstances, such as:

• Preventing a forced marriage from occurring;
• Handing over passports;
• Stopping intimidation and violence;
• Revealing the whereabouts of a person;
• Stopping someone from being taken abroad.

The Anti-social Behaviour, Crime and Policing Act (2014) made it a criminal offence to force someone to marry. This includes taking someone overseas to force them to marry, whether or not the forced marriage takes place; marrying someone who lacks the mental *capacity to consent to the marriage, whether they are pressured or not. The civil remedy of obtaining a Forced Marriage Protection Order through the family courts continues to exist alongside the criminal offence so victims can choose whether to pursue a case in the civil or criminal courts.

Further reading: HM Government (2014) *Multi-agency Practice Guidelines: Handling Cases of Forced Marriage*. Available at: https://www.gov.uk/government/uploads/system/uploads/attachment_data/file/322307/hmg_multi_agency_practice_guidelines_v1_180614_final.pdf.
HM Government (2014) *The Right to Choose: Multi-agency Statutory Guidance for Dealing with Forced Marriage*. Available at: http://www.gov.uk/government/uploads/system/uploads/attachment_data/file/322310/HMG_Statutory_Guidance_publication_180614_Final.pdf.

formal admission *See* COMPULSORY ADMISSION.

Form Fostering (CoramBAAF Form F [Fostering]) Used by social workers to complete a comprehensive assessment of applicants who want to become foster carers by pulling together a wide range of information about them such as individual profile, family and environmental factors, and present circumstances. *See also* FAMILY PLACEMENT TEAM; FOSTERING.

foster care *See* FOSTERING.

foster carer *See* FOSTERING.

foster home *See* FOSTERING.

fostering An arrangement where people approved for the purpose care for children who cannot live with their own parents. The term 'foster carer' refers to the individuals providing this care. In the past they were described as 'foster parents' but this was seen as misleading as the children cared for usually already have parents, and 'foster carer' more accurately reflects the often-temporary nature of a placement. Fostering is regulated by the Children Act (1989) and the Fostering Services (England) Regulations (2011). There are over 50,000 children in England who are placed with foster carers by children's services. Some of these children are able to return to their families within a matter of days. For many, returning home will take longer depending on their circumstances and the seriousness of the problems encountered. If a return to their family is not possible, a decision may be made to find them a permanent new family, through placement with a family member, remaining in foster care long-term, or *adoption. In the latter circumstances, sometimes a child is placed during the period of temporary *local authority care with foster carers who are also approved as adopters. If the court agrees that the child should be adopted and the adoption agency approves the 'match' between the foster carers as adopters and the child, the placement becomes an adoption placement. In the majority of cases children in foster care will retain regular *contact with their family of origin and their parents will continue to have responsibilities towards them while they are in foster care as they maintain a level of *parental responsibility. The backgrounds of children who require foster care are varied, with some needing to be looked after because of temporary incapacity on the part of a *birth parent. For example, they may need to be in hospital for a short time and there is no-one else to care for their children. Others may be children about whom the authorities have concerns regarding *significant harm, where it is not safe for them to remain in their families until the situation has been fully assessed (*see* SECTION 47 ASSESSMENT). Foster carers can be single people or couples, married or unmarried. They can be heterosexual, gay, or lesbian, and from a wide age range. People who wish to foster are assessed by a fostering agency, usually local authority children's services but sometimes by a private fostering agency. Children placed in foster care are assigned their own social worker and approved foster carers receive support from family placement services located within children's services or a private fostering agency. All foster carers are paid allowances for the children they look after. *See also* ACCOMMODATED CHILD; AGENCY DECISION-MAKER; CORAMBAAF; FAMILY PLACEMENT TEAM; FORM F; KINSHIP CARE; LEAVING CARE; LOOKED-AFTER CHILDREN; PERMANENCY PLANNING; PLACEMENT; PRIVATE FOSTERING; SPECIAL GUARDIAN.

(⊕) SEE WEB LINKS
• Official site of Foster Talk, which provides support for foster carers.

foster parent *See* FOSTERING.

fragmentation of roles and tasks There has been an increasing tendency to break down social work into a series of separate tasks, often completed by different social workers and/or teams. From a managerial perspective, functional specialization may be seen as increasing the efficiency and cost-effectiveness of the service by improving the 'throughput' of work, and providing greater control over different parts of the social work process. However, a social worker may find it frustrating to feel that s/he is only responsible for limited aspects of the *intervention. Most social work models and approaches encompass the stages of *assessment, intervention, *review, and evaluation, so restriction of the social worker's involvement to one or two stages can make it difficult for social workers to see their relevance or to perceive their role in the way it has been presented in their professional education. This may have an impact on their morale and job satisfaction. The person using the services might find the arrangements confusing, and might not be able to work out who has overall responsibility, and whom s/he should approach if there is a problem. Instead of experiencing social work as integrated, continuous, and coordinated, *service users can feel passed on from one social worker to another. Thus the fragmentation of roles and tasks undermines the *relationship-based components of social work. Yet engaging with issues such as an older person's life history, mental wellbeing, and social and emotional needs, or a young person's experience of *abuse, and wishes and feelings with regard to her/his future, is likely to depend on the formation of a relationship conducive to the exploration of sensitive and complex areas. The lack of time and opportunity to form these relationships, along with the perceived lack of relevance of relationships in some social work systems, are major barriers to *holistic assessment. In terms of intervention, the emphasis is often on the role of the practitioner as an intermediary—as a manager of services ensuring 'commodities' are delivered in *'care packages'—not on the social worker's deployment of skills in working with people. Fragmentation of roles and tasks ignores the extent to which relationships are central to the factors that give quality to people's lives. This applies to social work relationships as well as personal and social relationships, with relationships with social workers and service providers a central component in defining a quality service from the perspective of *service users. See also DEPROFESSIONALIZATION; DESKILLING; DIVISION OF LABOUR; FUNCTIONAL ANALYSIS; INTENSIFICATION OF (SOCIAL) WORK.

frailty In social work practice and much research and academic writing, frailty is related to physical deficits and *risk. This has significant implications for the ways in which policies and procedures are framed, particularly with regard to establishing *eligibility for services, how social work practice is constructed, and adults' experience of contact with services. Research on *service users' perspectives has shown that, in contrast with social work perspectives that emphasize service users' physical deficiencies, service users associate frailty with socially and emotionally defined experiences of feeling a *loss of control over their circumstances. The dominant social work construction of frailty ignores these experiences and prioritizes physical functioning. In so doing, it promotes simplistic forms of assessment that ignore social and emotional dimensions of the experience of frailty. Service *rationing and allocation are undertaken on the basis of the narrow physical construction of frailty, ignoring the way in which frailty is also structured by social and economic disadvantage. The dominant approach also sidelines individual and cultural *differences in the meaning and significance of physical frailty, and it implies negative attitudes and responses through its association with notions of pity, blame, or burden. See also AGEISM; SOCIAL MODEL OF DISABILITY.

Framework for Assessment of Children in Need and their Families
This was the national tool used by professionals to complete *initial assessments and *core assessments for children who were or might have been in need within the meaning of the Children Act (1989), including those who might have been in need of protection. It adopted an *ecological approach, enabling information to be collected under three domains: parental capacity to care for the child; the child's development needs; and wider family and environmental factors.

The *Munro Review recommended that the government should not prescribe national models for assessments and, accordingly, the national status of the *Framework for Assessment of Children in Need and their Families* was withdrawn. The model continues to exist as a reference point for all assessments under the Children Act (1989) (see ASSESSMENT [CHILDREN]). See also CHILD ABUSE AND NEGLECT; CHILD IN NEED; CHILD PROTECTION; COMMON ASSESSMENT FRAMEWORK; SAFEGUARDING CHILDREN.

Fraser competent (Fraser guidelines)
Taken from the name of one of the three Law Lords presiding in the Gillick case (see GILLICK COMPETENT), heard by the House of Lords in 1985, and used to describe a child under 16 who is considered to

be of sufficient age and understanding to be competent to receive contraceptive advice without parental knowledge or consent. Guidelines derived from the judgment in the case permit a doctor to give contraceptive advice or treatment to a person under 16 years without parental consent, provided the doctor is satisfied that:

- The young person will understand the advice;
- The young person cannot be persuaded to tell her/his parents or to allow the doctor to tell them that they are seeking contraceptive advice;
- The young person is likely to begin or continue having unprotected sex with or without contraceptive treatment;
- The young person's physical or mental health is likely to suffer unless s/he receives contraceptive advice or treatment.

The term is narrower than *'Gillick competent', though the two terms are often used interchangeably. *See also* ADOLESCENCE; TEENAGE PREGNANCY.

free nursing care *See* NHS-FUNDED NURSING CARE.

functional analysis 1. A system for analysing the way in which a particular form of behaviour operates and the purpose(s) it serves. It is based on breaking down the process within which the behaviour occurs:

Antecedents What happened before the person engaged in the behaviour?
Behaviour Exactly what occurred?
Consequences What happened after the behaviour?

Interventions can then be directed at reducing or eliminating the events that prompt the behaviour and/or reducing those consequences of the behaviour that serve to reinforce it. Functional analysis is often referred to as the ABC model. *See also* BEHAVIOURISM; BEHAVIOUR MODIFICATION.

2. A management approach to breaking down the components of a job into the functions performed. This approach has been widely used including to deconstruct and separate out what social workers do, as the basis for training and assessing them. The emphasis in functional analysis is on competence in the performance of tasks required by employers. *See also* FRAGMENTATION OF ROLES AND TASKS.

gardening An activity known to have substantial benefits. A growing body of research evidence demonstrates the variety of meanings people ascribe to interaction with the natural environment. *Older people and others speak of the benefits in terms of intellectual stimulation and interest, the pleasures of sight and smell, including the memories evoked by particular plants or activities in the garden, the value of physical activity, social exchanges based on the garden, including the giving and receiving of plants and produce, and the growing and eating of fruit and vegetables. Maintaining regular low-level physical activity, such as gardening, can have a valuable role in relation to *Alzheimer's disease and other conditions associated with old age. Gardens and gardening can also present some *risks, for example, from the psychological impact of being unable to maintain a garden or from *falls on uneven paths or steps. Social workers have often failed to include discussions of *service users' gardens in *assessments of their *capacity to live independently in their own homes. Gardening as a form of *group activity and/or therapy has been used in a wide variety of settings with a range of groups including offenders, disabled people, people with mental health problems, people living in *poverty, and older people. Benefits include increased social interaction and confidence as well as the satisfaction associated with growing, selling, and eating produce.

Further reading: Sempik, J., Aldridge, J. and Becker, S. (2005) *Growing Together: A Practical Guide to Promoting Social Inclusion through Gardening and Horticulture*, Policy Press.

(⊕) SEE WEB LINKS

• Official site of Thrive, a national charity that promotes the benefits of gardening for individuals and groups.

gatekeeping The role associated with controlling (granting or refusing) access to services because more people request or are referred for services than can be provided with them. In this context, the concern is with ensuring that only people whose needs are defined as satisfying certain policy criteria receive a service. As the gatekeepers of resources in these circumstances, social workers regulate, ration, and channel the distribution of services on behalf of the state through rules, regulations, and procedures. *See also* ELIGIBILITY CRITERIA.

gay and lesbian perspectives Social work has been influenced by the struggle for equal rights these perspectives represent, for example, in accepting gay and lesbian couples as foster carers and adopters. Social work has also been aligned with challenges to the pathologizing of gay men and lesbian women and young people, for example, in relation to young people coming out when being *looked after by *local authorities. However, social work with lesbian women and gay men can still be a marginalized area in practice, research, and teaching. *See also* ANTI-DISCRIMINATORY PRACTICE; ANTI-OPPRESSIVE PRACTICE; HETERONORMATIVITY; HETEROSEXISM; HOMOPHOBIA; QUEER THEORY.

Further reading: Cosis-Brown, H. and Cocker, C. (2011) *Social Work with Lesbians and Gay Men*, Sage.

gaze Refers to structured ways of viewing and interpreting the social world, derived from Foucault's (1926–84) work on surveillance. Using a metaphor derived from the philosopher Jeremy Bentham's design for prisons in the eighteenth century, the *panopticon, which allowed prisoners to be under the continuous gaze of their gaolers, Foucault argued that under the surveillance of the gaze of dominant *discourse, the subjects of that gaze do not have to be coerced; they regulate themselves by 'interiorizing' the gaze and engaging in self-surveillance. Foucault sees the gaze as enabling power to be exercised continuously. Some writers have regarded the development of the *welfare state as the refining of the gaze through the use of professional expertise, such as that of social workers. *See also* GOVERNMENTALITY; REPRESENTATION; TECHNOLOGIES OF THE SELF.

gender Socio-cultural characteristics that are attributed to women and men, through processes such as socialization, and that become associated with the differences between them. These differences are referred to in terms of *femininity and *masculinity. In contrast, 'sex' refers to the biological differences between women and men that make them *female and male. In short, the distinction made is that sex is anatomical but gender is acquired. This distinction was a crucial dimension of second-wave *feminism's analysis of power relations and how systems of patriarchal power were maintained and sustained. The consideration of gender in isolation has been criticized by writers who have insisted that femininity and masculinity are not constructed in isolation but in and through other social divisions such as age, *class, *disability, *ethnicity, *'race', and sexuality. *See also* DECONSTRUCTION; DIFFERENCE; DIVERSITY; FEMINIST SOCIAL WORK; GENDER DIFFERENTIATION; GENDER DYSPHORIA; GENDER IDENTITY; GENDER ROLES; INTERSECTIONALITY; SOCIAL CONSTRUCTIONISM.

gender differentiation Social processes through which biological differences between the sexes are used as the basis for social and cultural classification. A few years ago, an example in social work was that it was rare for male foster carers to attend meetings in foster placements because of the assumption that they were the 'breadwinners' and the female foster carer was the nurturer, and thus she was the only one who needed to be at meetings concerning the children being cared for in the placement. *See also* DECONSTRUCTION; FEMININITY; GENDER; GENDER IDENTITY; GENDER ROLES; MASCULINITY; SOCIAL CONSTRUCTIONISM.

gendered division of labour *See* DOMESTIC LABOUR.

gender dysphoria The discomfort or distress experienced by someone for whom there is a mismatch between their biological sex and gender identity. Also referred to as gender identity disorder, gender incongruence, or transgenderism.

gender identity The sense of self associated with one's *gender; the extent to which one identifies with being masculine or feminine. Some people may reject the gender associated with their biology and live as the other gender, or have surgery to change their bodily characteristics in line with their experience of their gender identity. *See also* DECONSTRUCTION; FEMININITY; GENDER; GENDER DIFFERENTIATION; GENDER DYSPHORIA; GENDER ROLES; MASCULINITY; SOCIAL CONSTRUCTIONISM.

gender roles The social expectations attached to gender and the sanctioning of ways in which gender should be expressed through forms of dress, types of posture, and particular gestures associated with either women or men. *See also* DECONSTRUCTION; FEMININITY; GENDER; GENDER DIFFERENTIATION; GENDER DYSPHORIA; GENDER IDENTITY; MASCULINITY; SOCIAL CONSTRUCTIONISM.

gender stereotyping (gender role stereotyping) Exaggerated generalizations of differences between the sexes that see certain attitudes, emotions, and behaviours as typifying what it means to be a woman or a man. The basis of much of the socialization of children and young people into their *gender identity. *See also* DECONSTRUCTION; FEMININITY; GENDER DIFFERENTIATION; GENDER DYSPHORIA; GENDER ROLES; MASCULINITY; SOCIAL CONSTRUCTION.

general duty *See* DUTY; TARGET DUTY.

general practitioner (GP) A qualified and registered doctor who provides general medical services (such as *diagnosis, referral to hospital, prescription of drugs), based in a surgery or medical centre in the *community, on the basis of being independently contracted (not employed) by the National Health Service. Some social workers are attached to general practices on a full- or part-time basis, though this mode of social work is rare.

genericism A general unspecialized form of social work in which social workers or social work teams (the precise arrangements varied) dealt with all service user groups. Genericism came to prominence with the establishment of *Social Services Departments, following the implementation of the Seebohm Report (1968) through the Local Authority Social Services Act (1970). The demise of genericism began with the implementation of the *community care reforms and later on the disbanding of Social Services Departments in the mid 2000s, with the setting up of separate adults' and children's services.

genogram A pictorial display of an individual's family relationships and *kinship network (see illustration). This is generated by using symbols representing gender and family status and connecting the people who appear by using a system of coded lines to define the nature of their relationships (see fig.). The system makes it possible to illustrate the individual's parental and *carer status, marital relationships, whether divorced or separated, whether children are birth children, adopted, or step-children. *Extended family and important wider social relationships are also likely to be included. A completed genogram will resemble a family tree but with all the different types of relationship included, and consequently provides a more detailed picture of the family it represents. Social workers and other professionals often construct and make use of genograms to make sense of the complex circumstances that characterize the lives of many of the children and families with which they work. It is a tool that may be used in *direct work with children and young people alongside other techniques such as *life story work. *See also* CHILD-CENTRED APPROACH; DIRECT WORK WITH CHILDREN; ECOLOGICAL APPROACH; ECO MAP; LIFE MAP; PLAY THERAPY.

genuineness *See* WARMTH.

geriatric medicine The medical specialism concerned with the treatment of *older people, led by a consultant geriatrician. *See also* AGEISM; ANTI-AGEIST PRACTICE; GERONTOLOGY; GRAY PANTHERS; THEORIES OF AGEING.

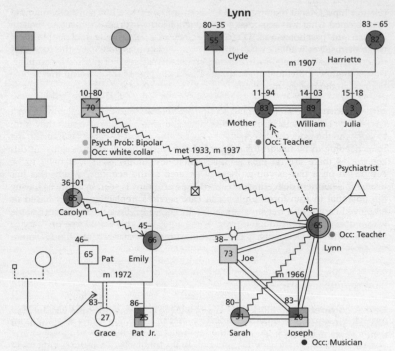

Genogram

gerontology Interdisciplinary subject area that focuses on ageing and *older people, drawing on biological, psychological, and social theories. In the 1970s it was primarily concerned with the individual older person and the processes associated with her/his ageing. Under the influence of social gerontology, this individually-focused approach developed into a wider concern with the political, economic, and social construction of ageing and what it means to be an older person. The status and portrayals of older people vary significantly in different societies and have varied in the same society in different historical periods. *See also* AGEISM; ANTI-AGEIST PRACTICE; GERIATRIC MEDICINES; GRAY PANTHERS; THEORIES OF AGEING.

((())) SEE WEB LINKS
• Official site of the British Society of Gerontology.

gestalt (therapy) [*German*: form, pattern, configuration, whole] Early twentieth-century gestalt psychology was concerned with the perception of coherent wholes, for example, demonstrating that wholes with a part missing were still perceived as wholes. From the 1940s onwards, Gestalt therapy transferred this emphasis on holistic analysis from the study of perception to an approach to people in which individuals are seen as complex wholes, constituted by their past influences, their present being, and their future aspirations, within the context of networks of wider relationships. Gestalt therapy was seen as contributing to a humanistic psychology that rejected what was regarded as the dogmatism and *reductionism of *behaviourism and *psychoanalysis. In contrast, it focused on how individual people could make themselves whole, experiencing personal growth as they filled the gaps they experienced as a consequence of the aspects of themselves that seemed incomplete. Gestalt therapy, individual or group-based, is underpinned by optimism that people can realize themselves more fully.

gig economy The sectors of the economy where workers seek employment on a day-to-day, task-to-task basis. Workers sign up online, stating the hours they want to work and the work they are willing to do, and the website matches workers to the roles needing to be filled. It is something of a misnomer to refer to 'jobs' in this context, as there are no jobs as such. There are simply tasks that need to be completed on a pay-as-you-go basis. One area of the economy where this has taken off is couriers delivering parcels. The gig economy is seen by some as having the potential to transform adult social care services, replacing agency-based or employed carers with freelance *personal assistants in direct contact with people who request services through an app. Some argue that this would free up *service users from the hassles associated with employing personal assistants directly (managing holiday and sick pay, pension contributions, national insurance, and tax—*see* DIRECT PAYMENTS). Others see problems with an unregulated workforce able to enter the homes of vulnerable people. *See also* AGENCY SOCIAL WORK; BUSINESS ORIENTATION; JUST-IN-TIME.

Gillick competent A Gillick competent child is a child under 16 who has the legal capacity to consent to medical examination and treatment, i.e. s/he is able to demonstrate that s/he has sufficient maturity and intelligence to understand and appraise the nature and implications of the proposed treatment, including the *risks and alternative courses of action. The term 'Gillick competent' is also often used to describe children who are capable of giving consent to other matters requiring their decision without parental consent, i.e. where they are capable of understanding what is proposed and can express their own wishes. It has a wider meaning than the term *Fraser competent, which specifically refers to contraceptive advice.

The concept arose from a legal case concerning whether a child under 16 has sufficient understanding to consent to medical treatment in her/his own right. The case was *Gillick v. West Norfolk Area Health Authority* (1986). The case began in 1982 when Victoria Gillick took her local health authority to court in an attempt to make it illegal for doctors to give contraceptive advice or treatment to her under-16-year-old daughter without parental consent. The High Court found in favour of the health authority. The Court of Appeal reversed the High Court's decision. The House of Lords ruled in favour of the High Court's original judgment. In its ruling, the House of Lords decided that an under-16-year-old could consent to medical treatment in her/his own right provided s/he had 'sufficient understanding to make informed decisions', recognizing that children's rate of development and maturity varied. (The guidelines derived from the House of Lords judgment are commonly referred to as the Fraser guidelines, after one of the Law Lords who presided in the case.) This principle was incorporated into the Children Act (1989), allowing a child who is Gillick competent to refuse to have a medical or psychiatric examination, even if it has been requested by a court. Subsequently it was established that refusal to consent could be overruled if it is deemed to be in the child's *best interests. Since the House of Lords' judgement, Gillick competency has been adopted more widely to help assess whether a child has the maturity to make her/his own decisions and to understand the implications of those decisions. For example, in the context of court cases, lawyers will want to ascertain whether children are Gillick competent and able to give their own instructions to the lawyers representing them. *See also* ADOLESCENCE; TEENAGE PREGNANCY.

glass ceiling A metaphor that conveys the invisible barriers that prevent women's career progression, even though the opportunities available to them ostensibly appear to be the same as those available to men. Sometimes used in relation to social work organizations in which social workers are predominantly women but men are over-represented in management posts.

global definition of social work (global definition of the social work profession) *See* INTERNATIONAL FEDERATION OF SOCIAL WORKERS.

globalization The increased openness of national economies to trade and financial flows, and the ensuing mobility of capital, investment, and production processes, underpinned by new forms of technology, particularly information technology. Though rooted in the world economy, globalization is not simply an economic phenomenon; it is also a political and ideological phenomenon associated with the rise of *neo-liberalism. One of its key aspects has been the subordination of social welfare measures within nation-states to the creation of conditions that will ensure international competitiveness, with a consequent diminution of autonomy for nation-states in determining social policy. Pressures are exerted on governments from business interests to accept responsibility for national competitiveness and to see the interests of business as the same as the national interest. Reappraisal of the *welfare state has thus been linked to maintaining the conditions necessary for profitability in order to avert capital flight and to attract new investment from multi-national corporations and international finance capital. Conservative, *New Labour, and Coalition governments have presented this as a struggle for survival in the global context. In this struggle, the ideas that underpinned the social democratic welfare state, including social work, have been seen as a barrier to national survival. They have been presented as outdated and inappropriate in a restless and uncertain global economy. Instead, neo-liberal ideas have been developed by governments that stress adaption to globalization as an uncontrollable phenomenon. These include the primacy of economic competitiveness; the subordination of social policy to the needs of a competitive national economy; more limited scope for government intervention; and stricter control over public expenditure. Globalization, and the need for national economic competitiveness in order to respond to its demands, is the macro-context within which governments have changed their *welfare regimes. Public services, such as social work, have been drawn deeper into managerial market-oriented ways of thinking and practising as an aspect of this much wider political rationale to reform services in response to the demands for competitiveness. As far as social work is concerned, the most influential dimensions of neo-liberal ideas have been: first, an emphasis on contracting-out service delivery from the *public sector to the *private and *voluntary sectors; secondly, applying ideas to public services that are drawn from private business management and that focus on securing more economic, efficient, and effective services; and, thirdly, the privileging of managers, rather than professionals, insisting on managers' brief to improve performance and bring about change, with emphasis placed on the achievement of targets. All of these trends have intensified in the context of *austerity. *See also* ECONOMY, EFFICIENCY, AND EFFECTIVENESS.

Gloucestershire judgment *See* ELIGIBILITY CRITERIA; UNMET NEED.

goal Anything that is an end result towards which work being undertaken with or for *service users is directed. The work itself is the means of reaching the goal(s).

goal displacement When an organization replaces the *goal(s) it is meant to achieve with other goals, for example, being dominated by the pursuit of narrowly defined targets rather than being concerned with the quality of social work practice, or simply when it loses sight of its goals and functions aimlessly or is motivated solely by ensuring its continued existence.

good-enough parenting Concept generally attributed to the paediatrician, psychiatrist, and psychoanalyst D. W. Winnicott (1896–1971), who originally identified the notion of the 'good-enough mother', whom he saw as laying down the foundations of a child's wellbeing through the 'ordinary loving care' of her child. He saw this care as associated with effectively meeting the physical needs of the child, including her/his requirements for nutrition and protection, and the provision of emotional warmth, love, care, commitment, and consistency. He also saw limit-setting in the form of establishing clear behavioural boundaries for the child as being associated with good-enough parenting. The major consideration was that all these aspects were provided consistently on a long-term basis, ensuring that the child grew up into an emotionally secure, fully developed, and competent adult.

In contemporary practice, the term is often used by professionals working in health and *child welfare to assess whether the care being provided to a child is sufficient to meet her/his needs. However, the expectations for what is seen as good-enough parenting are more modest than in Winnicott's original concept. They centre on meeting children's health and development needs, putting the children's needs first, providing routine and consistent care, acknowledging problems, and engaging with support services. The concept is of particular value when making judgements about the likelihood of *significant harm, especially when this is linked to concerns about possible neglect and emotional abuse of the child. The importance of the concept in this regard is in its implicit acceptance that to expect perfection of parents is unrealistic and that to do so may undermine the efforts of the majority of parents, who in all practical respects are doing enough to care reasonably for their children. However, applying the concept makes it possible to identify situations where parental care may not be 'good enough' and may be having a deleterious impact on the child. *See also* ATTACHMENT; CHILD ABUSE AND NEGLECT; CHILD DEVELOPMENT; PARENTING ASSESSMENT.

Further reading: Winnicott, D.W. (1991, orig. 1964) *The Child, the Family and the Outside World*, Penguin.

good practice There is a general legal expectation that social work organizations should not simply comply with legislation at a minimum level. The principles that have been established in *judicial reviews are consistent with what would be regarded as good practice in social work: being fair to people; listening to them; taking their expectations into account; having policies that can respond to individual circumstances. *See also* DISCRETION (LOCAL AUTHORITY); FETTERING DISCRETION.

governmentality Refers to the processes through which behaviour is controlled in personal life and social relationships. This approach to government, introduced in Foucault's (1926–84) work, is, therefore, not limited to formal government by the state and its various organizations. Rather, it is seen as running through the whole of society in the form of disciplinary power through which individuals acquire mind-sets, desires, and character traits by working on themselves. Foucault used the philosopher Jeremy Bentham's design for prisons in the eighteenth century as a metaphor for disciplinary power. The *panopticon enabled prisoners to be placed under the continuous *gaze of the warders. He argued that with modern developments, people regulate themselves through self-surveillance in accordance with dominant *discourses:

There is no need for arms, physical *violence, material constraints. Just a gaze. An inspecting gaze or gaze which each individual under its weight will end by interiorising to the point that he is his own overseer, each individual thus exercising this surveillance over, and against, himself. A superb formula: power exercised continuously and for what turns out to be at minimal cost (Foucault, M. (1980) *The History of Sexuality Vol. 1*, p.155).

The successful operation of disciplinary power results in people who act in conformity with what is considered to be socially appropriate without having to be subjected to coercive power from outside themselves. They identify with the *discursive formation and experience that identification as individual autonomy. The operation of governmentality through disciplinary power that is most relevant to social work is that identified by Foucault as the emergence of the 'psy-complex', characterized by experts in particular disciplines such as medicine, psychiatry, and psychology exercising disciplinary power. The psy-complex represents the refining of the disciplining gaze through professional expertise, such as that of social work, justified as necessary for people's wellbeing and given added impetus through the mechanisms of the *welfare state. *See also* REPRESENTATION; TECHNOLOGIES OF THE SELF.

government policy A statement of intention and direction by the government in power in relation to a particular sphere of operations, such as social work, or a more specific field within that sphere, such as *child protection, which is meant to shape decisions so that they are geared to the outcomes that the government is seeking to achieve. The detail of what is to be done and how it is to be done may not be included in policy statements but may appear in accompanying *guidance, procedures, or *codes of practice.

GP *See* GENERAL PRACTITIONER.

grand narrative Used by *postmodernists as a term to attack social theories that have a big theme, such as the idea that the development of social work resulted from increasing concern on the part of the state for the welfare of its citizens, or that it was an increasingly sophisticated means of ensuring their social control.

Gray Panthers An activist intergenerational organization that originally focused only on matters affecting *older people but increasingly developed into a progressive force campaigning on a wide range of issues. It was founded in the US in 1970 by Maggie Kuhn (1905–95), a retired social worker. The name was originally a nickname coined by a talk show producer. The national organization was built on local networks, or 'chapters', each of which had a convenor. The Gray Panthers' overarching organization has been dissolved but Gray Panthers networks still exist in the US and elsewhere. A new national organization in the US called the National Council of Gray Panthers Networks is still taking positions on issues and encouraging collective action, as well as offering support to local networks. *See also* AGEISM; ANTI-AGEIST PRACTICE.

⊕ SEE WEB LINKS
- Facebook page of the National Council of Gray Panthers Networks.

grief *See* BEREAVEMENT.

Griffiths Report *See* COMMUNITY CARE REFORMS.

grounded theory Developing theoretical ideas from data. Refers specifically to the process of analysing qualitative data by producing accounts of it that are tested repeatedly, as set out by Glaser and Strauss, originally in *The Discovery of Grounded Theory* (1967). Often mentioned in relation to social work research, but usually in a way that has come to mean simply that ideas have been generated from data, with the original rigour of Glaser and Strauss's method not having been employed.

group A number of individuals with a shared sense of *identity and/or who are bound together by interaction with each other. Closed groups have closely guarded boundaries with informal or formal criteria for membership, whereas open groups have loose boundaries that allow easy access to potential members. *See also* GROUP DYNAMICS; GROUP THERAPY; GROUP WORK; OUT-GROUP.

group dynamics The processes that occur within face-to-face groups. Tuckman's (1965) model of the stages that groups go through has often been used as a model within social work to understand the dynamics of service user groups and teams of social workers:

Forming Group members want to be accepted by the other members of the group and avoid controversy or conflict. Serious issues and feelings are avoided. This is a comfortable stage for a group to be in but the avoidance of conflict means that not much actually gets done.

Storming As issues start to be addressed, differences of view emerge and confrontations arise. These may relate to what the group should be doing, or how it should be operating, or be about the roles and responsibilities within the group. Some group members may relish getting into the issues; others may attempt to remain in the comfort and security of forming.

Norming As the group storms, the ground rules for the group start to be established. Having argued, group members understand each other better and have a better appreciation of each other's skills and experience. They listen to each other more, appreciate and support each other more, and are prepared to change pre-conceived views. As the norms become fixed, they feel they are part of a cohesive effective group.

Performing Not all groups reach this stage, when everyone knows each other well enough to be able to work together, and roles and responsibilities change according to what is required. Group *identity, loyalty, and morale are high and group members can concentrate on achieving the group's *goals.

Twelve years after identifying these four stages in the development of group dynamics, Tuckman added a fifth:

Adjourning The group reaches the end of its life and breaks up or has so many personnel changes that in effect a new group forms. Group members may recognize what they have achieved and move on. Others may primarily feel a sense of *loss, which has led some writers to term this stage 'mourning'.

The model should not be seen as suggesting that groups follow these stages in a linear process. As circumstances change in a group, it may move into a different stage. For example, a group may be norming or performing but a new member might take it into storming. *See also* GROUP; GROUP THERAPY; GROUP WORK.

Further reading: Tuckman, B. and Jensen, M. (1977). 'Stages of Small Group Development Revisited', *Group and Organizational Studies*, 2, 419–427.

group home A home for small numbers of *service users, usually adults with *learning disabilities or mental health problems, provided in an ordinary house or a purpose-built setting. There may be staff present on a permanent basis, or no staff presence, or a range of arrangements for staffing between these two extremes, such as staffing for part of the time or brief routine calls.

group therapy (group psychotherapy) In group therapy six to ten people meet with one or two qualified group therapists who set the ground rules for how the group will operate, emphasize the need to maintain *confidentiality about what happens in the group, and use *group dynamics to illustrate problems and initiate interventions. Although there are various approaches and purposes in group therapy and any therapeutic process that occurs in a group context can be seen as falling within group therapy (for example, dance therapy), the term most often refers to group psycho-therapy. The assumption underpinning group therapy is that when people come into a group and interact with other group members, they will replicate the problems that brought them to group therapy, and therefore the group's processes and dynamics can be used as mechanisms for change through the exploration of the interpersonal relationships within the group. A common technique is for members of the group to be encouraged to give *feedback to others. This involves individuals saying how they feel about what someone says or how someone behaves so that group members learn about how others see them and how they interact with others, becoming more self-aware in the process. The group can also be used to provide support to people who have shared similar experiences and can be used as an opportunity to try out new ways of behaving. With the assistance of the group therapist(s), the group can give support and offer alternatives so that the group becomes a place in which the problems displayed can be resolved. The group can provide a context in which someone can test out new ways of relating to people, for example, by being more assertive. In this way, relationships with other group members are used to assist with problem-solving. *See also* GROUP; GROUP DYNAMICS; GROUP WORK.

group work An approach to working with personal, and/or interpersonal, and/or social problems that can be directed by the group itself or that can be led or facilitated by an outside person such as a social worker. In what might be termed the classic conception of group work, in which social workers might be involved, the group's interaction is allowed to range widely and be largely self-determining with regard to the type of communication, the content of the discussion, the *goals of the group, and how they will be achieved. The social worker facilitates by focusing on the perspectives and abilities of group members and how these can be used to achieve their group's goal(s). S/he assists the group to see the strengths it has and the support it can provide to its members. There is a dual emphasis on the interaction of the group members, sometimes referred to as the maintenance or process function, and the group's agenda geared towards the achievement of its goals, sometimes referred to as the task or content function. Groups in which social workers are involved tend to be problem-focused, population-specific, and time-limited, for example, with abused children, women who have experienced *domestic violence, *older people with dementia, or young offenders. Groups primarily focused on support, for example, for *carers, might be more open-ended. Groups may be concerned with recovery, from mental health problems, or alcohol misuse, for example, or with building up social skills and confidence, such as groups for people with *learning disabilities. Group work used to be quite common but has become increasingly scarce in recent years. It is more common in the contemporary context in the recruitment of adoptive and foster parents, in services provided by *voluntary organizations, and in the *youth justice field. There is an increasing tendency to move away from classic group work in favour of scripted packages that provide everything needed to run a group on a particular topic (for example, *anger management or *parenting), session-by-session, with the social worker firmly in the role of group leader/tutor. *See also* GROUP; GROUP DYNAMICS; GROUP THERAPY.

Further reading: Whitaker, D. (2000, 2nd edn.) *Using Groups to Help People*, Routledge.

guardian *ad litem* *See* CHILDREN'S GUARDIAN.

guardianship (children) *See* SPECIAL GUARDIAN.

guardianship (mental health) A form of community compulsion authorized by Section 7 of the Mental Health Act (1983) for people 16 years and above:

The purpose of guardianship is to enable patients to receive care outside hospital where it cannot be provided without the use of compulsory powers... [It] provides an authoritative framework for working with a patient, with a minimum of constraint, to achieve as independent a life as possible within the community. Where it is used, it should be part of a patient's overall care plan.   (Department of Health (2015), *Mental Health Act 1983: Code of Practice*, p.342).

However, the powers of guardianship are limited and its use has tended to be infrequent and subject to considerable local variation. Applications for guardianship require two medical recommendations and the application is made to the *local authority, which decides whether to accept the application. Guardianship lasts up to six months, is renewable for a further six months and then yearly. The appointed guardian may be the local authority or a private individual approved by the local authority. In practice, private individuals rarely act as guardians. To satisfy grounds for guardianship the individual must be suffering from a mental disorder of a nature or degree that warrants reception into guardianship, and guardianship must be necessary in the interests of the individual's welfare or for the protection of other persons. The guardian has the power to require the individual to reside at a specified place; the individual to attend at specified places and times for the purpose of medical treatment, occupation, education, or training; access to the individual to be given, at any place where the individual is residing, to any medical practitioner, *approved mental health professional, or other specified person. There is no power to convey the person anywhere, except if s/he is absent without permission from any place s/he is required to reside, in which case the person may be taken into custody and returned to the specified place of residence. Guardianship does not provide statutory powers to make an individual accept treatment, such as medication, against her/his will. Individuals received into guardianship have the right to appeal to a *First-tier Tribunal. The *Mental Health Act (1983): Code of Practice* (2015) provides *guidance on when guardianship may be more appropriate than the use of a *Community Treatment Order or *leave of absence:

- It is social care-led and is primarily focused on patients with welfare *needs.
- The focus is on the patient's general welfare, rather than specifically on medical treatment.
- There is little risk of the patient needing to be admitted compulsorily and quickly to hospital.
- There is a need for an enforceable power to require the patient to reside at a particular place.

Guardianship has been declining in use for a number of years. In March 2015 there were 522 people in England subject to guardianship, and the number of new guardianship cases in 2014–15 was 212, a decline of 29 per cent compared to the previous year.

Further reading: Department of Health (2015) *Mental Health Act (1983): Code of Practice*, Chapter 30. Available at: https://www.gov.uk/government/uploads/system/uploads/attachment_data/file/435512/MHA_Code_of_Practice.pdf.

guidance In addition to being governed by legislation, social work is also subject to guidance from central government departments, usually the Department of Health for adults' services and the Department for Education for children's services. 'Statutory guidance' is given by a Secretary of State under Section 7 of the Local Authority Social Services Act (1970), which places a *duty on *local authorities to act on such guidance. Some guidance is referred to as 'policy guidance'. There is also 'practice guidance' which is not issued under Section 7. The courts have decided that in some circumstances local authorities have a statutory duty to follow policy guidance, whereas they only have to 'have regard to' practice guidance. The courts have tended not to rely on guidance in formulating their interpretation of legislation. In addition, there are *codes of practice, for example the *Mental Health Act (1983): Code of Practice* (2015). There is no legal duty to comply with such codes but there is an expectation that social workers will act in accordance with them and if they have not, they would be expected in any legal proceedings to have good reasons for not having done so. Similarly, circulars are issued by central government departments and while it would not be unlawful to ignore them, any actions that deviated from them would need to have good justification in any legal proceedings.

habitus A concept set out by Pierre Bourdieu (1930–2002) in *Outline of Theory and Practice* (1977) that describes a person's knowledge and understanding of the world, which are acquired from her/his *class position, expressed in thoughts, behaviours, and tastes, and manifested in patterned social and cultural practices. Bourdieu sees the habitus as, at least to some extent, malleable, leading some to argue that it has the capacity to encompass individual freedom. Others see it as an explanation for how ruling class domination is reproduced day-by-day at the micro level. Although Bourdieu used habitus in relation to a person's overall knowledge and understanding of the world, its use has been adapted to include what might be termed smaller-scale habiti. For example, the process of becoming a social worker (engaging in a course, undertaking placements, etc.) eventually produces a social work habitus, as forms of knowledge and understanding about the world of social work (and the wider world within which it is located) are acquired and expressed in ideas and behaviours that are seen as constituting what it means to be a social worker. *See also* CULTURAL CAPITAL; DISCOURSE; DOMINANT IDEOLOGY; GOVERNMENTALITY; HEGEMONY; TECHNOLOGIES OF THE SELF.

hallucination Distortion in a person's sensory perception experienced consciously in the absence of an external stimulus. Hallucinations can be experienced in any of the five senses and are typically accompanied by an intensely experienced and heightened sense of subjectively distorted reality. Auditory hallucination involves the sense of hearing, visual involves the sense of sight, olfactory involves the sense of smell, gustatory involves the sense of taste, kinaesthetic involves the sense of bodily movement, tactile involves the sense of touch, and somatic hallucination involves the perception of a physical experience within the body. Hallucinations are usually thought of as a symptom of mental disorder, but they may also be associated with drug use, sleep deprivation, neurological disorders, high temperature (fever), and delirium tremens. In the case of *schizophrenia, auditory hallucinations may take the form of benevolent voices, conveying positive messages to the person experiencing them, or they may be malicious or unpleasant. Visual hallucinations may accompany auditory hallucinations, and the person may believe they are being stared at, often with malicious intent. When experienced mildly, hallucinations are sometimes termed disturbances. They differ from *delusions in that delusions involve a deeply held belief that lacks an external stimulus, but can be given a bizarre significance. *See also* HEARING VOICES.

handicap *See* DISABILITY; SOCIAL MODEL OF DISABILITY.

harm minimization (harm reduction) An influential model informing work with drug users and some alcohol services, and potentially applicable to a wide range of public health issues. The model accepts that the use of drugs is common and that, although it has risks, the benefits the user perceives as arising from drug use have to be taken into account if services are to be effective. Harm reduction regards containment and reduction of the harm associated with drug use as a more realistic approach than abstinence. Accordingly, the use of drugs is accepted and no judgement is made that condemns or supports someone's use of drugs. The dignity and rights of the drug user are respected and services endeavour to be 'user-friendly', recognizing that, for many people, drug use is a long-term feature of their lives. The immediate priority is engaging *service users in seeking to achieve realistic *goals. The main focus of the approach is on reducing *risks so that harm can be reduced, with risk reduction primarily addressing the drug-taking behaviour of the drug user, for example, through heroin substitution or needle exchange programmes. There is no explicit goal of giving up drug use, although the harm reduction approach supports those who seek to reduce their drug use, or cease using drugs completely. *See also* ADDICTION.

hate crime (hate incident) The Association of Chief Police Officers defines a hate crime as: 'Any hate incident, which constitutes a criminal offence, perceived by the victim or any other person, as being motivated by prejudice or hate'. A hate incident is defined as: 'Any incident, which may or may not constitute a criminal offence, which is perceived by the victim or any other person, as being motivated by prejudice or hate'. Perpetrators of racially and/or religiously motivated hate crimes commit racially aggravated offences. Such offences receive more severe sentences than they would do if they were not racially aggravated (Crime and Disorder Act 1998). In addition, any offence that is motivated by hostility based on someone's *disability, sexuality, religion, or *'race' must have this element of the offence treated as an aggravating factor that makes the offence more serious, and the extra component in the sentence that is being given for this aggravating factor must be stated openly in court (Criminal Justice Act 2003).

Hawthorne effect An unintended modification of behaviour that results from being the subject of research or some other outside intervention. The source of the term was Hawthorne, a Chicago suburb where the Western Electric Company had a factory, which was the site for research in the 1920s into the effects on productivity of varying conditions at the workplace, such as changing the lighting, the hours of work, or the rate of pay. Regardless of what changes were made, and when they were reversed, productivity increased. The researchers concluded that the workers' receipt of attention from them had the effect of raising morale and increasing productivity.

Health and Care Professions Council (HCPC) A regulator that keeps a register of health and care professionals who meet its standards in relation to training, professional skills, behaviour, and health. It regulates arts therapists, biomedical scientists, chiropodists/podiatrists, clinical scientists, dietitians, hearing aid dispensers, *occupational therapists, operating department practitioners, orthoptists, paramedics, physiotherapists, practitioner psychologists, prosthetists/orthotists, radiographers, and speech and language therapists. Since August 2012 social workers in England have been regulated by the Health and Care Professions Council (HCPC). Social workers in *Wales, *Scotland, and *Northern Ireland are regulated by their respective Care Councils.

In addition to registration of social workers (and *protection of the title of 'social worker'), the HCPC has a two-fold impact on social work through the *Standards of Conduct, Performance and Ethics* that apply to all registrants, regardless of profession and the *Standards of Proficiency: Social Workers in England* that are specific to social work.

Standards of Conduct, Performance and Ethics

These state that registrants must:

- promote and protect the interests of service users and carers;
- communicate appropriately and effectively;
- work within the limits of their knowledge and skills;
- delegate appropriately;
- respect *confidentiality;
- manage *risk;
- report concerns about safety;
- be open when things go wrong;
- be honest and trustworthy;
- keep records of their work.

Each of these standards is fleshed out in detail. For example, the third standard—*working within the limits of knowledge and skills*—is broken down into two aspects: 'Keep within your scope of practice' and 'Maintain and develop your knowledge and skills'. What each aspect of each standard means is spelled out. For example:

3. Work within the limits of your knowledge and skills

   Keep within your scope of practice

   3.1 You must keep within your scope of practice by only practising in the areas you have appropriate knowledge, skills and experience for.

   3.2 You must refer a *service user to another practitioner if the care, treatment, or other services they need are beyond your scope of practice.

Standards of Proficiency: Social Workers in England

There are seventeen standards. Registered social workers must:

- be able to practise safely and effectively within their scope of practice;
- be able to recognize and respond appropriately to unexpected situations and manage uncertainty;
- be able to practise within the legal and ethical boundaries of their profession;
- be able to maintain fitness to practise;
- be able to practise as an autonomous professional, exercising their own professional judgement;
- be aware of the impact of *culture, equality, and *diversity on practice;
- be able to practise in a non-discriminatory manner;
- understand the importance of and be able to maintain confidentiality;
- be able to communicate effectively;
- be able to engage in inter-professional and inter-agency communication;
- be able to work appropriately with others;
- be able to maintain records appropriately;
- be able to reflect on and review practice;
- be able to ensure the quality of their practice;
- understand the key concepts of the knowledge base relevant to their profession;
- be able to draw on appropriate knowledge and skills to inform practice;
- understand the need to establish and maintain a safe practice environment.

Each of these standards is fleshed out in detail, for example, standard 7:

7. Be able to practise in a non-discriminatory manner

   7.1 Be able to work with others to promote social justice, equality, and inclusion.

   7.2 Be able to use practice to challenge and address the impact of discrimination, disadvantage, and *oppression.

See also CODE OF ETHICS; CODE OF PRACTICE; INTERNATIONAL FEDERATION OF SOCIAL WORKERS; KNOWLEDGE AND SKILLS STATEMENTS; PROFESSIONAL CAPABILITIES FRAMEWORK.

Further reading: *Standards of Conduct, Performance and Ethics.* Available at http://www.hcpc-uk.org/assets/documents/10004EDFStandardsofconduct,performanceandethics.pdf. *Standards of Proficiency: Social Workers in England.* Available at http://www.hpc-uk.org/assets/documents/10003B08Standardsofproficiency-SocialworkersinEngland.pdf.

(((⊕))) SEE WEB LINKS

• Official site of the Health and Care Professions Council.

Health and Social Care Trusts *See* JOINT FINANCE.

Health and Wellbeing Board The Health and Social Care Act (2012) established Health and Wellbeing Boards as fora where leaders from the health and social care system work together to improve the health and wellbeing of their local population and reduce *health inequalities, collaborating to understand their local *communities' *needs, agree priorities, and encourage commissioners to work in a more joined-up way, with the aim of producing more integrated NHS and *local authority services in the future. They became fully operational in April 2013 in 152 English local authorities with adult social care and public heath responsibilities. They are established and hosted by local authorities and bring together the NHS, public health, adult social care and children's services, councillors, and the local Healthwatch organization (a consumer body for health and social care) to plan how best to meet the needs of their local populations and tackle local inequalities in health. The Boards are a formal committee of the local authority, in most cases chaired by a senior councillor, charged with promoting greater integration and *partnership between bodies from the NHS, public health, and local government. The Boards have very limited formal powers. They are constituted as *partnership fora rather than executive decision-making bodies. However, they have a statutory duty, with *Clinical Commissioning Groups, to produce a Joint Strategic Needs Assessment and a Joint Health and Wellbeing Strategy for their local populations. The Joint Strategic Needs Assessment involves undertaking a comprehensive analysis of the current and future needs and assets of their areas. In the context of a JSNA, an asset can be anything that can be used to improve health outcomes and could include facilities such as a one-stop shop, green spaces, housing, education, local businesses, local providers with a specific expertise or capacity within the local *community, such as lunch clubs for isolated *older people. The JSNA includes needs and assets relevant to health, social care, and public health across the life course and includes an analysis of the wider determinants of health. Based on the JSNA, the Health and Wellbeing Board then develops a Joint Health and Wellbeing Strategy for their area to plan the delivery of integrated local services, based on the needs and assets identified in the JSNA, and collectively addresses the underlying determinants of health and well-being. This Strategy informs the *commissioning of services by Clinical Commissioning Groups and local authorities. *See also* JOINT FINANCE; JOINTLY COMMISSIONED SERVICE.

health assessment (looked-after children) Every *looked-after child must have a health assessment soon after becoming looked after by a *local authority and then at specified intervals, depending on the child's age. The first health assessment must be undertaken before the first placement, or, if not reasonably practicable, before the first review, unless one has been done within the previous three months. The first assessment must be undertaken by a registered medical practitioner. Subsequent assessments may be carried out by a registered nurse or registered midwife under the supervision of a registered medical practitioner. The health assessment should inform a health plan (also referred to as a health action plan), normally incorporated into a child's *care plan.

health inequalities Variations in people's health chances, as reflected in their life expectancy (mortality), their likelihood of suffering ill-health (morbidity), their quality of life, and access to health care when ill, which are all correlated with social divisions such as *class, *gender, and *ethnicity. Within countries, those in higher socio-economic groups live longer and have better health. Internationally, those countries with greater socio-economic equality and higher levels of social protection, for example, the Scandinavian countries, experience reduced inequalities in physical health when compared with countries like the US. Such disparities are most extreme in relation to the poorest countries in which life expectancy is substantially lower than in affluent countries, for example, several countries in sub-Saharan Africa have average life expectancies of below 40 years. Health inequalities may not seem to be an issue that would be of immediate concern to social work but as its *service users are predominantly members of *disadvantaged groups, who are living in relative *poverty, they are prone to experiencing poor health that results from socio-economic factors. While service users' poverty may have been the subject of longstanding concern because of social work's commitment to social justice, ill-health has only recently been recognized as a key aspect of the suffering that results from poverty. In addition, while social work has traditionally emphasized the importance of mental health, there is growing awareness that psychological and physical wellbeing are intertwined. Social services have been shown to contribute to improvements in people's health, but the narrowing of access to them through restrictive *eligibility criteria has reduced their positive potential in this regard. Similarly, welfare rights work (the maximization of take-up of service users' rights to social security benefits) has all but disappeared in social work, and this, too, is relevant to improvements in health. Notwithstanding these problems, there have been local initiatives by social workers who, with others, have secured designated funding to address health inequalities through more extensive interventions and greater *service user *participation. Self-help groups have also provided access to health and other information and given mutual support. *See also* HEALTH PROMOTION; INVERSE CARE LAW.

Further reading: Graham, H. (2009, 2nd edn.) *Understanding Health Inequalities*, Open
    University Press.
Pickett, K. and Wilkinson, R. (2010) *The Spirit Level: Why Equality Is Better for Everyone*,
    Penguin.

health promotion Defined by the World Health Organization as 'the process of enabling people to increase control over, and to improve, their health. It moves beyond a focus on individual behaviour towards a wide range of social and environmental interventions'. Although this is a wide definition, the focus in the UK has tended to be more narrowly on factors seen as lying within the immediate control of individuals, such as their individual health *choices and behaviours. Typically, health promotion activities have been targeted at changing people's lifestyles with regard to such issues as adopting a healthy diet, taking exercise, ceasing smoking, reducing alcohol use, and preventing heart disease. *See also* HEALTH INEQUALITIES.

Healthwatch Describes itself as 'the consumer champion for health and social care'. There is a local Healthwatch in every area of England. They are independent organizations that listen to the views of *service users/patients and 'share them with those with the power to make local services better'. Individual experiences of health and social care services can be reported directly to someone's local Healthwatch.

SEE WEB LINKS
• Official site of Healthwatch.

hearing impairment A generic term that refers to people with any type or degree of hearing loss, ranging from mild (difficulty hearing faint or distant speech), to severe (not being able to distinguish any sounds). The term 'deaf' is usually used to describe hearing *loss that cannot be improved by amplification and 'hard of hearing' is used for hearing loss that can benefit from amplification. Hearing loss either results from conditions occurring before or at birth (congenital) or it can be inherited or acquired. In medicine, four types of hearing loss are distinguished:

Conductive Caused by diseases, damage, or obstructions in the outer or middle ear that mean sound is not able to pass through.

Sensori-neural Results from damage to the inner ear or along nerve pathways to the brain.

Mixed Occurs when hearing loss is experienced in both the inner and outer or middle ear.

Central Results from damage to the central nervous system.

Audiological *assessments provide information about the degree and impact of hearing loss and its implications for receiving and producing verbal language. Some people can be assisted by hearing aids, or can have surgery to repair damage or augment the hearing they have. Children with hearing loss may be educated in a mainstream school with the assistance of interpreters and devices, or may be admitted to a special school where they will be taught through sign language. Many people decide to join the hearing population by whatever means available, such as a hearing aid or surgery. Others who do not have this option, prefer there to be no reference to 'hearing impairment' because they do not want to be primarily defined by their lack of or reduced hearing capacity, arguing that does not make them impaired as people. They prefer to be referred to as being 'deaf' or 'hard of hearing' but only when there is a need to refer to their hearing status, not as a primary way to identify them as people, when their hearing status is not relevant. Others use 'Deaf' to refer to themselves as people who are members of a cultural minority group/*community, as distinguished from the use of 'deaf' by the hearing to indicate a physical impairment. Such people may not want to overcome their deafness and become hearing, even if this were possible, identifying themselves positively as 'Deaf' and affirming the centrality of Deaf culture to their *identity, for example, through the use of sign language. This stance embraces 'deafness as *difference' and rejects the view of deafness as a medical condition. Although hearing impairment may be in the foreground of the reason someone has been referred to a social worker, the worker needs to avoid focusing exclusively on hearing loss and to consider the whole person within her/his situation. Given the range of perspectives, it also involves ascertaining how the person regards her/his hearing impairment/deafness/Deafness and the implications of her/his stance.

In addition to social work situations in which hearing impairment is foregrounded, age is the most significant *risk factor for all forms of sensory impairment, making hearing loss an issue for many *older people who may be seeing social workers for a range of reasons, but not for their difficulty in hearing. People who have become hearing impaired in later life are unlikely to use sign language, even if the social worker working with them happens to have this skill. Communication techniques may be as straightforward as speaking more slowly, articulating words clearly, facing the person, and not covering one's mouth. Many hearing impaired people find communicating difficult where there is background noise, so carrying out assessments in settings such as a day centre or hospital ward, or in the home when a number of people are present, may be problematic. Hearing impairment may cause embarrassment, loss of confidence, *depression, and avoidance of social contact. Conversation may demand a high level of concentration from the older person and be very tiring, so it is important to find out what helps and hinders communication for the person concerned. *See also* ACTION ON HEARING LOSS; BRITISH SIGN LANGUAGE; DISABILITY; SOCIAL MODEL OF DISABILITY.

hearing voices An auditory *hallucination, which is a common symptom of *schizophrenia and other *psychoses. The experience takes different forms. Some may experience hearing voices as though from an external source through the ears, even though there is no physical source. Some may experience voices as if they are spoken thoughts entering directly into the mind from somewhere outside themselves. The experience can be distressing and disturbing, and can significantly interfere with aspects of daily living. When schizophrenia or other psychosis is diagnosed, symptoms can be reduced or controlled with medication. Some individuals learn to accept their voices and regard them as a positive part of their lives. Self-help groups have gained ground in offering alternative solutions to medication and strategies for coping with hearing voices. Many consider the experience of hearing voices to be part of the range of human experience that is accepted in some cultures and is not necessarily seen as indicative of psychiatric disorder. *See also* HALLUCINATION; HEARING VOICES NETWORK.

Hearing Voices Network An organization with a telephone help-line and local self-help groups that provides information and support to people who hear voices and/or to the people who support them. It sees the psychiatric depiction of hearing voices as 'auditory hallucinations' as being limited and considers that there are many explanations for why people hear voices. As well as raising awareness of hearing voices, the organization gives people the opportunity to discuss their experiences and supports them in seeking to understand those experiences in their own way.

(⊕) SEE WEB LINKS
• Official site of the Hearing Voices Network.

hegemony A term introduced by the Italian Marxist Antonio Gramsci (1891–1937) to describe consent by the dominated to the social order and their own domination, through the *representation of the interests of the ruling class as being everyone's interests and there being no alternative to ruling class ideas. He distinguished this non-coercive form of social control through 'common sense' from direct *domination and the use of force under *capitalism and located hegemony predominantly in 'civil society', the non-state areas of personal and social life. Gramsci argued that hegemony was not fixed but represented a succession of unstable equilibria and, as a consequence, counter-hegemonic struggles could be waged against the prevailing hegemonic ideology. Gramsci described these struggles as 'war of position' in which the object of counter-hegemonic efforts was winning people's hearts and minds.

He saw intellectuals, a term he used in a very broad sense, as playing a central role in such battles over ideas. Some Marxists have identified social workers as intellectuals who can play such a role. In contemporary use, hegemony is often used to mean simply having considerable influence over. *See also* DISCOURSE; DOMINANT IDEOLOGY; GOVERNMENTALITY; HABITUS; MARXIST SOCIAL WORK; RADICAL SOCIAL WORK; TECHNOLOGIES OF THE SELF.

HelpAge International A worldwide alliance of over 80 organizations (such as *Age UK) in 50 countries that seeks to assist *older people in claiming their rights, challenging discrimination, and overcoming *poverty with the aim of their being able to lead more dignified, secure, active, and healthy lives.

(⊕) SEE WEB LINKS
• Official site of HelpAge International.

heteronormativity The assumption that heterosexuality is the default, preferred, 'normal' state for human beings because of the belief that people fall into one or other category of a strict *gender binary (*see* DECONSTRUCTION; OTHER). Thus it involves the further assumption that someone's biological sex, sexuality, gender *identity, and gender *roles are aligned. Such assumptions marginalize lesbian, gay, bisexual, and transgender people. Social work has been criticized for operating within heteronormative frames of reference, and developments in *fostering and *adoption by lesbian and gay couples can be seen as attempts to address such criticisms. However, questioning heteronormativity is relevant to all areas of social work practice. Heteronormativity is often associated with *heterosexism and *homophobia. *See also* ANTI-DISCRIMINATORY PRACTICE; ANTI-OPPRESSIVE PRACTICE; GAY AND LESBIAN PERSPECTIVES; HETEROSEXISM; HOMOPHOBIA; QUEER THEORY.

heterosexism Prejudiced attitudes, mistreatment, and discriminatory practices that are directed at people who are disadvantaged by imbalances of power in society on the basis of their sexuality (lesbian, gay, bisexual, transgender). It can be individual-to-individual, but is also institutionalized, embedded, systematic, pervasive, and routine. It involves invalidation, denial, or non-recognition of LGBT people. Its manifestations do not have to be extreme (for example, *hate crimes) in order for it to be present. For example, it includes day-to-day assumptions such as that everyone is heterosexual, or heterosexuality is the norm, or heterosexuality is superior. There are occasions when issues arise in relation to social work services that attract allegations of heterosexism. For example, the Equality Act (2006), implemented in England, *Wales, and *Scotland, outlawed discrimination in the provision of goods, facilities, and services on the basis of sexual orientation. There was wide media coverage of the demand from Catholic adoption agencies that they should be exempt from the change in the law that required them to work with gay and lesbian couples as prospective adopters in order to comply with the Sexual Orientation Regulations (2006). The adoption agencies were given a twenty-one-month transition period to adjust to the new regulations. Some of these cut their formal ties with the Church so that they could comply with the rules, while others ceased to operate. *See also* GAY AND LESBIAN PERSPECTIVES; HETERONORMATIVITY; HOMOPHOBIA; QUEER THEORY.

HIAs *See* HOME IMPROVEMENT AGENCIES.

hidden curriculum In the 1960s some writers in the sociology of education began to point out that as well as what is normally regarded as the curriculum (subjects such as geography, mathematics. etc.), schools had a hidden curriculum that consisted of inculcating certain values and character traits, such as accepting and respecting authority, and developing a sense of *competition with others. Under the impact of *neo-liberalism, what was once seen as hidden, and, when revealed, was often condemned, has become explicit in school life and foregrounded as a central aspect of schools' function in preparing students for the realities of life after school. *See also* DISCOURSE; DOMINANT IDEOLOGY; GOVERNMENTALITY; HABITUS; HEGEMONY.

hierarchy of needs (Maslow) Abraham Maslow's (1908–70) hierarchy of *needs is a conceptualization of motivation and personality that has been used extensively in social work education. Needs are seen as the requirements for survival and growth, and were arranged by Maslow in a pyramid structure according to their importance for survival and their power to motivate people. Basic physiological requirements, such as food and water, occupy the lowest level of the pyramid. Maslow argued that these needs have to be satisfied before needs higher up in the pyramid become important. The needs at the higher levels of the pyramid are oriented more towards psychological wellbeing and personal growth, and are seen as influenced by education and life experiences.

> *Physiological needs* Basic requirements for physical survival. When these needs are unmet, people will focus on satisfying them and will ignore higher needs.
> *Safety needs* Once people's basic physical needs are met, their needs for safety— for a sense of security and predictability—emerge and they try to maintain the conditions that allow them to feel safe. Maslow thought that emotional problems and *neuroses might result if these needs were not met satisfactorily.
> *Love and belonging needs* When people's physiological and safety needs are met, needs for love and belonging emerge. These needs include wanting an intimate relationship with another person, the need to belong to a group, and seeking acceptance.

Maslow's hierarchy of needs

    Esteem needs These include having a sense of self-esteem (feeling worthwhile) and being in receipt of the esteem of others (feeling respected).

    Self-actualization needs These are the needs associated with realizing people's full potential. As these needs emerge, people are geared to developing their interests and abilities as much as possible.

Maslow discussed other needs that did not fit into the pyramid, such as cognitive needs (for example, curiosity or interest in science) and aesthetic needs. He also put forward needs that extend beyond self-actualization at the top of the pyramid, which he called transcendence needs, such as making a contribution to the welfare of others and seeking meaning in life.

Despite the pyramid structure, Maslow acknowledged that it could not be applied rigidly. Although he maintained his position that lower needs must be satisfied in order for the person to pay attention to higher needs, he accepted that lower needs did not have to be completely satisfied and that most people would show a range of need satisfaction levels. Maslow also conceded that there might be situations in which lower needs might be ignored in favour of higher needs, for example, when a social work student sacrifices the security of a well-paid job in order to gain a qualification, although he regarded these circumstances as exceptions that did not invalidate the overall conceptualization.

The emphasis on positive aspects of human needs and behaviour in Maslow's hierarchy makes it an appealing framework to social workers seeking to understand behaviour from an alternative perspective to that of *individual pathology and *dysfunction, and wanting to allow for the possibility of growth and change. The pyramid provides a format for understanding human motivation in a range of settings that social workers encounter. However, the hierarchy has been criticized because it is difficult to research and evaluate as many of the issues that Maslow raised are subjective. The emphasis on a hierarchical ordering of human needs has not fared well either, as it can be seen that people can strive simultaneously, rather than sequentially, to satisfy needs for love, safety, and esteem, which are at different levels of the pyramid. Furthermore, people who have what Maslow sees as their lower needs met do not always seek the fulfilment of higher needs. This suggests that people are driven by a wide range of needs and motives, sometimes singly, sometimes in combination. Perhaps most significantly, Maslow's conceptualization is universalistic and does not acknowledge the extent to which people are shaped by the surrounding *culture and its values. For example, Maslow's conceptualization takes as its starting point an extremely individualistic conception of the self, which is derived from Western culture. A criticism of this has been that the hierarchy of needs is an account of the circumstances and values of twentieth-century, Western, white, middle-class men and as such it is not universally applicable. Despite these criticisms, the basic propositions of Maslow's conceptualization remain popular.

High Court (High Court of Justice) The court that hears civil cases in England and *Wales, above the levels of the magistrates' and county courts. It has three sections, known as 'divisions'. Two of these divisions have relevance to social work. The Queen's Bench Division includes within its remit the *judicial review of *local authority decisions. The Family Division's remit includes children and *divorce. *See also* FAMILY COURTS.

HIV/AIDS (human immunodeficiency virus/acquired immunodeficiency syndrome) A virus, HIV, which weakens the body's immune system, thus making someone more vulnerable to infections and their effects. It can lead to AIDS, a progressive and terminal condition, but survival rates have improved dramatically with advances in anti-retroviral drug treatments that delay the development of HIV. The HIV virus is spread by bodily fluids that are transmitted from an infected person to an uninfected person, principally through blood transfusions (a problem initially but now unlikely because of blood being screened), penetrative sex, and the sharing of needles in connection with using drugs, as well as being passed from a mother with HIV to her child in the womb or at birth. There is a test that shows whether the body has developed antibodies to HIV, which, if positive, shows that someone has been infected. However, there is a time delay with this test as it can take three months or longer for anti-bodies to be present after HIV has been contracted. Although the most extreme manifestations of animosity towards people with HIV or AIDS that characterized the early years after its discovery, such as reference to the 'gay plague' and violent attacks on gay men, have diminished (though not disappeared), stigma and discrimination are still encountered. *See also* NATIONAL AIDS TRUST.

holistic approach (holistic perspective) An approach that seeks to understand people within the context of their whole lives—past, present, and future—rather than seeing them only in relation to their role as *'service users' and recognizes the relationship between the individual and the circumstances that shape their lives. A holistic approach treats people as citizens with rights, rather than as dependent people in need of services. This means addressing the barriers that prevent their full *participation in the society of which they are members. It also means acknowledging their contributions as resources for, as well as recipients of, *welfare. Such an approach argues for social work addressing social, environmental, and economic inequalities that obstruct people's participation, as well as considering the emotional and interpersonal dimensions of their wellbeing.

However, there are obstacles in the path of adopting a holistic approach. First, a holistic approach depends on a holistic *assessment. Some progress has been made on this in children's services through the use of frameworks based on *ecological perspectives. In services for adults, despite policy rhetoric about the need for wide-ranging assessments to be undertaken, in practice assessments often come down to decisions about *eligibility for services based on physical functioning and self-care, neglecting someone's life history, interests, and social and emotional needs. This may vary in extent, with attention given to these aspects of people's lives with some service user groups, for example, in the use of *person-centred planning with people with *learning disabilities, and neglected with others, for example in 'routine' work with *older people. Whatever the precise local situation in a particular service setting, managerial requirements concerning the need to control resources will influence how people's *needs are assessed. The more that assessments are confined to narrow areas of people's physical functioning, the less of a holistic approach there will be and the wider the gap that will exist between what social workers have established on the basis of their assessments and the needs, views, and experiences of service users. Secondly, a holistic approach depends on good coordination of services. People do not compartmentalize their lives into different types of problems, such as health, housing, and social problems; these problems intermingle in their experience as whole people. If, for example, there are divisions between health and social services they can undermine a holistic response. Thirdly, the *fragmentation of roles and tasks within social work has resulted in people experiencing a form of social work that is often far from the integrated, continuous, and coordinated approach that would be associated with a holistic perspective, especially as such fragmentation undermines the *relationship-based aspects of the social work role. The lack of time and opportunity to form relationships is an impediment to 'whole person' assessment and responses.

home care service *See* DOMICILIARY SERVICES.

home help A person who used to undertake household tasks, such as cleaning and shopping, for those unable to do these chores for themselves (mainly *older people), usually between the hours of 8.00 am and 2.00 pm. This type of service was already in decline by the time of the *community care reforms but its decline was hastened with the reorientation of home-based services to the provision of more intensive services to those in greatest need. *See also* DOMICILIARY SERVICES.

Home Improvement Agencies (HIAs) Not-for-profit local organizations that usually receive some financial support from central government and *local authorities. There are nearly 200 HIAs in England, covering 82 per cent of local authorities. They help older, disabled, and vulnerable people to make modifications to their homes as their health and *needs change in order to enable them to 'stay put' in their own homes for longer. This may include major adaptations, such as fitting a downstairs bathroom, as well as small repairs, such as fitting door and window locks. HIAs also provide advice and guidance about housing repair issues, financial advice, for example, about applying for local authority grants or equity release, and technical help, for example, overseeing repairs and ensuring work is completed satisfactorily. They are sometimes known as 'Care and Repair' agencies or 'Staying Put' schemes. The relationship between health and housing is recognized through a growing number of joint initiatives. Schemes include those where HIAs carry out work to reduce the *risk of *falls within people's homes, for example, by fixing rails, securing carpets, and fitting brighter lights, and those that undertake repairs and adaptations necessary for safe *discharge from hospital. The cost of HIA intervention is low compared with other forms of domiciliary support, which suggests that it can be an alternative to the reactive approach of delivering services to help *older people address problems. Instead, proactively planning and designing the environment to promote *independence and wellbeing can enable older people to continue to live in ordinary housing. In addition to its physical dimensions the sense of being 'at home' can have significance for positive emotional wellbeing. Supporting older people to 'age in place' may enable them to retain integral components of their *identity as autonomous and *independent individuals. Later life may be a time of *loss and change, and in this context, home and environment can be a significant source of stability and continuity and a site of self-determination. Maintaining a safe and secure domestic space can be key to constructing and maintaining identity and providing a base from which older people can feel confident to engage in their neighbourhoods.

homelessness On the face of it, it would appear straightforward to define homelessness as the state of being without somewhere to live. However, in practice, it has proved difficult to identify the numbers who are homeless. The official figures cover only those people who have been accepted as being homeless by *local authority housing services, which are responsible for assisting them. These figures ignore all those who are homeless but do not present themselves to local authorities, and those who present themselves but whose *cases are rejected. Thus the official figures are a considerable underestimation of the extent of homelessness. The responsibility placed on local authorities to assist people who are homeless rests upon their having a connection with the local authority that they approach, such as: having lived there for three out of the last five years/six out of the last twelve months; having a close family member who has lived there for five years; being employed in the area; or other special reasons (for example, if it was the area in which someone grew up). If someone has a stronger connection with a different local authority than the one to which they apply, they can be referred there instead. In order to be owed a *duty under the Housing Act (1996) people have to fulfil four conditions. They have to be:

Eligible The local authority's duty to assist does not apply to people under immigration control.

Homeless This can include people who have somewhere to live but who cannot be reasonably expected to stay there because of the poor condition of the property, overcrowding, *violence, or the threat of violence.

In priority need Pregnant women, people with dependent children, those who are homeless because of an emergency such as fire or flood, 16 and 17-year-olds unless they are already the concern of children's services, young people aged 18 to 21 who have left care, and people who are vulnerable because of: old age, physical or mental disability; having been in the armed forces, prison, or local authority care; having left accommodation because of violence or threatened violence.

Not intentionally homeless Someone is intentionally homeless if they have done or failed to do something that has led to their losing their accommodation. The action or failure to act has to be deliberate.

People who meet all four of these conditions are owed a duty by the local authority to be accommodated. Those not meeting all four conditions should receive advice and assistance with finding accommodation.

Under the Homelessness Act (2002) local authorities have to publish their strategies for preventing homelessness in their areas.

Home Start *Voluntary organization with more than 300 local schemes covering many parts of the UK that provides support to parents with at least one child under five, who may be experiencing difficulties as a result of social isolation, family illness, *bereavement, or coping with the demands of a large family. After either self-referral to the scheme by the family or by a professional, a local organizer meets with the family and matches it with an approved volunteer. This is a person with parenting experience who will visit the family for two hours a week and offer both emotional and practical help. *See also* EARLY INTERVENTION; EXTENDED SERVICES; PREVENTION; SURE START.

(⊕) SEE WEB LINKS
• Official site of Home Start.

homonormativity *See* HETERONORMATIVITY; QUEER THEORY.

homophobia A term that originated in the 1970s, originally within psychology, to indicate extreme hatred and/or deep-seated fear of gay men, considered by some to stem from repressed or latent homosexuality. It has come to be used more generally to refer to individual dislike of or prejudice towards gay men or lesbian women, characterized by a range of intensity of feeling, as well as societal determinants and manifestations of the denigration of same-sex relationships. At the extreme, it may lead to intimidation and *violence, and has resulted in death (*see* HATE CRIME). Social work has played a role in combating homophobia through such developments as the approval of gay and lesbian couples as foster and adoptive parents, and recognition that the sexuality of *older people should not be assumed to be heterosexual, with consideration of the possible added isolation gay and lesbian older people may experience. *See also* GAY AND LESBIAN PERSPECTIVES; HETERONORMATIVITY; HETEROSEXISM.

honour-based violence (honour-based incident) An umbrella term to cover various offences dealt with under existing legislation. (There is no specific legislation in relation to honour-based violence.) It involves a violent crime or incident that has been committed to protect or defend the honour of a family or community. It is often perpetrated by family members, friends, or acquaintances who believe someone has brought shame on their family or *community by infringing traditional aspects of their *culture. Such infringements may include a woman having a boyfriend, rejecting a forced marriage, pregnancy outside marriage, engaging in an inter faith and/or inter ethnic relationship, seeking *divorce, or wearing (what is seen as) inappropriate dress or make-up. *See also* DOMESTIC ABUSE, STALKING AND HARASSMENT AND HONOUR BASED VIOLENCE RISK IDENTIFICATION, ASSESSMENT AND MANAGEMENT MODEL; DOMESTIC VIOLENCE.

(⊕) SEE WEB LINKS
• Official site of the Halo Project, a forced marriage and honour-based violence charity.

hospice A form of residential, day, or domiciliary provision for people who are terminally ill. Hospices developed in response to inadequacies in existing provision for people dying in hospitals, based on the beliefs that everyone matters throughout their life right up until they die, and that no one should die in avoidable pain or suffering. They have a dual focus on the management of pain through medication and support in facing the prospect of death. *See also* PALLIATIVE CARE.

(⊕) SEE WEB LINKS
• Site of the national charity Hospice Care.

hospital at home A service usually provided by a team of nurses, physiotherapists, and *occupational therapists with experience of working in an acute hospital environment. Typically, such a service provides short-term acute medical care (approximately one to five days) in people's own homes, as an alternative to admission to hospital, or so that discharge can take place earlier than would otherwise be the case. The patient's *general practitioner is informed of the involvement of a hospital at home team. The team will refer patients to, for example, *local authority *adults' services, community nurses, *community matrons, physiotherapy, or occupational therapy for continuing services after they are discharged by the hospital at home team. *See also* VIRTUAL HOSPITAL WARDS.

hospital discharge The Care Act (2014) guidance sets out the process for notifying a *local authority of a discharge from hospital when an adult requires an *assessment of her/his *care and support needs. When a local authority has not completed the necessary work by the day of discharge, the Care Act (2014) has amended the previous mandatory system (under the Community Care [Delayed Discharges] Act [2003]) of fining local authorities and reimbursing the National Health Service to a discretionary one.

The Department of Health's declared intentions for effective hospital discharge planning are:

- the safe discharge of patients from hospital care into local authority care and support;
- patients not being delayed in hospital when they are fit, safe, and ready for discharge;
- ensuring the wellbeing of the patient and delaying or preventing further care and support needs.

There is a 'discharge planning notification process' with the following stages:

Notice of Requirement of Assessment Issued by the NHS with as much notice as possible but not more than seven days prior to a patient's admission;

Assessment of Need Undertaken by the local authority, which has to be given a minimum of two days after the assessment notice or before the discharge date in which to complete the assessment;

Discharge Notification Issued by the NHS with as much notice as possible, a minimum of one day prior to the discharge date.

(Assessment notices and discharge notifications can be withdrawn by the NHS at any time.)

The NHS is required to issue an assessment notice to the local authority when it considers that a patient may need care and support on discharge from hospital. In order to ensure that any patients referred by the NHS receive the necessary care and support, locally agreed protocols are put in place between the NHS and local authorities that help NHS staff to identify when a patient should be considered to have care and support needs so that the NHS issues assessment notices consistently and appropriately. Before issuing an assessment notice, the NHS must consult with the patient and, where applicable, their *carer so that unnecessary assessments are not undertaken, for example if a patient wishes to make private arrangements for care and support without the involvement of the local authority. Before issuing an assessment notice, the NHS must complete an assessment of the potential continuing health care needs of the patient and, if applicable, make a decision on what services the NHS will be providing (*see* NHS CONTINUING HEALTH CARE). The assessment notice must state that it is given under paragraph 1(1) of Schedule 3 to the Care Act (2014). This alerts the local authority that it has to take steps to assess the patient and, where applicable, the patient's carer, and put in place any arrangements to meet the needs it proposes to meet. If the local authority fails to carry out such steps, it may be liable to pay the NHS for any delay in the patient being discharged.

On receiving an assessment notice, the local authority must carry out a *needs assessment of the patient and, where applicable, a *carer's assessment to determine whether the patient and/or carer has needs. If needs are identified, the local authority must decide whether any of them meet the *eligibility criteria and, if they do, how it proposes to meet them. The local authority must inform the NHS of the outcome of its assessment and decisions. To avoid any risk of having to pay the NHS because of a delayed discharge, the local authority must carry out a needs assessment and put in place any arrangements for meeting needs before the discharge date (as contained in the discharge notice) or within the minimum period of two days after receiving the assessment notice, whichever is the later. An assessment notice which is given after 2.00 p.m. is treated as being given on the following day. When the NHS has issued an assessment notice to a local authority, it must also give written notice of the proposed date of the patient's discharge, even if it included the proposed discharge date in the assessment notice. Where the discharge notice is issued after 2.00 p.m., it is treated as being given on the following day. The purpose of the discharge notice is to confirm the discharge date, as it may not have been known at the time the assessment notice was issued or may have changed since the assessment notice was issued. Patients and carers should be informed of the discharge date at the same time as or before the local authority. In addition, hospital staff may give the local authority an early indication of when discharge is likely as part of helping their planning. The NHS cannot seek any payment from the local authority for a patient's delayed discharge unless it has issued both an assessment notice and a discharge notice.

The Department of Health states that NHS bodies should not use payments by local authorities for delayed discharges as the first approach to addressing any local difficulties. If the NHS wants to seek payment from a local authority for a delayed discharge, it must have sent both an assessment notice and a discharge notice to the local authority, and the local authority must then either not have carried out an assessment or not put arrangements in place for meeting the patient's care and support needs and, where applicable, the carer's support needs, within a minimum of two days after the assessment notice or before the discharge date. It is then at the NHS's discretion whether to recover payments for delayed discharge days. The regulations set the level of payment at £130 per day for local authorities outside London and £155 per day for London authorities. The period for which liability for payment can be sought starts on the day after the date contained in the discharge notice or the minimum period of two days after the assessment notice was given. The period ends on the earliest date when any of the following occurs:

- The NHS withdraws either the assessment notice or the discharge notice.
- The local authority notifies the NHS that it has now carried out the assessment and put in place arrangements for meeting needs in respect of the patient or, where applicable, the carer.
- The local authority is no longer required to put arrangements in place either because the patient informs the local authority that s/he has made alternative arrangements for care and support and/or, where applicable, the carer informs the local authority that s/he has made alternative arrangements for support.
- The patient discharges her/himself.
- The NHS decides that the patient now needs to remain in hospital for a further course of treatment.
- The patient dies.

See DISCHARGE PLANNING; HOSPITAL SOCIAL WORK.

Further reading: Department of Health (2016) *Care and Support: Statutory Guidance*, Chapter 16 and Annex G. Available at: https://www.gov.uk/government/publications/care-act-statutory-guidance/care-and-support-statutory-guidance#person-centred-care-and-support-planning.

hospital managers' hearing (hospital managers' review) (mental health) One of two routes set out in the Mental Health Act (1983) by which psychiatric patients subject to detention under Part II of the Act (*see* COMPULSORY ADMISSION) and those under unrestricted *hospital orders (Section 37) may request a review of their detention. The route provides a framework for appeal and may result in discharge from detention. (The other route is a *First-tier Tribunal [Mental Health].) Compulsory detention under the Act is not merely a medical consideration but raises important issues concerning civil liberties. The hospital managers are the formal detaining authority under the Act and are legally responsible for detained patients. They are required to ensure that the patient's treatment, *care, and documentation are dealt with appropriately, and that the patient is not only informed of but also understands her/his rights, as far as is possible. Detained patients may request a review at any point during their detention. Managers have discretion to undertake a review at any time whether or not a request is made. They are required to undertake a review in relation to Section 20 (renewing detention) and Section 25 (where the *responsible clinician opposes the *nearest relative's application for a patient's discharge). The panel for a review comprises three authorized members. They might be committee or board members of the relevant health trust but they may not be employees. Continued detention can only be justified if it is a proportionate response to the perceived *risks that might occur should the patient be discharged. Risk can include psychological as well as physical harm. Managers must consider whether the original criteria for detention continue to be met and whether continued detention is lawful. The Mental Health Act (1983) gives hospital managers the power to discharge patients from compulsion. A decision to discharge can only be made if all three members are in agreement. The managers should be provided with written reports from the responsible clinician and other appropriate professionals. Reports should include professional recommendations for consideration. The patient should receive copies of all documentation. The *Mental Health Act 1983: Code of Practice* (2015) provides detailed guidance concerning *good practice in respect of managers' reviews, including the patient's right to support and representation during the process. Occasionally, professional or clinical views and recommendations may diverge. In these circumstances, the review panel may adjourn its decision while it obtains further advice.

Hospital managers' hearings also have the power to discharge *Community Treatment Orders under Section 23 and patients may request a hearing.

Further reading: Department of Health (2015) *Mental Health Act (1983): Code of Practice.* Chapter 37 provides guidance on the responsibilities of hospital managers under the Act, and Chapter 38 gives specific guidance on the exercise of their powers to discharge patients from detention under the Act. Available at: https://www.gov.uk/government/uploads/system/uploads/attachment_data/file/435512/MHA_Code_of_Practice.pdf.

Hospital Order (mental health) A court order, made under Section 37 of the Mental Health Act (1983) and based on the advice of two doctors, in respect of mentally disordered offenders who are not considered to pose a serious *risk to the public. It is imposed instead of a prison sentence. If an offender is sufficiently mentally unwell at the time of sentencing to require hospital admission, the Order ensures s/he receives treatment in hospital. An Order made solely under Section 37 is an unrestricted Order. If a Section 37 Hospital Order is made together with a Section 41 Restriction Order in order to protect the public from serious harm, the restrictions affect *leave of absence, transfer between hospitals, and discharge, all of which require the permission of the Ministry of Justice.

hospital social work There has been a long tradition of social workers placed in hospitals, going back to the nineteenth century, when they were originally referred to as 'almoners' and prone to being depicted as the 'handmaidens' of male doctors in much the same way as nurses were. Despite a long history, hospital social work has often struggled to achieve recognition in a setting dominated by other professions and the *medical model. The hospital is a complex setting in which to practise social work, as the multi disciplinary teams in which social workers are located have members with different training, professional backgrounds, status, and power. If the social worker espouses a social model of health, and stresses the centrality of the *service user and the necessity of her/his *participation, thus adopting a *holistic approach, this may be valued as a distinctive contribution to the team's work, or be seen as at odds with its *culture and as obstructing professional consensus. If it is the latter, in their concern with the whole person, social workers may be put in the position of having to point out the possibly deleterious consequences if someone is discharged too early. They may see other staff as adhering to a medical model that regards patients as bodies to be fixed, with little concern for what goes on outside the hospital. On the other hand, those staff may emphasize the danger of remaining in hospital with the *risk that infections such as MRSA imply and may stress that if someone is 'medically fit for discharge', s/he should leave hospital as quickly as possible. Despite the wide-ranging contribution that hospital social workers make to, for example, *palliative care, children in hospital, and services for people with *HIV/AIDS, the issue of their role in discharge of *older people has loomed large. After the implementation of the NHS and Community Care Act (1990), the already existing emphasis on social workers planning the discharge of patients intensified through to the implementation of the Care Act (2014) and since then this is the issue affecting hospital social work that has received the most attention. The pressures it has placed on hospital social workers have been compounded by the overall trend in discharging patients from hospital, which has meant that they have left, as one writer put it, 'quicker and sicker'. *See* DISCHARGE PLANNING; HOSPITAL DISCHARGE.

hostel Temporary residential provision that is provided for varying lengths of time for a wide range of *service user groups, such as homeless people, people with alcohol or drug misuse issues, ex-prisoners, people with mental health problems or *learning disabilities, young people leaving care, women and children who have experienced *domestic violence. The functions of hostels can be supportive, protective, or supervisory, or a combination of these elements. Some hostels provide ongoing access to social workers on the premises, and social workers may be involved in providing programmes of support and/or treatment. Others may have monitoring visits from social workers and others intermittent contact from social workers on request from residents. *See also* REFUGE.

household Usually people who share a living space, though also used to refer to someone living alone. It can encompass heterosexual, gay, and lesbian couples, *nuclear families, and *extended families, or groups of unrelated people. Often used in preference to 'family' because of its being capable of encompassing such wide variation, whereas 'family' can be open to interpretation as simply referring to the heterosexual nuclear family.

housing associations Not-for-profit organizations that build and then continue to be involved in the management of housing. Most of them are charitable companies (*see* CHARITABLE ORGANIZATIONS). They have occupied an increasingly significant role in housing provision, with the decline of *local authority-provided housing. Central government provides funds for building by housing associations through the Housing Corporation, which makes loans available to them. As well as providing general housing, housing associations have worked with local authorities to provide specialist accommodation for *older people, women and children who have experienced *domestic violence, people with mental health problems and *learning disabilities, people with alcohol and drug misuse issues, and young people leaving care. *See also* HOUSING AUTHORITY.

housing authority (housing department) The department of a *local authority that was traditionally responsible for building and managing public sector housing (or 'council houses'). The role of the housing department in the direct provision of homes declined significantly as a result of the Thatcher government's Housing Act (1980), which gave tenants of public housing the right to buy them and resulted in sales of around two million properties. However, local authorities were prevented from reinvesting the money realized from these sales in new public housing because of central government's stipulation that the receipts should not be used in this way. This led to a decline in the role of housing departments in providing housing that has continued until the present day and an increase in the role of *housing associations, which was the stated intention of the Conservative government, in addition to its wish to extend the reach of the private sector in providing homes to buy and to rent. A further measure was to bring council house rents up much closer to the market rate by including the costs of repair and maintenance in them, together with ongoing management costs. This led to significant increases in the level of rents. Under these pressures, many local authorities have transferred all or part of their housing stock to housing associations, which has been another factor in their increasingly prominent role. In some local authorities, the housing department has been merged with social services for adults.

housing problems *See* HOMELESSNESS.

humanitarian protection If awarded, this gives an *asylum seeker the right to remain, despite being not considered as satisfying the requirements for *refugee status. *See also* INDEFINITE LEAVE TO REMAIN.

human rights The Human Rights Act (1998) came into force in October 2000 and incorporated provisions of the European Convention of Human Rights, to which the UK had been a signatory since 1951. The Act requires that all UK legislation passed after October 2000 should be compatible with the Act. Furthermore, the interpretation of all pre-existing legislation has to give effect to Convention rights, wherever possible. The courts have the power to issue declarations of incompatibility in relation to any legislation. The government is then expected to respond by amending the law. The Act makes it unlawful for public bodies to act in a way that it incompatible with the Act, and there is a *duty on *local authorities to strive to prevent the infringement of human rights even where the local authority is not itself responsible for the infringement. Human rights are either 'absolute', 'qualified', or 'limited'. Limited rights can be restricted by specific limitations. Qualified rights can be infringed, provided there is sufficient justification. The rights under the convention are as follows:

Article 2 Protects right to life (but allows judicial death penalty) (Absolute).
Article 3 Prohibits torture, inhuman, or degrading treatment (Absolute).
Article 4 Prohibits slavery, forced, or compulsory labour (Absolute).
Article 5 Protects right to liberty and security of persons (Limited).
Article 6 Lays down minimum rules for fair hearings in courts and certain administrative processes where other convention rights are determined (Limited).
Article 7 Prohibits punishment without lawful authority (Absolute).
Article 8 Protects privacy, family life, home, and correspondence (Qualified).
Article 9 Protects freedom of thought, conscience, and religion (Qualified).
Article 10 Protects freedom of expression (Qualified).

Article 11 Protects freedom of assembly and association (Qualified).
Article 12 Protects right to marry (Absolute).
Article 13 Prohibits discrimination in enjoyment of convention rights (Qualified).

An illustration of the impact of the Human Rights Act (1998) is provided by its use in refining the *Deprivation of Liberty Safeguards (DoLS). The DoLS are intended to protect the human rights of people who lack the *capacity to consent to care or treatment, when they receive care that amounts to a deprivation of liberty, as defined by Article 5, Right to Liberty. Article 5 was a key factor in determining the *Supreme Court's judgment in the cases of *P v Cheshire West and Chester Council and another* and *P and Q v Surrey County Council*, which had a significant impact on decisions about arrangements made for the care and/or treatment of people who lack the capacity to consent to their living arrangements.

hyper-reality An assertion by Jean Baudrillard (1929–2007) that the saturation of everyday life by the mass media is such that reality loses its meaning as people cease to experience being participants in their own lives, become observers of media spectacles, and are defined by signs and representations of 'reality' to the extent that access to anything real is no longer possible.

hyphenated society *See* DEMOCRATIC-WELFARE-CAPITALISM.

hypochondriasis *See* HYSTERIA.

hysteria (hysterical disorder) In psychology and psychiatry, refers to physical symptoms that have a psychological rather than an organic cause, with the symptoms being subjectively experienced as real. Failure to find a medically-supported physical cause of symptoms can lead to *anxiety and *depression in the individual, exacerbating symptoms, and introducing new ones. Hysteria may be a *defence mechanism to avoid painful emotions by transferring distress to a sensory part of the physical body, for instance paralysis, blindness, or amnesia. Converting distress in this way is referred to as conversion disorder. Symptoms experienced in the digestive, reproductive, or nervous system are termed somatization disorder, which has replaced the term hypochondriasis. Hysteria is also associated with the outward expression of excessive or uncontrollable fear. Symptoms may mimic neurological and/or physical disorders, which must first be discounted before a *diagnosis of hysteria or hysterical disorder is made.

iatrogenic disease (iatrogenic illness) A concept, extended by Austrian philosopher and social critic Ivan Illich (1926–2002) beyond its original meaning, which referred to illness caused by the medical profession, to include the way in which people are encouraged to see themselves as needing medical interventions rather than drawing on their own capacity to respond to physical and emotional problems. *See also* MEDICAL MODEL.

ICD-10 See INTERNATIONAL CLASSIFICATION OF DISEASES.

ICT (information and communication technology) *See* COMPUTERIZATION.

ideal-type Producing a pure model of a phenomenon against which actual manifestations can be measured and discussed. For example, when Weber set out the ideal-type of *bureaucracy, he was not suggesting that any bureaucracy would have all of the features of the ideal-type. Rather, he was seeking to identify the key features of bureaucracy and their analytical importance through setting them out in an ideal form.

identity Usually seen as the unique and/or core essence of a person and often regarded as identified by a coherent set of traits and themes that are much the same throughout life. Identity has been of great concern within social work in a wide variety of services and settings, for example, concerns with the *loss of identity experienced by people with mental health problems or *learning disabilities in large institutions, the impact of disruption and inconsistency on children's identity formation, and the potential for entry to residential care to strip *older people of their identity. Traditionally, psychological and sociological accounts have relied upon different approaches to socialization as the routes to understanding the formation and maintenance of identity. Foucault's (1926–84) work on *discourse questioned this, as discourses are seen as shaping ways of knowing and talking about other people and ourselves. In this sense, people are inscribed by discourse. From this perspective, the material from which identity is constructed is seen as lying within discourses. When that material is taken up and 'lived in' by an individual, s/he forms a sense of identity. This questions the notion of identity as the core self or the 'real me', and replaces it with the idea that people can occupy multiple identities because different discourses offer different identity possibilities. It also opens up the prospect of linking individual identity with larger social divisions of identity such as age, *class, *'race', *gender, and sexuality (producing *gender identity, class identity, etc.) and the ways in which such social divisions are experienced and interwoven in people's lives. More recently, *postmodernists of differing persuasions have suggested that contemporary life either offers far greater opportunity for identity development (for example, they argue that people are able to reinvent themselves through *choices made as consumers) or, conversely, that identity is fragmented or lost as people are increasingly estranged from others and themselves. *See also* CONSUMERISM; IDENTITY CRISIS; IDENTITY MANAGEMENT.

identity crisis A concept developed by Erik Erikson (1902–94) during the Second World War to refer to those of his patients who no longer felt they were the same person and/or had no sense of continuity with their previous selves. Subsequently, he saw identity crisis as being common in the adolescent stage of development, when the young person is no longer a child but not yet an adult. In the intervening years the term has become part of everyday speech. *See also* ADOLESCENCE; IDENTITY; IDENTITY MANAGEMENT.

identity management A concept of Erving Goffman (1922–82) that encapsulated the complex ways in which people present themselves to other people. If a *service user wants to achieve a certain outcome from her/his contact with a social worker, the chances of success will be enhanced if her/his *identity is managed appropriately. For example, in the case of a parent wanting to have a child returned from care, the possibility will be strengthened if s/he is able to align her/his identity with that which the social worker deems to be the identity possessed by somebody to whom a child should be returned. *See also* DRAMATURGY; ENCOUNTERS; IDENTITY CRISIS.

identity management theory *See* THEORIES OF AGEING.

identity politics Basing politics on a sense of personal *identity as a woman, as gay, as *Black, etc., by 'naming and claiming'. Authority is claimed for particular experiences based on their articulation, identification with them, and coming together on the basis of them. During the 1980s it led to a proliferation of political groupings such as the *Disabled People's Movement and Stonewall's struggle for gay rights. Struggles for recognition of identities and negotiation of claims to social rights have been seen by some writers as introducing a cultural dimension to *citizenship that rests on three claims: the right to presence and visibility (versus marginalization); the right to dignifying representation (versus stigmatization); the right to identity and maintenance of lifestyle (versus assimilation). Cultural citizenship rests on a politics of identity and stresses the rights of citizens to be different, to revalue stigmatized identities, to embrace previously marginalized lifestyles, and to promulgate them openly. *See also* INTERSECTIONALITY; REFLEXIVE MODERNIZATION.

ideological state apparatuses A concept used by Louis Althusser (1918–90) alongside his parallel concept of 'repressive state apparatuses'. He argued that the state is maintained by both sets of apparatuses. Repressive state apparatuses—in the form of the army, the courts, the police, and the prison system—can punish and ensure conformity by force. In contrast, ideological state apparatuses—such as churches, trade unions, schools, the media (and social work might be added)—are outside the formal control of the state, but transmit the values of the state, and ensure that people think in ways that concur with the state's interests in order to maintain order in society, particularly with regard to reproducing capitalist social relations. To the extent that ideological state apparatuses are effective, repressive state apparatuses do not have to be brought into play. *See also* CIVIL SOCIETY; DISCOURSE; GOVERNMENTALITY; HABITUS; HEGEMONY; IDEOLOGY.

ideology A coherent body of ideas. Often used to refer to a set of ideas that justifies the *domination of one social group by another. For example, sexist ideology refers to a body of ideas about women, their alleged differences, and deficiencies, in a way that seeks to perpetuate men's domination on the basis of their gender. The origins of ideology as a concept are most closely identified with Marxism. Instead of seeing ideas as driving human history (as Hegel had done), Marx identified *class struggles as history's motor and in any particular age he saw the ruling ideas, or the ideas that achieved a pre-eminent position, as being those of the ruling class. He distinguished between the economic base of society, such as capitalism in a *capitalist society, and the ideological superstructure, suggesting that although sets of ideas are determined by the economic base they are distinguished from it. (Althusser referred to this as 'relative autonomy'.) These sets of ideas, Marx argued, obscure the exploitative nature of the economic base of society and the ways in which it benefits the ruling class. *See also* DISCOURSE; GOVERNMENTALITY; HEGEMONY; IDEOLOGICAL STATE APPARATUSES.

IEP *See* INDIVIDUAL EDUCATION PLAN.

IMCA (independent mental capacity advocate) *See* CAPACITY.

IMHA *See* INDEPENDENT MENTAL HEALTH ADVOCATE.

impaired insight *See* INSIGHT.

impairment *See* DISABILITY.

imprisonable offence *See* CUSTODIAL SENTENCE.

Improving Access to Psychological Therapies (IAPT) A UK-wide programme for making psychological therapies available to people with common mental health problems such as *anxiety and *depression, which commenced in 2009. IAPT services operate in the *primary health care sector, and provide psychologically based services (usually *cognitive behavioural therapy) to people on a time-limited basis. IAPT is meant to ensure that people receive timely evidence-based mental health support, while averting unnecessary and inappropriate referrals to secondary mental health services.

incapacity *See* CAPACITY.

incarceration The process of being placed in an institution such as a prison and being isolated from the wider society. *See also* DECARCERATION; DEINSTITUTIONALIZATION; INSTITUTION; INSTITUTIONALIZATION.

inclusion (education) This has been a long-standing principle in education, embraced to varying extents, that stresses the importance of meeting special educational needs in mainstream schools whenever possible, rather than in special schools or separate units within mainstream schools. Critics of the principle of inclusion argue that some students find it difficult to cope in mainstream schools, and that separate provision in special schools or units is more likely to result in their getting the education they need. The principle of inclusion was given added impetus by the *Office for Standards in Education through its extension to students who are marginalized or in danger of being marginalized within school, or who are excluded, or at *risk of being excluded. Included in Ofsted's concerns are children in need and children who are accommodated by *local authorities. The Education and Inspections Act (2006) went further and placed a *duty on schools to promote *community cohesion. The stress on inclusion of all children, fully participating in school life, sits uneasily with the far greater stress on competitiveness and selection and, by implication, exclusion in wider education policy, brought about through the use of performance/results tables and ranking of schools.

indefinite leave to remain The right to remain in the UK without a time limit, usually granted after a period of limited leave to remain, and giving the right to work, apply for housing, and obtain social security benefits. *See* HUMANITARIAN PROTECTION; REFUGEE.

independence (adults) The subject of competing definitions, the principal competition being between the dominant social work use of the term to mean reducing or eliminating an individual's use of services, and *service users' use of it to refer to their subjective feelings about their quality of life and being in control of their lives. Thus, a service user might have a high level of reliance on services *and* experience feelings of independence, for example an older person who feels more independent by using services that enable her/him not to be a 'burden' on her/his family. On the other hand, a service user might have a low level of reliance on services but not feel independent because that person does not feel s/he has any control over her/his life or her/his quality of life is poor because s/he does not feel valued. In practice, the dominant social work use of the term is often in evidence with the *goal of independence reduced to getting people off services rather than sensitive and collaborative consideration of service users' subjective sense of independence. The dominant view is accompanied by concern to reduce spending, seeing the promotion of independence as having this as a benefit. In addition to reducing service use, the dominant view encourages an individualistic conception of *need and responses to it, rather than reinforcing notions of *interdependence and reciprocity. Need is seen overwhelmingly as a product of individual characteristics and circumstances, services are provided through individual *'care packages', and service users are viewed solely as recipients of services rather than as contributors or potential contributors to their lives and those of people around them. *See also* INDEPENDENT LIVING; INDEPENDENT LIVING FUND.

independent advocacy *See* ADVOCACY (ADULTS).

independent domestic violence advisor (IDVA) A specialist worker who focuses on working predominantly with high-*risk victims (usually but not exclusively with female victims) of *domestic violence. They are usually involved from the point of crisis and offer intensive short- to medium-term support. They work in *partnership with *statutory and *voluntary organizations and mobilize resources on behalf of victims by coordinating the response of a wide range of agencies, including those working with perpetrators or children. There are differences in how IDVA services are delivered in local areas. *See also* SURVIVOR.

independent living An idea pioneered by the *Disabled People's Movement that symbolized living where they wanted, rather than where professionals thought was best, and having control over their own lives more generally. To realize greater autonomy, disabled people have employed *personal assistants as an alternative to being recipients of mainstream service provision. The availability of *direct payments has enabled the employment of personal assistants to become more widespread. *See also* INDEPENDENCE (ADULTS); INDEPENDENT LIVING FUND.

Independent Living Fund (ILF) A *non-departmental public body funded by the Department of Work and Pensions. It was a popular system of financial support that enabled 46,000 people to access *independent living between 1988 and 2015, when the fund closed and *local authorities assumed responsibility for supporting former ILF users under the Care Act (2014). *See also* CARE AND SUPPORT PLAN; INDEPENDENCE; NEEDS ASSESSMENT.

independent mental capacity advocate (IMCA) *See* CAPACITY.

independent mental health advocate (IMHA) A statutory role, the provisions of which are set out in Section 130 of the Mental Health Act (1983), as amended by the Mental Health Act (2007). An IMHA is a specialist advocate with specific roles and responsibilities towards certain categories of patients, including those subject to *guardianship or *Community Treatment Orders. Patients who are eligible for assistance from an IMHA are referred to as 'qualifying patients'. The main role of the IMHA is to help qualifying patients understand the legal provisions to which they are subject, and the rights and safeguards to which they are entitled. The role extends to: providing information about medical treatment being given, discussed, or proposed; the legal authority regarding medical treatment; the patient's legal rights and how their rights can be exercised; supporting qualifying patients in exploring options and decisions, and supporting them to articulate their views; speaking on behalf of the patient and representing them; and supporting the patient's *participation in decisions being made about their care and treatment. A person appointed to act as an IMHA must: have appropriate training or experience or both; be a person of integrity and good character; be able to act independently of any person who has requested an IMHA on behalf of a qualifying patient, and independently of any professionals involved in the patient's care and treatment. IMHAs have a right to: see and interview qualifying patients in private; meet and interview professionals involved in the patient's care; and, where the patient consents, see any records relating to her/his detention and treatment in hospital, and records relating to after-care services, including *local authority documents.

independent reviewing officer (IRO) A person responsible for chairing *case reviews for *looked-after children and ensuring that *local authorities are discharging their responsibilities with regard to care, planning and *review. The *Review of Children's Cases (Amendment) (England) Regulations* (2004) set out the procedure for the regular review of *care plans in seeking to ensure that they continue to meet children's *needs. The first review takes place within four weeks of the child being looked-after, the second review must be no more than three months after the first review, and subsequent reviews must take place at intervals of not more than six months. The Regulations place *duties on local authorities to seek the wishes and feelings of the child and parents and to give consideration to them, to inform parents of all important matters, to provide them with reports prepared for reviews and to invite them to reviews. The Children and Young Person's Act (2008) places a *duty on local authorities to appoint an IRO before the first looked-after review and a duty on IROs to monitor the performance of local authorities. An IRO is appointed under Section 26 (2A) of the Children Act (1989). The duties of the IRO are to:

- Participate in the review;
- Monitor the performance of the *local authority's functions in respect of the review;
- Refer the case to the *Children and Family Court Advisory Support Service, if considered appropriate.

Although IROs are appointed and paid by local authorities, their duty is to be completely independent of the authority, to ensure that the plan for each child meets her/his individual needs, and that the local authority carries out the plan. If exercised, their *power to refer to CAFCASS would have the effect of forcing a local authority to take action because CAFCASS is able to initiate proceedings in the *High Court.

The local authority independent reviewing functions discharged by IROs usually also extend to the chairing of *child protection conferences to ensure that an effective *child protection plan is made for children deemed to be at risk of *significant harm. As part of the child protection conference the IRO will make recommendations, in conjunction with the meeting attendees, that will assist in the development of the child protection plan as part of the *core group meetings.

The Children and Young Persons Act (2008) provides a *power to establish a national agency to recruit, train, appoint, and manage IROs. This is a reserve power that could be brought into play if there were doubts about IROs being independent from local authorities and questions about their working in the interests of children and seeking to obtain the best service for them from the local authority. *See also* ACCOMMODATED CHILD; CARE PLAN; CHILD ABUSE AND NEGLECT; CHILD PROTECTION; LOOKED-AFTER CHILDREN.

Further reading: Department for Education (2010) *IRO Handbook: Statutory Guidance for Independent Reviewing Officers and Local Authorities on their Functions in Relation to Case Management and Review for Looked After Children.* Available at: http://www.gov.uk/government/uploads/system/uploads/attachment_data/file/337568/iro_statutory_guidance_iros_and_las_march_ 2010_tagged.pdf.
The Review of Children's Cases (Amendment) (England) Regulations (2004). Available at: http://www.legislation.gov.uk/uksi/2004/1419/pdfs/uksi_20041419_en.pdf.

Independent Safeguarding Authority (ISA) *See* DISCLOSURE AND BARRING SERVICE.

independent sector A term that emerged with the introduction by the Thatcher government of *competition amongst service providers as part of the *community care reforms. The market arrangements were instigated by stipulating that *85 per cent of the funds transferred from central government's social security budget to local authorities for community care had to be spent on services provided by the 'independent sector', at that time a new way of referring to the *voluntary and *private sector within a single designation but one that has continued to the present day. One of the consequences of this designation is that it obscures the extent to which services have been/are being privatized.

independent visitor A volunteer who supports and advises looked-after children. Under Section 23 of the Children Act (1989) a *local authority has a duty to appoint an independent visitor for a *looked-after child where it appears that it would be in the child's *best interests to do so. The independent visitor makes regular visits to the child and maintains other contact, as appropriate. The main purpose of the visits and contacts is to befriend, advise, and assist the child.

indicative amount (indicative budget) After a *needs assessment has been conducted with an adult with *care and support needs or a *carer's assessment has been undertaken under the Care Act (2014), an 'indicative amount' (sometimes referred to as an 'indicative budget') is produced, which is an estimate of how much it will cost to meet the *needs identified. The indicative amount is used as a guide when planning care and support to meet *needs. It is one of the elements that the Care Act (2014) guidance stipulates must always be included in the final plan. Most *local authorities have 'tolerance levels' in relation to indicative amounts. These give social workers and front-line managers some leeway in the use of the indicative amount: for example there may be a tolerance of overspending the indicative amount by 15 per cent, together with a set cash maximum, per week. The process used to establish the indicative amount should be transparent so that people are clear how their indicative amount has been calculated and have confidence that the allocation is correct and that it is adequate to meet their needs. However, this amount is not an entitlement and, during the care and support planning process, different options of meeting the person's needs, including the ways that are most cost-effective, are given consideration. When the care and support and the costs have been agreed, the final *personal budget might be lower, higher, or the same as the indicative amount, depending on what has been seen as the best and most cost-effective way to meet someone's needs. The person, carer, or independent advocate (on the person's behalf) can challenge the local authority on the sufficiency of the final amount.

Further reading: Department of Health (2016) *Care and Support: Statutory Guidance*, Chapter 11. Available at: https://www.gov.uk/government/publications/care-act-statutory-guidance/care-and-support-statutory-guidance#person-centred-care-and-support-planning.

individual budget *See* PERSONAL BUDGET.

individual choice *See* CHOICE; CONSUMERISM.

individual education plan (IEP) Builds on the school curriculum that a child with *learning and/or physical disabilities is following and is designed to set out the strategies to be used to meet the child's identified needs. The plan is intended to focus on three or four targets chosen from those relating to the key areas of communication, literacy, mathematics, behaviour, and social. Plans should be discussed with parents and the child, wherever possible. Pupils who are in *School Action and *School Action Plus are likely to have an IEP that sets out short-term targets for the child, the teaching strategies to be used, the provision to be put in place, when the plan is to be reviewed, success and exit criteria, and *outcomes to be recorded when the plan is reviewed. The IEP is relevant to a looked-after child's *Personal Education Plan (PEP) but does not replace it. *See also* EDUCATION, HEALTH AND CARE PLAN; SPECIAL EDUCATIONAL NEEDS.

individualism Ideas that emphasize the importance of the individual, rather than the collective, and the primacy of the individual's interests, as in Margaret Thatcher's oft-quoted statement: 'There is no such thing as society.' In the current *neo-liberal context, the primacy of the individual is vociferously promoted and defended. The individual is seen as a figure made up of a collection of personal preferences who rationally chooses and calculatingly makes decisions in her/his own interests. This concern with individualism is most obviously present in *consumerism, with the notion of the individual defining her/himself through the purchase of commodities being held out as essential and desirable. This view of individualism has been imported into social work, most obviously through the implementation of the Care Act (2014) in services for adults. However, there remain stubborn gaps between the neo-liberal depictions of the individual and how people see themselves, often rejecting as untenable the idea that they are 'consumers' or 'customers' of social work. *See also* CONSUMERISM; INDIVIDUAL PATHOLOGY; RESPONSIBILIZATION.

individual pathology A perspective, which has exerted a powerful influence on mainstream social work practice, that explains the occurrence of problems in people's lives as arising entirely from within themselves (the result of their flawed psychological make-up) in a way that sets them apart from 'normal' people. From this perspective, social work is concerned with developing knowledge and forms of practice that have the capacity to control people who deviate from the 'normal', though such methods of control will usually be regarded as 'support' or 'treatment'. Individual pathology has been challenged by *radical social work and other forms of *anti-oppressive practice. Reliance on individual pathology as an explanation of people's problems has intensified in the current climate of *neo-liberal *individualism.

individual responsibility See CONSUMERISM; INDIVIDUAL PATHOLOGY; INDIVIDUALISM; RESPONSIBILIZATION.

individual service fund One of the options for using a *personal budget in implementing a *care and support plan: by having a managed account held by a third party, usually a *voluntary or *user-led organization, with support provided in line with the person's wishes.

Further reading: Think Local Act Personal (2015) *Individual Service Funds (ISFs) and Contracting for Flexible Support: Practice Guidance to Support Implementation of the Care Act (2014)*. Available at: http://www.thinklocalactpersonal.org.uk/_assets/Resources/SDS/TLAPISFsContractingFINAL.pdf.

individual utility See INDIVIDUALISM; RATIONAL CHOICE.

induction The process of introducing and orientating a social worker (or any worker) to her/his new job, identifying where the job fits into the organization, and giving an overview of its policies, roles, and functions. It may include an individual programme of visits to key people, organizations, and services with which the new starter will be working, and/or a formal training programme that will be attended with other new starters.

inequalities in health See HEALTH INEQUALITIES.

infantilization Treating an adult as a child. A powerful *discourse, fuelled by *ageism in the wider society, and encountered most often in the way *older people are treated by adults younger than themselves; encapsulated when older age is referred to as a 'second childhood'. Although it can occur anywhere, the infantilization of older people is more likely to occur when they move into settings where the people working with them have no knowledge of their previous lives. In these circumstances, their need for assistance is more easily associated with child-like status because staff may have no countervailing knowledge about the person, such as might be possessed in a family context. Infantilization can take many forms. Older people can be depicted as having behavioural characteristics that are associated with children, such as being impulsive, disruptive, and irrational. They may be spoken to in a tone of voice and manner that might be adopted with a child, such as being scolded for what are represented as their misdeeds. Assistance with *activities of daily living, such as dressing and eating, may be provided in a way that is reminiscent of how children are treated. They may be dressed inappropriately or not at all, remaining in pyjamas or a nightdress all day. They may be treated in a way that is over-casual and over-familiar for the situation they are in, such as being patted or kissed. Parties for birthdays may seem more like the kind of parties young children have. Although some instances of infantilization may have a malicious element, most are likely to be well-intentioned and continued by staff who may not have been provided with any other perspective on how to relate to older people. However, infantilization should not be seen simply in terms of the responses of individual staff. Consideration needs to be given to the way in which *ageism more generally and the *culture of a particular service or setting are contributing to the treatment of older people as children. *See also* AGE-APPROPRIATE; PATERNALISM.

infant mortality rate The number of infants who die within one year of their birth per thousand live births.

informal admission (mental health) An individual can be admitted to a psychiatric unit without the need for compulsion (sectioning) under the Mental Health Act (1983). The provisions for informal admission are set out in Section 131 of the Act and apply to at least half of all in patients, who are free to leave and retain the same rights of *consent to treatment as all other patients under medical care. Someone who is in this position is usually referred to as an 'informal patient', although sometimes the term 'voluntary patient' is used. Informal patients are those who have the *capacity to consent to admission and treatment, and who do not object. All patients who object to admission and/or treatment should be subject to the formal powers of the Mental Health Act (1983). Those who do not object, but who lack the capacity to consent, and where being in hospital amounts to a deprivation of their liberty, must be made subject either to the Mental Health Act (1983) or the *Deprivation of Liberty Safeguards.

informal care (informal carer, informal caring) *See* CARE; CARER.

informal patient *See* INFORMAL ADMISSION; COMPULSORY ADMISSION.

information and advice (adults) Under Section 4 of the Care Act (2014) a *local authority must: 'establish and maintain a service for providing people in its area with information and advice relating to *care and support for adults and support for *carers'. The *Care and Support Statutory Guidance* (2016) uses the term 'information' to mean the communication of knowledge and facts regarding care and support and 'advice' to mean helping a person to identify *choices and/or providing an opinion or recommendation regarding a course of action in relation to care and support. The *duty to provide information and advice relates to the whole population of a local authority's area, not just those with care and support needs. A local authority cannot, therefore, fulfil this universal information and advice service duty simply by meeting identified eligible needs (*see* ELIGIBILITY CRITERIA) because people may require information and advice before they need to access care or support services, to consider what actions they may take now to prevent or delay any *need for care, or how they might plan to meet the cost of future needs. A local authority must ensure that information and advice services not only cover basic information about care and support and the way the system operates but also include a wide range of care and support-related areas, for example prevention of care and support needs, finances, health, housing, employment, and *safeguarding. Also a local authority should not provide only 'blanket' advice. In fulfilling the duty, it should provide more personalized information fitted to a person's specific needs, pointing them towards the types of information and/or advice that may be particularly relevant to them. Furthermore, it should identify what is available and exactly what is needed locally in terms of information and advice, as well as how and where information and advice should best be provided. Whilst the local authority has to establish and maintain a service, it does not have to provide all of the elements of the service itself. It can make use of other *statutory, *voluntary, and *private sector information and advice resources available to people within its area. The information and advice service can be provided by a local authority directly or by another agency, including *independent providers.

The people who are envisaged as likely to need information and advice include:

- people wanting to plan for their future care and support needs;
- people who may develop care and support needs, or whose current care and support needs may become greater (*see* PREVENTION [ADULTS]);
- people who have not presented to a local authority for assessment but are likely to be in need of care and support. Local authorities are expected to take steps to identify such people and encourage them to come forward for an assessment of their needs (*see* PREVENTION [ADULTS]);
- people who are referred or who self-refer to a local authority for the first time, where an *assessment of needs is being considered (*see* NEEDS ASSESSMENT);
- people who are assessed by a local authority as currently being in need of care and support (*see* NEEDS ASSESSMENT). Advice and information must be offered to these people irrespective of whether they have been assessed as having eligible needs that a local authority must meet (*see* ELIGIBILITY CRITERIA);
- people whose needs for care and support a local authority considers to be eligible needs, whether it is paying for some, all, or none of the costs of meeting those needs (*see* CARE AND SUPPORT PLAN);
- people whose care and support plans are being reviewed (*see* MONITORING AND REVIEW);
- family members and carers of adults with care and support needs or those who are likely to develop care and support needs;
- people about whom there are safeguarding concerns (*see* SAFEGUARDING [ADULTS]);
- people who may benefit from financial information and advice on matters concerning care and support, helping them understand the costs of their care and support and where they can access independent financial information and advice;
- care and support staff who have contact with and provide information and advice as part of their jobs.

A local authority must recognize and respond to the specific requirements that *carers have for both general and personal information and advice. A carer's need for information and advice may be separate and distinct from information and advice for the person for whom they are caring or it may be possible to cover them together. Specific areas about which carers may need information and advice include:

- breaks from caring;
- the health and wellbeing of carers;
- caring and wider family relationships;
- carers' financial and legal issues;
- caring and employment;
- caring and education;
- a carer's need for *advocacy.

There will be some circumstances where impartial information and advice are particularly important and a local authority should consider when this may be best provided by an independent source, rather than by the local authority itself.

This is particularly likely to be the case when people are entering into a legal agreement with a local authority or other third party or they wish to question, challenge, or appeal against a decision of the local authority or other statutory body.

A local authority must ensure that information and advice are provided on:

- how the local care and support system works;
- how to access care and support available locally;
- types of care and support and the choice of care providers available in the local area;
- how to access independent financial advice on matters relating to care and support;
- how to raise concerns about the safety or wellbeing of an adult with care and support needs or a carer with support needs;
- available housing and housing-related support options;
- treatment and support for health conditions, including continuing health care arrangements (*see* NHS CONTINUING HEALTH CARE);
- health services;
- services that may help people remain independent for longer such as *home improvement agencies;
- befriending services and other services to prevent social isolation;
- *intermediate care;
- eligibility and applying for *disability and other types of *benefits;
- employment support for disabled adults;
- children's services and arrangements for *transition to adult services;
- carers' services and benefits;
- sources of independent information, advice, and advocacy;
- the *Court of Protection and *Enduring Power of Attorney;
- planning for future care costs;
- different types of *abuse and its *prevention.

In providing an information and advice service, a local authority must provide more than just leaflets and web-based materials. It should enable people to access what they need through a range of services. A local authority's development of an information and advice plan needs to include:

- engagement with *service users, carers, and family members to understand what is working and not working for them, their preferences, and how their information and advice needs can best be met;
- adopting a *co-production approach to the plan, involving service user groups and statutory, private and voluntary sector service providers;
- mapping the range of information and advice services, including independent financial advice and the different providers available;
- coordination with other statutory bodies with an interest in care and support, including local *Clinical Commissioning Groups and *Health and Wellbeing Boards;
- building into the plan opportunities to record, measure, and assess the impact of information and advice services rather than simply service *outputs;
- making the plan public once it is finalized.

In deciding the types of information and advice services to be provided, a local authority needs to analyse and understand the specific needs of its population. Some of the factors and circumstances that a local authority should consider in doing this will often be identified in the Joint Strategic Needs Assessment (*see* HEALTH AND WELLBEING BOARDS). These factors may include:

- the ethnic composition of the local area, including languages used;
- hard-to-reach groups;

- the split between those whose care and support is (or is likely to be) arranged or funded by the person her/himself and the state;
- demographic trends relating to health and care needs, age, and *disability;
- how people access information and advice at the moment and the quality of existing information and advice services;
- an appropriate balance between the needs of its local population for information and the needs people will have for access to advice;
- the current sufficiency of supply and the range of information and advice providers from different sectors (including their prospects for growth).

A local authority should review and publish information about the effectiveness of the information and advice service locally, including customer satisfaction, and may decide to build this into its local *Joint Health and Wellbeing Strategies.

Further reading: Department of Health (2016) *Care and Support: Statutory Guidance*, Chapter 3. Available at: https://www.gov.uk/government/publications/care-act-statutory-guidance/care-and-support-statutory-guidance#person-centred-care-and-support-planning.

information and communication technology (ICT) *See* CALL CENTRE; COMPUTERIZATION.

Information Commissioner's Office (ICO) An office set up to uphold information rights by promoting openness in access to information held by public bodies and protecting data privacy for individuals. The ICO rules on complaints, gives guidance to individuals and organizations, and can take action when the law is broken. The ICO enforces and oversees the following:

- Data Protection Act (1998);
- Freedom of Information Act (2000);
- Privacy and Electronic Communications Regulations (2003);
- Environmental Information Regulations (2004).

The ICO is responsible for data protection in England, *Scotland, *Wales, and *Northern Ireland, and for freedom of information in England, Wales, Northern Ireland, and UK-wide public bodies based in Scotland. Scotland has its own Environmental Information Regulations and the Freedom of Information (Scotland) Act (2002). These are regulated by the Scottish Information Commissioner. There are a number of tools available to the ICO in relation to organizations and individuals that collect, use, and keep personal information. They include criminal prosecution, non-criminal enforcement, and audit. The ICO also has the power to serve a monetary penalty notice (in effect, a fine) on a data controller. Under the Freedom of Information Act, Environmental Information Regulations, and associated codes of practice, the ICO's tools include non-criminal enforcement and assessments of *good practice. *See also* ACCESS TO RECORDS; CALDICOTT GUARDIAN; CONFIDENTIALITY; DATA PROTECTION; INFORMATION-GIVING; INFORMATION-SHARING.

(⊕) SEE WEB LINKS
- Official site of the Information Commissioner's Office.

information-giving Informing people about services was previously seen as an essential aspect of social work so that people would be able to access them when needed. For example, in the model of *care management that accompanied the *community care reforms, providing information was the first stage of the process. In the current context, providing *information and advice services for adults is a statutory *duty under the Care Act (2014), largely in the hope that this can replace or delay the need for services to be provided. In contrast, there is specific mention in the guidance to the Care Act (2014) of people who have not presented to a local authority for assessment but are likely to be in need of care and support, and local authorities are expected to take steps to identify such people and encourage them to come forward for an assessment of their needs. However, with demand perpetually outstripping supply, particularly since the onset of *austerity, it is difficult to imagine local authorities acting on this expectation. The exception to the ambivalence about publicizing services is the publication of information about services available to children or adults who may need to be safeguarded, given the ever-present anxiety of a tragedy involving *abuse. *See also* INFORMATION-SHARING.

information governance *See* ACCESS TO RECORDS; CALDICOTT GUARDIAN; CONFIDENTIALITY; DATA PROTECTION; INFORMATION COMMISSIONER'S OFFICE; INFORMATION-GIVING; INFORMATION-SHARING.

information-holding *See* DATA PROTECTION.

information-sharing In *collaborative working, one area of difficulty that arises for social workers is the sharing of information. There are a number of legal imperatives concerning the protection of data and the principle of *confidentiality. It is sometimes difficult to square these concerns with policy and practice requirements to collaborate closely with other agencies and professionals. Four models of information-sharing that strike different balances between protecting confidentiality and sharing information with other professionals and agencies have been identified (Richardson and Asthana 2006):

Ideal Information is shared appropriately but only when necessary.

Over-open Information is shared when this is not always necessary or appropriate. This model is likely to breach confidentiality but unlikely to lead to important information being withheld.

Over-cautious Information is withheld when it is necessary or appropriate to share it. This creates a high risk of failure to communicate necessary information but a low risk of breaching confidentiality.

Chaotic Sharing and withholding of information is indiscriminate, leading to high risks of both not communicating important information and breaching confidentiality.

Although there is limited evidence concerning the influence of professional *culture on information-sharing, it has been suggested that health professionals, influenced by the *medical model, may be more inclined to adopt an 'over-cautious' model, prioritizing the protection of confidentiality over the need to communicate with other professionals, while the police may adopt an 'over-open' approach, when communicating with health and social care agencies. In addition to professional culture, the level of trust between professionals is likely to have a strong bearing on their willingness to share information. Even when professional protocols regarding information-sharing are agreed and a working model is established, there remain practical difficulties in terms of the need for shared recording and information systems, with hardware and/or software in different agencies not being compatible. *See also* ACCESS TO RECORDS; CALDICOTT GUARDIAN; DATA PROTECTION; INFORMATION-GIVING; INFORMATION COMMISSIONER'S OFFICE.

Further reading: Richardson, S. and Asthana, S. (2006) 'Inter-agency Information-sharing in Health and Social Care Services', *British Journal of Social Work*, 36, 657–69.

informed consent An agreement to undergo medical or surgical treatment, to participate in an experiment or surgical trial, or to take part in a research project (including social work research). Essentially there is an ethical requirement that people should have sufficient information after learning about and understanding fully what they are about to participate in or undergo so that they are able to make an informed judgement about whether or not to go ahead.

in-group *See* OUT-GROUP.

initial assessment Previously an appraisal of a child referred to *local authority children's services, when it was necessary to establish whether s/he was a *child in need, had suffered, or was at risk of *significant harm, whether services were required, and whether a more detailed *core assessment was necessary. Initial assessments had to be completed by a qualified social worker within a maximum of ten days after the date of the referral, using the national *Framework for Assessment of Children in Need and their Families (see ASSESSMENT [CHILDREN]).

The *Munro Review recommended that the government should not prescribe national models for assessments and should replace *core and initial assessments with a single assessment. Accordingly, the national status of the *Framework for Assessment of Children in Need and their Families* was withdrawn, as were initial assessments. However, *Working Together* (2015) statutory guidance states that all assessments under the Children Act (1989) should be completed with reference to the three domains in the Assessment Framework (*see* ASSESSMENT [CHILDREN]). *See also* CHILD PROTECTION; SAFEGUARDING CHILDREN.

injunction A court order that instructs a person not to do or compels them to do specified acts. Although injunctions are made in civil proceedings, breach of an injunction is a criminal offence that can result in sanctions, including imprisonment. The police will respond where an injunction with a power of arrest is breached. *See also* DOMESTIC VIOLENCE.

insane asylum *See* ASYLUMS; INSTITUTIONALIZATION.

insanity Previously referred to serious mental disorder, or 'madness', but no longer used in mental health practice. It is still used in courts of law in cases where the defendant is either unfit to plead or deemed not guilty by reason of insanity. In legal proceedings, a mentally disordered defendant may assert unfitness to plead because of her/his mental disorder, though in practice the plea is very rare. Where the defence is not guilty by reason of insanity, the court has to establish that on the balance of probabilities, at the time of the offence, the defendant met the McNaughton Rules which establish that the defendant did not know or understand the act or its consequences. The McNaughton Rules were established in 1843 following the case of Daniel McNaughton, who was acquitted on the grounds of insanity after a failed attempt to shoot the prime minister, Robert Peel. Technically, the plea can be put forward for any offence but in practice it is rarely used and usually only in cases of murder or other serious offences. Evidence from at least two medical practitioners is required to return a verdict of not guilty by reason of insanity. If the verdict is reached, discretionary sentencing is likely to take place and the judge may order detention in hospital under the Mental Health Act (1983). *See also* HOSPITAL ORDER.

inscription (by discourse) *See* IDENTITY.

insight A change in someone's understanding of a problem, situation, or circumstances, particularly in relation to their causal factors or the influence of intra- or inter-personal dynamics. This may be because of having gained access to new material, for example, if someone who was previously looked after by a *local authority as a child is able to gain understanding of why that occurred because the person has accessed written records relating to that period of her/his life. Or, it may result from rearranging existing material, for example, when someone talks over a familiar problematic situation with a social worker and begins to understand it and/or her/his reaction to it in a different way to previously. For some people, gaining insight will be a significant component in enabling them to deal with and move on from what they experience as problematic aspects of their past or present lives. While the potential significance of insight for *service users may be readily recognized, it can also be important for social workers, who may experience 'breakthroughs' in thinking about their work with someone as a result of gaining fresh insight.

In psychiatry, insight refers to the individual's understanding of their illness, their understanding of how the illness affects their interactions with those around them, and their responses to the views held by others about their situation. This information is normally gathered during a *mental state examination and subsequent interviews. However, the concept of insight creates difficulties in this context because of its susceptibility to cultural bias and prejudice. An individual may be deemed to be lacking insight or having impaired insight, but this *assessment should not be based simply on whether or not the individual agrees with the doctor's *diagnosis. Further, different psychiatric disorders involve different mechanisms that may lead to insight being impaired. A patient who is displaying symptoms of *psychosis may exhibit an absence of insight into their condition. The degree of insight displayed by the individual should not be used as the sole indicator of *mental illness. The clinical value attached to an individual displaying 'good' or 'bad' insight may not be meaningful in relation to other symptoms or longer term *prognosis.

inspection Assessment by an outside body (an inspectorate) that decides whether an organization or a service is meeting required standards. The outside bodies concerned are the Care and Social Services Inspectorate in *Wales, the Regulation and Quality Improvement Authority in *Northern Ireland, the Care Inspectorate in *Scotland, and in England the Care Quality Commission (CQC) for adults' services and the *Office for Standards in Education (Ofsted) for children's services. *See also* AUDIT COMMISSION; PERFORMANCE MANAGEMENT.

inspectorate *See* INSPECTION.

instincts Aspects of thinking, feeling, and behaviour that are considered innate and naturally endowed, rather than learned. There is considerable controversy about which facets of human experience are instinctual and those that are learned, characterized as the *nature versus nurture debate.

institution 1. An established aspect of society through which certain concerns and interests are organized, such as the church or the family. Used in this sense, social work can be regarded as an institution.

2. Also used to describe closed forms of living arrangements such as long-stay psychiatric units or prisons, what Erving Goffman (1922–82) referred to as 'total institutions' (*Asylums* 1961), that closely control their inmates' behaviour in a regimented pattern of daily life, disregarding their interests in favour of the interests of staff, and stripping them of their pre-existing *identity.

3. Further used in a pejorative way to refer to residential care, implying that it possesses some of the characteristics of the total institution, as when homes for *older people are referred to as institutional care. *See also* DECARCERATION; DEINSTITUTIONALIZATION; INSTITUTIONALIZATION.

institutional care *See* INSTITUTION.

institutionalization This can mean the process of placing people in institutions, such as long-stay psychiatric units and prisons, and the psychological outcomes that can result for the people who are placed, which has also been referred to as 'institutional neurosis'. Institutionalization has become particularly and negatively associated with the segregation of people with mental health problems from the rest of society during the eighteenth, nineteenth, and twentieth centuries in Europe and North America. Long periods of confinement in institutions can result in dependency, *learned helplessness, hopelessness, social withdrawal, passivity, apathy, and extreme compliance. Institutionalization as a state strategy emerged strongly in the nineteenth century to deal with unproductive or vulnerable people who were seen as not fitting the requirements of a *capitalist society and were confined to workhouses, *asylums, or prisons. This view underpinned much of UK legislation and policy around large-scale asylum building and increased regulation of mentally ill people during the nineteenth century. In some quarters, religious or charitable asylums were run as benign and humane alternatives to the incarceration of mentally ill people in state asylums, workhouses, and unregulated private madhouses. The dominance of asylum provision persisted in the UK until the late 1950s and early 1960s when psychiatrists such as David Cooper (1931–86) and R. D. Laing (1927–89) challenged traditional coercive and institutional psychiatry with a sustained analysis and critique. Dubbed anti-psychiatrists, they called for services based on voluntary libertarian principles and psychological therapies. Sociologist Erving Goffman (1922–82) published his seminal work *Asylums* in 1961 in which he critiqued mental hospitals and termed them 'total institutions'. The 1950s also saw a pharmacological revolution as drugs were introduced to treat psychotic symptoms. A number of complex factors underpinned a gradual policy shift towards the closure of asylums in the UK, a process referred to as *deinstitutionalization. The concept of *community care was first introduced as a policy alternative to hospital and asylum-based provision in the 1950s but the wholesale closure of former asylums did not gather momentum until the 1980s. During the twentieth century, the development and organization of primary care, social services, and outpatient services gradually began to absorb the great majority of people suffering from *depression, *anxiety, and other common mental disorders. Today, secure psychiatric hospitals such as Ashworth, Broadmoor, and St Andrews are remaining examples of former asylums. *See also* ANTI-PSYCHIATRY.

institutional neurosis *See* INSTITUTIONALIZATION.

institutional racism *See* RACISM.

instrumental conditioning *See* BEHAVIOURISM; BEHAVIOUR MODIFICATION.

instrumentality *See* INTENSIFICATION OF WORK.

intake team Previously a group of social workers who took on all of the work referred to a *Social Services Department or to a smaller area within it, and who worked with people for a time-limited period, usually three or six months. With the reappearance of specialist services, this model declined substantially, but elements of it have been revived, for example in the development of *Multi-agency Safeguarding Hubs.

intellectual impairment A level of functioning that is below that of most people, usually established on the basis of *intelligence testing. It is regarded as a characteristic of the individual and not located within a wider perspective on how the impairment may be compounded by the social environment. The term *'learning disability' is probably preferable as it is able to encompass both the notion of impairment and the social barriers that construct what constitutes the extent of a person's disability. *See also* DISABILITY; SOCIAL MODEL OF DISABILITY.

intelligence testing The measurement of intellectual abilities. Traditionally this resulted in an IQ (intelligence quotient) score, expressed as a percentage worked out according to the formula: IQ = mental age ÷ chronological age x 100. There has been growing recognition that an IQ based on a single score does not represent the complexities and facets that constitute intelligence and assessments now typically focus on a range of domains thought to make up intelligence or multiple intelligences.

intensification of work (intensification of social work) *Performance management and *computerized systems have introduced ever more detailed stipulations concerning the content and process of social workers' practice through the use of performance indicators, and measurement of *outcomes against them, and compliance with the control exerted by IT system requirements. This has resulted in widespread intensification of the amount and pace of work. In many *local authorities social workers are cajoled and coerced to process as much work as possible in the shortest possible time. The intensification of work overwhelmingly stresses the quantitative aspects of social work, while at its heart are a series of small-scale qualitative interpersonal encounters between social workers and *service users. This stress on the quantitative has produced forms of practice that are increasingly instrumental in their focus on procedures, form-filling, and budgets, particularly as the environments in which social workers operate become more complex, highly resource-constrained in the context of *austerity, and subject to reorganizations and new legislation. Such intensified and instrumental social work exerts powerful pressure in the direction of divorcing social workers from the lived experience of service users. However, there are indications that many social workers strive to hang on to the importance of the qualitative aspects of their work and seek to maintain their commitment to advancing service users' interests. *See also* DEPROFESSIONALIZATION; DESKILLING; DIVISION OF LABOUR; FRAGMENTATION OF ROLES AND TASKS; FUNCTIONAL ANALYSIS.

intentionally homeless *See* HOMELESSNESS.

inter-agency working *See* COLLABORATIVE WORKING.

inter-country adoption The *adoption of children from other countries who are brought to live with their adopters in the UK. Such adoptions are restricted to *cases where:

- The child cannot be cared for in a safe environment in their own country.
- The adoption would be in the *best interests of the child and would not affect their internationally recognized human rights.
- The adopter has been assessed as eligible and suitable to adopt from overseas by an adoption agency in the UK.

See also ADOPTION; SAME-RACE PLACEMENT.

interdependence A concept that challenges the binary nature (*see* DECONSTRUCTION) of the discussion of *dependency and *independence in social work by stressing mutuality and reciprocity in relationships between people.

inter disciplinary practice *See* COLLABORATIVE WORKING.

inter generational contract The assumption that younger people would support *older people through their taxes and then, in their turn, would be supported by the next generation was one of the key founding principles of the post-war *welfare state. The increasing drive for individuals to take responsibility for their own welfare, rather than relying on the state (the agent responsible for executing the inter generational contract) has thrown the contract into question in the media and political discourse (*See also* DEMOGRAPHIC TIME BOMB).

Interim Care Order (ICO) At the first (initial) hearing in *care proceedings the court may decide that an Interim Care Order (ICO) is needed as a temporary measure to set out what should happen to the child during the proceedings, to allow investigations by the *local authority to continue and for plans to be made. The court can also give directions as to whether or not medical or psychiatric examinations or other assessments should be carried out, by whom, and how (*see* GILLICK COMPETENT). To make an ICO a court has to be satisfied that there are reasonable grounds for believing that the circumstances with respect to the child meet the *threshold criteria (Section 31(2) Children Act [1989]). An ICO was previously made initially for a maximum of eight weeks and thereafter for periods of four weeks at a time. These time limits were removed by the Children and Families Act (2014) and ICOs are now made to remain in place until discharged by the court or a final order is made. An ICO has the same effect as a full *Care Order while it lasts and the local authority therefore acquires *parental responsibility for the child under it. In some cases the child may continue living at home with the parents under specified conditions. However, if the child goes home and the conditions are not met, the local authority is able to intervene without having to obtain a full Care Order. If the child does not go home, s/he must be allowed reasonable *contact with her/his parents, guardians, or other persons who had parental responsibility prior to the making of an ICO, unless the court directs differently. *See also* FAMILY COURTS.

intermediate care (intermediate care services) A form of intensive, short-term support aimed at increasing people's *independence by improving their health and social functioning through the provision of integrated health and social care services that are intermediate, or a bridge, particularly between acute hospital care and care in the *community. The three main aims of intermediate care are to:

- Help people to avoid going into hospital unnecessarily;
- Help people to be as independent as possible after a stay in hospital;
- Prevent people from having to move into a care home until they really need to do so.

Provision of intermediate care depends on a comprehensive *assessment and a *care plan that identifies the need for some form of rehabilitative intervention. The planned outcomes must be related to the maximization of *independence and usually this will involve helping people to resume or continue living at home. The criteria limit the provision of intermediate care services to a maximum of six weeks, although this may sometimes be longer in specific circumstances (for example, following a *cardiovascular accident/stroke). The regulations stipulate that intermediate care services cannot be charged for, although this only applies to services provided for a period of six weeks or less.

Intermediate care services can provide intensive support in the home setting, for example through *rapid response teams, preventing the need for hospital admission. They can be provided immediately following discharge from hospital, for example through *'hospital at home' schemes, thus enabling people to be discharged from hospital more quickly. They can be offered on a day or residential basis between hospital care and discharge home, offering a period of *rehabilitation for people who might otherwise need admission to residential or nursing home care. The planning and provision of intermediate care requires *partnership working across professional and organizational boundaries. It is likely to involve collaboration between, for example, doctors, nurses, physiotherapists, *occupational therapists, and social workers. Younger adults may utilize intermediate care services but in practice the majority of users are *older people.

For intermediate care to be effective, an integrated whole-system approach is needed. Unless these services are supported by adequate and appropriate provision at other stages in the service pathway, including preventive and longer-term rehabilitative support, there is a danger that problems simply shift from one part of the system to another. A comprehensive and coherent strategy needs to be underpinned by fundamental principles throughout all levels and types of provision. The principles underpinning intermediate care (person-centred care, multi-agency working, and a *reablement approach) need to be integral across mainstream services, rather than being confined to a specialized, targeted, and time-limited intervention.

Further reading: Department of Health (2016) *Care and Support: Statutory Guidance* Chapter 2. Available at: https://www.gov.uk/government/publications/care-act-statutory-guidance/ care-and-support-statutory-guidance#person-centred-care-and-support-planning.

internalization The process by which people learn and accept as inevitable the values and norms of society, as applied to the positions they occupy within it. *See also* DISCOURSE; DOMINANT IDEOLOGY; HABITUS; HEGEMONY.

internal market A trading arrangement set up between different sections or units of *public sector organizations to buy and sell services between each other. This organizational development was instituted from the 1980s onwards by the Thatcher governments, with the most prominent example being the setting up of an internal market within the National Health Service. Under Conservative, *New Labour, and Conservative–Liberal Democrat Coalition governments, albeit with differing arrangements, *general practitioners have purchased services for their patients from hospitals. The intention was to make the NHS perform as though it was operating in private market conditions, the argument being that if it were compelled to do so, it would provide better quality services at a lower price. Another example of an internal market, which functions rather differently, is the *competition between schools, based on *inspection reports and league tables derived from students' aggregated examination results.

International Classification of Diseases (*ICD, ICD-10*) A diagnostic tool for classifying diseases and health problems. It is one of two reference texts containing standardized criteria for the classification of *mental disorder that are used in the UK by psychiatrists to assist the process of *diagnosis. The classification originates from the 1850s. The World Health Organization (WHO) adopted the *ICD* in 1948 when the classification was in its sixth edition. The *ICD* is now in its tenth edition. The *ICD* is mainly used in Europe. Unlike its counterpart, the *Diagnostic and Statistical Manual*, which uses an operational system based on meeting certain criteria, the *ICD* employs a diagnostic labelling system with guidelines on making definitive diagnoses. Classifications inform decisions about treatment and are used in predicting outcomes. In practice social workers do not use the *ICD* themselves but awareness of the use of it as a diagnostic tool by psychiatrists and familiarization with its features can aid their understanding of the process of diagnosis.

International Federation of Social Workers (IFSW) A global federation of national organizations of social workers. The IFSW approved a 'Global Definition of the Social Work Profession' in July 2014:

Social work is a practice-based profession and an academic discipline that promotes social change and development, social cohesion, and the empowerment and liberation of people. Principles of social justice, human rights, collective responsibility and respect for diversities are central to social work. Underpinned by theories of social work, social sciences, humanities and indigenous knowledge, social work engages people and structures to address life challenges and enhance wellbeing.

Recognizing the different circumstances in which social work is practised around the world, the Federation stated that this definition 'may be amplified at national and/or regional levels'. *See also* CODE OF ETHICS; CODE OF PRACTICE; HEALTH AND CARE PROFESSIONS COUNCIL; KNOWLEDGE AND SKILLS STATEMENTS; PROFESSIONAL CAPABILITIES FRAMEWORK.

((⊕)) SEE WEB LINKS
• Official site of the International Federation of Social Workers.

inter-organizational working *See* COLLABORATIVE WORKING.

inter-professional practice (inter-professional relationships, inter-professional working) *See* COLLABORATIVE WORKING.

intersectionality A concept that underpins much of the discussion within social work about *anti-oppressive practice, but is rarely named as such. It refers to the combined effects of positioning in different social divisions (age, *class, *disability, *ethnicity, *gender, *'race', sexuality) on people's lives, particularly with regard to the construction of their identities. It involves understandings of *identity that resist constructing a hierarchy of oppression and eschew the allocation of people to fixed categories, recognizing that not only is the experience of social divisions inter-related, it can also be fluid, varying over time and between different contexts. Thus, while social workers' understanding of people's lives and identities needs to be informed by knowledge about the implications of social divisions, no assumptions can be made about the precise way in which their different aspects interact in particular situations or about how they are experienced in people's lives, especially

given their mediation by other factors specific to individuals. *See also* IDENTITY
POLITICS; REFLEXIVE MODERNIZATION.

intervention Often used loosely in relation to almost anything a social worker
does following an *assessment (or even with reference to the assessment itself) that
involves action with a purpose, undertaken with or on behalf of a *service user.

interviewing A key component of day-to-day social work and the basis of work
undertaken with *service users. Before undertaking any interview, a social worker
needs to be as clear as possible about her/his role and the interview's purpose.
Careful consideration needs to be given to the pace of interviews, matching it to the
service user, and to ensuring that the service user understands what is happening,
for example, by pausing and summarizing the stage that has been reached, focusing
on what the service user has said. An interview may include the presence of an
advocate, to help represent the service user's wishes and interests, or an interpreter,
in order to allow a greater level and depth of *participation by the service user. Many
interviews are now shaped by particular formats, such as those associated with
assessing mental *capacity or care and support (*see* NEEDS ASSESSMENT). *See also*
COMMUNICATION SKILLS.

introversion and extroversion A way of classifying personality in terms of
being inward-facing or outward-facing. Introversion is seen as characterized by
reflection and responsibility, tending towards withdrawal, and extroversion by
sociability and impulsivity. Rather than seeing these as two compartmentalized
categories, with individuals fitting into one or the other, people have been regarded
as lying at different points on a continuum of personality types, with introversion
and extroversion at each end of the continuum.

inverse care law Formulated by Julian Tudor Hart in an article in *The Lancet* in
1971:

The availability of good medical care tends to vary inversely with the need for the population
served. This inverse care law operates more completely where medical care is most exposed to
market forces, and less so where such exposure is reduced. The market distribution of medical
care is a primitive and historically outdated social form, and any return to it would further
exaggerate the maldistribution of medical resources.

There is a great deal of evidence to support the inverse care law. The concern about
fairness, which underpins the law, arises from wider concerns about the distribution
of health. Inequalities in health arise not only from variations in access to health
services but also from variations in the quality of health care from area to area. They
also arise from factors outside the control of the National Health Service—wealth,
lifestyle, genetic, and environmental considerations all affect people's health. There
is considerable evidence that many populations, particularly those living in areas of
high socio economic disadvantage, suffer on all three dimensions: they use poor-
quality services, to which they have relative difficulty in securing access, and they
suffer multiple disadvantages. *See also* HEALTH INEQUALITIES.

involuntary service users People who do not want to have contact with social
workers but who are compelled to do so. Although there are *cases in which there
may be a clear legislative basis to compulsion, such as when someone is 'sectioned'
under the Mental Health Act (1983), involuntary service use is much broader than
this. For example, although there is no compulsion on parents to be involved with
social workers in relation to children who are *looked after by a *local authority, if

they wish to have their children returned to them, they will feel compelled to do so. An older person may feel compelled to accept *domiciliary services in order to avoid entering residential care. In circumstances of compulsion, social workers still attempt to recognize people's rights and enable them to participate in decision-making as far as possible. One of the ways in which this may be achieved is through the use of independent advocates. *See also* ADVOCACY; SERVICE USER PARTICIPATION.

involvement of service users *See* PARTICIPATION; SERVICE USER.

IRO *See* INDEPENDENT REVIEWING OFFICER.

irrelevant factors *See* RELEVANT FACTORS.

ISA *See* INDEPENDENT SAFEGUARDING AUTHORITY.

jargon Social work has a great deal of jargon, much of it based on acronyms, which functions as a kind of shorthand through which social workers communicate with each other or other professionals. While this is inevitable in any occupation, a key attribute of a good social worker is to be able to step out of using that jargon in her/his work with *service users and to be able to communicate with them clearly and effectively.

job evaluation Classifying jobs and determining the grades and pay attached to them according to their characteristics, rather than in relation to the person in the post, for example, the amount and nature of skill, responsibility, and discretion any holder of the job needs to possess.

joined-up working *See* COLLABORATIVE WORKING; COORDINATION OF SERVICES AND/OR STRATEGY.

joint commissioning *See* COMMISSIONING; JOINT FINANCE; JOINTLY COMMISSIONED SERVICE.

joint finance (joint financing) In principle any service could be jointly financed by any combination of organizations but joint finance is particularly associated with *local authorities and the National Health Service. Under *New Labour (1997–2010) financial changes were introduced to facilitate more effective working relationships between health and social services. The Health Act (1999) Section 31 allowed health and social services, to pool their budgets, designate a lead commissioner for particular services and share resources, including staff, in meeting their statutory obligations. The Health and Social Care Act (2001) went further in allowing the setting up of joint Health and Social Care Trusts through which health and social services for adults could be integrated. The August 2013 Spending Review established the Better Care Fund, which provides central government financial incentives for the integration of health and social care locally. It requires *Clinical Commissioning Groups and local authorities to pool budgets and to agree an integrated spending plan for how they will use their Better Care Fund allocations. Moves towards joint funding continued, with the *NHS Bodies and Local Authorities Partnership Arrangements (Amendment) Regulations* (2015) providing a legal framework for pooled budgets across the key health functions of Clinical Commissioning Groups and the health-related functions of local authorities, including social care. They underpin the operation of the Better Care Fund at local-level areas and developments like the Greater Manchester Authority taking on more devolved responsibility for health and social care. Greater financial integration is seen as having the potential to use resources more efficiently, in particular by reducing avoidable hospital admissions and facilitating early discharge. *See also* HEALTH AND WELLBEING BOARD; HOSPITAL DISCHARGE; JOINTLY COMMISSIONED SERVICE.

Joint Health and Wellbeing Strategy *See* HEALTH AND WELLBEING BOARD.

joint interview (joint visit) Although much of social workers' contact with service users is conducted on their own, there will be occasions when they undertake joint interviews, for example, with a police officer, a health visitor, an *occupational therapist, or a teacher. There are also occasions when two social workers undertake an interview together for safety reasons because there is a history and/or threat of *violence.

jointly commissioned service Two or more organizations, most commonly *local authorities and the National Health Service, assess needs together and identify gaps in services to meet them. Priorities are jointly agreed and decisions made about how services should be provided. Specifications for services are drawn up jointly to meet the priorities that have been agreed. Potential services are jointly appraised and commissioned. *See also* COMMISSIONING; HEALTH AND WELLBEING BOARD; JOINT FINANCE.

Joint Strategic Needs Assessment *See* HEALTH AND WELLBEING BOARD.

joint working *See* COLLABORATIVE WORKING, JOINT FINANCE.

Joseph Rowntree Foundation (JRF) A *charity that funds research and developmental work. It stresses that it has three concerns: to understand the root causes of social problems, to identify ways of overcoming them, and to show how social needs can be met in practice. The Foundation focuses on the circumstances of people experiencing *poverty and *disadvantage, the quality of their homes and *communities, and the kind of services and support available to them. In addition, the Joseph Rowntree Housing Trust (JRHT) is a registered housing association that manages around 2,500 homes and provides care services in York and north-east England. JRF and JRHT are two independent charities that share trustees and directors. Joseph Rowntree (1836–1925) was a Quaker, successful businessman, and philanthropist who developed the Rowntree confectionary company in York.

(((⊕))) **SEE WEB LINKS**
• Official site of the Joseph Rowntree Foundation.

Joseph Rowntree Housing Trust (JRHT) *See* JOSEPH ROWNTREE FOUNDATION.

judgement (adults' individual needs) The issue of judgement was central to the Gloucestershire case (*see* NEEDS ASSESSMENT). In the final ruling by the House of Lords, there was agreement that the professional judgements of social workers determine people's individual *needs. However, it was recognized that social workers make such judgements within *eligibility criteria, which were then variable between *local authorities but are now nationally determined under the Care Act (2014) (*see* ELIGIBILITY CRITERIA). The eligibility criteria constrain social workers' professional judgement in functioning as a *rationing mechanism for scarce resources. *See also* DISCRETION (LOCAL AUTHORITY); DUTY; ELIGIBILITY CRITERIA; EXCEPTIONS; FETTERING DISCRETION; GATEKEEPING. JUDICIAL REVIEW; NEEDS ASSESSMENT; POWER; REASONABLENESS; RELEVANT FACTORS; RIGID POLICIES; TARGET DUTY.

judicial review A court proceeding in which a judge reviews the lawfulness of a decision made by a public body, such as a *local authority, for example, in relation to its provision of a social work service, after it has been challenged in the High

Court. It is a procedure by which to challenge the way that a decision was made, rather than to question the actual decision that was reached. It is only concerned with whether or not the right procedures have been followed in reaching a decision. The courts have developed a set of principles of natural justice against which to judge whether the way that a particular decision has been made is legally flawed. These require public bodies to act within the law, in a fair manner and to arrive at a reasonable decision based upon the evidence. The court will overturn a decision if the public body failed to consider a relevant factor; considered an irrelevant factor; misunderstood or misapplied the law; or reached a decision that is so unreasonable that no reasonable authority could have come to it. *See also* DISCRETION (LOCAL AUTHORITY); FETTERING DISCRETION; GOOD PRACTICE.

Justice of the Peace *See* MAGISTRATES.

just-in-time A production system originating in Japan but embraced in many parts of the world that tries to deliver the exact quantity and quality of raw materials and components just in time for them to be used in production. It emphasizes the need for flexible methods of production, the ability to change rapidly the products produced and having networks of small companies that are contracted as suppliers. Its working principles are voiced in management circles in social work in terms of what can be learned from them and applied to the delivery of flexible personalized services. *See also* BUSINESS ORIENTATION; GIG ECONOMY.

key worker (mental health) *See* CARE COORDINATOR.

key worker (key worker role) Originally, and still sometimes, used to describe an identified member of staff within a residential or day care setting who is allocated to and forms a relationship with a particular *service user and who has special responsibility for ensuring that the service is meeting the service user's *needs as fully as possible, for example, by attending *case conferences or *reviews. In recent years, the term has also come to mean acting as the central point for communication about a particular service user or family, including facilitating communication with and between other professionals.

King's Fund A charitable organization that is primarily concerned with health services and how they can be improved. Its work includes research, leadership development, and service improvement. It offers a range of resources related to health services as a basis for sharing knowledge and ideas, including through its conferences. It was founded as the Prince of Wales Hospital Fund for London in 1897, changed its name to King Edward's Hospital Fund in 1902 after the Prince of Wales became Edward VII, and in 1907 became the King's Fund.

(((∰))) SEE WEB LINKS
• Official site of the King's Fund.

kinship assessment A process involving detailed appraisal of *kinship care arrangements lasting for longer than six weeks, culminating, if successful, in approval of the arrangements by a kinship panel. The assessment includes a home visit(s) by a social worker who checks that the environment is suitable for the child to live in, carries out police and other checks on every adult who lives in the home or regularly visits, and obtains a medical report from the care-givers doctor to ensure they are in good enough health to care for the child. The key considerations are that a prospective kinship carer(s) should be able to care adequately for the child and meet their needs. *See also* KINSHIP NETWORKS; PRIVATE FOSTERING.

kinship care 1. Care of a child by a relative or relatives from within the child's wider family, such as grandparents, instead of by her/his parents. It often has the advantage of children feeling less stigmatized about having to live away from their *birth family. Kinship care may be a short-term private arrangement between parents and relatives until the child can return to the parents. Where the arrangement is likely to last longer than six weeks, the *local authority will become involved and a social worker will assess the suitability of the kinship carer(s). To ensure greater permanency and security, a kinship carer may apply to a *family court for a *Child Arrangements Order, a *Special Guardianship Order or an *Adoption Order. In some circumstances a kinship carer may be assessed as a long-term foster carer for a child. Under the Children and Young Person's Act (2008), a local authority has the discretion to make payments to kinship carers to help cover the cost of the child's care. Kinship carers of *looked-after children will receive allowances from the local authority *fostering service and be supported by a fostering social worker.

2. Also, occasionally used to refer to the role of people caring for adults (*see* CARERS). *See also* KINSHIP ASSESSMENT; KINSHIP NETWORKS; PERMANENCY PLANNING; PRIVATE FOSTERING.

kinship networks Originated in anthropology as a means of describing systems that comprise people related by descent and marriage who belong to a social group where the obligations between the related people are stronger than those existing between strangers. However, not all ideas about kinship assume biological relationships between individuals and close associations can be emphasized instead. Kinship networks may be presented visually in the form of a *genogram, which is a pictorial display constructed by social workers to make sense of family relationships surrounding a child. *See also* DIRECT WORK WITH CHILDREN; ECO MAP; LIFE MAP.

kinship panel *See* KINSHIP ASSESSMENT.

kin-work The work involved in connecting related people in different households, mainly undertaken by women. It involves maintaining relationships, arranging celebrations, visits, telephone calls, presents, cards, and so on, and the mental work that accompanies these kinds of activities. When someone is receiving care from relatives, kin-work can be one of its dimensions. *See also* CARERS; DOMESTICITY; DOMESTIC LABOUR.

Knowledge and Skills Statements Statements that describe what a social worker should be able to do by the end of her/his first year in practice. They were published by the Department for Education (2014) for social workers in children's services and by the Department of Health (2015) for social workers in adults' services. Both statements are supplementary to the overarching *Professional Capabilities Framework, which sets out the generic standards for all social workers. The Knowledge and Skills Statements are designed to strengthen and enhance the Professional Capabilities Framework by setting out what is expected more specifically of newly qualified social workers working in adults' services and children's services. Each of the statements begins by providing an overview of the role of the social worker in her/his respective service setting, followed by more detailed information about specific knowledge and skills.

Social workers working with adults need:
to apply a wide range of knowledge and skills to understand and build relationships, and work directly with individuals, their families, and *carers to enable and empower them to achieve best *outcomes. This should include undertaking *assessments, planning *care and support, and making the best use of available resources to enable people to have better lives. Social workers should enable people to experience *personalised, integrated care and support them to maintain their *independence and wellbeing, cope with change, attain the outcomes they want and need, understand and manage *risk, and participate in the life of their communities. Social work should focus on the links between the individual, their health and wellbeing and their need for relationships and connection with their families, *community, and wider society. Social workers in adult social care must understand and be able to explain the role of social work as part of the system of health and *welfare support to individuals and families. They must understand the impact of *poverty, inequality, and *diversity on social and economic opportunities and how these relate to people's health and wellbeing as well as the functioning of their

families, particularly in connection with *child protection, adult *safeguarding, and also *empowering individuals who may lack mental *capacity.

More specific knowledge and skills are considered in relation to *person-centred practice; safeguarding; mental capacity; effective assessments and outcome-based support planning; direct work with individuals and families; *supervision, critical *reflection, and analysis; the organizational context; and professional ethics and leadership. The Statement concludes by considering the level of capability required of a social worker working in an adult setting at the end of her/his first year in employment and sets out the National Framework for the Assessment of Social Workers at the end of their *Assessed and Supported Year in Employment.

The child and family social worker will:

apply a wide range of knowledge and skills to help build family relationships, resources and *resilience so that the welfare of the child remains paramount; identify the full range of risks to children and help manage those risks; ensure proportionate *intervention, including securing and supporting alternative homes for children, including those in and beyond public care placed with family and friends and for *adoption; and provide care and support to young people as they move towards *independence and adulthood. Explain and critically evaluate the role of social work as part of a system of welfare support to children and their families, including parents as vulnerable adults, and how this relates to the social contract between *citizenship and the state and the role of family, *kinship and community; explain the impact of *poverty, inequality, and *diversity on social and economic opportunities and how that relates to child welfare, family functioning and the highest [*sic*] context of child protection.

More specific knowledge and skills are considered in relation to *child development; adult *mental ill-health, substance misuse, *domestic violence, physical ill-health, and *disability; *abuse and neglect of children; effective *direct work with children and families; child and family assessment; *analysis, *decision-making, planning, and review; the law and the family justice system; professional ethics; the role of supervision and research; and the organizational context. *See also* CODE OF ETHICS; CODE OF PRACTICE; HEALTH AND CARE PROFESSIONS COUNCIL; INTERNATIONAL FEDERATION OF SOCIAL WORKERS.

Further reading: Department for Education (2014) *Knowledge and Skills for Child and Family Social Work*. Available at: http://www.gov.uk/government/uploads/system/uploads/attachment_data/file/338718/140730_Knowledge_and_skills_statement_final_version_AS_RH_Checked.pdf.

Department of Health (2015) *Knowledge and Skills Statement for Social Workers in Adult Services*. Available at: https://www.gov.uk/government/uploads/system/uploads/attachment_data/file/411957/KSS.pdf.

Korsakoff's syndrome *See* DEMENTIA.

labelling (labelling theory) Primarily associated with the work of Howard Becker (1928–), labelling theory puts forward two principal propositions: deviant acts in which people engage are not of themselves deviant. *Deviance is an attribution of the onlooker, a judgement made about the act. Deviance is, therefore, not inherent in the act but is a property conferred by the societal reaction to the act. Second, once the deviant act has been attributed (primary deviation) and is labelled negatively by powerful social actors, people may become the deviants the labellers already thought they were. As a consequence, they will be denied opportunities and positive self-images in the conventional or mainstream world and may turn to a deviant sub-culture that will affirm their deviant identity and then commit more deviant acts. Secondary deviation, sometimes called career deviation, may result from societal labelling. Thus, whereas official accounts may see their labelling as simply identifying what is there, as when, for example, a social worker refers to someone as maladjusted or damaged, labelling theorists would stress that social workers, as the labellers, have the power to say what counts as deviance and in so doing push people to become the deviants they have labelled as such.

Labelling theory became very popular in the sociology of deviance in the 1960s and early 1970s and through the sociology of deviance exercised a presence in social work education, informing radical perspectives that shifted the focus from the *service user's *individual pathology to the definitional power and reaction of society and the state's oppressive institutions. It opened up in social work consideration of the ways in which definitional power and the social rules that underpinned it played a part in constructing social divisions such as age, *class, *disability, *gender, *'race', and sexuality. For example, rowdy behaviour in a town centre on the part of working-class young people may result in their detention overnight in police cells and possibly subsequent criminal charges, whereas similar acts engaged in by rich students at elite universities may be viewed as 'letting their hair down' or 'letting off steam'. Or a young woman who is convicted of the same crime as a young man may be punished more harshly because she is seen as not only having committed the crime but as having transgressed the rules concerning what it means to be a woman. *See also* DECONSTRUCTION; LEFT REALISM; OTHER.

Further reading: Becker, H. (2008, orig. 1966) *Outsiders: Studies in the Sociology of Deviance*, Simon and Schuster.

ladder of participation *See* ARNSTEIN'S LADDER.

laissez-faire (economics) An economic perspective that sees a competitive free *market as central to producing and allocating goods and services efficiently in a way that maximizes individual *choice and reduces the role of the state, either completely or as far as possible. Traditionally, this perspective was seen as located within the *private sector's market arrangements and the *public sector was seen as driven by a different dynamic (*see* DEMOCRATIC-WELFARE-CAPITALISM). However, the perspective has been drawn on increasingly as the basis for reforming the public sector, including social work, through *privatization and *quasi-market arrangements, for example, in the *community care reforms and the sustained emphasis in recent years on *service users acting as consumers or customers. *See also* CONSUMERISM.

Lasting Power of Attorney *See* CAPACITY.

later life *See* THEORIES OF AGEING.

lead professional *See* CARE AND SUPPORT PLAN; CARE PROGRAMME APPROACH; COMMON ASSESSMENT FRAMEWORK.

lead social worker (children) A designated professional member of staff from an agency with statutory powers for *safeguarding children (either *local authority children's services, or, more rarely, the *NSPCC) who is allocated to *cases where a *child protection conference decides that a child should be the subject of a *child protection plan. Such a designated worker is a requirement for every child who is the subject of a *child protection plan. Her/his responsibilities include making sure the outline child protection plan agreed at an initial *child protection conference is developed into a detailed inter-agency plan, and s/he plays a key role in the *core group, which is responsible for implementing the plan. (The child has to be seen, on their own and with other family members, at a minimum of every twenty working days, though not necessarily by the lead social worker.) *See also* CHILD ABUSE AND NEGLECT; SAFEGUARDING CHILDREN; SIGNIFICANT HARM.

league tables *See* PERFORMANCE MANAGEMENT.

learned helplessness A condition in which someone has learned to behave helplessly and feels powerless to alter her/his situation or condition, even if the opportunity presents itself. The concept was first developed in 1967 by psychologists Martin Seligman and Steven Maier, who observed that dogs subjected to inescapable electric shocks began to behave generally as though they were helpless. It was subsequently applied to human psychology as a descriptive and explanatory term. Learned helplessness describes passive behaviour that may follow exposure to uncontrollable events. It is also used to explain a cognitive process during which expectation of helplessness is learned following repeated or inescapable conditions or events, where any avoiding actions that are attempted are ineffective. Learned helplessness can be associated with many psychological and psychiatric conditions, such as *depression, *anxiety, *phobias, shyness, and loneliness. It has also been associated with *stereotyping, *labelling, and *stigmatization, and with processes that perpetuate social *oppression, leading to its internalization. Where external forms of definition are pervasive, collusive, negative, and imbued with power, they may dominate to the extent that the individual begins to identify with the meanings imposed upon them. Attributions of *otherness, *difference, and inferiority to which the individual is externally subjected may lead to the lowering of aspiration and self-esteem. The individual may feel or be powerless to alter or exert control over the situation and may begin to behave in a helpless manner, overlooking opportunities for change. Learned helplessness has been associated with the effects of *institutionalization, and can be associated with many situations in which the individual lacks power and control, or positive affirmation of self and *identity, such as *domestic violence.

learning difficulty *See* LEARNING DISABILITY.

learning disability Intellectual impairment that results in reduced functioning in ways that vary in nature and extent from one person to another. This term has steadily replaced 'learning difficulty' (which itself replaced 'mental handicap') in social work. In schools 'learning difficulty' is still used in relation to the assessment of special educational needs. Traditionally, learning disability has been crudely defined as existing if someone had an IQ below 70. However, this has been increasingly challenged on the basis that it says very little about a person's level of functioning in different areas of her/his life. The emphasis has shifted away from IQ and towards social functioning, understanding information, ability to learn skills, and the degree to which someone can live independently.

From the nineteenth century onwards, most of the provision for people with learning disabilities was in large institutions (*see* INSTITUTIONALIZATION) and an oppressive and stigmatizing system of medical classification was developed that categorized people as 'mongols', 'cretins', and so on, a system reflected in the Mental Deficiency Act (1913). There were periodic scandals concerning the abusive nature of institutional regimes but these public scandals probably represented only the tip of the iceberg of *abuse. These days many people with learning disabilities live independently or with minimal support in shared accommodation or in supported housing, or with their families. The service philosophy that pushed *deinstitutionalization forwards, originating with Wolf Wolfensberger (1934–2011), was *'normalization' (later shifting to *social role valorization), which, put simply, emphasizes that people with learning disabilities have the right to a normal life in the *community and need to adopt 'normal' behaviour if they are to be accepted, for example, not playing with toys or wearing age-inappropriate clothes. Normalization has clearly played an important part in humanizing service approaches to people with learning disabilities but the main criticism of it is that it simply accepts what exists and does not push the boundaries of normality. The emphasis is on the adaption of the person with learning disability, not on the part of the community, though challenges to the community can result from pursuing normalization, for example, when people do not want people with learning disabilities moving into their area. Although deinstitutionalization was seen as a progressive move towards 'care in the community' when it was initiated, the extent to which people with learning disabilities are accepted in their communities and are able to participate in them is often limited. In addition to changes to where people with learning disabilities live, there has been an increasing trend to close traditional day centres, because they were seen as segregating and stigmatizing people with learning disabilities, and to replace them with individual assistance so that people can access mainstream leisure, education, and work experience opportunities, if necessary, with support. The shift to individualization of service provision is underpinned by *person-centred planning, which seeks to establish what outcomes someone wants to achieve in her/his life and then to plan how those outcomes can be reached. A person with learning disability would typically have some form of *advocacy in the PCP process. *Direct payments have also been used by some people with learning disabilities. *See also* AGE-APPROPRIATE; DAY SERVICES.

learning log (reflective log) A tool used during social work qualifying and post-qualifying programmes and the *Assessed and Supported Year in Employment. The learning log is a form of self-assessment that is used by students and qualified social workers to record their thoughts and feelings as they engage in new learning experiences. Learning logs actively encourage self-reflection, help in recognizing personal and professional values and beliefs, and promote the use of critical reflective writing.

learning style (learning styles) Refers to an individual's preferred approach(es) to acquiring knowledge, utilizing certain methods or strategies. There are many different models for the consideration of learning styles but Honey and Mumford's model is often employed in social work education. Honey and Mumford identified four main learning styles, which they describe in much greater detail than is possible here:

pragmatists, who prefer a problem-solving approach and need to understand how things work in practice;

reflectors, who prefer to observe and evaluate alternative possibilities and think before taking any action;

theorists, who prefer to understand why a particular course of action is being undertaken;

activists, who prefer to try things out and feel comfortable thinking on their feet.

People's preferred learning styles are identified by the completion and scoring of a questionnaire.

Honey and Mumford acknowledge their debt to Kolb's experiential model of learning, in which he identified four stages of learning from experience: having an experience; reviewing the experience; concluding from the experience; planning the next step. They mapped their four learning styles onto Kolb's four stages of *experiential learning, according to which stages of experiential learning would be preferred by people with preferences for particular learning styles. *See also* REFLECTIVE PRACTICE.

Further reading: Honey, P. and Mumford, A. (2000) *The Learning Styles Helper's Guide*, Peter Honey Publications.

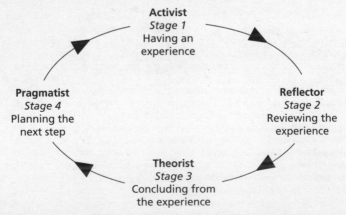

Honey and Mumford's Learning Styles and Kolb's Experiential Model of Learning

learning theory *See* BEHAVIOURISM; BEHAVIOUR MODIFICATION.

leaving care (services) (Sometimes referred to as after-care services.) The process of *looked-after children leaving *local authority care. As these young people approach the age of 18 years, when their status as a looked-after child will come to an end, local authority children's services are required by the Children (Leaving Care) Act 2000 to make provision for this important and challenging transition to be effectively negotiated. The Act requires that:

- A local authority assesses and meets the needs of young people aged 16 and 17 years who are in care or are care leavers. Wherever the young person lives, the duty rests with the local authority to keep in touch with care leavers until they are at least 21.
- Every eligible young person should receive a comprehensive *pathway plan when they turn 16, mapping out a clear route to *independence.
- Every young person should have a *personal advisor who will coordinate the provision of support and assistance. Particular emphasis is placed on helping the young person into education, training, or employment.
- An effective financial regime should be provided for care leavers by the local authority to ensure they receive comprehensive financial support.
- Continuing assistance is provided for care leavers aged between 18 to 21 years, especially with their education and employment, which will continue until the end of the agreed programme, even where this takes some young people past the age of 21 years, up to a limit of 24 years.

In response to these statutory requirements, local authorities have established care-leaving strategies, including the formation of leaving care social work teams, to support care-leavers. The legal responsibilities of local authorities towards looked-after children are set out in the *Care Leavers (England) Regulations* (2010).

See also ACCOMMODATED CHILD; DISABLED CHILDREN; FOSTERING; LOOKED-AFTER CHILDREN; PERSONAL ADVISOR; PLACEMENT.

Further reading: Department of Health (2009) *Care Leaving Strategies: A Good Practice Handbook* sets out the key issues to be considered by local authorities when developing integrated strategies to meet the support and housing needs of young people leaving care. Available at https://issuu.com/philayres/docs/leavingcarehandbook.

left realism A perspective that continues to be 'left' because it sees the origins of crime as lying in the inequalities inherent in *capitalist societies but is realistic about crime being directed mainly at working-class people and refuses to romanticize its perpetrators, as it alleges perspectives like *labelling theory have done.

legal duty *See* DUTY.

legal evidence *See* EVIDENCE.

legal power *See* POWER.

legitimation The process of making something seem right and/or acceptable. For example, *citizenship has been seen as the means of maintaining the social order in a *capitalist society by legitimating market-generated inequalities through according a status that attests to the formal equality of all citizens on the basis of their possession of the same civil, political, and social rights (*see* DEMOCRATIC-WELFARE-CAPITALISM). Another example would be that the increasing trend to shift responsibility from the state to social work's *service users themselves is legitimated by reference to this being in accordance with their seeing themselves as choice-making consumers.

letter before proceedings *See* PUBLIC LAW OUTLINE.

licence An arrangement under which an offender can be given early release from a prison sentence. While an offender is on licence, s/he can be recalled to custody. A licence can stipulate where an offender has to live and can include conditions about supervision.

life chances Now in common use but originally used by Max Weber (1864–1920) to refer to the distribution of power, made manifest in the ownership of property and access to goods and services in the market, which determines an individual's particular *class situation and hence her/his lot in life.

life course The processes of individual continuity and change from birth to death that stem from the interaction between biological, psychological, political, social, and economic events. From the 1990s onwards, 'life course' has been used increasingly in preference to 'life cycle' because the latter was seen as suggesting that people move through fixed stages that typify everyone's life, whereas the former emphasizes fluid and diverse processes in the interaction between biography and the social, political, and economic context that produces individual trajectories through life. Theorists of the life course differ in terms of whether they wish to retain the idea of life stages, although loosened up to take account of individual *differences in the transitions through them, or reject them in favour of a far greater emphasis on *choice as the means by which highly personalized pathways through life can be created. Life-course theory has been used in relation to *older people (*see* THEORIES OF AGEING). *See also* BIOGRAPHICAL APPROACHES; RESILIENCE.

life cycle *See* LIFE COURSE.

life map Used in *direct work with a child or young person to track her/his journey through life thus far, marking on it significant events and experiences, preferably with a symbol or picture for each selected event or experience and a label that identifies and dates it, at least roughly. Connectors can be used between events that show the order in which they happened. The connectors can also indicate how it felt moving from one event or experience to another, for example whether it felt as if a lesson was learnt or understanding was reached during this period of time. A life map operates in a similar way to a *life story book in assisting a child to make sense of what has happened to her/him but in a single pictorial representation rather than book form. It can be particularly helpful for *looked-after children, who may have experienced a great deal of change in their lives, to lay out everything in one place and be able to see the pattern of their lives as a whole, as well as exploring the significance of different stages within them. In this way it is a means of addressing a child's *identity in the here and now with reference to her/his past and the impact that changes and experiences have had on shaping who s/he is today. A child or young person can choose the format that s/he wants to use for a life map. Roads are a popular format, presumably because of the idea of journeying through life, and sometimes this is suggested as the format to use, in which case it may be called a life road map. Islands can be drawn with little boats travelling between each island, acting as the connectors. The possibilities are numerous: a diagram, a geographical

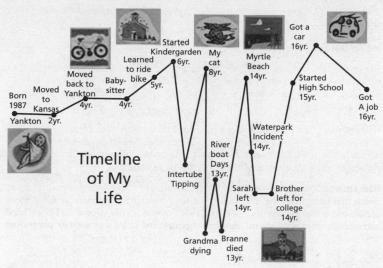

Timeline of My Life

Life map

map, a maze, a game of snakes and ladders, and so on. *See also* CHILD-CENTRED APPROACH; ECOLOGICAL APPROACH; ECO MAP; GENOGRAM; KINSHIP NETWORKS; PLAY THERAPY.

life story book (life story work) An approach used to assist a child who has been separated from her/his *birth family to make sense of her/his life and past experiences. This is particularly important for *looked-after children who may have experienced many changes in their lives and have had a number of social workers and care-givers. As a result, information about their origins and past may have become lost or forgotten. The work is usually undertaken through the compilation of a 'book' by the child and their social worker, foster carer, or adoptive parent. It records significant information and events for a child to keep and refer to as they grow up, including details of their *birth family, other significant people in their lives, and their care history. The book may be accompanied by a photo album, DVD, *genogram, and personal items and effects that relate to their previous experiences. The approach addresses disruption to the child's personal *identity and sense of self that may have occurred because of the changes and often traumatic experiences they have had. Its compilation provides an opportunity not only to generate a record the child can keep, but also, if old enough, to talk about those changes and experiences and their impact on the child. If the child was very young at the time they became looked after or adopted, a life story book commenced at the time by those responsible for their care can be referred to by the child as they grow up and enable them to find out more about their origins. *See also* CHILD-CENTRED APPROACH; DIRECT WORK WITH CHILDREN; ECOLOGICAL APPROACH; ECO MAP; GENOGRAM; KINSHIP NETWORKS; LIFE MAP; PLAY THERAPY.

Life story book

Further reading: Ryan, T. and Walker, R. (2007) *Life Story Work: A Practical Guide to Helping Children Understand their Past*, British Association for Adoption and Fostering.

listening (listening skills) Central to social work is the ability to hear and accurately understand what *service users say in a wide range of situations and when they are in many different emotional states. This involves social workers actively conveying to service users that they are listening carefully by their body posture and/or facial expression, summarizing what service users have said, and checking that they have correctly understood what was meant.

living will *See* ADVANCE DECISIONS.

local authority The unit of government that runs local services under the political leadership of elected *councillors. The amount of autonomy enjoyed by local authorities has been steadily eroded over the last forty years, with central government shaping structures, policies, and service provision at the local level to an increasing extent. The delivery of services, such as social work and other social services, is the responsibility of local authorities. The overall shape of services is determined by the legislation and policy of central government but the characteristics of particular local authorities, such as their political complexions, can influence priorities, funding, and the detailed design of services in their areas. Central–local political relationships have also shifted in recent years with *devolution. The administrations in the three countries of the UK with devolved powers (*Northern Ireland, *Scotland, and *Wales) now have substantial powers over local authorities that previously would have been exercised from Westminster. *See also* DISCRETION (LOCAL AUTHORITY); FETTERING DISCRETION.

local authority designated officer (LADO) The person involved in the management and oversight of allegations against people who work with children. Having a LADO is a requirement placed on *local authorities by Section 11 of the Children Act (2004). Her/his role is to give advice and guidance to employers and *voluntary organizations, liaise with the police and other agencies, and monitor the progress of *cases to ensure that they are dealt with as quickly as possible, consistent with a thorough and fair process.

local authority's duty to investigate *See* DUTY TO INVESTIGATE; SECTION 47 ENQUIRY.

Local Child Curfew *See* AGE OF CRIMINAL RESPONSIBILITY.

local government *See* LOCAL AUTHORITY.

Local Government Ombudsman (Commission for Local Administration) Someone who is dissatisfied with a *local authority service can make a complaint to the Local Government Ombudsman, whose function is to investigate maladministration and, where appropriate, make recommendations. (The Commission for Local Administration is the name of the official body that runs the Local Government Ombudsman service.) The complaint must usually be made within twelve months of the matter having occurred or within twelve months of the matter not having been resolved through the local authority's *complaints procedure. The Local Government Ombudsman is unlikely to investigate complaints where the complainant has a reasonably accessible legal remedy and will not accept a complaint for consideration unless it is clear that the local authority concerned has had a reasonable opportunity to deal with it first.

local protocol *See* ASSESSMENT (CHILDREN).

Local Safeguarding Children Board (LSCB) The key statutory mechanism for agreeing how relevant organizations in each local area will cooperate to safeguard and promote the welfare of children in the locality, and for ensuring the effectiveness of what they do. Relevant agencies include *local authority children's services, *health trusts, the police, *probation, *Children and Families Court Advisory and Support Service, *youth justice service, and the governor of any *secure training centre or prison in the area that detains young people. The functions of an LSCB are set out in the Children Act (2004) and defined in statutory guidance. They include establishing relevant safeguarding policies and procedures, including comprehensive inter-agency child protection procedures to which all professionals should adhere; having training strategies that equip professionals and others with the skills and knowledge needed to identify *child abuse and neglect, report their concerns, and properly manage allegations of *significant harm to children; and establishing arrangements for *child death reviews and *Serious Case Reviews. LSCBs superseded Area Child Protection Committees (ACPCs) in April 2005. By contrast ACPCs were non-statutory bodies, heavily criticized in the aftermath of the *child abuse inquiry into the death of Victoria Climbié, conducted by Herbert Laming, for often being ineffective and inconsistent in their performance. *See also* CHILD PROTECTION; SAFEGUARDING (CHILDREN).

Further reading: HM Government (2015) *Working Together to Safeguard Children: A Guide to Inter-agency Working to Safeguard and Promote the Welfare of Children*, Chapter 3. Available at https://www.gov.uk/government/uploads/system/uploads/attachment_data/file/419595/Working_Together_to_Safeguard_Children.pdf.

log *See* LEARNING LOG.

long-term placement *See* PLACEMENT; PERMANENCY PLANNING.

looked-after child (LAC) A child who is accommodated by a *local authority, a child who is the subject of an *Interim Care Order or *Care Order or *Emergency Protection Order, or a child in criminal proceedings who is remanded by a court into local authority accommodation or youth detention accommodation. (The last came into effect from 3 December 2012 as a result of the Legal Aid, Sentencing and Punishment of Offenders Act [2012] amending the Local Authority Social Services Act [1970] to bring such children into the definition of a looked-after child in the Children Act [1989].) Looked-after children may be placed with parents, foster carers (including relatives and friends), in *children's homes, in *secure accommodation, or with prospective adopters. It is a local authority's statutory duty (*see* DUTY [SPECIFIC]) to safeguard and promote the welfare of a looked-after child. *See also* LOOKED-AFTER CHILD (EDUCATION).

looked-after child (education) In recent years, greater emphasis has been placed on the educational attainment of *looked-after children because of the poor previous record in this regard. Regulations require that plans and *reviews (*see* LOOKED-AFTER CHILD REVIEW) pay particular attention to the child's educational needs and *local authorities have a specific duty to promote educational achievement under Section 52 of the Children Act (2004). In addition, looked-after children have first priority in school admissions. All looked-after children must have a *Personal Education Plan (PEP), which addresses any educational or developmental needs. The Plan considers the child's future aspirations through short- and long-term *goals. It is the responsibility of the social worker to ensure that the meetings to produce the Plan take place. Section 99 of the Children and Families Act (2014) requires local authorities to appoint an officer to promote the educational achievement of looked-after children, a person sometimes referred to as a Virtual School Head. *See also* CARE PLAN; EDUCATION, HEALTH AND CARE PLAN; INDIVIDUAL EDUCATION PLAN.

looked-after child review (looked-after child statutory review) Held at specified intervals for all *looked-after children. They are usually chaired by an *Independent Reviewing Officer and are designed to ensure that plans are in place to safeguard and promote the overall *welfare of the child and to make any recommendations that are necessary for changes to those plans. They are convened at the following intervals:

- Within twenty working days of the child becoming looked after;
- Then within three months of an initial looked-after child review;
- Then subsequent looked-after child reviews should be conducted not more than six months after any previous review.

Reviews of a looked-after child must take place sooner if the *Independent Reviewing Officer (IRO) requests one; a social worker's assessment is that a child's welfare is not being adequately safeguarded and promoted; a review would not otherwise occur before the child ceases to be detained in a *Youth Offenders Institution or a *Secure Training Centre, or accommodated on *remand; or the *local authority proposes to cease to provide accommodation for a child. The requirement to hold looked-after child reviews ends when the child ceases to be looked after or when the local authority has the authority to place a child for *adoption, in which case there is a requirement to hold adoption reviews.

loss Feelings of having been deprived that are associated with significant changes or separations. Although loss may be thought of mainly in relation to *bereavement, it can be an important element in many other situations that social workers encounter, for example, when a child is removed from her/his parents or when an older person moves into residential care. How someone reacts to a loss may be influenced by how they have experienced earlier losses in their life and how they dealt with them. The experience of loss is highly individual and may involve any of the following, either separately or in combination: anger, *anxiety, apathy, bewilderment, *depression, fear, hopelessness, panic, restlessness, tiredness. However, this is by no means an exhaustive list and individual responses will vary widely. Assisting children and adults to work through experiences of loss was traditionally seen as one of the central roles of social work but it is increasingly side-lined in contemporary practice. For example, whereas at one time a social worker might have spent time listening to an older person who had moved into residential care talking about what the loss of a home and neighbourhood and the associated friendships meant to her/him, and perhaps helping her/him to identify the strengths s/he had gained from other losses in life and how they might be brought to bear on the present loss, the role that is now likely to be occupied by a social worker in such a situation, which probably focuses heavily on practical arrangements, is liable to mean that this aspect of social work cannot be prioritized. *See also* DEATH AND DYING.

loyalty *See* VOICE.

LSCB *See* LOCAL SAFEGUARDING CHILDREN BOARD.

madness *See* INSANITY.

magical thinking Children thinking that they are responsible for things that happen in their lives. For example, social workers may encounter children who blame themselves for their parents separating or dying, or for the *abuse they have suffered. Particularly prevalent between the ages of four and eight, but can occur at other ages.

magistrates Lay people who hear cases in the magistrates' court, usually sitting as a panel of three. They have training for their role but are not legally qualified and are supposed to represent the local *community. The magistrates' courts deal with a high proportion of the criminal cases that come to trial. For young people under 18, there is a special magistrates' court called the *youth court. Magistrates can also hear *Care Proceedings cases.

magistrates' court *See* MAGISTRATES.

Makaton A language that uses signs and symbols to help people communicate. It is used to support spoken language, and whenever possible, the signs and symbols are used with speech in the same order as the spoken words. It is primarily used by and with people with *learning disabilities, although others who struggle to make themselves understood and to understand others can also use it to connect with people. The signs and symbols are pictorially based, and it is far simpler than *British Sign Language. Makaton can increase confidence and self-esteem, and when it assists in the development of speech, its signs and symbols can be gradually dropped.

(⊕) SEE WEB LINKS
• Official site of the Makaton Charity.

maladministration *See* LOCAL GOVERNMENT OMBUDSMAN.

management The processes of supervision, control, and coordination in organizations or the people employed to perform these functions, as in 'the management' or 'management won't like it'. Management literature stresses the range of tasks that managers undertake, for example, getting things done through people, setting objectives, deciding on the means to reach the objectives, and solving problems that frustrate their achievement. Typically, there is also an emphasis on communicating, motivating, monitoring, evaluating, delegating, and developing individual people and teams. Put like this, management could be interpreted and practised in many different ways but in recent years the dominant approaches have been shaped by *managerialism. Conventionally a distinction is made between 'line management', which is concerned with operational matters, and 'specialist management' (such as human resources, accountancy, legal advice, etc.) that supports operations. Social work organizations have a clearly identifiable line management system (or managerial hierarchy), with a designated line manager for every social worker. *See also* BUSINESS EXCELLENCE; BUSINESS ORIENTATION; EUROPEAN FOUNDATION OF QUALITY MANAGEMENT MODEL; MANAGERIAL CYBERNETICS.

managerial cybernetics A perspective on the process of *management that has been very influential in social work and the public sector generally. It advocates: identifying the organization's objectives; developing *performance indicators to reflect the objectives; and setting targets in relation to the performance indicators. Managers then choose actions to take and direct effort towards achieving the targets and progress is monitored against the performance indicators. For example, a *local authority children's services might have an objective to have more *looked-after children living in families. One of its performance indicators might be to have more children adopted than the average achieved by comparable local authorities. A target would then be set related to this performance indicator, for example, increasing the number of children adopted by 25 per cent during the next twelve months. Central to the cybernetic model of management is *feedback on what has been achieved against the performance indicators, and what will be achieved going forwards in the light of the *feedback. However, the literature notes that because the people involved can anticipate the way in which the performance indicators work, the use of the cybernetic model of management can have unintended consequences:

Tunnel vision An emphasis by management on phenomena that are quantified in the performance management system at the expense of unquantified aspects of performance.

Sub-optimization The pursuit of narrow local objectives at the expense of overall objectives.

Myopia The pursuit of short-term targets at the expense of long-term strategic objectives.

Measure fixation Despite a measure not fully capturing all of the dimensions of an associated objective, the pursuit of the reported measure rather than furthering the associated objective.

Misrepresentation The deliberate manipulation of data.

Misinterpretation The performance indicator system misinterpreting the data provided.

Gaming Minimizing the apparent scope for performance improvement to avoid increased expectations and higher targets in the future.

Ossification Organizational paralysis brought about by an excessively rigid performance evaluation system.

See also BEST VALUE; BUSINESS ORIENTATION; EUROPEAN FOUNDATION OF QUALITY MANAGEMENT MODEL; MANAGEMENT; MANAGERIALISM.

managerialism The *discourse concerning the transformative power of private business *management structures, systems, and techniques when they are applied to public services, such as social work, in pursuit of *economy, efficiency, and effectiveness. Managerialism has resulted in wide-ranging structural, organizational, and managerial changes in social work and other public (and also increasingly voluntary) services in recent years in many parts of the world. Some of the key features of managerialism are:

- Progress is seen as lying in the achievement of continuing increases in productivity;
- Increased productivity will come, in part, from the application of information technology;
- 'Management' is a separate and distinct organizational function;
- Measurement and quantification, for example, in the form of *performance indicators, are needed in order to provide *feedback to managers;
- *Markets or market-type mechanisms should be used to deliver services;
- Contractual relationships should be introduced wherever possible;
- Customer orientation should be at the forefront of services;
- The boundaries between the *public, *private, and *voluntary sectors should be blurred.

Underpinning all of these features of managerialism is the advocacy of granting greater power to managers, captured in the dictum that they have 'the right to manage'. Their role is seen as central to the improvement of organizational performance, which is to be achieved by limiting the *discretion of professionals, ostensibly in the interests of empowering the 'customer'. Managerialism is presented as technical, objective, and neutral, claiming to reveal the self-evident best way to do things. Accordingly, turning any problem into a managerial issue tends to obscure any political and/or ethical difficulties it may pose. For example, services for adults are now shrouded in technical language, the use of standardized forms and the application of *eligibility criteria. This aura of objectivity obscures the basis of decisions about how much to spend on services for *older people, people with *learning disabilities, and so on, what services to provide, and how to provide them. These decisions about how much to spend on which services and how they will be provided are decisions about priorities that are inextricably intertwined with political and ethical issues, even though these are obscured by managerialism. *See also* BEST VALUE; BUSINESS EXCELLENCE; BUSINESS ORIENTATION; BOUNDED RATIONALITY; MANAGERIAL CYBERNETICS; MARKET; NEO-LIBERALISM; NEW PUBLIC MANAGEMENT.

Further reading: Harris, J. (2003) *The Social Work Business*, Routledge.

managing authority *See* DEPRIVATION OF LIBERTY SAFEGUARDS.

manic depression *See* BIPOLAR DISORDER.

MAPPA *See* MULTI-AGENCY PUBLIC PROTECTION ARRANGEMENTS.

marginalization The process by which someone or some group, or their views, or contribution, are rendered marginal through the exercise of power. For example, a *looked-after child's views on her/his future might be marginalized by professionals. *See also* MORAL PANIC; OBJECTIFICATION; OTHER; OUT-GROUP.

market The arrangements for exchanging goods and services between buyers and sellers. The total amount of a particular good or service available for purchase is referred to as supply, and the total amount that people want to purchase is called demand. A number of theoretical assumptions are routinely made about markets, despite being rarely the case empirically. First, there is an assumption of perfect competition because there are supposed to be so many sellers and buyers that no one on either side has an undue influence in determining the market price. Secondly, that competition between sellers will lead to falls in prices for buyers. Thirdly, that markets mean the individual consumer is powerful as a consequence of distributing her/his income between goods and services, and so shaping what comes to the market. During the period of the post-war *welfare state, market arrangements were not applicable to public goods and services, which were seen as needing to be planned and allocated by the state, in accordance with principles derived from *citizenship. However, under the influence of *neo-liberalism, the assumption that public services should be driven by a different dynamic has been increasingly questioned, with the introduction of arrangements that resemble those of markets (*see* CARE MARKET; QUASI-MARKET).

market position statement *See* CARE MARKET.

market shaping *See* CARE MARKET.

Marxist social work The initial driving force in the development of *radical social work that from the late 1960s onwards repudiated the *psychodynamic *casework tradition with its concentration on *individual pathology in favour of highlighting the social fall-out from capitalism. As well as pointing to the individual and social devastation caused by the impact of *class-based inequality on life chances, Marxist social work highlights the lack of value accorded to those who are not involved in productive work, and the stigma and disadvantage that attaches to them. Capitalist *ideology locates the source of social problems within individuals who are seen as needing the attention of a wide variety of agencies, including social work, which are variously responsible for their supervision, control, treatment, and punishment, depending on whether they are seen, in Spitzer's (1975) graphic terms, as 'social junk' (dependent and needing to be cared for), or 'social dynamite' (dangerous and needing to be controlled). In contrast, Marxist social work draws attention to the collective basis for the problems people experience and advocates action by *service users and social workers to address the unjust social and economic conditions that create those problems. In addition, one strand of Marxist social work sees the day-to-day practice of social work as a site with openings for resistance and class struggle because of the contradictions that exist and the opportunities that exist to exploit them. Another strand sees social work as unequivocally part of the capitalist state's repressive *ideological apparatus, with social workers acting as its 'soft cops', and regards the potential for resistance as only existing through workplace trade unionism and radical action out of office hours. *See also* AGENTS OF SOCIAL CONTROL; RADICAL SOCIAL WORK.

masculinity (masculinities) While 'male' refers to being a certain physical sex, masculinity is the social practices and cultural representations that are associated with being a man. It is concerned with the social construction of men in the contexts in which they live, the positions they occupy, the characteristics that are attributed to them, and the way in which they exercise power in relationships and in society. Some prefer to refer to 'masculinities' in order to avoid the impression that there is one monolithic concept of what it means to be a man, and to emphasize that ways of being a man and cultural representations of men vary historically and culturally between different societies and between different men within the same society. This allows discussions of masculinity to acknowledge the way in which it intersects with other social divisions such as *class, *ethnicity, and sexuality, and the different forms it takes as a result. Social workers encounter a variety of masculinities in the course of their work, and they need to understand how they are constructed and played out in specific situations, such as *domestic violence. There is a consistent pattern of social work focusing on women, even if there are men around, because much of social work is concerned with areas of life that have traditionally been defined as part of women's caring role. This often results in women being blamed when things go wrong. For example, if a man abuses a child, the primary focus may be on a woman's 'failure to protect' the child. In some areas of social work, interventions have been developed with men that challenge their power, for example, by confronting and countering the rationalizing and minimizing strategies of perpetrators of *violence against women, and by providing *anger management programmes for male offenders. *See also* FEMININITY; GENDER; GENDER STEREOTYPING.

Maslow's hierarchy of needs *See* HIERARCHY OF NEEDS.

masquerade An adaptive response by individual *older people who are pressured to deny their experiences of their ageing selves and instead are constrained to present a youthful façade or masquerade, because of the hostility to and rejection of ageing by the wider society. *See also* THEORIES OF AGEING.

maternal deprivation *See* ATTACHMENT.

McDonaldization The process through which the principles of the fast-food restaurant come to dominate more and more sectors of society. George Ritzer argues that the fast-food restaurant symbolizes key elements of contemporary life that have resulted from social changes in recent years. He identifies four principles at the heart of the process: efficiency, predictability, calculability, and control through non-human technology. These principles have become widespread in the *management of a wide range of organizations including social work. *See also* ECONOMY, EFFICIENCY, AND EFFECTIVENESS; MANAGERIALISM.

Further reading: Ritzer, G. (2008, 5th edn.) *The McDonaldization of Society*, Pine Forge Press.

McNaughton Rules *See* INSANITY.

means test Determination of whether someone is eligible to receive a benefit or a service on the basis of drawing up a financial threshold and assessing whether her/his resources fall below the threshold, as in the *assessment of entitlement to some social security benefits (means-tested benefits), and when social workers complete assessments of financial resources as part of adults' *needs assessments. *See also* CHARGING FOR SERVICES.

mediation A non-adversarial process through which people involved in a dispute negotiate with each other with the assistance of a mediator (or sometimes two mediators), and seek to reach agreement. Mediation usually focuses on future rather than past behaviour, and is most often thought of in relation to family problems, such as when a relationship has broken down. In such circumstances, it can be used to consider any of the issues arising from the breakdown including financial arrangements, care of the children, and the future of the family home. However, mediation is also used in other ways, for example, to help resolve disputes between neighbours and in workplace situations. *See also* CHILD AND FAMILY REPORTER; PARENTING PLAN.

medical model The dominant paradigm in medicine since the nineteenth century that stresses the presence of an objectively identifiable disease or malfunction in the body, seen as a machine, with the patient regarded as the target for intervention by doctors using the latest drugs, technology, and surgical procedures. The reach of the medical model is now extensive. For example, there is a critique of the way in which childbirth has been medicalized, with women being subjected to extensive use of technology and intrusive practices. *See also* BIO-PSYCHO-SOCIAL MODEL; IATROGENIC DISEASE; MEDICAL MODEL (PSYCHIATRY).

medical model (psychiatry) The use of the *medical model in psychiatry is based on the physical sciences paradigm underpinning other branches of medicine. In psychiatry, the approach is rooted in a belief that the diagnosis of mental disorder is achieved by the accurate identification of an objective disease process. The medical model in psychiatry emerged from the mid-nineteenth century onwards, shifting previous moral and religious frameworks of explanation towards an illness framework. Early medical approaches focused on the premise that the causes of *mental illness were biological or physiological in origin, and could be treated in the same way as other physical illnesses. The research and treatment of mental illness, and the discipline of psychiatry grew in status with an accompanying locus of practice created by the widespread development of *asylums. The continued dominance of the medical model is reflected in the role that psychiatrists, hospitals, psychiatric units, health services, and pharmacological treatments still play in the management and treatment of mental health problems.

Criticisms of the medical model have arisen because it is argued that the scientific paradigm upon which the model is based is not supported by subsequent understandings of the causes of mental health problems. Nineteenth-century beliefs that mental illness was caused by physical disorders of the brain have been replaced by the understanding that mental illness consists of a disturbance in one or more areas of human functioning: thoughts, feelings, or behaviours. The classification systems used in the process of *diagnosis (*Diagnostic and Statistical Manual of Mental Disorders* and *International Classification of Diseases*) are modelled on the scientific paradigm, but there are no single diagnostic tests for mental illnesses such as there are for a large number of physical illnesses. Critics argue that professional *diagnoses are based instead on subjective interpretations of human emotions and behaviour, an *assessment of the patient's symptoms, and an evaluation of their *case history. Diagnosis can be influenced by the social, cultural, and political contexts in which psychiatric training takes place, differences of professional opinion can exist between and amongst psychiatrists, and psychiatric knowledge is constantly changing. Difficulties in achieving scientific certainty in respect of psychiatric diagnosis were illustrated in 1973 by sociologist David Rosenhan's study *On Being Sane in Insane Places*. Rosenhan sent a number of volunteers (pseudo-patients) to a psychiatric facility, reporting a variety of fake symptoms. All were given diagnoses of mental disorder and admitted to the facility; some were detained for months. Rosenhan revealed the experiment to the relevant authorities, and reversed his approach in a second study by asking staff to identify fake patients, though this time none had been sent. Alert to the first study, staff went on to identify a number of genuine patients as imposters. Rosenhan's findings created much controversy about the scientific status conferred on psychiatric diagnosis, and was a factor in a review of the classification of *schizophrenia in the *DSM*. The study also highlighted the issues of *labelling taking precedence over other observable problems and behaviours in the context of psychiatric care and treatment. This was illustrated when one pseudo-patient, arriving early for dinner, was described by staff as having an oral acquisitive nature. When pseudo-patients became aggressive, this was interpreted as a symptom of the disorder, rather than a rational response to coercive treatment.

Social theorists and some psychiatrists argue that emotions and behaviours referred to as symptoms are not pathological medical phenomena, but a meaningful and normal part of the human spectrum of experience. Pathologizing such outward human expressions by treating them as symptoms that need to be managed or controlled reinforces the perception that certain feelings and behaviours are socially or even politically unacceptable. The medical model has also been criticized for adopting a polarized understanding of mental illness. Lacking a multidimensional approach that captures the uniqueness of individuals, important information that might assist a fuller understanding of a person's mental distress might be overlooked. Advocates of the *social model of mental illness argue that social frameworks address some of the limitations of the medical model by introducing different perspectives that broaden an understanding of mental health problems. It is now common for mental health services to recognize the multifaceted nature of mental health difficulties by adopting a *biopsychosocial approach to treatment and intervention, rather than a purely medical model approach. *See also* HEARING VOICES; MENTAL DISORDER; MENTAL STATE EXAMINATION.

mental capacity *See* CAPACITY.

mental capacity assessment *See* CAPACITY; DEPRIVATION OF LIBERTY SAFEGUARDS.

mental disorder A generic term used to indicate a departure from the norm of mental health and wellbeing, and used broadly to describe a range of mental health problems, including severe disorders such as *schizophrenia and *bipolar disorder. This concept implies that the individual was once 'well-ordered' and requires care, treatment, and support to restore her/him to that state. There are several models of mental disorder, each framework reflecting a different conceptual understanding of mental disorder and how or if it should be addressed. The term is most commonly used in the legal context when considering issues of compulsion under the Mental Health Act (1983). Beliefs about mental disorder, as well as concepts of mental *capacity, free will, determinism, and social responsibility, combine to shape views about the role of law in this field. The definition of mental disorder is of central importance to the Mental Health Act (1983) because a diagnosis of mental disorder must be present in order for the scope and powers of the Act to apply to an individual. Section 1(2) of the Act, as amended by the Mental Health Act (2007), has removed specific classifications of mental disorders, leaving a broad and generic definition as 'any disorder or disability of the mind'. The amended definition means that the scope of the Act is much greater and includes disorders previously excluded. There has been considerable objection to and debate about the amended wider definition and its implications for practice, particularly because the Act has powers to deprive individuals of their civil liberties. The *Code of Practice to the Mental Health Act 1983* provides guidance on possible examples of mental disorder, for instance *affective disorders such as *depression and *bipolar disorder, *schizophrenia and *delusional disorders, organic mental disorders such as *dementia and delirium, mental disorders caused by brain injury, *personality disorders, *eating disorders, disorders caused by substance misuse, *autistic spectrum disorders, and *learning disabilities. While the process of *diagnosis is undertaken by doctors, judgements about mental disorder in the practice setting may be made by a range of people, for instance police, social workers, *magistrates, and *First-tier Tribunal members. By itself a diagnosis or belief of mental disorder is not sufficient to warrant detention under the Act. The nature or degree of disorder must be considered serious enough to warrant compulsion. *See also* MEDICAL MODEL; MEDICAL MODEL (PSYCHIATRY); MENTAL ILLNESS; MENTAL IMPAIRMENT.

mental handicap *See* LEARNING DISABILITY.

Mental Health Act Commission (MHAC) Established by the Mental Health Act (1983) to provide a safeguard for people detained in hospital under the powers of the Act. On 1 April 2009, the functions of the MHAC in England transferred to a combined regulator for health and adult social care, the *Care Quality Commission.

mental health assessment *See* DEPRIVATION OF LIBERTY SAFEGUARDS; MENTAL STATE EXAMINATION.

Mental Health Foundation Brings together knowledge from research and practice on a wide range of topics related to mental health, as well as initiating projects that address the issues raised.

(((∰))) SEE WEB LINKS
• Official site of the Mental Health Foundation.

Mental Health Review Tribunal (MHRT) *See* FIRST-TIER TRIBUNAL (MENTAL HEALTH).

Mental Health Task Force A *non-departmental public body set up in 2015 to create a national strategy for mental health for the National Health Service in England, which published a report, *Five Year Forward View for Mental Health for the NHS in England* (2016). The TaskForce was chaired by Paul Farmer of *MIND, and included people from health and social care, charities, and *experts by experience. The TaskForce's report was accepted by the government and the NHS, and the main recommendations included:

• Providing mental health support to an extra one million people by 2020–1;
• Ensuring people in crisis have access to mental health care twenty-four hours a day, seven days a week;
• Achieving parity of esteem between mental health and physical health care;
• Requiring all areas to have multi-agency *suicide prevention plans in place by 2017;
• Ensuring all hospital accident and emergency departments have psychiatric liaison services;
• Extending the provision of *evidence-based psychological services;
• Improving access of children and young people to high-quality mental health care;
• Ensuring more women have access to perinatal mental health care.

See also CHILD AND ADOLESCENT MENTAL HEALTH SERVICES.

mental illness A clinically diagnosed set of symptoms or behaviours associated with psychological distress and interference with aspects of daily living. Although it is intended to be understood in a specifically clinical sense, it is often used interchangeably with the broader concept of *mental disorder. Mental illness is commonly understood to refer to conditions that involve psychiatric intervention, including *affective (mood) disorders, *depression, *anxiety disorders, and *schizophrenia. The concept of severe or serious mental illness (SMI) is often encountered in practice, and while there is no universally agreed definition of SMI, it is generally understood to include psychotic disorders, schizophrenia, and *bipolar disorder. In the legal context, reference to mental illness in the Mental Health Act (1983) was removed with the amendments introduced by the Mental Health Act (2007) (*see* MENTAL DISORDER). However, no definition of mental illness was provided in the 1983 Act, in part because there was an assumption that the presentation of someone who is suffering from mental illness is obvious and the obvious did not need to be defined. This means that the definition of mental illness is established operationally by the clinical judgement made in each individual *case. *See also* BIO-PSYCHO-SOCIAL MODEL; *DIAGNOSTIC AND STATISTICAL MANUAL OF MENTAL DISORDERS*; *INTERNATIONAL CLASSIFICATION OF DISEASES*; MEDICAL MODEL; MEDICAL MODEL (PSYCHIATRY); MENTAL IMPAIRMENT; MENTAL STATE EXAMINATION.

mental impairment A condition that affects mental functioning, for example, *learning disabilities, *dementia, or certain mental health conditions. Mental functioning may include social, intellectual, interpersonal, and *cognitive functioning. Establishing the degree and nature of an individual's mental functioning can be extremely important in matters of law, for instance, signing contracts or criminal defence (*see* INSANITY). In legal frameworks the scope of mental impairment can be broad and might include *dementia, *insanity, delirium arising from physical injuries, intoxication, and the side-effects of medication. Impairment may be temporary or permanent. Entitlement to social security benefits and services may also be influenced by issues of mental impairment. The criteria in these *cases is often narrower, and the condition is usually expected to be permanent. A doctor's certification of mental impairment is usually required. Mental impairment and severe mental impairment were included as specific classifications of *mental disorder in the Mental Health Act (1983), in which they referred to *learning disabilities. They were defined as 'a state of arrested or incomplete development of mind, which includes significant impairment of intelligence and social functioning'. The categories were removed by amending legislation (Mental Health Act 2007) when a much broader definition of mental disorder was introduced (*see* MENTAL DISORDER). The Mental Capacity Act (2005) states that the inability to make a decision must be caused by an impairment of or disturbance in the functioning of the mind or brain. This includes psychiatric disorders, learning disabilities, dementia, brain damage, or confusion caused by toxic substances. *See also* CAPACITY; MENTAL ILLNESS; MENTAL STATE EXAMINATION.

mental incapacity *See* CAPACITY.

mental state examination (MSE) The principal psychiatric *assessment tool used during interviews with patients. Information is gathered concerning appearance, speech, mood, thought, cognitive state, and *insight. No single aspect of the MSE is by itself diagnostic, rather it is the combination of *symptoms and signs that might suggest a *diagnosis. The patient's own account of her/his situation is considered alongside information that may have been gathered from significant others and other professionals. During the MSE it is important that the doctor is aware of the cultural norms that are meaningful to the patient. *See also* MEDICAL MODEL; MEDICAL MODEL (PSYCHIATRY); MENTAL DISORDER; MENTAL ILLNESS; MENTAL IMPAIRMENT.

mentoring The process through which someone with relevant experience offers advice and/or support to someone else. For example, in work with young offenders, adult volunteers, who may come from similar backgrounds to the young offenders, spend time with them to give them the benefit of their experience. In social work, in addition to formal *supervision provided by a line manager, a newly qualified social worker may be mentored by a more experienced fellow social worker.

Merton-compliant *See* AGE ASSESSMENT.

methadone A synthetic opiate commonly used in liquid form with people addicted to opiates such as heroin as a substitute. It has to be medically prescribed and has the effect of preventing withdrawal symptoms for people who cease using or reduce the use of opiates. *See also* ADDICTION; COMMUNITY DRUG TEAM.

methodology The study of research methods that includes learning how to use particular techniques and theoretical questions, the basis for research, and how research should be undertaken. There has been a long-standing discussion about whether or not social research should (or even can) be 'positivist'; that is, whether it should follow the methods of the natural sciences as far as possible. There is also a commonly made distinction between quantitative methods, which are usually large-scale questionnaire-based approaches that produce statistical results, and qualitative methods, which are concerned with people's understandings and meanings, and are usually pursued through interviews and observation. *See also* ACTION-RESEARCH; APPLIED SOCIAL RESEARCH.

MHAC *See* MENTAL HEALTH ACT COMMISSION.

MHRT *See* MENTAL HEALTH REVIEW TRIBUNAL.

micropolitics The exercise of power in everyday life, which Michel Foucault (1926–84) conceptualized as operating in a capillary fashion, with a multiplicity of power relations at work in every situation, at every point in time. One of Foucault's interests was in the micropolitics of the relationships between experts and their clientele. This suggests that social workers encounter micropolitics in every aspect of their working lives, for example, in the office setting, in their relationships with *service users, and in service users' relationships with each other. *See also* DISCOURSE; GAZE; GOVERNMENTALITY.

milestones *See* CHILD DEVELOPMENT.

MIND A *charitable organization that provides information, support, and advice about mental health issues, and campaigns to promote and protect good mental health through improving policies for and attitudes towards people with mental health problems. In addition to the activities of the UK-wide organization, local MIND associations develop and run local services.

((⊕)) SEE WEB LINKS
• Official site of MIND.

mindfulness Being fully present and aware of experiences by observing them as they occur, being non-judgemental and accepting what is happening in the here and now. Mindfulness is learned and reinforced through sustained and regular practice of specific techniques that can be incorporated into daily life. There has been an explosion of interest in mindfulness generally and some argue that it has a place in social work for social workers and *service users. Advocates of mindfulness do not argue that practising its techniques will prevent stress occurring or magic it away when it occurs, but suggest that it can help social workers manage stress more effectively. *See also* DIALECTICAL BEHAVIOUR THERAPY; REFLECTIVE PRACTICE; REFLEXIVITY.

Further reading: Hick, S. (2009) *Mindfulness and Social Work*, Lyceum Books.

minimum intervention The practice of intervening as little as possible in response to crime because of *labelling theory's arguments concerning *deviancy amplification, i.e., that the formal attribution of a deviant *identity through prosecution, court appearance, and sentencing can increase the chances of someone reoffending. Minimum intervention has been most developed in the field of *youth justice where it is usually referred to as *'diversion' (from prosecution and custody). Although primarily associated with crime, similar arguments can be made about its use in relation to other issues, for example mental health problems, where formal attribution of a *mental illness label, and admission to a psychiatric unit may confirm someone's deviant (or, as Goffman put it, 'spoiled') identity. (*See* Rosenhan's experiment under MEDICAL MODEL [PSYCHIATRY] for a telling example.) *See also* DEVIANCE; MORAL CAREER; SYSTEM MANAGEMENT.

miracle question *See* SOLUTION-FOCUSED THERAPY.

missing from care A *looked-after child who is not where they are supposed to be living or not at some other place where they are expected to be such as school, and whose whereabouts are unknown.

missing patients *See* ABSENT WITHOUT EXPLANATION.

mixed economy of care (mixed economy of welfare) The provision of services from a variety of sources in the *public, *private, and *voluntary sectors through *quasi-market arrangements. The concept (and practice) first impacted on social work through the Conservatives' *community care reforms in the 1990s, but now has widespread support across the parliamentary political spectrum, not just for services for adults but also for children (for example, the mixed economy that now exists in the provision of foster carers). As a consequence of the mixed economy of care, the role of *local authorities in directly providing services has decreased significantly, while the roles of the *private and *voluntary sectors have increased accordingly. *See also* CARE MARKET; MARKET.

mobility The capacity to get around. Although *impairments in bodily functioning can place restrictions on people's mobility, the *social model of disability would point to the restrictions caused by the physical environment, such as problems with access to buildings and transport. *See also* DISABILITY; SOCIAL MODEL OF DISABILITY.

modelling *See* BEHAVIOUR MODIFICATION.

models of assessment (adults) *See* EXCHANGE MODEL OF ASSESSMENT.

modernization (modernization agenda) Literally the process of bringing something up-to-date. However, it is particularly associated with the *New Labour governments' (1997–2010) modernization agenda, which affected every aspect of central and local government. As far as public services like social work were concerned, they were depicted as rigid and outdated as a consequence of their origins in the post-war *welfare state. More individually attuned lifestyle-oriented consumers were said to demand services that were more in keeping with their experiences of consumer *culture in the rest of their lives. Accordingly, New Labour stressed the need for 'modernization', as a shorthand term for bringing the *public sector into line with the modern practices of *private-sector organizations. In seeking to achieve the changes it desired, New Labour defined social work's objectives at national level, set outcomes to be achieved locally, and monitored the results. An emphasis on local leadership, entrepreneurialism, and a strong performance culture with regard to standards and quality was pinned to the achievement of targets set by central government (*Modernizing Social Services*, Department of Health 1998). The *Quality Strategy for Social Care* (Department of Health 2000) laid out the tools for social work's modernization: national service frameworks, national standards, service models, and local performance measures against which progress within an agreed timescale would be monitored. The *Quality Strategy for Social Care* was explicitly keyed into the *Best Value programme and was meant to introduce 'a culture of continuous improvement'. Though subsequent governments have not had an all-embracing modernization programme on a par with New Labour's, the concept of modernization is still invoked as an argument in favour of policy and practice change. When this happens, modernization is presented as a neutral, technical, objective phenomenon that all right-thinking, progressive, and modern people will want to support. Thus the banner of modernization is presented as uniting the orientations and interests of all participants in change, obscuring any tensions, dilemmas, and contradictions that may be involved. *See also* CONSUMERISM; MANAGERIALISM; PERFORMANCE MANAGEMENT.

Further reading: Harris, J. and White, V. (2009) *Modernising Social Work: Critical Considerations*, Policy Press.

monitoring and review Social work activities that involve taking stock of how things are going in work with *services users. Monitoring is part of day-to-day social work and involves keeping a 'watching brief' on the service user's *needs, and the effectiveness of the service(s) being provided. A review goes beyond the ongoing checking involved in monitoring, and is a more formal and comprehensive mechanism for considering progress. Many aspects of social work have stipulated time intervals, some of them statutory, concerning the frequency with which reviews should take place, and reviews usually involve a meeting of all interested parties. Plans are updated, if necessary, at the end of the review. *See also* LOOKED-AFTER CHILD REVIEW; REVIEW OF CARE AND SUPPORT PLANS; REVIEW TEAMS.

mood disorder *See* AFFECTIVE DISORDER.

mood stabilizers A group of medicines that are prescribed in psychiatry to protect against mood swings. The main agents are lithium carbonate and carbamazepine, but anti-convulsant (anti-epileptic) medicines, and sodium valproate are increasingly used as alternatives. In the UK, these alternative drugs are not currently licensed for long-term use in *bipolar disorders. Blood tests are an integral part of lithium management to monitor kidney and thyroid function, and also lithium toxicity. Weight gain is a significant side-effect of lithium therapy. Carbamazepine can cause anaemia and annual blood tests are recommended.

moral career A concept developed by Erving Goffman (1922–82) (in *Stigma* 1963) to refer to the changes in character attributed to people who are stigmatized, a process not confined to their present *labelling, but extended to the reconstruction of a person's previous life so that it contains a narrative consistent with her/his current *deviance.

moral panic Coined by Stan Cohen (1942–2013) in his *Folk Devils and Moral Panics* (2002; orig. 1972) to describe an exaggerated societal reaction, fuelled by the media, to what begin as minor acts of *deviance. He studied 'mods' and 'rockers', gangs of youths with different youth *culture identifications, and the fighting in which they engaged at seaside resorts. The over-reaction to the initial skirmishes led to a process of *deviancy amplification that had the effect of attracting more participants. As well as seeing the societal response as an over-reaction, Cohen argued that it served the function of diverting attention from issues the dominant interests in society would rather obscure, and also reinforced a sense of social solidarity; 'they', the minority, were different from 'us', the majority. Since Cohen's work in the 1960s, the term has become more widely used and broadened to signify the process of stirring up social concern about an issue, for example the period during which *HIV/AIDS was depicted as the 'gay plague', and the periodic upsurges of horror about the ageing population expressed in terms like the 'rising tide' and *'demographic time bomb'. *See also* OTHER.

morbidity rate The incidence of a disease or disorder in a population usually expressed as the rate at which it occurs per 100,000 of the population.

motivational approach (motivational interviewing) An approach that can be used when *service users want to make changes in their lives. Its use has been most developed in drug and alcohol services but is capable of much wider application. Although the skills involved in using this approach in some situations need to be substantial, the basic principles are readily comprehensible. They involve getting across to the *service user that the social worker understands how things are for her/him; not getting into confrontations with the service user, but instead offering alternative explanations or ways of thinking; if the service user has tried to change previously and failed to do so, getting across that failing is not an inevitable consequence of change attempts in the future; and pointing out the disparities between where the service user is now and where s/he would like to be as a basis for setting her/his own *goals, which the social worker can support, rather than the social worker suggesting goals.

Further reading: Miller, W. and Rollnick, S. (2002, 2nd edn.) *Motivational Interviewing: Preparing People for Change*, Guildford Press.

mourning *See* BEREAVEMENT.

MSE *See* MENTAL STATE EXAMINATION.

Multi-agency Public Protection Arrangements (MAPPA) The mechanism through which agencies in local areas coordinate and discharge their statutory responsibilities to protect the public by managing violent and *sex offenders. Police, Prison, and Probation Services comprise what is referred to as the 'Responsible Authority' (RA) under the Criminal Justice Act (2003), and as such are charged with the duty to ensure MAPPA are established in their area, and responsibility is discharged for the identification, *assessment, and management of *risk in relation to all MAPPA offenders. Other agencies are under a duty to cooperate with the RA, including *local authority social work services and local *housing authorities, the latter providing accommodation for some offenders. MAPPA members meet on a regular basis at multi-agency public protection meetings to undertake and review risk assessments on violent and sex offenders, devise risk management plans, and review the progress of plans. *See also* PERSONS POSING A RISK TO CHILDREN; SCHEDULE 1 OFFENDER.

Further reading: Ministry of Justice, HM Prison Service and National Offender Management Service (2016) *Multi-agency Public Protection Arrangements Statutory Guidance*. Available at: https://www.gov.uk/government/publications/multi-agency-public-protection-arrangements-mappa-2.

multi-agency risk assessment conference (MARAC) A forum to assess and manage the *risk of adult perpetrators of *domestic abuse. *See also* DOMESTIC VIOLENCE.

multi-agency safeguarding hub (MASH) A multi-agency team set up in some *local authorities that is the first point of contact for all new *safeguarding referrals in order to ensure quicker and more effective information-sharing in relation to safeguarding vulnerable children.

multi-agency working *See* COLLABORATIVE WORKING.

multiculturalism In the 1960s, the mainstream political view was that immigrants should assimilate into UK society and become as much like the 'host' population as possible so that they could be fully integrated and absorbed. For example, when minority ethnic children were placed by social workers with foster or adoptive parents, it was usually seen as in their interests to place them with white families. Subsequently the assimilationist perspective was increasingly challenged, not least by *ethnic minority groups, to such an extent that seeking to integrate ethnic minority groups in the dominant (white) culture, through the *loss of their distinctiveness, is seen as oppressive. For example, social workers now usually seek foster or adoptive parents of the same *ethnicity as the child to be placed. In contrast to *assimilation, multiculturalism stands for the acceptance of cultural pluralism, and a political climate in which *difference (for example, linguistic and religious), and co-existence are valued. It is argued that positive images of *diversity and knowledge of other cultures helps to reduce *racism. *Anti-racist critiques of multiculturalism, in social work as elsewhere, have argued that it fails to address hierarchies of power. In addition, feminists have pointed out that the acceptance of other cultures advocated by multiculturalism can militate against women's interests in some of those cultures, because women's demands for greater freedom are not consistent with cultural tradition, and therefore, are not regarded as legitimate.

multidisciplinary working *See* COLLABORATIVE WORKING.

multiple child abuse *See* ORGANIZED CHILD ABUSE.

Multi-systemic Therapy (MST) A family- and community-based programme designed primarily for young people aged 12 to 17 with serious *anti-social or disruptive behaviour problems. It was developed at the Medical University of South Carolina (MUSC) during the 1990s. Today it is delivered under tightly controlled licensing arrangements in thirty-four US states and thirteen countries, including eight European countries (Belgium, Denmark, Iceland, the Netherlands, Norway, Sweden, Switzerland, the UK). The programme was developed from social ecology theory (*see* CHILD DEVELOPMENT), family systems theory (*see* FAMILY THERAPY), and the literature on behaviour problems in young people. MST addresses aspects of and issues in a young person's social ecology (family, peers, school, neighbourhood, and *community) that contribute to her/his *anti-social or disruptive behaviour. A therapist is on call twenty-four hours a day, seven days a week. The duration and frequency of sessions varies in accordance with changing circumstances, *needs, and the degree of progress being made. *Interventions are *case-specific, based on comprehensive *assessments of *child development and family and peer relations, and draw on a range of techniques and models. MST therapists operate in teams of no fewer than two and no more than four, and each therapist's caseload ranges from four to six families. The duration of a programme delivered to a family is usually three to five months. Therapists work with parents and other *care-givers to put them in a position of control; improve parenting skills and family bonding; reduce the young person's association with anti-social peers; improve the young person's school achievements; and engage the family's networks in order to support parents in their role and put the young person in a context that supports her/his renunciation of anti-social or disruptive behaviour. MST is marketed as an *evidence-based intervention that has been proven to work, producing positive results such as reducing out-of-home placements, keeping young people in school and/or out of trouble, reducing re-arrests, improving family relations and functioning, and decreasing adolescent psychiatric symptoms and *drug and alcohol use. Some researchers have questioned the evidence base that purports to support the success of MST. *See also* ECOLOGICAL APPROACH; FAMILY THERAPY; PARENTING CLASSES; YOUTH INCLUSION SUPPORT PANEL.

Further reading: Schnurr, S. and Slettebø, T. (2015) 'Programmes Crossing Borders: The International Travelling of Programmes in Social Work', *European Journal of Social Work*, 18, 4, 583–98.

(⊕⊕⊕) SEE WEB LINKS
• Official UK site of the Multi-systemic Therapy organization.

Munchausen's syndrome by proxy *See* FABRICATED AND INDUCED ILLNESS.

Munro Review In June 2010 the Conservative–Liberal Democrat Coalition government asked Professor Eileen Munro to undertake a review of *child protection in England. She produced three reports. The first report, *A Systems Analysis* (Department for Education, October 2010) sought to understand why previous reforms to the child protection system had not led to the anticipated improvements in outcomes and practice. She concluded that the previous changes, made in isolation, and in relation to specific children's deaths, had resulted in professionals having to be more concerned with procedures and regulations than with providing services that met the *needs of children and young people. The experiences of social workers and other professionals were highlighted in the report. They criticized the child protection system for being overly bureaucratic, too focused on meeting targets (put in place by the *New Labour government [1997–2010]), said that this had reduced the opportunities to spend time with children and young people, and impaired the exercise of their professional judgement. This theme was picked up in Munro's second report, *The Child's Journey* (Department for Education, February 2011), in which she emphasized again how targets, regulations, and *bureaucracy prevented social workers from doing what they should be doing with children. She also concluded that Ofsted's external evaluation of *Serious Case Reviews added to bureaucracy and inhibited learning from them. She recommended that Ofsted should be replaced by a national team of experts who would consider SCRs and make recommendations for improvements. The second report also emphasized the importance of having multi-agency services based in the community and ensuring that health staff, the police, and family support services could access social work advice when they were concerned about *child abuse and/or neglect. She stressed that experienced social workers should remain in front-line practice so that they could develop their expertise and supervise junior colleagues. She placed great importance on *prevention and *early intervention. In her final report, *A Child-centred System* (Department for Education, May 2011), Munro made fifteen recommendations designed to change the child protection system from a compliance to a learning culture. Her recommendations included: revising statutory guidance and modifying inspection to encourage professional judgement on how services should be provided to children and families; reducing targets, the demands of IT systems and removing set timescales, for example, for the completion of assessments; increasing the focus on preventive services; making early intervention services a statutory *duty for local authorities; improving the training and *continuing profes-sional development of social workers; changing the social work career structure to encourage the development of increasing expertise, thus keeping experienced social workers in practice; designating a principal social worker in each *local authority to report views and experiences from front-line practice; creating a Chief Social Worker for England to advise government ministers on how they can assist social workers in improving practice.

mystery shopper Someone who is employed to contact a social work service by, for example, ringing a *call centre and posing as a potential service user, then reporting back to the organization on the quality of the service provided to her/him in response to her/his enquiry. Originally a practice from the *private sector as, for example, when mystery diners take meals at restaurants, that has been adopted by some *local authorities. *See also* CONSUMERISM; CUSTOMER SATISFACTION.

narrative approaches Concerned with the individual and social meanings of the stories that people tell about themselves and their relationships with others. Drawing on *postmodernism's emphasis on the role of *discourse, narrative approaches focus on the accounts (or 'narratives') that individuals use to construct meaning about their lives, as people tell their own 'stories' based on their particular versions of 'reality'. (These stories are likely to vary between different places, times, and audiences.) Narrative approaches can help in grasping people's perspectives when a social worker is undertaking an *assessment. Attending to narratives in assessment—highlighting unhelpful narratives and uncovering and validating more helpful ones—is an example of how assessment can in itself lead to constructive change. They can also be a method of *intervention. Listening to narratives may open up alternative ways of making sense of situations, as people can be helped to tell more constructive 'stories', as a way of thinking about making changes, building on strengths rather than problems. For example, a social worker working with *older people might challenge narratives that reflect internalized *ageism and seek to replace them with narratives based on social rights. A social worker listening to a narrative needs to reflect on the influence of her/his own 'self' and social position on the story that is told and how it is interpreted. *See also* BIOGRAPHICAL APPROACHES; CONSTRUCTIVE SOCIAL WORK; SOCIAL CONSTRUCTION.

Further reading: Milner, J. (2001) *Women and Social Work: Narrative Approaches*, Palgrave.

NASS *See* NATIONAL ASYLUM SUPPORT SERVICE.

National Adoption Register *See* ADOPTION.

National AIDS Trust (NAT) A charity that champions the rights of people living with HIV, provides information, and campaigns for change. *See also* HIV/AIDS.

- Official site of the National Aids Trust.

National Asylum Support Service (NASS) The organization responsible for providing accommodation and financial support to *asylum-seekers. It was established by the Immigration and Asylum Act (1999), was originally located in the Immigration and Nationality Department of the Home Office, and is now in the UK Borders Agency. NASS has the power to refuse an application if someone does 'not claim asylum as soon as reasonably practicable after their arrival' (Section 55, Nationality, Immigration and Asylum Act 2002). Section 115 of the 1999 Act withdrew mainstream benefits entitlement from asylum-seekers, replacing it with subsistence support from NASS, at a level of around two-thirds of the subsistence level set in the social security system. Subsistence support is only provided when asylum-seekers are destitute or likely to be destitute within a specified time limit (Section 95), currently fourteen days, and until their claim to *refugee status is determined. Those whose claims are successful receive subsistence support for a further 28 days, while they find alternative accommodation and apply for mainstream benefits. Those who are unsuccessful receive support for a further 21 days after notification of the outcome of any appeal. Then, their support ceases (Section 9 of the Asylum and Immigration Act 2004), they have to leave NASS accommodation, and they lose the right to free health care (Borders, Citizenship and Immigration Act 2009). *See also* HUMANITARIAN PROTECTION; INDEFINITE LEAVE TO REMAIN; UNACCOMPANIED ASYLUM-SEEKING CHILDREN.

National Autistic Society (NAS) A charity for people with autism, including *Asperger's Syndrome, and their families that provides information, support, and services, as well as engaging in campaigning activities. *See also* AUTISM SPECTRUM.

(⊕) SEE WEB LINKS
• Official site of the National Autistic Society.

National Carers' Strategy *See* CARER.

National Children's Bureau (NCB) A charity that is focused on improving the lives of children and young people, especially the most vulnerable. It seeks to:
• be a strong independent advocate for children and young people;
• ensure that government policies and legislation have a positive impact on their lives;
• be a voice for practitioners and support them to deliver the best outcomes for children and young people;
• bring together groups and organizations, to achieve more by working in *partnership;
• involve children and young people so they are able to make a difference to their lives;
• provide evidence from research, *analysis, and practice to make the case for change.

(⊕) SEE WEB LINKS
• Official site of the National Children's Bureau.

National Council for Voluntary Organizations (NCVO) The largest umbrella body for the *voluntary sector in England.

(⊕) SEE WEB LINKS
• Official site of the National Council for Voluntary Organizations.

national eligibility criteria *See* ELIGIBILITY CRITERIA.

National Institute for Health and Care Excellence (NICE) An organization that provides guidance and advice on improving health and social care, including appraising the evidence on the efficacy of particular treatments. Its guidance sometimes proves controversial if it results in local decisions to withdraw treatments in the light of its findings.

(⊕) SEE WEB LINKS
• Official site of the National Institute for Health and Care Excellence.

National Society for the Prevention of Cruelty to Children (NSPCC) A charity founded in 1884 with Lord Shaftesbury (1801–85), the Victorian social reformer, as its first president. It is governed by a Royal Charter and by-laws granted in 1895 that make it the only children's charity with *statutory powers to safeguard children at risk of *abuse. It campaigns for the end of cruelty to children by raising public awareness of the issue. It also provides a range of services including Child-Line, a free confidential helpline for children and young people. Trained volunteers provide advice and support by phone and online, twenty-four hours a day. It has projects in local communities offering a variety of services for children at *risk of abuse and provides consultancy and advice for professionals working in the field of *child protection. The organization undertakes research and publishes a variety of materials to assist the public and professionals in preventing child maltreatment. *See also* CHILD ABUSE AND NEGLECT; SAFEGUARDING CHILDREN.

((⊕)) SEE WEB LINKS
• Official site of the National Society for the Prevention of Cruelty to Children.

National Vocational Qualifications (NVQ) The competence-based qualifications that are assessed in relation to work tasks or work-related tasks. NVQs are based on national standards for various occupations, including those in social care. The standards say what a competent person in a job at a certain level is expected to do. An assessor observes the worker carrying out her/his duties and questions her/him about the work. Knowledge and understanding is assessed as well as work performance. The assessor signs off individual NVQ units when a worker has reached the required standard.

nature versus nurture A longstanding and ongoing debate about the extent to which people are shaped by genetic factors or by the impact of the world around them, such as their upbringing. There is a wide range of perspectives in this debate, from those who see genetic make-up as determining a person's characteristics to those who see the influence of the surrounding environment as crucial. The debate continues and its ramifications are ever-present in social work. This can be illustrated by assuming that the extreme point on the nature end of the nature versus nurture continuum is correct. If that were so, in the case of a parent abusing a child there would be little point in working towards the child remaining with the parent. Most adopt a position in the debate that both nature and nurture contribute.

NCVO *See* NATIONAL COUNCIL FOR VOLUNTARY ORGANIZATIONS.

nearest relative (NR) Under Section 26 of the Mental Health Act (1983), the nearest relative has a number of important rights and functions in connection with the care and treatment of mentally disordered patients under the Act. The NR is not necessarily the same as the next-of-kin, even if the patient has identified their next of kin on nursing or medical notes. Instead, practitioners must follow the guidance given by the Act, which provides a list of persons who may act in this role. The person appointed as the NR must be the highest in that list, starting with any spouse, or if there is none, son and daughter, and so on. The NR has the right to apply for admission to hospital, though in practice the majority of applications are made by an *approved mental health professional. The NR also has the right to block an admission for treatment, the right to discharge a person from compulsion, and the right to certain information about the patient. The rights of the NR do not apply to restricted patients who are in the criminal justice system under part III of the Act. In 2000 the UK government was found to be in breach of Article 8 of the Human Rights Act (1998) because under the then existing legislation there was no provision for a patient to object to the choice of the NR or request a change in their appointment as defined by the Act. Therefore, the Mental Health Act (2007) amended Section 23 of the Mental Health Act (1983) by introducing a new right for a patient to apply for an order, under Section 29, to displace the NR on the same already-existing grounds provided to other applicants, who include an approved mental health professional, another relative of the patient, and someone living with the patient. Those grounds for an application to displace the NR were, and are, circumstances where the patient has no NR; where the NR is too ill to act; where the NR unreasonably blocks admission; and where there are concerns that the NR has discharged, or is likely to discharge, the patient without due regard. An additional ground was introduced, that the NR is unsuitable to act as such, and was made available to all applicants including the patient. Section 23 of the Mental Health Act (1983) has also been amended to provide courts with the power to appoint any other person to act as the NR, if in their view the designated NR is not suitable. These provisions are intended to protect patients whose NR as defined by the Act is unlikely to act in their *best interests, or where the NR has abused, or caused harm to the patient. The patient may apply to nominate another person to act as the NR instead and if the court considers the nominated person to be suitable, and upholds the application to displace the NR, the nominated person will be made the acting NR. The 2007 Act also amended the provisions for determining the NR in Section 26 to include civil partners amongst the list of relatives in accordance with the Human Rights Act (1998). *See also* COMPULSORY ADMISSION.

need An essential requirement. How need is defined is critical for *service users (and social workers) as it constitutes the dividing line between the responsibilities of the state (and social work) on the one hand, and those of the individual (with differential access to the *market, *carers, etc.) on the other. Its definition is influenced by particular social, cultural, and historical contexts and, in those contexts, the way it is defined results from conflict and negotiation about what counts as need and who has needs. For example, the introduction of the post-war *welfare state was explicitly targeted at addressing people's needs in response to five issues: want, disease, squalor, idleness, and ignorance. However, an influential analysis of human needs by Doyal and Gough rejects a solely relativist view of need. They begin from the premise that the preconditions for all human action and interaction are health and autonomy. From this, they develop four propositions in relation to 'common human needs': first, people can be seriously harmed by social circumstances that can be changed; secondly, social justice exists in inverse proportion to serious harm and suffering; thirdly, social progress occurs when there is social change that minimizes serious harm; fourthly, when serious harm is not minimized, the interests of those harmed are in conflict with the social circumstances. They acknowledge that common human needs will have different manifestations according to the culture in which they are located and that there are culturally specific needs in addition to universal needs. These culturally specific needs are put forward by those who experience them and, sometimes, by those working with them, in recognition of people's *differences above and beyond common human needs. For example, in social work, the need for a child to be safe from physical harm is a common human need but this does not mean that social workers should neglect to understand cultural differences in child-rearing or, if a child is removed, not recognize the need for her/him to have continuing contact with cultural reference points.

Even within a specific cultural and historical context, ways of defining need vary. Bradshaw developed an influential 'taxonomy of need' that distinguished four different ways of defining need:

Felt need refers to need that an individual experiences (but does not necessarily express). It should not be assumed that if a need is not expressed, the need does not exist. For example, in the past the low take-up of services by Black and minority ethnic *communities was attributed to simplistic, but often erroneous official assumptions about the availability of social support within these communities that reduced the level of felt need. Where felt need exists, there are a number of reasons why it may not be expressed. For example, people from Black and minority ethnic communities may not seek help with difficulties they experience because of lack of information about the services available, language barriers, or because services are seen as culturally insensitive or inappropriate to their needs. When considering 'expressed need' it is worth considering the nature and level of felt need that may not find expression in the form of requests for help.

Expressed need is need that an individual publicly acknowledges; it may or may not be the same as felt need. For need to be expressed in the form of a request for help, the individual has not only to experience it, but to perceive it, and be able to translate it into service terms. People's conceptions of their needs relate to their expectations, their view of what can and should be provided, what it is legitimate to ask for and their knowledge of the services available. Need may not be expressed if it is believed that the service will not be provided. When people express their needs, they may be obstructed in getting them heard and understood by, for example, restricted *assessment agendas or 'tick-box'-style formats that adopt a narrow focus. Also, there may be obstacles for social workers in hearing and understanding expressed need.

Normative or prescribed need is defined according to an agreed standard established by an expert or professional; it may differ significantly from an individual's felt and expressed needs. Normative definitions of need change over time. For example, the provision of *home helps to assist with cleaning and tasks around the house was widely accepted up until the mid-1980s. While home care support, normally for *personal care needs, is still arranged, the sort of low-level assistance previously given by home helps now falls outside *local authorities' normative definition of need. Assistance with household tasks is seen as need that can be met through arrangements made by the individual.

Comparative need refers to what is perceived as a need relative to that of other groups or individuals; it is likely to influence an individual's felt and expressed need as well as how normative need is defined. When deciding whether to seek help, people will be influenced by their evaluation of their own perceived need compared with that of others. Comparative need is also pertinent to a social worker, who will make decisions about an individual's level of need and *risk in the context of awareness of the needs and circumstances of other service users and potential service users.

It is primarily normative need that forms the basis of assessment in social work. Despite numerous statements to the effect that service users should be involved in the assessment process and treated as experts on their own needs, it is clear that, ultimately, normative need prevails when determining the need for services and that social workers are expected to be arbiters of normative need. *See also* ELIGIBILITY CRITERIA; HIERARCHY OF NEEDS; THRESHOLD CRITERIA (CHILDREN).

Further reading: Bradshaw, J. (1972) 'A Taxonomy of Social Need', *New Society*, March, 640–3. Doyal, L. and Gough, I. (1991) *A Theory of Human Need*, Macmillan.

needs assessment (adults) An *assessment of adults under the Care Act (2014) is undertaken if someone *appears* to need *care and support, regardless of her/his financial situation or whether s/he is thought to have eligible needs (*see* ELIGIBILITY CRITERIA). The assessment considers the most relevant aspects of wellbeing to the person being assessed, how her/his *needs impact on those aspects of wellbeing, and how care and support, or other services or resources in the local *community, can help her/him to achieve the *outcomes s/he seeks. The process is intended to be *person-centred and should enable someone to have as much *choice and control as possible. It is not only the gateway to care and support but a significant intervention in its own right that can help people to understand their situation and the needs they have; to reduce or delay the onset of greater needs; and to access support when they require it. Assessment helps people to understand their strengths and capabilities and the support available to them from services, networks, and community resources. The process should be flexible and adapted to fit a person's needs, wishes, and *goals, ranging from an initial contact that helps a person with low-level needs to access support in their local community to an ongoing process that requires the input of a number of professionals. A number of possible assessment formats are envisaged:

Online or telephone assessment may be used when a person's needs are not complex or where a person is already known to the *local authority and an assessment is following a change in her/his needs or circumstances;

Face-to-face assessment may be undertaken by the local authority;

Self-assessment, using the same assessment format as a face-to-face assessment, with the local authority checking that it provides an accurate reflection of a person's needs;

Joint assessment, with agencies working together to avoid someone undergoing multiple assessments;

Combined assessment, where an adult's assessment is combined with a *carer's assessment and/or an assessment relating to a child so that interrelated needs are properly considered.

The assessment process is intended to enable a person to:

- develop an understanding of the assessment process;
- develop an understanding of the implications of the assessment process for her/his condition(s) and situation;
- understand her/his own needs, the impact of her/his needs on her/his wellbeing, and the outcomes s/he wants to achieve, so that s/he engages effectively with the assessment process;
- begin to identify the options that are available to her/him to meet those outcomes and to support her/his *independence and wellbeing;
- understand the basis on which decisions are reached.

To help someone with needs for care and support to prepare for an assessment, the list of areas to be covered in the assessment should be provided in advance in an accessible format so that s/he can think about what her/his needs are and the outcomes s/he wants to achieve. Information is also given about the assessment process itself, as early as possible, including details about what to expect during the process, such as the format and timescale of assessment, *complaints processes, and access to independent *advocacy.

Assessment identifies the full extent of a person's needs before considering the person's eligibility for care and support and what types of care and support would help to meet those needs. The process takes a *holistic view of a person's needs in the context of her/his support network, considering how s/he, her/his support network, and the wider community can contribute towards meeting the outcomes s/he wants to achieve. Decisions about whether a person's needs are eligible for care and support from the local authority are made on the basis of the assessment and determining eligibility does not take place until the assessment has been completed, except when urgent needs have to be met by an immediate response, for example if someone has a condition that deteriorates rapidly or s/he has an accident. In these circumstances, a more detailed needs assessment then follows the initial response.

Early or targeted interventions such as a period of *reablement or providing equipment or minor household adaptations (*see* AIDS AND ADAPTATIONS) can delay an adult's needs from progressing. Someone's first contact, which triggers the assessment, may be followed by a pause in the assessment process to allow such interventions to take place and any resulting benefit to be taken into account in the subsequent assessment.

A person whose needs are under consideration is at the centre of the assessment process because s/he is best placed to judge what her/his own wellbeing involves. Any *carers are also included, as well as any other person whose involvement is requested by the person being assessed. These other perspectives and experiences can add to the understanding of a person's needs, outcomes, and wellbeing. Any difficulty in communicating, whether as a result of a *disability or because English is not a person's first language, should be addressed and a specialist worker or interpreter should be used where needed. If someone is unable to engage effectively in the assessment process, somebody else is sought who can assist her/him in engaging with the process and help her/him to articulate her/his needs and preferred outcomes. If a person has substantial difficulty in being involved in her/his assessment in terms of understanding the information provided, retaining the information, using or weighing up the information, or communicating her/his views, wishes or feelings, someone appropriate and independent supports and represents the person in order to facilitate her/his involvement. Where there is a family member or friend who is willing and able to facilitate a person's involvement effectively, and who is acceptable to the person and judged appropriate by the local authority, s/he may be asked to support the individual in the assessment process. Where there is no one appropriate for this role (either because there is no family member or friend willing and available, or if the person does not want her/him to be involved), an independent advocate is appointed (*see* ADVOCACY [ADULTS]). If someone is unable to request an assessment or struggles to express her/his needs, an assessment of *capacity is carried out under the Mental Capacity Act (2005). Anyone who lacks capacity needs extra support to identify and communicate her/his needs and make subsequent decisions and may need an Independent Mental Capacity Advocate (*see* CAPACITY).

When someone expresses a need or identifies challenges and difficulties that s/he faces, their impact on the person's day-to-day life is established. The ways her/his needs impact on her/his wellbeing, beyond the ways that s/he has identified, and the bearing her/his needs have on her/his desired outcomes are also considered. All of a person's care and support needs are taken into account, regardless of any support provided by a carer. Information on the care that a carer is providing is included in an assessment but it does not influence decisions about a person's eligibility for care and support. If a carer is willing and able to meet any of a person's needs, this is recorded in the assessment so that the full extent of a person's needs are identified and an appropriate response can be made if a carer feels unable or unwilling to carry out some or all of the caring that s/he has previously provided. When an assessment results in a decision that someone's needs are eligible, the care a carer is providing is taken into account during the planning of care and support.

A person's needs may fluctuate and at the time of the assessment they may not be indicative of her/his needs more generally. Consideration is given to whether someone's current level of need is likely to fluctuate and what her/his ongoing needs for care and support are likely to be. This is the case both for short-term fluctuations, which may be over the course of the day, and longer-term changes in the level of the person's needs. Account is also taken of what fluctuations in need can be reasonably expected based on the experience of others with a similar condition(s). Furthermore, the assessment considers a person's wider care and support needs. This may include types of care and support the individual has received in the past and her/his general medical history, which may be indicative of her/his current care and support needs. When assessing particularly complex or multiple needs, the support of an expert may be needed in order to ensure that the person's needs are fully identified. Where the person undertaking the assessment does not have the necessary knowledge of a particular condition or circumstance, s/he consults someone who has relevant expertise to ensure that s/he asks the right questions relating to the condition and interprets the condition appropriately in identifying underlying needs. During an assessment, consideration is given to what else other than the provision of care and support might assist a person in meeting the outcomes s/he wants to achieve. In considering what else might help, someone's strengths and capabilities and the support available from her/his wider support network or within the *community is included. Any suggestion that support could be available from family and friends is considered in the light of their appropriateness, willingness, and ability to provide any additional support and the impact on them of doing so. It must also have the agreement of the person in question.

People may have needs that are met by various bodies, and a *holistic approach to assessment that brings together all of a person's needs may require the input of a number of professionals. A needs assessment may be undertaken jointly with another body carrying out another assessment in relation to the person concerned, provided that the person agrees. For example, where a person has both health and care and support needs, the local authority and the NHS can work together to produce a coordinated assessment. This is an example of how assessment processes can be integrated in order to fit better around the person's needs. An integrated approach may involve working together with relevant professionals on a single assessment. It may also include putting processes in place to ensure that the person is referred for other assessments. Where more than one body is assessing a person, they need to work closely together to prevent that person having to undergo a number of assessments at different times, thus minimizing distress and confusion.

Someone who may have care and support needs may refuse to have an assessment, in which case an assessment will not be carried out, unless the person concerned lacks mental *capacity and carrying out an assessment is in her/his *best interests. A similar judgement about someone's best interests being served by having an assessment can be made when someone is experiencing, or is at *risk of experiencing, *abuse or neglect (*see* SAFEGUARDING ADULTS). When someone has refused a needs assessment but later requests an assessment, this is provided. When an individual has previously refused an assessment and it is established that her/his needs or circumstances have changed, offering an assessment at that point will be considered, unless the person continues to refuse to have one.

Following an assessment, a person is given a record of her/his needs assessment. A copy is shared with anybody else that the individual asks for a copy to be shared with. Where an independent advocate, an Independent Mental Capacity Advocate (*see* CAPACITY), or an *Independent Mental Health Advocate is involved, the advocate is kept informed so that s/he can support the person in understanding the outcome of the assessment and its implications.

A decision will be made about whether someone is eligible for services following the assessment (*see* ELIGIBILITY CRITERIA) and, if s/he is eligible, a *care and support plan will be drawn up. *See also* CARER'S ASSESSMENT; ELIGIBILITY CRITERIA; NEEDS-LED ASSESSMENT.

Further reading: Department of Health (2016) *Care and Support: Statutory Guidance*, Chapter 6. Available at: https://www.gov.uk/government/publications/care-act-statutory-guidance/care-and-support-statutory-guidance#person-centred-care-and-support-planning.

needs-led assessment An *assessment that is concerned with an individualized bespoke response to someone's *needs, rather than slotting the person into what is on offer from existing 'one-size-fits-all' services. The origins of the term lie in the rhetoric accompanying the implementation of the *community care reforms through the NHS and Community Care Act (1990), which depicted the reforms as being driven in large part by the need for a significant shift in this direction, modelled on demonstration *care management projects that had allocated budgets to social workers to spend on alternatives to existing services (*see* CARE MANAGEMENT). (Subsequently, needs-led assessment was a concept widely espoused across *service user groups.) However, when care management was adopted nationally, needs-led assessments were difficult to achieve because budgets were not devolved to social workers, and so they did not have the freedom to purchase services that social workers in the demonstration projects had had, and the prioritization of *risk, through the use of *eligibility criteria, meant that resources for low-level needs associated with, for example, leisure pursuits or supporting links with family and friends, were not available. *Personalization emerged as a revamped version of needs-led assessment with similar claims that needs would be uncovered and met in an individualized and responsive manner, and such assessments were advocated in *needs assessments undertaken following the Care Act (2014).

negative reinforcement *See* BEHAVIOUR MODIFICATION.

neglect *See* CHILD ABUSE AND NEGLECT.

negotiated order A concept that regards organizations as consisting of people negotiating with each other through their ongoing interaction, rather than that they exist as static structures. It points to the way in which organizations change in response to the time and context in which they exist and to their being characterized by constant processes of segmentation and fragmentation. This does not imply that all are equally powerful in negotiating an organization's order. Differences in organizational status, and position and location in social divisions such as *class, *disability, *gender, *'race', and sexuality will influence the extent and nature of the power that individuals and groups have in negotiation processes.

neighbourhood social work *See* BARCLAY REPORT (1982); DECENTRALIZATION.

neo-liberalism An economic and political ideology at the centre of which are two propositions: that governments should not seek to intervene in the economy, because the *market is an efficient and effective mechanism if left to its own devices; and that individuals should be responsible for themselves and run their own lives, though most variants of the ideology accept that there is a role for the state as a 'safety-net', providing a level of subsistence support when someone reaches the *poverty line. Liberalism (in this sense, not in the sense of philosophical values of tolerance and acceptance) had its origins in the *laissez-faire economics of early capitalism in the nineteenth century. It continued to be the dominant ideology until the establishment of the post-war *welfare state. Thereafter, the welfare state took on the role of modifying the impact of market forces through the provision of a range of benefits and services 'from the cradle to the grave'. In so doing, it was seen as a means of attempting to stabilize capitalism and regulate, at least to some extent, its impact on people's lives (*see* DEMOCRATIC-WELFARE-CAPITALISM).

Accordingly, the private commercial context of the *market and the public service context of the state were seen as analytically distinct. This distinction between the operation of the market on the one hand, and the welfare state on the other rested on social democratic ideas that enjoyed a broad measure of support across the parliamentary political spectrum, often referred to as the *'post-war consensus'. At the heart of the consensus was the idea that citizens had collective obligations for each other's welfare through the agency of the state, as a corrective to life chances based purely on market-based outcomes. Such was the level of support for these social democratic ideas that they became a 'common-sense' way of thinking and some commentators referred to them as representing the 'end of ideology'.

However, when the first Thatcher government came to power in 1979, influenced by *New Right ideas emerging from think-tanks such as the Institute of Economic Affairs, there was a resurgence of interest in liberalism and how it could be revised and revamped in a different economic, social, and political context from that of the nineteenth century; hence neo-liberalism, whose core elements of market freedom and the sovereignty of the individual were entirely consistent with those of nineteenth-century liberalism. The Conservative (1979–97), *New Labour (1997–2010), Conservative–Liberal Democrat Coalition (2010–15) and Conservative (2015–) governments have all espoused variants of neo-liberalism, and it has long replaced social democratic ideas as the parliamentary political consensus, usually presented as being non-political and simply the 'truth'. In addition to extolling the virtues of the market and the *private sector as dynamic, innovative, and responsive, neo-liberal ideas have been applied to public services, which have been enjoined to model themselves on the private sector. They have been brought as close to market conditions as possible through the use of *privatization and *quasi-markets. For example, in social work this involved many *local authorities 'floating off' residential care for *older people and there are quasi-markets in areas of provision as diverse as *community care services for adults and *fostering services for children. More generally, *public sector organizations, including social work, have been under pressure to change and become like private sector organizations and this has resulted in *managerialism being widely advocated and adopted.

Neo-liberalism has had an impact around the world first through its status as the orthodoxy of international economic bodies such as the International Monetary Fund and the World Bank, which have applied neo-liberal prescriptions to developing countries, and secondly, it has developed in tandem with *globalization, under the impact of which economic power has been denationalized and diffused. In the global context, the more a national government is attached to neo-liberal ideas, or coerced by them, the more primacy will be given to placing the country advantageously in relation to global economic forces, creating the conditions for international competitiveness by lowering trade barriers, opening up its national economy to multi-national companies, and encouraging mobility of capital, investment, and production processes. The leanness and efficiency of the public sector is seen as an important element in national competitiveness and the changes in *welfare regimes that result have an important bearing on how social work develops and the roles it plays. The financial crash of 2007-8 did not lead to a questioning of neo-liberalism in official policy but to its even more enthusiastic embrace as a solution to problems stemming from the crash and advocacy of *austerity policies that have impacted on social work. *See also* BUSINESS ORIENTATION; NEW PUBLIC MANAGEMENT.

network The patterns in which individuals are connected by kinship, friendship, and other ties. Although there are a number of approaches to network analysis, social work tends to concentrate on egocentric network analysis, which focuses on how the network is seen from the position of the *service user, for example a *looked-after child. *See also* ECO MAP; GENOGRAM; NETWORKING.

network analysis *See* ECO MAP; GENOGRAM; NETWORK.

networking Linking people together. Traditionally this referred to a role played by social workers in identifying or initiating and strengthening contacts between individuals and groups in the *communities in which they worked in order that they could further their interests, share information, knowledge, and resources, and give each other support. In contemporary social work, networking usually refers to initiating, maintaining, and improving links with and between other professionals, either at a general level on matters of shared interest, for example, through an area-based professional forum, or specifically in relation to the professional network around a *service user, for example, the *core group seeking to protect a child, often referred to as 'the team around the child'. In addition, a service user's networks are identified and considered when undertaking an *assessment, such as a child's family *network or an adult's network of family, friends, and neighbours when a *needs assessment is undertaken. *See also* COLLABORATIVE WORKING.

neurosis A psychological disorder (literally meaning 'nerve disorder') in which there is subjective distress, for example sadness or worry, without clear organic or physiological cause and where an individual's connection with reality is preserved. It has become predominantly associated with symptoms of *anxiety and with an underlying personality (neurotic) that leads to symptoms of anxiety. The term is little used in current clinical practice and was removed from the *Diagnostic and Statistical Manual of Mental Disorders* in 1980. Before reclassification, categories of neurosis included anxiety neurosis, depressive neurosis, obsessive-compulsive neurosis, hysterical neurosis, and a wide range of *phobias.

neutralizing (neutralization) Anticipation of the condemnation of others and attempting to neutralize the expected condemnation, for example neutralizing by denying responsibility—'I would never have attacked the child if I hadn't been drunk. I'm not myself when I've been drinking'; and by blaming the victim—'She was asking to be hit.'

New Labour After eighteen years of Conservative governments (1979–97) that had been shaped by *New Right thinking, the Labour Party, with Tony Blair as prime minister, distanced itself from the 'old Left' of its past and from the New Right of its predecessor. It did so by depicting itself as New Labour, adopting the *'Third Way', geared to steering a middle course through any of the issues that it had to confront. However, there were substantial areas of overlap between the Conservative governments and New Labour in terms of the primacy accorded to *globalization, the restructuring of the economy and society that were seen as necessary in response to its impact, and the changes required in established practices and ways of working as a basis for *capitalism's future prosperity, in particular the imperative towards low costs and flexible forms of working. In its representation of the *neo-liberal consensus and in its approach to social policy, including social work, New Labour's Third Way was strongly influenced by the *reflexive modernization theses of Ulrich Beck and, especially, Anthony Giddens. These theses suggested that new political responses were needed to meet the challenges posed not only by globalization but also by the decline in the influence of tradition and a heightened sense of *risk in society. They asserted that these forces undermined the social democratic *welfare state, as traditional *class identities dissolved and there were changes in the labour market, *gender relations, and *household forms. In the politics of New Labour that emerged from the influence of these theses, self-conscious citizens were stressed and their concerns were depicted as *consumerism, personal *identity, and 'life politics'. New Labour expected individuals to be active in meeting their *needs, with the state's primary role seen as strengthening the capacity of individuals to act on their own behalf in supportive communities. As *'community' achieved a new prominence, a key aspect of New Labour's political project was a stress on *communitarianism, which was used to mark out New Labour's difference from the Conservative governments, in its commitment to a set of social values that promoted togetherness and trust or, in the term New Labour usually preferred to adopt, 'social inclusion'. However, its version of communitarianism was criticized as morally prescriptive, economically liberal, and socially conservative, and as being top-down and authoritarian, rather than bottom-up and solidaristic, driven by central government and statute, with the 'community' often functioning as a code word for the state. The relevance of New Labour's communitarianism for social work was that it involved strict *regulation of public services and revisioning government as the guardian (but not the direct implementer) of the social interest. This was reflected in the top-down policing of professional performance in a way that powerfully reinforced and developed the message that professionals could not be trusted.

New Labour's emphasis on social inclusion, from communitarianism, was combined with the drive for *modernization and *'Best Value'. New Labour presented this combination as both empowering and requiring public sector workers, such as social workers, to identify with the organization because the organizational context was represented as embodying New Labour's attempts to secure social inclusion. Organizations, such as *Social Services Departments, as the delivery mechanisms for New Labour's political agenda, were seen as the carriers of corporate values that symbolized a common purpose. Managers were, therefore, not simply to be concerned with managerial control, but were seen as guardians of New Labour's political agenda. This version of *managerialism was presented as 'empowering' everyone; it was represented as an apolitical, self-evidently 'good thing'. In particular, this empowering managerialism purported to speak for *service users and any resistance to managerialism by social workers was attacked as simply élitist professional attempts to avoid accountability to them and to thwart the updating of services to match the expectations of modern consumers. In its take on managerialism, New Labour was also concerned with applying private business formulae to the operation of public sector services. The public sector was enjoined to deliver services within the discourses of *quality management and customer service, which demanded continual improvements to services, and to break traditional models of service provision, becoming more like the *private sector. New Labour placed considerable emphasis on quality management and customer service principles and techniques being applied to social work and linked into *'Best Value'. The *Quality Strategy for Social Care* (Department of Health 2000) laid out a framework to 'drive change at all levels in social care organizations through a shift to a culture of continuous improvement'. The impact of New Labour on social work was lasting and profound. *See also* PERFORMANCE MANAGEMENT; REGULATION.

Further reading: Harris, J. (2003) *The Social Work Business*, Ch 5, Routledge.

new public management An outworking of *neo-liberalism, initiated by the *New Right, that is a generic model of *management involving a shift away from administration in the *public sector to proactive management based on two principles: first, minimizing as far as possible the extent to which the public sector is different from the *private sector; secondly, freeing up public sector managers from procedures and enabling them to be more innovative and entrepreneurial, thus giving them the 'right to manage'. In many countries, this has stemmed from governments stressing national competitiveness in response to *globalization and seeking to maintain economic conditions that are attractive to private sector companies in order to avert capital flight and to attract new investment. In such contexts, public expenditure on social services has usually been depicted as a burden that needs to be, at least, contained and, preferably, reduced. In parallel to concerns about costs, proponents of new public management are critical of the way in which publicly-provided services have been run, alleging that they have been inflexible and inefficient. They have claimed that a more discerning public has emerged that experiences high levels of service in the market and demands correspondingly high levels of service from public and voluntary social services. Although some have argued that the contexts and purposes of private businesses are very different from those of social services, the political enthusiasm for this generic model of management has been widespread.

The main characteristics of new public management are transparent accounting, with detailed attribution of costs; viewing organizations as a series of principal/agent contractual relationships (*see* AGENCY THEORY); disaggregating the planning and provision of services so that the provision of services is through *quasi-market arrangements; contracting out service delivery from the public sector to the private and *voluntary sectors, and encouraging competition between the public, *private, and voluntary sectors; and giving service users more *choice and scope to swap service providers. Most writers no longer regard new public management as a unified global body of ideas, policies, and practices but as a broader and more general trajectory of change, pursued by different countries for different reasons and along different routes, as they pick different combinations of items from the menu offered by it. Accordingly, in order to make sense of this variation in the forms taken by new public management, it is important to pay attention to the significance of national institutions and local conditions. *See also* CONSUMERISM; MANAGERIALISM.

Further reading: Harris, J. (2003) *The Social Work Business*, Routledge.

New Right Discourse on the right of political ideas, which was marginalized during the *post-war consensus, but came to prominence because of its influence on Conservative governments (1979–97) through the work of a variety of right-wing writers and organizations. It was designated as 'new' because although it was on the right of the political spectrum it departed from mainstream Conservative ideas up to that point in support of the *post-war consensus on the *welfare state, which had lasted until the mid-1970s. It was a consensus built around social democratic ideas, which ran across the parliamentary political spectrum, about the importance of state intervention in the economy, the need for high levels of public expenditure, and the rights of citizens to state-provided benefits and services. During the consensus, the political parties shared an overarching assumption that the provision of welfare by the state was an unchallengeable commitment, and the arguments between them were about how to improve, adjust, or manage more efficiently the existing structures. The consensus was never complete but it was the mainstream political ideology concerning the welfare state that was adhered to by both Conservative and Labour governments, and it rested on the presumed permanence of the welfare state.

The consensus was challenged forcefully with the revival of ideas to the right of social democracy through the Conservative party, driven by philosophers such as Friedrich Hayek (1899–1992) and economic theorists such as Milton Friedman (1912–2006). The right-wing think-tanks in which the ideas were debated and consolidated were the Institute of Economic Affairs, the Centre for Policy Studies (founded by Margaret Thatcher and Keith Joseph in 1974), and the Social Affairs Unit. The core underpinning ideas coming from the New Right were: government spending has deleterious economic and social consequences; state provision is inherently inefficient; the *market is central and must operate free of government constraint; the consumer is sovereign. The welfare state, in general, and at times social work in particular, were central themes in the debates initiated by the New Right. Social work was caught up in the maelstrom and in many ways was seen to embody everything that was wrong with the welfare state. Some asked whether social work could survive.

In order for a major ideological shift to take place, ideas are needed and these were supplied by the New Right. Powerful personalities are also needed to realize those ideas by leading governments in a new direction. This aspect of the ideological shift away from the post-war consensus was provided by the Conservative governments under the leadership of Margaret Thatcher, from 3 May 1979 onwards. However, before governments can bring about an ideological shift, events are needed that are conducive to that ideological shift. A series of events favoured the New Right's ascendancy. First, in the 1970s, there was 'stagflation' (the combination of a low growth economy and inflation), unemployment rocketed, the balance of payments worsened, and the value of the pound declined. Secondly, decisions by the Organization of Petroleum Exporting Countries (OPEC) led to a quadrupling of oil prices in 1973, followed by economic recessions in Western countries. Thirdly, in 1976 the International Monetary Fund agreed to grant the Labour government a loan on condition there were cuts in public expenditure and a policy of wage restraint. Fourthly, the ensuing cuts and wage restraint led to the 'Winter of Discontent' (1978–9), with widespread strikes against the policies being implemented, and the Labour government seemed to have lost control. Therefore, when the first Thatcher government came to power in 1979, there was a widespread perception of social and economic crisis.

The response to the crisis was wide-ranging: strict control of the money supply; *privatization of state-owned enterprises such as telecommunications and public utilities; reducing public expenditure (except on defence); cutting direct taxation; introducing *quasi-markets into the public sector; and reducing the rights of trade unions and their members. In addition, the era of Thatcherism introduced three main themes from the New Right that had consequences for the welfare state and for social work as part of it:

Rolling back the state The state was presented as having expanded too far and as interfering in matters that should be left to individuals making their own decisions. State provision was seen as reducing the scope of the individual to make choices, by subjecting the individual to uniform provision in education, health, and social services. The state needed to be rolled back to free individuals to make their own decisions. Society should be seen as an aggregation of individuals who should enjoy 'freedom under the rule of law'. (Margaret Thatcher famously stated: 'There is no such thing as society; only individuals and their families'.) Rolling back the state was a *philosophical criticism* of the post-war welfare state.

Costs of welfare Excessive spending on the welfare state was seen as a major cause of Britain's poor economic performance. What was regarded as excessive spending required excessive taxation and the limits of taxation were considered to have been reached. The state's borrowing to pay for the welfare state fuelled inflation. Resources were diverted from productive profit-making economic activities into unproductive non-profit-making activities. Taxation made people less willing to be economically active, investors reluctant to invest, and workers less inclined to work. Individual economic initiative was, it was argued, stifled by the state's excessive taxation to pay for the welfare state. The cost of welfare was an *economic criticism* of the post-war welfare state.

Effects of welfare The welfare state was alleged to create dependency, weaken individual morality, and undermine the family because people had come to rely on the state to meet their needs. They had lost the capacity or the will to take care of themselves. The gap between benefits and earned incomes was too narrow. The effects of welfare was a *moral criticism* of the welfare state in which the New Right saw social work as deeply implicated. As far as social work was concerned, the overhaul of its failings was meant to be accomplished through the *Barclay Report (1982).

The political context of the early 1980s, in which these criticisms were made and developed, meant that much of the New Right attack organized against the welfare state by Thatcherism identified the Labour Party as the main architect of its expansion. But the criticisms were also addressed to the errors of other post-war Conservative governments and their acceptance of the post-war social democratic consensus. Although the New Right attack was aimed at gaining political advantage over the Labour Party, it also undertook a thorough reassessment of the whole of post-war politics and sought the overthrow of the assumptions of all political parties, including the Conservatives' own, in order to correct the perceived failings of the post-war consensus (*see* WELFARE STATE). However, the biggest achievement of the New Right was not in moving the Conservative Party to the right, but in moving the Labour Party to the right and creating a new consensus in which what had been the far right came to be seen as the new middle ground on which political battles had to be fought thereafter, up until the present day.

Further reading: Harris, J. (2003) *The Social Work Business*, Chs 3–4, Routledge.

NHS continuing health care (CHC) Care which is arranged and funded solely by the National Health Service for people not in hospital who have ongoing health care needs.

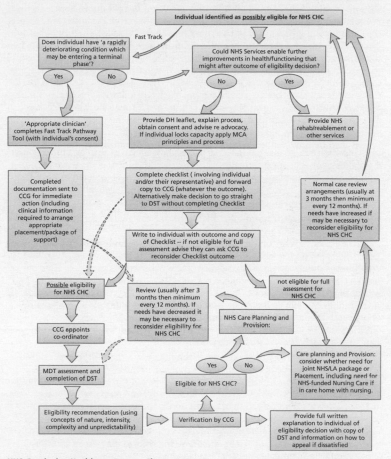

NHS Continuing Healthcare Process Chart

Department of Health (2012) *National Framework for NHS Continuing Healthcare and NHS-Funded Nursing Care*, p. 23

A number of ombudsman investigations in the 1990s highlighted various restrictive practices of health authorities that prevented people who should have been receiving continuing health care from accessing it. A significant Court of Appeal ruling in 1999, the Coughlan judgment, held that the NHS should accept responsibility for funding nursing care if it is primarily the person's health need that gives rise to the need for care. It held that *local authorities can only legally accept responsibility for nursing care where this is 'merely incidental or ancillary to the provision of accommodation'. This is determined by considering the type and level of nursing care needed. Despite the Coughlan Test for determining when continuing care should be provided and the issuing of various sets of guidance and directions, clear *eligibility criteria for the provision of continuing health care did not materialize and there was wide geographical variation in the criteria used. After the introduction of free nursing care bandings in 2007 (*see* NHS-FUNDED NURSING CARE) there was concern that assessment at the high band was being used when individuals met continuing health care criteria and should be having the total costs of care met by the NHS. This issue was tested in the Grogan case in 2006, which challenged the refusal of continuing health care by Bexley Care Trust. The High Court found that the Coughlan Test had not been used and that the Trust had unlawfully refused continuing health care on the basis that nursing costs could be met through the nurse care banding. The Grogan ruling reaffirmed the need to consider, on the basis of the totality of someone's needs, whether there is a primary need for health care.

CHC can be provided in any setting, including a person's own home or a care home. It is free, unlike *care and support provided by local authorities, for which a *means-tested financial charge is made. If someone receives CHC in their own home, the NHS not only pays for health care services (for example, from a community nurse or physiotherapist) but also for the costs of any associated social care needs (for example, help with bathing, dressing, or food preparation). If someone receives CHC in a care home, the NHS pays for their fees, including board and accommodation.

Anyone over 18 years of age assessed as having a certain level of care needs may be entitled to CHC. It is not dependent on having particular diseases, *diagnoses, or conditions, nor on who provides the care or where the care is provided. If the overall assessment of someone's care needs shows that s/he has a 'primary health need', s/he is eligible for CHC. Once CHC funding is agreed, it is regularly reviewed (after three months initially and then at least once a year) and if the person's care needs change, the funding arrangements can also change.

Whether someone has a 'primary health need' is assessed by considering their care needs in relation to four indicators:

Nature The characteristics and type of the needs and the overall effect these needs have on the person, including the type of interventions required;

Complexity How the needs present and interact and the level of skill required to monitor the symptoms, treat the condition, and/or manage the care;

Intensity The extent and severity of the needs and the support required to meet them, including the need for sustained/ongoing care;

Unpredictability How hard it is to predict changes in needs that might create challenges in managing them, including the risks to the person's health if adequate and timely care is not provided.

The first step in the process of deciding whether someone is eligible for CHC is completion of the Checklist Tool, a screening device to enable health and social care staff to judge whether it is appropriate to undertake a full assessment for eligibility for CHC. The Checklist is usually completed when someone is assessing or reviewing health and/or social care needs. If the Checklist Tool has been completed and indicates there is a need to carry out a full assessment of eligibility for CHC, the person who has completed the Checklist Tool will contact the *Clinical Commissioning Group (CCG), which will arrange for a multidisciplinary team of two or more health or social care staff to carry out an assessment. The assessment, with the person's permission, involves contributions from all of the health and social care staff involved in her/his care and in some cases the multidisciplinary team asks for more detailed specialist assessments. The multidisciplinary team uses the information from the assessment to complete a 'Decision Support Tool'. The Decision

Support Tool considers a range of factors that have a bearing on eligibility for CHC funding, and these are taken into account in reaching the decision. The Tool records under twelve 'care domains'. The domains are subdivided into statements of need, representing low, moderate, high, severe, or priority levels of need, depending on the domain. The care domains are behaviour, cognition, psychological and emotional needs, communication, mobility, nutrition, continence, skin, breathing, drug therapies and medication, altered states of consciousness, and other significant care needs.

The purpose of the tool is to help decide on the nature, complexity, intensity, and unpredictability of the needs (see above) and whether the person has a 'primary health need'. The multidisciplinary team then makes a recommendation to the CCG as to whether the person is eligible for CHC. The CCG usually accepts the recommendation unless there are exceptional circumstances.

If someone needs urgent care due to a rapidly deteriorating condition, which may be terminal, the 'Fast Track Tool' may be used instead of the Decision Support Tool to determine eligibility for CHC funding. If this is the case, a doctor will complete the Fast Track Tool and send it directly to the CCG, which will arrange for care to be provided as quickly as possible. A CCG may arrange for a review of needs and completion of a Decision Support Tool after immediate support has been provided following the completion of the Fast Track Tool.

Following every assessment or review, the person is sent a written decision as to whether s/he is entitled to CHC with reasons for the decision.

Where the NHS has a clear legal responsibility to provide a particular service, it is unlawful for a local authority to do so. This statutory position is intended to maintain the legal boundary between the NHS and local authority responsibilities. However, there is an exception to this general rule, in that the local authority may provide some limited health care services as part of a package of care and support, but only where the services provided are 'incidental or ancillary' (that is, relatively minor, and part of a broader package of care) and where the services are the type of support that a local authority could be expected to provide. However, decisions made about eligibility for CHC reveal the blurred and shifting boundaries between the definition of 'social care' needs and 'health care' needs. This allows plenty of scope for conflict between the NHS and local authorities in determining their respective responsibilities. The decisions that result are significant because of the impact they have on whether people have to pay for the care they need. *See also* CHARGING FOR SERVICES (ADULTS); ELIGIBILITY CRITERIA; NEEDS ASSESSMENT.

Further reading: Department of Health (2012) *National Framework for NHS Continuing Healthcare and NHS-funded Nursing Care.* Available at: http://www.gov.uk/government/uploads/system/uploads/attachment_data/file/213137/National-Framework-for-NHS-CHC-NHS-FNC-Nov-2012.pdf.

Department of Health (2016) *Care and Support: Statutory Guidance*, Chapter 15 and Annex J5. Available at: https://www.gov.uk/government/publications/care-act-statutory-guidance/care-and-support-statutory-guidance#person-centred-care-and-support-planning.

NHS-funded nursing care Funding from the National Health Service to homes providing nursing care in order to support the provision of that nursing care by a registered nurse. The New Labour government (1997–2010) introduced free nursing care under the Health and Social Care Act (2001, Section 49) in response to a recommendation of the Royal Commission on Long-term Care. Any nursing care required by someone in residential care is therefore the responsibility of the NHS and is provided free of charge to the resident. Free nursing care in care homes applies regardless of a person's financial circumstances. This means that even where a resident is paying their own care home fees, that part of the care that is 'registered nursing care' will be provided free of charge, as it is paid for by the NHS. 'Registered nursing care' is defined as care provided by a registered nurse. This includes nursing and health care that is planned, supervised, monitored, delegated, or directly provided by a registered nurse. For people in care homes with nursing, registered nurses are employed by the care home and, in order to fund this nursing care, the NHS makes a payment direct to the care home. There is a standard-rate contribution towards the cost of providing registered nursing care for those residents who are eligible. In all cases people should be considered for eligibility for *NHS continuing health care before a decision is reached about the need for NHS-funded nursing care. Residents within a care home that is registered to provide nursing care who do not qualify for NHS continuing health care have to have been assessed as requiring the services of a registered nurse. Residents will not need to have a separate assessment for NHS-funded nursing care if they have already had an assessment for NHS continuing health care, as this process will give sufficient information to judge whether there is a need for NHS-funded nursing care. However, if an assessment is needed, the *Clinical Commissioning Group will arrange it. If someone is eligible for NHS-funded nursing care, the payment is made directly to the care home and the care home's fee to the person is reduced accordingly. If a decision is made not to offer NHS-funded nursing care, the resident can ask the CCG for the decision to be reviewed and/or use the CCG complaints process. Since October 2007 NHS-funded nursing care has been based on a single band rate. Previously there were three different payment bands for nursing care. Anyone who was on the high band of NHS-funded nursing care under the previous three-band system is entitled to continue on this band until s/he no longer has nursing needs; or no longer lives in a care home that provides nursing care; or her/his nursing needs have reduced so that they do not qualify for the high band any more (s/he would move onto the single band rate instead); or s/he has become entitled to NHS continuing health care.

Further reading: Department of Health (2012) *National Framework for NHS Continuing Healthcare and NHS-funded Nursing Care*. Available at: http://www.gov.uk/government/uploads/system/uploads/attachment_data/file/213137/National-Framework-for-NHS-CHC-NHS-FNC-Nov-2012.pdf.

Department of Health (2016) *Care and Support: Statutory Guidance*, Chapter 15 and Annex J5. Available at: https://www.gov.uk/government/publications/care-act-statutory-guidance/care-and-support-statutory-guidance#person-centred-care-and-support-planning.

NICE *See* NATIONAL INSTITUTE FOR HEALTH AND CARE EXCELLENCE.

night shelter Overnight basic accommodation for homeless people that may not provide any facilities, and is not available for use during the day. Some shelters do, however, provide meals, baths, and have clothing available. Almost all night shelters are provided by registered *charities, with some provided by or linked to religious organizations such as the Salvation Army.

no fixed abode *See* HOMELESSNESS; VAGRANT.

nominated person *See* DIRECT PAYMENT.

non-departmental public body (NDPB) Also, and originally, referred to as a *QUANGO, an NDPB is a body that has a role in the processes of government, but is not a government department or part of a government department and so it operates to a greater or lesser extent at arm's length from government ministers. NDPBs have different roles. Some advise ministers; others carry out executive or regulatory functions. All NDPBs work within a strategic framework set by ministers, and ministers are ultimately responsible to Parliament for the bodies sponsored by their departments.

non-means-tested benefits *See* UNIVERSAL BENEFITS.

non-verbal communication Forms of communication that do not rely on the spoken or written word, and include bodily mannerisms, postures, and facial expressions that can be interpreted as unconsciously communicating somebody's feelings or psychological state. *See also* COMMUNICATION SKILLS.

no order principle One of the key principles of the Children Act (1989) is that a *family court will only make an order in respect of a child if it is better than making no order. In making this decision, a court will use the *welfare checklist to assist in its deliberations. An example of the use of the no order principle is when a *case is subject to *Care Proceedings and the court decides that there is no need for a *Supervision Order or *Interim Care Order to be in place, pending a decision as to whether a final order is required, because the parents are committed to working with the *local authority. The no order principle underlines the importance of local authorities working in *partnership with parents wherever possible and securing agreement to voluntary arrangements unless to do so would place the child at risk of *significant harm. In *private law cases the principle underlines the importance of the adults involved reaching agreement on issues relating to the care of their children rather than the court deciding the issue by making a court order. *See also* CARE ORDER; CHILD ARRANGEMENTS ORDER; CONTACT; PARAMOUNTCY PRINCIPLE; RESIDENCE.

no refusals assessment *See* DEPRIVATION OF LIBERTY SAFEGUARDS.

norm An expectation of behaviour that has connotations of what is desirable and acceptable, and can be a powerful means of securing conformity. Similar to rules in that they prescribe what someone should do or not do but without having a formal status. Behaviour that departs from norms may be *labelled as deviant.

normalization A perspective developed by Wolf Wolfensberger (1934–2011) in relation to people with *learning disabilities that advocates their living in 'normal' settings and having 'normal' lifestyles because this is in their interests and will foster their acceptance by the wider society. While this was a huge step forwards in terms of dignity and choice, when compared to the institutional conditions in which many people with learning disabilities were ghettoized, the perspective subsequently attracted criticism because conformity to what is seen as 'normal' was viewed as contentious. Others have argued that there are some benefits to people with learning disabilities in having the opportunity to be with each other because at such times they are released from the pressures they may experience in the rest of their lives. Proponents of the *social model of disability have argued that normalization smacks of the ways in which people with physical *disability were seen as needing to adapt to society before the model shone a spotlight on barriers to *participation created by the environment around them. *See also* SOCIAL ROLE VALORIZATION.

normative order (normative power) A system of shared or imposed expectations that govern a particular social situation or organization. For example, in social work organizations in which the normative order is *managerialism, control, performance, and efficiency are likely to be the basis for the exercise of normative power by managers. The normative power of managerialism sets out the terms of reference by which the organization will function, with anything that falls outside of these terms of reference not being part of the normative order. For example, when *eligibility criteria are used by social workers in their practice with adults, they are operating within a managerial normative order and as agents of normative power. *See also* BOUNDED RATIONALITY; DISCOURSE.

Northern Ireland Social work in Northern Ireland displays both elements of divergence and convergence with social work in England, *Scotland, and *Wales. Responsibility for policy, legislation, and the delivery of social work has long been a devolved function and was so during the development of statutory social work services between 1948 and 1971. It operated in the system of administrative devolution under direct rule from Westminster between 1971 and 1999. Since the restoration of devolution in 1999, health and social care continue to be a devolved matter, largely in line with Scotland and Wales.

Health care in Northern Ireland is almost entirely provided by the National Health Service. The current national system of publicly funded health care was created in 1948 at the same time as its counterparts in Scotland and in England and Wales, incorporating a principle that services would be kept in parity. However, structurally, the system in Northern Ireland is markedly different from in the rest of the United Kingdom. Since the 1970s it has operated an integrated system of health and social care with no direct *local authority involvement. Indeed the system in Northern Ireland has been described as one of the most structurally integrated and comprehensive modes of health and personal social services in Europe. Provision of health and social care has historically been maintained at generally the same scale and standard as in Great Britain. Funding for health and social care is determined by the Northern Ireland government from the block grant allocated by the UK Treasury. Standards of professionalism, education, training, regulation, inspection, registration, and practice are also traditionally kept in line with those in Great Britain.

A major review of public administration (RPA) led to the reconfiguration of health and social services in 2007. This strengthened integration with the establishment of five fully integrated Health and Social Care Trusts responsible for delivering all health and social care provision and one central health and social services authority (the Health and Social Care Board) responsible mainly for commissioning and performance management. Within this system, social work is integrated with both primary and secondary health in a unified structure. A key objective of the RPA was to maintain the integrated system, thereby preserving and developing the advantages of combining *medical and social models of *analysis of people's needs. In 2016 the health minister announced plans to abolish the Health and Social Care Board and all commissioning, planning, and monitoring powers were to be transferred to the Department of Health. In practice the detailed commissioning of domiciliary social care was carried out by the five Health and Social Care Trusts.

In Northern Ireland integration in the delivery of services is largely achieved through a programme of care approach at Trust level. This usually involves identifying the programmes and amalgamating resources under a focused management structure. At its most developed this encompasses a whole-systems approach to service delivery in hospital and community services. Integrated working is facilitated by the internal structures and budget arrangements of Trusts, and the use of resources is not constrained by artificial boundaries between health and social care.

Throughout the Trusts, the major programmes of care follow a broadly similar pattern for *older people, mental health, *learning disability, and physical *disability. Child care programmes tend to reflect less integration than adult social care as there are legal requirements that mean the programmes and teams are often staffed exclusively by social workers. Thus, even within the integrated structure of Northern Ireland, children's services are set apart. The programme of care management teams operates on a multidisciplinary basis. However, the degree of professional integration does vary between the programmes and the level of *need. Mental health and learning disability are the most fully integrated professionally, although it appears that the multidisciplinary model is more extensive in mental health than learning disability at the delivery level. There are increasing examples of specialist integrated teams, for example *child and adolescent mental health teams. Older people's teams are more social work-based, but they or specialist subgroups may include nursing, physiotherapists, *occupational therapists, and care workers. The person responsible for coordinating *assessment and leading teams can be anyone who has a professional or social care qualification. This method of working is a defining feature of the integrated system.

Alongside inter-professional working another distinctive feature of this integrated system is the single employing organization. This means that there is a single set of aims and objectives providing the context for close working relationships. Integrated Trusts also avoid the issue of a 'lead' partner or pressure for professional domination by one partner or the need for pooled budgets. Social services in Northern Ireland highlight the advantages of a 'one-stop shop' or 'no wrong door' approach—that is, there is one front door for anybody who needs health and personal social services and *service users can be appropriately dealt with or referred within the one organization and possibly within the one building. The one-stop shop/single door is a means of avoiding some still remaining perceptions of stigma attached to social work offices, particularly in encouraging some people at *risk to attend. Integrated care teams mean that only one assessment is needed to access a range of services, including *child protection, family *intervention, and those for complex needs or chronic health conditions. The single point of access and pathway into local services means older and vulnerable people do not have to move between organizations and significantly reduces the risk of their slipping through the net. Developments have included the introduction of Wellbeing and Treatment Centres as one-stop shops for health and social care provision. To date the evidence base for achievements and benefits from Northern Ireland's integrated system presents a mixed picture. Progress with closure of institutional care for people with mental health problems and learning disabilities and moving towards *community care has been slow. Performance in discharging patients from hospital is patchy. It can be argued that the full potential of integration has not been realized and structural integration does not automatically equate to a seamless service. Concern at the effectiveness of the integrated structures and the limited engagement by *general practitioners led to an initiative in 2014 called Integrated Care Partnerships, as networks within Trusts, which were created to focus on frail older people and some chronic health conditions. Also it is important to remember that while health and social care are integrated into one structure, education and social housing are in a totally separate administrative system.

Social work and poverty In Northern Ireland as in other parts of the UK, social work practice plays a potentially important role in alleviating *poverty, addressing complex social problems, and promoting social justice and equality. Social workers are charged with intervening in the lives of some of the most impoverished and socially excluded people. In comparative studies of poverty and *disadvantage across the UK, Northern Ireland has the highest rates of social deprivation and exclusion, with poverty described as deeply entrenched. As a region, it is marked by higher concentrations of poor people, concentrated in a number of areas of pronounced deprivation. A broad range of indicators confirm that social work practice in these areas takes place against a bleak and challenging backdrop of high levels of social need coupled with persistent and severe disadvantage.

The first large-scale study of poverty and social exclusion in Northern Ireland, 'Bare Necessities' was undertaken in 2002–3 (Hillyard et al, 2003). Whilst local and regional statistics and indicators such as rates of unemployment, economic inactivity, and dependency on benefits had invariably confirmed that it was the most deprived or one of the most deprived regions of the UK, there was a lack of robust and reliable information on the nature and extent of poverty. This research concluded rates of poverty were higher in Northern Ireland than in either the Republic of Ireland or Great Britain. Overall measures revealed that there were 30.6 per cent of people in poor households compared to 28.2 per cent in the Republic of Ireland and 25 per cent in Great Britain. The region was described by the authors as one of the most unequal societies in the developed world.

In the last decade the Joseph Rowntree Foundation has commissioned research and published a number of detailed reports designed to measure and monitor poverty and social exclusion in Northern Ireland. These studies draw on a wide range of existing sources, including government statistics and Health and Social Care Trusts' data. In 2006 the first report revealed that on many indictors Northern Ireland compared unfavourably with all of the nine English regions as well as with Scotland and Wales. The entrenched and persistent nature of child poverty was again highlighted in a Joseph Rowntree report on poverty in 2009 (Horgan and Monteith, 2009). It used data from the first longitudinal analysis of four years of the Northern Ireland Household Panel Survey (NIHPS), which revealed that at some stage in this four-year period, 48 per cent of children were living in poverty (before housing costs) and 21 per cent were in persistent poverty, i.e. in poverty for at least three of the four years. Therefore, the proportion of children in Northern Ireland who were poor at some point (48 per cent) was considerably higher than the comparable figure for Great Britain (38 per cent). Even more alarming, the rate of persistent poverty in Northern Ireland (21 per cent) was over twice that of Great Britain (9 per cent). The JRF report in 2016 concluded that 20 per cent of the population was in poverty, after housing costs, around the same as in Great Britain. The composition of those in poverty had changed between 2010 and 2015. There are more working-age adults (particularly young people), more private renters, and fewer pensioners in poverty. The overall employment rate was 5 per cent lower than in Great Britain and weekly pay remained lower (New Policy Institute, 2016).

The terms of the St Andrew's Agreement of 2006 placed a legal duty on the Northern Ireland Executive to 'adopt a strategy setting out how it proposed to tackle poverty, social exclusion and patterns of deprivation based on objective need'. The strategy, entitled 'Lifetime Opportunities', was published in 2006. In 2014 a *judicial review held that whilst the Executive had adopted the 'architecture and principles' of 'Lifetime Opportunities', there was no evidence that it had crafted a road map to deal with these endemic issues. It concluded that this should be dealt with as a matter of urgency with an agreed definition of objective need underpinning a *holistic strategy with a robust action plan (Heenan and Anderson, 2015). By the summer of 2016, no progress had been made on these issues. The target to end child poverty by 2020 has been abandoned by government and little or no discussion has taken place on how to address these failings. Child poverty has actually increased in both absolute and relative terms to 23 per cent and 25 per cent respectively in 2013–14.

Children's services The integrated structure means that children's social services are integrated with adult social services and also with primary and secondary health care. There is no direct connection with education where departmental and local administrative responsibility rests with separate bodies. This is a division which has had an influence on delaying and limiting the development of early years strategies. Despite the integrated structure some 2,000 staff are graded as child and family care workers. In 2015 some 24,000 children were known as children in need, 17 per cent of whom were disabled, half of whom had learning disabilities.

Northern Ireland had the largest numbers on *child protection registers of the four UK countries, until in 2013 it was overtaken by Wales. The number of *looked-after children is on a par with England per 10,000 population, with a total of 2,169 in 2015. Despite the differences in organization and separate Northern Ireland legislation, the broad range of children's services is similar to those in the rest of the UK, although some practices and procedures vary. For example, Northern Ireland has 'case management reviews', instead of *Serious Case Reviews, a multidisciplinary assessment initiative operates called *Understanding the Needs of Children in Northern Ireland*, and 'Gateway' operates as the first point of contact for all new referrals to children's social work services. Northern Ireland is unlikely to follow England in having a more mixed economy of provision in relation to children's services. It continues to have a probation service in which all probation officers must be qualified social workers, holding a degree in social work. All are employed by the Northern Ireland Probation Board, a *non-departmental public body, and, unlike England, no probation function has been outsourced to the *independent sector.

Social work and conflict Social work in Northern Ireland has operated in the context of deep community divisions, with civil disturbances and varying degrees of *violence. The basic division into Protestant and Catholic communities on a 60:40 per cent ratio has strong components of religious affiliation and belief, ethnic and national *identity, *prejudice, and segregation particularly along residential and educational lines. The delivery of social work services has been affected by both the prevalence of sectarianism and the impact of violence.

Sectarian factors have influenced social work practice in a number of ways, including interpersonal relationships. Social workers may regularly encounter the expression of sectarian attitudes, whether mooted generally or directed at them personally. Delivering social work in segregated neighbourhoods has presented a range of barriers amidst a dynamic that sustains sectarian attitudes and antagonisms. Such neighbourhoods and housing estates may be under the control of paramilitary organizations, and there have been examples of social workers requiring police escorts. The existence of peace walls in Belfast to separate communities physically can present barriers to accessing social work offices and social care facilities. One consequence can be the need to duplicate facilities within relatively small geographical areas. The problems of sectarianism and social work began to be addressed more specifically by government, the profession, and training bodies in the mid-1990s with the development of ideas about anti-sectarian practice that included examining the attitudes of social work staff. The principles developed for training and education were closely related to the principles of *anti-oppressive practice developed in Great Britain. With an increase in European migration and rising levels of *hate crime in Northern Ireland the anti-sectarian approach has been linked to *anti-racist strategies and this has also included strategies for working with travellers.

Over a lengthy period, from 1969 to 1995, Northern Ireland experienced extensive and intense levels of violence, with bombings, shootings, riots, intimidation, community disturbances, political violence, security measures, and clampdowns. This violence resulted in 3,700 deaths and 43,000 injuries, with major damage to property and population movements in some areas. Despite the ceasefires since the mid-1990s and the political agreement of 1998 on a devolved power-sharing government, there has been continuing sporadic violence, intimidation, and *community tensions. Most of the violence has been concentrated in specific areas and there is evidence of a high correlation of violence with levels of poverty and social deprivation (Morrissey and Smyth, 2002). The main consequences for social work have been the direct emergency impact of violence and population displacement, the impact of violence on mental health, and some disruption to service provision.

The emergency response following bombings, large-scale shootings, damage to homes, and intimidation has involved social work contributions. Until the 1990s the response by statutory social work agencies was loosely structured and even ad hoc. However, work by a Principal Social Worker in Belfast, Marion Gibson, on the theme of responding to disasters was to become influential in improving training and preparation. Gibson (2006) used a typology of staged interventions to emergencies and considered different forms of responses from social services. Crisis support teams were developed in the late 1990s in the statutory boards covering social work. The approach sought to involve local communities and the services of *voluntary organizations. Following the ceasefires and the peace process, social service emergency teams have remained, but now largely deal with the needs of people evacuated from their homes owing to intimidation or now more occasional violent incidents.

Social service responses developed with a major focus on *counselling support to complement social care. The nature of the violence was seen to have had a major impact on mental health and largely accounted for higher rates of *mental illness than those in England or Scotland. There was increasing research evidence of *post-traumatic stress disorder among those affected by the violence. In 1998 the Social Services Inspectorate produced a report, 'Living with the Trauma of the Troubles' (SSI, 1998), aimed at developing further services to meet the social and psychological needs of individuals seriously affected by the violence and improve awareness, understanding, and coordination of provision and training. The emphasis on trauma became more important after the Omagh bombing in 1998, Northern Ireland's worst single terrorist atrocity, in which twenty-nine people died and over 200 were injured. All of the Health and Social Service Boards established a Trauma Advisory Panel chaired by a senior social worker. There has also been research evidence from a number of studies of the long-term impact of stress related to the violence. The focus on trauma was accompanied by a more high-profile concern for the *needs of all victims of 'the Troubles'. The Belfast Health and Social Care Trust operates a Trauma Resource Centre and a regional specialist centre, the Northern Ireland Centre for Trauma and Transformation. This was set up after the Omagh bombing. It provides advice and care as well as developing and delivering training and undertaking research. A Social Services Inspectorate report (SSI, 2004) on the role of social work in mental health noted the continuing impact on social work practice of violent incidents, inter-communal violent behaviour, chronic stress, and related *addictions. Evidence shows that those who experienced a traumatic event related to the conflict are more likely to have a mental illness at some point. Despite the peace process there has been a continuing degree of paramilitary activity, creating what the Bamford Review at the time of its publication identified as a thinly veiled undercurrent of violence and intimidation (Department of Health, Social Services and Public Safety 2009).

While the conflict, sectarianism, and violence have had a unique impact on social work provision, it is important to note that the delivery of the great bulk of social care has not been affected, and dealing with conflict-related problems has taken up a small component of social workers' time in most locations throughout Northern Ireland. The violence and conflict did at times, however, disrupt more mainstream operations as well as create the unique needs that have been described.

In recent years, assessments of the role played by social work in the conflict and how this could translate more generally into the area of conflict resolution and care of *victims are beginning to emerge. As a consequence, there has been a growth in the number and range of these services across the statutory, community, and *voluntary sectors. As with other professional groups, social work has had to adapt to a changing policy landscape in relation to victims and *survivors of the conflict.

Adaptation to modernization themes In Great Britain debates about the modernization of social work have been dominated by the integration, *personalization, and *participation agendas. These have been endorsed by the previous and current UK governments and the devolved governments in Scotland and Wales. With the obvious exception of integration, Northern Ireland has been slow to adopt policies and strategies from these agendas, with little pressure or discussion coming from the Department of Health, Social Services and Public Safety, the Northern Ireland Assembly, the Health and Social Care Board, or the Health and Social Care Trusts. Northern Ireland did follow Great Britain in enacting legislation to introduce *direct payments, which allowed social service agencies to make payments to people to purchase and organize their own *care and support rather than rely entirely on statutory services. However, the uptake and development of these provisions in Northern Ireland have been slow and the total number of direct payments per annum has remained low. There is only one major source of voluntary support for people wishing to take direct payments in Northern Ireland, the Centre for Independent Learning, compared to a wide range of organizations in Great Britain. Commitment to the personalization agenda has remained weak, uptake of direct payments is low, and even knowledge of the scheme among social workers can be sketchy. Personalization has been given little priority as a strategy.

*Service user participation has been a significant aspect of the *modernization agenda in Great Britain, but again has not received the same priority in Northern Ireland. The system of governance for social work is totally integrated structurally with health and means that social work commissioning, planning, and delivery are the responsibility of nominated public bodies or *quangos, which are either centralized or very large in terms of population. There is, therefore, no local democratic control or local councillor involvement with social care and social work. Mechanisms for public involvement have not been developed much beyond formal public consultations. While the five Health and Social Care Trusts have produced public involvement strategies, the rationales have been limited to forms of public consultation or even interpreted as meaning participation by *voluntary organizations. Official documentation shows little awareness of the debates in England, Scotland, or Wales concerning such ideas as *co-production, strengthening *advocacy, and user involvement in the commissioning and delivery of services. The main mechanism for public involvement is a Patient and Client Council, which is a single body covering social care and health for the whole of Northern Ireland. It has very limited functions or powers and was set up on the *quango model of an appointed board. This means that it has no representative basis or formal localized structure. There has been little action to engage users and carers in the planning, delivery, and evaluation of social work and social care services. Research by Duffy (2008) found the development of user involvement in social work uneven across agencies in Northern Ireland. Whilst there were some examples of *good practice, many of those consulted had negative experiences of involvement with large-scale social work providers. Some progress has been made in the area of social work education, where users have been involved in practice assessment, teaching, student selection, curriculum design, and course review. Work has also been undertaken to enable social work students to understand better the needs of victims and survivors by developing innovative pedagogical approaches involving case studies and service users. Despite the rhetoric, and the formulation of Health and Social Care Trusts' public involvement statements, user participation in health and social care is relatively limited as far as *user-led organizations are concerned and is concentrated in the mental health field.

Mental health In 2002, in response to growing concerns about the nature and scale of mental illness, the then health minister established the most comprehensive review of mental health and learning disability to date in Northern Ireland, which became known as the Bamford Review (Department of Health, Social Services and Public Safety 2009). This review emphasized the need to place service users at the heart of the process and enable them to shape the design, delivery, and evaluation of support. Controversially, however, despite this statement of intent, the review was dominated by medical professionals, and service users were not involved at the outset. A number of groups expressed anger at what they viewed as being included later as a means to authenticate findings, rather than being engaged in a meaningful way to shape recommendations.

The conclusions of the Review presented a damning portrait of mental health services in Northern Ireland with a history of significant underinvestment in this area. Service users and *carers were described as poorly supported and insufficiently involved in the design and delivery of services. The process resulted in the publication of over ten substantial reports with over 700 recommendations but implementation has been disappointingly slow. Despite the evidence that this is a particularly significant issue in this post-conflict society, mental health and learning disability services have not been prioritized and remain inadequate. Recent research has highlighted concerns about the transgenerational mental health impact of years of violence, highlighting the conflict's legacy on subsequent generations (O'Neill et al, 2015). Suicide rates have doubled over a ten-year period and are once again the highest in the UK at 15.7 deaths per 100,000 population and 35.6 deaths in the most deprived areas.

Development of the social work profession Northern Ireland has emulated England, Scotland, and Wales in undertaking a wide-ranging review of the role and tasks of social workers. The underpinning analysis was undertaken by the Northern Ireland Social Care Council and this led to a ten-year strategy document for social work in Northern Ireland 2010–20 (Department of Health, Social Services and Public Safety 2010). The content had some similarity with the work in England, Scotland, and Wales, and was built on what the Chief Social Services Officer in Northern Ireland referred to as recognition that the context of social work was evolving. It was suggested that social work should build on developing the integrated structure, as well as the values of fairness and justice, and become more person-centred.

The Department of Health, Social Services and Public Safety's strategy paper put its main focus on the social work profession and its future development (Department of Health, Social Services and Public Safety 2010). It emphasized factors such as support for increasing the confidence of social workers, promoting public understanding, improving professional leadership, addressing workforce issues (including the number of social workers), and developing social work services around the needs of the people who use them. The paper had gaps and weaknesses compared to the papers produced in England, Scotland, and Wales.

In 2013 a consultation paper was published on the reform of adult care and support, entitled 'Who Cares?' (Department of Health, Social Services and Public Safety 2013). This consultation paper examined the costs of residential care but the paper was strongly criticized and there was no subsequent government action. There was also a lack of detailed discussion of engagement with users and the public; support for carers; the personalization agenda, including developments with *personal budgets; giving people more control; and the potential of the integrated structure in Northern Ireland. Despite the concerns in Northern Ireland in relation to child protection standards, children *leaving care, and early years social care, these issues were also not discussed.

Following the *devolution settlement, new separate devolved structures for registration, education, and inspection of social work were established. The Northern Ireland Social Care Council has responsibility for a registration scheme, the promotion and development of education and training for the social services workforce, the accreditation of social work qualifying and post-qualifying training, *codes of practice for social care workers and employers, and bursaries for social work students.

Future pressures The financial crises of the late 2000s (*see* AUSTERITY) resulted in the deepest and most sustained cuts to public expenditure since the inception of the *welfare state. Within health and social care in Northern Ireland, social work provision has been disproportionately affected by budget cuts. This may be viewed as a reflection of the low priority given to social care by politicians in the devolved institutions and the dominant position of health and the acute sector in the integrated structure, leaving social care in a Cinderella position. Expenditure per head on social care is now lower in Northern Ireland than in Scotland and Wales and just above the figures for England. Most domiciliary care is now provided by the *independent sector and about one-third of service users receive intensive care, but the numbers and amount of care hours delivered in *care packages have declined, as has the number of residential care places.

The Department of Health, Social Services and Public Safety and the Health and Social Care Trusts have not produced documentation similar to recent papers in Scotland and Wales covering additional themes of inequality, sustainability, and collaboration, or in England on meeting the cost of adult social care. A series of reviews have been undertaken relating to both health and social care, with an emphasis on ensuring a sustainable, cost-effective system of health and social care (Appleby 2011). This work stressed the need for a seismic shift in Northern Ireland's health and social care landscape, towards a system focused on primary and *community care. In 2011, the health minister announced a major review of health and social care to examine the future provision of services, including acute hospital configuration, the development of primary health care services and social care, and the interfaces between the sectors. The subsequent report 'Transforming Your Care' (Department of Health, Social Services and Public Safety 2011) stressed the need for a significant shift from provision of services in hospitals to provision of services in the community. Services are to be designed in conjunction with service users to meet their needs, rather than the preferences of those delivering the services. This review was described as the most radical shake-up of health and social care to date and one which would fundamentally alter the design and delivery of services, including social work services.

The reform process in Northern Ireland has been hampered by the ongoing *austerity agenda, which has resulted in a growing funding gap, alongside a system of health and social care that overinvests in an inefficient hospital sector whilst underinvesting in community-based care. In 2014, when Sir Liam Donaldson was asked to undertake a review of the governance of critical incidents in health, his work validated the recommendations of 'Transforming Your Care' concerned with moving towards community care but called for action not words with a new costed timetable for reform (Donaldson 2014). In 2016 the reform agenda was continued when a clinically led panel with local, national, and international expertise was established to consider the best options for health reform. There is a renewed political commitment to continue the process of reform in Northern Ireland. However there is frustration at the slow pace of change and the seemingly relentless focus on acute care, with social care and mental health care languishing far behind, and the continuing absence of new social care legislation to mirror that in England, Wales, and Scotland.

Further reading: Appleby, J. (2011) *Rapid Review of Northern Ireland Health and Social Care Funding Needs and the Productivity Challenge* 2011/12–2014/15, King's Fund.

Birrell, D. (2009) *The Impact of Devolution on Social Policy*, Policy Press.

Department of Health, Social Services and Public Safety (2009) *Delivering the Bamford Vision Action Plan 2009–2011*, DHSSPS.

Department of Health, Social Services and Public Safety (2010) *A Ten Year Strategy for Social Work in Northern Ireland 2010–2020*, DHSSPS.

Department of Health, Social Services and Public Safety (2011) *Transforming Your Care: A Review of Health and Social Care in Northern Ireland*, DHSSPS.

Department of Health, Social Services and Public Safety (2013) *Who Cares? The Future of Adult Care and Support in Northern Ireland*, DHSSPS.

Donaldson, L. (2014) *The Right Time and the Right Place*, Department of Health, Social Services and Public Safety.

Duffy, J. (2008) *Looking Out from the Middle: User Involvement in Health and Social Care in Northern Ireland*, Report 18. Available at: http://www.scie.org.uk/publications/reports.

Gibson, M. (2006, 3rd edn.) *Order from Chaos: Responding to Traumatic Events*, Policy Press.

Heenan, D. and Anderson, C. (2015) *No-one Left Behind*, Heenan-Anderson Independent Commission.

Hillyard, P., Kelly, G., McLaughlin, E., Parsius, D., and Tomlinson, M. (2003) *Bare Necessities: Poverty and Social Exclusion in Northern Ireland*, Democratic Dialogue.

Horgan, G. and Monteith, M. (2009) *What Can We Do to Tackle Child Poverty in Northern Ireland?*, Joseph Rowntree Foundation.

Morrisey M. and Smyth, M. (2002) *Northern Ireland after the Good Friday Agreement*, Pluto Press.

New Policy Institute (2016) *Monitoring Poverty and Social Exclusion in Northern Ireland*, Joseph Rowntree Foundation.

O'Neill, S. (2015) *Towards a Better Future: The Trans-generational Impact of the Troubles on Mental Health*, Commission for Victims and Survivors.

Social Services Inspectorate Northern Ireland (1998) *Living with the Trauma of the Troubles*, SSINI.

Social Services Inspectorate Northern Ireland (2004) *Inspection of Social Work in Mental Health Services*, Department of Health, Social Services and Public Safety.

NR *See* NEAREST RELATIVE.

NSPCC *See* NATIONAL SOCIETY FOR THE PROTECTION OF CRUELTY TO CHILDREN.

nuclear family A unit traditionally seen as consisting of heterosexual parents and their dependent children. It has been much idealized, presented as biologically 'natural', and socially as the *'norm' in terms of reproduction, child-rearing, and socialization of children, particularly on the political right. However, *household forms and functions are shaped by ideological, political, and economic processes and the rise of alternatives to the heterosexual nuclear family, shaped by these processes, means that social workers encounter a wide range of *household structures. This has led some to suggest that the nuclear family no longer has any validity as a term because it only captures one arrangement among many, while others have wanted to broaden the term so that, for example, a nuclear family can describe a household with a same sex couple or a single parent and her/his children. *See also* EXTENDED FAMILY; HETERONORMATIVITY.

nurseries A range of day care locations for pre-school children provided by *public, *private, and *voluntary sector organizations. Nurseries have to comply with the *early years foundation stage and are inspected by Ofsted. Predominantly associated with children who require care while their parents work, but there are also more specialist services for children and families with more complex needs who require support, usually as part of a range of provision. Nursery schools are distinguished from nurseries by their provision including education. *See also* CHILDREN'S CENTRES; EARLY YEARS SERVICES; EXTENDED SERVICES; FAMILY INFORMATION SERVICE; SURE START.

nursing care *See* NHS-FUNDED NURSING CARE.

NVQ *See* NATIONAL VOCATIONAL QUALIFICATIONS.

objectification A process by which a powerful group establishes and/or maintains its dominance over a less powerful group by regarding the subordinate group as less than human, as like an object. This eliminates the possibility of the powerful group sympathizing or identifying with the less powerful group. For example, pornography treats women as objects to serve men and is an extreme example of a range of ways in which women are objectified. On an interpersonal level, objectification can be a way of dealing with stressful situations and social workers need to be alert to the possibility of objectifying service users as a way of coping with the demands of the job. *See also* DECONSTRUCTION; OTHER; OUT-GROUP.

observation 1. An essential task in social work, for example when observing a *child's development, or a *contact between a parent and a child, or the circumstances in which an adult is living.
   2. An *assessment tool that is utilized on qualifying and post-qualifying social work programmes. It involves a student's or newly qualified social worker's practice with a *service user being observed, their performance being evaluated, and *feedback being given to them.

obsessive compulsive disorder (OCD) A psychiatric condition characterized by intrusive persistent thoughts that cannot be controlled, from which the individual cannot escape, and which cause distress, *anxiety, apprehension, and fear. The term can be broken down to represent the two aspects of the disorder. Obsessive refers to intrusive, alien, and unpleasant thoughts, and compulsive refers to behaviour engaged in to seek temporary relief from obsessive and anxiety-provoking thoughts. Therefore, symptoms of OCD are usually recognized by the behavioural aspect, such as repetitive hand-washing, hoarding, or repeating an action several times in a particular way. These compulsive rituals can be time-consuming and destructive, and can cause immense distress to the individual, who is usually aware that the behaviour is irrational. Many people can experience disquieting thoughts that might be unpleasant or seem out of character. The distinction with OCD is that extraordinary significance becomes attached to the thoughts. OCD is clinically distinct from obsessive compulsive personality disorder in which the individual rationalizes their thoughts and behaviour and is not distressed by them. Similarly, compulsive gambling or overeating are not classified as OCD because pleasure is experienced from these acts. Individuals with OCD do not wish to engage in their ritualized behaviours and gain no pleasure from feeling compelled to do so. OCD is treated with *cognitive behavioural therapies and medication can help reduce symptoms. *See also* PERSONALITY DISORDER.

occupational socialization Being inducted into and learning the attitudes and behaviours that are associated with a particular occupation. For example, social workers are socialized into thinking of their work in terms of *'cases' of particular kinds that have particular characteristics. Although formal training plays a part in occupational socialization, informal work *norms and *peer group values and relationships are powerful shapers of attitudes and behaviours, as can be seen in the workplace *culture of social work. A term in French—*déformation professionnelle*—captures the end-product of occupational socialization; the tendency to see things from the ('deformed') perspective of one's profession. It is a play on words: *formation professionnelle* means 'professional training'. The implication is that occupational socialization produces a form of tunnel vision through which the world is viewed. *See also* HABITUS.

occupational standards *See* KNOWLEDGE AND SKILLS STATEMENTS; PROFESSIONAL CAPABILITY FRAMEWORK.

occupational therapist (OT) A specialist in *rehabilitation who seeks to maintain or improve someone's level of physical and/or psychological functioning. OTs are employed by the National Health Service and *local authority adults' services and the latter work particularly closely with social workers, assessing *service users in relation to what are often referred to as *activities of daily living and arranging for *aids and adaptations to be provided in response to the *needs revealed. In doing so, they may participate with social workers in *needs assessments conducted under the Care Act (2014) or they may undertake a separate specialist assessment that feeds into a social worker's needs assessment. Depending on the setting in which they work, OTs can also be involved in teaching skills that will improve someone's functioning and therapeutic activities that may include, for instance, arts and crafts. For example, in a mental health setting, OTs assess functioning in relation to daily living skills and in order to improve those skills may provide training programmes in work, recreational, and social skills.

OCD *See* OBSESSIVE COMPULSIVE DISORDER.

offender manager *See* COMMUNITY SENTENCES.

offending behaviour Term that has tended to replace 'crime' or 'criminal activity' in professional parlance.

offending behaviour programmes Aimed at confronting and changing attitudes towards offending. Such programmes are offered in prisons and in institutions for young offenders, as well as in community settings through the *Probation Service and *Youth Offending Teams or under *outsourcing arrangements they have with other organizations. Attending such a programme can be a requirement of a *community sentence. Some programmes are concerned with offending in general. Other are more specific, for example, focusing on *anger management or *substance misuse.

Office for Standards in Education, Children's Services and Skills (Ofsted) A non-ministerial inspectorate that reports directly to parliament. It inspects schools and academies, *early years services, child care (including *childminders and *nurseries), *children's centres, *children's homes; *family centres; *adoption and *fostering agencies, the *Children and Family Court Advisory Support Service, children's services in *local authorities, initial teacher training, further education colleges, a range of work-based learning and skills training, and education and training in prisons and other secure establishments. The responsibility for inspecting local authority children's services includes services for *looked-after children, *safeguarding, and *child protection.

• Official site of the Office for Standards in Education, Children's Services and Skills, where publicly available reports of its inspections can be found

Office of the Public Guardian *See* CAPACITY.

old age *See* THEORIES OF AGEING.

older people The preferred term in social work rather than 'the elderly' or 'old people' because it retains the personhood of older people and recognizes the slipperiness of the concept of older age and when it begins. Someone may be regarded as an older person on the basis of chronological age, or by reference to signs of physical ageing, or by taking account of health, abilities, and/or behaviour. Or, the emphasis may be placed on subjective self-perceptions; whether or not someone sees themselves as old. If chronological age is used to define someone as an older person, it is important to remember that a wide age range can be encompassed. For example, defining the threshold of old age at 65 means that the category of 'older people' may span three or four decades. To deal with this, some studies distinguish a category of the 'older old', for example, those aged over 75 or 80, suggesting that particular social and psychological processes may characterize this phase of later life but even amongst the 'older old', chronological age may indicate very little beyond being a process of general social categorization. In response to the problems of defining an 'older person' simply in relation to the numbers of years lived, it is tempting to regard biological ageing as an alternative starting point for defining old age and to see this as more objective and scientific. However, the rate of biological ageing is influenced by social and economic conditions. For example, older people from certain *ethnic minority groups tend to experience premature biological ageing and poorer health, illustrating how dimensions of *inequality encountered at earlier stages in the *life course can impact on biological processes and the lived experience of later life. Notwithstanding the limitations involved, research studies and official categorizations of older people, such as those used in social work, often adopt a chronological definition of old age, usually people who are over the age of 65.

Even though 'older people' may be adopted in preference to 'the elderly' or other terms now considered outdated, there is still a danger of essentializing older people, of assuming that everyone is the same, obscuring differences by implying a fixed social category. However, in some cases, those within the category of older people will have a stronger sense of sharing key aspects of *identity with people outside the category as much as, or more than, with those within it. For example, a Black or disabled identity may be more salient for a person's sense of self than being an 'older person'. Sources of *difference and *diversity amongst older people arise from location within other social divisions such as *class, *disability, *ethnicity, *gender, and sexuality. For example, ethnic inequalities in health and income increase considerably with advancing age. Another example is provided by the increasing number of older people with *learning disabilities but, as their overall number remains a small proportion of the total number of older people, there is a danger that their specific needs are neglected. Another dimension of difference amongst older people is the discrimination and the obstacles that historical *oppression and social disapproval of same-sex relationships present in terms of older people feeling able to declare their sexuality if they are gay or lesbian. As a consequence, there is a danger of isolation for lesbian women and gay men as they age and experience the *loss of partners, friends, and/or mobility. They may particularly fear residential care, as even if staff members are *anti-oppressive in their practice, some residents may be homophobic. These are illustrative examples of areas of difference amongst older people that demonstrate how diverse the category is. There are many other aspects of diversity that interrelate with age that are likely to be significant for social workers working with older people. For example, social workers may work with: older people in prison; older people who are homeless; older people who have problems related to misuse of alcohol or drugs. For these older people, there will be areas of commonality with younger age groups in terms of how difficulties have arisen, are experienced, and are managed, but there will also be differences associated with particular factors related to ageing.

If age is seen as a social division that is cross-cut by other social divisions, such as class, disability, ethnicity, gender, and sexuality, those who have been disadvantaged earlier in the life course are likely to experience a continuation or exacerbation of inequality in later life, leaving some sections of older people much more vulnerable to *poverty. For example, the lower lifetime earnings of women compared with men contribute to their high rates of poverty in later life, resulting in the income of women who have recently retired being only about half of that received by men in the same situation, with twice as many women as men relying on *means-tested benefits. Women are less likely to belong to an occupational pension scheme and when they do, this is often worth on average less than a third of that received by men. The impact of inequalities over the life course related to ethnicity is also significant. Within a broad pattern of disadvantage in older age experienced by ethnic minority groups there are differences between ethnic minority groups. For example, there is evidence that Chinese and Vietnamese older people fare worse than either African Caribbean or South Asian older people in terms of income in later life.

While social workers need to take into account the impact of social divisions in their understanding of the experiences of older people, recognizing and valuing diversity amongst older people as an important component of *anti-oppressive practice, no assumptions can be made about the precise way in which different aspects of inequality interact in particular situations or about how they are experienced by the individuals concerned. The impact of social divisions is mediated by more personal influences such as *life course experiences, *personality, attitudes, and values. However, concentrating solely on individual differences can obscure shared interests, weakening the potential for older people to acquire strength through uniting against common sources of injustice and exclusion, with people from diverse backgrounds seen as unified on the basis of their shared experience of marginalization and devalued identities.

If there are dangers and limitations to using 'older people' as a social category, with the potential to create and consolidate ageist assumptions and practices, and to ignore the multiple and cross-cutting differences of those so categorized, there are also dangers of lapsing into 'agelessness', denying the changes that accompany ageing and what the years someone has lived signify, stripping older people of their history. There are a number of ways in which age is significant. First, there are physiological processes associated with ageing. The body does age, with inevitable physical changes occurring, albeit in different ways and at varying rates for different individuals. Engaging with older people's experiences of ageing means acknowledging the significance of these changes. Secondly, there are specific social and economic processes that shape the experience of later life, for example, retirement and pension policies, and social services provision. Thirdly, chronological age is related to membership of generational cohorts and this is linked with particular life experiences, attitudes, and values. Social workers need to reach an understanding of an older person's current situation within the context of their *life course as a whole and the meanings this has for them. Steering a course between not making assumptions because someone belongs to the category of 'older people' and not propounding the myth of agelessness, involves social workers acknowledging the potential significance of age and the ageing process, but not letting this prejudice their *assessments or *interventions. It means social workers anchoring their understanding of older people's situations in knowledge and awareness of physiological changes, social and economic processes, and generational influences but at the same time moving beyond this level of understanding to exploring the meaning and significance of these factors for the individuals concerned. This second tier of understanding involves engaging with individual biographies, attitudes, values, beliefs, understandings, and practices. Social workers need to recognize that each situation is unique, diverse, complex, and constantly changing yet, at the same time, is influenced by physiological, social, and structural factors. Being an older person is both personal and located in an economic, social, and political context. *See also* AGEISM; BIOGRAPHICAL APPROACHES; INTERSECTIONALITY; MASQUERADE; NARRATIVE APPROACHES; SAFEGUARDING ADULTS; THEORIES OF AGEING.

Older People's Advocacy Alliance (OPAAL UK) A registered *charity that promotes access to independent *advocacy for *older people, seeks enhanced standards, and increases the involvement of older people themselves.

((⊕)) SEE WEB LINKS
• Official site of the Older People's Advocacy Alliance.

ombudsman Investigator of complaints of maladministration made against official bodies. *See* LOCAL GOVERNMENT OMBUDSMAN.

one-stop shops Locations at which members of the public can make initial contact in relation to any of the services provided by their *local authority. They can be situated in shopping areas or in local authority premises such as libraries. *See also* ADVICE CENTRES.

one-way mirror (one-way screen) Used by a consultant or team of consultants to observe therapeutic sessions, for example, a family therapist working with a family. The consultant may offer suggestions for *interventions, either through an ear-piece, while the session is taking place, or to the therapist during a break in the session, or at the conclusion of the session in relation to how the next session might be approached. Or the consultant may meet with the therapist and family for part of the session and engage directly by initiating an intervention in response to what has been observed from behind the one-way screen. *See also* FAMILY THERAPY.

online government *See* ELECTRONIC GOVERNMENT.

OPAAL UK *See* OLDER PEOPLE'S ADVOCACY ALLIANCE.

open adoption *Adoption where the birth mother and adoptive family know who each other is and may even have contact with each other. It can also be used to describe situations where the birth mother has some choice in the placement and is involved in selecting the adoptive parents of the child, even if there is to be no further contact. This is in contrast to the practice of closed adoption whereby placements, usually those involving babies and very young children, were traditionally made on the basis of a birth mother having limited or no knowledge of the adoptive parents, having no contact with the adopters or the child, and very limited involvement in the selection process. As the trend towards older children being adopted has grown, open adoptions have become more common, but even in these circumstances the legal rights of the *birth parent are ended and the adoptive parents become the child's legal parents. Whether contact takes place and in what form will be decided on the basis of what is judged to be in the *best interests of the child and the nature of the particular circumstances that led to their adoption. In the sense that all adoptive parents are now encouraged by adoption agencies to be open with the children placed with them about their origins and the circumstances that led to the adoption, and that birth parents are likely to be involved in some way in identifying a suitable placement, whether the child is older or very young, such as in the case of an unwanted pregnancy, the process of contemporary adoption may be described as being 'open' in this broader sense. Undertaking, or sharing previously undertaken, *life story work with adopted children is one way in which this approach may be promoted for the benefit of the child. *See also* CHILD-CENTRED APPROACH; INTER-COUNTRY ADOPTION.

open questions *See* QUESTIONS.

operant conditioning *See* BEHAVIOURISM; BEHAVIOUR MODIFICATION.

oppression *See* ANTI-OPPRESSIVE PRACTICE.

oral history History that exists in memories of experiences and that is passed on to others, often in audio or transcribed form. Mainstream history has often focused on famous people and landmark events and has neglected ordinary people's perceptions of those events and of everyday events. As well as emphasizing that everyone has a story to tell about their life, oral history has pointed to the voices that are often omitted from history, such as those of working-class people (*see* CLASS), people with disabilities, and members of *minority ethnic communities, and seeks to make history more inclusive. *See* BIOGRAPHICAL APPROACHES; NARRATIVE APPROACHES; REMINISCENCE GROUP.

oral medication The administration of medication by mouth that may include a tablet, capsule, solution, liquid, syrup, or elixir.

ordinarily resident (ordinary residence) Whether a person is deemed to live in a particular *local authority's area decides which local authority is liable for paying for services provided. This can be particularly significant in relation to the provision of services to adults under the Care Act (2014). The local authority is only required to meet needs in respect of an adult who has *eligible needs and is 'ordinarily resident' in their area (or is present there but has no settled residence). A person's ordinary residence is where the person lives, or where their main home is, and this determines which local authority will assess their *needs and potentially fund any *care and support. If someone has moved, there can be a dispute about which local authority should take financial responsibility: the authority in which the person currently resides and receives services or the authority where the person lived previously. Guidance states that disputes about ordinary residence should only take place after an *assessment and the provision of services so that the *outcome of an assessment is not prejudiced by residence considerations. Guidance also states that if a local authority places an adult in a home in another local authority's area, the first local authority retains financial responsibility. However, if someone has made their own arrangements to live in a home in another area or has moved to another area to live with relatives, and subsequently requires local authority support, the authority in the area to which they have moved is responsible. Exceptions may be adults who are at *risk, in hospital, or homeless.

organized child abuse Harm to children that is characterized by *abuse involving a number of abusers and a number of children, where the abusers concerned may be acting in concert to abuse children, sometimes acting in isolation, or may be using an institutional framework, such as a *children's home, or a position of authority, for example, a head teacher or police officer, to recruit children for abuse. Government guidance refers to this form of *child abuse variously as complex, organized, or multiple abuse, and it invariably requires highly sophisticated and well-coordinated forms of detection and investigation by *child protection agencies. The term may be used to refer to child sexual abuse rings where groups of paedophile men procure, groom, and abuse often large numbers of children. *See also* CHILD PROTECTION; CHILD SEXUAL EXPLOITATION; CHILD TRAFFICKING; PAEDOPHILIA; SAFEGUARDING CHILDREN; SIGNIFICANT HARM.

OT *See* OCCUPATIONAL THERAPIST.

other (othering) Placing a person or a group outside and/or in opposition to what is considered to be the norm. A concept developed by Simone de Beauvoir (1908–1986) in *The Second Sex* (1972) to analyse how women are constructed by patriarchal culture as not simply different from men but as negative, inferior, and abnormal in comparison with men. While men are 'the One', beings in and of themselves, women are 'the Other', being defined only in relation to men; they are what men are not, for example, men are rational, women are emotional. She saw this as a pervasive myth on which men build society and which women internalize, accepting their otherness: 'One is not born a woman; one becomes one.' In recent years, the concept has been extended in social work (and elsewhere) in relation to a range of other social divisions, such as age, *disability, *ethnicity, and sexuality. The processes by which people are made to contrast sharply with 'us', such as *marginalization and denigration, are often referred to as 'othering'. *See also* DECONSTRUCTION; MORAL PANIC; OBJECTIFICATION; OUT-GROUP; PATRIARCHY.

outcome 1. The impact or end results of services on a person's life. Wherever possible, social workers seek to engage *service users in identifying the outcomes they would like to see achieved, for example when undertaking *care and support planning with adults.
2. Used in managerial *discourse to refer to the impact that a change in policy or to the structure of an organization has had in terms of the end results the change was meant to achieve.

out-group Originally a sociological term but came into widespread use and reflects the sense of security people derive from their own group (the in-group) and their antipathy to what is seen as the competing or opposing group (the out-group). In-group/out-group dynamics are often a feature of attempts to develop *collaborative working. *See also* MARGINALIZATION; MORAL PANIC; OBJECTIFICATION; OTHER; REFERENCE GROUP.

out-of-hours duty team *See* EMERGENCY DUTY TEAM.

outreach Approaches that try to get services to people who need them but would not otherwise access them. The original model of *care management envisaged outreach as the first stage of the process but this was not pursued because of fears of creating demand for services that could not be met. *Advice centres and *voluntary organizations often have outreach campaigns to publicize benefits and services to those who may be entitled but are not in receipt of them. For an example of taking services to people in the field of mental health, *see* ASSERTIVE COMMUNITY TREATMENT.

outsourcing Obtaining goods or services under contract from an outside supplier that were previously provided within the organization. The *community care reforms resulted in large-scale outsourcing of services for adults, such as residential and *domiciliary services that had previously been provided by *local authorities, a process that is even more pronounced under the Care Act (2014). A parallel process has occurred more recently with the trend towards outsourcing of foster parents, with local authorities purchasing *fostering services from private *agencies. *See also* AGENCY THEORY; COMMISSIONING; CONTRACT STATE; MARKET; MIXED ECONOMY OF CARE; QUASI-MARKET.

overseas adoption *See* INTER-COUNTRY ADOPTION.

PACE beds Commonly used to refer to the transfer of children and young people up to 17 years old from police custody to *local authority accommodation under Section 38(6) of the Police and Criminal Evidence Act (1984) (PACE) and the related requirement in Section 21(2) of the Children Act (1989) with regard to the care of children who have been charged with an offence and have been denied bail. Section 38(6) requires that when a child or young person is detained after charge, the police custody officer must seek to transfer them to local authority accommodation pending appearance at court, unless either it is impracticable to transfer them or, in the case of someone aged 13 or over, no secure accommodation is available and other local authority accommodation that is available would not be adequate to protect the public from the possibility of serious harm. When a local authority receives a request from the police to accommodate a child or young person, they have a *duty, under Section 21(2) of the Children Act (1989), to do so. *See also* REMAND TO LOCAL AUTHORITY ACCOMMODATION.

package of care *See* CARE PACKAGE.

packages, use in group work *See* GROUP WORK.

paedophilia As a formal diagnosis or condition, describes behaviours and thinking in adults and adolescents that are characterized by a primary or exclusive sexual preference for children of pre-pubertal or early pubertal age. Within the media and in public *discourses about child sexual abuse, it has come to be used to refer to any sexual interest in children or sexually abusive acts, with any individual demonstrating these traits described as a paedophile. There is debate about whether it is accurate to see it as a psychiatric disorder or the consequence of serious distortions in thinking and behaviour induced by a range of psychosocial factors, including the possible impact of individuals' life experiences. In response to this, treatment for *sex offenders is likely to include *cognitive-behavioural interventions aimed at addressing distorted thinking about women and children, and work on exploring and changing the thought processes and behaviours that lead up to the individual's offending behaviour. In general, treatment *outcomes for sex offenders are uncertain. Men who may be more accurately described as paedophiles because of formal *diagnosis in terms of exclusivity of sexual preference are likely to be less amenable to change than other sex offenders, given the deeply entrenched nature of their thinking and behaviour. Paedophiles have increasingly used the Internet to obtain pornography involving children, and have been able to exploit children through the growth of sex tourism abroad. The police has established a Child Exploitation and Online Protection Centre as a response to this kind of crime. *See also* CHILD ABUSE AND NEGLECT; MULTI-AGENCY PUBLIC PROTECTION ARRANGEMENTS; ORGANIZED CHILD ABUSE; PERSONS POSING A RISK TO CHILDREN; SCHEDULE 1 OFFENDER.

🌐 SEE WEB LINKS
• Official site of the Child Exploitation and Online Protection Centre.

palliative care A *holistic approach to the *prevention and relief of suffering for people with advanced progressive illnesses that emphasizes identification, *assessment, and treatment of pain and responsiveness to psychosocial issues. It is provided through specialist teams that can include nurses, social workers, doctors, counsellors, *occupational therapists, and physiotherapists, working in people's homes, hospitals, or *hospices, or some combination of these settings. It takes a stance that is life-affirming and that regards dying as a normal process, seeking neither to hasten death nor postpone it. It enhances quality of life by assisting people to live as fully as possible when they are terminally ill. It usually also provides support to family members during someone's terminal illness and following her/his death. *See also* BEREAVEMENT; DEATH AND DYING.

Further reading: Reith, M. and Payne, M. (2009) *Social Work in End of Life and Palliative Care,* Policy Press.

panopticon First used by the philosopher Jeremy Bentham (1748–1832) in the late eighteenth century for his design of workhouses, asylums, and prisons that had a circle of single cells around a central tower for constant surveillance of the cells' inmates (see fig.). Michel Foucault (1926–84) analysed the panopticon as a means of making power function automatically because inmates knew that they always visible to their overseers, thus rendering unnecessary constant coercive power on the part of the overseers. He developed the panopticon as a metaphor for the increasing surveillance exercised by institutions (such as social work) in modern society as an alternative to explicit coercion, as a consequence of which individuals become more disciplined and controlled, and come to regulate themselves. *See also* GAZE; GOVERNMENTALITY; SELF-SURVEILLANCE.

parallel plan (parallel planning, twin-track plan, twin-track planning) Considering a contingency plan for a *looked-after child at the same time as pursuing the primary plan for the child. As part of *permanency planning for looked-after children, parallel plans are drawn up to ensure that alternative plans have been explored and are available without delay, if the preferred permanent *outcome proves unachievable. An example would be having a contingency plan for *adoption of a looked-after child if the primary plan of returning the child to her/his parent(s) fell through. The intention is to minimize disruption and delay, in this example by having alternative plans for adoption in place if the option of returning the child to her/his parent(s) is not successful. *See also* FOSTERING; PATHWAY PLAN; PLACEMENT ORDER.

paramountcy principle The duty laid on courts in Part I of the Children Act (1989) when determining any question with respect to the upbringing of a child, or the administration of a child's property, or the application of any income arising from it. Under this provision, the child's welfare must be the court's paramount consideration, and it must have regard to factors set out in the *welfare checklist when making decisions. The court must also have regard to the general principle that delay in making decisions is likely to prejudice the welfare of the child. The paramountcy principle is widely seen as the central tenet of professional practice with children and families. *See also* CARE ORDER; CHILD ASSESSMENT ORDER; CHILD PROTECTION; CHILDREN AND FAMILY COURT ADVISORY AND SUPPORT SERVICE;

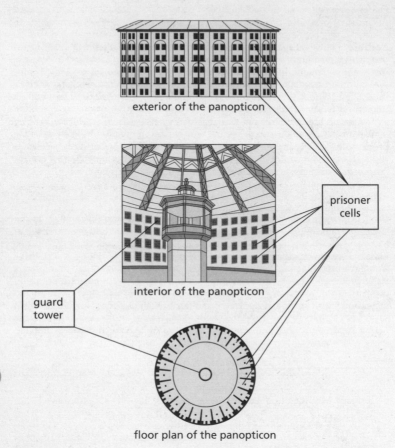

exterior of the panopticon

interior of the panopticon

guard tower

prisoner cells

floor plan of the panopticon

Panopticon

CONTACT ORDER; EMERGENCY PROTECTION ORDER; INTERIM CARE ORDER; NO ORDER PRINCIPLE; RESIDENCE ORDER; SAFEGUARDING CHILDREN; SIGNIFICANT HARM; SUPERVISION ORDER.

paranoia In psychiatry refers to an exaggerated unfounded distrust of others that sometimes manifests as *delusions of persecution. Individuals who are paranoid can be deeply suspicious of the motives of those around them, believing that certain people or people in general intend them harm. They may feel that others are discussing them behind their backs and intense feelings of distrust can lead to hostility. Paranoia is often a psychotic feature of *bipolar disorder, paranoid *schizophrenia, and schizo-affective disorder. Paranoid *personality disorder may be diagnosed if symptoms of schizophrenia are absent but the individual's personality is driven by paranoia. Individuals affected by paranoia may change their actions and behaviour to address the perceived threat. Manifestations of paranoia include *self-referential thinking*, a belief that other people, including strangers, are always talking about the individual; *thought broadcasting*, the belief that others can read the individual's thoughts; *magical thinking*, the sense that the individual's thoughts can influence the thoughts and behaviour of others; *thought withdrawal*, the sense of thoughts being stolen by others; *thought insertion*, the belief that others are putting thoughts into the individual's mind; and *ideas of reference*, where the individual believes that electrical appliances such as the television and radio are directly addressing the individual.

Symptoms of paranoia might also be associated with neurological disorders such as *dementia, Huntington's disease, and Parkinson's disease. Some prescribed medications can cause symptoms of paranoia, as well as illegal drugs such as cocaine, ecstasy, amphetamines, LSD, and marijuana. Excessive alcohol use can also cause symptoms of paranoia. Individuals displaying symptoms of paranoia should be thoroughly assessed to establish the cause. Symptoms of paranoia can be difficult to treat because the sense of mistrust that is felt is often directed at professionals involved in care and treatment. Medication may be viewed suspiciously and engaging in a treatment plan may be more difficult if the individual lacks awareness of the disorder. Because of the nature the condition, individuals with symptoms of paranoia may become subject to detention under the Mental Health Act (1983) so that they can be treated. Where mental disorder is established as the underlying cause, individuals may be treated with *anti-psychotics. If the underlying *diagnosis is a mental disorder such as schizophrenia, paranoid symptoms are considered likely to be a lifelong condition. *Cognitive behavioural therapy (CBT) may help the individual to learn to interpret the intentions of others more accurately, although mistrust of the therapist can create barriers. Support groups may help individuals and their family and friends.

parasuicide An apparent attempt at *suicide in which the intended outcome is not death. Parasuicide includes any deliberately inflicted non-fatal, self-injurious behaviour such as a drug overdose or self-inflicted harm. A universally agreed definition has not been established and some studies include in parasuicide suicide attempts in which death was intended but not achieved. Incidents of parasuicide are treated seriously as studies show they are a long-term predictor of suicide.

parental responsibility The term used in Section 3 of the Children Act (1989) to describe all the rights, duties, powers, and responsibilities conferred on a parent by law in relation to the child and her/his property. It also includes the rights, powers, and duties an appointed guardian has in relation to the child and their property. Parental responsibility is automatically held by: the mother and father of a legitimate child from birth; the mother of an illegitimate child from birth; the father of an illegitimate child on his marriage to the mother; the father of an illegitimate child who is registered as the child's father on the register of births after 1 December 2003. Same-sex parents, if civil partners or married, both have parental responsibility. Parental responsibility may be acquired by the father of an illegitimate child or a child's step-parent through a written agreement with a mother (Parental Responsibility Agreement), or through an order of the court (Parental Responsibility Order); by individuals appointed through a *Child Arrangements Order or *Special Guardianship Order; by appointment as a guardian; through *adoption, which is the only way that parental responsibility conferred at birth can be extinguished as it vests all rights, duties, and responsibilities in the adoptive parents. A *local authority may acquire parental responsibility through a *Care Order or *Emergency Protection Order. The local authority's acquisition of parental responsibility does not result in the child's parents relinquishing their parental responsibility. However, that acquired by the local authority gives it the decisive power to make decisions about the day-to-day care of the child, albeit in consultation with the child's parents as far as possible. Major decisions about the child's care will also need to have the approval of the court. The retention of parental responsibility also holds good for individuals who have parental responsibility after adopting a child or who have had a special guardianship order made in their favour. By contrast, a person who acquired parental responsibility through a *Residence Order loses this status on the making of a Care Order because this has the effect of discharging the Residence Order (*see* CHILD ARRANGEMENTS ORDER; CONTACT ORDER 1). A number of people can share parental responsibility for a child. *See also* FAMILY COURTS.

parental rights *See* PARENTAL RESPONSIBILITY.

parent and child placement *See* PLACEMENT.

parenting assessment An appraisal of a parent's or other *care-giver's parenting capacity to determine if s/he is able to offer appropriate care to a child and consistently meet her/his needs. The *assessment may recommend *intervention that would assist the parent in offering appropriate care. *See also* ASSESSMENT; GOOD ENOUGH PARENTING; KINSHIP ASSESSMENT; VIABILITY ASSESSMENT.

parenting classes (parenting interventions, parenting programmes) Programmes for parents whose children are exhibiting or at *risk of displaying anti-social or criminal behaviour that focus on gaining skills and confidence. Parents whose children have been excluded from school or have been truanting may also be required to attend. Attendance is usually a condition of a *Parenting Order, a measure designed to hold parents to account for the behaviour of their children. Classes seek to promote positive parenting based on warmth, respect, and consistency, good communication, and *empathy. Information is provided for parents on what to expect at each age, how to handle behavioural problems, and manage discipline, school, and education. *See also* EXCLUSION FROM SCHOOL; FAMILY THERAPY; GOOD-ENOUGH PARENTING; MULTI-SYSTEMIC FAMILY THERAPY; PARENTING ASSESSMENT; PARENTING CONTRACT; PARENTING SKILLS; SCHOOL ATTENDANCE.

parenting contract Section 19 of the Anti-social Behaviour Act (2003) enables a local education authority or a school governing body to enter into a voluntary agreement with a parent where a child is not attending school regularly, or is excluded, or behaving in a manner that is likely to lead to exclusion. The parents must agree to comply with specific stipulations and the *local authority agrees to provide specified support to enable a parent to comply. The objective is to try to resolve attendance/behaviour issues at an early stage. There are no sanctions for failure to comply and contracts are unenforceable. Nevertheless, a court can take a breach of a parenting contract into account if the local education authority applies for a *Parenting Order. *See also* EDUCATION SUPERVISION ORDER; EXCLUSION FROM SCHOOL; GOOD-ENOUGH PARENTING; PARENTING ASSESSMENT; PARENTING CLASSES; PARENTING SKILLS; SCHOOL ATTENDANCE.

Parenting Order A court order, made under the Crime and Disorder Act (1998), that lasts for up to three months, which holds parents responsible for a child's behaviour and assists them to improve it. It usually involves parents or *care-givers in attending *parenting classes (sometimes called parenting programmes or *interventions). Parents may also be ordered to meet other conditions such as making sure their child stays at home at certain times or attending meetings with their child's teachers. The Order can be made when a child has been excluded from school for serious bad behaviour, either permanently or for the second time in twelve months. They can also be applied for by a *local authority as a result of persistent truanting or when a child or young person has displayed or is at risk of displaying anti-social or criminal behaviour, and when parenting is considered to be a factor in the child's behaviour. *See also* EDUCATION SUPERVISION ORDER; EXCLUSION FROM SCHOOL; GOOD-ENOUGH PARENTING; PARENTING CLASSES; PARENTING CONTRACT; PARENTING SKILLS; SCHOOL ATTENDANCE; TRUANCY.

parenting plan Sets out arrangements that separating parents make covering all aspects of the child's life in order to ensure that the child remains well cared for and supported through the difficult transition associated with the separation of her/his parents. The *Children and Families Court Advisory and Support Service provides a detailed guide for parents on how to make these plans, and sets out where parents can go for further help and support. Developing a parenting plan is seen as a useful tool in facilitating *mediation between separating and divorcing parents. *See also* CHILD AND FAMILY REPORTER; FAMILY COURTS.

Further reading: Children and Family Court Advisory and Support Service (2015) *The Parenting Plan*. Available at: https://www.cafcass.gov.uk/ media/190788/parenting_plan_final_web.pdf.

parenting programmes *See* PARENTING CLASSES.

parenting skills Encompasses the behaviours and attitudes necessary to promote the healthy physical, emotional, social, and intellectual development of a child from infancy to adulthood. It refers to the activity of caring for and raising a child, and thus applies to biological or *birth parents, step-parents, guardians, adoptive and foster parents, and other individuals who may be the child's primary *care-giver(s). *See also* ATTACHMENT; CHILD DEVELOPMENT; GOOD ENOUGH PARENTING; PARENTING CLASSES.

parole The release of someone from prison before the end of her/his sentence as a result of a decision of the Parole Board. The Board is an independent body that acts under directions issued by the Justice Secretary, which emphasize that the main basis of the Parole Board's decisions must be the *risk of someone re-offending. The Parole Board is only concerned with the cases of prisoners who are imprisoned for the protection of the public or who have been sentenced to life imprisonment (Criminal Justice Act 2003). However, it still deals with other long-term prisoners who were sentenced before the implementation of this provision of the Act.

Parole Board *See* PAROLE.

participation *Service users' and *carers' involvement in matters that affect them. Participation has been around in social work and service user *discourses for many years. However, it first received official endorsement as a key objective in children's and adult social services in New Labour's (1997–2010) White Paper *Modernizing Social Services* (Department of Health, 1998). Its remit was seen as including involvement of service users and carers in planning services, in tailoring individual *care packages, and in their having recourse to effective mechanisms for making complaints. Participation has been presented as offering service users a key role in shaping the services they use, even if they are using services involuntarily, as, for example, is often the case in relation to *child protection issues. It is seen as a principle that represents a trend in contemporary social work practice (for example, it is stressed throughout the statutory guidance on the Care Act [2014]), away from a previous era in which it was more likely that social workers would have thought of themselves as knowing what was best for service users, with service users having little influence on what happened. However, sometimes the shortcomings of the past and the advances of the present can be exaggerated. For example, in the case of a child protection conference, the participation of parents may be limited to the social worker sharing her/his report with the parents immediately beforehand, with other participants bringing their reports to the conference, limiting the opportunity for parents to participate because they have not been able to think about their responses in advance. (Of course, there is also a massive imbalance of power in such situations.) Participation is used to describe a wide range of practices with regard to service user involvement. Service users may participate individually at times when decisions are being made, for example, at case conferences or reviews of *care plans. In residential and day care settings they may be involved as a group in residents' or service users' committees. They may be involved collectively in consultation events when a social work organization wants to canvass service user opinion. They may be asked to represent service user opinion on a committee or a working party or as members of an inspection team that is reviewing a particular service(s). They may be actively involved in scrutinizing services and providing *feedback on how they are experienced and should be developed through membership of service user or carer organizations.

At one end of a continuum, participation can consist of a one-off event, for example, filling in an evaluation form at the end of a period of social work contact. At the other end, it can be an ongoing and intensive dialogue between service users and social work organizations. Beresford identifies a number of principles for increasing participation, based on understanding and valuing service users' experience:

- Listening to what people say;
- Seeking to develop *empathy with the perspectives and situations of others;
- Working to be open-minded and non-judgemental, and challenging *discrimination in ourselves and other people;
- Recognizing what we do and don't 'know';
- Valuing people's direct experience;
- Accepting the possibility that there are knowledges different from our own;
- Being prepared to accept something we may not fully understand instead of rejecting it without consideration;
- Being willing to move out to people, meet people on their own territory, and see how things are for them;
- Acting upon knowledge that is based on direct experience—not just saying that we accept that this is how it is for someone else, but also being prepared to work with them to change it (active knowledge);
- Involving people with direct experience (for example, service users) in the development and provision of professional education and training;
- Valuing the direct experience of service users in health and social care, and encouraging the recruitment of service users as workers;
- Increasing access to research training for people with direct experience and supporting their involvement in research so that they can influence the process of knowledge production.

See also ARNSTEIN'S LADDER; CONSUMERISM; PARTNERSHIP (WITH SERVICE USERS).

Further reading: Warren, J. (2007) *Service User and Carer Participation in Social Work*, Learning Matters.

partnership (with other professionals/organizations) *See* COLLABORATIVE WORKING.

partnership (with service users) The trend towards *service user *participation derives from legislation and policy, professional responsibilities and values, and the demands and actions of service users themselves. Working in partnership with service users goes further than service user participation, and implies a levelling out of the balance of power between the partners. The feasibility of this needs to be questioned. Social workers, as (most often) agents of the state, are invested with massive amounts of power compared with users of social work services, who are likely to be drawn from *oppressed and *marginalized social groups. In this sense, 'partnership working' with service users can never be based on an equal distribution of power.

PASA (PASAUK) *See* PRACTITIONER ALLIANCE FOR SAFEGUARDING ADULTS.

pastoral support Those functions of school that attend to the wider emotional, psychological, and physical welfare of pupils, and the role that teachers and other staff, parents, and governors play in the promotion of these dimensions of learning and development. One of these functions is the prevention of *bullying in schools. The National Association for Pastoral Care in Education is an organization that seeks to establish links between educational professionals who have an interest in pastoral care. *See also* EDUCATION SOCIAL WORKERS.

(((())) SEE WEB LINKS
• Official site of the National Association for Pastoral Care in Education.

patch-based social work Social work in a small geographical area. *See also* BARCLAY REPORT; COMMUNITY SOCIAL WORK; NEIGHBOURHOOD SOCIAL WORK.

patch system (patch team, patch work) A social work team serving a small geographical area. *See also* BARCLAY REPORT; COMMUNITY SOCIAL WORK; NEIGHBOURHOOD SOCIAL WORK.

paternalism Protecting people as though they were children so that they are not able to exercise freedom or responsibility, on the basis that others know what is best for them. This approach was widely adopted in health and social services in the past, for example, in relation to *older people and people with *learning disabilities. It was regarded as the exercise of kindness and thought best for those on its receiving end. Nowadays, it would be regarded as a reflection of inequality in the exercise of power, a means of controlling people and preserving the power of professionals. There is a need to be on guard for its appearance in current contexts, for example, in discussions and decisions with *service users (such as older people and people with learning disabilities) in relation to their *risk-taking. *See also* AGE-APPROPRIATE; INFANTILIZATION.

pathology The study of the nature of diseases, their causes, development, and consequences. 'Pathological' can be used with negative connotations to mean unreasonable, unnatural, or abnormal as in 'pathological child abuser'. *See also* INDIVIDUAL PATHOLOGY.

pathway plan (pathway planning) A statement that *local authorities must develop and agree with all *looked-after children aged between 16 and 17 years who are approaching the point of *leaving care, which is a requirement of the Children (Leaving Care) Act (2000). Following an assessment of the young person's needs, the plan describes how these will be met by the local authority and other agencies in assisting the young person to make the transition from being 'in care'. The plan must take into account the young person's wishes and feelings, and state the support, advice, and assistance s/he will receive. The plan is reviewed every six months or upon the request of the young person, social worker (if the young person is under 18) or *personal advisor. *See also* PARALLEL PLAN.

patriarchy Literally meaning the rule of the father and originally referred to societies and communities structured around the authority exercised by the male heads of households. It has been widely used within feminist perspectives to mean domination by men in general. *See also* BIOLOGICAL DETERMINISM; FEMINISM.

PAVA *See* PRACTITIONERS ALLIANCE FOR SAFEGUARDING ADULTS.

PCP *See* PERSON-CENTRED PLANNING.

peer group (peer group pressure) A group of people with similar status and interests. Although the term can be used in relation to any such group, for example, when referring to a social worker's peer group, it is most often encountered through attention and concern focused on peer groups of young people, particularly with regard to these groups' impact on attitudes and behaviour, which is often referred to as peer pressure. Such concern has resulted in policy interventions against *anti-social behaviour.

penalty notice *See* UNAUTHORIZED ABSENCE.

people-processing Lipsky's work on *street-level bureaucracy identifies a mentality through which front-line workers (such as social workers) can adapt to their work settings by following procedural models of working unreflectively. A number of commentators claim that this mentality is increasingly prevalent in social work as it has become more proceduralized and *commodified, with a diminution in social workers' *discretion. *See also* FRAGMENTATION OF ROLES AND TASKS; ROUTINIZATION.

percentile chart *See* CENTILE CHART.

performance culture The ethos pertaining in an organization and the wider environment in which it operates that stems from the application of *performance management. It is a culture in which the primary determinant of the *goals of an organization and its members' activities is complying with the requirements of the performance management system. *See also* DASHBOARD; MANAGERIAL CYBERNETICS; MANAGERIALISM.

performance indicators *See* DASHBOARD; MANAGERIAL CYBERNETICS; PERFORMANCE CULTURE; PERFORMANCE MANAGEMENT.

performance management Measuring the performance of an organization, or a particular service, or both by quantifying aspects of performance and then seeking to maintain that level of performance, if it is already at a high level, or improve performance, if it is not at the level required. In the period from 1945 to 1978, Labour and Conservative governments placed faith in professionals as guarantors of the performance of *welfare state services, including social work. The Conservative governments (1979–97) eroded professionals' responsibility for safeguarding performance and introduced performance management, seeking to change *local authority managerial and professional *cultures, particularly via the pressure applied by the activities of the *Audit Commission and, in the case of social work, through the Social Services Inspectorate, as well as through the combination of the two bodies in inspections by the Joint Reviews Team. These regulatory organizations stressed the extent to which performance was giving 'value for money', underpinned by advocacy of the three 'e's (*economy, efficiency, and effectiveness), as a means of judging performance. Standardized performance indicators were developed against which social work (and other) services were measured and competition between *local authorities was encouraged by publishing comparative data, which included *benchmarking, believing that all local authorities would want to attain the levels set by the best performers.

When it came to power, *New Labour (1997–2010) shared a key assumption with the previous Conservative governments that predisposed it to retain and intensify performance management: it did not think that professionals would provide high quality, cost-efficient services without external monitoring against targets. Accordingly, New Labour took over the terminology and activities of performance management, such as the setting of explicit targets for services and monitoring performance against them, and extended them further, with more measures and greater attention to using performance management in pursuit of its policy *goals. Detailed definition at national level of social work's objectives was introduced, with the setting of targets to be met locally and central monitoring of the results. This generated a strong *performance culture with local authority politicians and managers expected to concentrate on achieving New Labour's targets as a way of ensuring that central government programmes were delivered by social workers. These expectations were reinforced by the production of 'naming and shaming' reports and league tables. Exposing performance in this way was assumed to stimulate continuous improvement. (*Best Value provided an added stimulus to performance management.)

The management, measurement, evaluation, and improvement of performance became the dominant concern. Public Service Agreements between central and local government were introduced, with SMART (specific, measurable, achievable, relevant, timed) targets to fine-tune the attainment of central government priorities at the local level, later measured through Comprehensive Performance Assessments of local councils devised by the Audit Commission. (One impact of devolution was that *Wales and *Scotland developed performance management frameworks that were less prescriptive and less intrusive than those in England, relying to a greater extent on self-assessment.) In social work, specific performance elements were set out in the *Quality Strategy for Social Care* (Department of Health 2000), and included national service frameworks, national standards, service models, and local performance measures against which progress within an agreed timescale was monitored. The *Strategy* gave the Social Services Inspectorate the responsibility for setting and monitoring standards for each local authority's social services functions. These were specific to each inspection and were intended for use by local authorities in their own audit and review processes. Following the *Strategy*, a Performance Assessment Framework was developed and a system of star ratings became the way of 'badging' a local authority's social services performance as follows:

- Three stars—excellent.
- Two stars—good.
- One star—adequate.
- Zero stars—inadequate.

The policies and actions of the Conservative and New Labour governments were crucial in establishing performance management in social work and elsewhere. It has remained an integral part of organizational culture at all levels, from the overall performance of the organization to the performance of social work teams and that of individual social workers (*see* DASHBOARDS). Despite its largely taken-for-granted nature, in the literature a number of issues have been raised about the use of performance management:

- Performance measurements tend to be 'top-down' in nature, reflecting the perspectives and values of senior management, and neglecting the positions of other groups;
- The emphasis on quantifiable measures of performance means there is a danger that aspects of service quality that are particularly valuable to service users will be underplayed;
- The difficulty in capturing broader effects and impacts that may be of particular concern to local *communities;
- The limits to the degree to which equity considerations can be captured through quantitative indicators;
- Performance measurement has particular limits in the context of multi-agency *partnership working where it may be difficult to ascribe *outcomes to individual agency effort;
- There are limits on the extent to which factors that have contributed to process factors in organizational performance can be captured quantitatively;
- Performance measurement systems provide a partial picture of what is happening; they do not provide an understanding of why it is happening and, therefore, contribute little to a culture of organizational learning.

In addition, performance management is essentially concerned with quantitative data but the core of everyday social work remains essentially qualitative and small-scale in nature. There is tension between the qualitative nature of everyday social work and the quantitative performance management environment in which it is located, as social work is reduced to a series of service transactions, translated into categories for judgement, for the purposes of performance management. In the process, social work is represented as a neutral machine for the production of services, divorced from wider questions about equity and social justice. In this way performance measurement 'creates' social work practice in that it determines the specific forms of practice that count, and are therefore authorized, by drawing them into the framework of accountability. This is particularly the case when social work organizations manage performance in advance, in anticipation of and in preparation for performance measurement.

Performance management presents measures of performance, and identification of the extent to which they have been met, as readily identifiable through the use of what is portrayed as a technical, objective, neutral approach. In the process, the politically, ethically, and morally charged nature of social work, and the many interests and goals at play when social work's performance is considered, are obscured. The power relations of different participants, as well as their different interests in and perspectives on performance, are ignored. *See also* DASHBOARD; MANAGERIALISM; MANAGERIAL CYBERNETICS.

Further reading: Harris, J. and White, V. (eds) (2009) *Modernizing Social Work: Critical Considerations*, Policy Press.

performance measurement *See* DASHBOARD; MANAGERIAL CYBERNETICS; PERFORMANCE CULTURE; PERFORMANCE MANAGEMENT.

permanence *See* PARALLEL PLAN; PERMANENCY PLAN.

permanence report *See* CHILD'S PERMANENCE REPORT.

permanency *See* PARALLEL PLAN; PERMANENCY PLANNING.

permanency plan (permanency planning) The process for achieving for a *looked-after child, within a timescale that meets the child's *needs, a permanent *outcome that will provide security and stability for the child throughout her/his childhood. Wherever possible, permanence is achieved through a return to the parents' care or a placement within the wider family but where this cannot be achieved within a timescale appropriate to the child's needs, plans may be made for a permanent alternative family placement, which may include *adoption or a Special Guardianship Order (*see* SPECIAL GUARDIAN). The objective of permanency planning is to provide a child with a safe, stable home environment in which to grow up, provided by an individual or individuals committed to providing a lifelong relationship. *See also* ACCOMMODATED CHILD; ADOPTION; FOSTERING; LOOKED-AFTER CHILD; PARALLEL PLAN; PLACEMENT; PRIVATE FOSTERING.

Further reading: Department for Education (2015) *The Children Act 1989 Guidance and Regulations. Volume 2: Care Planning, Placement, and Case Review.* Available at https://www.gov.uk/government/uploads/system/uploads/attachment_data/file/441643/Children_Act_Guidance_2015.pdf.

permanency team *See* FAMILY PLACEMENT TEAM.

personal advisor Individual who provides advice, information, and support to a young person *leaving care, following assessment of their needs and the drawing up of a *pathway plan that specifies the services that will be provided to meet those needs. This person must be independent of the *local authority. There is a range of arrangements in place in different local authority areas to meet this requirement, which is set out in Section 23D of the Children Act (1989).

personal assistant Someone employed to carry out specific tasks under the direction of a service user. *See also* DIRECT PAYMENTS.

personal budget An amount of money allocated by a *local authority that is sufficient to meet the cost to the authority of meeting the person's *needs, which it is under a *duty to meet (*see* ELIGIBILITY CRITERIA), or has exercised its *power to meet. Initially an *indicative amount is calculated on the basis of a person's *needs assessment. This is an approximate indication of what it might cost to meet the person's needs as indicated in their *assessment. Following completion and authorization of a *care and support plan, a personal budget is calculated that provides the amount of money considered to be needed to provide the care and support identified in the plan, which is then allocated to the person concerned. A personal budget is available to any adult who has been assessed by a local authority as having eligible needs for care and support or to carers who have been assessed as having eligible needs for support, under the national *eligibility criteria (Care Act (2014)). In addition, young people aged 16–25 with special educational needs or *disabilities who have an *education, health, and care plan have the right to request a personal budget, which may contain elements of education, social care, and health funding.

A personal budget, in conjunction with a care and support plan (for an adult with care and support needs) or a support plan (for carers), is seen as enabling a person, others s/he may wish to involve such as family and friends, and her/his *advocate if s/he has one, to exercise more *choice and control over how their care and support needs are met. The personal budget gives the person clear information regarding the money that has been allocated to meet the needs identified in her/his assessment and recorded in her/his plan. The indicative amount is shared with the person, and anybody else involved, at the start of the planning process, with the final amount being confirmed when the process is completed, and the detail of how the personal budget will be used is set out in the finished plan. At all times, the wishes of the person should be considered and respected. For example, people should not be forced to accept specific options, such as moving into care homes, against their will because they are the cheapest. There are four options for managing a personal budget:

- *__Direct payment__* The personal budget is paid into an account set up for that purpose by the person and is used by her/him to purchase directly what they need to meet their identified *outcomes, rather than using services arranged by the local authority.
- *__Individual service fund__* The personal budget is paid into the account of a third-party individual or organization that holds the money for the person and purchases support on her/his behalf and under her/his instruction.
- __Local authority-managed personal budget__ The personal budget is managed by the local authority and the support a person receives is from local authority-commissioned services.
- __Mixed personal budget__ A combination of any of the above options.

The arrangements that are made for the personal budget can be adjusted subsequently, if the person wishes.

The overall personal budget is broken down into the amount the person must pay, following the *financial assessment, and the remainder of the budget that the local authority will pay. The personal budget may also set out other amounts of public money that the person is receiving, such as money provided through a personal health budget or from other funding streams, such as housing, and the local authority considers any request from a person who wants their personal budget set out in this way. Where budgets are integrated, a lead organization agrees to monitor all of the budgets the person is receiving.

Where the local authority is meeting the *eligible needs of a person whose financial resources are above the limit, but who has requested the local authority to meet their needs, a charge may be made for putting in place the arrangements to meet needs (*see* SELF-FUNDER). When this occurs, the information is set out for the person in an accessible format. This fee is not part of the personal budget, because it does not relate directly to meeting needs, but it is presented alongside the budget to help the person to understand the total charges to be paid.

Where the person or a third party on their behalf, such as a relative, is making an additional payment (or a 'top-up') in order to be able to secure the care and support of the person's choice, when this costs more than the local authority would pay, the additional payment does not form part of the personal budget, because the budget indicates the costs to the local authority of meeting the needs. However, the information about the additional payment is presented so that the total amount of charges being paid is clear and the link to the personal budget amount can be understood.

*Intermediate care (including *reablement) is a free universal service for the first six weeks (Care and Support [Charging and Assessment of Resources] Regulations [2014]) and so the cost of the provision of intermediate care and reablement services is excluded from the person's personal budget. A person who has intermediate care or reablement services but no other forms of care and support does not have a personal budget. However, s/he still has a plan describing what is being provided, by whom, and for how long, to help her/him understand what is being provided to meet her/his needs.

The person, as well as her/his *carer, if s/he has one, and her/his independent advocate, if s/he has one, is made aware of how her/his personal budget is calculated, so that s/he knows the amount at a stage that enables her/him to engage effectively in planning and can have confidence that the amount includes all relevant costs and is sufficient to meet her/his identified needs in the way set out in her/his plan. The initial indicative amount can be increased or decreased depending on the decisions made during the development of the plan. Three principles apply to both the indicative upfront amount and the final signed-off personal budget that forms part of the care and support plan:

Transparency The budget allocation processes are publicly available as part of the general information on offer from the local authority (*see* INFORMATION AND ADVICE). Each person with a plan also has the budget allocation process explained in relation to their plan in a format accessible to them so that the person can understand how their personal budget has been calculated, both in the indicative amount and the final personal budget allocation.

Timeliness Making an upfront allocation in an indicative budget enables the person to plan how the needs are met. After refinement during the planning process, this indicative amount is adjusted to the amount that is sufficient to meet the needs which the local authority is required to meet or decides to meet (*see* ELIGIBILITY CRITERIA). This adjusted amount is the personal budget recorded in the care plan.

Sufficiency The amount calculated as the personal budget is sufficient to meet the person's needs that the local authority is required to meet or decides to meet and takes into account reasonable preferences about meeting needs as set out in the plan.

The personal budget equates to the cost to the local authority of meeting the person's needs. In establishing the 'cost to the local authority', consideration is given to local *market conditions and to ensuring that local quality care that meets needs can be obtained for the amount specified in the budget. The cost assumptions are shared with the person so they are aware of how their personal budget was calculated. Consideration is also given to whether the personal budget is sufficient where needs will be met via direct payments, especially with regard to other costs that may be required to meet needs or to ensure people are complying with legal requirements associated with becoming an employer (*see* DIRECT PAYMENTS).

Consideration can be given to how choice can be increased by people pooling their personal budgets. This can include pooling budgets of people living in the same household, such as a person with care and support needs and a carer, or pooling budgets of people within a *community with similar needs.

A carer's need for support can be met by providing care to the person they care for. However, decisions about for whom a particular service is to be provided affect whether the service is chargeable and who is liable to pay any charges. It has to be made clear whose needs are intended to be met by a particular type of support, to whom the support will be provided directly, and therefore who pays any charges due. Where a service is provided directly to the person needing care, even though it is to meet the carer's needs, then the person needing care is liable to pay any charge and must agree to do so. Such a charge cannot be imposed on the carer. Therefore, decisions about which services are provided to meet carers' needs, and which are provided to meet the needs of the adult for whom they care, will impact on which individual's personal budget includes the costs of meeting those needs. These decisions are made as part of the care planning process in discussion with the individuals concerned, and this includes consideration of whether joint plans (and therefore joint personal budgets) may be beneficial. Where possible, personal budgets are aligned when they are meeting the needs of both the carer and the person needing care at the same time. Where a person has eligible needs for care and support and has a personal budget and a care and support plan in their own right, and the carer's needs can be met in part or in full by the provision of care and support to the person needing care, then this kind of provision is incorporated into the plan and personal budget of the person with care needs, as well as being detailed in the support plan for the carer. The carer's personal budget is an amount that enables the carer to meet their needs to continue to fulfil their caring role and takes into account the outcomes that the carer wishes to achieve in their day-to-day life. This includes their wishes and/or aspirations concerning paid employment, education, training, or recreation if the provision of support can contribute to the achievement of those outcomes. The manner in which the personal budget is used to meet the carer's needs is agreed as part of the planning process. If someone being cared for does not have eligible needs and so does not have their own care plan and personal budget, the carer has a support plan that covers their needs and how they will be met but the person needing care does not receive a personal budget or care plan. However, the person requiring care is involved in the decision-making process so that agreement can be reached on the intended course of action. The decisions taken by the carer and the person requiring care and the charging implications are agreed and recorded in the carer's support plan. In *cases other than replacement care, the personal budget that the carer receives specifies the costs to the local authority and the costs to the carer. *See also* CARER'S ASSESSMENT; CHARGING FOR SERVICES.

Further reading: Department of Health (2016) *Care and Support: Statutory Guidance*, Chapter 11. Available at: https://www.gov.uk/government/publications/care-act-statutory-guidance/care-and-support-statutory-guidance#person-centred-care-and-support-planning.

personal care Meeting intimate *needs of adults, such as assisting with going to the toilet, bathing, dressing, and undressing. Personal care is regarded as a social need, and individuals are subject to a *means test to determine the charge they should pay for services to meet these needs, unless they fall under provisions for *NHS continuing health care or *NHS-funded nursing care. As a consequence, personal care has increasingly been referred to as social care, even though it involves care of the body. *See also* CHARGING FOR SERVICES.

personal data *See* DATA PROTECTION.

personal education plan (PEP) A plan that supports *looked-after children at school. It provides essential information for schools and *care-givers, and encourages communication between social workers, care-givers, and schools in order to seek the achievement of the best educational *outcomes for the child. It is a statutory requirement for all looked-after *school age children. The plan identifies areas of strength and areas where extra support may be necessary. The PEP document is regularly reviewed. In order to be effective it will:

- Include all relevant personal information regarding school history;
- Identify areas for educational development and ensure access to services and support;
- Have recent attendance and exclusion records;
- Act as a record of the young person's progress and achievements, academic and others;
- Establish clear targets for the young person relating to academic achievements. Personal and behavioural targets will also be identified;
- Include a consideration of improving access to out-of-school-hours activities;
- Identify who will action the plan with timescales for action and review;
- Consider school transitions and specify any additional support required for a successful transition.

See also ACCOMMODATED CHILDREN; EDUCATION, HEALTH AND CARE PLAN; INDIVIDUAL EDUCATION PLAN; PATHWAY PLAN; PERSONAL ADVISOR; SCHOOL ACTION; SCHOOL ACTION PLUS; SPECIAL EDUCATIONAL NEEDS.

personal expenses allowance *See* CHARGING FOR SERVICES.

personality Refers to the assumption that there is a consistent set of characteristics that distinguishes one person from another, and that such characteristics can be observed and assessed by others, such as social workers. These characteristics are assumed to operate across different situations and in different circumstances, and are seen as underpinning attitudes and behaviour. *See also* IDENTITY.

personality disorder A generic term that describes a group of psychiatric disorders characterized by pervasive, ingrained, and enduring patterns of behaviour, cognition, and inner experience which interfere with the person's ability to make and sustain personal and social relationships, and cause significant distress. Personality disorders are often associated with maladaptive coping strategies that fall outside society's *norms and expectations. They differ from conditions such as *schizophrenia, *bipolar disorder, and *depression since they are not viewed as *mental illnesses as such and in general are not amenable to treatment with psychiatric medication. This has in the past led to people with personality disorders being excluded from mental health services on the basis that they were 'not treatable'. In recent years there has been wider recognition of the suitability of psychological treatment for many types of personality disorder. There is a range of categories of personality disorder included in the *Diagnostic and Statistical Manual of Mental Disorders* and the *International Classification of Diseases*, which include *paranoid, schizoid, anti-social, borderline, *obsessive-compulsive, *anxious (avoidant), narcissistic, histrionic, and dependent. In the UK, anti-social personality disorder (ASPD) and borderline personality disorder (BPD) have particular public and mental health policy relevance. ASPD is characterized by disregard for and violation of the rights of others. It is associated with patterns of aggressive and irresponsible behaviour that emerge in childhood or early *adolescence. It is considered that individuals with ASPD account for a disproportionately large proportion of *crime, *violence, and suicidal behaviour. BPD is characterized by elevated levels of personal and emotional instability, leading to significant impairment in the ability to form and sustain relationships, and is associated with *self-harm and suicidal behaviour. *Diagnosis can be controversial because the concept of personality disorder has been criticized for relying on subjective opinions and judgements about behavioural traits. In addition the attachment of the label of personality disorder (particularly anti-social personality disorder) to someone may be unwelcome because of the stigma associated with it. Nevertheless, the subjective distress and poor coping skills of individuals diagnosed, as well as the impact of their behaviour on others and society, have caused the concept of personality disorder to become centrally rooted in mainstream psychiatry and service provision. Although medication may be used to treat symptoms of personality disorders such as agitation and distress, it is usual for those deemed suitable to be offered psychological interventions such as *dialectical behavioural therapy (DBT) and *cognitive behavioural therapy (CBT).

personalization Making services more individually attuned to the needs of their users. This *goal dates from at least the Conservatives' (1979–97) *community care reforms, with their emphasis on the social worker/care manager arranging services to meet the needs of a particular person, rather than requiring the person to fit whatever services were already available. *New Labour (1997–2010) presented 'personalization' as its contribution to the goal of achieving individually-attuned services in order to take *consumerism to new levels of sensitivity and responsiveness. This was depicted as necessary because of higher and still-rising consumer expectations of public services and, as part of that trend, the existence of a greater appetite for *choice and personalization, with New Labour portraying users of services as ever more refined and discriminating customers. Personalization offers an implicit and tantalizing vision of public services being experienced as akin to 'high-end' consumerism in the *market place; the sort of consumerism that does not just provide choice but also personalizes its products and services. A milestone in the shift towards personalization was the Adult Social Care Green Paper, *Independence, Well-Being, and Choice* (Department of Health, 2005), which saw increasing the use of *direct payments and introducing *personal budgets as the principal routes to its achievement. The Green Paper's proposals were taken forward in the White Paper, *Our Health, Our Care, Our Say* (Department of Health, 2006), which indicated that proactive approaches were necessary in order to increase the take-up of *direct payments by requiring social workers to discuss them as the first option with everyone at every assessment and review. Similarly, the need to develop *personal budgets was also emphasized. *Putting People First* (2007) brought together New Labour's themes in the Green and White Papers in stressing that personalization involved the reduction of the role of the state in the provision of services and individuals taking on greater responsibility for their own lives. When the Conservative–Liberal Democrat Coalition government (2010–15) came to power, its *Vision for Adult Social Care* (2010) emphasized personalization even more strongly than New Labour in the context of cuts in public expenditure (*see* *AUSTERITY) and rooted it in the principles of responsibility, freedom, and fairness, urging greater community involvement in providing support, in a way that was consistent with the *'Big Society'.

Personalization has been a key theme in the implementation of the Care Act (2014). It is meant to emphasize putting people at the centre of understanding their *care and support *needs, choosing the services they receive and having control over their lives so that they can live independently and actively in their *communities. Personalization is often associated with *direct payments and personal budgets, which enable people to choose the services they receive. It also includes the provision of improved *information and advice on care and support for adults and *carers, investment in services to prevent, reduce, or delay people's need for care and support, and the promotion of *independence and self-reliance among individuals, carers, and communities. The aim of the personalization agenda is to improve the lives of adults and their carers by arranging support that focuses on the adults and carers' own individual needs, aspirations, strengths, and *outcomes. The challenge is to ensure that all people, for example including those with *dementia and mental health problems who lack *capacity, also benefit. The declared intention is that adults should be able to self-assess their own needs, with or without support, play a full part in drawing up a wide-ranging support plan, and directly purchase or choose the services they want. As a result of personalization, *local authorities have created roles to support adults in carrying out these tasks or have commissioned external organizations to do so, including *user-led organizations. The role of commissioner (*see* COMMISSIONING) has changed as a result of personalization. Instead of purchasing services in bulk from available providers and fitting adults who are eligible into those services that best meet their needs, commissioners now shape the social *care market to promote the availability of a range of services from which adults, and their carers, can choose. This envisages adults and carers as individual commissioners, specifying and purchasing their own support. Personalization also requires a change in approach from care providers. As local authorities devolve purchasing responsibility to adults and their carers, they are using framework agreements rather than block contracts, under which providers are accredited to provide services of a particular quality at an agreed price but are not guaranteed business, as decisions on whether to use them rest with service users. This is intended to make providers more responsive to service users' needs. *See also* CARE AND SUPPORT PLAN; CARER'S ASSESSMENT; NEEDS ASSESSMENT.

Further reading: Gardner, A. (2011) *Personalisation in Social Work*, Learning Matters.

personal narratives *See* BIOGRAPHICAL APPROACHES; NARRATIVE APPROACHES; ORAL HISTORY.

personal social services A term that is gradually falling into disuse. Traditionally it was used to refer to social work and other social services focused on individuals. It developed as a residual category within the *welfare state to cater for those services falling outside the social policy 'giants' of housing, health, social security, and education. The personal social services cater for children needing support or protection, *older people, people with mental health problems, disabled people, and people with *learning disabilities. Social work is a part of the overall activity of the personal social services.

person-centred counselling *See* COUNSELLING; UNCONDITIONAL POSITIVE REGARD; WARMTH.

person-centred planning (PCP) Utilizes a range of tools and approaches that plan *with* a person. As such, PCP is an alternative to conventional planning that involves professionals assessing *need, allocating services, and making decisions *for* people. It originated in the 1980s as a way of enabling children and adults with *learning disabilities to move out of segregated schools, hospitals, and residential and day care settings and into mainstream schools and communities. It seeks to empower people who have traditionally been disempowered by 'specialist' or segregated services, and tries to hand control over to them. It is a means of considering the ways in which people with learning disabilities can move towards their own *goals. It begins from a detailed consideration of the person and what it is s/he wants to realize in her/his life. The tools are used to help the person think about what is important in their lives now and what they would like to happen in the future. Careful attention needs to be paid to assisting people to communicate what they think so that they are not reflecting what they think professionals want them to say. *Advocacy may be helpful in this regard. PCP builds on a person's circle of support and includes the people who are important in her/his life. It embraces the value of inclusion and considers what support a person needs to be included and involved in her/his *community.

Further reading: Cambridge, P. and Carnaby, S. (eds) (2005) *Person-centred Planning and Care Management with People with Learning Disabilities,* Jessica Kingsley Publishers.

personhood *See* DEMENTIA.

persons posing a risk to children Individuals convicted or cautioned for offences against children. Previously referred to as *Schedule 1 offenders, this has become the preferred term because of anomalies in the offences covered by Schedule 1 of the Children and Young Persons Act (1933). Some new offences against children had not been added to this list while many of the older offences had been removed. There was also inconsistency in the use of the list. For example, conviction for a Schedule 1 offence did not always trigger any statutory action in relation to *child protection issues. Moreover, the label 'Schedule 1 offender, took no consideration of the circumstances of the offence and made no assessment of the actual *risk that an individual might pose. For these reasons, the Home Office issued a circular in 2005 directing that the old term should no longer be used and instead the focus should be on those identified as presenting a risk or potential risk to children. This circular included a list of offences that should trigger consideration of whether a person poses a risk to children. It is a comprehensive list including offences that have been superseded by new legal definitions and new offences introduced by legal changes. Agencies in many local areas have established protocols for identifying and managing persons posing a risk to children, which sit alongside interagency child protection procedures developed by *Local Safeguarding Children Boards and *Multi-agency Public Protection Arrangements. *See also* CHILD ABUSE AND NEGLECT; ORGANIZED CHILD ABUSE; PAEDOPHILIA; SEX OFFENDERS REGISTER.

perverse incentive A concept employed by the political right in relation to criticisms of welfare provision, most often in relation to the social security system. For example, arguing that unemployment is encouraged because benefits fail to provide an incentive to work, as they are not set sufficiently below the minimum wage, or that when a situation is supported by benefits, it is more likely to occur, or that providing benefits for lone mothers makes it more likely that women will choose to be lone mothers. The concept can also be used more generally to analyse the undermining of a policy direction. For example, in 1980 the Conservative government introduced an arrangement whereby the social security system paid for residential care for people with assets of under £3,000. For many years there had been a policy of *community care but there was now a perverse incentive acting against it because of people being placed in residential care rather than being provided with community-based services in their own homes. This was because the system the Conservatives had introduced meant that in many circumstances the easiest service provision to arrange for a person who needed day-to-day support was to find a place in a *private sector home at central government's expense. Resources that could have been used for care in the community were locked up in costly residential provision, as central government stimulated the development of private sector residential care through this social security-funded arrangement for payment. *See also* POVERTY TRAP.

philanthropy The giving of assistance or money to the poor or those in trouble, as a moral duty to improve the lives of others and as a way of maintaining social order and deference, whose origins lie in the nineteenth century. This combination of *care and control was influential in the development of social work in the work of the *Charity Organisation Society, and the tension between the caring and controlling elements of social work, which originated in philanthropy, has continued to pose dilemmas through to the present day. *See* CHARITABLE ORGANIZATION; CHARITY.

phobia A strong, unrelenting, irrational fear of and desire to avoid a situation, activity, or thing that poses little or no actual danger. There are many specific phobias: for example, arachnophobia is a fear of spiders, acrophobia or altophobia is a fear of heights, agoraphobia is a fear of public places, and claustrophobia is a fear of closed-in places. People with phobias try to avoid what they are afraid of. If they encounter what they fear they may experience panic, rapid heartbeats, difficulty breathing, shaking, sweating, nausea, and the urge to run away. *Interventions with phobias can include medication and therapy. Desensitization (*see* BEHAVIOUR MODIFICATION) involves gradually exposing someone, with support, to the situation, activity, or thing about which they are phobic. *Cognitive behavioural therapy seeks to reduce the onset of phobic reactions by helping someone change her/his way of thinking. It usually has three elements: educating the person about phobias, setting up positive expectations for the sessions, and promoting the cooperation of the person; identifying the thoughts and assumptions that influence the person's behaviour, particularly those that may be directly related to her/him being phobic; teaching the person more effective thinking and behaviour as strategies that can be used in phobic reaction-inducing situations. *See also* ANXIETY DISORDER.

physical abuse *See* CHILD ABUSE AND NEGLECT.

physical disability *See* DISABILITY; SOCIAL MODEL OF DISABILITY.

placement 1. A range of arrangements whereby children are placed by a *local authority either in *children's homes or with substitute *care-givers who have been assessed and approved by a social worker.

Emergency placement A foster or residential placement that involves caring for a child or young person who needs somewhere safe to stay immediately or at very short notice. This placement is likely to be of short duration with the child moving somewhere else after a few days. Emergency placements are likely to include situations where a parent becomes suddenly incapacitated and there is no other family member to care for the child, or where a child assessed as being at grave *risk of *significant harm needs to be removed from home in the interests of her/his safety and there is no suitable alternative option within the wider family.

Short-term placement A foster or residential placement that provides a child with a temporary place to stay until the child is able to return to her/his own family, move into a long-term foster or residential placement, or an adoptive family. This is likely to last for a few weeks but may develop into something longer if the child's needs require this and the foster carer agrees to the placement being extended.

Long-term placement Refers to situations where a child cannot return home and a decision has to be made to find her or him a permanent family. This may mean *adoption or, particularly for older children likely to remain in contact with their *birth family, long-term foster care or residential placement. Children in long-term foster care remain a legal part of their original family, but live with long-term foster parents until they are ready to live independently. These situations may eventually lead to the foster carers applying to the *family courts for a *Child Arrangements Order or a *Special Guardianship Order, both of which are designed to provide the child and the placement with greater permanency.

Parent and child placement Arrangements where it is appropriate to place the parent or parents and their child with a foster carer while assessments take place regarding the parent's suitability to continue to care for the child.

Respite placement Involves a child spending short periods of time with a foster family to give their own family or other foster carers with whom they mainly reside a break, usually for a weekend or a week or two. This arrangement may be used for *disabled children or children with *learning disabilities.

Placement may also be used in the context of *adoption to refer to the child's adoptive placement.

See also ACCOMMODATED CHILD; BRITISH ASSOCIATION FOR ADOPTION AND FOSTERING; FOSTERING; LEAVING CARE; LOOKED-AFTER CHILD; PERMANENCY PLAN; PLACEMENT ORDER; PLACEMENT PLAN; PLACEMENT PLANNING MEETING; PRIVATE FOSTERING.

Further reading: Department for Education (2015) *The Children Act 1989 Guidance and Regulations. Volume 2: Care Planning, Placement, and Case Review.* Available at: https://www.gov.uk/government/uploads/system/uploads/attachment_data/file/441643/Children_Act_Guidance_2015.pdf.

2. A period of assessed practice undertaken by a social work student.

Placement Order A court order, made under Section 21 of the Adoption and Children Act (2002), that gives authority to a *local authority to place a child with prospective adopters. It can only be made in relation to a child who is the subject of a *Care Order or where the *threshold criteria for a Care Order are satisfied or where there is no parent or guardian. Parental consent to the Placement Order may be dispensed with by the Court under Section 47 of the Adoption and Children Act (2002) on the grounds that the parent cannot be found or is incapable of giving consent or the welfare of the child requires parental consent to be dispensed with. A Placement Order has the effect of suspending a Care Order. If the Placement Order is subsequently revoked, the Care Order is reinstated. The Placement Order continues until it is revoked or until an Adoption Order is made or until the child is 18, marries, or enters a civil partnership. Only a local authority can apply for a Placement Order and such an Order is required before a child can be placed for adoption with prospective adoptive parents unless parental consent has been given to the placement. Prospective adopters acquire *parental responsibility for the child as soon as the child is placed with them, to be shared with the *birth parents and the adoption agency making the placement.

placement plan A written statement describing the arrangements and agreements that should be in place when a child or young person becomes *looked-after, such as essential names and addresses, immediate arrangements for contact, agreement for the child to be looked after and to receive medical treatment, and details of the child's social worker. It should also define the aims and objectives of the placement. A placement plan should be completed whenever a child or young person becomes looked-after, even in an emergency. *See also* ACCOMMODATED CHILD; FOSTER CARE; PLACEMENT; PLACEMENT PLANNING MEETING.

Further reading: Department for Education (2015) *The Children Act 1989 Guidance and Regulations. Volume 2: Care Planning, Placement, and Case Review*. Available at: https://www.gov.uk/government/uploads/system/uploads/attachment_data/file/441643/Children_Act_Guidance_2015.pdf.

placement planning meeting Should be undertaken in relation to all looked-after children after they move to a new *placement. Thereafter a placement planning meeting provides an opportunity to consider whether the *placement plan for a looked-after child continues to be appropriate. In the event of an emergency placement or other significant event in relation to a child placed in a *children's home, foster home (*see* FOSTERING), or secure accommodation, an emergency placement planning meeting should be convened. *See also* PERMANENCY PLAN.

place of safety In mental health practice, refers to a hospital, a police station, or any other suitable place where someone may be taken in order to undergo *assessment under the Mental Health Act (1983). Section 135 of the Act allows an application for a warrant to be made to a justice of the peace (magistrate) by an *approved mental health professional authorizing any constable to enter any premises specified in the application to remove a mentally disordered individual to a place of safety. The individual must be suffering ill-treatment or neglect, or must be unable to adequately care for her/himself, and be living alone. The individual may be kept in a place of safety for up to seventy-two hours or until the assessment is completed. The assessment will conclude whether an application for admission to hospital under the Act is necessary. In practice, there are regional variations in what is considered to be a place of safety. The *Code of Practice to the Mental Health Act 1983* indicates that police stations should only be used in exceptional circumstances, for example, if *risk of danger to self or others is considered too great to manage in a different setting. The Code advises that a health care setting is most appropriate, and that residential care homes, or the home of a friend or relative of the person, if they are willing to accept her/him, should also be considered. *See also* EMERGENCY PROTECTION ORDER.

play therapy Techniques that aim to help children understand difficult events and experiences, and work through the feelings associated with them. Rather than having to explain what is troubling them, as with adult therapy, the techniques enable children to use play to communicate at their own level and pace without feeling they are being interrogated or threatened. They help children in a variety of ways: giving emotional support, learning more about their feelings and thoughts, playing out traumatic events to make sense of their past and cope better with the future. This therapy may also help children to learn to manage relationships and conflicts in more appropriate ways. Other possible outcomes may be lower levels of anxiety, improved self-esteem, and positive changes in behaviour. *See also* CHILD-CENTRED APPROACH; DIRECT WORK WITH CHILDREN; ECO MAP; GENOGRAM; LIFE STORY WORK.

Further reading: Axline, V. (1990, orig. 1964) *Dibs in Search of Self: Personality Development in Play Therapy*, Penguin.

(((●))) SEE WEB LINKS

• Official site of the British Association of Play Therapists.
• Official site of the UK Society for Play and Creative Arts Therapies.

police protection Referred to in Section 46 of the Children Act (1989) as the removal and accommodation of children by police in cases of emergency, this provision permits a constable, who has reasonable cause to believe that a child would otherwise be likely to suffer *significant harm, to take her/him to suitable accommodation or take steps to prevent a child's removal from hospital, or other place in which s/he is being accommodated. After taking a child into police protection following authorization by an officer of the rank of inspector, the police are required to inform the *local authority, which must then make enquiries under *Section 47 of the Act in accordance with its *duty to investigate concerns of actual or likely *significant harm. A child may not be kept in police protection for a period exceeding seventy-two hours. A police station should be used as a place of safety for a child who is the subject of police protection only as a last resort. *See also* EMERGENCY PROTECTION ORDER; SECTION 47 ENQUIRY; STRATEGY DISCUSSION; STRATEGY MEETING.

policy guidance *See* GUIDANCE.

politics of identity *See* CITIZENSHIP; IDENTITY POLITICS; POLITICS OF RECOGNITION; REFLEXIVE MODERNIZATION.

politics of recognition Struggles by excluded and *marginalized groups against systematic disrespect of their *cultures, ways of life, and status as people, and for achievement of a position of equal worth. *See also* CITIZENSHIP; IDENTITY POLITICS.

Poor Law The Poor Law Amendment Act (1834) introduced a system that replaced the Elizabethan Poor Law of 1601. The new system was based on the principle of 'less eligibility': 'The situation of the pauper shall not be made really or apparently so eligible as the situation of the independent labourer of the lowest class'. The principle was premised on the belief that work could be found if someone looked hard enough and was prepared to accept the wages on offer. In this way less eligibility was designed to force people into the labour market, and to deter others by reminding them what would happen if they needed assistance from the state. If this strategy failed, assistance was pitched at a level that would prove someone was utterly without independent support and was destitute, and therefore s/he would accept any conditions to avoid starvation. The principle of less eligibility was embodied in the workhouse as a test of destitution. It had a harsh and punitive living regime and its inmates were put to hard and repetitive labour. The workhouse meant that no one had to decide whether a pauper was genuine. The beauty of the 'workhouse test' was that it operated on a self-selecting basis. The 1834 Poor Law was one of the most significant and enduring developments in the history of social policy. *See also* CHARITY ORGANISATION SOCIETY; DESERVING POOR.

positive action (positive discrimination) Policies and practices that seek to combat the inequalities and disadvantages that have been experienced, for example, in education and employment, by sections of the population, usually *ethnic minority groups or women. Positive action seeks to give assistance to people from the identified sections of the population in order to bring them up to the requirements for a particular sort of job or a particular educational programme so that they are on a level playing field with other applicants. Positive discrimination sets aside some or all of the requirements in order to ensure that disadvantaged individuals can benefit.

postmodernism A term found in a wide range of disciplines that highlights the relationship between knowledge and power, and questions the existence of 'universal truths' associated with the belief in progress and reason during the period of modernity, roughly from the seventeenth to the late twentieth century. It sees the role of language in creating meaning, not simply reflecting it, as very significant. Power relations influence what is defined through language as knowledge and 'truth', and thereby result in particular frameworks that are used for understanding and explaining situations. While there are many 'knowledges' and interpretations available, some *discourses, through their connections with relationships of power, become dominant; they are heard more often and carry more weight than others. Dominant discourses may be accepted by those with less power or they may be challenged or resisted.

The postmodernist understanding of knowledge has implications for the sources of knowledge that are seen as relevant to understanding social work and for how this knowledge is used. Knowledge is not just theories contained in social work textbooks. Postmodernist approaches emphasize that there are multiple truths in any situation and stress the validity of the many different types and sources of knowledge. In particular, practitioners are encouraged to value 'ways of knowing' from their own practice and to uncover and value the *marginalized discourses of *service users. For social workers, this indicates the need for an inclusive approach to what is regarded as valid knowledge for understanding the situations they encounter. However, postmodernist approaches have been criticized. They have been seen as over-emphasizing subjectivity to the point where the individual's relationship with the social structure is ignored. This, it is argued, seriously restricts the emancipatory potential of social work in terms of challenging inequality and *oppression, understood in structural terms.

An alternative position, critical postmodernism, seeks to reconcile individual agency and social structure. It builds on the *insights gained from postmodernist approaches about the significance of subjectivity and individual agency, but combines this with *analysis of the impact of social structure on people's lives, thereby accepting a reality outside that of individual subjectivity. However, society is seen as complex, with numerous influences in any situation, such that simple explanations in terms of cause-and-effect relationships are spurious. Social structure is also not seen as determining individual experience, since individuals have the capacity to think, act, change, and resist. Rather, social structure is regarded as creating tendencies and part of the social worker's role is to understand and explain these tendencies. Once these tendencies are understood, it is argued, they can be challenged. *See also* CONSTRUCTIVE SOCIAL WORK; DECONSTRUCTION; SOCIAL CONSTRUCTION.

post-traumatic stress disorder (post-traumatic stress syndrome) (PTSD, PTSS) A range of symptoms developed in response, often delayed, sometimes for many years, to being deeply and enduringly shocked by an event such as a major disaster, an experience of war, or being involved in or seeing a road accident, a mugging, or a sexual or physical assault. Any event or experience outside someone's control that induces fear or horror can result in ongoing problems. Some contest the appropriateness of using 'disorder' in this context because far-reaching reactions to disturbing events or searing experiences are understandable. Initially, there may be a feeling of numbness but then other indications of PTSD may include suicidal feelings; *anxiety; *depression; being irritable and/or aggressive; nightmares; distress when there are reminders of what happened; inability to concentrate; being startled easily; thoughts being monopolized by going over the event; flashbacks in which it feels like the event is happening again; being unable to express affection. Many people who have experienced a traumatic event find that these sorts of symptoms fade quite quickly. Only if they last for a month or more and/or are particularly severe will they be seen as indicative of PTSD. The *National Institute for Health and Care Excellence recommends the following treatments:

Cognitive-behavioural therapy

Eye movement desensitization and reprocessing While recalling the traumatic event, making rhythmic eye movements that stimulate the information-processing system in the brain so that the processing of the traumatic events is speeded up.

Rewinding After being put into a relaxation state, the person imagines her/himself watching a film of the traumatic event, thus distancing her/himself from the memory.

Anti-depressants These may relieve some of the symptoms and/or assist people in benefiting from other treatments.

Further reading: Stein, D., Friedman, J., and Blanco, C. (eds.) (2011) *Post-traumatic Stress Disorder*, Wiley-Blackwell.

post-war consensus *See* DEMOCRATIC–WELFARE-CAPITALISM; WELFARE STATE.

POVA *See* SAFEGUARDING ADULTS.

poverty A distinction is usually made between absolute and relative poverty. Absolute poverty is the state of an individual who does not have sufficient resources for subsistence, as in some parts of the world. Definitions of relative poverty are usually used in Western societies. These refer to an individual's or group's disadvantaged position when compared with other members of society. They vary in precisely how this is defined but are united in seeing poverty as relative to the standards regarded as those needed to live an adequate life in a particular society. Relative definitions of poverty draw a poverty line below which people are poor and above which they are not, and there is considerable controversy about where this line should be drawn. *See also* PERVERSE INCENTIVE; POVERTY TRAP.

Further reading: Backwith, D. (2015) *Social Work, Poverty and Social Exclusion*, Open University Press.

poverty trap The situation that can be faced by individuals or families when they take up paid employment after being on benefits or when they move on to a higher income having been on a combination of a low income and benefits. The trap occurs when the loss of benefits and/or income tax payments are equal to or exceed any additional earnings so that the individual or family is no better off or is worse off than previously. *See also* PERVERSE INCENTIVE; POVERTY.

power (legal) Legislative provision that is permissive rather than mandatory. A body such as a *local authority *may* take a particular course of action but does not have to do so. However, just because something does not have to be done, it cannot necessarily be ignored. If an Act gives a power, consideration has to be given to using it. A local authority should not fetter its *discretion by having a policy that is so inflexible that it is impossible to make decisions with regard to an individual on the merits of her/his *case. Thus, a policy that states a specified group of people is not eligible for a service in any circumstances will fetter discretion because there will never be the possibility of any decision having to be made. The unfairness that could result from such a policy means it is open to legal challenge. In order to ensure that the discretion given by a power is used fairly, there will usually be a written policy concerning its use. *See also* DISCRETION (LOCAL AUTHORITY); DUTY; FETTERING DISCRETION; JUDICIAL REVIEW; TARGET DUTY.

power of attorney *See* LASTING POWER OF ATTORNEY.

practice educator A registered social worker who takes responsibility for support-ing, supervising, and assessing social work students on periods of assessed practice or for qualified social workers undertaking post-qualifying professional development and learning, including the *Assessed and Supported Year in Employment.

practice wisdom *Tacit knowledge that social workers draw on to make judge-ments and decisions, drawn from sources such as colleagues, training courses, and their own direct experience, and fashioned, often unconsciously, into working principles and practices.

Practitioner Alliance against Abuse of Vulnerable Adults (PAVA) *See* PRACTITIONER ALLIANCE FOR SAFEGUARDING ADULTS.

Practitioner Alliance for Safeguarding Adults (PASAUK) Formed in 1997 as Practitioner Alliance Against Abuse of Vulnerable Adults (PAVA), the name change in 2011 reflected current terminology and the thinking underpinning it, namely *safeguarding adults whose circumstances may make them more at *risk of *abuse, neglect, and exploitation. PASAUK works to bring together practitioners engaged in safeguarding adults. It includes as practitioners all paid staff and volunteers who have an adult safeguarding function contained in their job descrip-tion or responsibilities. It seeks to support practitioners: by increasing public awareness of abuse and neglect of adults who need safeguarding and of the need for a professional response; by promoting multi-agency and cross-professional working and collaboration in the development of safeguarding policies, procedures, and practice; by facilitating the development of virtual and local fora to debate dilemmas encountered in practice and multi-agency working; and by promoting *outcomes that are practical and reflect the interests, wishes, and *needs of adults at risk of abuse, neglect, or exploitation. In addition, it seeks to assist in developing and responding to legislation, policy, and practice changes from a *human rights and *citizenship perspective.

(((🌐))) SEE WEB LINKS
• Official site of the Practitioner Alliance for Safeguarding Adults.

praxis Used in Left politics and in some quarters of *radical social work to refer to the process (often struggle) of uniting theory and practice in action and reflection.

precedent *See* CASE LAW.

preferences These are contrasted with *needs in relation to services for adults. *Local authorities have a statutory *duty to meet eligible needs but not preferences. This can lead to conflict with other policies. For example, *personalization stresses that social workers should discover *service users' aspirations for their lives but service users may then be told that these are preferences rather than eligible needs and therefore that they cannot be met. *See also* ELIGIBILITY CRITERIA.

prejudice Bias and/or preconceived opinion in favour of or against individuals or groups, though it is almost always used to refer to negative responses. Prejudice relies on stereotypes that stem from the use of someone's or some group's feelings or perspectives as a basis of generalization.

pre-proceedings agreement *See* PRE-PROCEEDINGS MEETING.

pre-proceedings letter *See* PRE-PROCEEDINGS MEETING.

pre-proceedings meeting An important requirement of the *public law outline whereby a *local authority is required to inform parents in plain language of the concerns it has about their children, usually in relation to the children experiencing *significant harm, and the fact that *care proceedings are being considered. A pre-proceedings letter in a prescribed format must be sent to the parents setting out these concerns and informing them what they need to do to avoid the local authority taking care proceedings. Parents are invited to a meeting to discuss the concerns and are advised to bring a solicitor. They have legal aid for their solicitor's help at the meeting and in any negotiations with the local authority. If the parents accept the concerns of the local authority and are prepared to cooperate, they are asked to sign a pre-proceedings agreement. Compliance with the agreement is monitored and a timescale set for its review. The public law outline requires that the local authority should file a record of important discussions with the parents if and when care proceedings are issued.

pre-sentence report (PSR) A document prepared under Section 158 of the Criminal Justice Act (2003) by a professional from either the *probation or *youth justice services, depending on the age of the offender, that is intended to assist a court in determining the most suitable method of dealing with her/him after s/he has pleaded guilty or been found guilty of an offence. The criminal courts are required to obtain such a report or a Specific Sentence Report (SSR) before imposing a *custodial or *community sentence. The report includes an assessment of the nature and seriousness of the offence and its impact on the victim, and is disclosed to the offender or her/his legal representative. If the offender is under 18 years old the court must give a copy to her/his parent or guardian. *See also* ASSET; DETENTION AND TRAINING ORDER; REHABILITATION ORDER; SECURE ACCOMMODATION; SECURE ACCOMMODATION ORDER; SECURE TRAINING CENTRE; YOUNG OFFENDER'S INSTITUTION.

presenting needs (adults) *See* ELIGIBILITY CRITERIA.

prevention A practice that seeks to identify and avert a potential problem. The success of a preventive strategy is evidenced by a reduction in the incidence and prevalence of a specific problem. Prevention is often used alongside the term *early intervention. The two are distinguished by the latter referring to responding at as early a stage as possible to difficulties that have already emerged rather than preventing them in the first place. In reality, differentiating between preventive and early intervention programmes may be difficult as either of them may perform both functions at the same time. There has been much professional and policy debate about the potential benefits and challenges of investing significant resources in prevention rather than putting them into early intervention. In response, attempts have been made to explore the latter in more depth and define the balance to be achieved between the two. There has been a persistent failure in general across the range of social work services to shift substantial resources into preventive services.

prevention (adults) Section 2 of the Care Act (2014) states that *local authorities must intervene early to support adults and *carers in order to prevent, delay, or reduce needs wherever possible. (This is sometimes referred to as the prevention *duty.) The *care and support system is seen as needing to intervene early to support individuals, help people retain or regain their skills and confidence, and prevent *need or delay deterioration wherever possible. The local authority's responsibilities for preventing, delaying, and reducing needs apply to all adults, including:

- people who do not have any current needs for *care and support;
- adults with needs for care and support, whether their needs are eligible and/or met by the local authority or not;
- *carers, including those who may be about to take on a caring role or who do not currently have any needs for support, and those with needs for support which may not be being met by the local authority or other organizations.

The term 'prevention' can cover many different types of support, services, facilities, or other resources. There is no single definition and it can range from wide-scale whole population measures aimed at promoting health to targeted individual interventions aimed at improving the skills or functioning of one person or a particular group or lessening the impact of caring on a carer's health and *well-being. Prevention is often broken down into three general approaches: primary (prevent), secondary (reduce), and tertiary (delay).

Primary prevention (prevent) Aimed at people who have no current specific health or care and support needs, this covers services, facilities, or resources provided or arranged that may help people to avoid developing needs for care and support, or help a carer avoid developing support needs, by maintaining *independence and good health and promoting wellbeing. They are generally *universal services, which may include:

- providing access to good-quality information;
- supporting safer neighbourhoods;
- promoting healthy and active lifestyles;
- reducing loneliness and isolation;
- encouraging early discussions in families or groups about potential changes in the future, for example conversations about potential care arrangements or suitable accommodation should a family member become ill or disabled.

Secondary prevention (reduce) More targeted interventions aimed at individuals who have an increased risk of developing needs, where the provision of services, resources, or facilities may help slow down or reduce deterioration or prevent other needs from developing. Some early support can help stop a person's life tipping into crisis, for example helping someone with a *learning disability manage their money, or support for a family carer who is caring for an older relative. Early interventions could include:

- a *falls prevention service;
- adaptations to housing to improve accessibility or provide greater assistance (*see* HOME IMPROVEMENT AGENCY);
- handyperson services;
- short-term provision of wheelchairs or *telecare services.

In order to identify people likely to benefit from such targeted services, local authorities could undertake screening (*see* CARE MANAGEMENT) or *case finding, for instance to identify individuals at *risk of developing specific health conditions or experiencing certain events (such as strokes or falls), or those who have needs for care and support that are not currently met by the local authority. Targeted interventions should also include identifying carers, including those who are taking on new caring roles, so that they can benefit from support.

Tertiary prevention (delay) Interventions aimed at minimizing the effect of impairment or deterioration for people with established or complex health conditions, (including progressive conditions, such as *dementia), supporting people to regain skills and manage or reduce need where possible. Tertiary prevention could include, for example, the rehabilitation of people who are severely sight-impaired. Local authorities must provide or arrange services, resources, or facilities that maximize *independence for those already with such needs, for example:

- meeting a person's needs in their own home;
- *reablement services, including *aids and adaptations;
- joint care management for people with complex needs.

Tertiary prevention services can also improve the lives of carers by enabling them to continue to have a life of their own alongside caring, for example through *respite care, peer support groups, or stress management classes. This can help carers develop an awareness of their own physical and mental health needs.

In assessing whether an adult has any care and support needs (*see* NEEDS ASSESSMENT) or a carer has any needs for support (*see* CARER'S ASSESSMENT), a local authority must consider whether the person concerned would benefit from the preventive services, facilities, or resources provided by the local authority or which might otherwise be available in the *community. This is regardless of whether the adult is assessed as having any care and support needs or the carer any support needs. As part of the *assessment process, the local authority considers the capacity of the person to manage their needs and achieve the *outcomes which matter to them, and allows for access to preventive support before a decision is made on whether the person has eligible needs. Regardless of whether or not a person is ultimately assessed as having either any needs at all or any needs that are to be met by the local authority, the authority must provide *information and advice in an accessible form about what can be done to prevent, delay, or reduce her/his needs. Where a person has some needs that are eligible and some other needs that are not deemed to be eligible, the local authority must provide information and advice on services, facilities, or resources that would contribute to preventing, reducing, or delaying the needs that are not eligible.

Although the Care Act (2014) and the accompanying statutory guidance (2016) are at pains to highlight the benefits of prevention, the context of *austerity has limited the extent to which local authorities are able move towards a substantially greater emphasis on prevention in practice.

Further reading: Department of Health (2016) *Care and Support: Statutory Guidance*, Chapter 2. Available at: https://www.gov.uk/government/publications/care-act-statutory-guidance/care-and-support-statutory-guidance#person-centred-care-and-support-planning.

Primary Care Trust An organization that commissioned health services before the introduction of *Clinical Commissioning Groups.

primary health care Front-line community-based health services provided by *general practitioners, practice nurses, community nurses, health visitors, etc. It is not a setting within which social workers usually operate in providing services for adults (*see* SOCIAL WORK IN), but the Care Act (2014) guidance stresses that it plays an essential role in services for adults and should be dovetailed with *local authority provision.

primary health care, social work in The practice of locating social workers in *primary health care settings (usually general practices). Locality-based studies have consistently demonstrated significant benefits for *service users, notably *older and disabled people, in settings where this has happened. These include enhanced rates of self-referral and referral of patients by health care personnel for social services, improved access to benefits advice and previously unclaimed state benefits, and increased chances of preventive social services input. However, this remains a relatively undeveloped form of social work, because of the failure to provide state funding to underwrite its expansion.

primary health need *See* NHS CONTINUING HEALTH CARE.

principal-agent relationships (principal-agent transactions) *See* AGENCY THEORY.

private fostering An arrangement where a child under the age of 16 years (under 18 if disabled) is cared for by someone who is not their parent or a close relative. It is a private arrangement made between the parent and the *care-giver for twenty-eight days or more. Close relatives are defined as step-parents, grandparents, brothers, sisters, uncles, and aunts whether of full blood, half-blood, or by marriage. A person who has looked after someone else's child for twenty-eight days or more, and others who may have been involved in making the arrangement or are aware of it, are required by law to notify their *local authority, which will arrange for a social worker to visit the home to assess the suitability of the arrangement. Thereafter, the local authority will monitor the situation and provide support as necessary. Private fostering is different from other forms of *fostering because the latter are arrangements made by a local authority to ensure a child is cared for by approved individuals when the child cannot live with their parents. It is different from *kinship care because the private foster carer is not a close relative. *See also* ACCOMMODATED CHILD; FOSTERING; KINSHIP NETWORKS; LOOKED-AFTER CHILD; PLACEMENT.

private law This either does not involve a public body, such as a *local authority, or if it does, the public body is acting like a private individual and does not have any special *powers or *duties. For example, in a case involving a disputed contract over the sale of goods, even if the purchaser of the goods is a public body, it is still a private law matter.

The private law cases most commonly encountered by social workers are where parents have split up and there is a disagreement about with whom the children should live and have *contact. A range of different types of court order can be applied for, including a *Child Arrangements Order and a *Special Guardianship Order. *See also* PUBLIC LAW.

private sector The organizations providing services that are run to make profit and are in the hands of individuals or companies. Historically, such organizations played little part in social services provision but the *community care reforms opened up a *mixed economy of care in day, residential, and *domiciliary services for adults. Subsequently, the private sector became increasingly involved in children's services, with substantial growth in the number of private children's homes and private fostering agencies. For many years, governments have presented the private sector in an idealized form as the fount of wisdom and the provider of high standards of service. The private sector is depicted as knowing best, doing things better, and being a model for the improvement of the public sector. Governments have argued that by learning lessons from the private sector, the public sector will produce better and more desirable services, more in tune with what the users of those services want. Incorporating the discipline of the *market, managerialist beliefs, and business practices from the private sector in the *public sector has been presented as the key to success, particularly in *local authority services. More recently private sector organizations have moved into the provision of social work services. The first example of a privately owned profit-making company taking on the provision of statutory adult social work functions was Richard Branson's Virgin Care taking over adult social work services (and children's community health and continuing health care) in Bath and North East Somerset. This was agreed by the Council and the local *Clinical Commissioning Group in November 2016, to take effect from April 2017. *See also* BUSINESS EXCELLENCE; BUSINESS ORIENTATION; MANAGERIALISM.

privatization The transfer of responsibilities and undertakings from the *public sector to the *private sector. It can take many different forms, from the sale of energy utilities, previously owned by central government, to private companies to the 'floating off' of *domiciliary services from *local authorities into the *private sector, as in the *community care reforms. It can also refer to a trend, rather than an identifiable event, in which there is a gradual transfer from the public to the private sector. For example, though the community care reforms represented a landmark transfer of assets from local authority social services to the private sector, in subsequent years there has been a gradual and largely unpublicized shift towards private sector provision in many areas of social services.

Probation Service The statutory organization that provides reports to criminal courts, supervises offenders on *community sentences, and provides a welfare service in prisons. It emerged from the work of Police Court Missionaries in the nineteenth century. Up until the 1990s, the probation service was seen as primarily having a social work function to 'advise, assist, and befriend' offenders and probation officers undertook social work training courses in preparation for their role. Probation then moved out of social work education and became a specialism in its own right with its own distinct professional qualification. The predominant stress currently on managing *risks associated with offenders has led many to claim that the service has shifted a long way from its social work origins. *See also* NORTHERN IRELAND; SCOTLAND.

problem family A pejorative term used to describe families regarded in popular *culture as 'chaotic' and 'feckless', and seen as requiring essentially punitive *interventions to modify their *'anti-social' and 'irresponsible behaviour'. The term is often linked to the notion of an *'underclass' comprising the poorest, most socially *disadvantaged, and excluded members of society whose circumstances are often attributed, at least in part, to perceived deficiencies in their moral character. The *labelling of a group in society as 'undeserving' is not a new phenomenon (*see* DESERVING POOR). It dates back to Victorian times and was arguably implied in the notion of the *cycle of deprivation that emerged in the UK during the late 1970s and early 1980s to explain the persistence of *poverty.

In recent social work practice with children and families there has been a contrasting emphasis on a strengths-led approach to addressing difficulties, which aims to build positively on the capabilities and resources of families and avoid *interventions that are experienced as stigmatizing. However, while such an approach may be appropriate and possibly successful for most families experiencing difficulties, social workers encounter a dilemma when working with parents who are resistant, even hostile, to professional interventions aimed at keeping children safe. This has led to debate about the balance to be struck between the provision of social support to families with complex needs, and 'authoritative child protection practice' as advocated in the *Serious Case Review conducted after the death of Peter Connolly in 2007. Based on an analysis of professional practice in this *case, which was unsuccessful in preventing the catastrophic harm caused to the young child by his *care-givers, the approach is predicated on a need to maintain a clear and insistent focus on promoting the health and safety of children, a low threshold of concern in relation to children who have already experienced harm at the hands of their parents, and high expectations of parents in terms of the care they provide and in relation to the services provided to them. This approach appears to be underlined by the findings of earlier *child abuse inquiries, which have consistently demonstrated that social workers and other professionals need to be alert to deceptive behaviour and a lack of cooperation with *child protection plans by some parents. The need to avoid an over-optimistic view of parents' progress and capabilities, and to recognize non-compliance in both its overt and disguised forms have been stressed. *See also* CHILD POVERTY; CHILD WELFARE.

procedural model of assessment *See* EXCHANGE MODEL OF ASSESSMENT.

pro-choice *See* ABORTION.

production of welfare model *See* CARE MANAGEMENT.

profession An occupation that has traditionally been regarded as having a number of characteristics: a code of ethics/conduct; a regulatory body; a knowledge base; and control over new entrants. There has been debate about the extent to which social work possesses these characteristics, leading some to argue that it should be regarded as, at best, a semi-profession. Given that the duties of social work are undertaken on behalf of the state, it is the state context that draws the parameters of the spaces within which the problems and possibilities of the social work (semi-)profession are located. Terence Johnson's well-known analysis of professional work, *Professions and Power* (1972), views professions as occupational power structures that can be classified into three categories: collegiate, patronage, and mediated. In the case of mediated professions, an agency, usually a state organization, acts as mediator between the profession and its clientele in deciding with whom the profession will work, and what should be provided for those people with whom the profession engages, within the parameters of legal frameworks and resource allocation. Through this process, power is delegated to the professionals concerned and their status is legitimated by the functions they perform on behalf of the state. Social work is located within just such a state-mediated professional organizational structure as the base within and through which social workers operate. *See also* BUREAU-PROFESSIONAL REGIME; PROFESSIONALISM; PROFESSIONALIZATION.

Professional Capabilities Framework (PCF) A single career structure for social work that was introduced by the then College of Social Work. Since the demise of the College of Social Work in 2015, the *British Association of Social Workers has managed the PCF as the way for social workers to think about and plan their careers and professional development. It applies from enrolment on a social work qualifying course, through attainment of a social work qualification, and on to *continuing professional development after qualification. It divides capabilities into nine domains:

Professionalism Identify and behave as a professional social worker committed to professional development.

Values and ethics Apply social work ethical principles and values to guide professional practice.

Diversity Recognize diversity and apply *anti-discriminatory and *anti-oppressive principles in practice.

Justice Advance human rights and promote social justice and economic wellbeing;

Knowledge Apply knowledge of social sciences, law, and social work practice theory.

Judgement Use judgement and authority to intervene with individuals, families, and communities to promote *independence, provide support, and prevent harm, neglect, and *abuse.

*Critical reflection and *analysis* Apply critical reflection and analysis to inform and provide a rationale for professional decision-making.

Contexts and organizations Engage with, inform, and adapt to changing contexts that shape practice. Operate effectively within your own organizational frameworks and contribute to the development of services and organizations. Operate effectively within multi-agency and inter-professional settings.

Professional leadership Take responsibility for the professional learning and development of others through supervision, mentoring, assessing, research, teaching, leadership, and management.

On the basis of these capability domains, the framework sets out expectations of what a social worker should be able to do at each stage of her/his career and professional development. It specifies 'capability statements' for each career stage so that as social workers become more experienced, they deepen their knowledge and increase their skills, and this is reflected in their capability to take on more complex, specialist, challenging, and risky work. The career stages are:

- Social work qualifying programmes:
    Entry to qualifying programmes
    Readiness for practice
    End of first placement
    End of last placement
- End of qualifying programmes
- Assessed and Supported Year in Employment
- Social Worker
- Experienced Social Worker
- Advanced: Advanced Practitioner/Professional Educator/Manager
- Principal Social Worker.

The framework is seen as assisting employers with appraisal and workforce planning, making clear to the public and other professions what social workers do, and resulting in greater priority being given to ongoing learning and development.

Some have welcomed the emphasis on capability in the PCF as a move forward from the previous stress on *competence. Whereas competence is concerned with whether or not someone can do something, capability supplements this with the future potential for learning and thus has a more developmental approach. Others have argued that what students learn about the nature of social work through the PCF and what occurs in practice are radically different.

The PCF applies to all social workers in England in all roles and settings. For social workers in *Northern Ireland, *Scotland, and *Wales, the National

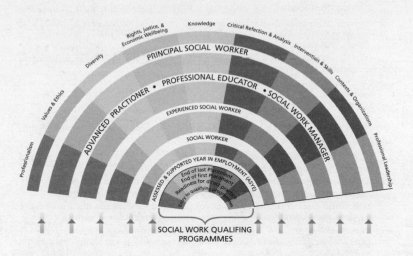

Professional Capabilities Framework

Occupational Standards still apply. The Standards are published by the UK Commission for Education and Skills and were revised in 2011. *See also* CODE OF ETHICS; CODE OF PRACTICE; HEALTH AND CARE PROFESSIONS COUNCIL; INTERNATIONAL FEDERATION OF SOCIAL WORKERS; KNOWLEDGE AND SKILLS STATEMENTS.

Further reading: *The National Occupational Standards.* Available at: https://www.gov.uk/government/publications/national-occupational-standards
The Professional Capabilities Framework. Available at: https://www.basw.co.uk/resource/?id=1137

professional discretion *See* DISCRETION (SOCIAL WORKERS').

professional identity *See* PROFESSION.

professionalism The orientation to work as a professional is stereotypically depicted as an unselfish devotion to the work in hand, the esoteric nature of professional knowledge as it is employed in reaching expert judgements, and the professional's concern with performing tasks to the best of her/his ability and thus being worthy of a high degree of trust. Critics see this as a gloss that covers professions' pursuit of their own interests. It could be argued that a form of professionalism has traditionally existed in social work that has had nothing to do with the grandiose aspirations to the elite status and professional self-determination associated with the established professions. It might be termed 'parochial professionalism'. This involves supervisors and social workers attempting to construct a shared view of good professional practice in social work as a key aspect of their working relations, a form of professional consultation and dialogue that is an alternative to purely line management-based supervision. Parochial professionalism has come under increasing strain with the greater prominence accorded to managerial surveillance of social workers' practice. *See also* BUREAU-PROFESSIONAL REGIME; PROFESSION; PROFESSIONALIZATION.

professionalization The establishing of control over a sphere of operations enabling an occupational group to exercise power, to enhance its status, and increase its remuneration. This process is sometimes referred to as the pursuit of a professional project. The mainstream professional project of social work in the UK was to seek incorporation into the state as the occupation officially recognized as dealing with problematic areas of people's lives. *See also* BUREAU-PROFESSIONAL REGIME; PROFESSION; PROFESSIONALISM.

professional values *See* VALUES.

prognosis A prediction, based on medical knowledge, of the expected course and outcome of a disease, and hence the likelihood of recovery from a disease.

Prohibited Steps Order Prohibits a person with *parental responsibility from carrying out a particular act in relation to a child (Section 8, Children Act [1989]).

pro-life *See* ABORTION.

promoting wellbeing (adults) Under Section 1, local authorities must promote wellbeing when carrying out any of their duties under the Care Act (2014). This is sometimes referred to as 'the wellbeing principle' because it is a guiding principle that puts wellbeing at the heart of *care and support for adults. The purpose of adult care and support is to help people to achieve the *outcomes that matter to them in their lives. Underpinning all of the processes, activities, or responsibilities that a *local authority performs under the Act, is the authority's *duty to promote wellbeing. The wellbeing principle applies in all cases where a local authority is carrying out a care and support function or making a decision in relation to a person. It applies equally to adults with care and support needs and their *carers. In some circumstances, it also applies to children, their carers, and to young carers when they are subject to transition assessments (*see* TRANSITION TO ADULT CARE AND SUPPORT).

Wellbeing is a broad concept, which the Care Act (2014) and the statutory guidance (2016) do not define. Instead, wellbeing is described as relating to the following areas in particular:

- personal dignity (including treatment of the individual with respect);
- physical and mental health and emotional wellbeing;
- protection from abuse and neglect;
- control by the individual over day-to-day life (including over the care and support provided and the way it is provided);
- *participation in work, education, training, or recreation;
- social and economic wellbeing;
- domestic, family, and personal relationships;
- suitability of living accommodation;
- the individual's contribution to society.

Promoting wellbeing involves actively seeking improvements in aspects of wellbeing (set out above) when carrying out a care and support function in relation to an individual at any stage of the process, from the provision of *information and advice, to *assessment (*see* CARER'S ASSESSMENT; NEEDS ASSESSMENT), to *care and support planning, to *reviewing a care and support plan. Wellbeing covers a broad range of aspects of a person's life and encompasses a wide variety of specific considerations depending on the individual. A local authority should consider what the person wants to achieve and how the action that the local authority is taking will promote the wellbeing of the individual. The focus on wellbeing signifies a shift from duties on local authorities to provide particular services to the concept of 'meeting needs', recognizing that everyone's *needs are different and personal to them. In terms of promoting wellbeing, local authorities must consider how to meet each person's specific needs rather than simply considering what service(s) s/he will fit into (*see* PERSONALZATION).

During the assessment process, the local authority should explicitly consider the most relevant aspects of wellbeing to the individual concerned and assess how their needs impact on them. Taking this approach allows for the assessment to identify how care and support, or other services or resources in the local *community, could help the person to achieve their outcomes. During care and support planning, when agreeing how needs are to be met, promoting the person's wellbeing may mean making decisions about particular types or locations of care (for instance, to be closer to family).

The wellbeing principle applies equally to those who do not have eligible needs but come into contact with the care and support system in some other way (for example, via an assessment that does not lead to ongoing care and support) as it does to those who go on to receive care and support and have an ongoing relationship with a local authority. The principle should also inform delivery of *universal services provided to all people in the local population, as well as being considered when meeting eligible needs. Although the wellbeing principle applies specifically when the local authority performs an activity or task or makes a decision in relation to a person, it should also be considered by the authority when it undertakes broader, strategic functions, such as planning, which are not in relation to one individual. Wellbeing should, therefore, be seen as the common theme around which care and support is built at both local and national levels.

There are a number of other key principles and standards to which the local authority must have regard in promoting wellbeing in its functions under the Care Act (2014):

Beginning with the assumption that the individual is best placed to judge her/his wellbeing. The local authority should assume that the person her/ himself knows best her/his own outcomes, *goals, and wellbeing. Local authorities should not make assumptions as to what matters most to the person; there should be an assumption that the individual is best placed to understand the impact of her/his condition/s on her/his outcomes and wellbeing.

The individual's views, wishes, feelings, and beliefs. Considering the person's views and wishes is critical to a person-centred system. Local authorities should not ignore or downplay the importance of a person's own opinions in relation to their life and their care. Where particular views, feelings, or beliefs (including religious beliefs) impact on the choices that a person may wish to make about their care, these should be taken into account. This is especially important where a person has expressed views in the past, but no longer has *capacity to make decisions themselves.

Preventing or delaying the development of needs for care and support and the importance of reducing needs that already exist. At every interaction with a person, a local authority should consider whether or how the person's needs could be reduced or other needs could be delayed from arising. Effective interventions at the right time can stop needs from escalating, and help people maintain their *independence for longer (*see* PREVENTION [ADULTS]).

Decisions are made having regard to all the individual's circumstances and are not based on her/his age or appearance, any condition s/he has, or any aspect of her/his behaviour that might lead others to make unjustified assumptions about her/his wellbeing. Local authorities should not make judgements based on preconceptions about the person's circumstances, but should in every case work to understand her/his individual needs and goals.

The individual participating as fully as possible in decisions about her/him and being provided with the information and support necessary to enable her/him to participate. Care and support should be personal, and local authorities should not make decisions from which the person is excluded.

The importance of achieving a balance between the individual's wellbeing and that of any friends or relatives who are involved in caring for the individual. People should be considered in the context of their families and support networks, not just as isolated individuals with needs. Local authorities should take into account the impact of an individual's needs on those who support her/him, and take steps to help others access information or support.

The need to protect people from *abuse and neglect. In any activity which a local authority undertakes, it should consider how to ensure that the person is and remains protected from abuse or neglect. (*See* SAFEGUARDING ADULTS).

The need to ensure that any restriction on the individual's rights or freedom of action is kept to the minimum necessary. Where a local authority has to take actions which restrict rights or freedoms, it should ensure that the course followed is the least restrictive necessary.

All of the matters listed above must be considered in relation to every individual, when a local authority carries out a function under the Care Act (2014). A person's life should be looked at *holistically, considering their needs in the context of their skills, ambitions, and priorities, as well as considering the other people in their life and how they can support the person in meeting the outcomes they want to achieve.

Promoting wellbeing is not always about local authorities meeting needs directly. It is just as important for them to put in place a system where people have the information they need to take control of their care and support and choose the options that are right for them. People can request their local authority support in the form of a *direct payment that they can then use to buy their own care and support using this information.

Further reading: Department of Health (2016) *Care and Support: Statutory Guidance*, Chapter 1. Available at: https://www.gov.uk/government/publications/care-act-statutory-guidance/care-and-support-statutory-guidance#person-centred-care-and-support-planning.

prosecution of parents for their children's irregular attendance at school *See* SCHOOL ATTENDANCE (PROSECUTION OF PARENTS).

protection of title Since 1 April 2005, the title 'social worker' has been protected in England by Section 61 of the Care Standards Act (2000). Individuals who are not registered on the Social Care Register maintained by the *Health and Care Professions Council (HCPC) are in breach of Section 61 of the Care Standards Act, if they:

- Describe themselves as a social worker; or
- Describe themselves in a way which implies registration with the HCPC; or
- Hold themselves out as registered with the HCPC

and, by doing so, they intend to deceive another person. All social workers in England must register with the HCPC and maintain their registration in order to be able to practise. Prosecutions can result in the person gaining a criminal record and a fine of up to £5,000.

Protection of Vulnerable Adults (POVA) *See* SAFEGUARDING ADULTS.

protective factor (child protection) Any influence, irrespective of source, that has the capacity or potential to offset or diminish the impact of a *risk factor and contribute to a positive *outcome for a child.

proxy measures A measure that stands in for and is taken to represent evidence of something else, such as using *outputs as measures of *outcomes. For example, if a social work organization decides that a measure of the quality of an assessment process will be a social worker giving a copy of the resulting written assessment to the *service user, then if social workers confirm that they have given a service user a copy of her/his assessment, this will be taken as a measure of the quality of the assessment itself. This example illustrates the flaw in the use of proxy measures: the assumption that they can indicate when beneficial outcomes are being achieved. In the example, a service user could have experienced the assessment as a poor outcome but as long as the social worker complied with the output requirement and gave a copy of the assessment to the service user, a quality outcome would be assumed to have taken place. *See also* MANAGERIAL CYBERNETICS; PERFORMANCE MANAGEMENT.

PSR *See* PRE-SENTENCE REPORT.

psychiatry A branch of medicine dealing with the *diagnosis and treatment of *mental disorders, which has been largely regarded as an applied natural science. There are inherent tensions in this association as many aspects of mental health care do not resemble traditional scientific activity. A doctor who works in psychiatry is termed a psychiatrist and is medically qualified to prescribe medication as well as recommend other forms of treatment. Psychiatrists have tended to adopt the *medical model in their approach to mental disorder, but their reliance on the subjective experience of patients in order for a diagnosis to be made undermines the scientific paradigm that emphasizes objective observation and data collection. *See also* ANTI-PSYCHIATRY.

p

psychoanalysis Developed originally by Sigmund Freud (1856–1939) over a century ago, there has since been considerable development in its theory and practice, but key ideas have maintained their place, including:

- Extensive aspects of psychological functioning are unconscious and have a profound impact.
- Unconscious conflict is a major feature of this functioning.
- When human beings become involved in relationships with others they bring deep influences from early childhood situations.
- The centrality of sexuality and *aggression in mental life, with key aspects of this established in childhood.

The application of these principles has seen psychoanalysis become a major method of psychological help, seeking to remove conflicts that can block healthy psychological development and act as a barrier to a more fulfilling life. It was most influential on social work in the 1950s and 1960s but was criticized for emphasizing the importance of the inner worlds of individuals while underplaying the impact of wider social influences on *human development, such as *poverty, *disadvantage, and other forms of *oppression. However, in drawing attention to the influence of early experience, particularly those of a traumatic nature, it has provided social workers and other professionals with useful insights into *child development, *attachment, and the impact of *child abuse and neglect. Awareness of the ways in which individuals construct subjective realities and how these influence their behaviour towards their own children can be of considerable value to those working in the field of *child welfare. The Institute of Psychoanalysis and the British Psychoanalytical Society are responsible for the training of psychoanalysts in the UK. *See also* PSYCHODYNAMIC CASEWORK.

Further reading: Bower, M. (2005) *Psychoanalytic Theory for Social Work Practice: Thinking under Fire*, Routledge.

psychodynamic casework The dominant method of social work from the end of the Second World War until the early 1970s, which was broadly based on psychoanalytic concepts in order to explain what was happening in people's lives. Such explanations were couched in terms of the influence of early childhood experiences, the structure of the personality, *defence mechanisms, and the role of the unconscious. The conditions of state social work in the UK made the practice of psychodynamic casework in its original form difficult, given its origins in private practice in the US, but it nevertheless provided what were regarded as powerful explanations. In UK practice there was a modified form of psychodynamic casework with an emphasis on current coping mechanisms, the social worker's analysis of the problem(s), and the *service user achieving change through *insight into the problem(s), and ventilation of feelings aroused by that insight, as s/he worked with the social worker. This approach to social work chimed with the wider context. The *welfare state was supposed to have addressed wide-scale social problems so any individual problems that remained could be seen as the result of the intra-personal processes experienced by malfunctioning citizens. Although easy to deride from a historical distance because of its emphasis on the social worker's esoteric knowledge and its neglect of the material circumstances of service users' lives, psychodynamic casework represented a more humanistic and optimistic approach when compared with what had gone before (*see* CHARITY ORGANISATION SOCIETY). It can be seen as a progressive shift away from moralizing that took service users' inner worlds seriously, as social workers sought to form constructive relationships based on a sense that something could be done. In addition, psychodynamic casework performed an important role in social work's striving to become a profession, as it provided a body of knowledge that set apart the qualified social worker from the 'unenlightened' who did not have access to this knowledge. Although few of today's social workers would claim to practise psychodynamic casework, the sediment deposited by this period is found in some of the terms that are still used by social workers, who may be unaware of their origins (for example, insight, acting out, resistant, manipulative, transference, projection, testing out). *See also* PSYCHOANALYSIS.

psychopath A term no longer used in *psychiatry but widely used in a lay sense. The term *psychopathic disorder was a legal term found in the Mental Health Act (1983), which included individuals with a persistent disorder or disability of the mind who displayed abnormally aggressive or seriously irresponsible conduct. It was removed by the Mental Health Act (2007). The third edition of the *Diagnostic and Statistical Manual of Mental Disorders* replaced the term with that of anti-social *personality disorder in 1980.

psychopathology The study of the causes, processes, and manifestations of mental and behavioural disorders.

psychosis A generic term used in psychiatry to describe symptoms whereby the individual experiences an alternative perception of reality and is unable to distinguish personal subjective experience from the external world. The most common types of psychosis are *hallucinations and *delusions. Psychosis is a feature of particular types of mental disorder, such as *schizophrenia, *delusional disorder, and some *affective disorders. It can also occur in certain physical illnesses and as a result of drug or alcohol use.

psy-complex *See* GAZE; GOVERNMENTALITY; TECHNOLOGIES OF THE SELF.

puberty *See* ADOLESCENCE.

public choice theory The study of politics, policy-making, and policy implementation from an economic perspective that has been deeply influential in the critique of public services through its questioning of the values and practices of *service*. Instead, it assumes that everyone involved in public services, such as social workers, is pursuing self-interest and is concerned with maximizing her/his own return, and that because distribution systems are not governed by price, they are inherently inefficient. It argues that this results in policies and practices that are not in the interests of citizens or economic efficiency. The power of public servants, such as social workers, is seen as needing to be curtailed by the introduction of *competition for the provision of services, which it is argued will also render services more economically efficient. *See also* ECONOMY, EFFICIENCY, AND EFFECTIVENESS.

Public Guardian *See* CAPACITY.

public inquiry An investigation into an issue or incident about which there is public concern, usually undertaken by a senior judge who takes evidence from those with an interest, cross-examines them (or has counsel representing the inquiry who does so), produces findings on where responsibility lies, and makes recommendations for improvements and the avoidance of similar occurrences in the future. The report from a public inquiry goes to the relevant government minister who decides whether and to what extent to act on its contents. A succession of public inquiries has been set up to report on the deaths of children as a result of child abuse and they have been influential in shaping subsequent policy and practice. *See also* CHILD ABUSE INQUIRIES.

public law Involves the legal relationship between the state and the individual, for example, the duty of a *local authority to intervene when a child is at risk of *significant harm (*Section 47, Children Act [1989]). It refers to both legislation and procedural rules that are used to enforce rights or defend actions taken or not taken. All *local authority social workers' relationships with service users are subject to public law. *See also* CASE MANAGEMENT HEARING; PRIVATE LAW; PUBLIC LAW OUTLINE.

Public Law Outline Government guidance that came into force on 1 April 2008 aimed at improving case preparation, promoting active case management, and the early identification of the key issues requiring determination and cooperation in advance of *public law cases coming before the *family courts. The guidance seeks to enable those involved in court proceedings that may lead to the making of a *Care Order or *Supervision Order to reach timely decisions for the child and reduce unnecessary delay. A key aspect is the sending by the local authority of a Letter before Proceedings to parents with a view to deflecting proceedings. The letter sets out the areas for change in the care of the child that need to be demonstrated to avoid legal action by the *local authority. *See also* CASE MANAGEMENT HEARING; CHILD PROTECTION; CHILD WELFARE; PRE-PROCEEDINGS MEETING; SAFEGUARDING CHILDREN; SIGNIFICANT HARM.

public sector The totality of services provided by the state. Traditionally, the mainstay of social services provision but increasingly services have been provided by the *voluntary and *private sectors in a *mixed economy, with the state in the roles of funder and commissioner. This transition is sometimes masked by referring to the provision of public *services*, as opposed to previous provision of services by the public *sector*, because this term enables the use of 'public' to refer to private sector provision. *See also* COMMISSIONING; PRIVATIZATION.

public service agreements *See* PERFORMANCE MANAGEMENT.

punishment *See* BEHAVIOURISM; BEHAVIOUR MODIFICATION.

pupil referral unit (PRU) A school, or unit within a school, run by a *local authority to provide education for children who cannot be maintained in mainstream education. Such provision is required under Section 19 of the Education Act (1996). Such units are often thought of as a place where badly behaved children are sent, but they cater for a wide range of children and young people, including those who cannot attend school because of medical problems, teenage mothers, pregnant students, children who have been assessed as school phobic, and those awaiting a school place. PRUs also provide education for those who have been excluded or who are at risk of *exclusion. Children who attend a PRU because of behavioural problems are not taught alongside those who are there for other reasons. For most, the main focus of the unit is on returning them to a mainstream school. *See also* EDUCATIONAL PSYCHOLOGIST; EDUCATION SOCIAL WORKERS; EDUCATION SUPERVISION ORDER; INDIVIDUAL EDUCATION PLAN; SCHOOL ACTION; SCHOOL ACTION PLUS; SCHOOL PHOBIA; SPECIAL EDUCATIONAL NEEDS; TEENAGE PREGNANCY.

p

purchaser *See* AGENCY THEORY; COMMUNITY CARE REFORMS; CONTRACT STATE.

purchaser–provider split *See* AGENCY THEORY; COMMUNITY CARE REFORMS; CONTRACT STATE.

qualifying patients *See* INDEPENDENT MENTAL HEALTH ADVOCATE.

quality assurance (quality control, quality improvement) Improving the quality of services has been a mantra in social work for some time and has been much emphasized from *New Labour's *modernization programme onwards. Although there are many definitions of quality, they share an emphasis on the customer's expectations being met and being met at a level that is beyond the bare minimum. (The reference to 'customer' stems from the business context in which the concern with quality originated; it has been imported into social work along with the quality agenda.)

Quality can be defined in one or more of the following ways: 'fitness for purpose' (whether a service does what it is supposed to do); 'specification conformity' or 'compliance' (whether the service meets the specifications laid down for it); or 'customer satisfaction' (often discussed in terms of the customer being delighted with the service received). Quality is depicted as a technical and value-free activity that is applicable in any context and hence can be utilized in public services such as social work. However, there are features of services such as social work that strain this applicability. When shifting towards a concern with quality, the motivation for *private sector businesses was market competition; they wanted to give more attention to the quality of goods and services in order to increase their market share. In social work, shortage of resources usually means that social workers are enjoined to *ration services (*see* AUSTERITY), not stimulate the demand for them. In addition, many aspects of social work are concerned with statutory *duties to protect and safeguard children and adults and/or *service users are receiving services under coercion. For example, however 'well' a child is removed from a parent against her/his will, it is unlikely that the parent will regard themselves as having received a quality service. These factors mean that the fit between quality concerns and social work is often strained. This is rarely acknowledged because the emphasis on the improvement of quality through universally applicable technical systems predominates, despite the managerial selection of indicators of quality and design of systems by which it is to be measured, reflecting particular values about what matters in social work practice.

'Quality assurance' had its origins in manufacturing industry, but is a term now encountered in social work. Another term that is encountered is 'quality control' and the two terms are often used interchangeably. However, within the quality *discourse, quality control is the monitoring of services against the standards set for them so that high-quality services can be identified and emulated and the causes of poor quality services can be addressed. Quality control is seen as a central component in improving quality but as only one aspect of quality assurance, which is represented as an all-embracing commitment to establishing an organizational culture of continuous improvement. Such a culture is seen as typified by a focus on the customer, efficient and effective use of available resources, and staff commitment to delivering high-quality services. In quality assurance, the use of *outcome criteria is advocated, which describe results in terms of exactly what happens when a quality service is delivered, rather than simply counting *outputs (what services were delivered to how many people) but outputs are often taken as *proxy measures of outcomes.

Three issues associated with the use of quality assurance systems in social work are, first, that even if they were to work perfectly and result in high-quality services, they would only help those using services. All the attention is focused on current service users and the situation of those refused a service is ignored. Secondly, these systems close down discussion of the sources of service users' problems. They reduce social work to a series of service transactions, representing it as a neutral machine for the provision of services, divorced from wider questions about equity and social justice, and separated from the lived experience of service users. Such questions are atomized in the values base of the social workers providing the services. Thirdly, the insistence that quality assurance systems embody a technical, objective neutral perspective masks the extent to which there are many interests and *goals at play when quality is considered. For example, managers, social workers, and service users all have their views on what constitutes quality. It is just that political and managerial interests obscure the views and interests of others, maintaining the power relations that the definition and measurement of quality embody. *See also* BEST VALUE; BUSINESS ORIENTATION; CONSUMERISM; ECONOMY, EFFICIENCY, AND EFFECTIVENESS; EUROPEAN FOUNDATION OF QUALITY MANAGEMENT MODEL; PERFORMANCE MANAGEMENT.

Further reading: Hafford-Letchfield, T. (2007) *Practising Quality Assurance in Social Care*, Learning Matters.

quango (quasi-non-governmental organization) An agency, such as the *Care Quality Commission, that implements policies and carries out tasks set down by government. The term is falling into disuse and being replaced by *non-departmental public body.

quasi-markets Originally introduced into social work through the *community care reforms initiated by the Thatcher government, with the assumption that this was a desirable development because *market arrangements were seen as more economical, efficient, and effective than the *public sector in providing services (*see* ECONOMY, EFFICIENCY, AND EFFECTIVENESS). This assumption stemmed from the belief that competition between service providers produces efficient services in which prices decrease while quality increases. Radical changes in social work were encapsulated by this belief in quasi-market arrangements with cash-limited budgets, *purchaser-provider splits, *outsourcing, and more widespread charging for services. *Local authorities became primarily funders, allocating budgets to suppliers. Subsequently quasi-markets were extended from residential and *domiciliary services for adults to other areas of provision such as *fostering and *children's homes.

Quasi-markets differ from 'pure' markets in a number of important respects. On the supply side there is competition between service suppliers but, in contrast with 'pure' markets, suppliers are not necessarily privately owned nor are they necessarily required to make profits. On the demand side, consumer purchasing power is not inherent in the individual. For example, in services for adults, following assessment a *personal budget is allocated to be spent by the service user through *direct payments, or by a third party or the *local authority on the service user's behalf.

The shift to quasi-markets has been significant for a number of reasons. First, it has bolstered the political legitimation of central government on social work issues and priorities because market outcomes are presented as neither fair nor unfair. They are seen as either the result of the operation of impersonal market forces or stem from the decisions of social workers and their local authority employers as they *gate-keep the access to the market. As such, central government can deflect responsibility for the outcomes of its policy elsewhere. Secondly, quasi-markets undermined the sense in which social services had represented a counterbalance to market values during the post-war consensus on welfare (*see* DEMOCRATIC-WELFARE-CAPITALISM). Thirdly, they introduced competition amongst service providers. Local authorities were made responsible for setting clear service specifications, stimulating provision by the *voluntary and *private sectors, and floating off some of their own services to those sectors. Fourthly, they embodied aspects of *agency theory in the instigation of the purchaser-provider split. In this arrangement, control resides with the purchaser of services, with providers having to comply with the purchaser's requirements. This has centralized strategic control in the local authority, while decentralizing responsibility for service delivery, underpinned by the use of contracts. Fifthly, what had previously been reciprocal relationships between local authorities and the *voluntary sector were changed. *Voluntary organizations that received grants from local authorities to pursue wide-ranging interests and functions, such as campaigning, were restructured to make their functions as specific as possible and render them contractable services to social work. Local authorities then controlled the allocation of contracts for services with tightly specified activities or *outputs. The voluntary sector's sense of distinctiveness—in terms of its nature, purpose, and autonomy—was eroded as voluntary organizations accommodated to this reconstructed relationship with local authorities. *See also* CARE MARKET; CONTRACT STATE; MIXED ECONOMY OF CARE.

quasi-non-governmental organization *See* QUANGO.

queer theory Initially arising out of an activist movement involving alliances between gay men and lesbian women in the United States in the 1980s that argued for declarations of gay and lesbian visibility by appropriating derogatory terms such as 'queer' and 'dyke', thus celebrating identities that were normally stigmatized and derided. Subsequently the academic field that developed tended to be referred to as lesbian and gay studies, within which some variants of queer theory argued that there was a need to incorporate into the study of sexuality issues associated with *'race', *gender, *class, *ethnicity, *disability, and age. Other strands of queer theory have highlighted the limitations of liberal approaches to achieving equal rights, such as gay and lesbian marriage and the *fostering and *adoption of children by lesbian and gay couples, on the basis that such approaches incorporate gay men and lesbian women into relationships that are modelled on the conventional norm, a process sometimes referred to as homonormativity or *heteronormativity. In critiquing the limitations of liberal approaches, Foucault's three-volume work on *The History of Sexuality* has been influential in queer theory's consideration of the production of sexual *identity through discourse. *See also* ANTI-DISCRIMINATORY PRACTICE; ANTI-OPPRESSIVE PRACTICE; GAY AND LESBIAN PERSPECTIVES; HETEROSEXISM; HOMOPHOBIA.

Further reading: Hicks, S. and Jeyasingham, D. (2016) 'Social Work, Queer Theory and After: A Genealogy of Sexuality Theory in Neo-liberal Times', *British Journal of Social Work*, 46, 8, 2357–73.

questioning model of assessment *See* EXCHANGE MODEL OF ASSESSMENT.

questions Asking questions is central to social work. There are some obvious pitfalls for social workers to avoid, such as asking leading or unclear questions, or running together two or three questions into a 'mega-question'. The main distinction is between open and closed questions. Open questions are intended to give *service users as much scope as possible to put their thoughts and feeling into their own words. However, social workers need to be aware that some service users may feel overwhelmed by open questions such as 'where would you like to start?' It is important not to rush to fill an initial silence or hesitant reply with suggested responses to an open question. Closed questions require either factual answers, such as someone's address, or can be answered 'yes' or 'no'. Asking closed questions inappropriately in relation to matters that are more complex and not amenable to yes/no responses may leave the service user feeling that they are not being taken seriously or are being slotted into pre-defined compartments. This can be the effect of tick-box *assessment formats in which intimate personal aspects of people's lives may be addressed through short pointed questions that reduce the potential complexity of the issues to formulaic responses. In situations like this, social workers can resist this dehumanizing process by asking open questions about the relevant areas of people's lives and then providing the information in the form that the assessment requires. *See also* COMMUNICATION SKILLS.

q

'race' Originally used for the now widely discredited idea (except on the far right of the political spectrum) that people could be divided into distinct biological groups with fixed characteristics, in an ordered hierarchy that made some groups inferior to others. Skin colour was the overwhelmingly significant factor that was drawn on in propagating this view. In recent years, 'race' has re-emerged in a new guise in relation to the monitoring of equal opportunities policies, for example, in relation to job applications, when applicants are asked to choose to locate themselves as belonging to one of a number of 'racial' categories. In order to recognize the artificial, though well-intentioned, use of the concept in such circumstances, it has become customary to use inverted commas in order to signify that the writer is aware that the concept of 'race' is essentially problematic. This indicates that the writer acknowledges that it needs to be employed on occasions but is being used with reservations, with awareness that it is socially constructed and without connotations of racial stereotyping. *See also* MARGINALIZATION; OTHER; RACIALIZATION; RACISM; WHITENESS.

racialization 1. The social processes by which a group is categorized as a *'race'.
   2. A means of indicating that a social problem has been (wrongly) designated as a 'racial' issue.

racially aggravated offences *See* HATE CRIME.

racism Values, beliefs, ideologies, or behaviour that distinguish people's characteristics and abilities and justify discrimination against them on the basis of their 'membership' of a 'racial' group, most often on the basis of skin colour, but also can be on the basis of their country of origin or their *culture. Racism has often resulted in vicious treatment of people; asserting extreme and unalterable differences between 'races' allows the dominant group to think of the subordinated group as 'not like us' and not fully human. Until the 1990s, racism was conceived of in policy and practice as an individual or group phenomenon. The formula often quoted was that racism resulted from a combination of *prejudice plus power. However, a public enquiry into the Metropolitan Police concluded that it was characterized by 'institutional racism', which was defined as the collective failure of an organization to provide an appropriate service to people because of their colour, culture, or ethnic origin. It was found to be detectable in processes, attitudes, and behaviour that amounted to discrimination, even if the intent was not consciously to discriminate, as a result of unwitting prejudice, ignorance, thoughtlessness, and racist stereotyping. Some have taken exception to the concept of institutional racism, arguing that it is too woolly and that the focus needs to be kept on individuals who are overtly racist. However, the concept of institutional racism has been used in social work to reflect on the ways in which actions may have inadvertent and unintended consequences. For example, if a social work team states that it does not discriminate against anyone and its services are available to all in the *community in which it is located, but only provides information in English and any images it uses are only of white people, it can be seen to be institutionally racist. There is no deliberate intention to discriminate but in practice discrimination will result. The concept also warns of the danger of assuming that policies and practices are automatically working by acknowledging that the operation of an organization may be having effects that are other than those intended. *See also* MARGINALIZATION; OTHER; 'RACE'; RACIALIZATION; WHITENESS.

radical right *See* NEW RIGHT.

radical social work In the late 1960s and 1970s, in the wider context of movements of students, workers, and others, and a burgeoning in critical social science, there was a movement of social workers and academics that rejected the social work tradition of seeing people's problems in terms of *individual pathology in favour of structural explanations rooted in the unequal nature of society, particularly the impact of *class on people's lives. This initial emphasis on class was subsequently augmented by a number of critical perspectives that highlighted *oppression stemming from other social divisions such as age, *disability, *gender, *'race', and sexuality, though there is still debate about the extent to which these other perspectives were embraced by the radical social work movement. Diverse though these perspectives were, they were united in seeing (what were experienced and presented as) personal problems as political issues. Within radical social work there was a division between those who regarded social work's role on the part of the state as unequivocally one of social control on behalf of the ruling class, and those who saw the *welfare state as a balance of oppressive and progressive forces, partly serving the interests of the ruling class but also providing benefits and services that had been won by working class struggles. The latter standpoint emphasized the potential for further struggle within the welfare state in a progressive direction in pursuit of radical objectives. Those who saw social work as an unambiguous tool of state power considered that there was little point in attempting to develop such forms of radical practice. For example, they argued that it did not matter if children were taken into care by a radical social worker or a traditional psychodynamic caseworker, they were still taken into care. They stressed that social workers were workers, not professionals, and should concentrate their efforts on radicalizing their trade unions. While also stressing social workers' involvement in the trade union movement, those who regarded the welfare state as having the potential for more progressive forms of social work advocated *consciousness-raising (or *conscientization)—exploring with *service users the structural basis for the problems they were experiencing—as well as *group work and *community work to repudiate *psychodynamic casework's basis in individual pathology. The radical social work movement was caught up in the 'Winter of Discontent' (1978-9) in which there was extensive and prolonged trade union action against the Labour government's policies on pay restraint and cuts in services at the behest of the International Monetary Fund, from which the government had been forced to request a loan in 1976.

At the end of this period of militancy, a *neo-liberal Conservative government under Margaret Thatcher came to power (May 1979). Social work initially found itself under attack as a failed profession and then was reconstructed through the introduction of *markets and *managerialism. In this changed climate radical social work dwindled, leaving behind, however, a commitment to *anti-discriminatory and *anti-oppressive practice in mainstream social work, at least rhetorically. In recent years, there has been a resurgence of interest in radical social work, led by the *Social Work Action Network (SWAN), as a consequence of social workers' dissatisfaction with markets and managerialism. SWAN seeks to identify the potential for *resistance to neo-liberalism in social work and advocates collective campaigning that is allied with service users, trade unions, and the labour movement more generally. *See also* AGENTS OF SOCIAL CONTROL; MARXIST SOCIAL WORK.

Further reading: Turbett, C. (2014). *Doing Radical Social Work*, Palgrave Macmillan.

rankings *See* MANAGERIAL CYBERNETICS; PERFORMANCE MANAGEMENT.

rapid response (children) The combined actions of a group of key professionals who come together for the purpose of enquiring into and evaluating a sudden and unexpected or unexplained death of a child in the locality for which they are responsible. It is part of the processes established for the purpose of *child death review under the Children Act (2004). When a rapid response is initiated, the subsequent investigation is led by the police and a paediatrician, with appropriate involvement by other agencies. A case review meeting takes place on conclusion of the investigation at which all the information on the child's death is shared. The process is intended to achieve the objectives of supporting the child's parents, establishing as far as possible what led or contributed to the child's death, and determining what further action may be needed in the *case. It precedes the consideration of the case that is eventually conducted by the Child Death Overview Panel established by the relevant *Local Safeguarding Children Board. *See also* SERIOUS CASE REVIEW; SUDDEN UNEXPECTED DEATH IN CHILDHOOD.

Further reading: HM Government (2015) *Working Together to Safeguard Children: A Guide to Inter-agency Working to Safeguard and Promote the Welfare of Children*, Chapter 5. Available at: https://www.gov.uk/government/uploads/system/uploads/attachment_data/file/419595/Working_Together_to_Safeguard_Children.pdf.

rational choice *Consumerism's introduction into social work was meant to change the way in which social workers conceived of *service users and service users conceived of themselves. Service users acting as customers on the basis of rational choice has been presented as best for them in a wide range of policy documents. This view is rooted in rational *choice theory, which originated in economics. It asserts that actors will seek to achieve the best outcomes for themselves and when faced with a choice an actor will seek the best deal that maximizes her/his utility. As a consequence of this theory's influence across the *public sector, service users have been depicted as competent economic and social actors, capable of pursuing their best interests in the *market place of services. This is a *neo-liberal approach to service users that sees society as made up of atomized individuals rather than being constituted by bonds of mutuality and reciprocity that go beyond instrumental transactions. It sees people as entrepreneurial, individualistic, autonomous, competitive, self-interested, rational, and informed. In this neo-liberal *discourse, service users have only their individual interest in getting the best deal they can. Some writers have argued that this conception of service users bears little relationship to the circumstances in which many service users come into contact with social work or to the situations in which they find themselves, and ignores the existence of rationalities other than maximizing individual utility.

rationing Restricting the allocation of resources in the context of rising demand has become an increasingly prominent feature of social work. For example, there is an established trend of a continuing reduction in the number of people receiving *domiciliary services, as these services are concentrated on those in greatest need. *See also* ELIGIBILITY CRITERIA; GATEKEEPING.

reablement (reablement service) Provision in adult services that enables people to lead an independent life in their own home for as long as possible by supporting and encouraging them for a specific period of time, usually six weeks. Reablement can be considered for anyone who is over 65 and who could benefit from a short period of intensive and focused support to maximize independent living. Reablement services are often helpful to people recovering from an illness or a *fall or who are experiencing a major life change. Those who may not benefit from reablement services, and who may be excluded from them, include people with advanced *dementia, complex neurological/cognitive deficits, high levels of *risk, terminal illness, and drug and alcohol problems. Referrals may come from *information and advice services, *hospital discharge teams, *general practitioners, or social work teams following initial *assessment.

The service is provided by staff, either individually or in combination, with a range of different roles, such as *occupational therapist, *care manager, *community care worker, and *rehabilitation officer, who visit during the six-week period. It focuses tailored support to individuals in regaining, maintaining, or developing daily living skills and instilling the confidence to carry them out independently. The intention is to support *service users in taking greater control of their lives and remaining independent, thus eliminating or minimizing the need for further *intervention. This involves focusing on people's strengths and abilities, working alongside them to see how they can best get around areas where they are struggling, and seeing if *aids and/or adaptations can help them overcome difficulties. They are encouraged to do as much as possible for themselves; reablement has a 'do with' not 'do for' emphasis in order to assist people in rebuilding skills and confidence and gaining new skills. Progress against individual *goals is tracked by regular visits from team members. At the end of the initial period, ongoing support may continue to be provided, if required.

Reablement services are free for up to six weeks regardless of people's financial status or whether they meet the threshold set by the national *eligibility criteria. Whilst reablement is usually a time-limited intervention, in some *cases it does not have a strict time limit, since the period of time for which the support is provided depends on the *needs of and *outcomes for the individual. When it is provided beyond six weeks, it can be charged for but it can continue to be provided free of charge if there are clear benefits to the person and a reduced risk of hospital admission.

If a person who has already begun the process of assessment is considered likely to benefit from reablement, the assessment can be put on hold to allow time for the benefit of a period of reablement to be realized so that the final assessment of need and decision about eligibility for *care and support is based on the remaining needs that have not been met through reablement. *See also* INTERMEDIATE CARE.

Further reading: Department of Health (2016) *Care and Support: Statutory Guidance*, Chapter 2. Available at: https://www.gov.uk/government/publications/care-act-statutory-guidance/care-and-support-statutory-guidance#person-centred-care-and-support-planning.

reactive depression (exogenous depression, situational depression) A transient experience of *depression precipitated by a stressful life event that can include the birth of a baby, *divorce, *death of a loved one, or harassment at work. The experience is usually a short-term reaction to the event and can be manifested in feelings of low mood, hopelessness, unfairness, or being burdensome to others. Sleeplessness, over-sleeping, and suicidal thoughts are not uncommon. Unlike other forms of depression, the individual usually acquires coping skills to deal with the stressful event but low feelings can last from a few weeks to six months. If symptoms persist beyond six months or if they worsen, the *diagnosis is reviewed as other types of depression may need to be considered. Because the experience of reactive depression is similar to other types of depression, the value of making the distinction may not be very significant, as treatment for reactive depression is similar to treatment for other types.

reality orientation (reality therapy) An approach that seeks to maintain memory in *older people who are suffering from memory *loss, such as those with *dementia. It uses written and spoken reminders of current events to connect them to contemporary life. It claims to reduce mental disorientation and confusion, and to increase self-esteem. It may involve group work, with a board displaying information about the day, date and location. Group members undertake a series of tasks that provide mental stimulation and reinforce the time, the place, and the people involved in the group. As well as being a distinct activity, reality orientation is used day-to-day in some residential and day care settings. For example, there may be a board in the entrance that says 'Welcome to Sunny Centre. Today is Monday 10th June'. *See also* REMINISCENCE.

reasonable adjustment *See* DISABILITY DISCRIMINATION; DISABLED CHILDREN.

reasonableness A concept that occurs frequently in legislation that gives *local authorities leeway within which to take decisions as long as the actions they take are reasonable. Unreasonableness is one of the key issues raised by judges in relation to local authority decisions in *judicial reviews. *See also* DISCRETION (LOCAL AUTHORITY); FETTERING DISCRETION; RELEVANT FACTORS; RIGID POLICIES.

reassessment *See* ASSESSMENT; CARER'S ASSESSMENT; NEEDS ASSESSMENT; REVIEW; REVIEW TEAMS.

recidivism (recidivist) A recidivist is someone who reoffends. Recidivism is usually measured in terms of the percentage of people reoffending, usually categorized according to the type of offence, over a set period of time.

recording Documenting activities such as *assessments, *care plans, *reviews, meetings, and visits plays a central role in social work. Recording almost always takes the form of inputting information in a standardized form on a *computerized system, which then generates reports in a prescribed format. These systems are designed primarily to meet the managerial demands of organizations and to enable the monitoring and extraction of data required by *inspection and *performance management systems. However, they also require social workers to share copies of documents such as assessments and care plans with *service users and *carers. In this context, there can be tension between what social work agencies require from records for managerial purposes and service users' and carers' requirements. Service users and carers are likely to value records that are presented in a clear and easily accessible format and written in straightforward language. Computer-generated reports that aim to convey information seen as necessary by the organization and other professionals may bear little relationship to how someone perceives her/his own situation. There may be a gulf in understanding and language between professionals and service users. What are everyday terms for social workers—such as *'need', 'assessment', and 'eligibility'—may be alien concepts to service users. *Professional language can provide an easy shorthand for professionals, but act as a barrier to work with service users, so social workers can find themselves acting as interpreters between professional and service user languages and *cultures. In addition, the need to demonstrate that difficulties are *'eligible needs' in adult services can lead to social workers concentrating exclusively on problems, which can result in service users feeling discredited and demoralized. While the practice of giving copies of reports to service users may be seen as commendable in principle, questions have to be asked about how the receiving of reports is experienced by service users in practice, unless recording is clear, positive in tone, and conveys strengths as well as difficulties and needs. For example, rather than stating that 'Mr Smith is immobile', it might be preferable to say 'Mr Smith has full use of his arms and hands, but he needs help to walk.' Writing in a way that is both clear and incorporates strengths does not mean that difficulties cannot be detailed as well. Much of what is needed involves describing what someone can and cannot do, rather than using a label, such as 'immobile', as in the example.

Concerns about recording in children's services have centred on the complexity of the electronic systems in use and the large amount of time social workers spend processing and loading information relative to the time they are able to spend working directly with children and families. This was a major theme in the *Munro Review of Child Protection in England conducted during 2010–11, which sought to identify and recommend steps to reduce the bureaucratic burdens on social workers that were barriers to the effective exercise of professional judgement. Professor Munro also criticized the *Framework for Assessment of Children in Need and their Families (Department of Health 2000), the government template then used for collating and recording information about children and families, suggesting that it was inefficient and cumbersome, overly prescriptive in terms of the timescales for completion of assessments it stipulated, and was in need of reform. Her approach contrasted with that of the two previous government reviews of child protection in England conducted by Lord Laming, following the deaths of Peter Connolly in 2008 and Victoria Climbié in 2000. The Laming reviews sought to apply more prescriptive approaches to *safeguarding work in order to eliminate *risk and uncertainty, an objective Munro has described as unrealistic due to the complexities of *child protection work. Irrespective of the systems used, sound recording in children's social work remains essential to clearly identifying concerns about children and their needs, and providing a firm basis for planning and decision-making. The compilation of case *chronologies that provide in systematic terms a full history of the family, particularly when children have experienced complex, chronic, and in some situations, intergenerational *abuse and neglect, is another important facet of recording practice, which is central to the effective analysis of *risk.

Further reading: Munro. E (2011) *The Munro Review of Child Protection: Final Report: A Child-centred System*, Department for Education.

recovery (mental health) An approach to mental ill-health and distress that emphasizes the individual's potential for recovery through an ongoing process of 'living well' that may involve accepting and learning to live with particular aspects of the experience of mental ill-health. It evolved directly from the experiences of mental health service users about what helped them to live a meaningful life, in particular from *service user movements in the US in the 1980s and 1990s that emphasized the importance of self-help, *empowerment, and *advocacy. There is no accepted definition of the concept, although common principles apply. These include the capacity to live a personally meaningful and satisfying life; self-determination and self-growth; self-awareness; self-acceptance; and a shift away from the sick role, helplessness, and *dependency. Central components of user-led understandings of recovery pose fundamental challenges to traditional psychiatric approaches that are premised on notions of medical control, patient deficit, incapacity, and pessimistic *prognosis. While *psychiatry is oriented primarily to the control or removal of 'symptoms', recovery is about achieving a good quality of life, whether while living with a mental health 'problem' or in its aftermath. The *goal of recovery is not 'cure', 'remission', or restoration to a pre-illness state. Recovery may mean changing certain behaviours but it may also include accommodating to experiences such as *hearing voices, periodic episodes of low mood, or self-harming behaviours. Recovery incorporates strategies to deal with the social reaction to *'mental illness', for example, *social exclusion and *stigma, and associated experiences of *poverty, unemployment, and isolation. It also encompasses recovery from professional and service responses to mental distress, such as deprivation of liberty, harmful side-effects of medication, and experiences of invalidation. While acknowledging the social, political, and economic determinants of mental health, the recovery model requires individuals to take responsibility for their own wellbeing. This means reaching an understanding of the past and developing strategies to achieve personal growth and fulfilment. Recovery cannot be imposed or directed by anyone else but is rooted in individual self-management. However, the need for a supportive environment is central to the recovery model. Recovery is therefore not just a matter of developing individual strategies, but also about accessing mechanisms for peer learning and support, *community involvement, and working in *partnership with professionals and services. Hope, a belief that recovery is possible, and that individuals are able to take charge of their lives, underpins the recovery model and this positive orientation has to be shared by the individual and all those within the support network. The personal experiences and narratives of other *'survivors' play a key role in developing and sustaining hope. There are particular approaches to planning for recovery. One is the WRAP approach (Wellness Recovery Action Planning), developed by people with experience of mental health problems. The WRAP approach involves setting personal goals and devising an action plan, usually based on small achievable steps. A recovery model does not preclude the use of medication or hospital treatment, as long as these form part of the individual's chosen recovery strategies. For practitioners, the model requires a focus on individual potential, rather than on the restrictions and limitations imposed by symptoms, and realistic life goals and supporting individuals to achieve them, rather than managing the illness and focusing on symptoms and pathology.

Although the recovery approach was initiated by service users, it has been adopted within mainstream mental health *discourses and policy agendas. *New Labour introduced the concept of recovery to the mental health policy agenda with its publication of the *Guiding Statement on Recovery* (2005), which set out principles for the delivery of recovery-oriented mental health services. These principles include a *holistic and integrated approach to treatment and recovery based on a strengths model that emphasizes hope, *independence, realization of life roles, culture, spirituality, socialization, and educational needs. While, on the one hand, continuing official recognition of recovery principles can be seen as a positive development, attesting to the increased influence of user-centred values and practices, there is concern that key recovery principles become diluted and distorted as they are appropriated within policy agendas. For example, the emphasis on self-management could be reinterpreted as people not needing formal services and a focus on recovery could marginalize people who are seen as not having the potential to 'recover'. The key to ensuring that the recovery model continues to promote the mental wellbeing of service users is for service users to remain at the heart of how the model is understood, practised, and developed.

Further reading: Information about the WRAP selfmanagement and recovery system. Available at: http://mentalhealthrecovery.com

Slade, M. (2009) *Personal Recovery and Mental Illness: A Guide for Mental Health Professionals*, Cambridge University Press.

Recovery Order A direction to produce a child who is under *police protection or who is the subject of an *Emergency Protection Order, *Interim Care Order, or *Care Order, or to disclose her/his whereabouts. The Order authorizes a constable to enter specified premises and search for the child using reasonable force if necessary (Section 50, Children Act [1989]).

reductionism (reductionist) A strategy for reducing complex phenomena and individual variation between instances of the same phenomena to a basic simpler form. For example, if a burnt-out social worker developed a *routinized approach to cases of *child abuse on the basis of treating them all in the same way, s/he would reduce the complexity involved in particular circumstances and not recognize differences between *cases. *See also* BURN-OUT; OBJECTIFICATION; PEOPLE-PROCESSING; ROUTINIZATION.

re-enablement (re-enablement service) *See* REABLEMENT.

reference group A group that is characterized by attitudes, beliefs, and behaviours that supply a set of *norms for individuals who belong to it and provide a way of making judgements about people outside it. Although often associated with adolescent groupings, reference groups operate in a wide range of contexts. For example, a social work team may function as a reference group that exerts a strong influence on how social workers think about and carry out their work, and may generate attitudes to others outside the reference group such as teachers or nurses. *See also* MARGINALIZATION; OBJECTIFICATION; OTHER; OUT-GROUP; PEER GROUP.

referral Notification to a social work organization that there is a potential *service user who may need the services it provides. This notification can come from the potential service user her/himself, her/his family or friends, a stranger, a local *councillor, or another professional such as a *general practitioner. Although the process of referral and becoming (or not becoming) a service user is usually taken for granted, it is embedded in social processes that shape the organization's response. Whether a referral results in provision of a service can depend on: the influence and/or persistence of the person making the referral; how good the information is in the referral; the vagaries involved in the *screening of referrals; the quality of an initial *assessment; the perception of *risk; how social workers interpret and apply the organization's policies. *See also* DISCRETION (SOCIAL WORKERS').

Referral Order Involves referral of a young offender to a *Youth Offender Panel by a *Youth Court for a period of between three and twelve months. First introduced by the Youth Justice and Criminal Evidence Act (1999) when these orders were required for all those appearing before a youth court for the first time who pleaded guilty, unless they were given an absolute discharge or a *custodial sentence. However, courts can now make a Referral Order for a second conviction, if there

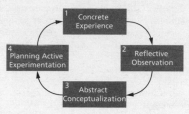

Kolb's experiential learning model

has not been a previous Referral Order. If there has, a second order can only be made in exceptional circumstances (Criminal Justice and Immigration Act 2008). *See also* ASSET; COMMUNITY SENTENCES; PRE-SENTENCE REPORT; REPARATION ORDER; YOUNG OFFENDER; YOUTH JUSTICE SERVICE; YOUTH JUSTICE SYSTEM; YOUTH OFFENDING TEAM; YOUTH REHABILITATION ORDER.

reflective log *See* LEARNING LOG.

reflective practice A term increasingly heard in social work education that refers to the process of learning from experience by 'hovering above' and thinking about one's own practice, and applying knowledge to it. This can be seen, for example, in items requiring reflection that have to be completed by social work students for inclusion in practice placement portfolios. Critical reflection goes further and is concerned not only with the immediate processes that constitute practice but also involves examining the power dynamics of the situation and the wider structures that shape practice. Additionally, *reflexivity contributes a social worker's awareness of self and her/his impact on practice, integrating personal knowledge and understanding with professional knowledge and understanding. A popular way of thinking about reflection is to see it as part of a cycle of learning from experience (Kolb): social workers experience practice, reflect on that experience, conceptualize the experience by analysing and theorizing their actions/feelings, and move on to plan how to act in future on the basis of what they have learned. For learning to be fully effective, reflection is seen as needing to be consolidated in the succeeding stages of the learning cycle. *See also* LEARNING STYLES; MINDFULNESS.

Further reading: Gardner, F. (2014) *Being Critically Reflective*, Palgrave Macmillan.

reflexive modernization A concept devised by Ulrich Beck (1944–2015) in *Risk Society: Towards a New Modernity* (1992), and developed by Anthony Giddens (*Beyond Left and Right: The Future of Radical Politics* [1994]), amongst others, through whom it came to have an important impact on the thinking of *New Labour. It describes the process in contemporary societies by which people create their own *narratives and *biographies through choosing between a wide range of *identities, opinions, values, lifestyles, groups, and sub-cultures. As a consequence, attachments to families, neighbourhoods, and social classes are weakened. *Diversity is prized and *differences in age, *ethnicity, and *gender provide the basis for *identities and lifestyles that replace *class identifications. *See also* IDENTITY POLITICS; INTERSECTIONALITY.

reflexivity Social workers 'putting themselves into the picture'. This requires social workers not only to think things over and evaluate, as in *reflective practice, but also to monitor their reactions, the impact of their involvement on *service users, and the effect the involvement is having on themselves. Reflexivity assumes that people's understanding of their social context is part of that context. Social workers do not just occupy social spaces: they partly create them through their assumptions, understandings, and influence. Accordingly this means social workers remaining open to alternative ways of understanding, and being willing to question what they know and how they know it.

reframing Developing a different perspective on events, situations, or circumstances, or seeing a problem in a new way. For example, it can be used to produce a more positive slant on something that has happened, perhaps highlighting a person's strengths in dealing with a particular situation s/he found stressful.

refuge Temporary accommodation for women, and their children, who have been the subject of *violence by men. *See also* CHILDREN AND DOMESTIC VIOLENCE; DOMESTIC VIOLENCE; WOMEN'S AID.

refugee The United Nations Convention Relating to Refugees (1951, as amended 1967) defines a refugee as:

A person who owing to a well-founded fear of being persecuted for reasons of race, religion, nationality, membership of a particular social group, or political opinion, is outside the country of his nationality and is unable or, owing to such fear, is unwilling to avail himself of the protection of that country; or who, not having a nationality and being outside the country of his former habitual residence as a result of such events, is unable or, owing to such fear, is unwilling to return to it.

As the UK is a signatory to the Convention, this is the definition that is supposed to govern applications for asylum in the UK. *See also* ASYLUM-SEEKER; HUMANITARIAN PROTECTION; INDEFINITE LEAVE TO REMAIN; NATIONAL ASYLUM SUPPORT SERVICE; UNACCOMPANIED ASYLUM-SEEKING CHILDREN.

refusal of treatment (mental health) *See* COMPULSORY TREATMENT.

registered intermediary (RI) A professional communications specialist who has been recruited, selected, and accredited by the Ministry of Justice, and whose details are recorded on the Intermediary Register, the Witness Intermediary Scheme's national database. Provided under the special measures introduced by the Youth Justice and Criminal Evidence Act (1999), RIs play an important role in enabling vulnerable witnesses and victims with communication needs to participate in the justice system. They assist with communication and understanding so that witnesses and victims can give their best evidence during an investigation and at trial.

registered nurse (registered nursing care) *See* NHS-FUNDED NURSING CARE.

register of disabled people Under Section 77 of the Care Act (2014), a *local authority must establish and maintain a register of sight-impaired and severely sight-impaired adults who are *ordinarily resident in its area. In addition, a local authority may establish and maintain one or more registers of adults who are ordinarily resident in the local authority's area and who:

• have a *disability;
• have a physical or mental impairment which is not a disability but which gives rise, or which the authority considers may in the future give rise, to needs for *care and support;

- come within any other category of people the authority considers appropriate to include in a register of those who have, or may in the future have, needs for care and support.

Whilst there is no legal requirement for a local authority to establish such a register(s), if established, the purposes of such a register are planning service provision to meet needs for care and support and monitoring changes over time in the number of adults in the local area with needs for care and support, and the types of *needs for which care and support are required. *See also* SOCIAL MODEL OF DISABILITY; VISUAL IMPAIRMENT.

regulation A general term for a range of activities that is focused on influencing and controlling policy and practice at the local level. *See* AUDIT COMMISSION; INSPECTION; PERFORMANCE MANAGEMENT.

Regulation 24 Sets out the process for placing *looked-after children with *connected persons who are not already approved as foster carers (Care Planning, Placement and Review [England] Regulations [2010]).

regulations Also referred to as statutory instruments, regulations are secondary legislation made under Acts of Parliament as the primary legislation. For example, the rules concerning *direct payments are contained in regulations. *See* TABLE OF LEGISLATION, REGULATIONS, AND CODES OF PRACTICE.

rehabilitation Originally the restoration of someone to their previous or optimal level of functioning following an accident, other trauma, or illness through the intervention of doctors, nurses, physiotherapists, *occupational therapists, social workers, etc. Still used in this sense, but also now used more widely to include work with offenders and people with drug and/or alcohol problems. *See also* REABLEMENT; YOUTH REHABILITATION ORDER.

Rehabilitation Order *See* YOUTH REHABILITATION ORDER.

reimbursement policy *See* HOSPITAL DISCHARGE.

reinforcement (reinforcers) *See* BEHAVIOURISM; BEHAVIOUR MODIFICATION; TOKEN ECONOMY.

relapse The worsening of symptoms after a period of improvement. In mental health it can be important to identify signs and symptoms of relapse as *early intervention may help prevent a new episode. These can include becoming withdrawn from friends, family, and significant others; neglecting personal care; losing interest in food; becoming more suspicious, wary, or distant; or talking in a strange or incoherent manner. For example, in *bipolar disorder, an episode of mania is often preceded by losing one or two nights' sleep and increased irritability; alternatively, someone may become unusually happy and energetic, more talkative, and more active generally. Relapse is sometimes triggered when people stop taking their prescribed medication and can happen gradually over a period of weeks or months.

relapse plan *See* RISK ASSESSMENT.

relationship-based practice Advocated by Eileen *Munro as part of her review of *child protection, particularly in the second report (*The Child's Journey* 2011), in which she emphasized social workers' engagement with children's views and opinions as priority areas for reform in the child protection system. Work undertaken for the review found that children need to be seen and understood, to have a continuous relationship with a trusted social worker, and for processes to be clearly explained to them. Munro emphasized developing the expertise of social workers and addressing the training and *supervision they need in order to work to make children safe, along with reducing *bureaucracy. This chimed with the feelings of social workers about being unable to devote sufficient time to *direct work and building relationships with children. *See also* RECORDING.

relative deprivation Given that people's expectations are in part generated by comparisons with others, whether and how deprived people feel will not just stem from their circumstances, but from their perceptions of those with whom they compare themselves. *See also* NEED; POVERTY.

relative poverty *See* POVERTY.

relevant factors In their decision-making, local authorities must take account of relevant factors and not include irrelevant factors. Failure on either or both counts can be the basis for *judicial review. *See also* DISCRETION (LOCAL AUTHORITY); FETTERING DISCRETION; REASONABLENESS; RIGID POLICIES.

relevant person representative *See* DEPRIVATION OF LIBERTY SAFEGUARDS.

remand An interim measure available to courts during criminal proceedings, for example, while a defendant is waiting for her/his case to come to trial, or when s/he has been convicted and sentencing has been adjourned for the preparation of reports. People can be remanded in the *community on *bail or in *custody.

remand to local authority accommodation All children remanded other than on bail can only be dealt with by a remand to *local authority or youth detention accommodation under the Legal Aid, Sentencing and Punishment of Offenders Act (2012). Local authority accommodation means any accommodation that is provided by or on behalf of a local authority. It has a wide definition and can include the homes of relatives. *See also* PACE BEDS.

reminiscence group (reminiscence therapy, reminiscence work) The process of *older people recalling and talking about the past, usually in a group, and often found in residential and day care settings. The initial stimulus for this type of activity was provided by an American gerontologist and psychiatrist, Robert Butler (1927–2010). In the 1960s he used the term 'life review' to describe the process he went through in his practice with individual older people, who talked about their past lives and gained a sense of perspective about them. This was consistent with work by Erik Erikson, who depicted the final phase life as presenting a psychological conflict between a sense of integrity and despair (*see* THEORIES OF AGEING). Butler's work can be seen as seeking to assist older people to resolve that conflict in the direction of achieving a sense of integrity about their lives.

In reminiscence work, older people's memories of their life experiences are seen as the basis of their *identities. Such memories enable older people to have a sense of who they are and, when shared, they allow others to have a greater sense of who someone is. The facilitator of a reminiscence group typically uses prompts from the past, such as music, photographs, or artefacts (such as household items), to encourage group members to talk about the memories stimulated by them. There are also reminiscence 'kits' that can be used by facilitators. For example, there are some materials that move through a succession of historical periods. More recently touch-screen software has been developed that supports communication and inter-action, and has the potential to draw on thousands of digital media items, such as photographs, television shows, music, and film clips. While some of the memories stimulated by these activities can be anecdotal and light-hearted, other themes roused by the prompts—such as family, friendship, love, *loss, disappointment—can produce powerful emotions or even lead to reliving previous trauma.

The *goals for reminiscence groups vary but may include one or more of: providing a social activity; improving someone's mood; fostering a sense of self-worth; and improving communication, for example, they can provide a way for people with short-term memory loss to interact with others based on their long-term memory. In a wider sense, reminiscence work can result in the realization of the goals of the life reviews Butler undertook, if older people come to terms with the disappoint-ments and losses in their lives, and have pride in what they have accomplished. *See also* AGEISM; BIOGRAPHICAL APPROACHES; NARRATIVE APPROACHES; REALITY ORIENTATION.

Further reading: Kunz, J. A. and Gray Soltys, F. (2007) *Transformational Reminiscence: Life Story Work*, Springer.

Reparation Order Introduced by the Crime and Disorder Act (1998), the Order requires a young offender (under 18) to perform up to 24 hours of tasks in repayment for the offence within three months of an Order being made, such as work for the victim of her/his crime or for the benefit of the *community generally. *See also* ASSET; COMMUNITY SENTENCES; PRE-SENTENCE REPORT; REFERRAL ORDER; RESTORATIVE JUSTICE; YOUNG OFFENDER; YOUTH JUSTICE SERVICE; YOUTH JUSTICE SYSTEM; YOUTH OFFENDING TEAM; YOUTH REHABILITATION ORDER.

representation 1. In everyday speech, it means to act or to speak for, as when a social worker as a *Children's Guardian represents a child's interests in court. *See also* ADVOCACY.

2. It also refers to the ways in which speech and the written word construct their subject matter. Meaning is not a reality that is simply reflected in written and spoken representations: it is constructed by them. For example, a social worker who undertakes an *assessment of an *older person can subsequently represent that person in a way that either recreates and thus endorses stereotypical ideas about old age and *older people or that challenges them. Representations can be deconstructed by asking questions such as: Who constructed the representation? For what purpose? For what audience? For example, a social worker may produce an assessment of an older person that highlights problems, dependency, powerlessness, and *risk in order to secure expensive services because s/he knows that this stereotypical representation of an older person will play well with a *resource panel. *See also* ADVOCACY; DECONSTRUCTION; GAZE; GOVERNMENTALITY; SOCIAL CONSTRUCTION.

repressive state apparatuses *See* IDEOLOGICAL STATE APPARATUSES.

reprimand Under the Crime and Disorder Act (1998), reprimands replaced *cautions for young offenders (under 18). A decision about a reprimand is at the discretion of the police and can only be used for a minor first offence that is admitted. A further offence may result in a *final warning or a court appearance. *See also* ASSET; COMMUNITY SENTENCES; PRE-SENTENCE REPORT; REFERRAL ORDER; REPARATION ORDER; YOUNG OFFENDER; YOUTH JUSTICE SERVICE; YOUTH JUSTICE SYSTEM; YOUTH OFFENDING TEAM; YOUTH REHABILITATION ORDER.

research-mindedness The quality possessed by social workers who are know-ledgeable about research findings and apply them to their practice. It can also mean the development of research knowledge and skills by social workers themselves. *See also* EVIDENCE-BASED PRACTICE.

residence A stipulation of where a child will live, usually following *divorce or separation by her/his parents. In circumstances where parents are unable to agree on arrangements for their children's residence, the *family courts may decide to make a *Child Arrangements Order to determine where the child will live. The Children Act (1989) replaced the previous term *'custody' with residence. *See also* CONTACT.

Residence Order Has been replaced (*see* CONTACT ORDER). *See also* CHILD ARRANGEMENTS ORDER; CONTACT; PARENTAL RESPONSIBILITY; RESIDENCE.

residence requirement Stipulates that an offender has to live in a specific place. Such a requirement can be part of a suspended sentence or a *community sentence.

residential assessment A *parenting assessment completed in a centre where children and parents live together, enabling a high level of monitoring of the parents' care. *See also* ASSESSMENT; PLACEMENT.

residential care Accommodation that provides in-house support for personal and social care *needs for any groups of *service users. Residential care may be provided in small units, where a few individuals are supported in a lifestyle as close as possible to living independently in the community, or in larger specialist units, where complex physical, emotional, or health needs result in the pursuit of econ-omies of scale. In larger facilities, substantial provision may be made to meet residents' needs for social activities, development, and interaction. However, prin-ciples and standards for *good practice encourage continuing interactions with a wide range of community-based activities, services, relationships, and opportunities.

resilience An individual's capacity to cope with stress and adversity. It is usually understood as a process rather than an individual trait and located in theories of psychosocial development. These theories see human growth and development in terms of the operation of *risk and *protective factors at each stage of the *life cycle and crucially at points of critical transition. The success or otherwise of such transitions will influence the development of adaptive strategies, problem-solving skills, and the individual's sense of self-efficacy. However, the pathways through these processes are regarded as complex and multi-faceted, and considered unlikely to be characterized by a steady linear progression. Rather, they are more likely to emerge in response to a series of events and short-term sequences that may sometimes appear random and unrelated. Moreover, resilience is not static: it emerges over time and assumes different characteristics and outcomes at different stages. For example, a child may do poorly during a critical life transition such as entering secondary education, but experience problems that are less severe than would be anticipated given the many risk factors the child might have faced up to that point. Additionally, an individual who appears to have coped well with chal-lenges encountered during the life cycle and in response to critical transitions may at other points flounder. What is likely to be crucial to these outcomes is the presence of protective factors, which prove effective in counteracting or diminishing risk factors. The impact of a potentially vast range of factors, whether genetic, derived from the impact of early experience on neurological development and *attachment, social, psychological, or cultural, or linked to the impact of social and economic disadvantage and discrimination on individuals, *communities, and the wider society, will play their part in the acquisition of resilience. In social work with children and families and vulnerable adults most of the approaches used are likely to be based on interventions that seek to build up protective factors, identified within the circumstances of individuals, families, neighbourhood, and communities, and ameliorate risk factors, with a view to strengthening resilience by generating a relationship between the identified risk and protective factors that favours the latter. The situations that are likely to pose the greatest challenge to the resilience and welfare of children and adults and make this relationship more difficult to achieve are when risk factors accumulate to the point at which they permanently predominate. *Domestic abuse, adult and *child abuse and neglect, poor mental health, and *drug and alcohol misuse, have been identified as particularly damaging risk factors in an individual's circumstances, especially when one or more appear together.

There has been criticism of the increasing emphasis on individual resilience as another aspect of neo-liberal thinking in which the responsibility for solving social problems is seen as belonging to the individual. For example, the concept of resilience in relation to bullying has been seen as situating the governance of human behaviour within a neo-liberal framework, locating accountability and responsibility within the individual in the here and now. Thus resilience in relation to bullying is seen in terms of individual empowerment, responsibility and 'manning up'—skills that can be taught and acquired. *See also* CHILD ABUSE AND NEGLECT; CHILD DEVELOPMENT; CHILD POVERTY; CHILD WELFARE; CYCLES OF DEPRIVATION; ECOLOGICAL APPROACH; GOOD-ENOUGH PARENTING; INDIVIDUALISM; LIFE COURSE; NEO-LIBERALISM; PROBLEM FAMILY; PSYCHOANALYSIS; RESPONSIBILIZATION.

Further reading: Jensen, J. and Fraser, M. (eds.) (2011) *Social Policy for Children and Families: A Risk and Resilience Perspective*, Sage.

Sims-Schouten, W. and Edwards, S. (2016) '"Man up!" Bullying and Resilience within a Neoliberal Framework', *Journal of Youth Studies*, 19. 10, 1382–400.

resistance In the case of social workers, refusal to go along with or be incorporated into dominant trends that seem inimical to social work, such as *managerialism, and seeking to further *service users' interests in any discretionary spaces they have in their work and/or by working through organizations such as trade unions and the *Social Work Action Network. At an individual level, resistance may be manifested in reluctant and minimal compliance, maintaining a critical distance, or open scepticism, as social workers experience the gaps between dominant *discourses and the evidence of their everyday working lives, such as the gap between the rhetoric of *consumerism and shortfalls in services. For service users, individual and collective resistance may be directed against dominant discourses that represent them in particular ways, for example, in objectifying models of *'mental illness.' A range of service user groups and movements have sprung up to resist others' definitions of the nature of their 'problems' and the explanations given for them, *See also* OBJECTIFICATION.

resource panels Began to proliferate in local authorities following the *community care reforms because of anxiety about the level of resourcing involved in options such as *residential care for *older people. They are usually composed of senior managers and sometimes have social worker representation. The panels take the *gatekeeping role away from social workers by receiving their *assessments and identifying, comparing, and keeping a watching brief on people who are a high priority and have *needs for similar resources. They allocate resources as these become available to the people on the waiting list who have been prioritized as having the greatest needs. The statutory guidance on the Care Act (2014) refers to them as 'approval panels' and warns about their possible impact on the timeliness and *bureaucracy introduced into the planning process. In some cases panels are seen as an appropriate mechanism to sign off large or unique *personal budget allocations and/or plans. However, the guidance states that local authorities should refrain from creating or using panels that seek to amend planning decisions, micro-manage the planning process, or are in place purely for financial reasons.

Further reading: Department of Health (2016) *Care and Support: Statutory Guidance*, para. 10.85. Available at: https://www.gov.uk/government/publications/care-act-statutory-guidance/care-and-support-statutory-guidance#person-centred-care-and-support-planning.

respite care (respite placement, respite service) A short-term *placement of a child or adult away from where they usually live in order to give parents or *carers a break, for example, as part of a support programme to families, for children with disabilities, or for *older people. Placements can be in hospital, *residential care, or with other families. (More rarely, respite can be provided in a *service user's own home by using live-in support staff.) In addition to giving parents or carers a break, there is increasing attention being paid to the importance of making the break a positive experience for the person in the placement.

responsible clinician (RC) A role introduced by the Mental Health Act (2007) that replaced the former role of responsible medical officer (RMO). The responsible clinician will be an *approved clinician (AC) who is designated as having overall responsibility for a patient's treatment. In most cases this role will be undertaken by a patient's psychiatrist but the legislation allows a range of professionals to exercise the functions set down in the Act, and it can be undertaken by a psychologist, specialist nurse, *occupational therapist, or social worker. Responsible clinicians have statutory responsibilities that include renewing detention, authorizing leave, and discharging patients. However, if the role is not undertaken by a psychiatrist, the responsible clinician cannot make decisions about medication and must refer such decisions to an approved clinician who is a psychiatrist.

responsible medical officer *See* RESPONSIBLE CLINICIAN.

responsible officer The person who administers a *community sentence, usu-ally a *probation officer or a member of a *youth offending team, but in the case of *electronic tagging it could be someone working for a security firm.

responsibilization Making individuals responsible for functions and risks that were previously the responsibility of the state, for example, through the use of *direct payments. Such initiatives have emphasized their emancipatory potential but the other side of the coin is the responsible managerial role that is required of *service users in relation to carrying out tasks previously undertaken by the state and in being accountable for their outcomes. This is described by some writers as the 'managerialization of the self' because being made responsible means service users have to manage public money, keep records that have to be available for inspection/audit, achieve the *outcomes agreed in the *care plan, and possibly become employers of people supporting them. It becomes the service user's responsibility to make what they can of their support arrangements, finding sup-port, monitoring *quality, managing *risks, and ensuring *value for money. The increasing emphasis on responsibilization has raised questions from some commentators about the implications of this trend for those service users unable to take over the state's former role. *See also* RESILIENCE.

restorative justice A specific form of *restorative practice using measures through which offenders are encouraged to make amends for harm they have caused. This is the principle at the centre of the *Reparation Order but it has also been introduced as an element in a range of other sentences, as well as being acted upon through a number of other mechanisms. For example, *family group conferences have been used to divert young offenders from the courts by negotiating informal agreements about what should happen to them that can include their making amends. Restorative justice has also been central to offender–victim mediation schemes in which the offender meets the victim of her/his crime in a supervised context. *See also* COMMUNITY SENTENCES.

restorative practice Helping to build and maintain healthy relationships, remove barriers, resolve difficulties, and repair harm, for example where there has been conflict, and seeking to create shared accountability and positive change. It is an approach that has broad applications, for example in *family group conferencing and *restorative justice.

Restraining Order *See* DOMESTIC VIOLENCE.

Rethink Mental Illness A mental health charity whose overall *goal is a better life for people with *mental illness. It provides information and advice, organizes services and groups, and undertakes campaigns. It has a wide range of informative factsheets on its website.

(((⊕))) SEE WEB LINKS
• Official site of Rethink Mental Illness.

retirement community (retirement village) A form of housing for *older people with provision on site that can include a cafe, bar, restaurant, craft room, workshop, gym, greenhouse, hairdresser's, beauty salon, laundrette, library, or IT suite. As well as catering for people who have retired from full-time employment, the *'community' comes from people within a certain age range living in a geographically defined area, and from elements of collective living such as participating in shared activities and using shared facilities. These settings have been reported as giving older people a sense of autonomy alongside a feeling of security, as well as optimism that they provide a new beginning, recapturing the neighbourliness they felt was lacking in their previous homes. Because of the size of retirement communities, it is possible to provide facilities that are more cost-effective and more flexible. While facilities such as fitness centres and cafés are not focused on providing *'care', they address aspects of social, recreational, and educational needs, with associated benefits to health and wellbeing. There is some evidence of benefits to local health and social services. For example, resources are saved by being able to deliver services (such as GP visits and health promotion activities) to older people living in one location and there is some evidence that access to on-site care and support reduces the need for hospital admission, and facilitates early discharge from hospital. The potential benefits of retirement communities have been identified as: their function as an alternative to *residential care; the extension of *choice and the potential to meet diverse needs and preferences; the support opportunities for people with *dementia; and their role in community regeneration and support.

However, places in retirement communities are not readily available and affordable. There has been concern that this form of specialist provision should not be promoted at the expense of support to enable older people to live in ordinary housing, when this is their choice. *See also* SHELTERED ACCOMMODATION.

retrenchment Cutting expenditure. Often used as in 'retrenchment of resources' or 'a climate of retrenchment', in preference to the simpler and more honest reference to 'cuts'. *See also* AUSTERITY.

reverse discrimination *See* POSITIVE DISCRIMINATION.

review *See* MONITORING AND REVIEW.

review of care and support plans (adults and carers) Reviews of *care and support plans (for people with care and support needs) or support plans (for *carers) take place under Section 27 of the Care Act (2014). These reviews are an opportunity to reflect on what is and is not working, and what might need to be changed in a person's plan. They are a way of ensuring that plans are kept up to date and relevant to a person's needs and aspirations, and they can reduce the *risk of people entering a crisis situation. Without regular reviews, plans can become out of date, resulting in people not obtaining the care and support required to meet their *needs. Plans may also have identified *outcomes that the person wanted to achieve which were progressive or time-limited so a periodic review ensures that the plan remains relevant to the person's *goals and aspirations.

A review of the plan is undertaken at least every twelve months, following an initial 'light-touch' review six to eight weeks after the plan has been signed off. The latter ensures that the arrangements put in place are working and that there are no issues that have arisen in the interim that need to be addressed. A 'light-touch' review is also undertaken after revision of an existing plan to ensure that the new plan is working as intended.

The review process is intended to be person-centred, outcome-focused, accessible, and proportionate to the needs being met. The process involves the person needing care, the *carer, where feasible, and consideration is given to whether to involve an independent advocate (*see* ADVOCACY [ADULTS]). If the person's needs have changed, the review can lead to a reassessment (*see* NEEDS ASSESSMENT). It also identifies if other circumstances have changed and ensures that the person is not at risk of *abuse or neglect. When a review is being undertaken and a person has a carer, consideration is given to whether the carer's support plan also requires review.

There are different routes to reviewing a plan including:

- a planned review, the date of which was set with the person during the planning process or through general monitoring (*see* MONITORING AND REVIEW);
- an unplanned review that results from a change in needs or circumstances, for example a *fall or a hospital admission;
- a requested review, when the person with the plan, or their carer, family member, advocate, or other interested party makes a request that a review should be conducted. This may be as a result of a change in needs or circumstances.

If a request for a review is made by the person or someone acting on the person's behalf, a review will usually take place. The right to request a review applies not just to the person receiving the care, but to others supporting them or interested in their wellbeing. For example, a person with advanced *dementia may not be able to request a review, but a relative or a neighbour may want to draw deterioration in the person's condition to the attention of the *local authority. Such a request is considered even if it is not made by the adult or their carer. When a decision is made not to conduct a review following a request for one, the reasons for not accepting the request are set out in a format accessible to the person, along with details of how to pursue the matter if the person remains dissatisfied.

A review should cover the following elements, which should be communicated to the person in advance of the review:

- Have the person's circumstances and/or care and support needs or the carer's support needs changed?
- What is working in the plan, what is not working, and what might need to change?
- Have the *outcomes identified in the plan been achieved or not?
- Does the person have new outcomes s/he wants to meet?
- Could improvements be made to achieve better outcomes?
- Is the person's *personal budget enabling her/him to meet her/his needs and the outcomes identified in her/his plan?
- Is the current method of managing the person's personal budget still the best one for what s/he wants to achieve—for example, should *direct payments be considered?
- Is the personal budget still sufficient?
- Are there any changes in the person's informal and *community support *networks that might impact negatively or positively on the plan?
- Have there been any changes in the person's needs or circumstances that might mean s/he is at risk of *abuse or neglect?
- Is the person/carer/independent advocate satisfied with the plan?

When a decision is made that a revision of the plan is necessary, the person, or a person acting on her/his behalf, is informed of the decision and what this will involve. Where the person has substantial difficulty in being actively involved with the review, and where there are no family or friends to help her/him in the process, an independent advocate is involved.

Wherever possible, the revision of a plan should follow the processes used in assessment and care and support planning. If the circumstances have changed in a way that affects the plan, a *needs and/or *carer's assessment and financial assessment are carried out and the plan and personal budget are revised accordingly. The assessment process following a review does not start from the beginning of the process but picks up from what is already known about the person and is proportionate. In some cases a complete change of the plan may be required, whereas in others only minor adjustments may be needed. When there is an urgent need, interim *care packages can be put in place to meet urgent needs while the plan is revised.

Further reading: Department of Health (2016) *Care and Support: Statutory Guidance*, Chapter 13. Available at: https://www.gov.uk/government/publications/care-act-statutory-guidance/care-and-support-statutory-guidance#person-centred-care-and-support-planning.

review teams (reviewing teams) In services for adults, teams are often set up that have the sole function of reviewing *service users' *care packages. This will happen on a regular basis at designated intervals. Reviews may cause considerable *anxiety to service users as they fear having services reduced or removed. In addition to this regular reviewing activity, at times when cuts are being made to services, all service users' care packages will need to be reviewed in order for any cuts to be made to service users whose *needs have not changed (*see* UNMET NEED). *See also* AUSTERITY; MONITORING AND REVIEW; RETRENCHMENT.

revolving door syndrome A pattern of short-term readmissions to psychiatric units owing to repeated cycles of recovery and improvement in hospital, followed by *relapse upon discharge. The concept became a familiar term in policy debates in the UK in the 1990s following a number of high-profile *cases (such as Christopher Clunis, who murdered Jonathan Zito, and Ben Silcock, who was mauled to death by a lion at London Zoo, both in 1992) in which *community care arrangements were criticized. The government considered that a small number of patients required additional measures and more community supervision than was then available. Supervised after-care (also known as supervised discharge) was introduced by the Mental Health (Patients in the Community) Act (1995). Similar to *guardianship, the measures included additional powers to convey someone to hospital and were intended to be health-driven rather than the province of social work. Supervised after-care was subsequently replaced by *supervised community treatment (SCT), introduced by the Mental Health Act (2007). Although the term SCT is not present in the Mental Health Act (2007), it was used in the Explanatory Notes to the Act and in the original accompanying Code of Practice to refer to the *Community Treatment Order (CTO) provisions in Sections 17A–G of the Act. The current Code of Practice (2016) now uses the term CTO in place of SCT. A CTO obliges patients to continue treatment and maintain contact with mental health services after a compulsory detention period in an attempt to attenuate the revolving door syndrome.

rights Often seen as natural and/or universal, as in *human rights, but they emerge in particular contexts at particular junctures and are often associated with *citizenship. They enable individuals to ask to be treated in a certain way, or to be protected, or to lay claim to a particular benefit or service as a consequence of the existence of a declaration, law, or *code of practice. In social work, *service users' rights to, for example, *participation and *partnership have been increasingly emphasized in a more general sense.

rights-based advocacy *See* ADVOCACY.

right to manage *See* MANAGERIALISM.

rigid policies Local authorities have to have policies with enough flexibility to cater for exceptions so that individual *needs can be met. Rigid policies may be grounds for *judicial review on the basis of *fettering discretion. *See also* DISCRETION (LOCAL AUTHORITY); REASONABLENESS; RELEVANT FACTORS.

riot An outbreak of collective *violence, often against property, or more directly aimed at people in authority, for example as in the riots that occurred between 6 and 11 August 2011, when thousands of people rioted in several London boroughs and in cities and towns across England, following the shooting to death by police of Mark Duggan from Tottenham. Those against whom riots are aimed, for example aspects of the state, will usually say that riots are no more than extreme examples of law-breaking, often presented as under the control of a 'small group of troublemakers' or a 'lunatic fringe'. In contrast, sociological studies of riots have regarded them as the explosion of unresolved social tensions.

risk Identifying and responding to risk can place social workers in the midst of conflicting values and responsibilities, on the one hand, to promote *independence and rights and, on the other hand, to protect people (both *service users and others) from harm—thus bestowing on social work both *care and control functions. At the intersection of these dual responsibilities lies risk. Identifying and managing risk has gained an increased profile in social work in recent years. Contributory factors include the drive for improved 'evidence' and 'certainty' as the basis of practice and the culture of 'blame' that leads to practitioners 'covering their backs', rather than taking risks for which they will be held accountable.

The significance of risk in contemporary social work can also be related to wider political and policy developments. Whereas the *welfare state was premised on the provision of universal services to meet collective need, much of this responsibility has now devolved to individual citizens. For example, *older people are encouraged to age 'well' and 'successfully' by working for as long as possible, volunteering, being responsible members of their *communities, and careful guardians of their own health and wellbeing. The state then has a residual role, targeting intervention at particular individuals who have 'failed' to discharge effectively their personal responsibility for managing risk. Much *assessment work in the *statutory sector is centrally concerned with risk. A complicating aspect of risk is that for many users of services risk is depicted with overwhelmingly negative connotations. Society may be prepared to condone or even extol risk-taking when it involves young men, but finds it hard to accept risk-taking by, for example, older people or people with *learning disabilities. The construction of service users as vulnerable, dependent, and powerless can lead to risk being seen as something to be avoided at all costs. The internalization of such views may contribute to feelings of passivity and dependency, and it is important that social workers are aware of their own power to influence decision-making about risk. For example, service users may reduce or avoid risk in order to allay the concerns of their families, even if this runs counter to their own wishes, and social workers can play a role in supporting their *choices. The social work role may entail encouraging people to examine their own thoughts and feelings about risk, and assisting them to reach a decision that is compatible with these, rather than following unquestioningly the recommendations of others. A thorough assessment of risk cannot be undertaken 'objectively' by identifying various risk factors in an individual's situation. It also has to engage with the values of the person concerned and with their understanding of the implications and meaning of risks and the different options for addressing them. Sometimes, if professionals or families or *carers are arguing in favour of a risk-averse option that the service user does not want, it may be necessary to involve an advocate to help determine and represent the person's interests (*see* ADVOCACY).

Although risk is often seen in negative terms—the likelihood of unwanted outcomes occurring—a social worker's *assessment of risk means weighing up potential benefits as well as potential harms or losses; taking risks involves deciding that the potential benefits of a proposed act outweigh the potential drawbacks. For example, admitting an older person to a care home may be seen as a 'safe' option, compared with supporting her/him at home, but while this option may reduce some risks, such as self-neglect and loneliness, it may increase other risks, such as disorientation, *depression, *loss of social contacts, and *abuse. Making judgements about risk is ultimately a subjective process, since individual values influence how different *outcomes are evaluated and the degree of risk that is felt to be legitimate in order to achieve a desired *goal. For example, older people who place a premium on personal privacy and autonomy may be prepared to tolerate a high level of risk to remain living in their own home. Given that social workers are involved in decisions concerned with risk, they need a framework for assessing and managing it. Brearley's framework (*Risks and Social Work: Hazards and Helping*, 1982) is often used as the basis for models of risk assessment. This is not a way of removing uncertainty in decision-making, but a means of structuring the knowledge, ideas, and values involved in the process. Coherent and detailed risk assessment will clarify value issues, but not remove them. Brearley sees risk analysis as involving two key tasks:

Estimation of risk The consideration of probability: how likely is it that a particular outcome will occur?

Evaluation of risk The value attached to the outcome: how serious are the consequences deemed to be?

Furthermore, he argues that risk assessment must take account of:

Hazards The factors that increase the possibility of a negative outcome; a greater number of hazards will increase the likelihood of danger.

Strengths The factors that reduce the likelihood of a negative outcome.

Brearley highlights the importance of distinguishing hazards (that is, the factors likely to increase risk) from dangers (i.e. the feared outcomes themselves). For example, an older person may be said to be 'at risk of falling'. This indicates something about the feared outcome (a *fall), though not its potential consequences, but nothing about the factors that will increase or reduce the likelihood of it occurring. Yet it is through enhancing strengths and reducing hazards that risks can be managed. For example, in relation to someone 'at risk of falling', greater clarity and precision would result from starting to analyse risk in the following way:

The *danger* (feared outcomes): broken limbs; threats to physical health through lying unattended and being unable to summon help; death;

The *hazards*: steep stairs; poor mobility; poor eyesight; loose rugs;

The *strengths*: a stair rail; an alarm pendant; a neighbour who calls in twice a day.

Each danger can be assessed in terms of the likelihood of it occurring (*estimation*) and, if it does happen, the likely severity of the consequences (*evaluation*). The assessment would take account of both the hazards and strengths present in the situation. This sort of detailed risk assessment would help in the formulation of a plan to manage the risks, which is likely to involve a combination of interventions to decrease the hazards on the one hand, and increase the strengths on the other. A basic principle in managing risk is to look for the least disruptive change that will appropriately manage the risk; managing risk does not necessarily mean eliminating it.

In social work with children and families, particularly where there are concerns that children are at risk or likely risk of *significant harm, the need to identify, quantify, and analyse the sources and nature of the risks is essential to keeping children safe. This can be seen as the basis of effective decision-making and planning. However, aspects of government guidance present an altogether more ambivalent and, arguably, for practitioners, confusing approach to risk assessment, sometimes choosing not to refer to risk at all but to reframe the concept exclusively and more ambiguously in terms of *'need'. However, it has been pointed out that need and risk are different sides of the same coin, and failure to address both adequately can result in incomplete assessments of children and families and plans that do not fully address the seriousness of a child's situation. A clear and unequivocal focus on risk makes it possible for social workers and other *child protection professionals to keep the child firmly in view, an aspect of practice consistently criticized as inadequate in numerous *child abuse inquiries, with catastrophic implications for the children concerned. Moreover, such a focus also makes it possible for professionals to be clearer with parents and *care-givers about their concerns and what needs to change to ensure their children are brought up safely and in good health. The *Munro Review of Child Protection in England* (Munro 2011) asserted that since child protection work is characterized by uncertainty, the key is to manage risks to children effectively, rather than necessarily seeking to eradicate them altogether. Munro's analysis underlines the importance of having in place for social workers the sound principles for risk assessment cited in her review. The review also lends weight to the need to have clear pathways through which professional judgements are reached that are designed specifically to assist effective risk analysis in child protection. *See also* AT RISK; CONSUMERISM; DANGEROUSNESS; INDIVIDUALISM; NEO-LIBERALISM; PROTECTIVE FACTOR; RESILIENCE; RESPONSIBILIZATION; RISK ASSESSMENT (MENTAL HEALTH); RISK FACTOR; SAFEGUARDING ADULTS; SAFEGUARDING CHILDREN; STRENGTHS-BASED APPROACH.

Further reading: Munro, E. (2011) *The Munro Review of Child Protection: Final Report: A Child-centred System,* Department for Education.

Tuck, V. (2004) 'Analysing Risk in Child Protection. A Model for Assessment' in White, V. and Harris, J. (eds.) *Developing Good Practice in Children's Services,* Jessica Kingsley Publishers.

risk assessment *See* RISK.

risk assessment (mental health) The formal evaluation of *risk undertaken in mental health services with individuals subject to the *Care Programme Approach (CPA). The risk *assessment is usually undertaken by the individual's *care coordinator. It is used to gather information about risks of *violence, self-harm, self-neglect, harm towards others (for example, family, staff), accidental harm, and harm from others. The assessment considers the individual's history and personal circumstances. It often includes a *relapse plan that provides information and guidance about how to act in the event of a deterioration in the individual's mental health. The relapse plan may include information about signs and *symptoms that might indicate or trigger a relapse, such as ceasing to take medication, the use or increased use of drugs or alcohol, the influence of others in the individual's life, anniversaries of bereavements, *suicidal thoughts, becoming withdrawn, or increases in stress or pressure. The assessment is intended to be part of an ongoing process of risk management and should be reviewed regularly. Where possible the risk assessment should be shared with the person concerned and, where consent is given, with significant others who can provide support and monitoring. The individual might disagree with information contained in the assessment and should be provided with the opportunity to discuss any concerns with the *care coordinator. Risk assessment documentation is retained on the case file held by the team that coordinates care, but other care providers and support agencies will often require access to the assessment, for instance, upon inpatient admission, or as part of the referral process to housing agencies and support groups. It is usual for a copy of the risk assessment to be sent to someone's *general practitioner.

Further reading: Langan, J. and Lindow, V. (2004) *Living with Risk: Mental Health Service User Involvement in Risk Assessment and Management,* Policy Press.

risk factor (child protection) Any influence, irrespective of source, that has the capacity or potential to cause or contribute to a damaging or harmful outcome for a child. *See also* PROTECTIVE FACTOR.

risky-shift The possibility that people will make decisions that are more risky when they are in groups than when they are alone. For example, a young person may be more willing to engage in risk-taking behaviour in a *peer group, or a social worker may be willing to contemplate a higher level of *risk as a result of participating in decisions taken in a *child protection *case conference than s/he would if the decisions were taken in isolation.

role Assuming the beliefs, attitudes, mannerisms, and patterns of behaviour that are associated with a particular position and/or status, for example, being a social worker. One view of roles is that they only make sense when they interact with each other. For example, the social worker role only makes sense in relation to the *service user role, because each role is defined by the expectation of the other, and the roles may be modified in the interaction between them. It is unlikely that the roles will be dramatically changed, however, as the concept of role conveys strong social expectations and *norms to which most people will conform. 'Role-distance' may be one of the responses to stress in social work, with a social worker seeking to play her/his role with a degree of internal detachment in order to protect her/himself from excessive emotional strain. People may experience 'role conflict' from competing expectations. For example, a social work team manager may be pressured by senior managers to allocate more work to social workers because of the number of people awaiting *assessments, while being reluctant to do so because of her/his awareness of the pressures the social workers are already under. *See also* HABITUS; OCCUPATIONAL SOCIALIZATION.

routinization The process by which actions or activities that have been repeated many times can be performed with less and less attention. While this is beneficial in enabling people to get through mundane matters with the minimum of effort, it has its dangers in other areas. For example, a social worker who has done a great many *assessments or *reviews may carry these out in a routinized manner that risks missing important information about individual *service users. *See also* BURN-OUT; OBJECTIFICATION; PEOPLE-PROCESSING; REDUCTIONISM.

Royal National Institute for Blind People (RNIB) A charity providing information, support, and advice to blind and partially sighted people. As well as helping with *Braille and talking books, information is provided on eye conditions, and support and advice is provided on sight *loss. It also funds research into sight loss and wider eye health issues. *See also* REGISTER OF DISABLED PEOPLE.

((()) SEE WEB LINKS
• Official site of the Royal National Institute for Blind People.

Royal National Institute for Deaf People *See* ACTION ON HEARING LOSS.

safeguarding adults Encompasses a range of activities undertaken by professionals and agencies that are focused on the protection of adults from maltreatment. Section 42 of the Care Act (2014) sets out a *local authority's responsibility to ensure enquiries are undertaken into cases of *abuse and neglect. The accompanying Care and Support Statutory Guidance (2016) sets out the key principles of safeguarding and what constitutes abuse and neglect. It also emphasizes making safeguarding personal, with the person being involved from beginning to end. The Care Act (2014) provides a legislative framework for safeguarding adults for the first time, replacing the previous multi-agency statutory guidance, *No Secrets* (2000), as the basis for practice.

The Care Act (2014) requires that a local authority must:

- set up a *Safeguarding Adults Board;
- make enquiries, or cause others to do so, if it believes an adult is experiencing, or is at *risk of, abuse or neglect. An enquiry should establish whether any action needs to be taken to prevent or stop abuse or neglect, and if so, by whom;
- arrange, where appropriate, for an independent advocate to represent and support an adult who is the subject of a safeguarding enquiry or a *Safeguarding Adults Review where the adult has 'substantial difficulty' in being involved in the process and where there is no other suitable person to represent and support her/him (*see* ADVOCACY [ADULTS]);
- cooperate with relevant partner organizations in order to protect the adult.

The aims of adult safeguarding are to:

- prevent harm and reduce the *risk of abuse or neglect to adults with *care and support needs;
- stop abuse or neglect wherever possible;
- safeguard adults in a way that supports them in making *choices and having control about how they want to live;
- concentrate on improving life for the adults concerned;
- raise public awareness so that *communities as a whole, alongside professionals, play their part in preventing, identifying, and responding to abuse and neglect;
- provide information and support in accessible ways to help people understand the different types of abuse, how to stay safe, and what to do to raise a concern about the safety or wellbeing of an adult;
- address what has caused the abuse or neglect.

The Care Act Statutory Guidance (2016) provides an illustrative guide to different types of abuse and neglect: physical abuse; *domestic violence; sexual abuse; psychological abuse; financial or material abuse; modern slavery; discriminatory abuse; organizational abuse; neglect and acts of omission; self-neglect. The Guidance sets out six principles as underpinning practice in safeguarding adults:

Empowerment People being supported and encouraged to make their own decisions;

Prevention Where possible, taking action before harm occurs;

Proportionality The least intrusive response appropriate to the risk presented;

Protection Support and representation;

*Partnership Local solutions through services working with their communities;

Accountability Accountability and transparency in delivering safeguarding.

In addition to these principles, the Guidance stresses that adult safeguarding arrangements are there to protect individuals with different preferences, histories, circumstances, and lifestyles. Accordingly safeguarding should be person-led and *outcome-focused, deciding with the person concerned how best to respond to the situation in a way that enhances involvement, choice, and control as well as improving quality of life, wellbeing, and safety. The circumstances surrounding any actual or suspected case of abuse or neglect will inform the response. For example, abuse or neglect may be unintentional and may arise because a *carer is struggling to care for the person. This makes the need to take action no less important, but in such circumstances, an appropriate response could be a support package for the carer and *monitoring. However, the primary focus must still be on how to safeguard the adult. In any circumstances where safeguarding concerns arise from abuse or neglect, it is necessary to consider immediately what steps are needed to protect the adult and whether to refer the matter to the police in order to consider whether a criminal investigation is required or is appropriate. Although a local authority has the lead role in making safeguarding enquiries, where criminal activity is suspected, the early involvement of the police is likely to be needed. Behaviour that amounts to abuse and neglect can also constitute specific criminal offences. In addition, the Mental Capacity Act (2005) created the criminal offences of ill-treatment and wilful neglect in respect of people who lack the ability to make decisions. The offences can be committed by anyone responsible for an adult's care and support—paid staff, family carers, or people who have the legal authority to act on an adult's behalf.

A local authority's safeguarding *duty applies to an adult who:

- has needs for care and support (whether or not the local authority is meeting any of those needs);
- is experiencing, or at risk of, abuse or neglect;
- as a result of those care and support needs is unable to protect her/himself from either the risk or the experience of abuse or neglect.

The safeguarding duty is also a legal responsibility placed on other organizations, for example the National Health Service and the police. Safeguarding means protecting an adult's right to live in safety, free from abuse and neglect. Organizations are expected to work together to prevent and stop both the risk and experience of abuse or neglect, while at the same time making sure that the adult's wellbeing is promoted. Practitioners from the organizations work with the adult to establish what being safe means to her/him and how it can best be achieved.

The objectives of an enquiry into a specific case of abuse or neglect are to:

- establish the facts;
- ascertain the adult's views and wishes;
- assess the needs of the adult for protection, support, and redress and how they might be met;

- protect from the abuse and neglect, in accordance with the wishes of the adult;
- make decisions as to what follow-up action should be taken with regard to the person or organization responsible for the abuse or neglect;
- enable the adult to achieve resolution and recovery.

When undertaking a safeguarding enquiry, the practitioner concerned should record:

- the concern;
- the adult's views and wishes;
- any immediate action taken;
- the reasons for those actions.

The purpose of the enquiry is to decide whether or not the *local authority or another organization or person should do something to help and protect the adult.

Enquiries need to be handled in a sensitive and skilled way to ensure distress to the adult concerned is minimized and to support her/him in realizing the outcomes s/he wants. It can be difficult and complex to assess and intervene in situations of abuse or neglect in relationships within community settings. For example, an adult may make a choice to be in a relationship that involves emotional abuse because this outweighs for her/him the unhappiness that would result from not maintaining the relationship. If an adult has the mental *capacity to make informed decisions about her/his safety, s/he can decide that s/he does not want any action to be taken in response to abuse or neglect. (This capacity for self-determination in situations of abuse or neglect makes safeguarding adults very different from *safeguarding children.)

A local authority, in its lead and coordinating role, should ensure that a safeguarding enquiry satisfies its duty under Section 42 of the Care Act (2014) to decide:

- what action (if any) is necessary to help and protect the adult;
- by whom;
- to ensure that such action is taken when necessary.

Once enquiries are completed, the outcome should be notified to the local authority, which should then determine with the adult what, if any, further action is necessary and acceptable. It is for the local authority to determine the appropriateness of the outcome of the enquiry. One outcome of the enquiry may be the formulation of agreed action for the adult, which should be recorded on her/his care plan. This should set out:

- what steps are to be taken to ensure the adult's safety in the future in relation to the identified risks;
- the provision of any support, treatment, or therapy, including ongoing *advocacy;
- any modifications needed in the way services are provided;
- how best to support the adult through any action they take to seek justice or redress;
- any ongoing risk management strategy;
- any action to be taken in relation to the person or organization that has caused the safeguarding concern.

See also PRACTITIONER ALLIANCE FOR SAFEGUARDING ADULTS; SAFEGUARDING ADULTS BOARD.

Further reading: Department of Health (2016) *Care and Support: Statutory Guidance*, Chapter 14. Available at: https://www.gov.uk/government/publications/care-act-statutory-guidance/care-and-support-statutory-guidance#person-centred-care-and-support-planning.
Mantel, A. and Scragg, T. (eds.) (2011, 2nd edn.) *Safeguarding Adults in Social Work*, Learning Matters.

Safeguarding Adults Board (SAB) The Care Act (2014) requires that a *local authority must set up an inter-agency Safeguarding Adults Board (SAB). The main objective of a SAB is to ensure that local safeguarding arrangements and partners act to help and protect adults in its area. A SAB has three core duties:

- publishing a strategic plan for each financial year that sets how it will meet its main objective and what its members will do to achieve it. The plan must be developed with local *community involvement. The plan should be *evidence-based and make use of all available evidence and intelligence from the partnering organizations;
- publishing an annual report that details what the SAB has done during the year to achieve its main objective and implement its strategic plan, and what each member has done to implement the strategy, as well as detailing the findings of any *Safeguarding Adults Reviews and subsequent action;
- conducting *Safeguarding Adults Reviews.

See also PRACTITIONER ALLIANCE FOR SAFEGUARDING ADULTS; SAFEGUARDING ADULTS.

Safeguarding Adults Review (SAR) The Care Act (2014) requires that a *Safeguarding Adults Board (SAB) must arrange a Safeguarding Adults Review (SAR) when an adult in its area dies as a result of abuse or neglect, whether known or suspected, and there is concern that partner organizations could have worked more effectively to protect the adult. An SAR must also be arranged if an adult has not died but the SAB knows or suspects that the adult has experienced serious *abuse or neglect. SARs may also be used to explore examples of *good practice where this is likely to identify lessons that can be applied to future *cases. *See also* PRACTITIONER ALLIANCE FOR SAFEGUARDING ADULTS; SAFEGUARDING ADULTS.

safeguarding children Encompasses a broad range of activities undertaken by professionals and organizations that are concerned with the protection of children from maltreatment; preventing impairment of children's health and development; ensuring that children are growing up in circumstances consistent with the provision of safe and effective care; and undertaking these roles so as to enable children to have optimum life chances and enter adulthood successfully. The term is often expanded in government guidance to 'safeguarding children and promoting their welfare' in order to reflect this broad conceptualization. *Child protection is a part of safeguarding and promoting welfare, and refers to the activity that is undertaken to protect specific children who are suffering or are likely to suffer *significant harm. Guidance issued by government to practitioners emphasizes that effective child protection is essential as part of wider work to safeguard and promote the welfare of children, but states that all agencies and individuals should aim proactively to safeguard and promote the welfare of children so that the need to protect children from harm is reduced. Those supporting this approach would contend that protecting children from maltreatment in itself may be insufficient to ensure that children are growing up in circumstances consistent with the provision of safe and effective care. A counter view is that this approach to safeguarding children leads to the net being cast too widely when viewing children's circumstances, leading to a loss of focus on actual and potential threats to children's immediate and long-term health and safety. It is contended that, as a result, the *risks to children posed by their parent(s), *care-giver(s), or others may easily be overlooked, inadequately assessed and acted upon. The findings of reviews into child deaths have been cited as evidence of this loss of focus, even though public, media, and political reaction in the aftermath of such tragedies has emphasized the overriding need to secure the safety of children as the first priority of professional intervention. *See also* CHILD ABUSE AND NEGLECT; CHILD ABUSE INQUIRIES; CHILD DEVELOPMENT; CHILD IN NEED; CHILD SEXUAL EXPLOITATION; CHILD TRAFFICKING; CHILD WELFARE.

Further reading: HM Government (2015) *Working Together to Safeguard Children: A Guide to Inter-agency Working to Safeguard and Promote the Welfare of Children*. Available at: https://www.gov.uk/government/uploads/system/uploads/attachment_data/file/419595/Working_Together_to_Safeguard Children.pdf.

Safeguarding Children Board *See* LOCAL SAFEGUARDING CHILDREN BOARD.

Samaritans A confidential emotional support service that is available twenty-four hours a day for people who are experiencing distress or despair, including feelings that might lead to suicide. Volunteers respond to phone calls, emails, and letters, and meet with people face-to-face.

(⊕) SEE WEB LINKS
• Official site of the Samaritans.

same-'race' placement Foster or adoptive placements where children are placed with *care-givers from the same ethnic and cultural background as opposed to substitute carers of different ethnic and cultural origins. The latter almost always refers to situations where *Black and minority ethnic children are placed with white families rather than the opposite. A great deal of controversy has surrounded this issue with advocates of same-*'race' placements arguing that it is essential that Black and minority ethnic children are able to grow up in a family which, in sharing the child's background, is best able to meet their general and specific physical and emotional needs, including equipping them with a positive sense of their own *identity. The importance of this is seen in terms of Black children encountering racist and discriminatory attitudes outside the home. This aspect of their experience, and the support they need in relation to it, is considered unlikely to be sufficiently addressed if they are placed with white care-givers. Advocates of transracial *fostering and *adoption take the view that same-'race' placement policies often result in unjustifiable delay in finding suitable long-term placements for accommodated children from Black and minority ethnic backgrounds. They argue that treating the need for a same-'race' placement as the paramount consideration runs the *risk of children drifting into residential care, with the attendant prospect of their experiencing poorer *outcomes than children who are placed in long-term substitute care more swiftly. For many years, in most local authorities priority was given to same-'race' placements. However, more recently, Section 1(5) of the Children Act (1989) was repealed, with the declared aim that *differences in *ethnicity, religion, culture, or language were not to be given 'undue emphasis or prominence'. *See also* ACCOMMODATED CHILD; ADOPTION; FOSTERING; LOOKED-AFTER CHILD; PERMANENCY PLANNING; PLACEMENT.

Sarah's Law *See* CHILD SEX OFFENDERS POLICE DISCLOSURE SCHEME.

scaling questions *See* SOLUTION-FOCUSED THERAPY.

scapegoating A process by which a person or group is blamed for things that go wrong and comes to bear the brunt of *aggression. The process can occur in families when one of its members is seen as the source of all of its problems. On a wider scale, *ethnic minority groups can be the victims of scapegoating, being seen as the cause of problems such as unemployment.

Schedule 1 offender Previously, individuals whose offending history posed a *risk to children, as set out in a list of offences in Schedule 1 of the Children and Young Persons Act (1933). Superseded, but still heard, in 2005 by *'person posing a risk to children'. *See also* MULTI-AGENCY PUBLIC PROTECTION ARRANGEMENTS; PAEDOPHILIA.

schizophrenia Coined in 1911 by the Swiss psychiatrist Eugen Bleuler (1857–1939). Literally translated, it means 'splitting of the mind'. First classified as a distinct mental disorder in 1887 by the German psychiatrist Emil Kraepelin (1856–1926), who named it *dementia praecox* (premature or early onset dementia). Kraepelin and Bleuler both studied patients in whom patterns of behaviour and clusters of symptoms bore similarities. Kraepelin drew the first distinction between *dementia praecox* and manic depression (*see* BIPOLAR DISORDER). However, Bleuler observed that the mental deterioration associated with senile (older-age) dementia, upon which Kraepelin had based his conclusions, was not present in many of his own studies of younger patients. He believed that this signified evidence of an entirely different disorder. Central to his perception of the disorder was a loss of association between thought processes and perception, and the *loss of association between thought, emotion, and behaviour. He therefore replaced the term *dementia praecox* with schizophrenia to convey the literal meaning of an impairment (splitting) of the cognitive processes (mind). His term was not meant to convey the idea of split or multiple personality, which has since become a widespread misconception. Since Kraepelin and Bleuler, there have been relatively few modifications of the concept of schizophrenia. Subsequent variations (for example, paranoid schizophrenia, schizo-affective disorder) largely represent refinements of the disorder. In the 1930s, the German psychiatrist Kurt Schneider (1887–1967) further differentiated schizophrenia from other types of *psychosis. He designed a diagnostic tool that became known as 'Schneider's first-rank symptoms' consisting of specific types of *delusions and *hallucinations. His model still has an influence on current diagnostic criteria. In the early 1970s, concern grew about the wide variations in psychiatrists' diagnoses of schizophrenia. This led to the development of operational criteria to try to standardize *diagnosis. Since 1994, the two main classification systems used worldwide are *DSM-5* (American Psychiatric Association) and *ICD-10* (World Health Organization), which is used primarily outside North America.

In psychiatric practice, schizophrenia is understood as a chronic mental health condition that is manifested in a range of symptoms. These include disorder of thought or hallucinations (hearing, seeing, or smelling things that do not exist), and disorders of perception or *delusions (believing in things that are untrue). Hallucinations and delusions are usually referred to as psychotic symptoms. (*Psychosis refers to a state in which a person is not able to distinguish between reality and their imagination.) Hallucinations and delusions are also often described as 'positive' (i.e. active) symptoms. In addition, schizophrenia is associated with long-term 'negative' symptoms, such as flattening of mood, lethargy, and social withdrawal. These symptoms are less amenable to treatment than positive symptoms.

Whether or not schizophrenia can be classified as a disease has been long debated (*see* ANTI-PSYCHIATRY). Within *psychiatry it is now often considered as a collection of illnesses rather than a single entity. It currently has the status of a syndrome. A syndrome is not a disease but a disorder for which there is no objective test or pathology, and which is identified by a characteristic cluster of symptoms that last for a certain time. The exact cause of schizophrenia is unknown. However, most experts hold that the condition is best understood by considering a combination of genetic, biochemical, psychological, and social/environmental factors.

School Action Further assessment, additional or different teaching materials, or a different way of teaching provided to pupils who require educational provision over and above that which can be provided by 'differentiation' of the curriculum. It involves the tailoring of teaching approaches to suit an individual child's or young person's particular learning *needs and styles. Most children with special educational needs will have these met by their school through School Action or *School Action Plus. *See also* INDIVIDUAL EDUCATION PLAN; PERSONAL EDUCATION PLAN.

School Action Plus Steps taken in education when *School Action has not helped a child or young person to make adequate progress, and the school requests assistance from the support services provided by *local authority children's services. This could include the involvement of health and social work professionals, a speech therapist, or an *occupational therapist, each offering suggestions as to how to work differently with the child in class. It might require sharing information about the child's home circumstances that helps explain changes in the child's behaviour and her/his attitude to learning, which in turn can help the school to work with others to resolve the situation. Most children with *special educational needs will have these met by their school through School Action or School Action Plus. *See also* INDIVIDUAL EDUCATION PLAN; PERSONAL EDUCATION PLAN.

school attendance Sometimes used as shorthand for the measures set in place by government and enacted by schools and local authorities to reduce absence from school. *Education social work services have a particularly important role to play in addressing problems associated with poor school attendance, though in some local authorities these services have been cut in response to *austerity. *See also* COMPULSORY SCHOOL AGE; EDUCATION SOCIAL WORKERS; EDUCATION SUPERVISION ORDER; EXCLUSION; PARENTING ORDER; SCHOOL ATTENDANCE ORDER; SCHOOL ATTENDANCE (PROSECUTION OF PARENTS); SCHOOL PHOBIA; TRUANCY.

school attendance (prosecution of parents) Section 444 of the Education Act (1996) makes it an offence for parents to fail to secure regular attendance at school of a registered child. The Act was amended to create two separate offences. Failing to secure regular attendance is punishable by a fine. However, a parent who knows the child is not attending school and fails without reasonable justification to cause him/her to attend commits an offence that is punishable by a fine and/or six months imprisonment. For a parent to be guilty of an offence, the local education authority only has to show that a registered child has failed to attend, even on one occasion. In order to avoid a conviction the parent has to show:

- The absence was agreed by school staff.
- The pupil was ill or prevented from attending by any unavoidable cause.
- The absence was on a day exclusively set aside for religious observance by the religious body to which the parent belongs.

- The school is not within walking distance of the child's home and the LEA has made no suitable arrangements for transport, boarding, or an alternative school.

Before issuing proceedings, the local education authority is required to consider whether it would be appropriate (instead of or as well as instituting the proceedings) to apply for an *Education Supervision Order with respect to the child (Section 447, Education Act 1996). This means that the local education authority has to consult with social work services before issuing proceedings. *See also* COMPULSORY SCHOOL AGE; SCHOOL ATTENDANCE; SCHOOL ATTENDANCE ORDER.

School Attendance Order Gives a local education authority (LEA) power to try to ensure that children attend school. The Order is not intended for irregular attenders but for children who are not registered with a school. The LEA can serve a notice requiring parents to satisfy it within a specified time (not less than 15 days) that a child is receiving suitable education. If the parents fail to satisfy the LEA, it can serve a School Attendance Order on the parents requiring that the child is registered at a school named in the Order (Section 437, Education Act 1996). The LEA must consult with the named school and the parents have the opportunity to name an alternative school, subject to a disputes procedure. It is an offence to fail to comply with a School Attendance Order (Section 443, Education Act 1996). *See also* COMPULSORY SCHOOL AGE; SCHOOL ATTENDANCE; SCHOOL ATTENDANCE (PROSECUTION OF PARENTS).

school exclusion *See* EXCLUSION.

school phobia Complex and extreme form of *anxiety about going to school (not restricted to going to one particular school), which may manifest itself in stomach aches, nausea, fatigue, shaking, frequent visits to the toilet, and other symptoms. Younger children suffering from the condition may experience separation anxiety, finding it difficult being parted from their parent(s) or *care-giver(s). Older children are more likely to experience the condition in the form of a social phobia where they are anxious about their performance in school or some aspect of it such as games, mental arithmetic, having to read aloud, or answer questions in class. The condition may also be associated with the child experiencing *bullying and/or *cyber-bullying at school. Children with anxieties about going to school may suffer panic attacks if forced to attend, which may make them fearful of having further attacks. The spiral of *anxiety that emerges is often very difficult for parents to manage and may lead to problems with *school attendance and possible *truancy. Children experiencing the condition are likely to become involved with an *education social worker and possibly referred to an *educational psychologist. A referral to *Child and Adolescent Mental Health Services may also be made to assist the child and their family with the problem. *See also* INDIVIDUAL EDUCATION PLAN; PERSONAL EDUCATION PLAN; SCHOOL ATTENDANCE.

Scope A charity that supports disabled people and their families, offering services for disabled children and adults, mainly for those who have complex support *needs that are not met elsewhere. It also seeks to raise awareness, change attitudes, and influence government policy.

 SEE WEB LINKS

- Official site of Scope.

Scotland Social work and social care and health services are devolved functions of the Scottish Parliament. Day-to-day responsibility for social work and social care functions is located with *local authorities. There are currently thirty-two local authorities, although there is ongoing debate about whether having so many units of government makes strategic decisions difficult to take.

The 2011 census gives the population of Scotland as 5,295,000—the highest ever and a rise of around 200,000 over the past ten years. Around 3.5 million of this population live across the Central Belt, which includes the two main cities, Edinburgh and Glasgow. Historically, the Central Belt was home to the heavy industries of coal, steel, and shipbuilding, but since the 1980s these have either disappeared or been reduced to a fraction of their previous size and importance. The closure of these industries has contributed to a range of social problems—long-term unemployment, *poverty, chronic sickness, and *disability. Such problems are particularly apparent in Glasgow, which has the highest mortality rates in the UK.

The re-establishment of the Scottish Parliament in 1999 and subsequent political directions of travel have seen growing divergence between social work and social welfare more generally in Scotland and other nations of the United Kingdom. Differences can be identified as centring around a greater sense of *collectivism than might be apparent in England, and a predisposition to look to broadly educational and *community-based rather than individualized responses to social problems. What follows provides an overview of salient historical moments in Scottish social welfare, indicating how these have been reflected in policy and practice, offering some pointers as to how social work might develop within a rapidly evolving political landscape.

History Social work in Scotland has been shaped, in large measure, by its particular religious past and by the maintenance, even during political union with England, of its own legal and education systems. The Scottish Reformation of 1560 is important in understanding many of Scotland's social attitudes. The Reformation was strongly doctrinal, based on Calvinist principles. The country inherited from the Reformation a distinct set of political and moral preferences, a social ethos that has been described as 'secular Presbyterianism' or *communitarianism. Structures within the Reformed Church were, on the one hand, socially authoritarian but, on the other hand, were influenced by a notion of 'militant democracy' and, in many ways, were strikingly *egalitarian. The Reformation also placed the onus of providing social welfare on parish communities, which assumed responsibility for the care of the sick, orphans, and those who had fallen on hard times. To ensure the Calvinist imperative, that everyone should have unmediated access to the Bible, the Kirk assumed responsibility for education. A school was established in each parish and an educational ideal became rooted in Scottish life. Education and social welfare, therefore, had common roots in the parish system. Parishes adopted primarily community-based approaches to social welfare. The preferred way of responding to orphan or destitute children, for instance, was for them to be 'boarded out' with respectable families. 'Outdoor' or community-based relief, rather than institutional provision, was common. However, the levels at which outdoor relief was granted were persistently austere.

Political and intellectual developments The union of Scotland and England in 1707 made provision for the continuation of separate Scottish educational and legal systems, as well as maintaining the Church of Scotland as the established church. This arrangement kept the cornerstones of social welfare provision intact within the new political settlement and, while the political centre of gravity moved to London, this allowed the development of a vibrant civic culture in Edinburgh. This was manifest in the particular flavour of the Scottish Enlightenment, which stressed collectivist and, ultimately, relational understandings of social issues.

The demographic and social changes wrought by industrialization and urbanization strained what had until then been a predominantly rural and small-town parish system of poor relief. The established church was considered to have become increasingly comfortable and complacent. Prompted by disputes over patronage, a group of evangelical ministers broke from the Church of Scotland to form the Free Church of Scotland in the Disruption of 1843. A number of figures in the Disruption became key players in the development of a social welfare response to the needs of the new cities. Foremost among these social reformers was Dr Thomas Chalmers. Chalmers was committed to the idea that a revitalized parish ministry should cater for people's spiritual but also their material needs. Scotland's poor relief system during this period continued to be independent of England and *Wales. Chalmers saw charity as a neighbourly responsibility and encouraged the poor to become independent by working hard. Organized poor relief, he argued, diminished their determination to lift themselves out of *poverty. The new Scottish Poor Law of 1845, however, overturned Chalmers' preference for voluntarism, introducing a system whereby local taxes could be raised to fund poor relief.

Victorian period and the early twentieth century Workhouse provision expanded in Scotland from around 1844, largely as a result of urbanization and the breakdown of the parish system. This development also saw an increased adoption of the doctrine of 'less eligibility', derived from the English *poor law. Institutional care was still frowned upon, however, on the very pragmatic grounds that *prevention was considered better than cure, an early manifestation of the current vogue for *early intervention. At a point in English history where the family was considered a contaminating influence on a child, Scottish thinking produced the novel argument that children attending industrial schools (which in Scotland were, predominantly, day rather than residential facilities) might return home to their parents at night and pass on some of their day's learning.

During the first half of the twentieth century, the Local Government Act (1929) transferred the administration of the Poor Laws from parish councils to county, city, and burgh councils, and renamed the service 'public assistance', although public parlance still spoke of the 'puirs house' or the 'pairish'. A preference for outdoor relief persisted, although provision remained niggardly. Poor houses operated in towns and cities, generally providing little more than austere batch living, although examples of smaller and more imaginative provision did exist in pockets.

Post-war years The immediate post-Second World War years gave the UK government the opportunity to implement the recommendations of the *Beveridge Report (1942), which aimed to address the five giants of want, disease, ignorance, squalor, and idleness through the introduction of the *welfare state. The Report led to the National Assistance Act (1948), which founded the National Assistance Board and established *means-tested benefits for the uninsured.

The years following World War Two also witnessed specific advances in respect of children's services. The findings of the 1946 Report of the Committee on Homeless Children (the Clyde Report), mirrored the parallel Curtis Report (1946) in England, reflecting unease about the effect of large-scale institutional provision on children's emotional development, and advocated smaller homes based on a 'family' model. The impetus generated by these reports led to the passage of the Children Act (1948), which established Children's Departments in each local authority.

The mid-twentieth century exemplified a tendency for separate Acts of Parliament in Scotland, containing largely similar measures to those in English and Welsh legislation. Services, however, were generally less well-developed in Scotland than in England and Wales. While departments existed throughout the country for child care and welfare work, many operated little more than notionally, being poorly staffed and supported. They provided very basic services for *older people and people with disabilities. Services for children were generally rather better developed. *Probation was also among the better-developed services, being used more for children than adults. The opportunity to absorb the probation service into a new welfare-based system for children in trouble paved the way for the next stage in the development of Scottish social work, one that saw it depart significantly from the situation in England and Wales.

Kilbrandon Report (1966) In response to one of the periodic outbreaks of political concern over juvenile *delinquency (as it was then called), Lord Kilbrandon, the country's foremost law lord, was commissioned in 1961 'to consider the provisions of the law of Scotland relating to the treatment of juvenile delinquents and juveniles in need of care or protection or beyond parental control'. His committee, reporting in 1964, concluded that similarities in the underlying situation of juvenile offenders and children in need of care and protection 'far outweigh the differences' and that 'the true distinguishing factor . . . is their need for special measures of education and training, the normal upbringing processes having, for whatever reason, fallen short' (para. 15). In reaching these conclusions the committee might be thought to have been tapping into an existing educational tradition in Scotland.

Kilbrandon's conception of education extended beyond the classroom, to encompass what he termed social education, 'education in its widest sense'. His remedy for those occasions when children's upbringing process had fallen short was additional measures of education for the child, and where appropriate for the parents, in order to strengthen 'those natural influences for good which will assist the child's development into a mature and useful member of society' (para 17). *Needs rather than deeds were to be the touchstone for intervention, and it was this principle that underpinned the proposal for children's hearings to consider community responses to children who had offended or were deemed to be in need of care and protection. Kilbrandon's proposal was for such hearings to comprise child care professionals. The matching field organization to support this proposed social education function was identified as a Social Education Department to be located in local authorities under the Director of Education and staffed by social workers. Thus, social work with children and families was conceived of as broadly educational and was to take place within a universal education system.

Social work and the community Many of the principles and provisions of the Social Work (Scotland) Act (1968), Scottish social work's foundational legislation, stem from the Kilbrandon Report (1966) and the report is often regarded as the progenitor of modern Scottish social work. The lineage, however, is not quite that simple. The 1960s marked the high point of welfare consensus. A powerful social work lobby, with visions of cradle-to-grave welfare services, was growing in influence. Social work as a profession was asserted to be a positive and radical force for social change. In this climate, Kilbrandon's idea of social education was considered too limiting. The Association of Child Care Officers proposed a vision of social work that went beyond the boundaries of social education, arguing that all the social services should be concentrated in one department. This more radical view held sway and was incorporated into the White Paper *Social Work and the Community*

(1966), which adopted some of Kilbrandon's ideas, but located them within generic Social Work Departments. The proposals set out in the White Paper became enshrined in the Social Work (Scotland) Act (1968), enacted in 1971.

Social Work (Scotland) Act (1968) Section 12 of the 1968 Act placed a broad duty on *local authorities to promote social welfare, which remains in place today. It was more ambitious than contemporaneous legislation in England and Wales, which shied clear of such a wide-ranging duty. England and Wales also failed to bring all of the various branches of social work under the one legislative and professional umbrella, as was the case in Scotland. Specifically, the Probation Service continued as a separate entity in England and Wales. In place of Kilbrandon's proposed Social Education Department, all social work services were brought together in new generic Social Work Departments. One of the innovative changes to flow from the 1968 Act was the creation of a system of children's hearings to address the problems faced by children who offend and those deemed to be in need of care and protection. Reflecting Kilbrandon's conclusions, the underlying needs of both groups were considered to be largely similar. The key player in the children's hearings system is the Reporter to the Children's Panel or Children's Reporter. The Reporter may come from a variety of professional backgrounds (although mostly, and increasingly, law), and her/his role is both as the initial gatekeeper to the system and the person who ensures its proceedings comply with the law. Children and young people can be referred to the Reporter from a number of sources, including police, social work, education, and health. They are referred because some aspect of their life is giving cause for concern. The legal grounds for referral incorporate both offending and a range of care and protection concerns.

The Reporter's primary role is to decide whether a child may require compulsory measures of care. To assist her/him in this decision, the Reporter may ask for a social work report. If, following receipt of this report, a decision is taken that a child may require compulsory measures of care, then the child (and her/his parents) are required to attend a children's hearing. A hearing consists of three lay panel members, who are part-time volunteers, thus emphasizing a community responsibility for children in trouble. Panels receive background reports prepared by social workers but the child and her/his family are included as key participants in the decision-making process. Following a full discussion of the circumstances of a *case, panel members can decide to take no further action, suggest voluntary measures of support, or impose a supervision requirement, which may involve a child remaining at home subject to social work supervision, or could include particular conditions, such as the requirement to live in a foster home or residential care. Hearings are, in legal terms, tribunals and proceed by consent. If a child or her/his parents do not accept the grounds of referral or if they dispute the outcome of a case, they have recourse to the Sheriff Court either to have the grounds proved in a court of law or to reverse the hearing decision.

The years following the enactment of the 1968 Act represent the high point in Scottish social work, which, with the inception of large regional authorities following local government reorganization in 1975, enjoyed a place at the top table in the local authority hierarchy. Social work services reflected a commitment to high-quality universal public services with a strong welfarist ideology, shored up by the dominance of the Labour Party in local and national politics. A strand of *radical social work, linking a structural analysis of *service users' problems to an imperative to act to address them, raised questions about the profession's role as operating both in and against the state. A collective dimension was apparent in the growth of *community social work, especially in the west of Scotland. The children's hearings system, under the guidance of some impressive founding Reporters to the Children's Panel, brought a genuinely 'whole child' perspective to deliberations about how best to deal with children in trouble or in need of care. Developments in social work reflected other strands in Scottish *public sector changes around this time, including comprehensive schooling, community education, youth work, and community development, all of which stressed links between the social and economic circumstances faced by children and families and subsequent educational or social *outcomes. There were, however, other strands in social work's development. The profession continued to be influenced by psychosocial traditions and practice developed primarily along *casework models. Responses to social problems within such models took the form of individual or family *interventions.

Thatcher years The generally fair political wind that social work had enjoyed over the course of the 1970s changed with the election in 1979 of a Conservative government in Westminster, buttressed by *neo-liberal political and economic *ideologies that were played out in increasingly managerial approaches to practice. The effects of this became manifest in a number of ways. The focus of children and families social work, at a UK level, shifted from being an essentially welfarist one to reflecting a predominant concern with investigative and procedural *child protection.

In adult services, UK-wide legislation—the NHS and Community Care Act (1990)—wove together anti-institutional ideology with a concern for reducing the costs of care. It introduced the notion of social workers as *care managers, thus de-emphasizing the relationship-building aspects of the social work role. It also introduced the *purchaser—provider split, promoting a *mixed economy of care that involved local authorities in *commissioning services from the *voluntary and *private sectors.

Criminal justice social work was also pulled in a different direction. From the 1970s until the mid-1990s, it had, in Scotland, followed a different trajectory from a number of other countries, owing to its continued commitment to what commentators have called penal-welfare values, where the primary focus of work was the *rehabilitation of offenders. Over the course of the 1990s, it began to reflect some of the populist punitive stance that is a hallmark of neo-liberal thinking. National Objectives and Standards (NOS) were introduced in 1991, imposing centralized Scottish Office control over practice and a concern for greater *accountability within a burgeoning 'what works' paradigm (*see* EVIDENCE-BASED PRACTICE).

Another feature of neo-liberal political ideology was the increased recourse to law and legalism. The 1990s witnessed a growth in rights *discourses, generally restricted, however, to a narrow legal and contractual version of rights rather than broad social and cultural rights envisaged by United Nations source documents, and indeed by the children's rights discourse which developed in Scotland over the course of the 1960s and 1970s. The Children (Scotland) Act (1995), which replaced the child care provisions of the Social Work (Scotland) Act (1968), whilst maintaining a broadly welfare approach to child care decision-making, also introduced a greater justice orientation, in which legal principles were uppermost. It also compromised the *'best interests of the child' principle by allowing claims of *risk and community safety to compete with it. In criminal justice, rights became reduced to little more than due process, as prison populations rose steadily.

The increasing specialization of practice over the course of the 1990s led to the demise of *generic social work, which had formed the underpinning rationale of the 1968 Act, and the separation of practice into the three main domains of children and families, community care, and criminal justice, the last being funded directly from the Scottish Office. For the most part, policy and practice mirrored developments elsewhere in the UK, although civil servants in what was then the Scottish Office contrived to mitigate the more radical elements of Thatcherism, and sought to accommodate the views of the professions in policy development and implementation.

New Labour and the modernization agenda The New Labour government, elected in 1997, sought to chart a *'Third Way' in respect of public services, promising to remove these from political ideology, asserting that what mattered was what worked. Their 'governance' agenda was concerned with 'modern', efficient, and accountable public services, and *partnership with other professionals, and it claimed to represent the voices of users and carers. These aspirations were set out in a Scottish context in the White Paper *Aiming for Excellence* (1999), which set the scene for subsequent political engagement with social work. The political forum for such engagement shifted with the re-establishment of the Scottish Parliament in 1999.

Scottish Parliament One of the early acts of the New Labour administration elected in 1997 was to legislate for *devolution across the nations of the UK. A Scottish Parliament with powers over significant areas of domestic policy, including social services, was re-established and inaugurated in Edinburgh in 1999. Its executive arm was called just that, the Scottish Executive. From then until 2007, Scotland was governed by a Labour/Liberal Democrat coalition with Donald Dewar as the inaugural First Minister. Dewar died suddenly the following year, and Henry McLeish took over as First Minister. McLeish's legacy was the introduction of free personal care for older people, a policy not without its difficulties in terms of sustainability, but indicative nonetheless of a commitment to principles of social welfare. McLeish's stay in office, however, was brief. Jack McConnell, his successor, presided over a period of policy convergence with developments in England, reflecting the *'modernization' and *managerialism that were hallmarks of New Labour at UK level.

New Labour added grist to the mill of Conservative *managerialism through its adoption of *target-setting and *performance management systems. It further reduced professional *discretion and imposed greater central government control. A centralizing and populist tendency was particularly evident in the field of criminal justice, which witnessed a proliferation of new institutions that, overall, had the effect of strengthening central government control over criminal justice policy. These new bodies included *youth justice teams; local criminal justice boards; drug and alcohol action teams; community justice authorities; the Police Services Authority; the Scottish Crime and Drug Enforcement Agency; specialist domestic violence, drugs, and youth courts; and the risk management authority. National Objectives and Standards were set for youth justice (2002) and victim support (2005). The National Youth Justice Standards were subsequently updated by *Preventing Offending by Young People: A Framework for Action* (2008), to take account of the more child-centred *Getting it Right for Every Child* (GIRFEC) model (see below). The multi-agency aspect of these developments was exemplified in *Multi-Agency Public Protection Arrangements (MAPPA) (2007). The fundamental purpose of MAPPA is public safety and the reduction of serious harm, and it aims to provide a consistent approach to the management of offenders across all local authority and police force areas, providing a framework for assessing and managing the risk posed by some of those offenders. McConnell's administration focused much of its attention on questions of youth crime, introducing a *Ten-Point Action*

Plan (2002), which included an increase in the number of beds in secure accommodation, and the introduction of *electronic tagging as an alternative to secure accommodation. A new field of youth justice developed organizationally, in many respects recreating the distinction between youth offending and care and protection that Kilbrandon had eschewed.

The partnership agenda set out in *Aiming for Excellence* was taken forward in respect of adult services by the *Joint Futures* initiative, which encouraged joint working across health and social work to improve access to both services and led to Local Partnership Agreements between local authorities and Health Boards. In children's services the *For Scotland's Children* (2001) report called for better integration of children's services across different disciplines. Organizationally, this saw local authorities merge previously discrete departments such as education with the children and families functions of social work, while adult social work services began to work more closely with Health Boards.

For Scotland's Children, with its call for greater interdisciplinary working, paved the way for the 2004 GIRFEC policy. The thrust of this was similar to the *Every Child Matters* policy in England, with the focus on providing adequate levels of support for all children and for considering the needs of children with additional support needs within this universal framework of children's needs. GIRFEC identified a number of wellbeing indicators for children, specifying that they ought to be: safe, healthy, active, nurtured, achieving, respected and responsible, and included. The GIRFEC practice model offers three main tools to guide practitioners' *assessments and interventions with children and their families: the My-World Triangle, the Wellbeing Wheel, and the Resilience Matrix. The GIRFEC agenda dovetailed with the main educational development in recent years, the implementation of *Curriculum for Excellence* (2004). This identified the aspiration of the Scottish education system to seek to promote a broad and flexible conception of education, picking up, to some extent, on generalist educational traditions. It aimed to develop four capacities in children: that they might become successful learners, confident individuals, responsible citizens, and effective contributors.

Regulation and inspection A major strand of New Labour's interface with social work was its implementation of legislation to regulate care across the different UK jurisdictions. In Scotland this was enacted by the Regulation of Care Act (2001), which established the Scottish Social Services Council (SSSC), to regulate the social care workforce and to create *codes of practice, and the Care Commission, charged with setting standards for the provision of care and inspecting service providers against them. The provisions of the Regulation of Care Act form but one layer of the regulatory apparatus that has grown up around social work. The *Changing Lives* report (2006) (see below) noted that 'Social work is currently regulated and inspected by: Social Work Inspection Agency; Scottish Social Services Council; Care Commission; Mental Welfare Commission; Audit Scotland; Joint Future Unit; HM Inspectorate of Education; and, from 2006, the proposed Community Justice Authorities.' The scope of regulation has grown massively since the establishment of the SSSC. The regulated workforce in Scotland is currently almost as large as it is in England despite Scotland having only around one-tenth of its population.

The Crerar Review (2007), established on the back of *Changing Lives*, identified some of the dysfunctional consequences of inspection and recommended substantial reductions and even cessations in inspection schedules. In response to the Review, separate inspection functions were brought together in 2011 under a new body, Social Care and Social Work Improvement Scotland (SCSWIS), which became known by its working title, the Care Inspectorate. The purpose of the care regulation legislation was argued to be the improvement of services and safeguarding the public. There is little evidence that it has done either. Excessive regulation has resulted in a proliferation of legislation, regulation, and *guidance, which has arguably reshaped the social work role away from the development of relationships towards a primary emphasis on procedures and administration. It has also sought to monitor and control workers' behaviour through codes of professional conduct and fitness-to-practise directives.

Changing Lives (2006) Two high-profile cases in the early 2000s, in which social workers were severely criticized, prompted the Scottish Executive to institute what it termed a 'fundamental review of social work' in 2004. In Edinburgh, a baby was killed by his mentally impaired father, while in the Scottish Borders three adult males abused a woman with *learning disabilities over a period of time. The Review reported in 2006 as *Changing Lives, the 21st-Century Review of Social Work*, confirming a picture of social work well-recognized by practitioners as a profession lacking in confidence and uncertain about its role and identity and one that had lost touch with its core purpose. It also recognized the risk-averse and process-driven nature of much contemporary practice. In a climate where questions were being asked about the very existence of social work as a discrete profession, many social workers welcomed *Changing Lives*' findings. It asserted a role for social work, concluding that it was and should remain a single generic profession and that social workers possessed a distinctive set of knowledge, skills, and values. It also reasserted the importance of the social work relationship. In other ways *Changing Lives* positioned social work firmly within a consumerist model, claiming that: 'As demanding consumers of goods and services, users of social work services will increasingly expect the same variety, *choice, and flexibility that they expect from the business sector' (*see* CONSUMERISM). Its central idea was that of *'personalization', any definition of which was, at best, left loose. This was, nevertheless, put at the heart of the reimagined social work task.

Legislative developments in post-devolution Scotland

Adult services Significant legislation since devolution relates to adult services, with four main pieces of legislation: the Adults with Incapacity (Scotland) Act (2000), the Mental Health (Care and Treatment) (Scotland) Act (2003), the Adult Support and Protection Act (2007), and the Social Care (Self-directed Support) (Scotland) Act (2013). These four Acts can be seen as modernizing legislation by reflecting contemporary understandings about how to intervene in the lives of adults who are vulnerable, in need of protection, or at risk of harming themselves or others, in ways that are least restrictive, of benefit to individuals, and take into account their wishes.

Adults with Incapacity (Scotland) Act (2000) provides a framework for safeguarding the welfare and managing the finances of adults who lack *capacity owing to mental disorder or a *disability or an inability to communicate, by putting in place arrangements for a 'proxy' to make certain decisions (welfare and/or financial) on behalf of a person with incapacity. Those who may be deemed to lack capacity include people with *dementia, a *learning disability, an acquired brain injury, severe and chronic *mental illness, and those with severe sensory impairment. The Act is intended to remedy previous legislation in which capacity was seen as an 'all-or-nothing' concept. Now, incapacity must be seen as person- and situation-specific and the Act provides a range of powers for intervention: for example a person with dementia may be able to decide on the level of support s/he would want for day-to-day living, but may struggle to manage her/his finances. In such a case, a financial intervention may be all that is needed. In other circumstances a combination of welfare and financial measures may be necessary.

Individuals with capacity can give powers of attorney covering both welfare and financial matters to any individual of their choice. However, if an individual no longer has capacity, anyone with an interest in the adult, normally a family member, close friend, or the local authority, can apply to the Sheriff Court to become a welfare and/or financial guardian. A *Guardianship Order gives authority to act and make certain decisions over the long term and is monitored through the *Office of the Public Guardian.

Mental Health (Care and Treatment) (Scotland) Act (2003) is the second major piece of legislation and repealed and replaced the Mental Health (Scotland) Act (1984). The Act followed on from and ran alongside developments in thinking about mental health and wellbeing. The Millan Committee, chaired by former Scottish Secretary Bruce Millan, was set up just prior to devolution to review the Mental Health Act (1984). The Committee's report, released in 2001, presaged a more collaborative, fair, and respectful approach to mental health service users and their families. It also included a discussion about the development of public campaigns to tackle the *stigma attached to mental health.

From 2001, Scottish mental health work centred round the work of the National Programme for Improving Mental Health and Wellbeing, which ran from 2001 to 2006. The National Programme aimed to raise awareness and promote ideas of mental health and wellbeing, challenge stigma and *discrimination, prevent *suicide, and promote *recovery. The idea of recovery has become a central one in relation to mental health. It borrows from the experiences and voices of the service user movement. Recovery is considered to be best brought about through harnessing an individual's own knowledge and experiences of coping with mental illness and working towards mental wellbeing. The effect of this has been an ideological and service-level shift away from primarily medical understandings of mental health and ill-health. The Scottish Recovery Network (SRN), launched in 2004, grew out of the National Programme. It works to develop an understanding of recovery for those who have experienced mental ill-health, practitioners, and the public more generally. A major piece of its work has been the Narrative Research Project, which has collected together narratives of recovery from people who have experienced mental ill-health and recovery, and sought to identify the factors that have assisted their recovery.

In legislative terms, the 2003 Act extended the role of the Mental Health Officer (MHO), placing a duty on local authorities to appoint sufficient MHOs for their area. MHOs are officers of a local authority and must meet certain requirements in respect of qualifications, training, and experience. Unlike England, where the Mental Health Act (2007) widened the range of those eligible to act as *Approved Mental Health Professionals with statutory duties in relation to compulsory measures, the Mental Health Officer in Scotland must be a qualified social worker with a post-qualifying award. One important MHO function is to prepare a Social Circumstances Report (SCR) in cases where a *Compulsory Treatment Order (CTO) is considered. Before the introduction of CTOs, compulsory measures authorized the detention and/or treatment of a person in hospital. The Scottish legislation introduced an option (not widely accepted by service user groups) of a community-based Compulsory Treatment Order. This can impose requirements on the person concerned, for example that they reside at a specified location or attend a specific place for treatment.

The 2003 Act established a new national body, the Mental Health Tribunal for Scotland ('the Tribunal'). Tribunals take decisions in a wide range of situations, for example on an application for a Compulsory Treatment Order. A Tribunal consists of three categories of member: legal, medical, and general. A 'named person', chosen by the detained person, has the right to all documentation, to be consulted about treatment and planning, and to attend Tribunals. The 'named person' may or may not be a relative.

The 2003 Act also extended the duties of the Mental Welfare Commission for Scotland. This has specific powers and duties in relation to carrying out visits to patients, investigations, interviews, medical examinations, and inspecting records. It also has *powers and *duties to publish information and guidance, and to give advice or bring matters to the attention of others in the mental health law system.

Adult Support and Protection Act (2007) Addresses concern over historical scandals in learning disability hospitals, and more recent concerns over abuse of older people that have prompted government action to *safeguard adults who may be at risk of harm or in need of protection. The Act imposes a statutory duty on local authorities to make inquiries about a person's wellbeing, property, or financial affairs, if they know or believe that the person is at risk, and that they might need to intervene to take protective action. Council officers (who have been social workers to date) have the power to carry out investigations through visits and interviews, and through examination of financial or other records. Where certain conditions are met, officers can pursue Protection Orders, including in situations where an individual has capacity but refuses to cooperate and where there is evidence of 'undue pressure' from a third party. Public bodies have duties to cooperate with a local authority making enquiries under the Act through *participation in multi-agency Adult Protection Committees and to report to the local Committee when they know or believe that someone is an adult at risk of harm and when action is needed to protect her/him.

The overarching principles of this Act are that any intervention in an individual's affairs should benefit the individual and should be the least restrictive option needed to achieve the purpose(s) of the *intervention. Interventions take into account the wishes and feelings of the adult deemed to be at risk, and those of other significant individuals, such as immediate relatives or carers, emphasizing the importance of the adult taking an active part in the functions under the Act.

Social Care (Self-directed Support) (Scotland) Act (2013) builds on previous provision for *direct payments. Consistent with the emphasis placed on personalization within *Changing Lives*, the preferred approach to adult social care delivery in Scotland is now that of self-directed support (SDS). The aim of SDS is to support people to live independently by providing individual budgets. It is claimed that these offer greater flexibility, choice, and control over the support arrangements people need to live their lives. A common expression of self-directed support is where individuals buy support from a service provider or employ a *personal assistant (PA). Support is available through dedicated *voluntary organizations to help people set up and run their *care packages, and to provide training about being an employer.

From 2010 local authorities were expected to have an SDS strategy. Subsequently, the Social Care (Self-directed Support) (Scotland) Act (2013) came into effect in April 2014. This provides options ranging from direct payments to the local authority continuing to provide services, or a mix of different options. While SDS is most often thought of as applying to adults with learning disabilities, the intention is that anyone who needs social support should be able to access SDS. While few would argue with the principle of individuals having greater control over the type of services they wish to use, the reality of SDS is rather more complicated than might first appear, especially in a context of financial stringency when local authorities are being forced to reduce spending, and where increasing numbers of vulnerable people are living in the community. In this climate, SDS can coincide with cuts in services and deterioration in the working conditions of *carers supporting individuals.

Children's services While there has been significant activity relating to children since devolution, most of this has been in terms of policy rather than legislation, as exemplified by GIRFEC and Curriculum for Excellence. A Scottish government consultation on *child protection, completed in 2011, identified a clear link between child protection and GIRFEC, and sought to embed child protection within the wider GIRFEC framework, thus potentially bringing child protection back from its predominantly investigative and procedural role, and locating it within an overall understanding of children's needs. Specific legislation in recent years includes:

Adoption and Children (Scotland) Act (2007) This act repealed and replaced the Adoption (Scotland) Act (1978). It introduced Permanence Orders and allowed for both partners in an unmarried couple to adopt jointly. The Act maintains existing adoption services and local authorities continue to have a duty to provide adoption services. People directly affected by adoption have a right to pre- and post-adoption services.

Children's Hearings (Scotland) Act (2011) While maintaining the basic principles of the children's hearings system, this Act sought to modernize it through instituting a new national body, Children's Hearings Scotland, under a Chief Executive, in place of locally based children's panels. This body sets standards and ensures consistency across Scotland.

Children and Young People (Scotland) Act (2014) This major piece of legislation involved the introduction of a duty on the Scottish Ministers to have due regard to the *United Nations Convention on the Rights of the Child (UNCRC) when exercising any of their functions across a range of policy contexts. More specifically, it contains provision for offering additional early learning and child care services, facilitating better *permanency planning by giving young people *looked after in foster care, *kinship care, or residential care the entitlement to stay in their care placement until their twenty-first birthday, and to extend the *after-care support available to those *leaving care up to their twenty-sixth birthday. It also enshrines the *Getting it Right for Every Child* (GIRFEC) approach in law, ensuring additional support to children who need it within a framework of universal services. The Act also legislates for what has become the 'named person' scheme, whereby a single point of contact (generally a child's health visitor or head teacher) is identified to coordinate support to children who need it. This has become controversial, with claims that it mandates the state to intrude into the 'private' sphere of the family.

Developments in criminal justice social work As noted above, one of the defining features of Scottish social work is its retention of a criminal justice function. Criminal justice practice has remained, rhetorically at least, rooted within social work values and principles. Previous National Standards have been updated by the National Outcomes and Standards for Social Work Services in the Criminal Justice System (2010). Registered social workers remain accountable for the provision of all reports to court hearings that could have an impact on an individual's liberty; the provision of all reports to the Victims, Witnesses, Parole, and Life Sentence division of government, as they could impact on public safety and/or on an individual's liberty; investigation, assessment, review, and implementation of *risk management plans; and the supervision of those subject to statutory supervision on release from prison. Social workers also undertake direct case management work in respect of those who are subject to statutory orders or licence, and who are considered to pose a high risk of serious harm. Previous probation or community service disposals are now incorporated within *Community Payback Orders, combinations of which can be imposed as an alternative to custody. Unlike England, the probation function remains a social work one.

In Scotland a number of *civil society initiatives have suggested the need to move away from the country's high use of imprisonment. The Scottish Government professes to want the most progressive justice system in Europe and claims to be committed to a radical reduction in the prison population. Rhetoric and reality have not yet converged around this aspiration, with prison rates still being among the highest in Western Europe.

Professional identity While there is little doubt that trends in the direction of social work are similar in Scotland to those of other parts of the UK, the fragmentation of services has proceeded at a slower pace. There is also relatively strong Scottish Government support for the profession compared with that in England. A consequence of this greater sense of political support is that there remains a greater sense of professional coherence in relation to social work's identity in Scotland. The Scottish branch of the British Association of Social Workers (BASW) has become the Scottish Association of Social Work (SASW) in response to members' calls for a stronger identification with the specific traditions and features of Scotland's social work system.

The Christie Commission on the Future Delivery of Public Services (2011) took forward this development of a 'Scottish model', arguing that Scottish approaches to welfare differ significantly from those in England. The report proposed four key objectives of a reform programme: public services built around people and communities, organizations working together more effectively, prioritization of preventive approaches, and a constant drive to improve performance and reduce costs.

Partly in response to developments in England and partly to review progress since *Changing Lives*, a Strategic Forum was established in 2013 to develop a vision and strategy for social services. The vision talks of a socially just Scotland with excellent social services that work with others to *empower, support, and protect people. It picks up other current policy themes around prevention, early intervention, and enablement. Running alongside this Forum, a *Review of Social Work Education* was initiated and completed in 2016. This has identified a system of social work education that is largely functioning well. Some of the more radical proposals for social work education evident in England are less apparent here. Specifically, the Review has reaffirmed a generic qualifying education.

Political developments The 2007 elections to the Scottish Parliament are likely to be seen as a watershed in Scottish politics. These produced a Scottish National Party (SNP) minority government under the stewardship of Alex Salmond as First Minister. Its minority status precluded any significant political initiatives or changes in direction. It did, however, quickly change the name of the Scottish Executive to the Scottish Government, while on the social front it aspired to social democratic traditions with strong connections to those of Nordic countries. Signs of more socially progressive approaches were evident in its decision to remove university tuition fees, and to cut and subsequently eliminate prescription charges.

In recent years developments in social welfare have been inextricably intertwined with a rapidly unfolding political situation. In 2011, the Scottish National Party won a landslide victory, which afforded them a mandate to hold a referendum on Scottish Independence in September 2014. While the referendum resulted in a vote against Independence, the process of the referendum itself had a profound impact on Scottish *culture, encouraging a spirit of civil activism. The group Women for Independence, for instance, was involved in the decision not to proceed with the building of a new women's prison. A vibrant alternative media is also instrumental in providing a forum for progressive values and practices to be discussed and taken forward. Politically, the SNP went on to win 56 out of 59 Westminster seats in the 2015 General Election. Some of this massive political change has been reflected in initiatives in the fields of education and social welfare being employed to support a process of what might be thought of as 'nation building', which seeks to distinguish between what is happening in Scotland and the rest of the UK, or at least England. Socially progressive rhetoric, however, is not always mirrored in actual policies.

Should it be so minded, the Scottish government, in its pursuit of a Scottish model, might do worse than to reconnect with the basic principles outlined in the Kilbrandon Report but never wholly realized. The idea of social education proposed by Kilbrandon might resonate with the growing interest in European models of *social pedagogy. Interest in social pedagogy is apparent across the UK, but perhaps has a particular resonance in Scotland, where its ideas might be thought to chime with those of social education. Asquith et al., in their literature review on the role of the social worker undertaken for *Changing Lives, The Role of the Social Worker in the 21st Century* (2005), suggested that Kilbrandon in his proposals for social education had a vision of a service akin to social pedagogy. They suggested that social pedagogy emphasizes direct relationship-based work with people, which is consistent with the core values and practices of social work.

Scottish Executive (Scottish government) *See* SCOTLAND.

screening referrals *See* CARE MANAGEMENT.

SCT *See* SUPERVISED COMMUNITY TREATMENT.

seamless services *See* COLLABORATIVE WORKING; COORDINATION OF SERVICES AND/OR STRATEGY.

second opinion appointed doctor (SOAD) A registered medical practitioner and experienced psychiatrist who provides an independent opinion in respect of consent to treatment under Part IV of the Mental Health Act (1983). *See also* COMPULSORY TREATMENT.

section (sectioned, sectioning) *See* COMPULSORY ADMISSION.

Section 7 Report Requested by a court in private family proceedings involving divorcing or separating parents where the court requires the *Children and Family Court Advisory and Support Service or the *local authority to comment on the particular issue or issues affecting the welfare of the child that are before the court, for example the people with whom a child should reside or have *contact under a *Child Arrangements Order. The Report derives its name from Section 7 of the Children Act (1989). A Section 7 Report needs to contain background information and the key facts and evidence that the child's *needs have been considered in accordance with the *welfare checklist. The Report collates all of the available evidence and information about the child's situation and sets it out in the form of a comprehensive report advising the court of the child's wishes and feelings and what the social worker considers to be in the *best interests of the child.

Section 12 approved doctor A registered medical practitioner who has special experience in the *diagnosis and treatment of mental disorder and has specific functions under the Mental Health Act (1983). One of the two medical recommendations for *compulsory admission under the Act must be made by a Section 12 approved doctor. All *approved clinicians (AC) are deemed to be approved for this role, but the approved doctor may also be the *responsible clinician (RC) if the RC is a registered medical practitioner.

Section 20 accommodation (Section 20 admission of a child) *See* CHILD ACCOMMODATED BY A LOCAL AUTHORITY.

Section 31A Plan Where *family court proceedings have begun that might result in a *Care Order being made with respect to a child, the *local authority must, within a timescale decided by the court, prepare a *care plan for the future care of the child (Section 31A, Children Act [1989]). While the proceedings are pending, the authority must keep the care plan under review and if some change is required, revise the plan or make a new plan. *See also* CARE PROCEEDINGS.

Section 47 enquiry In Section 47 of the Children Act (1989) the 'local authority's *duty to investigate' refers to the statutory responsibility of *local authority children's services to make such enquiries as they consider necessary when information is received that a child in their area may be suffering or is likely to suffer *significant harm. Such enquiries are also necessary if the child is the subject of an *Emergency Protection Order or is placed under *police protection. The local authority is required to use the information generated by the enquiry to decide on any action that is needed to safeguard the child or promote her/his welfare. In reality 'local authority' will mean the local children's social work team responsible for investigating allegations of abuse in respect of children living in its area. If there is a possibility that a criminal offence has been committed against the child, the team will discuss the situation with the local police, usually a dedicated *child protection team of specially trained officers. A judgement will be reached on whether a joint investigation is needed by social workers and police or whether a single agency enquiry is to be undertaken. The enquiry will establish what has happened to the child and what further action is needed in response to the allegations. A *strategy discussion or *strategy meeting will take place for this purpose, with other professionals involved as appropriate. The strategy meeting or strategy discussion will agree: when and where the child will be seen; when and where the allegations will be put to the alleged perpetrator; whether the child will be interviewed under the requirements of government guidance for the conduct of recorded interviews with child witnesses; the timing and location of any medical examination that may take place as part of the enquiry/investigation. Investigative and welfare issues relating to any siblings will also be considered. Children's teams will 'at an early stage of enquiries' undertake background checks with other agencies to establish what information is held on the child and family by professionals, and whether there have been other concerns. If the child is assessed to have experienced or be at *risk of experiencing significant harm, a *child protection conference will take place within fifteen days of the strategy meeting or strategy discussion and the need for a *child protection plan will be considered. Not all children subject to a Section 47 enquiry will be considered to be at continuing risk of harm, but they may require services as a *child in need to assist them and their family. *See also* ACHIEVING BEST EVIDENCE; ASSESSMENT (CHILDREN); CHILD PROTECTION; SAFEGUARDING CHILDREN.

Further reading: HM Government (2015) *Working Together to Safeguard Children: A Guide to Inter-agency Working to Safeguard and Promote the Welfare of Children*, Chapter 1, pp. 39–42. Available at: https://www.gov.uk/government/uploads/system/uploads/attachment_data/file/419595/Working_Together_to_Safeguard_Children.pdf.

secure accommodation *See* DETENTION AND TRAINING ORDER; SECURE CHILDREN'S HOMES; SECURE TRAINING CENTRE; YOUNG OFFENDERS' INSTITUTION.

Secure Accommodation Order Issued by a *family court under Section 25 of the Children Act (1989), its effect is to place a child in secure accommodation with powers to prevent her/him from leaving. For an Order to be made, the requirements of Section 25 must be met. They are:

- that the child has a history of running away and is likely to run away from accommodation which is not secure; and
- if s/he runs away, s/he is likely to suffer *significant harm; or
- if s/he is not in secure accommodation, s/he is likely to injure her/himself or someone else.

See also DETENTION AND TRAINING ORDER; SECURE CHILDREN'S HOMES; SECURE TRAINING CENTRE; YOUNG OFFENDERS' INSTITUTION.

secure attachment *see* ATTACHMENT.

secure children's homes Closed accommodation that accommodates the most vulnerable young offenders whose problems are thought to have contributed to their criminal behaviour. They may have been previously in care or have mental health problems. Those in secure children's homes tend to be younger than those in *secure training centres or *young offenders' institutions. *See also* CUSTODIAL SENTENCE; DETENTION AND TRAINING ORDER; SECURE ACCOMMODATION ORDER.

secure training centre (STC) Provides secure accommodation for offenders up to the age of 17, usually smaller than a *young offenders institution, and provides education and vocational training, as well as addressing young offenders' behaviour. People in these centres receive up to thirty hours of education each week, aimed at equipping them with skills and qualifications. *See also* CUSTODIAL SENTENCE; DETENTION AND TRAINING ORDER.

secure unit A psychiatric facility that provides *assessments, treatment, and secure accommodation for patients who require higher levels of supervision in order to prevent them harming themselves or others. There are three categories of secure hospital, referred to as high, medium, or low. High secure hospitals (formerly Special Hospitals) were established by the National Health Service Act (1977) in order to detain and treat mentally disordered individuals considered dangerous and violent, including those who have committed violent offences. These are run under Home Office rules. Before admission, mental disorder must be established, the individual must be liable to detention under the Mental Health Act (1983), and *risk to others must be present. Admission must be justified in that the highest level of security is required, and the individual would pose a grave and immediate risk to the public without a high-security regime. There are three high secure units: Ashworth, Broadmoor, and Rampton hospitals.

There is a far greater number of medium secure units. Before admission to a medium secure unit, the presence of mental disorder and liability to detention under the Mental Health Act (1983) must be established, but risk posed to others does not have to be grave or immediate. Patients have a range of other difficulties, often behavioural, that pose a level of risk to themselves or others that cannot be managed by mainstream psychiatric hospitals.

Low secure units (also known as intensive care, or intensive treatment, or high dependency units) are often attached to mainstream psychiatric hospitals. They provide higher levels of security than open wards, with locked doors, perimeter fencing, and higher staffing levels. They provide more intensive monitoring of patients whose challenging or disturbed behaviour cannot be managed on an open psychiatric ward, or on an acute admission ward. Low secure units are not appropriate for long-term inpatient care because their objective is not therapeutic. They are designed to manage short-term crises, for instance, when a patient is highly psychotic or agitated on admission, or where the risk of *suicide appears significant.

Seebohm Report (1968) *See* GENERICISM; SOCIAL SERVICES DEPARTMENT.

self-advocacy *See* ADVOCACY.

self-funder (self-funding) Someone who can pay for their own *care and support in full. The Care Act (2014) provides for self-funders to receive an *assessment and *care and support plan from the *local authority and enables a self-funder to ask the authority to arrange care and support on her/his behalf. There is no difference in practice between the assessment and care and support planning process for self-funders and for people receiving financial support from the local authority. The local authority may enter into a contract with a self-funder's preferred provider or may broker the contract on behalf of the person. The local authority should ensure contractual arrangements are in place that clearly set out where responsibilities for costs lie and ensure that the self-funder understands the arrangements. A local authority can charge an arrangement fee to a self-funder, though the cost of this may be offset if the local authority is able to get cheaper rates than if a self-funder were arranging services for themselves. In addition to their role with individual self-funders, local authorities have a more general responsibility for providing *information and advice, including to self-funders.

self-harm Behaviours that cause harm, injury, or damage to a person's body, often as an expression of personal distress. Self-harming behaviour might include cutting, burning, head-banging, hitting, biting, pinching, severe scratching, swallowing objects, and self-poisoning. There are different perspectives on self-harming behaviour, depending on the nature of intent and the context in which it takes place. A broad perspective might apply to many culturally acceptable behaviours that can result in self-inflicted physical or psychological damage, such as cigarette smoking, recreational drug use, long-term alcohol use, over-eating, and dieting. Some religious practices may be considered to involve self-harm, for instance self-flagellation. Deliberate self-harm refers to acts that are specifically intended to cause injury and that are associated with psychological or emotional distress. Some acts of self-harm can occur that are not within an individual's control or awareness, for instance, children who have been abused may harm themselves in a dissociative (or trance-like) state.

People self-harm for many different reasons including: self-punishment, to gain feelings of control, to attempt to end life, to communicate with others, or to obtain help or relief from a difficult or overwhelming situation. Self-harm for some need not be a plea for help, and can be an important way of coping with extremely painful or difficult emotions and experiences, such as sexual abuse. For such individuals, self-harm can be a way of avoiding *suicide or of relieving suicidal feelings, though this is not always easily understood by practitioners. Repeated acts of self-harm can escalate, becoming physically and psychologically addictive. This is because adrenaline is released and gives immediate relief from emotional pain. Self-harm behaviour can be difficult to stop once it has become an ingrained coping mechanism. The risk of *suicide is greater in general for individuals who self-harm, and many individuals who have committed suicide have a history of self-harming behaviour. *Depression is commonly diagnosed in individuals who self-harm. It is important to avoid assumptions created by previous knowledge of the individual's motives. Each incident should be assessed separately and the individual's feelings should be explored carefully to determine the underlying motivation as motives and intentions can change.

self-surveillance *See* GAZE; GOVERNMENTALITY; TECHNOLOGIES OF THE SELF.

senile dementia *See* DEMENTIA.

Sense A charity supporting, providing information, working with, and campaigning for children and adults with *dual sensory (combined sight and hearing) impairment. It also provides advice and information for families, carers, and professionals who work with them.

(⊕) SEE WEB LINKS
• Official site of Sense.

sensory impairment *See* DUAL SENSORY IMPAIRMENT; HEARING IMPAIRMENT; VISUAL IMPAIRMENT.

separation anxiety *See* SCHOOL PHOBIA.

Serious Case Review (SCR) A requirement that *Local Safeguarding Children Boards (LSCB) make arrangements for a review whenever a child dies (including death by suicide) and *child abuse and neglect is known or suspected to be a factor in the child's death. Such a review also has to be considered in circumstances where a child has sustained a potentially life-threatening injury through abuse or neglect, serious sexual abuse, or permanent impairment of health and development through abuse or neglect, and the *case gives rise to concerns about the way in which local professionals and services have worked together to safeguard and promote the welfare of the child. The Children Act (2004) established LSCBs and empowered the Secretary of State to make regulations setting out their functions. The regulations that were issued require LSCBs to undertake SCRs and *Child Death Reviews. Guidance that sets out the particular duties and processes to be undertaken to carry out SCRs is contained in *Working Together to Safeguard Children and their Families* (2015), issued under the Children Act (1989). Agencies with involvement in the case are required to submit an individual management review detailing their involvement to the LSCB, which arranges for these to be drawn together in an overview report designed to highlight lessons that arise from the case. This report includes recommendations made to the LSCB and organizations with a view to improving practice where this is necessary. It should also highlight *good practice. This process is to be distinguished from a Child Death Review that is concerned with looking at the circumstances of children in a locality who die for reasons other than abuse and neglect. However, a Child Death Review and *rapid response may reveal circumstances that lead to an SCR. There is increasing reluctance to undertake SCRs routinely and some LSCBs are only using them in the most serious cases.

Further reading: HM Government (2015) *Working Together to Safeguard Children: A Guide to Inter-agency Working to Safeguard and Promote the Welfare of Children*, Chapter 4. Available at https://www.gov.uk/government/uploads/system/uploads/attachment_data/file/419595/Working_Together_to_Safeguard_Children.pdf.

service user A widely-used term for someone receiving social work and/or social services. It has largely replaced the term *'client', though this term is sometimes still heard, because client was thought to have connotations of seeing a solicitor or other such professional, thus implying that the social worker was in the role of a distant expert. Under the influence of *consumerism, there have been widespread attempts to replace service user with 'consumer' or 'customer', with some social work organizations issuing edicts to staff dictating which of these terms should be used. There is evidence of service users not being comfortable with either term and the credibility of their use in many situations is stretched to breaking point. For example, is it realistic to refer to parents in court facing the *risk of having their children removed from them as customers of the *local authority seeking to remove them? Given the difficulties of finding a term that fits the wide range of people with whom social workers come into contact in a wide range of situations, service user is seen by many as the least worst alternative. *See also* EXPERT BY EXPERIENCE; PARTICIPATION; PARTNERSHIP; SURVIVOR.

service user involvement *See* PARTICIPATION; PARTNERSHIP.

service user organizations *See* USER-LED ORGANIZATIONS.

service user participation *See* PARTICIPATION.

sexism Attitudes and actions that discriminate against and oppress women on the basis of their sex or *gender. Sexism is evident at institutional as well as individual and group levels. For example, the majority of social workers are women but more men than women are managers. There can also be examples of sexism in social work practice, for example, if assumptions are made about women as *carers of *older people and children. The individual *identity of a woman caring for children may disappear within the social work process as she comes to be simply referred to as 'Mum' by social workers. Sexism intersects with *oppression based on other social divisions such as *'race', sexuality, and *disability. *See also* ANTI-DISCRIMINATORY PRACTICE; ANTI-OPPRESSIVE PRACTICE; INTERSECTIONALITY.

sex offender Someone convicted of a sexual offence, for example, rape or incest. *See also* MULTI-AGENCY PUBLIC PROTECTION ARRANGEMENTS; PAEDOPHILIA; PERSON POSING A RISK TO CHILDREN; SCHEDULE 1 OFFENDER; SEX OFFENDERS REGISTER.

Sex Offenders Register Offenders who have been cautioned or convicted for specified sexual offences have to notify police of their address and if they plan to go abroad. They have to register initially with the police within three days of being cautioned or convicted and thereafter each year. Periods for registration can be between one year and for life, depending on their sentence. Despite 'Sex Offenders Register' having become the standard term in use, there is no register as such. There is simply a category for recording such offenders on the Police National Computer. *See also* MULTI-AGENCY PUBLIC PROTECTION ARRANGEMENTS; PAEDOPHILIA; PERSONS POSING A RISK TO CHILDREN; SCHEDULE 1 OFFENDER; SEX OFFENDER.

sexual abuse *See* CHILD ABUSE AND NEGLECT.

sexual division of labour *See* DOMESTIC LABOUR.

sexually inappropriate behaviour A child's behaviour of a sexual nature that appears to be inappropriate for the child's age, stage of development, and the level of understanding of sexual issues that would reasonably be expected of children of that age. This is in contrast to sexual exploration by children, which would generally be regarded as a usual part of *child development. While the distinction between the two is not always clear and may rely on a degree of subjective judgement, the behaviour exhibited is likely to be such as to lead to professional concern about the wellbeing of the child concerned and other children in contact with her or him, including the possibility of the child who is behaving in a sexually inappropriate way causing harm to other children. Children exhibiting sexually inappropriate behaviour are often first identified in school, where referral to appropriate services, for example, children's social work services or *Child and Adolescent Mental Health Services, will lead to attempts to work with the child and their parents/carers to identify the reasons for the behaviour, of which there may be many, and how it might be best addressed.

Shared Society *See* BIG SOCIETY.

sheltered accommodation (sheltered housing) Usually flats but can be small houses or bungalows, with a paid warden who lives in the complex or nearby and who is available to assist residents. Originally designed primarily for *older people, sheltered accommodation has also been provided for people with physical disabilities, *learning disabilities, and mental health problems. When it was introduced for these latter groups, it represented an advance on living in long-stay institutional settings and was seen as a shift to community living. There is now criticism of what was once seen as progress, not least from *service user movements because such settings still embody an element of segregation. *See also* RETIREMENT COMMUNITY.

short-term placement *See* PLACEMENT.

sign *See* SIGN LANGUAGE; SYMPTOM.

significant harm The threshold that justifies compulsory intervention in family life in the best interests of the child. Introduced by *Section 47 of the Children Act (1989), the concept places on local authorities the *duty to make enquiries (or investigations, as defined in the Act) in order to decide whether action should be taken to *safeguard or promote the welfare of a child who is suffering, or likely to suffer, significant harm. There are no absolute criteria on which to rely when judging what constitutes significant harm. *Child protection practitioners give consideration to the severity of ill-treatment when making this judgement, taking account of the degree and extent of physical harm, the duration and frequency of *abuse and/or neglect, the extent of premeditation, and the presence of a degree of threat, coercion, sadism, bizarre, or unusual elements. Each of these aspects of abuse has been associated with more severe effects on the child, and relatively greater difficulty in helping children overcome the adverse impact of maltreatment. Sometimes a single traumatic event may constitute significant harm, for example, a violent assault, suffocation, or poisoning. More often significant harm is a compilation of significant events, both acute and longstanding, which interrupt, change, or damage the child's physical and psychological development. Some children live in family and social circumstances where their health and development are impaired. For them it is the corrosiveness of long-term emotional, physical, or sexual abuse that causes impairment to the extent of significant harm.

In understanding and identifying significant harm, practitioners also weigh the capacity of the parents to adequately meet the child's needs, including any special needs such as a medical condition or *disability, and the wider family and environmental context. Under Section 31(9) of the Children Act (1989), as amended by the Adoption and Children Act (2002), 'harm' means ill-treatment or the impairment of health or development, including impairment suffered from seeing or hearing the ill-treatment of others. This amendment was made to capture the impact of *domestic violence on children (*see* CHILDREN AND DOMESTIC VIOLENCE). Under Section 31(10) of the Children Act (1989), the question of whether harm suffered by the child is significant turns on the child's health and development, comparing this with that which could reasonably be expected of a similar child. 'Development' means physical, intellectual, emotional, social, or behavioural development. 'Health' means physical or mental health. 'Ill-treatment' is not just physical; it includes sexual abuse and forms of ill-treatment that are not physical. Family courts may make a *Care Order if satisfied that a child is suffering or likely to suffer significant harm and this harm is attributable to a lack of adequate parental care or control. *See also* CHILD ABUSE AND NEGLECT; CHILD DEVELOPMENT; CHILD PROTECTION; GOOD-ENOUGH PARENTING; SECTION 47 ENQUIRY; DUTY TO INVESTIGATE; PARENTAL RESPONSIBILITY; PARENTING SKILLS; THRESHOLD CRITERIA.

sign language *See* BRITISH SIGN LANGUAGE; MAKATON.

signs and symptoms *See* SYMPTOM.

silo culture *See* CALL CENTRE.

situational depression *See* REACTIVE DEPRESSION.

Skills for Care An independent charity that is the strategic body for workforce development in adult social care, working with employers to set standards and qualifications for social care workers.

 SEE WEB LINKS
• Official site for Skills for Care.

smart home *See* TELECARE.

SMART targets *See* PERFORMANCE MANAGEMENT.

Social Care Institute for Excellence (SCIE) A charity that brings together and shares knowledge relevant to social work and social care by producing practical resources, learning materials, and services aimed at improving the knowledge and skills of those working at all levels in services.

(⊕) SEE WEB LINKS

• Official site of the Social Care Institute for Excellence.

social citizenship T. H. Marshall's (1893–1981) concept that was included in his model of *citizenship, alongside the earlier-established civil and political rights. He regarded social citizenship as characteristic of a collective approach to the provision of social rights through *state social welfare after 1945. *See also* BEVERIDGE REPORT; DEMOCRATIC-WELFARE-CAPITALISM; WELFARE STATE.

social class *See* CLASS.

social construction (social constructionism) A perspective that focuses on how issues become and remain social problems. It involves adopting a critical approach towards everyday ways of seeing issues and treating the way in which they are presented and the responses that are made to them as not immediately obvious and 'common sense'. Instead, it stresses that nothing in the social world is given or has a fixed nature. It cultivates a questioning approach to how social problems come to be constructed as such, emphasizing that they are specific to particular times, places, and *cultures. In addition, it contends that there is a great variety of knowledge and understanding that exists or can be brought to bear on an issue. Accordingly, the definition of social problems is seen as coming about through negotiations between different knowledges and understandings of issues, some of which are more powerful than others and can be made to 'stick'. *See also* DECONSTRUCTION; DISCOURSE; SOCIAL MODEL OF DISABILITY; SOCIAL MODELS.

social exclusion A broad way of conceptualizing deprivation and disadvantage predominantly in terms of severance of links with the wider *community or society. Under *New Labour particularly, the language of social exclusion increasingly displaced that of *poverty, with a tendency either to marginalize the impact of lack of material resources or to include it as simply one among many factors contributing to exclusion.

social institution *See* INSTITUTION.

social model of disability Sees *disability as caused by the way society is organized, rather than by a person's impairment. *'Impairment' refers to someone's functional limitation and 'disability, refers to the socially created restriction and *oppression experienced by people living with impairment in a society shaped by and for non-disabled people. It opposes the *medical model, and 'expert' perspectives on disability in general: first, because that model assumes that disability is a personal tragedy, with the difficulties experienced by disabled people being caused directly by their impairments; and secondly, because its view of functional limitations leads to its seeing disability as requiring emotional adjustment on the part of the disabled person and compensatory interventions. The social model is thought to have had its origins in the work of the Union of the Physically Impaired Against Segregation (UPIAS) in the mid-1970s. It was adopted and developed by the *Disabled People's Movement and by academics in the field of disability studies. It has proved influential in relation to public policy and professional practice in some areas of health and social care. While a considerable amount of early work gave attention to the negative impact on disabled people of a wide range of social factors, activists and academics sought to bring about a much more fundamental change in ways of understanding disability through the social model. They were

S

concerned to shift the definition of disability from the intrinsic to the extrinsic, from a personal and individual problem to a solely public issue requiring social and political solutions. It was seen by some as crucial to establish that individual characteristics were not restricting in themselves, and that there was no inevitable causal relationship between impairment and disability. While the social model has provided an inspirational and influential point of reference for many and has been the basis for collective struggles for social justice and *citizenship, it has also been contested. Some have criticized the social model for being an over-socialized way of understanding disability. Some critics have also pointed out that it becomes true by definition: once it is accepted that disability is extrinsic to the individual, only those things which are extrinsic to the individual are defined as disabling. Some disabled activists and academics have continued to hold the view that impairment must not be conceded to have any bearing on the difficulties that disabled people experience. This position has been challenged by others who recognize the debilitating impact of hostile material and ideological environments but who do not necessarily agree that their impairments have no bearing on the restrictive, sometimes painful, aspects of their lives. *See also* DECONSTRUCTION; INDIVIDUAL PATHOLOGY; SOCIAL CONSTRUCTION; SOCIAL MODELS.

Further reading: Oliver, M., Sapey, B., and Thomas, P. (2012, 4th edn.) *Social Work with Disabled People*, Palgrave Macmillan.

social models A range of social perspectives that have been developed to offer explanations about the inter-relationships between problems experienced by individuals and wider social and environmental factors. Social models have come to represent alternative perspectives to the *medical model, particularly in the fields of mental health and *disability. There is no universally agreed definition of what constitutes a social model, and it can be more usefully seen as a number of overlapping perspectives. These perspectives have been developed within a wide range of disciplines including sociology, psychology, psychotherapy, social *psychiatry, behavioural *family therapy, and transcultural psychiatry. Social perspectives have also emerged from civil rights and user movements, for instance, the *women's movement and lesbian and gay movements have developed *discourses about the impact of *patriarchy, *heterosexism, systematic *oppression, and *discrimination on issues such as mental health. The *Disabled People's Movement has campaigned for a greater acknowledgement of alternative models of understanding to those generated by dominant medical frameworks. Mental health user networks and critics of psychiatry and the medical model have argued for symptoms to be understood as part of a normal and meaningful spectrum of human experience. The *recovery movement maintains that recovery is less about being free from symptoms and more about restoring or developing a socially valued lifestyle. Because there is a plurality of perspectives, there is no single clear social model of practice in social work. Nevertheless, the underlying values can influence approaches to practice. This can include valuing and respecting the individual's own definitions of their problems, rather than imposing an explanation or *diagnosis; valuing and accepting the individual's *identity and experience, rather than reinforcing pathological frameworks that emphasize individual differentness and separateness; and employing *holistic approaches that seek to integrate a much broader understanding of the individual's subjectively experienced life, rather than objectifying issues in attempts to recognize patterns of behaviour. Social perspectives are also important in recognizing dynamics of power and systematic oppression, and are thus perceived to support *anti-oppressive and empowering approaches to practice. *See also* INDIVIDUAL PATHOLOGY; SOCIAL CONSTRUCTION; SOCIAL MODEL OF DISABILITY.

social pedagogy A professional and academic discipline that focuses on the *holistic education and personal development of people and their integration into society, with variants in a number of continental European countries. It is not characterized by a single theory or approach to practice but instead includes a diverse range of thinkers who share a conceptual foundation and attitude based on respect for individuals and the belief that everyone has the ability to change and to participate in society, given the right support, knowledge, and opportunities for individual development. Although social pedagogy has a long tradition in continental Europe, many of those who are now considered key thinkers did not use the term 'social pedagogy' themselves, as it was only coined towards the end of the nineteenth century. Social pedagogy is not deficit-oriented but regards all human beings as needing guidance to reach their full potential. Therefore, there is little or no stigma attached to people being clients of social pedagogues in continental Europe and much of the work takes place within the *community and the everyday life of the individual. The central aspect of practice is the relationship between the social pedagogue and the client. Social pedagogues strive to build authentic trusting relationships with their clients as the medium through which they can offer learning situations that *empower clients to become more competent in managing their lives. This can take many different forms and the practitioner chooses the most appropriate method for the situation, often integrating her/his personal interests such as sports, art, or theatre in her/his work with the *client. Social pedagogic practice is very interactive and the practitioner usually takes part in the activities. Whilst social pedagogues work with individuals or groups, their orientation encompasses society as a whole and the integration of the individual into it. By offering learning opportunities and helping the individual to master her/his everyday life, social pedagogues build *resilience and empower individuals to participate fully in society.

In continental Europe social pedagogues are educated to degree level and work in a wide range of settings including all areas of social care and welfare, the *voluntary sector, youth work, adult education, and business corporations. In comparison, the interest in social pedagogy in the UK is very recent, starting in the early 1990s in academic circles and in the late 1990s in policy. It can be argued that while the use of the term social pedagogy is very recent, there are people like Robert Owen (1771–1858) and Thomas *Barnardo (1845–1905) and organizations like the Camphill-Steiner Schools, as well as the Scottish tradition of welfare (*see* SCOTLAND), that reach much further back and are social pedagogical in nature. In order to develop a UK interpretation of social pedagogy it is useful to build on existing traditions like *patch social work, *relationship-based practice, *systemic approaches, and *youth work. Such traditions link well with social pedagogy. They have been less valued in recent years, under the impact of *managerialism, but social pedagogy is rediscovering them and re-evaluating what they have to offer.

In the UK, social pedagogy was initially adopted in the fields of residential care and *fostering through pilot programmes, hiring German and Danish social pedagogues and training existing members of staff. Foundation and undergraduate degrees in social pedagogy have been established and make a positive contribution to support and care workers' skill levels, as well as to qualifying programmes for youth and community workers. In addition, individual practitioners and organizations working in all areas of social work have been meeting to share ideas and connect practitioners who are using social pedagogy. Social pedagogy is still a relatively small niche within UK social work but one that has grown in recent years. The launch of the Social Pedagogy Professional Association is another step towards social pedagogy having a bigger presence in the UK.

(()) SEE WEB LINKS

• Official site of the Social Pedagogy Professional Association.

social role valorization A development from and beyond *normalization which argues that people with *learning disabilities should be able to fulfil roles that have value in society. The approach is based on five principles: *community presence, community *participation, *choice, *competence, and respect.

Further reading: Wolfensberger, W. (2000) 'A Brief Overview of Social Role Valorization', *Mental Retardation* [*sic*] 38, 2, 105–123.

Social Services Department Following the recommendations of the *Seebohm Report (1968), the Local Authority Social Services Act (1970) required every *local authority in England and *Wales to establish a Social Services Department, which brought together all the social work services previously provided in separate local authority departments (Children's Departments, Welfare Departments, and Mental Welfare Departments). The SSDs were gradually disbanded in England following the introduction of organizationally separate services for children and adults in the 1990s. However, the term 'social services' (often used originally to refer to Social Services Departments) is still common in everyday use. Social Services Departments have remained in existence in Wales. *See also* GENERICISM.

Social Work Action Network (SWAN) A radical campaigning organization of social work and other practitioners, students, *service users, *carers, and academics that considers social work is being undermined by *managerialism and *marketization, by the stigmatization of service users, and by welfare cuts and restrictions. While it recognizes that social work is one of the mechanisms through which the state controls people in *poverty, it believes that social work can, nevertheless, assist people to address the problems and difficulties in their lives. It sees many of these difficulties as rooted in inequality and *oppression, and regards social work as needing to confront the structural and public causes of private troubles. *See also* AUSTERITY; RADICAL SOCIAL WORK.

(()) SEE WEB LINKS

• Official site of the Social Work Action Network.

social work in primary health care *See* PRIMARY HEALTH CARE, SOCIAL WORK IN.

solution-focused therapy (solution-focused brief therapy) (SFT) An approach that focuses on solutions rather than problems, is concerned with the future, rather than going over the past, and identifies concrete realistic *goals towards which practice is directed. It is based on the assumption that everyone has some idea of what would make her/his life better, and that everyone who has accepted that s/he needs assistance has some level of ability to work towards solutions. The latter forms the core of solution-focused therapy; practice is built around identifying and realizing someone's vision of a solution(s). Accordingly, techniques are concerned with identifying solutions and clarifying how they can be put into place.

The questions asked usually centre on the present and the future, focusing on what is working and how the person would like their life to be, rather than going over problems. For example, a question might be: 'How will next week look if you're continuing to make progress?' Compliments are seen as important because they endorse what someone is already doing well, and looking for previous solutions acknowledges someone's existing problem-solving capacity and encourages ideas about how to solve current problems. A question might be: 'Have there been times when this was less of a problem?' If the answer is 'yes', a follow-up question might be, 'What did you do that helped?' If there are no examples of previous solutions, or as an addition to them, someone's attention may be drawn to examples of exceptions to their problem, situations in which the problem could have occurred but something else happened instead. A question might be: 'What happens during times when this is less of a problem?' These techniques—use of compliments, identifying previous solutions, and singling out exceptions to the problem—are important in themselves but also provide stepping stones towards trying to get someone to do more of what is working or has worked.

Two techniques used in solution-focused therapy have been widely publicized: scaling questions and the miracle question. Scaling questions are used so that people can assess their own situations, review their progress, or decide how others might rate them on a scale of 0 to 10. They can be used in relation to virtually any topic, for example, confidence, motivation, hope, *depression. Once a point on the scale has been identified, the person can be asked what they would need to do to get to the next point on the scale. The miracle question is a means of identifying small steps that can be taken towards a solution. The person is asked to imagine that in the middle of the night there is a miracle and the problem is solved. However, because this happens while s/he is sleeping, the person does not know that a miracle has occurred and the problem is solved. The person is asked to say what, on waking, would be the first small sign that would make her/him realize the problem had gone. S/he is then taken through the signs that would indicate the problem had gone, a step at a time, and encouraged to identify the changes that the person would need to make in order for those signs to come about.

Although solution-focused therapy has its origins in therapeutic practice in the US, models of practice based on it have been used in UK social work. *See also* BRIEF INTERVENTION; CONSTRUCTIVE SOCIAL WORK; STRENGTHS PERSPECTIVE; TASK-CENTRED APPROACH.

Further reading: de Shazer, S. and Dolan, Y. (2012) *More than Miracles: The State of the Art of Solution-focused Brief Therapy*, Routledge.

Milner, J. and O'Byrne, P. (2002) *Brief Counselling: Narratives and Solutions*, Palgrave.

somatization disorder *See* HYSTERIA.

special educational needs (SEN) *See* EDUCATION, HEALTH AND CARE NEEDS ASSESSMENT; EDUCATION, HEALTH AND CARE PLAN.

Special Guardian Introduced under Section 115 of the *Adoption and Children Act (2002) as an amendment to the Children Act (1989), this status may be conferred by *family courts on non-parents who are caring for or who wish to care for a child in a long-term secure placement. It is intended for those children who cannot live with their *birth parent(s) and who would benefit from living in a legally secure placement, usually *looked-after children, but can be non-looked-after children who are cared for by a relative. A Special Guardianship Order has the effect of discharging any existing *Care Order on a child and confers *parental responsibility on the applicant(s). It is a more secure order than a *Child Arrangements Order because a birth parent cannot apply to discharge it unless they have the permission of the court to do so. It falls short of an Adoption Order because it does not end the legal relationship between the child and her/his birth parents. It may be the most effective means of conferring permanency on a family placement. Examples of those most likely to apply for a Special Guardianship Order are any guardian of a child; a foster carer with whom a child has lived for one year immediately preceding the application; an individual who has a Child Arrangements Order in respect of a child. *See also* FOSTERING; KINSHIP CARE; PERMANENCY PLANNING; PLACEMENT; PRIVATE FOSTERING.

Special Guardianship Order *See* SPECIAL GUARDIAN.

special hospital *See* SECURE UNIT.

Specific Issues Order Granted under Section 8 of the Children Act (1989) to resolve specific issues concerning the upbringing of a child, for example in relation to the child's religion or education, when those with parental responsibility cannot agree. The Order is not available to local authorities.

spot contract *See* BLOCK CONTRACT.

Standards of Conduct, Performance, and Ethics *See* HEALTH AND CARE PROFESSIONS COUNCIL.

Standards of Proficiency for Social Workers *See* HEALTH AND CARE PROFESSIONS COUNCIL.

statement (statemented, statementing) *See* EDUCATION, HEALTH AND CARE NEEDS ASSESSMENT; EDUCATION, HEALTH AND CARE PLAN.

Statement of Special Educational Needs *See* EDUCATION, HEALTH AND CARE NEEDS ASSESSMENT; EDUCATION, HEALTH AND CARE PLAN.

Statutory Assessment of Special Educational Needs *See* EDUCATION, HEALTH AND CARE NEEDS ASSESSMENT; EDUCATION, HEALTH AND CARE PLAN.

statutory duty *See* DUTY (SPECIFIC); TARGET DUTY.

statutory instruments *See* REGULATIONS.

statutory power *See* POWER.

statutory review *See* LOOKED-AFTER CHILD REVIEW.

statutory sector Collective term for all of the social work organizations that are obliged by legislation to provide or commission services. In practice this means all *local authorities that provide social work services for children and adults. *See also* SOCIAL SERVICES DEPARTMENT.

statutory services Services that are provided under legislation, for example, protecting a child from *abuse or assessing an *older person for *care and support services.

statutory setting A location in a *local authority from which services are provided or *commissioned under legislation, for example a *fostering team or a team for *older people.

staying put initiatives (staying put schemes) *See* HOME IMPROVEMENT AGENCIES.

stereotype (stereotyping) Negative inflexible assumption(s) about an individual or group, usually based on appearance and/or social role, for example, age, *class, *disability, *ethnicity, marital status, religion, sexuality. These assumptions are used to justify *discrimination and *oppression towards the individual or group targeted. For example, the stereotyping of *older people, and especially older women, as vulnerable, dependent, and powerless leads to physical *risk being seen as something to be avoided at all costs. Stereotypes can be internalized by the people subjected to them. For example, older people's internalization of ageist stereotypes may contribute to feelings of passivity, dependency, and low sense of self-worth, and cause them to acquiesce to others making decisions for them. Social workers frequently encounter *service users who have been stereotyped and have internalized stereotypes, and an important aspect of their practice is to signal that they do not share such views and actively seek to counter them. *See* ANTI-DISCRIMINATORY PRACTICE; ANTI-OPPRESSIVE PRACTICE; STIGMA.

stigma Severe condemnation of someone because of what are regarded as negative characteristics that distinguish them from others. Erving Goffman (1922–1982) is regarded as having produced the classic work on stigma (*Stigma: Notes on the Management of Spoiled Identity* 1968) in which he defines stigma as 'the process by which the reaction of others spoils normal *identity'. He identified three kinds of stigma: physical deformity, *mental illness, and being associated with a particular religion, nationality, or 'race'. Stigma attacks people's identity or 'spoils' it, in Goffman's terms. People either internalize their stigmatization or reject it and challenge its validity. Social workers meet many service users who have been stigmatized and the fact that they are seeing a social worker may add to their stigmatization in their own estimation and that of others. *See also* ANTI-DISCRIMINATORY PRACTICE; ANTI-OPPRESSIVE PRACTICE; STEREOTYPE.

stimulus-response *See* BEHAVIOUR MODIFICATION; BEHAVIOURISM.

strategy discussion Initiated following a *referral that indicates that a child may be suffering or likely to suffer *significant harm, the purpose of this discussion, usually conducted by social workers and the police on the telephone, is to share information; agree the conduct and timing of any criminal investigation; decide whether a *Section 47 enquiry should be initiated; plan how a Section 47 enquiry should be conducted; agree what action is required immediately to safeguard the child; determine what information from the strategy discussion will be shared with the family, unless such information might place the child at increased *risk of harm or jeopardize police investigations into any alleged offences; determine if legal action is required. In more complex and/or serious situations, a *strategy meeting will take place, usually involving a wider range of agencies with knowledge of the child and her/his family. *See also* CHILD ABUSE AND NEGLECT; CHILD PROTECTION; CHILD PROTECTION CONFERENCE; CHILD PROTECTION PLAN; EMERGENCY PROTECTION ORDER; POLICE PROTECTION.

strategy meeting A meeting initiated following a *referral that indicates a child may be suffering or likely to suffer *significant harm. The purpose of this meeting is to bring together, as a minimum, children's social work services and the police to share information; agree the conduct and timing of any criminal investigation; decide whether a *Section 47 enquiry should be initiated; plan how the Section 47 enquiry should be conducted; agree what action is required immediately to safeguard the child; determine what information will be shared with the family unless such information may place the child at increased risk of harm or jeopardize police investigations into any alleged offences; determine if legal action is required. The decision to hold a strategy meeting, rather than simply to have a *strategy discussion, will be influenced by the complexity and/or seriousness of the allegations and concerns about the child. The strategy meeting should involve all agencies that are working with the child in order to ensure that they are party to decision-making at an early stage of a Section 47 enquiry. *See also* CHILD ABUSE AND NEGLECT; CHILD PROTECTION; CHILD PROTECTION CONFERENCE; CHILD PROTECTION PLAN; EMERGENCY PROTECTION ORDER; POLICE PROTECTION.

street-level bureaucracy *See* DISCRETION (SOCIAL WORKERS').

strengths-based approach Working collaboratively with *service users and taking account of their capacities, strengths, skills, and expertise; an assets-based approach that recognizes *resilience and ability to change. *See also* CONSTRUCTIVE SOCIAL WORK; EXCHANGE MODEL OF ASSESSMENT; RISK.

stroke *See* CARDIO-VASCULAR ACCIDENT.

Stroke Association A charity supporting research, providing information and support services, and campaigning, for example the FAST campaign, which it developed to help people recognize the signs of a stroke and take emergency action. This was subsequently taken up by the Department of Health and promoted to millions of people. *See also* CARDIO-VASCULAR ACCIDENT.

(⊕) SEE WEB LINKS
• Official site of the Stroke Association.

structured dependency theory *See* THEORIES OF AGEING.

subject access *See* DATA PROTECTION.

subsistence level *See* POVERTY.

substance abuse *See* ADDICTION; ALCOHOLISM; COMMUNITY DRUGS TEAM; DRUG AND ALCOHOL PROBLEMS.

substitute family care *See* ADOPTION; FOSTERING; KINSHIP CARE; PERMANENCY PLANNING; PLACEMENT; PRIVATE FOSTERING; SPECIAL GUARDIAN.

sudden infant death syndrome (SIDS) *See* SUDDEN UNEXPECTED DEATH IN CHILDHOOD.

sudden unexpected death in childhood Has replaced 'sudden infant death syndrome' to reflect the expansion of the original concept in response to developments in policy and practice following implementation of *child death review and *rapid response. Most protocols developed by *Local Safeguarding Children Boards for enquiring into these *cases now define the condition as sudden, unexpected, or unexplained deaths in infants under the age of two years, often referred to colloquially as 'cot deaths', and also sudden, unexpected, or unexplained deaths of all children up to eighteen years of age, excluding still-births and planned terminations of pregnancy carried out within the law. Government guidance defines an unexpected death of a child as a death that was not anticipated as a significant possibility, for example, 24 hours before the death, or when there was an unexpected collapse, or incident leading to or precipitating the events which led to the death.

Further reading: HM Government (2015) *Working Together to Safeguard Children: A Guide to Inter-agency Working to Safeguard and Promote the Welfare of Children*, Chapter 5, pp. 85–91. Available at: https://www.gov.uk/government/uploads/system/uploads/attachment_data/file/419595/Working_Together_to_Safeguard_Children.pdf.

suicidal ideation Having thoughts about committing *suicide. Suicidal ideation is commonly associated with *depression and *bipolar disorder. Thoughts may include a formulated plan, though most individuals experiencing suicidal ideation do not go on to commit suicide. Suicidal ideation is often accompanied by other symptoms such as insomnia, severe *anxiety, feelings of hopelessness, difficulty concentrating, and panic attacks.

suicide The deliberate act of causing one's own death. Many factors can contribute to the act of suicide, including feelings of despair, *depression, hopelessness, *alcoholism, substance misuse, overwhelming financial difficulties, and difficulties in coping with interpersonal relationships. Suicide rates have been rising and men are three times more likely than women to take their own lives. It is the main cause of premature death in people with a mental disorder. *Schizophrenia, depression, and *bipolar disorder are associated with the highest *risk of suicide overall. In *psychiatry, suicide *risk assessments are undertaken in clinical interviews and a variety of rating scales are used. This process also includes an exploration of an individual's feelings. In mental health practice, the *Care Programme Approach provides a framework for suicide risk assessment in the *community, though risk may need to be regularly reviewed to monitor changes in the person's mental well-being. Some physical health conditions are also associated with a higher risk, such as heart disease, cancer, visual impairment, and some neurological disorders. Suicide has become a major public health concern in recent years.

supervised after-care (mental health) *See* COMMUNITY TREATMENT ORDER.

supervised community treatment (SCT) (mental health) A term that, although it is not present in the Mental Health Act (2007), was used in the Explanatory Notes to the Act and in the original accompanying Code of Practice to refer to the *Community Treatment Order provisions in Sections 17A—G of the Act. The current Code of Practice (2016) now uses the term Community Treatment Order in place of SCT.

supervised contact *See* CONTACT.

supervised discharge (mental health) *See* COMMUNITY TREATMENT ORDER.

supervision In general terms the overseeing of one person's work (or other activities; *see* SUPERVISION ORDER) by another person. In social work it has a particular connotation as an ongoing supervisory relationship, between a social work student and practice assessor during training and after qualification between a social worker and her/his line manager, that involves setting time aside to discuss work without interruption. Alfred Kadushin's identification of the three functions of supervision has been widely used to describe the content of such supervision sessions: *administrative*—the promotion of good standards of work, coordination of practice with agency policies, maintaining an efficient work setting; *educational*—the professional development of each social worker; *supportive*—the provision of personal support and the maintenance of harmonious working relationships. Many view the development of *performance management as undermining the capacity of supervision to balance these three functions as the administrative function has become more managerial and has predominated in connection with the pursuit of targets and ensuring the throughput of work.

Further reading: Kadushin, A. and Harkness, D. (2014, 5th edn.) *Supervision in Social Work*, Columbia University Press.
Wonnacott, J. (2012) *Mastering Social Work Supervision*, Jessica Kingsley Publishers.

Supervision Order (children) Made under Section 35 of the Children Act (1989) by a court if it is satisfied that a child is suffering or likely to suffer *significant harm, and the harm is attributable to the care given to or withheld from the child, or the child is beyond parental control. Under this provision a designated *local authority is required to advise, assist, and befriend the supervised child. Distinguished from a *Care Order because it does not confer *parental responsibility for the child on the local authority. *See also* FAMILY COURTS; PARAMOUNTCY PRINCIPLE; PUBLIC LAW OUTLINE; SAFEGUARDING CHILDREN; WELFARE CHECKLIST.

Supervision Order (mental health) If someone is found not guilty of a crime by reason of insanity, a court can make a Supervision Order. This requires the person to be under the supervision of a *local authority social worker or probation officer for the period specified in the Order (up to two years). An Order may require the supervised person to submit, during the whole of the period or part of it as specified in the Order, to treatment by or under the direction of a registered medical practitioner (Criminal Procedure [Insanity] Act [1964] Schedule 1A).

supervisory body *See* DEPRIVATION OF LIBERTY SAFEGUARDS.

support plan (carers) *See* CARE AND SUPPORT PLAN.

Supporting People A government-funded programme, introduced by *New Labour in 2003, that unified a number of funding streams in order to provide accommodation-related support services. The programme covers different groups such as *older people in *sheltered accommodation or living in their own homes, women who have left their homes because of *domestic violence, young people who are *homeless, and people with mental health problems. *Local authority Supporting People teams are responsible, in *partnership with others from the *voluntary and *private sectors, for developing strategy and services in their areas. Some services provide accommodation while support is being given, such as domestic abuse *refuges, homeless hostels, and supported housing projects. For people who already have a home that suits their needs, but who need accommodation-related assistance, there are services that provide support where people already live. Most significant in this regard are 'floating support services' that visit people's homes. This may be to stop people losing a tenancy, provide assistance in understanding bills and with budgeting, or help with access to other services. Community alarm services are also usually available as well as *home improvement schemes. Supporting People does not offer care services. The programme only covers accommodation-related support.

Supreme Court The highest court in the UK legal system. It takes appeals on criminal law from England, *Wales, and *Northern Ireland, and on *civil law from the whole of the UK. The Supreme Court replaced the Law Lords in the House of Lords in 2009, following the implementation of the Constitutional Reform Act (2005).

Sure Start A programme, introduced by *New Labour (1997–2010), with the stated intention of delivering the best start in life for every child by bringing together early education, child care, health, and family support. It initially covered a wide range of service provision, both universal and targeted at particular local areas or *disadvantaged groups within England, with slightly different versions in *Northern Ireland, *Scotland, and *Wales. This included the establishment of *children's centres. Sure Start's geographical coverage and the range of services it provides have shrunk in the context of *austerity. *See also* EARLY INTERVENTION; EARLY YEARS FOUNDATION STAGE; EARLY YEARS SERVICES; EVERY CHILD MATTERS; EXTENDED SERVICES; FAMILY INFORMATION SERVICE; HOME START; PREVENTION; UNDER-FIVES PROVISION.

survivor Used by some people and some services in preference to 'victim', for example, to refer to women who have been sexually assaulted or who have experienced *domestic violence, or people who have been inpatients in psychiatric units. Unlike 'victim', which conveys a picture of someone who is powerless and passive, survivor implies someone who has had the strength to come through a terrible experience and who is, therefore, deserving of respect.

symptom Within the *medical model, a sensation experienced by a patient that is described to the doctor, who then makes a *diagnosis based on her/his clinical knowledge and judgement concerning the evidence of a physical or *mental illness that the symptom is most likely to indicate. Symptoms are sometimes referred to in combination with signs, as in 'signs and symptoms'. Signs refer to the objective evidence of the existence of a disease, for instance a rash, where the reported symptom is itching.

systematic review (systematic literature review) Provides an overview of a particular field or issue by bringing together information from the literature relating to it. The review should indicate: what question(s) the review was trying to answer; the criteria used to decide which literature to include; how the search for the literature was carried out; the criteria used to judge the quality of the literature; and the *outcomes and how they relate to the question(s). The *Social Care Institute of Excellence provides systematic reviews on a range of social work topics.

systems approach (systems perspective, systems theory) An influential approach in the 1970s, still encountered in social work education, that was imported from the US. It located social work, social workers, and *service users in a wider social context. The text that had the most impact was Allen Pincus and Anne Minahan's *Social Work Practice: Model and Method* (1973). In it they constructed a conceptual framework for social work consisting of four systems: the client system (individuals, groups, families, communities seeking assistance); the change agent system (social workers and the organizations within which they work); the target system (the focus of the change agent system's efforts); and the action system (the system with which the change agent system is engaged to achieve its objectives). The popularity of the systems approach can be seen as a response to two parallel developments. First, social work organizations were increasing in size, and both they and their activities lent themselves to a broader framework of analysis. For example, the popularity of the systems approach coincided with the establishment of *Social Services Departments. Secondly, social work methods were becoming increasingly compartmentalized into fields of practice concerned with work with individuals, *group work, and *community work. The systems approach was capable of encompassing all of these methods because it was concerned with individual, group, *community, and societal systems, and their functioning. Thus, it was not only a broader framework of analysis but also a more coherent one, often referred to as integrated and/or unitary by its proponents.

Three main criticisms were raised against the systems approach. First, it often merely described existing work in new terms, producing little of value. For example, if a social worker (as the change agent system) was engaged in psychodynamic casework with an individual *service user, that service user was simultaneously the client, target, and action systems. Secondly, it offered no basis on which to choose particular methods of work, allowing anything to be undertaken within its framework. Thirdly, it tended to be pragmatic in seeking to make connections between systems and achieve their effective functioning, assuming that systems were just there, with no analysis of the political, economic, and social factors that shaped them, though there were isolated examples of *radical social work writers identifying ways in which they thought the systems approach might be adapted for use in conjunction with more critical perspectives. Perhaps the most significant example of the impact of the systems approach on UK practice is to be found in *systems management.

systems management Particularly during the 1980s and 1990s, this strategic development was very influential in the *youth justice system. It involved applying the thinking behind the *systems approach to the operation of youth justice, with the objectives of reducing the use of custodial sentences for those already in the system and keeping as many young people as possible out of the system. Detailed monitoring of trends and processes was undertaken and inter-professional cooperation was strengthened. Mechanisms were set up to divert young people from the system at an early stage. *See also* DEVIANCE; DIVERSION; LABELLING; MINIMUM INTERVENTION.

S

tacit knowledge (tacit understanding) The routine, taken-for-granted, and usually unquestioned knowledge that people use in their everyday lives and in specific contexts within them, which gives a sense of coherence, for example, the tacit knowledge that social workers draw on to guide how they carry out social work. *See also* HEGEMONY; PRACTICE WISDOM.

tagging *See* ELECTRONIC TAGGING.

take-up rate The number of people receiving a particular social security benefit compared with the number of people who are eligible to receive it.

tardive dyskinesia *See* DEPOT MEDICATION.

target culture *See* MANAGERIAL CYBERNETICS; PERFORMANCE MANAGEMENT.

target duty A requirement on a public body that is created by statute and framed in general terms. Many legal duties require public bodies, such as *local authorities, to provide services or act in a particular way towards groups or individuals and if they fail to do so, a group or individual affected can enforce their rights through the courts (*see* DUTY [SPECIFIC]). In contrast, target duties are aspirational in nature and the duty placed upon the public body is to attempt to carry out the duty. An example of a target duty in relation to adults' services is Section 1 of the Care Act (2014), which states that a local authority has a general duty to promote an individual's wellbeing. In children's services, Section 17 of the Children Act (1989) provides an example. It states that it is the general duty of every local authority to safeguard and promote the welfare of children within their area who are in *need and, so far as is consistent with that duty, to promote the upbringing of such children by their families by providing a range and level of services appropriate to those children's needs. A local authority, as a public body, has latitude in deciding the extent to which it will carry out target duties such as these. It may take into account its financial and other resources provided it also considers the consequences of not carrying out the duty. Essentially, despite the latitude, it must act reasonably (*R v London Borough of Barnet ex parte G[FC]* 2003). Thus there is recognition that there may be good reason why a public body is unable to meet a target duty. If the public body does not fulfil a target duty, generally speaking an individual who is affected by that failure is not entitled to enforce the duty through the courts. *See also* DISCRETION (LOCAL AUTHORITY); FETTERING DISCRETION; REASONABLENESS; RELEVANT FACTORS; RIGID POLICIES.

targeting (services) Selecting and defining the types of need and situations, which are likely to result in services being provided, for example in the case of adult service users through the application of *eligibility criteria.

targets *See* MANAGERIAL CYBERNETICS; PERFORMANCE MANAGEMENT.

tariff The scale of sentences in the *youth justice system and the expectation of the points on the scale that will be used for particular sorts of crimes, taking into account offenders' previous criminal records.

task-centred approach (task-centred casework, task-centred method) A structured and time-limited approach, initially formulated by Reid and Epstein (*Task-centred Casework* 1972), that is focused on the present and based on working in *partnership with the *service user. It begins by considering the areas the service user regards as problematic. The service user is closely involved in selecting the problems to be addressed, prioritizing goals in seeking to resolve the selected problems, setting tasks in order to reach the chosen *goals, and reviewing progress. It aims to develop the ability of the service user to resolve her/his own difficulties, developing her/his knowledge, confidence, and skills in problem-solving by agreeing tasks that are carefully graded and achievable. Not every piece of work involving tasks to be accomplished means that a task-centred approach has been, or should be, used. It also needs to be used critically, taking account of issues that the method may not adequately address. For example, a task-centred approach may ignore issues of an emotional/psychological nature in favour of a focus on concrete tasks with more easily measurable outcomes. The focus on the latter can also lead to lack of attention to wider structural or *diversity issues that are less easily addressed through specific tasks. *See also* BRIEF INTERVENTION; CONSTRUCTIVE SOCIAL WORK; SOLUTION-FOCUSED THERAPY; STRENGTHS PERSPECTIVE.

Further reading: Marsh, P. and Doel, M. (2005) *The Task-centred Book*, Routledge.

team Once seen as the core *collective unit for the delivery of social work in response to the *needs of a defined local geographical area. The team has increasingly less significance with the development of function-based specialisms, offices with large staff groups serving much bigger geographical areas, and social workers working individually from home. *See also* AREA TEAMS; BARCLAY REPORT; COMMUNITY SOCIAL WORK; DECENTRALIZATION; NEIGHBOURHOOD SOCIAL WORK; PATCH-BASED SOCIAL WORK; SOCIAL SERVICES DEPARTMENT.

team around the child A range of different practitioners coming together to help and support an individual child. This is not a multidisciplinary team that is located together or that works together all the time. It is a group of professionals working together only when necessary to help one particular child. *See also* COLLABORATIVE WORKING.

technologies of the self The techniques and interventions for managing behaviour and thinking that discipline people and render them governable. Practitioners, such as social workers, apply these techniques to others, but citizens also govern themselves through self-regulation by using technologies of the self. Such self- and practitioner-assisted surveillance, geared to her/his compliance with the social order, renders direct coercion of the citizen unnecessary. *See also* DISCOURSE; GAZE; GOVERNMENTALITY.

technology *See* CALL CENTRE; COMPUTERIZATION; TELECARE.

teenage pregnancy A pregnancy occurring before someone's eighteenth birthday. Most young women in this situation will not have completed their secondary education and are likely to be financially dependent on their parents or *care-givers.

In 1999, the New Labour government pledged to halve these pregnancies by 2010 but this proved difficult to achieve despite a national teenage pregnancy strategy being put in place. This strategy, linked to the *Every Child Matters* agenda, aimed not only to reduce the under-18 conception rate, but also to increase the proportion of teenage parents in education, training, or employment to reduce their *risk of long-term *social exclusion. Among the components of the strategy was the provision of sexual advice services and youth services in local areas but this suffered dramatically following extensive cuts to the youth service by the Conservative-Liberal Democrat Coalition government elected in 2010. *See also* ADOLESCENCE; FRASER GUIDELINES; GILLICK COMPETENCY.

telecare The use of technology in supporting people to live at home. Telecare equipment and services include community alarm systems that act as emergency response mechanisms; sensors in the home to detect and monitor movement; devices to detect falls, fire, or gas, and trigger a warning at a response centre; lifestyle monitoring systems that provide warning of a change or deterioration in an individual's normal pattern of behaviour; and telemedicine that monitors vital signs such as blood pressure and transmits the information to a response centre. These mechanisms have been combined in smart homes that have small computers positioned around the house, enabling systems and devices to communicate with each other. For example, it is possible to dial into a smart house from outside so that lights and heating can be turned on in advance of returning home; smoke detectors can automatically trigger a call to the fire brigade; a motion detector can automatically turn on lights for someone who gets up in the night; and in the morning, a single switch can turn on lights, draw back curtains, and run a bath. Telecare is seen as having the potential to:

• Reduce the need for residential and nursing care.
• Reduce acute hospital admissions.
• Reduce accidents and *falls that occur in the home.
• Contribute to *preventive services.
• Provide support to people who wish to die at home.
• Increase *service users' *independence and choice.
• Give more relief and freedom to *carers.

Telecare has been used predominantly with *older people who may feel more secure if they know monitoring systems are in place. The availability of systems to respond to difficulties if they arise through the triggering of alarms may enable older people to live their lives more freely, without worrying so much about *risks, and they may feel more independent if they are managing with less direct assistance from others. However, they may find telecare systems intrusive, both into their personal privacy and their home environment. *Carers may feel reassured that there is a way of keeping an eye on things when no-one is with the older person and this may give them times when they are freed up to do other things. However, both carers and older people may be concerned about the decrease in human contact that such systems encourage. *Local authorities, as funders of services, often see telecare as a cost-effective option that has beneficial *outcomes for older people. Although there are initial outlay costs for telecare, the ongoing running costs are likely to be low compared with the staffing costs involved in *domiciliary services. Providers of services might be concerned that telecare will enable funders of services to cut back on contracts with them for the purchase of services involving direct assistance from paid carers.

The Department of Health commissioned a study on the effectiveness of telecare. The Whole System Demonstrator Project reported in 2013 on its research into the experiences of 2,600 people from over 200 *general practitioner practices in three local authority areas who had been randomly allocated into two groups, one that received telecare as well as 'traditional' care and one that received 'traditional' care without telecare. These two groups were followed up after twelve months to find out if telecare produced better outcomes for those who received it. No statistically significant differences were found between the two groups in terms of mortality, proportions admitted to permanent residential or nursing care, number of weeks over which domiciliary social care was provided, number of inpatient hospital admissions, length of inpatient hospital stays, the number of contacts with *general practitioners or the costs met by hospitals, social care services, and general practices. By the time the findings were published, many local authorities had already invested heavily in telecare, believing that it offered better and more cost-effective outcomes, and significant investments in telecare continue to be made. *See also* AIDS AND ADAPTATIONS; ASSISTIVE TECHNOLOGY.

Further reading: Department of Health (2005) *Building Telecare in England*. Available at: http://webarchive.nationalarchives.gov.uk/+/http://dh.gov.uk/prod_consum_dh/groups/ dh_digitalassets/@dh/@en/documents/digitalasset/dh_4115644.pdf.
Loader, B., Hardey, M. and Keeble, L. (2009) *Digital Welfare for the Third Age: Health and Social Care Informatics for Older People*, Routledge.
Poole, T. (2006) *Telecare and Older People*, King's Fund.

terminal care *See* PALLIATIVE CARE.

termination *See* ABORTION.

Thatcherism *See* NEW RIGHT.

theories of ageing These perspectives can be grouped together in terms of whether they focus mainly on the individual, the economic and social structure or subjectivity and meaning.

Focus on the individual

Biological theories seek to understand the process of ageing in terms of biological and physiological changes that occur as people grow older. Biological theories include those that view ageing as a result of harmful environmental influences or internal defects, and those that view it as an inevitable pre-programmed developmental deterioration. Biological theories adopt a predominantly negative view of ageing as a time of *loss of function and decline and, though individualistic in emphasis, offer universalistic explanations that often fail to take account of individual *differences and social, cultural, and environmental influences, marginalizing individuals' experience of the process of ageing and ways in which they adapt to physical changes. Because of their status as 'scientific', biological theories have been very influential in shaping attitudes and beliefs about ageing. In particular, biological theories of ageing have contributed to negative cultural attitudes towards *older people through the association of ageing with frailty and incapacity. These negative constructions also impact on the attitudes and self-perception of *older people themselves. Signs of physical ageing become something to be feared or disguised, or are accepted as part of an 'aged' *identity but with negative implications for the self. Another facet of biological understandings is that passive acceptance of the 'problems' of ageing is legitimated. Thus, professionals, *carers, and older people themselves may 'explain' problems such as

Life stage	Conflict	Ego functioning
Infancy	Basic trust/mistrust	Hope
Childhood (1)	Autonomy/doubt	Will
Childhood (2)	Initiative/doubt	Purpose
Childhood (3)	Industry/inferiority	Competence
Adolescence	Ego identity/role confusion	Fidelity
Young adulthood	Intimacy/role confusion	Love
Adulthood	Generativity/stagnation	Care
Old age	Integrity/despair	Wisdom

Erikson's developmental stages

memory loss, incontinence, or declining mobility in terms of 'it's just his/her/my age', thereby excluding the possibility of *interventions that may treat or alleviate the difficulties.

Erikson's psychological theory sees *personality as developing across the life span and distinguishes eight stages. Each stage is seen as characterized by a particular psychological conflict that has to be negotiated. Depending on how the conflict is resolved, a particular quality of ego functioning is developed in each stage. The stages are interrelated in that how conflicts are resolved at each developmental stage has implications for the subsequent stages.

The conflict to be negotiated in later life is between integrity and despair. To achieve ego integrity, an individual reaches an acceptance of the life lived, a sense of 'keeping things together', and a feeling that the life lived has coherence. There is an acceptance of past *losses and failures, and a feeling that there are no 'loose ends'. In contrast, a state of despair results from regret about unresolved issues, feelings of discontinuity, and a fear of death. Satisfactory resolution of the conflict between integrity and despair results in the ego quality of wisdom that may be passed on to other generations.

Erikson's developmental theory connects later life with the rest of the life course and, unlike many previous psychological theories, acknowledges that learning and development are not confined to childhood but also feature in later life. However, a number of criticisms have been made of his life cycle model. First, it is seen as Western-centric, accepting uncritically the cultural norms of society at the time (the US in the 1950s). It takes as 'normal' and generalizes from conventional expectations about life stage progression. Departure from these expectations is not seen as reflecting *diversity in terms of behaviours that are different but of equal value, but rather as representing unresolved conflicts that have negative consequences for later development. Secondly, while Erikson's model is based on traditional expectations about progression through particular life stages, there is now enormous diversity in terms of the stages in the life course at which various life events or experiences occur. For example, people may have children, develop new relationships, or return to education in later life. Erikson's model fixes aspects of development in particular stages rather than allowing for multiple developmental pathways, with various conflicts and challenges arising or resurfacing at different stages. *Identity issues, for example, are not only encountered in *adolescence but may recur in later life through experiences such as unemployment and *divorce. Erikson's theorizing also remains essentially child-centred, with interest in the final two life stages being more concerned with the conditions for successfully raising children, namely passing on care and wisdom, than with understanding the subjective experiences of adulthood and later life.

Activity theory is based on the notion that continued involvement in social roles, relationships, and activities can enhance wellbeing in later life. Although activity theory predated disengagement theory (see below), it was developed further in efforts to repudiate disengagement theory. The dimensions important for quality of later life are seen as the same as those for earlier in the *life course, in contrast with disengagement theory, where later life is seen as a distinct phase, with different requirements. Both theories are, however, based on a consensual view of society. In activity theory, it is assumed that society's need for active and hard-working citizens is matched by the needs and wishes of older people to remain active. Whereas there is limited *empirical support for disengagement theory, activity theory is consistent with research evidence that suggests that older people do strive to maintain personal interests, activities, and relationships. Not only is this what many older people want, there is also evidence that social activity plays an important role in sustaining their wellbeing.

Whereas disengagement theory legitimates not responding or responding negatively to difficulties in retaining activities, roles, and relationships, activity theory can promote positive *intervention, including with older people traditionally seen as incapable of participating in social activity. In work with people with *dementia, for example, occupation is seen as an important dimension for retaining *personhood. A review of research on *rehabilitation and dementia notes that activities can improve communication and mental and emotional wellbeing, if activities are selected and adapted to accommodate someone's level of cognitive impairment. However, activity theory does have potential pitfalls. Older people want and benefit from continued engagement not in any activity, but in social activities that are personally meaningful and rewarding to them. The whole notion of 'activity' is more complex than its presentation in activity theory. We need to allow for the *diversity of meanings that activity may have for older people; for example, older people may interpret it to include activities such as taking naps, watching television, gambling, and day-dreaming.

Both disengagement and activity theories are prescriptive in that they are putting forwards a view about how older people *should* behave. Establishing a direct causal relationship between activity and older people's wellbeing is problematic. Indeed, one study suggests it is the social relationships as an intrinsic part of most activities that are the significant factor in promoting wellbeing, rather than activity itself.

Continuity theory asserts that older people manage changes and choices by seeking to preserve both internal continuity, that is, continuity of ideas, preferences, skills, etc., and external continuity, that is, continuity of their physical and social environment. While continuity theory has been criticized by those who argue that later life is characterized by constant change and fluidity, its supporters have argued that continuity does not necessarily mean that things remain exactly the same but rather that change is negotiated within an overall framework of continuity that connects the individual with her/his past life. This is supported by longitudinal research, which found continuity in the life themes of people over the age of 80, with family relationships being the themes' main sources. Research has also demonstrated the importance to older people of maintaining habits and routines, and the significance of continuity of the physical environment of home and locality. However, while there is empirical support for some aspects of continuity theory, it tends to attribute problems encountered to individual deficits rather than social factors. For example, if people cannot meet their own needs because they are disabled or poor, some writers see this as 'pathological ageing'. Similarly, continuity has been seen as maladaptive when someone lacks the physical or mental capacities that are necessary to retain continuity. The assumption is that it is the functioning of individuals that is pathological or maladaptive, rather than that environmental barriers are preventing older people from realizing their aspirations. (*See* SOCIAL MODEL OF DISABILITY.)

Focus on the economic and social structure
Disengagement theory was developed in the US in the late 1950s and published in the early 1960s by Cumming and Henry. As in Erikson's model, old age is understood in the context of an 'end of life' stage; while for Erikson this is about tying up loose ends, for Cumming and Henry it is about social withdrawal. Disengagement theory links the needs of ageing individuals with the needs of the social system, seeing the two as compatible. Older people are seen as disengaging from social roles and relationships in a process that is 'natural' and beneficial for them, releasing them from social expectations, and this process is regarded as of equal value for society, freeing up opportunities for younger people. Ageing is represented as a process involving mutual disengagement between the older person and others. Thus disengagement is presented as an inevitable, central, and universal aspect of ageing, seen from the perspective of a consensual view of society. This theory has been subject to substantial criticism on a number of counts.

First, it conveys an uncritically negative view of old age as a time of stagnation and withdrawal. Secondly, the theory is contradicted by research findings that reveal high levels of activity and engagement amongst many older people. While there may be some loss of social roles and activities, new roles and activities can take their place; there can be a process of reorientation or accommodation, instead of disengagement. Rather than disengagement being inevitable, cross-cultural studies show that in many developing countries older people retain a very active role in their *communities. Thirdly, it is assumed that disengagement is a positive choice for older people and this is contradicted by the evidence. Being able to engage in hobbies and activities is an important dimension of quality of life, as defined by older people. Rather than disengagement being a positive *choice, social, economic, and political processes mean that in many cases older people have no option but to disengage. There is evidence to suggest that those who do choose to disengage in later life are those inclined by personality to more socially isolated lifestyles. Fourthly, disengagement theory suggests that in later life the needs and wishes of older people take a different turn and are distinct from their expectations and requirements earlier in the life course. Again, this is not supported by research evidence. Finally, the theory can be criticized for its negative implications for policy and practice. Through portraying disengagement as a beneficial and inevitable process, the *marginalization of older people, for example, through retirement policies, segregated accommodation, and 'closed off' forms of *residential care, is justified. However, on a more positive note, it has been argued that while there has been little support for disengagement theory itself, it has been of value in stimulating debate and theorizing that offer alternative perspectives.

Structured dependency (or **political economy**) **theory**'s main emphasis is that social and economic conditions create conditions of *dependency in older people (*see also* SOCIAL MODEL OF DISABILITY.) The focus is shifted from biological/ individual to social/structural determinants of ageing. Instead of seeing older people as a homogeneous group, the focus is on the differential experience of ageing according to social *class, *ethnicity, and the role played by social policy in contributing to the dependent status of older people. Attention is drawn to compulsory retirement policies that exclude older people from the labour market, pensions policies that relegate older people to lives of *poverty, and, when they can no longer survive these conditions, to institutional care that segregates and isolates them, creating further dependency.

A criticism of structured dependency theory is that, at least in earlier versions, the emphasis placed on the significance of employment and pensions policies was more relevant to the situations of older men than older women. Structured dependency theory has also been criticized for being too deterministic and not allowing enough scope for the individual and collective agency of older people in challenging and resisting oppressive policies and conditions. For example, some older people take an active role in saving and planning for their future to avoid reliance on a state pension. Also, retirement and residential care may be positive choices for some older people, rather than outcomes foisted upon them. In other words, it is important to see older people as having the potential to be active agents, rather than simply seeing them as passive victims. Linked with this, it is also argued that structured dependency theory pays insufficient attention to how individuals interpret and give meaning to their situations. For example, there is no direct correlation between objective and subjective assessments of quality of life. Individuals in adverse social conditions may evaluate their lives and situations positively and vice versa. For example, 'old older people' have been noted to reconstruct their situations in order to maintain a positive outlook. It has been argued that is not enough, therefore, to adopt a structural model to understand the experience of ageing; the individual meaning of ageing and subjective factors should also be included.

Focus on subjectivity

Life course theory's approach to ageing draws attention to the connections between an individual's past life, her/his life as currently lived, and her/his aspirations for the future. The emphasis is not so much on preserving continuity as a way of managing the ageing process, but rather on understanding experiences of ageing within the context of the *life course as a whole. This perspective is based on the premise that experiences of ageing can only be understood in the context of the whole life course because the life that has been lived gives meaning to old age. Life course theories do not represent the life course as a series of fixed stages, as in Erikson's view, but as characterized by changing and diverse processes. In terms of the implications of this perspective, it highlights the significance of understanding an older person's past life in order to understand their current needs and plan appropriate service provision. While there is a danger of insufficient attention being given to the significance of social, economic, and political factors in shaping life experiences, it is possible to adopt a life course perspective and take account of ways in which a life course has been moulded by structural factors.

Identity management theory is a theoretical perspective based on a *postmodernist understanding of society as complex, rapidly changing, and allowing multiple opportunities for individuals to construct and reconstruct identities of their choice through *consumerism. *Identity is viewed as fluid, rather than fixed, and individ-uals are seen as exercising agency in responding to changing social situations and conditions by making particular lifestyle choices. There is recognition that the body places restrictions on the ability of individuals to choose their identity; in later life, the self cannot entirely escape the constraints imposed by an ageing body. There are different views about the nature of the tensions between self, body, and social responses, and about how these tensions are managed. One view is that a self perceived as youthful is trapped inside an ageing body; society responds to the individual in terms of the visible aged body, or 'mask of ageing', creating tension for the inner youthful self. An alternative view is that in later life the individual is forced to deny their experience of an ageing self, and instead present a youthful façade or masquerade, because the social space is hostile to and rejects ageing. These two interpretations of how identity is managed in later life suggest different social responses. While the 'mask of ageing' indicates the need to recognize the older person's youthful inner self and help them to express this, 'masquerade' suggests the need to create social environments that are accepting and supportive of the ageing self. These understandings and interventions are not, of course, mutually exclusive. The focus on individual agency in these perspectives can underplay the significance of constraints on choice arising from structural factors, such as restricted access to resources and opportunities. However, it has been argued that in emphasizing the fluidity and individuality of experiences of ageing, these theories allow for multiple layers of diversity. Identity management theories also make a valuable contribution in recognizing the ways in which the ageing body constrains individual subjectivity and triggers negative social responses.

Further reading: Tanner, D. and Harris, J. (2008) *Working with Older People*, Ch. 1, Routledge.

theory (theory and practice) A set of ideas that explains why something has occurred and/or predicts when and how something may occur in the future. Traditionally, it has been seen as the product of scientific knowledge and associated with objectivity, rationality, neutrality, and detachment. However, Kuhn (*The Structure of Scientific Revolutions*, 1970), amongst others, has argued that the processes by which certain sets of ideas come to be seen as legitimate are located within particular historical and social contexts, and these processes are embedded in networks of interests and relations of power.

The relationship between theory and practice in social work is often regarded as fraught, with the application of theory to practice seen as problematic. This often stems from a view that theory is supposed to be taken from a textbook and applied to practice in a straightforward way. Then, if theory does not fit practice, it is tempting to conclude that either theory is irrelevant to practice or that it has been understood inadequately. However, theory cannot provide simple answers that tell us 'how to do' practice in the same way that a recipe tells us how to cook a particular dish. Theory can only guide and inform. In addition, the relationship between theory and practice is often thought of as a one-way relationship in which theory informs practice. However, practice can generate, challenge, develop, and transform theory so rather than thinking in terms of the application of theory to practice, theory and practice can be seen as influencing each other. Theories, as sources of knowledge and under-standing, need to be shaped in relation to a particular situation and the ideas from theory need to be adapted and developed as they are used in practice.

*Postmodernism has criticized the privileging of certain sorts of knowledge, high-lighting the relationship between knowledge and power. It argues that power rela-tions influence what is defined through language as knowledge and, therefore, the particular frameworks that are used for understanding and explaining situations. From this perspective, knowledge is not just the theory contained in textbooks but consists of many different types and sources of knowledge put forward by a wide range of people who would like to see their ideas used to make sense of the world around them. Thus those on the receiving end of what we traditionally think of as theories can resist them, reformulate them, or come up with theories of their own.

Further reading: Healy, K. (2014, 2nd edn.) *Social Work Theories in Context: Creating Frameworks for Practice*, Palgrave Macmillan.

therapeutic community A residential setting involving use of the group as the therapeutic resource in which residents are actively and continuously involved in their own therapy, and the power differential between staff and residents is reduced, though sometimes this can mask the operation of power in more subtle ways. There are regular *group meetings in which the interaction in the group is discussed and analysed.

Think Ahead A fast-track social work qualification scheme for graduates who wish to specialize in mental health. Participants undertake a year-long placement in a mental health setting, interspersed with taught days and a short contrasting learning experience with children. They qualify as social workers after year one and work towards completing their *Assessed and Supported Year in Employment and a master's degree in the second year of the programme. Participants are assessed and mentored by an experienced 'Consultant Social Worker'.

third sector *Collective classification for organizations that are not part of the state and are not in the business of making profits. The sector includes *voluntary organizations, *community groups, cooperatives, social enterprises, and not-for-profit organizations. New Labour (1997–2010), Conservative–Liberal Democrat Coalition (2010–15), and Conservative governments (2015–) have all extolled the value of the third sector and its contribution to *civil society. It has played an increasing role in service provision.

Third Way A key set of ideas when New Labour governments were in office (1997–2010) that were meant to capture the ideological indifference of *New Labour, as it steered a middle course, distanced from 'Old Labour' and the *New Right. However, there were substantial areas of overlap between the Conservative governments of the previous eighteen years and New Labour in terms of the primacy accorded to globalization, the restructuring of the economy, and society in response to its impact and the changes required in established practices and ways of working as a basis for capitalism's future prosperity, in particular the imperative towards low costs and highly flexible forms of working. Four shared themes were: the primacy of economic competitiveness; the subordination of social policy to the needs of a competitive national economy; the limited or reduced scope envisaged for government intervention or direction; and a central concern with control over public expenditure. New Labour stressed that priority needed to be given to economic performance, growth, and low inflation. Within the Third Way, the role of social policy was delineated as follows:

- Social policy should function for capital. The state should promote permanent innovation and flexibility in a relatively open economy and seek to use social policy to strengthen economic competitiveness.

- Social policy should be subordinated to the demands of labour market flexibility and economic competitiveness.
- In social policy, increasing importance should be attached to non-state mechanisms compensating for *market failures and delivering state-sponsored policies.

The Third Way was strongly influenced by the *reflexive modernization theses of Beck (*The Risk Society* 1992) and especially Giddens (*Beyond Left and Right: The Future of Radical Politics* 1994). These theses suggested that new political responses were needed to meet the challenges posed not only by globalization, but also by social reflexivity, detraditionalization, and a heightened sense of *risk in the late modern world. The theses asserted that these forces undermined the social demo-cratic *welfare state, as traditional *class identities dissolved and there were changes in the labour market, *gender relations, and *household forms. In the Third Way politics and policies of New Labour, the influence of these theses can be seen in the stress on self-conscious citizens, who were depicted as concerned with *consumer-ism and the market, with *identity, and with 'life politics'. *See also* IDENTITY POLITICS.

Further reading: Harris, J. (2003) *The Social Work Business*, Ch. 5, Routledge.

thought disorder In *psychiatry this refers to a disturbance of speech, commu-nication, or thought content and is often a symptom of *psychosis. The concept is not straightforward as the disorder is inferred from disordered speech or, more rarely, writing, giving rise to the assumption of underlying problems with thought processes. Many symptoms of thought disorder, therefore, refer to disorganized speech. Common terms in mental health practice include pressure of speech, which refers to speaking quickly and incessantly, often associated with mania; flight of ideas, which refers to switching topic in mid-sentence; thought-blocking, which refers to a sudden cessation of speech that recommences later or is replaced by an entirely different topic; retardation of thought, which is opposite in form to pressure of speech, and refers to thoughts appearing to be slow, often a symptom of *depression; and poverty of thought, which refers to a sudden interruption in spontaneous speech, perceived to represent an absence or deprivation of thought. There are many other manifestations of thought disorder. Thought disorders are particularly associated with *schizophrenia, *dementia, and mania. Disordered thinking is fundamental to the clinical *diagnosis of *schizophrenia and is a key feature in the *mental state examination. Evidence of thought disorder is sometimes associated with *delusions and some view delusions themselves as another mani-festation of thought disorder. There is a clinical distinction present in respect of the manifestation of thought disorder in functional disorders (i.e. *mental illness) and organic disorders (for example, dementia or delirium). Mentally disordered people usually lack awareness or *insight into their disordered thinking, whereas people with organic illnesses are often aware of their disorganized thinking and may express concern about being confused or unable to think clearly.

three 'e's *See* ECONOMY, EFFICIENCY, AND EFFECTIVENESS.

threshold criteria (adults) The threshold that must be crossed in order for a *local authority to have a *duty to meet *care and support needs (or support needs of *carers) under the Care Act (2014) is set out in national *eligibility criteria. A local authority can decide to meet *needs that do not reach this threshold but this is unlikely in the context of *austerity.

threshold criteria (children) The legal test under Section 31(2) of the Children Act (1989) that must be satisfied before a court can make a *Care Order or *Supervision Order in respect of a child. A *local authority must establish that:

• The child is suffering or likely to suffer *significant harm.

It must also establish that the harm or likelihood of harm must be attributable to one of the following:

• The care being given or likely to be given by the parent(s), if the Order were not made, falls below the standard that it would be reasonable to expect a parent to give;
• The child is beyond parental control.

Even if the court decides that the local authority has demonstrated this threshold, the court does not have to make an Order. It will only do so if this is deemed to be in the *best interests of the child. Outside the court context, the term has come to assume wider and unrelated usage in situations where practitioners make decisions regarding an appropriate level of *intervention in a family or provision of a service. For example, when a *referral from another agency is received by a social worker requesting a service for a child, a decision will be made, depending on the circumstances reported, as to whether this warrants a *Section 47 enquiry or an *assessment as a potential *child in need. It may lead to a decision that none of the threshold criteria have been met, in which case the child may be referred to another agency deemed to be capable of providing a more appropriate service, or a decision may be made that no further action should be taken. *See also* CARE PROCEEDINGS; CHILD ABUSE AND NEGLECT; FAMILY COURTS; INTERIM CARE ORDER; NO ORDER PRINCIPLE; PARAMOUNTCY PRINCIPLE; PUBLIC LAW OUTLINE; WELFARE CHECKLIST.

time-out (time-out from positive reinforcement) Removing a child from a situation because of her/his behaviour and placing her/him somewhere where s/he receives no attention. *See also* BEHAVIOURISM; BEHAVIOUR MODIFICATION.

token economy (system) A form of *behaviour modification geared to increasing desired behaviour and decreasing undesirable behaviour through the use of tokens. Tokens are given immediately after someone has displayed desired behaviour. When a stipulated numbers of tokens have been collected, they can be exchanged for a reward.

Token economies are used in *institutional settings* to manage aggressive or unpredictable behaviour; *home settings* to teach desired behaviour and social skills; *education* for children with *learning disabilities, *hyperactivity attention deficit disorder, or behaviour problems; and *rehabilitation programmes*. Token economies can be used with individuals or in groups.

The key elements in a token economy are:

Tokens Commonly used items include stickers, points, or pretend money. Tokens have no value of their own. They are collected and later exchanged for rewards. Tokens can be lost for displaying undesired behaviour. Loss of tokens is sometimes referred to as 'response cost'.

Clearly defined target behaviour Desired and undesired behaviour is set out in simple specific terms. The number of tokens awarded or lost for particular behaviour is specified.

Reinforcers The rewards received in exchange for tokens, for example toys, extra free time, or trips.

System for exchanging tokens A designated time and place for purchasing reinforcers with tokens. It is seen as important to preset the value of the reinforcers carefully. If their value is set too low, people will be less motivated to earn tokens. If the value is set too high, people may become discouraged.

System for recording performance Changes in behaviour, as represented by tokens awarded, are recorded. This information is used to measure individual progress, as well as the effectiveness of the token economy. Information about the exchange of tokens is also recorded.

Consistent implementation by staff All staff have to reward the same behaviours, using the correct amount of tokens.

Initially tokens are awarded frequently and in higher amounts but as individuals learn the desired behaviour, opportunities to earn tokens decrease. (The amount and frequency of token dispensing is sometimes called a 'reinforcement schedule'.) By gradually decreasing the availability of tokens (sometimes called 'fading') people eventually learn to display the desired behaviour independently, without the use of tokens. Reinforcers that individuals would normally encounter, such as verbal praise, accompany the awarding of tokens to aid in the withdrawal of tokens.

Although the use of token economies in a home setting to encourage desired *goals may not be seen as problematic, for example when encouraging a child with learning disabilities to use the toilet, there have been concerns about the use of comprehensive token economy systems as the basis for regimes in institutional or residential settings. These include criticisms that any gains in token economy systems do not generalize to other settings; token economy systems do not focus sufficiently on individual care, support, or treatment plans; participating in a token economy system is humiliating; and token economy systems are oppressive. *See also* BEHAVIOURISM; FUNCTIONAL ANALYSIS; INSTITUTION.

tokenism *See* ARNSTEIN'S LADDER.

tolerance The body's gradual adaption to taking a drug so that increasing amounts are needed in order to gain the desired effect. *See also* ADDICTION.

top-up fees (topping-up fees) (adults) *See* CARE AND SUPPORT PLAN; CHARGING FOR SERVICES; PERSONAL BUDGET.

total institution *See* INSTITUTION.

total quality management (TQM) An influential approach, originally from the business world, which is concerned with maximizing the quality of the services provided. It involves considering four dimensions: goals, organization, processes, and people. Its dictum is 'ensuring that the right things are done right first time'. It is 'total' because it covers all aspects and activities of an organization, not just direct service delivery. There are eight principles of total quality management:

Customer-focused organization Organizations depend on their customers and therefore should understand current and future customer *needs, meet customer requirements, and strive to exceed customer expectations.

Leadership Leaders establish unity of purpose, direction, and the internal environment of the organization. They create the environment in which people can become fully involved in achieving the organization's objectives.

Involvement of people People at all levels are the essence of an organization and their full involvement enables their abilities to be used for the organization's benefit.

Process approach A desired result is achieved more efficiently when related resources and activities are managed as a process.

System approach to management Identifying, understanding, and managing a system of interrelated processes for a given objective contributes to the effectiveness and efficiency of the organization.

Continual improvement A permanent objective of an organization.

Factual approach to decision-making Effective decisions are based on the logical and intuitive analysis of data and information.

Mutually beneficial supplier relationships (between the organization and its suppliers). Enhance the ability of both to create value.

The way in which these principles are expressed is deeply influenced by the business context from which they originate, with the emphasis on increasing customers, for example. TQM has been used in the public sector in which the concern is likely be with restricting access to services by *rationing what is available, but the language and practices of TQM are not modified to reflect this very different context. TQM is assumed to be universally applicable. *See also* BUSINESS ORIENTATION; EUROPEAN FOUNDATION OF QUALITY MANAGEMENT MODEL; MANAGERIALISM; PERFORMANCE MANAGEMENT.

transformational discourse A prominent *discourse in social work and other public sector organizations that stresses the need for dismantling allegedly outdated structures and ways of thinking, and driving forwards change in order to produce organizations that are 'fit for purpose' in today's world. Advertisements for managers in social work organizations almost always represent the organizations as progressive and innovative, or as wanting to move further in that direction, with a dynamic role needing to be played by the manager appointed. The emphasis is on rapid radical change brought about by business ways of thinking and managing. *See also* BUSINESS ORIENTATION; MANAGERIALISM; TOTAL QUALITY MANAGEMENT.

transgenderism *See* GENDER DYSPHORIA.

transition assessment (transition planning) *See* TRANSITION TO ADULT CARE AND SUPPORT.

transitions *See* HUMAN DEVELOPMENT.

transition to adult care and support The process that supports young people (and their families) to move from services they have received as a child to those that they need when they become an adult.

The Care Act (2014) contains provisions to help with preparation for adulthood for three particular groups of people: children, *young carers (*see also* ASSESSMENT [CHILDREN]), and children's *carers. In the context of transition *assessment and planning, a *child* is a young person in their teenage years preparing for adult life, a *young carer* is someone under 18 who is caring for an adult while preparing for adulthood themselves, and a *child's carer* is an adult carer of a child preparing for adulthood. Each group has its own specific transition assessment: a child's needs assessment, a young carer's assessment, and a child's carer's assessment. (Here 'transition assessment' is used for all three.)

The Care Act (2014) places a *duty on a *local authority to assess a child, young carer, or a child's carer before they turn 18 in order to help them plan, if they are likely to have *needs once they (or the child they care for) turn 18 and if it will be of 'significant benefit'. The consideration of 'significant benefit' is not related to the level of a young person's or carer's needs, but rather to the timing of the transition assessment. The point at which a transition assessment will be likely to be of significant benefit will be when needs for care and support as an adult can be predicted reasonably confidently but may also depend on other factors including (but not limited to):

- the stage the young person has reached at school and any upcoming exams;
- whether the young person or carer wishes to enter further/higher education or training;
- whether the young person or carer wishes to get a job when they become an adult;
- whether the young person is planning to move out of their parental home into their own accommodation;
- whether the young person will have care leaver status when they become 18;
- whether the carer of a young person wishes to remain in or return to employment when the young person leaves full-time education;
- the time it may take to carry out an assessment;
- the time it may take to plan and put in place adult *care and support;
- any relevant family circumstances;
- any planned medical treatment.

The duty to conduct a transition assessment applies when someone is likely to have needs for care and support (or support as a carer) under the Care Act (2014) when s/he, or the person s/he cares for, transitions to the adult system. Transition assessment and planning is based around the individual needs, wishes, and *outcomes that matter to that person (*see* CARE AND SUPPORT PLAN; NEEDS ASSESSMENT). A whole family approach has been advocated as an important part of the assessment and support planning process. A guidance document (Department of Health et al. [2015] *The Care Act and Whole-Family Approaches*) sets out four key steps for practitioners:

- step one—think family;
- step two—get the whole picture;
- step three—make a plan that works for everyone;
- step four—check it's working for the whole family.

Transition to adult care and support comes at a time when other changes can be happening in a young person's life, including changes to the support they receive from education and health or involvement with new agencies such as those providing support with housing, employment, or further education and training. Some of the issues that matter for young people approaching adulthood (and their families) may include (but are not limited to):

- paid employment;
- health;
- completing exams and/or moving to further or higher education;
- independent living (*choice and control over one's life and housing options);
- social inclusion (friends, relationships, and *community).

The provisions in the Care Act (2014) relating to transition to adult care and support are not only for those who are already receiving children's services, but for anyone who is 'likely to have needs' for adult care and support after turning 18. These needs may not be just those needs deemed eligible under the Care Act (2014). It is likely that young people and carers who are in receipt of children's services would be 'likely to have needs' in this context, and local authorities should therefore carry out a transition assessment for those who are receiving children's services as they approach adulthood, so that they have information about what to expect when they become an adult.

For young people with special educational needs who have an *Education, Health and Care Plan (under the Children and Families Act [2014]), preparation for adulthood must begin from year 9 (see *Special Educational Needs and Disability Code of Practice*, 2107). The transition assessment should be undertaken as part of one of the annual statutory reviews of the EHC Plan and should inform a plan for the transition from children's to adult care and support. For care leavers, local authorities should consider using the statutory *pathway planning process as the opportunity to carry out a transition assessment, where appropriate.

A young person or carer, or someone acting on their behalf, has the right to request a transition assessment. The local authority must consider such requests and whether the likely needs and significant benefit conditions (see above) apply and, if so, it must undertake a transition assessment. If the local authority thinks these conditions do not apply and refuses an assessment, it must provide its reasons for this in writing in a timely manner, and it must provide *information and advice on what can be done to prevent or delay the development of needs for support. Where someone is refused (or they themselves refuse) a transition assessment, but at a later time makes a request for an assessment, the local authority must again consider whether the likely needs and significant benefit conditions apply and carry out an assessment if they do.

Most young people who receive transition assessments will already be known to local authorities under the Children Act (1989). However, local authorities have to consider how they can identify young people who are not receiving children's services but who are likely to have care and support needs as adults. Examples include:

- young people with degenerative conditions;
- young people (for example with autism) whose needs have been largely met by their educational institution, but who, once they leave, will require their needs to be met in some other way;
- young people detained in the *youth justice system who will move to adult custody;
- young carers whose parents have needs below the local authority's *eligibility criteria/threshold but may nevertheless require advice or support to fulfil their potential, for example a child with deaf parents who is undertaking communication support;
- young people and young carers receiving *Children and Adolescent Mental Health Services (CAMHS) may also require care and support as adults even if they did not receive children's services from the local authority.

Even if they are not eligible for services, a transition assessment with information and advice about support in the community can be helpful for these groups.

The local authority must assess the needs of an adult carer where there is a likely need for support after the child being cared for turns 18 and it is of significant benefit to the carer to be assessed. For instance, some carers of *disabled children are able to remain in employment with minimal support while the child is in school. However, once the young person leaves education, it may be the case that the carer's need for support increases and additional support and planning is required from the local authority to allow the carer to stay in employment.

The local authority must also assess the needs of young carers as they approach adulthood. For instance, many young carers feel that they cannot go to university or enter employment because of their caring responsibilities. Transition assessments and planning must consider how to support young carers to prepare for adulthood and how to raise and fulfil their aspirations. The local authority must consider the impact on other members of the family (or other people the authority may feel appropriate) of the person receiving care and support. This will require the authority to identify anyone who may be part of the person's wider *network of care and support. Young carers' assessments should include an indication of how any care and support plan for the person(s) they care for would change as a result of the young carer's change in circumstances. For example, if a young carer has an opportunity to go to university away from home, the local authority should indicate how it would meet the *eligible needs of any family members that were previously being met by the young carer.

The transition assessment should support the young person and their family to plan for the future, by providing them with information about what they can expect. All transition assessments must include an assessment of:

• current needs for care and support and how these impact on wellbeing;
• whether the child or carer is likely to have needs for care and support after the child in question becomes 18;
• if so, what those needs are likely to be, and which are likely to be eligible needs;
• the *outcomes the young person or carer wishes to achieve in day-to-day life and how care and support can contribute to achieving them.

Transition assessments for young carers or adult carers must also specifically consider whether the carer:

• is able to care now and after the child in question turns 18;
• is willing to care now and will continue to after 18;
• works, or wishes to do so;
• participates in or wishes to participate in education, training, or recreation.

In all cases, the young person or carer in question must agree to the assessment where they have mental *capacity and are competent to agree. Where a young person or carer lacks mental capacity or is not competent to agree, the local authority must be satisfied that an assessment is in their *best interests. The local authority must undertake an assessment if it suspects that a child is experiencing or at *risk of *abuse or neglect. For young people below the age of 16, local authorities will need to establish a young person's competence using the test of '*Gillick competent' (whether they are able to understand a proposed treatment or procedure). Where the young person is not competent, a person with *parental responsibility will need to be involved in their transition assessment or an independent advocate provided if there is no one appropriate to act on their behalf (either with or without parental responsibility). The Care Act (2014) places a *duty on local authorities to provide an independent advocate to facilitate the involvement in the transition assessment where the person in question would experience substantial difficulty in understanding the necessary information or in communicating their views, wishes, and feelings (*see* ADVOCACY [ADULTS]). This duty applies for all young people or carers who meet the criteria, regardless of whether they lack mental capacity under the Mental Capacity Act (2005).

The local authority may combine a transition assessment with any other assessment it is carrying out, or it may carry out assessments jointly with, or on behalf of, another organization. For example, transition assessments should be combined with existing EHC needs assessments unless there are specific circumstances to prevent it. The power to join up assessments also applies, so, for example, if an adult is caring for a 17-year-old in transition and a 12-year-old, the local authority could combine:

- the child's needs assessment of the 17-year-old under the Care Act (2014);
- any assessment of the 17-year-old's needs under Section 17 of the Children Act (1989);
- any assessment of the 12-year-old's needs under Section 17 of the Children Act (1989);
- the child's carer's assessment of the adult under the Care Act (2014).

Many people value having one designated person who coordinates assessments and transition planning across different agencies, and helps them to navigate through numerous systems and processes that can sometimes be complicated. Often there is a natural lead professional involved in a young person's care who fulfils this role and the local authority may consider formalizing this by designating a named person to coordinate transition assessment and planning across different agencies. It may also consider setting up specialist posts to carry out this coordination function for people who are preparing for adulthood. This coordinating role, sometimes referred to as *'key working' or *'care coordination', can not only help to deliver person-centred integrated care but also help to reduce *bureaucracy and duplication for local authorities, the NHS, and other agencies. Care coordinators are also often able to build close relationships with young people and families and can act as a valuable provider of information and advice both to the families and to local authorities. Care leavers will have *personal advisors to provide support, for example by providing advice or signposting the young person to services. The personal advisor will be a natural lead in many cases to coordinate a transition from children's to adult care and support.

Having carried out a transition assessment, the local authority must give an indication of which needs are likely to be eligible needs (and which are not likely to be eligible) once the young person in question turns 18 (*see* ELIGIBILITY CRITERIA), to ensure that the young person or carer understands the care and support they are likely to receive and can plan accordingly. There is a particularly important role for local authorities in ensuring that young people and carers understand their likely situation when they reach adulthood. The different systems for children's and adult care and support mean that there will be circumstances in which needs that were being met by children's services may not be eligible needs under the adult system. Where the transition assessment identifies needs that are likely to be eligible, local authorities should consider providing an indicative *personal budget, so that young people, carers, and their families are able to plan their care and support before entering the adult system. For any needs that are not eligible under the Care Act (2014), local authorities must provide information and advice on how those needs can be met and how they can be prevented from getting worse.

The local authority and relevant partners should consider building on a transition assessment to create a person-centred transition plan that sets out the information in the assessment, along with a plan for the transition to adult care and support, including key milestones for achieving the young person or carer's desired outcomes. An advantage of a transition plan is that it is easier to update and refine without undertaking a new assessment. Transition assessments and plans should be reviewed regularly to take account of changes both in circumstances and in desired outcomes. The local authority should accept reasonable requests from young people and their families to review transition plans (*see* REVIEW OF CARE AND SUPPORT PLANS).

In the case of an adult carer, if the local authority has identified needs through a transition assessment which could be met by adult services, it may meet these needs under the Care Act (2014) in advance of the child being cared for turning 18. In deciding whether to do this, the local authority must have regard to what support the adult carer is receiving under children's legislation. If the local authority decides to meet the adult carer's needs through adult services, as for anyone else under the adult legislation, the adult carer must receive a support plan and a *personal budget, as well as a financial assessment if they are subject to charges for the support they will receive (*see* CHARGING FOR SERVICES; PERSONAL BUDGET). A local authority can not meet an adult carer's needs for support under the Care Act (2014) by providing care and support to the child cared for. This will always happen under children's legislation.

There is no obligation on the local authority to move someone from children's services to adult care and support as soon as someone turns 18. Very few moves take place on the day of someone's eighteenth birthday. For the most part, the move to adult services begins at the end of a school term or another similar milestone, and in many cases should be a staged process over several months or years. Prior to the move taking place, the local authority must decide whether to treat the transition assessment as a *needs assessment or a *carer's assessment under the Care Act (2014). If the local authority will meet the young person's or carer's needs under the Care Act (2014) after they have turned 18 (based either on the existing transition assessment or a new needs assessment, if necessary), the local authority must then undertake the care planning process as for other adults, including creating a *care and support plan and producing a personal budget. However, if adult care and support is not in place on a young person's eighteenth birthday, and they or their carer have been receiving services under children's legislation, the local authority must continue providing services until the 'relevant steps' have been taken, so that there is no gap in provision.

The 'relevant steps' are if the local authority:

- concludes that the person does not have needs for adult care and support;
- concludes that the person does have such needs and begins to meet some or all of them (the local authority will not always meet all of a person's needs—certain needs are sometimes met by carers or other organizations);
- concludes that the person does have such needs but decides they are not going to meet any of those needs, for instance because their needs do not meet the *eligibility criteria under the Care Act (2014).

Where young people aged 18 or over continue to have Education, Health and Care Plans under the Children and Families Act (2014) and they move to adult care and support, the care and support aspects of the EHC Plan will be provided under the Care Act (2014). The statutory care and support plan must form the basis of the care element of the EHC plan. In the case of care leavers, local authorities may choose to extend foster placements beyond the age of 18. For some people with complex special education and care needs, local authorities may decide that children's services are the best way to meet a person's needs, even after they have turned 18. Both the Care Act (2014) and the Children and Families Act (2014) allow for this. The latter enables local authorities to continue children's services beyond the age of 18 and up to 25 for young people with Education, Health and Care Plans if they need longer to complete or consolidate their education and training and achieve the outcomes set out in their plan. Where a person over 18 is still receiving services under children's legislation through their EHC Plan and the EHC Plan ceases, the transition assessment and planning process must be undertaken. Where this has not happened at the point of transition, the requirement under the Care Act (2014) to continue children's services (see above) applies.

*Clinical Commissioning Groups determine what ongoing services people aged 18 years or over should receive under *NHS continuing health care provision. They should ensure that adult NHS continuing health care is assessed at all transition planning meetings for all young people who may be potentially eligible. The timing is as follows:

- Children's services should identify young people with likely needs for NHS continuing health care and notify the relevant CCGs when such a young person turns 14.
- There should be a formal referral for adult NHS CHC screening at 16.
- There should be a decision in principle at 17 so that a package of care can be in place once the person turns 18 (or later, if agreed more appropriate).

Further reading: Department of Health (2016) *Care and Support: Statutory Guidance*, Chapter 16. Available at: https://www.gov.uk/government/publications/care-act-statutory-guidance/care-and-support-statutory-guidance#person-centred-care-and-support-planning.

transracial adoption and fostering (transracial adoption and fostering placement) *See* SAME-'RACE' PLACEMENT.

trickle-down effect Despite evidence to the contrary, the view that if the activities of the rich are unrestrained in an unequal society, economic growth will result and will benefit the whole of society, as the impact of increased wealth percolates down the *class structure, thus rendering unnecessary state intervention to address *poverty. *See also* NEO-LIBERALISM; NEW RIGHT.

truancy Persistent non-school attendance. By law all children of *compulsory school age (5 to 16 years) are required to receive a suitable full-time education. For most parents this means registering their child at a school, although some choose to make other arrangements to provide a suitable full-time education, in some cases educating their children at home. Once a child is registered at school, the parent is legally responsible for making sure s/he attends regularly. Parents who fail to do this may be prosecuted by the *local authority. *Education social work services will become involved with children and families where truancy emerges as a problem and will work with the parents and child to identify and overcome the issues that may be contributing to the situation, avoiding wherever possible recourse to legal proceedings. In the most serious *cases, the *local authority can make an application for an *Education Supervision Order. *See also* PARENTING ORDER; SCHOOL ATTENDANCE; SCHOOL PHOBIA.

Tuckman's model (Tuckman's model of stages in group development) *See* GROUP DYNAMICS.

twin-track (twin-tracking) *See* PARALLEL PLAN.

unaccompanied asylum-seeking children (UASC) The Home Office (UK Border Agency) defines an unaccompanied asylum-seeking child as 'a person under 18 years of age or who, in the absence of documentary evidence establishing age, appears to be under that age', and who 'is applying for asylum in their own right; and is separated from both parents and not being cared for by an adult who by law or custom has responsibility to do so'.

In 2014 UNICEF reported that globally an estimated 230 million children were living in areas that were affected by armed conflicts and that in the previous ten years around 10 million children had been killed as a result of war. Continued armed conflicts around the world have given rise to an increasing number of people seeking refuge and *asylum outside their home countries. For Western governments, these demographic changes are socially and politically controversial, as these nations are regarded as the preferred destinations for *refugees. Within these migratory flows exists an exceptionally vulnerable group of young refugees who are unaccompanied minors. These are children under the age of 18 who arrive in a foreign country without a parent or adult *care-giver. They receive little practical or emotional support and are often forced to face extremely stressful situations alone. These children have commonly come to be known as unaccompanied asylum-seeking children. The United Nations Committee on the Rights of the Child has identified a number of factors that result in the separation of children from their parents. These include the persecution of children and/or their families; trafficking, including the sale of children by parents; civil war; international conflicts; famine; and *poverty.

In 2016, England had 4,210 unaccompanied minors being *looked after in *local authority care, representing 6 per cent of the looked-after children population. These young people have been exposed to high levels of *violence, disrupted social lives, and personal *loss. These experiences can increase the risk of psychiatric disorders such as *depression, *post-traumatic stress disorder, or other *anxiety-related difficulties. *Early intervention in addressing these psychological conditions is regarded as crucial for an individual's mental wellbeing and future social integration. While there is some evidence of what constitutes effective psychological intervention with these children, little is known about how social work is responding to them. However, it appears that *local authorities are becoming increasingly overwhelmed by the need for services but unclear on how best to offer them in order to promote UASC's interests and wellbeing.

Debates surrounding UASC are politicized and polarized between the state and those campaigning on behalf of *asylum-seekers and *refugees. Central to these competing arguments is the issue of how the legal position of UASC is regarded. This has created a tension, on the one hand, between recognizing the paramountcy of the rights of the child (under human rights legislation) and the *'best interests of the child' principle (under child care law) and, on the other hand, regarding these children as first and foremost defined by their asylum status in the UK and, therefore, seeing asylum and immigration legislation as taking precedence over child care law. As a consequence, some have argued that there is no appropriate legal framework for considering children's asylum applications, resulting in UASC being treated as asylum-seekers first and children second. This has led to controversy about the detention of UASC and highlighted three key issues. First, that all UASC should be afforded protection and they should be considered separately from the asylum context. Secondly, the need to balance increased immigration controls with the 'best interests of the child' principle. Thirdly, advocates for UASC argue for a radical overhaul of the current asylum system and the creation of a new system with the best-interests principle as its cornerstone. The Hillingdon Judgment (2003), considered as a landmark ruling, stated that local authorities have a *duty of care to asylum-seeking children. This ruling reasserted the 'best interests of the child' principle as paramount in dealing with UASC.

UASC are the responsibility of the local authority in which they present themselves. The main legislative framework and guidance to be followed is the Children Act (1989), the Hillingdon Judgment and Local Authority Circular 2003 (13). These embody the statutory duty of social workers to support all UASC on arrival under Section 20 of the Children Act (1989) until a full assessment of *need is determined. Depending on assessed need, accommodation is likely to be required and should be provided, also under Section 20, and most UASC are entitled to *leaving care services. In exceptional cases, Section 17 can be used to provide support to an UASC as a *'child in need', where the *assessment of an unaccompanied asylum-seeking child identifies that if s/he were to be designated as *looked-after, this would not be in her/his best interests. For example, this could occur if a child expresses a strong aversion to becoming looked after. In addition, it is unusual for a local authority to admit UASC to the care system if they are over 16 years of age, as they can be supported in the community as 'children in need'. This is similar to the services offered to other young people through the leaving care system, recognizing the need for transitional planning towards adulthood for 16- to 18-year-olds and their need for more *independence.

A local authority should undertake a full assessment of all children's needs and the unaccompanied asylum-seeking child should be provided with a copy of the assessment in their own language. Where age is disputed, i.e. an unaccompanied asylum-seeking young person says that s/he is under 18 years of age but his/her appearance strongly suggests s/he is over 18 years, an *age assessment must be undertaken with the assistance of a skilled interpreter. The case of *R. v Merton LBC* (2005) provides guidance on age assessments. *See also* PARAMOUNTCY PRINCIPLE.

((())) SEE WEB LINKS

- Official site of Children and Families Across Borders.
- Official site of the United Nations High Commission for Refugees.

unauthorized absence (from school) Being away from school without the school's agreement. The law regards the parent as legally responsible for a child's attendance at school, and the parent of a child who is absent from school without its permission can be found guilty of an offence (Education Act 1996). This can include parents who take their children on holiday during term-time without authorization from the school. If action is taken against parents, they can be issued with a penalty notice as an alternative to being taken to court. Penalty notices can be issued by *local authorities, the police, or head teachers, who can delegate this power to deputy and assistant head teachers. The penalty is £50, rising to £100 if not paid within 28 days. Payment of the penalty counts as conviction for the offence. If parents fail to pay a penalty within 42 days of a notice being issued, they can be prosecuted. *See also* SCHOOL ATTENDANCE.

unconditional positive regard The stance, initially identified by the counsellor Carl Rogers (1902–87) in his non-directive person-centred approach, according to which parents/significant others and, he argued, the therapist or counsellor, accept a person for what s/he is. Thus, he advocated that positive regard should not be withdrawn if someone does something wrong or makes a mistake as this enables her/him to feel that they can try things out. In contrast, conditional positive regard is where approval depends on, for example, a child behaving in ways that the parent(s) thinks are correct. The child is not accepted for the person s/he is and approval is conditional on her/his behaving only in ways acceptable to the parent(s)

unconditioned response (unconditional response) *See* BEHAVIOURISM; BEHAVIOUR MODIFICATION.

unconscious, the *See* PSYCHODYNAMIC CASEWORK.

underclass A concept referring to a group that is depicted as dangerous and dependent and outside the mainstream of society. There has been considerable debate concerning its existence, and the nature and causes of its marginalization. Charles Murray (1943–) initially advanced the underclass thesis in the US (*Losing Ground* 1984) and argued that welfare dependency was causing the break-up of the family and the development of an alternative *culture that despises work and fosters dependency and criminality. Murray has tended to see the underclass as the purveyor of its own misfortune, whereas his critics have contended that inequality *disadvantages certain social groups, for example, the Black population in the US. Although consideration of the nature and extent of the underclass originated in the US and has been extensively debated there, the ideas generated have been found in discussion of welfare dependency in the UK. Murray himself has argued that the same trends are at work in the UK as in the US and that it is simply that in the US the trends are more pronounced at present, but the UK is heading in the same direction (*The Emerging British Underclass*, 1990; *Underclass: The Crisis Deepens*, 1994). Some have argued that the concept of the underclass brackets together a range of diverse people and that its value has been its availability for deployment in political rhetoric rather than its effectiveness in social *analysis. The political right has used the term to castigate those depicted as morally lacking and unwilling to work because they have grown up in single-parent families in an ethos of reliance on social security benefits. The political left has either eschewed the term or accepted that it describes a group or groups of people who are systematically disadvantaged by inequality. Social work is placed within these debates because much of its work is with those designated as belonging to the 'underclass'. Thus the political right often presents social workers as conniving with the underclass and contributing to its demoralization, and elements of the political left see social workers as reinforcing the marginalized position of the underclass by explaining problems they experience in terms of *individual pathology. *See also* CYCLE OF DEPRIVATION; DESERVING POOR; NEW RIGHT; WELFARE.

under-fives provision The range of services and settings operating in the *private, *public, and *voluntary sectors that cater in a variety of ways for pre-school children. A term that is falling out of use in favour of *early years services. *See also* CHILDREN'S CENTRES; CHILDMINDERS; EXTENDED SERVICES; FAMILY INFORMATION SERVICE; NURSERIES; SURE START.

undeserving poor *See* DESERVING POOR.

Union of the Physically Impaired Against Segregation (UPIAS) *See* SOCIAL MODEL OF DISABILITY.

unitary approach *See* SYSTEMS APPROACH.

United Nations Convention on the Rights of the Child An influential expression of *children's rights that was adopted by the UN in November 1989. It comprises 54 articles setting out nation states' obligations to children and young people up to the age of 18 years within four categories: survival rights, developmental rights, protection rights, and *participation rights. In 2000, two optional protocols were added to the UNCRC. One asks governments to ensure that children under the age of 18 are not forcibly recruited into their armed forces. The second calls on them to prohibit child prostitution, child pornography, and the sale of children into slavery. A third optional protocol was added in 2011. This enables children whose rights have been violated to complain directly to the UN Committee on the Rights of the Child. To date, 194 countries have signed up to the Convention, with only two countries not having done so. Its ratification by the UK government in December 1991 resulted in children having specific rights including the right to life, survival, and development; to have their views respected; to have their best interests considered at all times; to live in a family environment or alternative care; and to have *contact with both parents wherever possible. Health and welfare rights are set out, including rights for *disabled children, as well as rights to education, leisure, *culture, and the arts. These rights apply to all children and young people. The Convention has been seen as useful by some of those supporting children's rights because it can be used to put pressure on governments. The Children's Rights Alliance for England is a non-government body that produces annual reviews on how well the government is performing in relation to the Convention. Its implementation worldwide is monitored by the UN's Committee on the Rights of the Child. *See also* CHILD-CENTRED APPROACH; CHILD POVERTY; CHILD WELFARE.

Further reading: UNICEF (n.d.) *Fact Sheet: A Summary of the Rights under the Convention on the Rights of the Child*. Available at: https://www.unicef.org/crc/files/Rights_overview.pdf.

((⊕)) SEE WEB LINKS
• Official site of the Children's Rights Alliance for England.

universal benefits *Benefits that are available to all who meet the stipulations laid down for receiving them because they are not dependent on a person's financial resources and thus are not *means-tested.

universalism (feminism) The perspective that all women, regardless of *class, *ethnicity, *'race', or sexuality, have a fundamental commonality and a universal experience of *oppression that is a basis of their unity. Universalism has been attacked by Black and lesbian feminists who have asserted the significance of *differences between women. Some within and beyond *feminism have called for forms of politics that can account for and address the claims of different groups under the banner of 'differentiated universalism'. In this formulation, universalism refers to the equal value and inclusion of all, and differentiation challenges the inequality and/or exclusion of some groups drawing on people's self-definition of their *diversity and seeking solidarity based on respect for *difference. In *feminist social work, a version of this debate has focused on the extent to which women social workers and women service users have common interests.

universalism (service provision) The principle that a service should be available to all, the most celebrated example of which is the National Health Service. There have been arguments in favour of making social work a universal service, the most notable of which was in the Seebohm Report (1968), which established *Social Services Departments. It recommended:

a new local authority department, providing a community-based and family-oriented service, *which will be available to all*. This new department will, we believe, reach far beyond the discovery and rescue of social casualties; it will enable the greatest possible number of individuals to act reciprocally, giving and receiving service for the well-being of the community (para. 2, our emphasis).

However, this lofty aspiration was not realized and social work has remained overwhelmingly focused on poor and *disadvantaged people.

universal services (adults) A term introduced with the implementation of the Care Act (2014) to describe services for adults that are available to all, which may include, but are not limited to, interventions and advice that provide access to information, support safer neighbourhoods, promote healthy and active lifestyles (for example, exercise classes), and reduce loneliness or isolation (for example, befriending schemes or community activities). In the Care Act Statutory Guidance (2016), these services are presented as having the potential to reduce the need for *care and support arranged by *local authorities. This is debateable, as they are catering for different *needs from those assessed as eligible under the Care Act (2014) by local authorities (*see* ELIGIBILITY CRITERIA). They may, however, dovetail with care and support services or delay the provision of them. Also needing to be taken into consideration is that with the onset of *austerity universal services have been under greater pressure at a time of reduced resources.

unmet need A *need that is identified by an *assessment but is not met, usually because the resources to meet it are not available. When the *community care reforms were introduced in 1991, *local authorities were issued with guidance by central government that advocated the separation of the assessment of need from decisions about what services were provided. Assessment was to be needs-led, with services shaped to people's needs, rather than deciding what people's needs were in the light of the services that happened to be available. The guidance also encouraged local authorities to require social workers to record any unmet needs following assessments of *service users so that service shortfalls could be aggregated and tracked. Subsequently, a circular (1992) from the Chief Inspector at the Social Services Inspectorate, Herbert Laming, warned social workers not to record needs unless they were confident they could supply services to meet them because of fears that recording needs would create a legal obligation to meet them. This led away from the concept of 'needs-led assessment', promoted by the community care reforms, and towards local authorities using *eligibility criteria to ration services in line with the resources they had available.

A significant legal case, the Gloucestershire judgment (1997), confirmed that local authorities could act lawfully in taking into account resources when deciding whether it was necessary to meet needs, and this was set out in the *Fair Access to Care Services Guidance* (Department of Health 2002). However, such decisions had to be taken on the basis of an assessment or reassessment of need, had to be made in relation to eligibility criteria, resources could not be the sole consideration, and decisions had to be reasonable, taking account of the right to life and right to family life and home under the *Human Rights Act (1998). This led to a situation in which social workers fought shy of the recording of 'wants' that fell outside definitions of need in eligibility criteria because of the legal obligation to meet needs that fell within them. This was despite the distinction made in the *FACS* guidance between presenting needs and eligible needs and the statement that local authorities should monitor presenting needs that were not assessed as eligible needs. The implementation of the Care Act (2014) has replaced the FACS guidance with national *eligibility criteria, which operate in a similar way.

Therefore, it is entirely legitimate to identify and record unmet need in the sense of presenting needs that are not eligible needs. However, all needs assessed as eligible must be met. In addition to fears about the legal obligations that may be invoked by recording unmet needs, another explanation for the lack of their recording is that they are simply not identified in the first place. Social workers may restrict the needs they consider to those they know can be met, and unmet needs will then remain uncovered.

Failure to record unmet need has significant implications for service development because it becomes detached from local issues and needs. Therefore, on the one hand, unmet needs in terms of presenting needs that do not fall within eligibility criteria should be recorded and monitored. On the other hand, failure to meet need that has been assessed as eligible constitutes a breach of statutory *duty. If the preferred means of meeting the need is not available, other avenues to meet the need should be pursued. Clarity about the legal status of unmet need and about the broader purpose of *assessment—helping individuals to reach a better understanding of their situation and to identify options for dealing with difficulties—are important for social workers and their employing authorities. This broader purpose should encourage them to be concerned with need as perceived and expressed by people ('presenting needs') rather than just need for which they know help will be provided ('eligible needs'). It should also reinforce the identification and recording of unmet need as a key mechanism for *monitoring the nature and level of overall needs so that this can be used to inform the planning and *commissioning of services. This is reinforced in the Care Act Statutory Guidance (2016), which states that local authorities must consider how to identify unmet need, whether it is not being met by the local authority or anyone else. Understanding unmet need is seen as crucial to developing a longer-term approach to *prevention that reflects the needs of the local population. *See also* NEEDS ASSESSMENT.

Further reading: Department of Health (2016) *Care and Support Statutory Guidance* para. 2.30. Available at: https://www.gov.uk/government/publications/care-act-statutory-guidance/care-and-support-statutory-guidance#general-responsibilities-and-universal-services.

unpaid work Previously known as 'community service', work that is performed by offenders after sentencing under various orders that set out how many hours of work have to be completed. *New Labour referred to unpaid work as 'community payback', though this is not a legal term, and introduced bright orange jackets for those undertaking unpaid work with 'community payback' prominently displayed. *See also* COMMUNITY SENTENCES; VOLUNTEER.

unreasonableness *See* REASONABLENESS.

use of self As social work is undertaken person-to-person, the social worker's use of self has always been seen as central and involves a social worker being aware of her/his strengths and weaknesses in her/his work with *service users. This requires the social worker to be aware of how s/he impacts on others and how others impact on her/him—an awareness of the self in action. The skilled use of self also requires that a social worker is able to engage in awareness and appraisal of the knowledge and *values that s/he brings to each situation. *See also* REFLECTIVE PRACTICE; REFLEXIVITY.

use of technology *See* COMPUTERIZATION; TELECARE.

user *See* SERVICE USER.

user empowerment *See* EMPOWERMENT; PARTICIPATION; PARTNERSHIP; SERVICE USER PERSPECTIVES.

user involvement *See* EMPOWERMENT; PARTICIPATION; PARTNERSHIP; SERVICE USER PERSPECTIVES.

user-led organization (user-controlled organization) Just because an organization works with *service users, it is not necessarily a user-led organization. Many such organizations are *for* service users, whereas ULOs are organizations *of* service users. They are run and controlled by people who use services, including disabled people, *older people, people with *learning disabilities, and people with mental health problems (often referred to in ULOs as mental health *survivors). The ULO Shaping Our Lives carried out a consultation about developing and sustaining ULOs. It stated that values, power, and knowledge had to be demonstrated in a ULO:

- A ULO is an organization based on clear *values* of *independence, involvement, and peer support.
- Unlike other *voluntary sector organizations, in ULOs people who use services control (hold *power* in) the organization.
- ULOs are identified by their *knowledge*, which is based on direct lived experience.

Typical activities undertaken by ULOs include:

- *information and advice;
- *advocacy;
- peer support;
- support in using *personal budgets and *direct payments;
- support to recruit and employ *personal assistants;
- support with *recovery and *rehabilitation;
- assistance with self-assessment, support planning, and care *reviews;
- equality training;
- campaigning;
- employment and return to work support;
- *partnership activities with local agencies, such as *civil society organizations and health and social services.

ULOs are sometimes regarded as a relatively recent phenomenon but they are the outcome of struggles by health and social care service users for many years to have their voices heard. The early struggles united service users on the basis of their disempowering experiences and desire for greater control over their own lives and the services they used. The civil rights movements from the 1960s onwards, for example in relation to *gender and *'race', had an impact on service user activism. Service users made the same arguments as those used by the civil rights movements that society ignored, excluded, and discriminated against them and they demanded to be treated as equal citizens. The political and social climate that emphasized rights and *citizenship was fertile ground in which people who used services could also fight for their voices to be heard. These early struggles by service users led to the ULOs that make their voices heard today as '*experts by experience'.

SEE WEB LINKS
• Official site of Shaping Our Lives, a national network of service users and disabled people.

user participation *See* EMPOWERMENT; PARTICIPATION; PARTNERSHIP; SERVICE USER PERSPECTIVES.

user perspectives *See* SERVICE USER PERSPECTIVES.

vagrancy (vagrant) Traditionally, someone who was homeless, without an income, and who moved from place to place, though the idea of having to be on the move is no longer necessarily associated with the term and someone may be receiving benefits, though establishing entitlement to benefit is a difficult process. A person may be sleeping rough or using *night shelters, or alternating between the two. To refer to a 'vagrant' can have nineteenth-century-like judgemental connotations of someone who has brought *homelessness on themselves. Therefore, *charities and campaigning organizations have eschewed the term in favour of placing the emphasis on homelessness as a problem produced by social and economic factors. There are periodic episodes of *moral panic about begging, and at such times, calls are heard for the use of the provisions available in the Vagrancy Act (1824) for the punishment of 'idle and disorderly persons', 'rogues', and 'vagabonds'.

value for money *See* AUDIT COMMISSION; ECONOMY, EFFICIENCY, AND EFFECTIVENESS.

values Principles or ideals that shape people's attitudes and behaviour. In the context of social work, such principles are included in the Health and Care Professions Council's *Standards of Conduct, Performance and Ethics.*

Statements of values often do not reflect the complex and contested nature of social work. For example, there can be an awkward fit between values exhorting social workers to *empower people, while they are required to implement policies that maintain forms of social injustice and restrict the use of resources to improve people's lives. Value conflicts also arise from the requirement on social workers to be *person-centred, focusing on the interests of the child or adult, when, at the same time, they have to take account of the potentially competing interests and conflicting *needs of other family members, the *goals of other professionals and agencies, and the interests of their employing organizations. These two examples illustrate the value conflicts social workers can experience as different responsibilities and concerns come into play.

In addition, there may be competition between different social work values themselves, for example, service user self-determination and protecting service users from harm. Value conflict may also arise when the rights and freedom of one individual are in opposition to the 'the wider society', for example, an *older person may choose to live with very low standards of cleanliness within her/his home but this may have environmental health consequences for those living nearby. Furthermore, there may be conflict between personal values and professional social work values, for example, a particular social worker might have a personal value that adult children should look after their older parents, but social work values include being non-judgemental and respecting the wishes and values of others. Or, a value conflict may entail a clash between personal and/or professional values and organizational values and practices, for example, personal and professional values may support the position that society should promote the wellbeing of people with disabilities, but this may be undermined by policies and practices related to the application of stringent *eligibility criteria.

Social workers constantly have to negotiate and manage such value conflicts. Despite the conflicts and constraints that are an inevitable and intrinsic part of social work, there is much that social workers can do to seek to ensure that their practice upholds social work values. Often this will be achieved in day-to-day encounters with service users but social work's role is also to question and challenge policies and practices that compromise social work values. This has been pointed up in recent years by the dominance of the *neo-liberal agenda in social work as it has often *commodified and depersonalized services. In the face of neo-liberal challenges to social work values, it has been argued that the elements of its agenda that appear to have a surface resemblance to social work values and appear to be in sympathy with them, such as its promotion of *choice and *empowerment, need to be carefully interrogated and placed within the *market context of *consumerism from which they emerge. *See also* CODE OF ETHICS.

Valuing People A White Paper published in 2001 by the New Labour government (1997–2010) that was concerned with how the lives of people with *learning disabilities, their families and *carers, could be improved. This was the first major policy initiative for people with learning disabilities since *Better Services for the Mentally Handicapped* in 1971. *Valuing People* set out eleven objectives, with a chapter on each. The first chapter is concerned with issues affecting children with learning disabilities and the objectives in the remaining ten chapters focus primarily on adults with learning disabilities:

- Objective 2: Transition into Adult Life.
- Objective 3: More *Choice and Control.
- Objective 4: Supporting *Carers.
- Objective 5: Good Health.
- Objective 6: Housing.
- Objective 7: Fulfilling Lives.
- Objective 8: Moving into Employment.
- Objective 9: *Quality.
- Objective 10: Workforce and Planning.
- Objective 11: *Partnership Working.

Valuing People laid out a five-year action plan for improving services and support for people with learning disabilities, from birth to old age, based on four principles, that people with learning disabilities should:

- Have equal legal and civil rights;
- Be given the chance and the means to lead more independent lives;
- Have more choice and be able to express and achieve their preferences;
- Be included in mainstream society.

*Goals for realizing these principles were set out in relation to employment, transport, education, housing, health, and social services. The White Paper also aspired towards people with learning disabilities being less *marginalized and being active in their local *communities. *Local authorities had to set up Learning Disability Partnership Boards, which had to write proposals about how *Valuing People* would be implemented in their local area. The government set up the Learning Disability Task Force to review progress on the *Valuing People* initiatives and established the

Valuing People Support Team to provide assistance with implementation. Although the government initially set out a five-year period to move towards the goals in the White Paper, subsequently, in 2009, the New Labour government published *Valuing People Now*, a three-year strategy for 'delivering the vision' contained in the original proposals of *Valuing People*, while also adding a *human rights perspective and promoting *personalization. However, when New Labour left power in 2010, this initiative was left, as one organization in the field of learning disability put it, to 'wither on the vine'. Despite the decline in government interest in the aims that underpinned *Valuing People* and *Valuing People Now*, the contents of these documents are still drawn upon and articulated by learning disability organizations.

ventilation The expression of feelings that may bring a sense of relief and acknowledgement if a *service user has not been able to express them to anyone previously and may give a feeling afterwards of her/his being able to move on to tackling issues facing her/him.

verbal communication *See* COMMUNICATION SKILLS.

viability assessment A preliminary *assessment process, usually required when a *local authority is seeking to identify alternative care arrangements for a child. It is intended to be a concise, informative assessment that gathers all the necessary information in a short period of time to determine the suitability of an adult(s) as a *care-giver. A common circumstance in which a viability assessment is necessary is when alternative care arrangements need to be considered for a child and a member(s) of the child's wider family has put themselves forward as a care-giver for the child. The viability assessment will determine the prospective care-giver's capacity to meet the child's needs in the long-term, as well as more immediately. Following the completion of a positive viability assessment, it may be necessary for a more extensive assessment (such as a Special Guardianship assessment) to take place, if the placement might be made long-term. *See also* CORE ASSESSMENT; FOSTERING; KINSHIP CARE; KINSHIP NETWORKS; PARENTING ASSESSMENT; PERMANENCY PLANNING; PLACEMENT; PRIVATE FOSTERING; SPECIAL GUARDIAN; SPECIAL GUARDIAN.

victim personal statement A written statement by a victim of a criminal offence that describes the impact that the offence has had on her/him to the court after the offender is found guilty and before sentencing. *See also* VICTIM SUPPORT; VULNERABLE WITNESS.

Victim Support A national *charity with local branches in England and *Wales that provides free and confidential assistance to victims of crime, their families, and friends, as well as support to witnesses in criminal court cases. It also campaigns on issues affecting victims and witnesses. Victims do not have to report a crime to the police to receive assistance and there is no time limit on seeking help, even if the crime happened several years previously. *See also* VICTIM PERSONAL STATEMENT; VULNERABLE WITNESS.

(())) SEE WEB LINKS
• Official site of Victim Support.

violence Behaviour that threatens, attempts, or causes physical, emotional, or sexual harm to others or self. Whether people, groups, and organizations understand and classify a particular act as violent is shaped by the context in which it occurs and the sense that is made of it. This process of interpretation determines whether behaviour comes to the attention of someone authorized to intervene in relation to the perpetrator and/or help the person who is the victim. The interpretation of the act and the nature of any intervention in response to it will determine whether violence is seen as understandable or not, culturally acceptable or not, legal or illegal. The ability to make interpretations 'stick' depends on the power of the individuals, groups, or organizations to make their perspectives on what it or is not violence count. In other words, social processes involving individuals, groups, and organizations construct which acts are defined as violence and which acts of violence are seen as legitimate and illegitimate. *See also* CHILD ABUSE AND NEGLECT; CHILDREN AND DOMESTIC VIOLENCE; DOMESTIC VIOLENCE; SAFEGUARDING ADULTS; SAFEGUARDING CHILDREN; SOCIAL CONSTRUCTION.

Violent Offender Order Made under Sections 98–117 of the Criminal Justice and Immigration Act (2008), the Order imposes prohibitions, restrictions, or conditions that the court considers necessary for the purpose of protecting the public from the risk of serious violent harm caused by an offender. The prohibitions, restrictions, or conditions may prevent the offender:

- From going to any specified place or premises, either at all or between specified times;
- From attending any specified event;
- From having any, or any specified description of, contact with any specified person.

The Order can last for between two and five years. An Order can be made if someone is over 18 and has been convicted (including in other countries) of a specified offence (manslaughter; soliciting murder; wounding with intent to cause grievous bodily harm; attempting/conspiring to commit murder; malicious wounding) in respect of which a custodial sentence of at least twelve months was imposed, or a *Hospital Order (with or without restriction) was made; or has been found not guilty of such an offence by reason of *insanity, and the court made a Hospital Order or a *Supervision Order.

virtual hospital wards A hospital-like service to people living in their own homes. Potential patients considered to be most at *risk of unplanned hospital admissions are identified using a predictive model (usually the Combined Predictive Algorithm, developed by the King's Fund, Health Dialog and New York University) that uses *general practitioner, hospital inpatient, outpatient, and accident and emergency data. A list of people is then produced in order of risk so that extra support can be offered to those who are most at risk in order to avoid the need for emergency admissions. In aiming to prevent unplanned hospital admissions, virtual wards work just like an inpatient hospital ward, using the same staffing, systems, and daily routines, except that the people being cared for stay in their own homes throughout. A community matron usually leads the day-to-day clinical work of the ward and a ward clerk collects and disseminates information between patients, their families, GP and other practice staff, virtual ward staff, and hospital staff. On admission, the community matron conducts an initial *assessment in the patient's home. It is entered in a shared set of electronic ward notes, as is any future *recording. Before the assessment, a summary of information from general practitioner records is pasted into these ward notes to provide background information and avoid unnecessary duplication. The GP practice is informed of all significant changes. Virtual ward staff hold a *ward round each working day, discussing patients at different frequencies depending on their circumstances, with some staff participating by conference calls. In addition, weekly multidisciplinary team meetings are held, to which all of the *community professionals are invited, including GPs, district nurses, specialist nurses, physiotherapists, *occupational therapists, social workers, pharmacists, and the *intermediate care team. Virtual ward staff decide when a patient is ready to be discharged back to their GP practice. If this decision has not been made and a patient drops outside the parameters for those with the highest predicted risk, virtual ward staff will be prompted to discharge the patient. *See also* HOSPITAL AT HOME.

Virtual School Head *See* LOOKED-AFTER CHILD (EDUCATION).

visual impairment The overall term for people with sight problems. Under Section 77 of the Care Act (2014), a *local authority must establish and maintain a register of sight-impaired and severely sight-impaired adults who are *ordinarily resident in its area, and registration is on the basis of laid-down clinical criteria. When people see a consultant ophthalmologist, a form is completed that triggers the person's registration with the local authority. Through this registration process, the local authority should become aware that the person is someone who may have *care and support needs and for whom it may have a *duty to carry out a *needs assessment under the Care Act (2014). However, the *needs of people with visual impairments are often given low priority by *local authorities, though some do provide a range of specialist services. Studies with visually impaired people have shown that many have not experienced *holistic assessment of their needs or early responses that offered them support. Many are not in touch with any services. This may be for a number of reasons. First, people may feel that they have needs but do not express them if they do not know that services are available or they think that services will not help them. Secondly, there may be poor *communication between and within agencies responsible for providing support. Thirdly, it may be that an assessment is triggered through the process of registration but that the presenting needs of people with visual impairments are not regarded as 'eligible' in relation to *eligibility criteria. These problems can lead to visually impaired people lacking information about services, benefits, and low vision equipment, as well as having no access to *rehabilitation. As a result, they may lack support with household tasks and access to help with correspondence and bills, as well as being socially isolated. The *social model of disability's emphasis on the environmental barriers faced by disabled people is borne out in relation to visually impaired people. *See also* REGISTER OF DISABLED PEOPLE; ROYAL NATIONAL INSTITUTE FOR BLIND PEOPLE; SENSORY IMPAIRMENT.

voice One of three concepts outlined by Albert Hirschmann (1915–2012) in his influential *Exit, Voice, and Loyalty: Responses to Decline in Firms, Organizations, and States* (1970). He argues that members of any organization, for example, a work organization, have two responses available when they think that the organization is not delivering what it should or is not benefitting them. They can *exit* the organization or they can use *voice* and seek to improve the organization, for example, through communicating grievances or proposals for change. Similarly, when consumers are dissatisfied with purchases they have made, they can either decide to *exit* from purchasing from the seller in future, use *voice* to take up the issue by complaining to the seller, or both. The third concept identified by Hirschmann is *loyalty*, which he says can affect whether exit or voice come into play. Where there is loyalty to a product, service, or organization, the use of exit and voice may be reduced. Hirschmann's model has been used subsequently to describe and explain a wide range of political, economic, and social phenomena and processes, including its being applied to users of social services.

Conservative, New Labour, and Conservative–Liberal Democrat governments have argued that by extending market mechanisms into service provision (*see* QUASI-MARKETS), *service users become consumers and enjoy the power of exit; they can choose to take their custom elsewhere. This is what the Conservative government argued in relation to the *community care reforms, which encouraged sellers to provide social services for adults in competition with *local authorities in *market-like arrangements (a system that has continued), as a basis for service users becoming consumers and exercising *choice. However, the rhetoric outstrips the reality. For example, it is extremely difficult for an *older person who is unhappy with the residential establishment in which s/he is living to exit and move to another home. The construction of service users as consumers has been contested, not only on pragmatic grounds, such as the lack of alternatives that would allow people to exit, but also in principle, the contention being that services should be under democratic control with service users able to use voice if they are unhappy with what is provided. However, there has been wide discussion about the difficulties faced by service users in 'coming to voice' or 'finding their voice'. The embedding of certain *discourses in services often makes it difficult for individual service users or service user groups to speak in their own voices, to find words that describe and represent their experiences to powerful actors and organizations that impact on their lives. This is crucial to service users' capacity to combat *oppression because one of the mechanisms by which oppression works is through preventing people having access to an alternative discourse that is capable of expressing their experience. The existence of self-help groups and service user movements emphasizes that people can develop and voice their own discourses based on knowledge gained from experience, and these discourses can be the bases from which to challenge the tendency towards monopoly power exerted by professional knowledge. This points to the need to create dialogue between service user and professional discourses. In such dialogue, service user movements have stressed the need to democratize professional-service user relations, seeing themselves as active citizens with voice, pursuing collective concerns, rather than taking individualized action as represented by a consumer's use of exit. *See also* CONSUMERISM; EXPERTS BY EXPERIENCE; PARTICIPATION; PARTNERSHIP.

voluntary accommodation in care (**voluntary admission to care**) When a child who is looked after by a local authority with parental consent, under Section 20 of the Children Act (1989). *See also* CHILD ACCOMMODATED BY A LOCAL AUTHORITY.

voluntary admission (mental health) *See* COMPULSORY ADMISSION; INFORMAL ADMISSION.

voluntary organizations Agencies initially established by the coming together of people who were concerned about an issue or the welfare of a particular group of people. Many of the large ones now employ paid professional workers or a mix of both paid workers and unpaid *volunteers, while smaller ones may still rely mainly or solely on the work of volunteers. Traditionally, their *independence and flexibility were highly prized and their roles were to campaign publicly for change, to provide services that supplemented or added to the work of *statutory organizations, or to experiment with innovative responses and provision. In recent years, they have been drawn increasingly into providing a wide range of services under contract on behalf of *local authorities and in competition with *private sector organizations, a development that has required them to become more business like. With the advent of this contract culture, large national voluntary organizations with a history of service provision were better placed than smaller organizations engaged in *advocacy or self-help activities, such as much of the voluntary effort in *ethnic minority communities. In addition, those voluntary organizations which, in the pre-contract culture era, might have been pressuring public services by pointing to shortfalls in provision were now constrained to bid for contracts to provide services themselves. Some have argued that this shift in role has compromised their inde-pendence and muzzled their critical campaigning potential. The shift in role has resulted in voluntary organizations playing an increasingly significant part in pro-viding services, changing the balance of their activities and eroding their distinctive identity. However, their practices and *values may still have the potential to be more closely aligned with the needs of *service users than those within the *statutory sector. For ethnic minority groups in particular, voluntary organizations may act as an important link to other agencies, providing information and advice in accessible and acceptable forms, especially to people whose first language is not English. Minority ethnic voluntary organizations have often developed in response to their awareness of communication barriers and the lack of cultural awareness and competence within mainstream services, and as such have offered alternative sources of support. However, the consequence of many of the services provided by voluntary organizations being contracted by *statutory agencies, which, in effect, delegate their statutory functions to voluntary organizations, is that the *business orientation required to engage effectively in contracting can conflict with and eclipse the key values and practices that most endear voluntary organizations to service users. For example, the contracted work of a voluntary organization may be hemmed around by *performance indicators, *outputs, and *outcomes required by the statutory contractor, leading it to be more responsive to the contractor than to service users. *See also* CONTRACT STATE; COUNCIL OF VOLUNTARY SERVICE; INDEPENDENT SECTOR; OUTSOURCING; QUASI-MARKETS; VOLUNTARY SECTOR.

voluntary patient (mental health) *See* COMPULSORY ADMISSION; INFORMAL ADMISSION.

voluntary sector Collective term that covers the huge diversity of all *voluntary organizations and the work they undertake. *See also* COUNCIL OF VOLUNTARY SERVICE; COMPULSORY ADMISSION; INFORMAL VOLUNTEER.

voluntary sector agencies *See* VOLUNTARY ORGANIZATIONS.

volunteer Someone who works for a statutory or *voluntary organization without being paid. This can involve undertaking practical tasks or taking on befriending or *advocacy roles. With the arrival of the Conservative–Liberal Democrat Coalition government in 2010 and its advocacy of the *'Big Society', the roles of volunteers were represented as needing to expand considerably, with calls for increased levels of volunteering and its extension into areas not previously seen as the domain of volunteers, not least so that shortfalls in services as a result of cuts could be ameliorated.

Social work's origins lie in the work of volunteers in the nineteenth century. (*See* CHARITY ORGANIZATION SOCIETY.) *See also* AUSTERITY; COUNCIL OF VOLUNTARY SERVICE; VOLUNTARY ORGANIZATIONS; VOLUNTARY SECTOR.

volunteer bureau *See* COUNCIL OF VOLUNTARY SERVICE.

vulnerable adult *See* SAFEGUARDING ADULTS.

vulnerable witness A witness, usually a victim, in a criminal court who is considered to be vulnerable because of the type of offence, fear of giving evidence, age, or *disability. Such witnesses can be catered for by changing the way in which they give their evidence to the court. This can inclued use of a live video link or previously recorded video evidence, the removal of wigs and gowns, and the use of screens to prevent the person on trial being able to see the witness. *See also* VICTIM SUPPORT.

Wales One of the four constituent nations of the United Kingdom. It has a population of just over three million people, most of whom live in the urban conurbations of the north-east and south-east. The mountainous central belt of Wales has a sparse and declining population, bringing challenges of rurality to service provision. Demographically, Wales has a larger proportion of *older people, growing at a faster rate, than other parts of the UK. As well as an indigenous older population, Wales is a net importer of older people from other parts of Britain. In coastal parts of North Wales, for example, this produces additional demands on both health and social care services.

The Welsh economy of the twenty-first century is characterized by a greater dependence on public service employment than other parts of the UK. Manufacturing makes up a greater proportion of the Welsh economy than is the case for the economies of the other parts of the UK, but there is a very much diminished engagement in the traditional industries of coal and steel production. Throughout the twenty-first century large parts of Wales, in West Wales and the Valleys, have qualified for European Union Convergence Funding, the highest level of economic aid, available only to those parts of the European Union where gross domestic product is below 75 per cent of the EU average. In recent years, however, unemployment levels in Wales have been close to, or below, the UK average. The gap in levels of economic inactivity, where people of pre-retirement age no longer seek *participation in the workforce, has also narrowed significantly. Some Valley communities, however, continue to have substantial numbers of people of working age who do not seek employment because of long-term illness or *disability. Other indices of social distress, strongly associated with both worklessness and long-term life-limiting sickness, are consequently highly and powerfully spatially concentrated. *Child poverty in Wales, having dipped below the UK average during the most successful Blair years, then returned to at or above the UK figure. Indeed, half the improvement in the child poverty rate between the mid-1990s and the mid-2000s was lost from 2006 to 2011. In more recent years, further progress has been evident, with the rate of child poverty in Wales falling, in 2015, from 31 per cent to 29 per cent. Pensioner *poverty, as in the rest of the UK, has fallen substantially. In the 1990s some 26 per cent of pensioner households lived below the poverty line. By 2015 the figure had fallen to 13 per cent. By contrast, working families and young people in Wales are at greater risk of poverty in 2016 than was the case a decade ago.

In *class terms, Wales has a larger working class and a smaller middle class than both England and Scotland. It is also unique, in the UK, in having a pronounced preference for parties of the centre-left, ever since the first stirrings of universal suffrage in the early nineteenth century. Labour remains the dominant party at both Westminster and Assembly elections, albeit with a clear long-term shift towards greater pluralism in voting patterns.

Wales is a bilingual nation. Some 20 per cent of the Welsh population is able to speak the Welsh language. In contrast to powerfully-held *stereotypes, there are greater numbers of Welsh speakers in urban rather than rural Wales. Over the last quarter of a century, Welsh-speaking has grown more quickly amongst younger rather than older age groups. The expansion in Welsh medium education has been most pronounced in southeast Wales, where, otherwise, the language is at its weakest. Users in Wales have a right to receive services in either Welsh or English, as they choose, wherever they live. In terms of social work's service users, the Welsh language is particularly important amongst *older people, the very young, and in providing services for people with a *learning disability or mental health condition; but the right exists for all, and workforce planning has to take this into account.

Social services and devolution Since 1999 social services in Wales have been the responsibility of the National Assembly, which essentially is a social policy-making body. It has control over the domestic agenda of health, education, local government services (including social services), environment, transport, and leisure. Foreign affairs, defence and, to a diminishing extent, tax and benefit policy all remain the responsibility of the Westminster government. The Social Fund and Council Tax Benefit were both, against the wishes of the National Assembly, devolved to it during the period of coalition government (2010–15) at Westminster. From April 2018, for the first time since the Middle Ages, responsibility for aspects of taxation will also be devolved to Wales. The Assembly has both widened and deepened its sphere of responsibilities since it was established. Of direct relevance to social services, for example, has been the assumption by the Assembly of responsibilities for health and education services in prisons and the operation of the *Children and Family Court Advisory Support Service. A lively debate continues over the possible devolution of *youth justice responsibilities to Wales. In terms of deepening powers, following a successful referendum held in March 2011, the Assembly became a full legislature in its own right, with capacity to make laws in all its fields of devolved responsibility.

Operationally, the Assembly is divided between government and parliamentary sides. The Welsh government consists of a First Minister and up to eleven other full and deputy Welsh Ministers. *Gender balance has been a feature of both the Assembly and the executive throughout the devolution period.

Successive Welsh governments have pursued what has been called a 'clear red water' agenda in policy-making. Its core principles remain the basis on which public policy in Wales, and policy for social services in particular, have been carried forward. These include:

- Good government remains the best vehicle for solving common problems and securing collective benefits.
- Universal rather than *means-tested services are to be preferred wherever that is practical and possible.
- The relationship between the individual and the state is best shaped on the basis of *citizenship rather than *consumerism.
- Cooperation, rather than *competition, remains the best way of improving the quality of public services and high-trust, not low-trust, relationships are the best way of carrying out those services at the front-line.
- Finally, and most importantly of all, equality of outcome, rather than simply equality of opportunity (*see* EGALITARIANISM), remains the most important ambition for any nation that aims to combine economic success and social solidarity as the basis for its future.

Against that general background, three distinctive policy drivers can be seen at play in the Welsh context. First, the decision to preserve *local authorities as the core provider of services reflects a Welsh preference for services to be publicly-provided and delivered. Social workers in Wales generally work in unified *Social Services Departments. It is argued that within such departments social workers are better placed to mobilize the range of resources on which their users rely, if the departments remain within local authorities. In Wales, then, social workers continue to be regarded, essentially, as brokers who act between individual families on the one hand, and the services which those individuals need, if they are to fashion more successful lives, on the other. Being part of a local authority that also provides, for example, housing, environmental, and educational services places the social worker in a more powerful position to mobilize those resources on behalf of service users. Secondly, at the level of the individual worker, the Welsh view of social services is that such responsibilities are best discharged through well-trained staff members, motivated by a spirit of public service, and enabled to exercise independent *professional judgement. In practice, tensions remain between this ambition and the *bureaucratic demands, for example, of the all-Wales *child protection procedures. Thirdly, there has been a policy imperative in Wales to reorientate social services away from operating in rescue mode, in which intervention only takes place once social difficulties have reached a level where they can no longer be ignored, and towards repair-mode services, in which investment is made in those services that aim to prevent difficulties from developing in the first place.

All these characteristics were given new legislative force during the fourth Assembly term, using the full powers available for the first time. The landmark Social Services and Wellbeing (Wales) Act (2014) was the single most extensive piece of legislation to come before the Assembly during that period. Its companion Act, the Regulation and Inspection of Social Care Act, reached the statute book in the final months before the election of May 2016. Together they represented a major legislative effort to reform and remake social services for the needs of the twenty-first century and, in particular, to respond to the pervasive impact of *austerity on public services in Wales.

The 2014 Act was taken through the Assembly by the long-serving and highly respected Deputy Minister for Social Services, Gwenda Thomas. She described it, always, as a 'people's Act', designed to remove artificial barriers between services for children and older people and based unambiguously upon a model in which users of services and their *carers were to be regarded as equal partners in bringing about improvement.

This 'strengths', or 'asset-based', model underpinned the major thrust of the Act, a shift from intervention after the fact to *prevention. Local authorities were urged to design services that aimed to assist people to go on managing without them, rather than making long-term reliance inevitable. In place of 'What is the matter?', practitioners in multidisciplinary teams were urged to make 'What matters to you?' the first question to be asked of any new person seeking help.

The Act attracted criticicism from those who regarded it as a rowing back from the previous levels of assistance provided by the *welfare state as well as from *voluntary organizations anxious that a 'people's Act' would result in a dilution of service for their particular user groups. The former objections were rejected on the grounds that they were rooted in a deficit model in which volume of service was mistakenly equated with *quality and efficacy. The latter anxieties were addressed by the creation of new statutory *partnerships between social services departments and local health boards, formed around the areas of the seven LHBs, with needs being assessed and services planned in relation to these bigger geographical areas with larger populations. The Act came into force on 6 April 2016.

Within a few weeks of the election of the fifth Assembly, the referendum of 23 June 2016 had resulted in a decision to leave the European Union. Such an outcome had been strongly opposed by all levels of government in Wales, very largely because the least well-off *communities were clear net beneficiaries of European funding. The *Children's Commissioner for Wales, for example, expressed concern that the poorest children would suffer most from the Brexit decision. Beyond the direct financial benefits, Wales had also played a committed part in many of the regional networks that Europe provided, for example in healthy ageing and services for older people, opening up funding, research, and practice possibilities for Wales in the process. The reliance of social care services, in particular, upon workers from other parts of the European Union made free movement of people, as well as matters of funding, of real significance during the early months of the new Assembly term.

Policies for children Wales faces particular challenges in providing services for children, especially those with needs that bring them to the attention of Social Services Departments. The downside of a belief in 'active' government can be seen in the extent to which departments engage in substantial *intervention in the lives of families. At the end of March 2014 the Welsh rate of looked-after children stood at 91 per 10,000, compared with a rate of 60 per 10,000 in England. Moreover the rate at which children were removed from their families had risen, year on year in Wales for more than a decade, and the gap between English and Welsh practice in this area had grown, rather than diminished. The need to halt and reverse this trend has become an objective of policy in this area.

This stands in sharp contrast to the avowed purpose of policy-making in relation to children in Wales that has long emphasized a preference for a preventive approach, based on a set of rights for children. The rights-based approach has been especially prominent in the post-devolution period. Wales was, for example, the first of the UK nations to appoint a Commissioner for Children (the office being established in 2001) and the first to make compliance with the requirements of the *United Nations Convention on the Rights of the Child a statutory obligation on all public authorities in Wales, as established in the *Rights of Children and Young Persons (Wales)* (2011). It has been argued that the cumulative impact of policies designed to deal with child poverty—to improve *participation, amplify the *voice of the child in policy-making, and embed a rights-based approach in practice— amount to 'a distinctive Welsh policy space' as far as children are concerned.

Turning now to education services for children, Flying Start is a spatially targeted programme, aimed at 0–3-year-olds in the most disadvantaged communities in Wales. It is best understood as part of the continuum of 'progressive universalism' in Welsh policy-making in which, at one end of the spectrum, nursery education has been available for all Welsh children from the age of three since 2005, as part of the Foundation Phase. The Foundation Phase represents a radical redesign of *early years education, on a learn-through-play model, pioneered in Scandinavian nations. It aims, particularly, to encourage learning amongst those children who, in previous systems, have been the first to fall behind. At the other end of the continuum, Flying Start provides an additional set of services, available to all children and families in areas where economic and social difficulties are most concentrated. In that sense, it forms part of a continuum that includes universal nursery provision and *Sure Start programmes, which, in Wales, are provided by every local authority. The programme offers high-quality part-time child care for all two- and three-year olds within Flying Start areas, an enhanced health visitor service, and access to specially designed *parenting programmes. The scheme draws directly on international best evidence of what works in *early intervention services. It combines a set of short-term measurable *outcomes—such as increased rates of breast-feeding and childhood immunization rates—with longer-term ambitions to reduce the need for interventions as a result of things going wrong in the lives of young people through drug use, *truancy, involvement in the *youth justice system, and so on.

Aligned with Flying Start is the Welsh government's Families First programme. This programme operates more specifically within the social services domain but, in its targeted nature, it shares many of the characteristics of Flying Start. The government has described its key principles as being: *family-focused*, through involving the whole family; *bespoke*, in shaping services to meet individual family circumstances; **integrated**, in bringing together interventions from across organizations; *proactive*, in seeking early identification of those in need of assistance; *intensive*, in concentrating significant help on those most in need; and *local*, in developing ways of providing services which reflect the needs and identities of local communities. Families First aims to provide an injection of practical and emotional help in a way that provides both prevention and protection, without the drawbacks of *labelling and *deviancy amplification that have been so characteristic of analogous programmes in the past. If it works, it will reach out to families most at *risk of exclusion and build a series of bridges between them and the life of the *community around them. It provides a practical example of the policy thrust that has been developed in Wales since 1999 in which services are re-orientated towards creating the conditions for successful living, rather than picking up the pieces once things have gone wrong.

Policies for older people As noted earlier, Wales has a higher proportion of older people in its population than any other part of the UK, and that proportion is expected to grow from 18 per cent in 2008 to 26 per cent by 2033. In the post-devolution period, a set of *universal policies have been developed for older people, including free travel on buses and free swimming in local authority leisure centres for those aged over 60. In 2008, Wales appointed the first Older Persons Commissioner in the UK. The Commissioner draws on the work of the National Partnership Forum for Older People, which functions at an all-Wales level and is mirrored in 50-plus Forums that exist in each local authority. At this universal level, policies for older people in Wales are characterized by optimism about the contribution that people make in later life and the capacity of individuals to go on enjoying fulfilled independent lives, provided that ambition is properly supported through the services provided by different tiers of government. This policy approach is well summarized by the Older Persons Commissioner in her *Strategic Plan 2010–13* (2010):

We want to see a Wales in which respect for the rights and dignity of older people is a practical reality in all areas of life, where age *discrimination is a thing of the past and where a positive view of ageing and of older people prevails.

The older people who need the help of Social Services Departments are almost always more fragile and vulnerable than older people in general. As elsewhere in the UK, they are likely to have greater health needs, especially as *co-morbidity increases in the post-75-year-old age group. The interface between health and social services thus increases in importance with age, but also remains an area where practice is variable, both in nature and quality. Delayed transfers of care between (free) hospital services and (*means-tested) social care continue to be a feature in many parts of Wales. The border-zones between *residential, nursing, and *continuing health care also remain contested and, at the level of the individual, the cause of acrimony between users, family members, and service providers.

More generally, social services for older people in Wales are provided in a *mixed economy, albeit one in which local government remains a stronger direct provider of services than in other parts of the UK. Wales has been by no means immune from general patterns in which, for example, the number of hours of domiciliary care has risen over the last decade, but that help has been progressively concentrated on fewer and fewer individuals, each with high levels of need. *Direct payments are available in Wales, with eligibility extended considerably by the Social Services and Wellbeing Act (2014). *Personal budgets have not been adopted. In this area, as in others, the advantages of *collective provision continue to exercise a substantial influence on Welsh policy-making and service provision.

Residential care services provide for an older and frailer population than in the past. Over a quarter of a century such services have shifted from, in effect, a public service monopoly, where local authority homes dominated, to a position where the *private sector now occupies that same position. In recent times, actions have been taken by the Welsh government to promote the growth of not-for-profit providers of residential and nursing care in an attempt to rebalance the *market.

Taken together, this means that policy for older people in Wales, while clear enough in intention, remains in considerable flux in actual service delivery and is likely to remain so for the foreseeable future.

Governance The Care Standards and Social Work Inspectorate for Wales (CSSIW), established in 2002, is the organization that combines the regulation and inspection of a series of social care settings, bodies, and professional groups in Wales. Those settings include care homes for adults, *domiciliary care agencies, *children's homes, and fostering and adoption agencies in the *public, *voluntary and *private sectors, as well as all social services provided through unified local authority departments across Wales. Through its registration process it decides who can provide services. Through inspections it sets standards and reports on them, taking compliance and enforcement measures where necessary. When complaints are received, it has the power to investigate and take action. The Chief Inspector of Social Services is a post that reports to the Welsh government, but is separate from it. The Inspector has a set of independent powers that allows the post-holder to report publicly on any issue within the role's ambit, without needing to secure the consent of the Minister. Over time, the regulation and inspection regime in Wales has shifted towards one which is 'risk-based', aiming to calibrate the level of inspection to the established quality of provision. Inspection activity has retained a focus on the encouragement of improvement, innovation, and change, which sets it apart from regulatory regimes that have developed elsewhere in the UK. It works closely, for example, with the Social Services Improvement Agency for Wales, an organization jointly owned by the Welsh Local Government Association, the Association of Directors of Social Services, and the Welsh government, which assists local authorities in improving standards and performance across the range of social services.

The Health Inspectorate Wales (HIW), established in 2004, is the organization that carries out many of the same functions as CSSIW, but in the field of health. It is responsible for the quality and safety of the patient care that is commissioned and provided by health care organizations in Wales. It discharges its duties through a programme of inspection, production of reports, and other mechanisms designed to create a culture of continuous improvement. The Welsh NHS has been described as the service which, of all four UK nations, remains most true to the NHS's founding principles. Health services in Wales are delivered primarily through seven local health boards with responsibility for primary, community, secondary, and mental health services. The Welsh NHS makes minimal use of the private sector, providing services in-house rather than *out-sourcing. Since 2000, it has attempted to shift the balance in favour of primary, preventive, and public health services through initiatives such as abolishing prescription charges, being the first to initiate legislation to ban smoking in public places, and developing proposals to ban smoking in cars when children are passengers. This overall policy thrust received endorsement in the Wanless Review, completed for the Welsh government in 2004. It confirmed that a strategy based on attempting to grow supply, in order to meet burgeoning demand for health services, could never be successful in Wales. Rather, it recommended measures that improved the engagement of individuals in promoting their own health, supported by government action, to promote prevention and tackle *health inequalities. It proposed a reconfiguration of services, away from too many district hospitals, all trying to provide too many services, in too many parts of Wales. In its place would come an expanded primary care service, capable of providing a wider range of care closer to patients' homes. For the large number of Welsh patients suffering from chronic diseases, it endorsed the development of condition management programmes, aimed at involving patients in greater self-care and self-management. For planned operations, it concluded that more specialist secondary care services should be concentrated in fewer hospital settings, sometimes further away from patients' homes than had been the case hitherto. From a social services perspective this has a series of implications for closer joint working, for the joint management of a frailer, older population in the community, and for the sharing of information between services.

In relying on cooperation rather than *competition as the way of improving quality, the Welsh health service has also attempted to amplify the significance of collective patient *voice (rather than individual *choice) as a means of ensuring that users, as well as producers, of services are fully engaged in their design and delivery. The main vehicle for doing so has been the retention and extension of Community Health Councils, first established in 1974 as the voice of patients within the NHS. Popularly known as the patients' 'watchdog', CHCs are made up of nominees from local government, *voluntary organizations, and health authorities. They were set up to oversee services and assess local needs, to act as patients' advocate (providing assistance and advising on complaints), and to participate in health planning. In England, CHCs fell victim to the consumerist agenda pursued by the *New Labour Health Minister, Alan Milburn. He regarded CHCs as an example of the sort of outdated *collectivism that had been characteristic of post-war thinking. In their place he proposed a system of 'patient advisors' who would assist individuals to secure redress against the system when things went wrong. The decision in Wales to take the opposite course of action was an early test of the ability of a Labour-led administration in Cardiff to pursue a different agenda from that being developed by Labour politicians at Westminster. In the event, CHCs were retained and strengthened in Wales, providing them with new rights of entry to a wider range of NHS premises and a new set of responsibilities for representing patients in areas such as hospital cleanliness. In the aftermath of the Southern Cross scandal of 2011, calls have been made to extend the remit of CHCs still further, to include new rights to enter and inspect residential care settings. They remain an important fixture in the governance landscape of the Welsh health and social care services.

Communities First is often described as a 'flagship' policy of the Welsh Labour Party in the post-devolution period. Indeed, despite reservations expressed by other parties, it has survived through each and every Assembly administration since the programme was established in 2000. The original prospectus described Communities First as a 'bottom-up' *community development scheme, focused on the 100 most deprived council wards in Wales. It was to be long-term and led by local residents, as 'experts' in the needs of their own localities. From the outset, however, local *partnerships have employed community development workers, many of whom have been drawn from those with a social work qualification.

While primarily an area-based set of activities, the original Communities First designations also included a small number of 'communities of interest', *ethnic minority populations in Cardiff, for example, which extended the scope of the programme beyond an exclusive focus on geographical concentrations of disadvantage. Over the period in which it has been in existence, the programme has undergone a number of developments. In its earliest phase it focused heavily on capacity building, identifying local needs, and the ability of residents to respond to them. In the second half of its existence, the programme has taken a more active approach to 'programme bending', bringing pressure to bear on statutory services provided by local authorities, local health boards, and others, to reverse the *inverse care law and invest more directly in areas where need is greatest. At the same time, Communities First partnerships have developed a stronger focus on local community economic development, looking for ways in which employment opportunities can be generated within localities. Finally, some realignment of governance arrangements for local partnerships has been attempted. In part this responds to the varying levels of success that a 'bottom-up' approach inevitably produces between different local partnerships. It also aims to avoid a funding 'cliff edge' in which an area that succeeds in improving its circumstances could find itself cut off from the support that has helped make progress possible. A smaller number of geographically larger partnerships is the likely result, bringing some anxieties that the very local focus of the scheme may be compromised in the future.

Legislation Organizational arrangements and policy principles in relation to social services have emerged with distinctiveness in the post-devolution period in Wales. As the Assembly has gathered new powers, so this distinctiveness has begun to emerge in separate legislative arrangements for Welsh social services. In addition to measures already mentioned, a Mental Health Measure, passed in 2010, placed the arrangement of community mental health services and *advocacy services for inpatients on a new legislative basis. A Children's Rights Measure, passed into law in 2010, placed the United Nations Convention on the Rights of the Child on the statute book as far as social services for children in Wales are concerned. These are examples of how the degree of separation between Wales and other parts of the UK has increased and seems set to do so all the more in the future.

ward round A doctor's meeting with patients to review their *diagnosis, treatment, and progress. In general hospitals this usually consists of making a circuit of a doctor's patients in different wards and visiting patients at their bedsides, sometimes accompanied by medical students and nursing staff. In psychiatric hospitals, ward rounds involve meetings with the patient in a meeting room, usually weekly, that often include a large number of professionals. These might include members of the nursing team, social workers, psychologists, *occupational therapists, *approved mental health professionals, and any other relevant professional. The patient may be asked to attend for only part of the meeting during which s/he is interviewed by the doctor, before being asked to leave, not being present during professional discussions that then take place. If the patient consents, family members, friends, or significant others may also attend. The ward round can be intimidating to patients and they may not have met many of the professionals present. It is not usual practice for professionals who are present to introduce themselves, but a patient is entitled to request this. The ward round is important because it is often the only opportunity the patient has to meet the doctor. Patients can be encouraged to think about what they want to say in advance and to think about any questions they have. Patients can be represented or supported by advocates, for example, an *independent mental health advocate. Some hospitals have their own independent patient *advocacy services and some *voluntary organizations such as *MIND may provide support. Social workers can play a key role in ward rounds by advocating on the patient's behalf or by including important information about wider aspects of the patient's life and circumstances that might otherwise be overlooked.

wardship A power that resides with the High Court to assume responsibility for all aspects of the care of a child. When the High Court makes a child a ward no orders can be made or decisions or actions taken that affect the child without the permission of that court having first been obtained. The High Court effectively becomes the child's responsible parent. As the Children Act (1989) confers on courts, including the High Court, the power to make orders relating to children, wardship proceedings are used only in *cases where exceptionally complex decisions need to be taken in relation to the care of a child.

warmth One of the three qualities (the other two being *empathy and genuineness) that the American therapist Carl Rogers (1902-87) regarded as the core conditions of a helping relationship. *See also* UNCONDITIONAL POSITIVE REGARD.

welfare 1. The wellbeing of individuals or groups and service provision related to their wellbeing such as education, health, housing, social security, and social services. When the state takes a major responsibility for people's welfare, the totality of the provision and the institutional arrangements underpinning this, it is referred to as the *welfare state.

2. In recent years, particularly in the US, the term has become specifically associated with *means-tested benefits paid to those in *poverty and is used pejoratively, for example, when referring to 'welfare dependents', with the implication that where such benefits exist to support particular circumstances, those circumstances are more likely to occur. In the case of attacks on 'welfare', this has been argued particularly vociferously with regard to support for lone parents, which has been seen as encouraging women to choose to be single mothers. *See also* UNDERCLASS.

welfare checklist 1. The criteria (set out in Section 1(3) of the Children Act [1989]) that are used by *family courts when considering making a *Care Order or *Supervision Order under the Children Act (1989). The checklist is not meant to be exhaustive and there may be other factors for the court to consider in addition to those listed. Reports submitted by social workers and other professionals to assist courts in making judgements about a child's future will have regard to this checklist and the *paramountcy principle that underpins it:

(a) The ascertainable wishes and feelings of the child/children concerned
  (considered in the light of his/her/their age and understanding);
(b) His/her/their physical, emotional, and educational *needs;
(c) The likely effect on him/her/them of any change in his/her/their circumstances;

(d) His/her/their age, sex, background, and any characteristics of his/hers/theirs which the court considers relevant;

(e) Any harm which he/she/they has/have suffered or is/are at risk of suffering;

(f) How capable each of his/her/their parents, and any other person in relation to whom the court considers the question to be relevant, is of meeting his/her/their needs;

(g) The range of powers available to the court under the Children Act (1989) in the proceedings in question.

2. The criteria (set out in Section 1(4) of the Adoption and Children Act [2002]) that are used by family courts and adoption agencies in coming to a decision relating to the *adoption of a child or matters affecting the *placement. The *paramountcy principle underpins the adoption welfare checklist, with the addition of 'throughout his [*sic*] life' Section 1(2). A court or adoption agency must have regard to the following matters:

(a) the child's ascertainable wishes and feelings regarding the decision (considered in the light of the child's age and understanding);

(b) the child's particular *needs;

(c) the likely effect on the child (throughout her/his life) of having ceased to be a member of the original family and become an adopted person;

(d) the child's age, sex, background, and any of the child's characteristics which the court or agency considers relevant;

(e) any harm (within the meaning of the Children Act [1989]) which the child has suffered or is at risk of suffering;

(f) the relationship which the child has with relatives, and with any other person in relation to whom the court or agency considers the relationship to be relevant, including:

  i) the likelihood of any such relationship continuing and the value of the child of its doing so;

  ii) the ability and willingness of any of the child's relatives, or of any such person, to provide the child with a secure environment in which the child can develop, and otherwise to meet the child's needs;

  iii) the wishes and feelings of any of the child's relatives, or of any such person, regarding the child.

See also CARE PROCEEDINGS; CHILD-CENTRED APPROACH; CHILD DEVELOPMENT; PUBLIC LAW OUTLINE; SAME-'RACE' PLACEMENT.

welfare pluralism *See* MIXED ECONOMY OF WELFARE.

welfare principle *See* PARAMOUNTCY PRINCIPLE.

welfare provision *See* WELFARE; WELFARE REGIME; WELFARE STATE.

welfare regime An alternative to the use of the term the *welfare state that has the advantage of not assuming or implying that the state necessarily occupies the central role in welfare provision. The roles that social work plays, and how and by whom they are undertaken, will be shaped by the nature of the welfare regime in which it is located. There have been attempts to categorize different welfare regimes using *ideal-types, such as:

Corporatist Well-developed welfare provision primarily though the labour market.

Latin Limited welfare provision through churches and charitable foundations.

Residual Underpinned by the ideology that the state should not be the main provider of welfare with an emphasis on provision by families and the *market.

Social democratic *Universal provision of welfare to all citizens with the state as the main provider and little provision outside the state.

Such ideal-types can be used to analyse the extent to which actual welfare regimes in particular countries conform to or depart from them. Feminists have criticized formulations of ideal-types of regime for not considering the differential impact they may have on men and women and their neglect of the roles played by women in the informal sector of welfare, for example, as *carers in households.

welfare rights (welfare rights work) Seeking to ensure that an individual or group is receiving all of the social security benefits to which they are entitled. This involves: giving people information about benefits, sometimes through targeted campaigns, advising them about their entitlement and how to make claims; and advocating on behalf of people in support of claims or in appeals when claims have been rejected. In the 1970s it was commonplace for social workers to engage in welfare rights work, but it has dwindled to the point where it is now very rare to find social workers engaged in this sort of work. Some *local authorities employ welfare rights advisors, and organizations such as Law Centres and *Citizen Advice Bureaux undertake welfare rights work. Social workers can direct people to such organizations if they think that the *benefits received by a *service user fall short of her/his entitlement or simply want to give a service user the opportunity to have their benefits checked.

welfare state The totality of the service provision and the institutional arrangements underpinning it in a system that involves the state taking a major responsibility for people's *welfare in an attempt to improve their life chances and mitigate the worst excesses of inequality. In the UK, the welfare state was initiated by the Beveridge Report (1942) and introduced by the post-war Labour government (1946–1951) in response to the impact of the Second World War, economic collapse, and a range and depth of governmental response, during and after the war, that was shaped by a conception of the state as active and responsible. It involved state provision in education, health, housing, social security, and social services. The welfare state was based on the assumption that citizens had collective obligations for each other's welfare through the agency of the state, as a corrective to life chances based purely on market-based outcomes. If the *market was left unchecked, injustice would result because of capitalism's inability to guarantee the provision of services as a right to all citizens. Therefore, the inequalities of the *market had to be constrained by the state in order to promote social stability, balancing the socially divisive effects of market-based inequalities by the integrative experience of social solidarity provided by the welfare state (*see* DEMOCRATIC-WELFARE-CAPITALISM). T. H. Marshall (1893–1981) saw the welfare state as the final stage in the development of *citizenship, adding social rights to the civil and political rights that had been attached to citizenship in the eighteenth and nineteenth centuries respectively. As a consequence, in the policy, practice, and *analysis of the British post-war welfare state, a clear distinction was drawn between public non-commercial activities, which the welfare state was considered to exemplify, and private commercial activities, driven by the market's profit motive. The welfare state was seen as shouldering responsibilities that were intrinsically non-capitalist. Its *interventions, such as social work, were depicted as being driven by a very different dynamic and as protected from the vagaries of market forces. This distinction between the operation of the market on the one hand and the welfare state on the

w

other enjoyed a broad measure of support across the parliamentary political spec- trum in Britain from 1945 until the late 1970s, a phenomenon often referred to as the *post-war consensus. The consensus rested on the assumption that the provision of welfare by the state and its continuing expansion was an unchallengeable commit- ment. The consensus was fuelled by wider trends. For example, during the 1960s, gross domestic product increased, public expenditure and public services expanded, and average personal incomes rose, in the context of full employment, low inflation, and steady, if slow, economic growth.

The framework of the welfare state provided the primary vehicle for the expan- sion of social work. It was the source of social work's legal and moral authority as, ultimately, social workers implement legislation on behalf of the state, as an arm of social policy, rather than as an autonomous profession. The law sets out the *powers and *duties of social workers, on the one hand, and the rights and respon- sibilities of service users, on the other, in those socially problematic areas which have been accorded official recognition by the state. Although social work joined the post-war welfare institutions somewhat in the shadow of the major pillars such as the National Health Service and Social Security, from the end of the Second World War the dominant professional interests in Britain saw their struggle to secure social work's legitimacy as linked to its having a more central role in the welfare state. The range and responsibilities of social work grew through its location in different departments of local government, with administratively discrete, legis- latively specific, and professionally specialized services for children and families (Children's Departments), for people with mental health problems and *learning disabilities (Mental Welfare services under the auspices of Medical Officers of Health), and for *older people and people with physical disabilities (Welfare Depart- ments). In these organizational settings, social workers had a key role in identifying those citizens who required assistance and allocating state resources to them. This somewhat disjointed development of social work changed dramatically when social work broke out of its position as a relatively marginal and dispersed collection of roles and practices, located in separate social work services, and was transformed into a central and systematically organized element of state welfare as a result of the Seebohm Report (1968) and its implementation in the Local Authority and Allied Social Services Act (1970). The Act required *local authorities to establish *Social Services Departments.

If the establishment and consolidation of social work's position in the welfare state was the key to understanding its greater prominence, the destabilization of that niche is the key to social work's subsequent transformation. In the 1970s, inflation increased dramatically, unemployment reached inter-war depression levels, the balance of payments worsened, the value of the pound against the dollar declined, leading to economic conditions of low growth and high inflation— so-called 'stagflation'. Conditions of stagflation lent themselves to the portrayal of public services as non-productive and a drain on the wealth-producing parts of the economy. As a result, the post-war consensus on the welfare state came under siege, particularly in the wake of an economic crisis in 1976, following the quadrupling of oil prices in 1973 at the instigation of the Organization of Petroleum Exporting Countries. With Britain's currency reserves endangered by the mounting economic crisis, the International Monetary Fund granted a loan in 1976 on condition that severe cuts were made in public expenditure and that a policy of wage restraint was introduced. As part of the expenditure cuts, the Labour government set about reducing the total amount of local government spending. As the Labour govern- ment's strategy took effect, the winter of 1978/9 became infamous as the 'Winter of

Discontent', with massive trade union action, which included social workers, in response to the curbing of pay demands and cuts to the 'social wage' through public expenditure restraint.

This was the immediate context in which the first Conservative government led by Margaret Thatcher was elected in May 1979. It inherited and exploited a public perception of a social and fiscal crisis in welfare provision. The Conservatives' economic policy was to control the rate of monetary growth, bring down the public sector borrowing requirement, lower taxation with the aim of providing incentives for investment, and implement public expenditure cuts to allow reductions in borrowing and taxation. The critique of the *public sector was intense, with ferocious attacks on the welfare state on the following grounds:

Ideological The state had expanded too far. It was interfering in matters that should be left to individuals making their own decisions. State provision reduced the scope of the individual to make choices, by subjecting the individual to uniform provision in education, health, and social services. The state needed to be rolled back to free individuals to make their own decisions. Society is an aggregation of individuals who should enjoy 'freedom under the rule of law'.

Moral Criticisms about the effect of welfare focused on the welfare state creating dependency, weakening individual morality, and undermining the family. People had come to rely on the state to meet their needs. They lost the capacity or the will to take care of themselves. The work-shy were encouraged because the gap between benefits and earned incomes was too narrow.

Economic Excessive spending on the welfare state was a major factor in Britain's poor economic performance. Excessive spending required excessive taxation and the limits of taxation had been reached. The state's borrowing to pay for the welfare state caused inflation. Resources were diverted from productive profit-making economic activities into unproductive non-profit-making activities. Taxation made people less willing to be economically active, investors reluctant to invest, and workers less inclined to work. Individual economic initiative was stifled by the state's excessive taxation to pay for the welfare state.

The economic grounds were fuelled by the public perception of a fiscal crisis that enabled the Thatcher government to depict the existing welfare state as too expensive for the state's tax base to support, as squeezing out *private sector investment, and as undermining (through its demands for taxation support) entrepreneurial and managerial incentives. Accordingly, the welfare state was castigated as a prime contributor to Britain's economic decline through its misallocation of resources, sapping of individual responsibility, and production of dependent citizens. In attacking the welfare state as economically mismanaged, dependency-inducing, and needing to be trimmed if Britain were to succeed in the global economy, the Conservative government saw itself as correcting the failings of the post-war consensus on the welfare state, in which social work was considered to be deeply implicated.

The critique of the welfare state predisposed Thatcher governments to take a sceptical view of social workers and local authority Social Services Departments. Social work was a key component in the Conservatives' depiction of the welfare state's services as *bureaucratic and insensitive to individual *needs. In this context, it has been argued that social work became the metaphor for what was considered to be wrong with the welfare state and social work's critics questioned whether social work could survive as the 'nanny state' was demolished. Four themes were identified as essential to the transformation of social work:

- Introduction of *market mechanisms;
- Promotion of competition leading to efficiency gains and savings;
- Keeping state provision to a minimum;
- Pursuit of individualism and individual choice.

(These themes were also taken up by *New Labour when it came to power in 1997 [*see* MODERNIZATION].) As a consequence, the welfare state was drastically restructured and social work subsequently operated on a different basis within it.

Criticisms of the welfare state came not just from the Right. The Left saw it in one of two ways: either as a mechanism for pacifying and buying off the working class, thus deflecting it from demands for more fundamental change; or as embodying contradictions, protecting people from the worst excesses of capitalism, but also enabling capitalism to function and thus legitimating it. Feminists criticized the welfare state because it was rooted in the traditional family system, primarily aimed at supporting male *participation in the paid labour force, and therefore it was not neutral in relation to sexual divisions of labour. Other critics pointed out that the welfare state was also not neutral in its employment of *racialized norms or in how it dealt with *disability or sexuality. The essence of this range of criticisms was that rather than being a neutral arbiter of society's interests, the welfare state both reflected and reproduced social divisions in society, by assuming that people were homogenous and not recognizing and responding to the *differences that shaped the *diversity of their lives. Thus, the rules of welfare state *bureaucracies and the practice of professionals were seen as contributing to the reproduction of existing power relations based on *discrimination and *oppression. Social work was one of the sites on which these issues were played out (*see* ANTI-DISCRIMINATORY PRACTICE; ANTI-OPPRESSIVE PRACTICE). However, when the welfare state began to be restructured, most of these critics defended it, fearing that any changes were likely to intensify the characteristics of which they were critical. *See also* WELFARE REGIME.

wellbeing (adults) *See* PROMOTING WELL-BEING.

Welsh Assembly *See* WALES.

what works? *See* EVIDENCE-BASED PRACTICE.

whistleblowing The action of someone in an organization who reveals abusive attitudes and/or practices that are taking or have taken place. The Public Interest Disclosure Act (1998) seeks to protect whistleblowers from adverse consequences by dissuading employers from treating them detrimentally, for example, by dismissing them or reducing their pay.

whiteness A concept that problematizes white people as a racial category. It challenges the tendency of white people to view themselves as non-racial or race-neutral, identifies the privilege attached to whiteness, and sees it as a specific standpoint from which white people regard themselves and others.

whole person approach *See* HOLISTIC APPROACH.

Whole System Demonstrator Project *See* TELECARE.

withdrawal The process that follows ceasing to use a drug to which someone is addicted, which can involve nausea, cramps, diarrhoea, and convulsions. It can be undertaken with or without assistance from medication. *See also* ADDICTION.

witness protection *See* VULNERABLE WITNESS.

womanism Used by some Black feminists in preference to *'feminism' because feminism is seen as having (white) ethnocentric connotations.

women-centred (women-centred approach, women-centred social work) *See* FEMINIST SOCIAL WORK.

Women's Aid Grew out of the *women's movement in the 1970s, as the issue of *violence in the home and other forms of sexual and interpersonal violence towards women were highlighted. It began in 1974, providing practical and emotional support in a range of services to women and children who had experienced violence. It has a national 24-hour helpline and local groups and services that include *refuges. It also engages in campaigning and awareness-raising activities. Its position is that:

• Women and children have a right to live their lives free from all forms of violence and *abuse and society has a duty to recognize and defend this right.
• *Domestic violence is a violation of women's and children's human rights. It is the result of the abuse of power and control, and is rooted in the historical status of women in the family and in society.

Its aims are to:

• Empower women who have been affected by domestic violence.
• Meet the needs of children affected by domestic violence.
• Provide services run by women, which are based on listening to *survivors.
• Challenge the *disadvantages that result from domestic violence.
• Support and reflect *diversity and promote equality of opportunity.
• Promote cohesive inter-agency responses to domestic violence and develop *partnerships.

(⊕) SEE WEB LINKS
• Official site of Women's Aid.

women's movement The coming together of women to improve their position in society that is usually used to describe second-wave *feminism in the 1970s. (The first wave was in the nineteenth and early twentieth centuries and is usually thought of in relation to the struggle for the vote for women.) Also used to refer to specific campaigns addressing particular issues that bring together a movement of women.

working agreement 1. A document drafted by social workers when working with *service users, for example families who are experiencing difficulties, with the aim of defining the parameters and expectations on both sides of the work to be undertaken, its aims, and tasks, and the services to be provided, highlighting areas on which there is cooperation between the social worker and service user(s). It needs, as far as possible, to be the outcome of negotiation between both parties and to be expressed in readily understandable terms. It is intended to provide structure to the working relationship by agreeing aims, objectives, and targets, often linked to a time-scale for completion. The success of the agreement will be determined by the commitment of all parties and is likely to be most successful if the active *participation and agreement of the parents or *care-givers are given. While the emphasis is on achieving a *partnership between service users and practitioners in pursuance of agreed *goals, this may be more difficult to achieve in situations where service user participation is involuntary, for example when the document is drafted as part of a *child protection plan. The notion of partnership between family and practitioners is unlikely to apply in such circumstances, in contrast to situations where help was originally requested by the family and is more readily accepted. *See also* EARLY INTERVENTION; FAMILY GROUP CONFERENCE; FAMILY SUPPORT MEETING; LEAD PROFESSIONAL; PREVENTION; TASK-CENTRED CASEWORK.

2. A document drafted between a social work student on an assessed practice placement and her/his practice educator (and workplace supervisor, if applicable) that typically includes working and administrative arrangements; learning needs; proposed workload; theories and models; learning objectives; supervision arrangements; and how the student will be assessed.

workload management System(s) for allocating and reviewing the amount of work undertaken by a social worker. The most commonly used model allocates time allowances to each of the social worker's *'cases' and to any other activities in which s/he is engaged, for example attending meetings within the organization or with other organizations that are not connected with 'cases'. Time allowances can be allocated in advance or the amount of time a social worker spent on each element of her/his work in the previous month can be recorded in retrospect and adjustments can be made accordingly. A third system combines the first two, allocating time allowances in advance and then reviewing actual time spent. The intention of whatever system is used is to prevent social workers from becoming overloaded, with the possibility of *burn-out, and to manage the overall workload of a particular team. Although such systems work effectively in some places, in others they are regarded cynically by social workers because they can be over-optimistic about how quickly work can be completed, or because the norms they lay down are exceeded and social workers are overloaded anyway. *See also* CASELOAD MANAGEMENT.

Further reading: Edwards, K., Hallett, C., and Sawbridge, P. (2008) 'Working with Complexity: Managing Workload and Surviving in a Changing Environment', in S. Fraser and S. Matthews (eds) *The Critical Practitioner in Social Work and Health Care*, Sage.

written agreement *See* WORKING AGREEMENT.

YOT *See* YOUTH OFFENDING TEAM.

young carer Children and young people who provide help and assistance to family members and others who are physically or mentally ill, frail, *disabled, or who suffer from a substance misuse problem related to drugs or alcohol. Since the mid-1980s, young carers have been given varying degrees of attention by policy-makers, researchers, service providers, and the media. *Local authorities and *voluntary organizations across the UK have developed a range of young carers support projects, offering information, personal and practical support, and leisure activities. Young people who provided care and assistance to others became eligible for inclusion within the definition of a *'carer' under the Carers (Recognition and Services) Act (1995), and they can also be regarded as a *'child in need' under Section 17 of the Children Act (1989). Their recognition under the Carers Act (1995) has been replaced by provision under the Care Act (2014).

The Care Act Statutory Guidance (2016) highlights a young carer's vulnerability when her/his caring role impacts on her/his emotional and/or physical wellbeing or her/his prospects in education and life generally. This can include preventing the young carer from accessing education, for example, because an adult's needs for *care and support result in the young carer's regular absence from school, and preventing the young carer from building relationships and friendships. When a young carer is identified, a *needs assessment is offered to the adult who requires care and support and the young carer can also be referred for a young carer's assessment (Section 63 of the Care Act [2014]) or an assessment under the Children Act (1989). Adults' and children's services should work together in considering the impact of an adult's needs on a young carer and deciding whether any of the caring responsibilities the young carer is undertaking are inappropriate. Responsibilities are inappropriate if they are likely to impact on a young carer's health, wellbeing, or education or if they are considered unsuitable in the light of the young carer's circumstances. Such responsibilities may include personal care such as bathing and toileting; carrying out strenuous physical tasks such as lifting; administering medication; handling the family budget; and providing emotional support to an adult. The young carer's own views are taken into account in deciding whether the tasks they undertake are inappropriate. Consideration is given to how supporting an adult with needs for care and support can prevent a young carer from undertaking excessive or inappropriate caring responsibilities.

A local authority must also assess the needs of young carers as they approach adulthood. For instance, many young carers feel that they cannot go to university or enter employment because of their caring responsibilities. 'Transition assessments' and planning consider how to support young carers to prepare for adulthood and how to raise and fulfil their aspirations (*see* TRANSITION TO ADULT CARE AND SUPPORT). A young carer's assessment should indicate how any care and support plan for the adult s/he cares for would change as a result of a change in the young carer's circumstances. For example, if a young carer has an opportunity to go to university away from home, the local authority should indicate how it would meet the *eligible needs of an adult that were previously being met by the young carer.

The approach taken by the Care Act (2014) is in line with many of the perceived problems in young carers' lives that have been seen as being associated with having caring responsibilities. These include poor educational attainment; *stigma; isolation from their *peer group; lack of time and opportunity for the usual childhood activities; conflict between the caring role and their own *needs; a lack of recognition of their caring contribution; limitations on aspirations and *choices; *stress and worry; and physical problems resulting from lifting and assisting another person. Some children, however, have reported a sense of pride in what they do, and have emphasized the positive aspects of the relationship with the adult needing support and assistance. It has also been argued that defining children as 'young carers' or 'children in need' locks them into an inappropriate role that is detrimental and stigmatizing both for them and for their families. Accordingly, some have criticized the growth of specialist services for young carers and instead have demanded that support services should be made available to adults who need them so that they can live a more ordinary life without needing to rely on children for assistance or on specialist services for young carers. There have also been objections to what is seen as the problematizing of the relationship between disabled adults and their children. Any implication that children brought up within households with a disabled parent would inevitably experience a negative childhood has been strongly challenged.

In response to these perspectives, specialist young carers services now tend to emphasize *partnership and collaboration with parents and other family members, in addition to any *direct work undertaken with the children. At a formal policy level at least, the Care Act (2014) acknowledges the need both to be aware of the factors that may precipitate children into an inappropriate caring role and to make arrangements that avoid it. The Care Act Statutory Guidance (2016) has emphasized the positive consequences for children when adults are assessed in their own right for services to meet need, including those that support them in their parenting role. However, resource constraints and the way that *eligibility criteria are applied in most *local authorities severely limit the level of services available. This is likely to mean that some will continue to rely upon the help and assistance of children and that some of those children will continue to seek the support, information, and advice provided by specialized young carers services. *See also* ASSESSMENT (CHILDREN); CARE; CARE RECIPIENTS; CARER'S ASSESSMENT; CARERS UK.

Further reading: Dearden, C. and Becker, S. (2004) *Young Carers in the UK*, Carers UK.
Department of Health (2016) *Care and Support: Statutory Guidance* Chapter 16. Available at: https://www.gov.uk/government/publications/care-act-statutory-guidance/care-and-support-statutory-guidance#person-centred-care-and-support-planning.
Social Care Institute of Excellence (2005) *The Health and Well-being of Young Carers*, SCIE.

young offender Person aged between 10 and 17 years who is convicted or reprimanded (previously cautioned) in England and *Wales for a criminal offence. *See also* AGE OF CRIMINAL RESPONSIBILITY; CAUTION; REPRIMAND; YOUNG OFFENDERS' INSTITUTION; YOUTH JUSTICE SERVICE; YOUTH JUSTICE SYSTEM.

young offenders' institution Run by the Prison Service, these establishments hold male offenders aged 15–17 years on sites specifically set aside for them or on sites shared with but separate from Youth Offender Institutions for 18–20 year olds. Young female offenders are placed in self-contained units attached to existing institutions for women and these work in the same way as young offender institutions. Inmates receive up to twenty-five hours of education a week. Some female prisoners under the age of 18 may be placed in a designated wing of an adult female prison in exceptional circumstances for child care or medical reasons. *See also* CUSTODIAL SENTENCE; DETENTION AND TRAINING ORDER; SECURE TRAINING CENTRE.

Youth Inclusion Support Panel (YISP) A *multidisciplinary service aimed at addressing *anti-social behaviour and *risk of offending by young people aged 8–13, though some YISPs extend the age range as high as 17. A young person who is identified as involved in *anti-social behaviour and/or is considered to be at *risk of offending can be offered the chance to appear before a YISP. The panel consists of an ad hoc collection of professionals who are seen as relevant to the young person's *needs, typically their parents, teachers, *youth workers, social workers, *Child and Adolescent Mental Health Services workers, and other relevant people. The Panel makes a plan aimed at helping the child or young person with their behaviour, channelling them into constructive activities, and reducing the risk of offending. Other support such as *anger management programmes or *parenting classes may also be offered. *See also* ACCEPTABLE BEHAVIOUR AGREEMENT; ANTI-SOCIAL BEHAVIOUR ORDER; MULTI-SYSTEMIC THERAPY.

Youth Justice Service (YJS) Formerly called the Youth Offending Service, which was established in 1999 as a result of the Crime and Disorder Act (1998). The change in name represented the widening of the focus of the service to include work not only with young people who have committed or are at *risk of committing offences, but also parents and the *victims of crime. The service continues to bring together within every *local authority area professionals and others from key agencies in a coordinated multidisciplinary approach to youth offending. The agencies concerned are:

- Children's services;
- *Probation;
- Police;
- Education;
- Health;
- Drugs and Alcohol Misuse services;
- Housing.

These services work together throughout the different stages of the *youth justice system, parts of which will also require the involvement of the Crown Prosecution Service, solicitors, and the courts. *Young offenders are assessed by staff in *Youth Offending Teams using a national assessment tool known as *ASSET. Professionals operating in the service assist the courts in reaching judgments about the most appropriate way to deal with a young person convicted of criminal offences through the preparation of a *pre-sentence report. *See also* YOUTH JUSTICE SYSTEM; YOUTH OFFENDING TEAM.

youth justice system The combined organizations and processes used in England and *Wales to prosecute, convict, and punish young people aged between 10 and 17 years who commit criminal offences. Its principal stated aim is to prevent offending by children and young people and therefore a *young offender is in most circumstances likely to be dealt with differently from an adult offender. The system comprises a number of stages:

Prevention Work by those agencies which constitute the *Youth Justice Service to address the *needs of a young person who is at *risk of offending.

Pre-court Work by these agencies with a young person who commits a first or second offence and who admits guilt or who is behaving anti-socially.

Court Involvement of the youth justice service, police, and Crown Prosecution Service with a young person who is charged after committing further offences, or a young person charged with a more serious offence. This may lead to her or him being bailed or *remanded in *custody prior to appearing in a youth court, or if charged with a serious offence, the local Crown Court.

Sentencing Where a young person pleads guilty or is convicted of a charge and receives either a *community sentence or is sentenced to *custody.

End of sentence The *Youth Justice Service assists young people, particularly those sentenced to custody, to settle back into the community by providing the services required to achieve this. An example of this is the integrated resettlement support programme, which works with young people experiencing substance misuse problems both in custody and in the community.

When sentencing a young person, courts have a range of community and custodial options at their disposal. In deciding which option to select, courts will be guided by a *pre-sentence report prepared by either the probation service or Youth Justice Service. *See also* ASSET; COMMUNITY SENTENCES; DETENTION AND TRAINING ORDER; ELECTRONIC TAGGING; PARENTING ORDER; REHABILITATION ORDER; SECURE ACCOMMODATION ORDER; SECURE CHILDREN'S HOMES; SECURE TRAINING CENTRE; YOUNG OFFENDERS' INSTITUTION; YOUTH OFFENDING TEAM.

Youth Offending Service *See* YOUTH JUSTICE SERVICE.

Youth Offending Team (YOT) A multidisciplinary team in a local area that seeks to respond to the needs of *young offenders in a comprehensive way to prevent further offending. *See also* YOUTH JUSTICE SERVICE; YOUTH JUSTICE SYSTEM.

Youth Rehabilitation Order A sentence replacing the Curfew Order that came into effect on 30 November 2009 as a result of the Criminal Justice and Immigration Act (2008). It is a generic *community sentence for young offenders that combines a number of sentences under one provision. It is the standard community sentence used for the majority of children and young people who offend, simplifying sentencing for young people, providing flexibility in *interventions, and minimizing the use of *custody. The Order represents an individualized *risk and *needs-based approach to community sentencing, permitting the attachment of a variety of requirements deemed appropriate to the circumstances of the young person, for example activity, curfew, drug treatment, and education requirements. Non-statutory practice guidance for Youth Rehabilitation Orders has been produced. *See also* ASSET; COMMUNITY SENTENCES; PRE-SENTENCE REPORT; REFERRAL ORDER; REPARATION ORDER; YOUNG OFFENDER; YOUTH JUSTICE SERVICE; YOUTH JUSTICE SYSTEM; YOUTH OFFENDING TEAM.

Further reading: Youth Justice Board for England and Wales (2010) *The Youth Rehabilitation Order and Other Youth Justice Provisions of the Criminal Justice and Immigration Act 2008: Practice Guidance for Youth Offending Teams.* Available at: http://yjbpublications.justice.gov. uk/Resources/Downloads/Youth%20Rehabilitation%20Order%20and%20the%20Criminal% 20Justice%20and%20Immigration%20Act%202008.pdf.

youth work A spectrum of activities with young people that may include running a youth club; making contact with groups of young people in a particular neighbourhood; activities with young people sponsored by a religious group; and many others. A number of key principles have been identified that distinguish youth work:

- A focus on young people—a readiness to engage with young people and make sense of their experiences.
- An emphasis on the voluntary *participation of the young people concerned.
- Committing to association—joining together in companionship or to undertake a particular task.
- Being friendly, informal and approachable—the person or character of the worker is of fundamental importance.
- Concern with the education and welfare of young people.

Youth work was hard hit by the cuts in public spending introduced by the Conservative-Liberal Democrat Coalition government (2010–15) and has remained so in the context of ongoing *austerity.

y

Table of Legislation, Regulations, and Codes of Practice

LEGISLATION

Section 17	aids and adaptations; assessment (children); child abuse inquiries, child in need; child welfare; duty (specific); family support; target duty; transition to adult care and support; unaccompanied asylum-seeking children; young carer
Section 20	assessment (children); child accommodated by a local authority; unaccompanied asylum-seeking children; voluntary accommodation
Section 21	PACE beds
Section 22	looked-after children
Section 23	independent visitor; personal advisor
Section 25	Secure Accommodation Order
Section 26	advocacy; independent reviewing officer
Section 31	Care Order; care proceedings; Interim Care Order; Placement Order; significant harm; threshold criteria (children); Section 31A plan
Section 33	Care Order
Section 34	contact 2; Contact Order 2
Section 35	Supervision Order
Section 36	Education Supervision Order
Section 39	Care Order
Section 43	Child Assessment Order
Section 44	assessment (children); Emergency Protection Order
Section 46	assessment (children); police protection
Section 47	achieving best evidence; assessment (children); child abuse inquiries; child accommodated by a local authority; chronology; duty to investigate; Emergency Protection Order; family support; initial assessment; police protection; public law; Section 47 enquiry; significant harm; strategy discussion; strategy meeting; threshold criteria (children)
Section 50	Recovery Order
Children Act (2004)	child; Child Death Review; Children and Young People's Plan; coordination of services; *Every Child Matters*; Local Safeguarding Children Board; rapid response; Serious Case Review
Section 11	local authority designated officer
Section 52	looked-after children (education)
Children and Families Act (2014)	aids and adaptations; Care Proceedings; Child Arrangements Order; Custody Order; Education, Health and Care Needs Assessment; Education, Health and Care Plan; Interim Care Order; transition to adult care and support
Section 37	aids and adaptations
Section 99	looked-after child (education)
Children and Young People (Scotland) Act (2014)	Scotland
Children and Young Persons Act (1933)	persons posing a risk to children; Schedule 1 offender
Children and Young Person's Act (2008)	independent reviewing officer; kinship care
Children (Leaving Care) Act (2000)	leaving care (services); pathway plan
Children (Scotland) Act (1995)	Scotland

REGULATIONS

Privacy and Electronic Communications Regulations (2003)	Information Commissioner's Office
Review of Children's Cases (Amendment) (England) Regulations (2004)	care plan (children); independent reviewing officer
Sexual Orientation Regulations (2006)	heterosexism
Young Carers' (Needs Assessment) Regulations (2015)	assessment (children)

CODES OF PRACTICE

Deprivation of Liberty Safeguards (2008)	Deprivation of Liberty Safeguards
Employers of Social Care Workers (2002)	Code of Practice
Mental Capacity Act (2005)	capacity
Mental Health Act (1983)	after-care (mental health); guardianship (adults); hospital managers' hearing; mental disorder; place of safety
Mental Health Act (2007)	Community Treatment Order
Police and Criminal Evidence Act (1984)	appropriate adult
Social Care Workers (2002)	Code of Practice

Acronyms

ABC model	antecedents-behaviour-consequences (*see* FUNCTIONAL ANALYSIS)
AC	approved clinician
ACPC	Area Child Protection Committee
ACT	assertive community treatment
ADHD	attention deficit hyperactivity disorder
ADL	activities of daily living
ADP	anti-discriminatory practice
AEA	Action on Elder Abuse
AHL	Action on Hearing Loss
AMHP	approved mental health professional
AOP	anti-oppressive practice
ARP	anti-racist practice
ASBO	Anti-social Behaviour Order
ASPD	anti-social personality disorder
ASW	approved social worker [defunct] (*see* APPROVED MENTAL HEALTH PROFESSIONAL)
ASYE	Assessed and Supported Year in Employment
AWOL	absent without leave
BAAF	British Association for Adoption and Fostering (*see* CORAMBAAF)
BACP	British Association for Counselling and Psychotherapy
BASW	British Association of Social Workers
BEAT	Beating Eating Disorders (*see* EATING DISORDERS)
BFT	behavioural family therapy
BGOP	Better Government for Older People
BPD	borderline personality disorder (*see* PERSONALITY DISORDER)
BSL	British Sign Language
CAF	Common Assessment Framework
CAFCASS	Children and Family Court Advisory Support Service
CAMHS	Child and Adolescent Mental Health Services
CAO	Child Arrangements Order
CBT	cognitive behavioural therapy
CCG	Clinical Commissioning Group
CDR	Child Death Review
CDT	Community Drug Team
C4EO	Centre for Excellence and Outcomes in Children's and Young People's Services
CIC	community interest company
CHC	Community Health Council (*see* WALES)
CHC	Continuing Health Care (*see* NHS CONTINUING HEALTH CARE)
CMHN	Community Mental Health nurse

CMS	Child Maintenance Service
COS	Charity Organisation Society
CPA	Care Programme Approach
CPD	continuing professional development
CPN	Community Psychiatric Nurse
CPR	Child Permanence Report
CPS	Crown Prosecution Service (*see* DOMESTIC VIOLENCE)
CQC	Care Quality Commission
CRB	Criminal Records Bureau [defunct] (*see* DISCLOSURE AND BARRING SERVICE)
CSA	Child Support Agency [defunct] (*see* CHILD MAINTENANCE SERVICE)
CSE	child sexual exploitation
CSSIW	Care Standards and Social Work Inspectorate for Wales (*see* WALES)
CTO	Community Treatment Order
CVA	cardio vascular accident
CVS	Council of Voluntary Service
DBS	Disclosure and Barring Service
DBT	dialectical behavioural therapy
DFG	Disabled Facility Grant (*see* AIDS AND ADAPTATIONS)
DHSSPS	Department of Health, Social Services and Public Safety (*see* NORTHERN IRELAND)
DOLS	Deprivation of Liberty Safeguards
DP	direct payments
DPAC	Disabled People Against Cuts
DSA	Down's Syndrome Association
DSM* or *DSM 5	*Diagnostic and Statistical Manual of Mental Disorders 5*
DTO	Detention and Training Order
DVF	Domestic Violence Forum
DVPN	Domestic Violence Protection Notice
DVPO	Domestic Violence Protection Order
EBP	evidence-based practice
ECM	*Every Child Matters*
ECT	electroconvulsive therapy
EDT	emergency duty team
EFQM	European Foundation of Quality Management
EHC	Education, Health and Care Plan
EHRC	Equality and Human Rights Commission
EPO	Emergency Protection Order
ESO	Education Supervision Order
FACS	Fair Access to Care Services [defunct] (*see* ELIGIBILITY CRITERIA)
FDAC	Family Drug and Alcohol Court
FGM	female genital mutilation
GIRFEC	*Getting it Right for Every Child* (*see* SCOTLAND)
GP	general practitioner
GRO	General Register Office

GSCC	General Social Care Council [defunct] (*see* HEALTH AND CARE PROFESSIONS COUNCIL)
HCPC	Health and Care Professions Council
HIA	Home Improvement Agencies
HIV/AIDS	human immunodeficiency virus/acquired immunodeficiency syndrome
HIW	Health Inspectorate Wales (*see* WALES)
IAPT	Improving Access to Psychological Therapies
ICD or ICD-10	*International Classification of Diseases 10*
ICO	Information Commissioner's Office
ICO	Interim Care Order
ICT	Information and communication technology (*see* CALL CENTRE; COMPUTERIZATION)
IDVA	independent domestic violence advisor
IEP	individual education plan
IFSW	International Federation of Social Workers
ILF	Independent Living Fund
IMCA	independent mental capacity advocate (*see* CAPACITY)
IMHA	independent mental health advocate
IRO	independent reviewing officer
ISA	Independent Safeguarding Authority [defunct] (*see* DISCLOSURE AND BARRING SERVICE)
JRF	Joseph Rowntree Foundation
JRHT	Joseph Rowntree Housing Trust
JSNA	joint strategic needs assessment
KSS	Knowledge and Skills Statements
LAC	looked-after child
LADO	Local Authority Designated Officer
LEA	Local Education Authority
LGBT	lesbian, gay, bisexual, transgender
LSCB	Local Safeguarding Children Board
MAPPA	Multi-agency Public Protection Arrangements
MARAC	Multi-agency Risk Assessment Conference
MASH	Multi-agency Safeguarding Hub
MHAC	Mental Health Act Commission
MHRT	Mental Health Review Tribunal
MSE	mental state examination
MST	Multi-systemic therapy
NAS	National Autistic Society
NASS	National Asylum Support Service
NAT	National Aids Trust
NCB	National Children's Bureau
NCVO	National Council for Voluntary Organizations
NDPB	non-departmental public body
NICE	National Institute for Health and Care Excellence
NIHPS	Northern Ireland Household Panel Survey (*see* NORTHERN IRELAND)
NISCC	Northern Ireland Social Care Council (*see* NORTHERN IRELAND)

NOS	National Objectives and Standards (*see* SCOTLAND)
NR	nearest relative
NSPCC	National Society for the Prevention of Cruelty to Children
NVQ	National Vocational Qualifications
OCD	obsessive compulsive disorder
Ofsted	Office for Standards in Education, Children's Services, and Skills
OPAAL	Older People's Advocacy Alliance
OT	occupational therapist
PACE	Police and Criminal Evidence Act (1984) (*see* APPROPRIATE ADULT)
PASAUK	Practitioner Alliance for Safeguarding Adults
PCF	Professional Capabilities Framework
PCP	person-centred planning
PEP	personal education plan
PLO	public law outline
PRU	pupil referral unit
PSR	pre-sentence report
PTSD/PTSS	post-traumatic stress disorder/syndrome
quango	quasi-non-governmental organization
RA	responsible authority (*see* MULTI-AGENCY PUBLIC PROTECTION ARRANGEMENTS)
RC	responsible clinician
RNIB	Royal National Institute for Blind People
RO	responsible officer
RPA	review of public administration (*see* NORTHERN IRELAND)
SAB	Safeguarding Adults Board
SAR	Safeguarding Adults Review
SASW	Scottish Association of Social Work (*see* SCOTLAND)
SCIE	Social Care Institute of Excellence
SCR	Serious Care Review
SCR	Social Circumstances Report (*see* SCOTLAND)
SCSWIS	Social Care and Social Work Improvement Scotland
SCT	supervised community treatment
SEN	special educational needs (*see* EDUCATION, HEALTH AND CARE ASSESSMENT)
SFBT	solution-focused brief therapy
SFT	solution-focused therapy
SIDS	sudden infant death syndrome (*see* SUDDEN UNEXPECTED DEATH IN CHILDHOOD)
SMI	serious mental illness
SNP	Scottish National Party (*see* SCOTLAND)
SOAD	second opinion appointed doctor
SSI	Social Services Inspectorate (*see* NORTHERN IRELAND)
SSSC	Scottish Social Services Council (*see* SCOTLAND)
STC	secure training centre
SWAN	Social Work Action Network
TQM	total quality management
UASC	unaccompanied asylum-seeking children

ULO	user-led organization
UNCRC	United Nations Convention on the Rights of the Child
UPIAS	Union of the Physically Impaired Against Segregation (*see* SOCIAL MODEL OF DISABILITY)
WRAP	Wellness Recovery Action Planning (*see* RECOVERY)
YISP	Youth Inclusion Support Panel
YJS	Youth Justice Service
YOT	Youth Offending Team

Oxford Quick Reference

A Dictionary of Psychology
Andrew M. Colman

Over 9,000 authoritative entries make up the most wide-ranging
dictionary of psychology available.

'impressive ... certainly to be recommended'
Times Higher Education Supplement

'probably the best single-volume dictionary of its kind.'
Library Journal

A Dictionary of Economics
John Black, Nigar Hashimzade, and Gareth Myles

Fully up-to-date and jargon-free coverage of economics. Over 3,400
terms on all aspects of economic theory and practice.

'strongly recommended as a handy work of reference.'
Times Higher Education Supplement

A Dictionary of Law

An ideal source of legal terminology for systems based on English law.
Over 4,200 clear and concise entries.

'The entries are clearly drafted and succinctly written ... Precision for the
professional is combined with a layman's enlightenment.'
Times Literary Supplement

A Dictionary of Education
Susan Wallace

In over 1,250 clear and concise entries, this authoritative dictionary
covers all aspects of education, including organizations, qualifications,
key figures, major legislation, theory, and curriculum and assessment
terminology.

Oxford Quick Reference

A Dictionary of Sociology
John Scott

The most wide-ranging and authoritative dictionary of its kind.

'Readers and especially beginning readers of sociology can scarcely do better ... there is no better single volume compilation for an up-to-date, readable, and authoritative source of definitions, summaries and references in contemporary Sociology.'

A. H. Halsey, *Emeritus Professor, Nuffield College, University of Oxford*

The Concise Oxford Dictionary of Politics
Iain McLean and Alistair McMillan

The bestselling A–Z of politics with over 1,700 detailed entries.

'A first class work of reference ... probably the most complete as well as the best work of its type available ... Every politics student should have one'

Political Studies Association

A Dictionary of Environment and Conservation
Chris Park and Michael Allaby

An essential guide to all aspects of the environment and conservation containing over 8,500 entries.

'from *aa* to *zygote*, choices are sound and definitions are unspun'
New Scientist

Oxford Quick Reference

Concise Medical Dictionary

Over 12,000 clear entries covering all the major medical and surgical specialities make this one of our best-selling dictionaries.

'"No home should be without one" certainly applies to this splendid medical dictionary'

Journal of the Institute of Health Education

'An extraordinary bargain'   *New Scientist*

A Dictionary of Nursing

Comprehensive coverage of the ever-expanding vocabulary of the nursing professions. Features over 10,000 entries written by medical and nursing specialists.

A Dictionary of Dentistry
Robert Ireland

Over 4,000 succinct and authoritative entries define all the important terms used in dentistry today. This is the ideal reference for all members of the dental team.

A Dictionary of Forensic Science
Suzanne Bell

In over 1,300 entries, this new dictionary covers the key concepts within Forensic Science and is a must-have for students and practitioners of forensic science.

Oxford Quick Reference

A Dictionary of Chemistry

Over 4,700 entries covering all aspects of chemistry, including physical chemistry and biochemistry.

'It should be in every classroom and library ... the reader is drawn inevitably from one entry to the next merely to satisfy curiosity.'

School Science Review

A Dictionary of Physics

Ranging from crystal defects to the solar system, 4,000 clear and concise entries cover all commonly encountered terms and concepts of physics.

A Dictionary of Biology

The perfect guide for those studying biology — with over 5,500 entries on key terms from biology, biochemistry, medicine, and palaeontology.

'lives up to its expectations; the entries are concise, but explanatory'

Biologist

'ideally suited to students of biology, at either secondary or university level, or as a general reference source for anyone with an interest in the life sciences'

Journal of Anatomy

Oxford Quick Reference

The Concise Oxford Companion to English Literature
Dinah Birch and Katy Hooper

Based on the best-selling *Oxford Companion to English Literature*, this is an indispensable guide to all aspects of English literature.

Review of the parent volume:
'the foremost work of reference in its field'

Literary Review

A Dictionary of Shakespeare
Stanley Wells

Compiled by one of the best-known international authorities on the playwright's works, this dictionary offers up-to-date information on all aspects of Shakespeare, both in his own time and in later ages.

The Oxford Dictionary of Literary Terms
Chris Baldick

A best-selling dictionary, covering all aspects of literature, this is an essential reference work for students of literature in any language.

A Dictionary of Critical Theory
Ian Buchanan

The invaluable multidisciplinary guide to theory, covering movements, theories, and events.

'an excellent gateway into critical theory'

Literature and Theology

Oxford Quick Reference

The Kings and Queens of Britain
John Cannon and Anne Hargreaves

A detailed, fully-illustrated history ranging from mythical and pre-conquest rulers to the present House of Windsor, featuring regional maps and genealogies.

A Dictionary of World History

Over 4,000 entries on everything from prehistory to recent changes in world affairs. An excellent overview of world history.

A Dictionary of British History
Edited by John Cannon

An invaluable source of information covering the history of Britain over the past two millennia. Over 3,000 entries written by more than 100 specialist contributors.

Review of the parent volume
'the range is impressive ... truly (almost) all of human life is here'
Kenneth Morgan, *Observer*

The Oxford Companion to Irish History
Edited by S. J. Connolly

A wide-ranging and authoritative guide to all aspects of Ireland's past from prehistoric times to the present day.

'packed with small nuggets of knowledge' *Daily Telegraph*

The Oxford Companion to Scottish History
Edited by Michael Lynch

The definitive guide to twenty centuries of life in Scotland.
'exemplary and wonderfully readable'

Financial Times

OXFORD